MW00993659

West Academic Publishing's Law School Advisory Board

JESSE H. CHOPER
Professor of Law and Dean Emeritus,
University of California, Berkeley

JOSHUA DRESSLER
Distinguished University Professor, Frank R. Strong Chair in Law
Michael E. Moritz College of Law, The Ohio State University

YALE KAMISAR
Professor of Law Emeritus, University of San Diego
Professor of Law Emeritus, University of Michigan

MARY KAY KANE
Professor of Law, Chancellor and Dean Emeritus,
University of California, Hastings College of the Law

LARRY D. KRAMER
President, William and Flora Hewlett Foundation

JONATHAN R. MACEY
Professor of Law, Yale Law School

ARTHUR R. MILLER
University Professor, New York University
Formerly Bruce Bromley Professor of Law, Harvard University

GRANT S. NELSON
Professor of Law Emeritus, Pepperdine University
Professor of Law Emeritus, University of California, Los Angeles

A. BENJAMIN SPENCER
Professor of Law,
University of Virginia School of Law

JAMES J. WHITE
Robert A. Sullivan Professor of Law Emeritus,
University of Michigan

THE LAW AND POLICY OF SENTENCING

Tenth Edition

■ ■ ■

Lynn S. Branham
Distinguished Visiting Scholar
Saint Louis University School of Law

AMERICAN CASEBOOK SERIES®

WEST
ACADEMIC
PUBLISHING

The publisher is not engaged in rendering legal or other professional advice, and this publication is not a substitute for the advice of an attorney. If you require legal or other expert advice, you should seek the services of a competent attorney or other professional.

American Casebook Series is a trademark registered in the U.S. Patent and Trademark Office.

COPYRIGHT © 1973, 1981, 1986, 1991, 1997 WEST PUBLISHING CO.
© West, a Thomson business, 2002, 2005
© 2009, 2013 Thomson Reuters
© 2018 LEG, Inc. d/b/a West Academic
      444 Cedar Street, Suite 700
      St. Paul, MN 55101
      1-877-888-1330

West, West Academic Publishing, and West Academic are trademarks of West Publishing Corporation, used under license.

Printed in the United States of America

ISBN: 978-1-68328-680-6

Dedicated,

with love and gratitude,

to

My parents,

Ray and Thais Sanders.

Models for marriage . . . and life

PREFACE

For those who wish to practice criminal law proficiently and effectively, learning about sentencing law and policy is a must. But, as will become evident when reading the materials in this book, sentencing law and policy affect not just those who work in the criminal-justice system or are processed through it. They affect us all, with each of us having a stake in the purposes, legality, costs, and effects of sentencing-related decisions. Learning more about sentencing will redound then, most assuredly, to the benefit of all.

This casebook enables law schools and criminal-justice programs to ensure that their course offerings include this pivotally important area of law and policy. Like earlier editions of this book, the current edition includes seminal Supreme Court cases bearing on the subject of sentencing law and highlights other significant issues percolating in the courts. Interwoven into the book are statutes, court rules, sentencing guidelines, article excerpts, model standards, policy statements, statistics, questions, and problems that are designed not only to impart knowledge, but to provoke thought, discussion, and debate about how the law and policy of sentencing should evolve.

Because of the heightened centrality of sentencing law and policy to criminal justice and the burgeoning number of sentencing-related policy issues of which students and others should be aware, I have made the decision to no longer combine materials for two discrete courses—one on sentencing and the other on the rights of those who are incarcerated (often termed "prisoners' rights")—in one casebook. The tenth edition of this book therefore concentrates exclusively on sentencing law and policy. Doing so has allowed more expanded coverage of sentencing-related developments and ideas. Examples include:

- A more in-depth overview of restorative justice and restorative practices

- Research findings on factors contributing to racial and ethnic disparity in the people subject to correctional supervision

- More details about day fines

- Research findings on the effects of requiring people convicted of crimes to pay fees to defray the costs of criminal-justice operations and correctional programs

- A discussion of options to eliminate the "correctional free lunch" under which states pay the full costs of imprisonment

v

- Augmented information about the "enmeshed penalties" (also known as "collateral consequences") that attend a criminal conviction, including steps being taken to limit their adverse impact

- The inclusion, as principal cases, of additional Supreme Court decisions

Within the book, footnotes, citations, and some section headings in cases have been omitted without so specifying. When footnotes have been included, the numbers from the original sources have been retained. All letter footnotes contain information added by the author.

I would like to express my appreciation to the publishers and authors who granted permission to reprint the book and article excerpts whose inclusion in the book has greatly enhanced its pedagogical value. I am also grateful to all those with whom I have worked over the years to improve the functioning of the criminal-justice system and from whom I have learned so much.

LYNN S. BRANHAM

February 2018

SUMMARY OF CONTENTS

TABLE OF CONTENTS

TABLE OF CASES

The principal cases are in bold type.

THE LAW AND POLICY OF SENTENCING

Tenth Edition

CHAPTER 1

INTRODUCTION TO SENTENCING

∎ ∎ ∎

A. SENTENCING: YESTERDAY AND TODAY

Winston Churchill once said: "The mood and temper of the public with regard to the treatment of crime and criminals is one of the most unfailing tests of the civilization of any country." Marvin E. Frankel, Criminal Sentences: Law without Order 9 (1973). We should at times, therefore, stop and ask ourselves: "How civilized is our country's response to crimes and those who have committed them? And, from a practical perspective, how effective are our efforts to control crime and to hold people accountable for the harm their crimes have caused individuals and their communities?"

It is obvious, when comparing the sentencing systems of today in our country with the modes of punishment employed in earlier years, that punishment practices have changed dramatically. In colonial times, for example, individuals who had committed such offenses as not observing the Sabbath and being in the company of drunkards often had their legs immobilized in stocks, which were set up in a public place. Pillories, wooden frames used to immobilize individuals' heads and hands, were also frequently used as a form of punishment, and as an added touch, people sometimes had their ears nailed to the wood on either side of the holes through which their heads were stuck. Members of the community often gathered at the site of stocks and pillories to ridicule these hapless individuals and throw objects such as stale eggs, potatoes, and excrement at them.

Public humiliation was a common element of other types of punishment as well. Many people were required to wear letters sewn on their clothes or branded on their bodies publicizing their malefactions. An "A" signified that an individual had committed adultery, a "B" that he or she had uttered blasphemous words, and a "D" that the person had been drunk.

During these times, women, particularly women who scolded their husbands, often were singled out for punishment. A type of stick that pinched the tongue sometimes was affixed to the tongue of a scolding wife, or the wife was placed in a ducking stool and then immersed in water. The ducking stool was also used for other purposes. Married couples who

1

quarreled too much or too loudly, for example, were tied back to back at times and dunked in the water together.

Whipping was another popular form of punishment during the early years of this country, one employed for such offenses as stealing a loaf of bread, lying, and name-calling. Other forms of physical punishment were common as well. People sometimes had their ears cut off, their nostrils slit, a hole bored through their tongues, or their cheeks, foreheads, or other parts of their bodies branded as punishment for an assortment of crimes. For more information about punishment practices in earlier years in this country, see The Oxford History of the Prison: The Practice of Punishment in Western Society (Norval Morris & David J. Rothman eds., 1995) and Alice M. Earle, Curious Punishments of Bygone Days (1968).

Penitentiaries came into use in this country in the late 1700s as part of a reform movement designed to alleviate the harshness of some of the forms of punishment described above. Penitentiaries were viewed, as their name suggests, as places where people could contemplate the error of their ways, become penitent, and seek God's forgiveness for their sins. This reform process, it was felt, could be accomplished through a regimen of compulsory Bible reading and enforced silence to protect prisoners from bad influences exerted by other prisoners. John W. Roberts, Reform and Retribution: An Illustrated History of American Prisons 26–27, 31–33 (1997).

We now have moved into another punishment phase in this country. Although prisons today are hardly characterized by pervasive silence and Bible reading, incarceration is still a popular form of punishment in the United States. In 2015, 458 of every 100,000 residents were in prison, over four times more than the historical average of 110. Bureau of Justice Statistics, U.S. Dep't of Justice, Prisoners in 2015, at 8 (2016) [hereinafter Prisoners in 2015]; Comm. On Causes & Consequences of High Rates of Incarceration, Nat'l Research Council, The Growth of Incarceration in the United States: Exploring Causes and Consequences 34 (Jeremy Travis et al. eds., 2014). The per-capita incarceration rate, a figure which includes individuals confined in jails, was still higher—660 per every 100,000 residents. Bureau of Justice Statistics, U.S. Dep't of Justice, Correctional Populations in the United States, 2015, at 12 (2016) [hereinafter Correctional Populations in 2015]. This incarceration rate is one of the highest in the world, far eclipsing the rate in other industrialized nations. See Inst. for Criminal Policy Research, World Prison Brief, Highest to Lowest—Prison Population Rate, at http://www.prisonstudies.org/highest-to-lowest/prison_population_rate?field_region_taxonomy_tid=All (reporting, on February 13, 2018, incarceration rates (a rate that includes pretrial detention) of 77 in Germany, 101 in France, 114 in Canada, and 143 in England and Wales). And since the per-capita imprisonment and incarceration rates recounted above include residents who are children and since children typically are not incarcerated in prisons or jails, these statistics considerably mask the prevalence of incarceration in the United States. See Prisoners in 2015, at 8 (imprisonment rate of 593 per 100,000 U.S. residents 18 and older compared to a rate of 458 per 100,000 residents of all ages); Correctional Populations in 2015, at 12 (incarceration rate of 860 per 100,000 U.S. residents 18 and older versus 660 per 100,000 residents of all ages).

At the same time, probation is a widely imposed sentence in the United States. For example, in 2015, there were more than twice as many people on probation than in prison. Correctional Populations in 2015, at 2 (3,789,800 on adult probation compared to 1,526,800 in prison). Over 6.7 million adults, approximately one of every thirty-seven adults, were under correctional supervision in the country—in prison or jail or on probation or parole. Id. at 1. In addition, other community-based sentencing options, such as fines, restitution, community service, home confinement, electronic monitoring, and day-reporting centers, are being used with increasing frequency as criminal-justice policymakers and practitioners strive to find the most appropriate and cost-effective responses to crimes—responses that are neither overly lenient nor overly punitive.

B. SENTENCING PURPOSES

In assessing the soundness and efficacy of prevailing approaches to sentencing in the United States, a number of questions must be addressed, including the following: First, for what purpose or purposes are sentences to be imposed? Second, what types of conduct should be subject to criminal sanctions? Third, what sentencing options should be available and employed? Fourth, what constraints should be placed on their use in terms of amount, duration, and other conditions? And fifth, what steps should be taken and procedural safeguards put in place to ensure that an appropriate sentence is imposed on a particular individual? After answering all of these questions, two more questions then must be addressed: What are the costs of the sentencing system we are contemplating, and are we willing to pay them? For if we are not, then we must reexamine our answers concerning the direction to be taken by this part of our nation's criminal-justice system.

Set forth below are some of Professor Wayne LaFave's observations regarding the first question posited above: What are the purposes of criminal sentences? Then follows a case, United States v. Bergman, 416 F.Supp. 496 (S.D.N.Y.1976), in which the court considered these purposes in deciding the appropriate sentence to impose on a defendant.

WAYNE R. LaFAVE, CRIMINAL LAW

(6th ed. 2017). Reprinted with permission of West Academic Publishing.

* * *

Purposes of the Criminal Law—Theories of Punishment

The broad purposes of the criminal law are, of course, to make people do what society regards as desirable and to prevent them from doing what society considers to be undesirable. Since criminal law is framed in terms of imposing punishment for bad conduct, rather than of granting rewards for good conduct, the emphasis is more on the prevention of the undesirable than on the encouragement of the desirable.

* * *

The criminal law is not, of course, the only weapon which society uses to prevent conduct which harms or threatens to harm these important interests of the public. Education, at home and at school, as to the types of conduct that society thinks good and bad, is an important weapon; religion, with its emphasis on distinguishing between good and evil conduct, is another. The human desire to acquire and keep the affection and respect of family, friends and associates no doubt has a great influence in deterring most people from conduct which is socially unacceptable. The civil side of the law, which forces one to pay damages for the harmful results that his undesirable conduct has caused to others, or which in appropriate situations grants injunctions against bad conduct or orders the specific performance of good conduct, also plays a part in influencing behavior along desirable lines.

(a) Theories of Punishment. How does the criminal law, with its threat of punishment to violators, operate to influence human conduct away from the undesirable and toward the desirable? There are a number of theories of punishment, and each theory has or has had its enthusiastic adherents. Some of the theories are concerned primarily with the particular offender, while others focus more on the nature of the offense and the general public. These theories are:

(1) Prevention. By this theory, also called *intimidation*, or, when the deterrence theory is referred to as general deterrence, *particular deterrence*,[a] criminal punishment aims to deter the criminal himself (rather than to deter others) from committing further crimes, by giving him an unpleasant experience he will not want to endure again. The validity of this theory has been questioned by many, who point out the high recidivism rates of those who have been punished. On the other hand, it has been observed that our attempts at prevention by punishment may enjoy an unmeasurable degree of success, in that without punishment for purposes

---

[a]   This penological purpose also is commonly referred to as "specific deterrence."

of prevention the rate of recidivism might be much higher. This assumption is not capable of precise proof, nor is the assertion that in some instances punishment for prevention will fill the prisoner with feelings of hatred and desire for revenge against society and thus influence future criminal conduct.

(2) Restraint. The notion here, also expressed as *incapacitation*, *isolation*, or *disablement*, is that society may protect itself from persons deemed dangerous because of their past criminal conduct by isolating these persons from society. If the criminal is imprisoned or executed, he cannot commit further crimes against society. Some question this theory because of doubts that those who present a danger of continuing criminality can be accurately identified. It has also been noted that resort to restraint without accompanying rehabilitative efforts is unwise, as the vast majority of prisoners will ultimately be returned to society. The restraint theory is sometimes employed to justify execution or life imprisonment without chance of parole for those offenders believed to be beyond rehabilitation.

(3) Rehabilitation. Under this theory, * * * we "punish" the convicted criminal by giving him appropriate treatment, in order to rehabilitate him and return him to society so reformed that he will not desire or need to commit further crimes. It is perhaps not entirely correct to call this treatment "punishment," as the emphasis is away from making him suffer and in the direction of making his life better and more pleasant. The rehabilitation theory rests upon the belief that human behavior is the product of antecedent causes, that these causes can be identified, and that on this basis therapeutic measures can be employed to effect changes in the behavior of the person treated. Even when there has been more of a commitment to the "rehabilitative ideal" than to other theories of punishment, much of what is done by way of post-conviction disposition of offenders is not truly rehabilitative. Perhaps this is why the theory of reformation has not as yet shown very satisfactory results in practice.

* * *

(4) Deterrence. Under this theory, sometimes referred to as *general prevention*, the sufferings of the criminal for the crime he has committed are supposed to deter others from committing future crimes, lest they suffer the same unfortunate fate. The extent to which punishment actually has this effect upon the general public is unclear; conclusive empirical research on the subject is lacking, and it is difficult to measure the effectiveness of fear of punishment because it is but one of several forces that restrain people from violating the law.

It does seem fair to assume, however, that the deterrent efficacy of punishment varies considerably, depending upon a number of factors. Those who commit crimes under emotional stress (such as murder in the heat of anger) or who have become expert criminals through the training and practice of many years (such as the professional safebreaker and pickpocket) are less likely than others to be deterred. Even apart from the nature of the crime, individuals undoubtedly react differently to the threat of punishment, depending upon such factors as their social class, age, intelligence, and moral training. The magnitude of the threatened punishment is clearly a factor, but perhaps not as important a consideration as the probability of discovery and punishment.

(5) Education. Under this theory, criminal punishment serves, by the publicity which attends the trial, conviction and punishment of criminals, to educate the public as to the proper distinctions between good conduct and bad—distinctions which, when known, most of society will observe. While the public may need no such education as to serious *malum in se* crimes, the educational function of punishment is important as to crimes that are not generally known, often misunderstood, or inconsistent with current morality.

(6) Retribution. * * * By this theory, * * * punishment (the infliction of suffering) is imposed by society on criminals in order to obtain revenge, or perhaps (under the less emotional concept of retribution) because it is only fitting and just that one who has caused harm to others should himself suffer for it. Typical of the criticism is that this theory "is a form of retaliation, and as such, is morally indefensible."

However, the retribution theory, when explained on somewhat different grounds, continues to draw some support. Some contend that when one commits a crime, it is important that he receive commensurate punishment in order to restore the peace of mind and repress the criminal tendencies of others. In addition, it is claimed that retributive punishment is needed to maintain respect for the law and to suppress acts of private vengeance. * * *

* * * Today [the retribution theory] is commonly put forward under the rubric of "deserts" or "just deserts" * * *[43] Those who favor the theory claim it "provides an important check against tyranny, for a person is punished only when he deserves it; and the opposite is also true—that he is not punished if he does not deserve it." * * *

(7) Restoration. Yet another theory of punishment, one which has been the subject of considerable discussion and debate in recent years, usually goes under the title of "restorative justice." Restorative justice, it is said, "creates an avenue to bring criminals and their victims together rather than keep them apart. * * * It gives crime victims the opportunity

---

[43] It "is likely to include two princip[al] assertions. First, the primary object of criminal sanctions is to punish culpable behavior. Although punishment may result in certain utilitarian benefits, notably the reduction of criminal behavior, the justification of punishment does not require such a showing; for it is moral and just that culpable behavior be punished. Second, the severity of the sanctions visited on the offender should be proportioned to the degree of his culpability." F. Allen, The Decline of the Rehabilitative Ideal 66 (1981). * * *

to meet with the criminals who harmed them—to discuss the pain and disruption crime has caused their lives. * * *" A primary objective "is making amends for the offending, particularly the harm caused to the victim, rather than inflicting pain upon the offender. Accountability is demonstrated by recognizing the wrongfulness of one's conduct, expressing remorse for the resulting injury and taking steps to repair the damage."

* * *

Restorative justice has been "championed as an alternative to traditional punishment theories, particularly retributivism," which it is said "largely neglect the needs of those directly injured by crime and the resulting damage done to social relationships within an interconnected community." Its advocates "claim that restorative practices are more cost effective, more likely to reduce crime rates and recidivism, and more humane than traditional criminal justice, American-style." But, restorative justice also has its critics. It is argued that restorative justice theory "would allow disparate treatment of otherwise identical offenders, could encourage arbitrary decision-making, and may pay insufficient heed to society's overriding interest in punishing crime." * * *

(b) Conflict Between the Theories. For many years most of the literature on the subject of punishment was devoted to advocacy of a particular theory to the exclusion of others. Those who espoused the rehabilitation theory condemned the rest, those who favored the deterrence theory denied the validity of all others, and so on. But in recent years the "inclusive theory of punishment" has gained considerable support; there is now general agreement that all (or, at least most) of the theories described above deserve some consideration.

This has given rise to another difficult problem, namely, what the priority and relationship of these several aims should be. This problem must be confronted, as it is readily apparent that the various theories tend to conflict with one another at several points. The retribution, deterrence, and prevention theories call for presenting the criminal with an unpleasant experience; but the chances for rehabilitation are often defeated by harsh treatment. The rehabilitation theory would let the criminal go when (and perhaps *only* when) he had been reformed. This may be a substantially shorter period of time (or a substantially *longer* period of time) than can be justified under the deterrence and retribution theories, which would vary the punishment in accordance with the seriousness of the crime. * * *

It is undoubtedly true that the thinking of legislators, judges and juries, and administrative officers who have a part in fixing punishment, as well as the thinking of the expert criminologist and non-expert layman whose views tend to influence those officials, varies from situation to situation. Sometimes the retribution theory will predominate; most of us share the common feeling of mankind that a particularly shocking crime should be severely punished. Where, for example, a son, after thoughtfully taking out insurance on his mother's life, places a time bomb in her suitcase just before she boards a plane, which device succeeds in killing the mother and all forty-two others aboard the plane, we almost all feel that he deserves a severe punishment, and we reach this result with little reflection about influencing future conduct. Likewise, when a less serious crime is involved and it was committed by a young person who might be effectively reformed, the rehabilitation theory rightly assumes primary importance. And the deterrence theory may be most important when the crime is not inherently wrong or covered by moral prohibition. Illustrative are income tax violations, as to which deterrence is especially important because of our reliance on a system of self-assessment.

* * *

<h1 style="text-align:center">UNITED STATES V. BERGMAN</h1>
United States District Court, Southern District of New York, 1976.
416 F.Supp. 496.

FRANKEL, DISTRICT JUDGE.

Defendant is being sentenced upon his plea of guilty to two counts of an 11-count indictment. The sentencing proceeding is unusual in some respects. It has been the subject of more extensive submissions, written and oral, than this court has ever received upon such an occasion. The court has studied some hundreds of pages of memoranda and exhibits, plus scores of volunteered letters. A broad array of issues has been addressed. Imaginative suggestions of law and penology have been tendered. A preliminary conversation with counsel, on the record, preceded the usual sentencing hearing. Having heard counsel again and the defendant speaking for himself, the court postponed the pronouncement of sentence for further reconsideration of thoughts generated during the days of studying the briefs and oral pleas. It seems fitting now to report in writing the reasons upon which the court concludes that defendant must be sentenced to a term of four months in prison.[1]

I.   Defendant and His Crimes

Defendant appeared until the last couple of years to be a man of unimpeachably high character, attainments, and distinction. A doctor of divinity and an ordained rabbi, he has been acclaimed by people around the world for his works of public philanthropy, private charity, and leadership in educational enterprises. Scores of letters have come to the court from across this and other countries reporting debts of personal

---

[1]   The court considered, and finally rejected, imposing a fine in addition to the prison term. Defendant seems destined to pay hundreds of thousands of dollars in restitution. The amount is being worked out in connection with a state criminal indictment. Apart from defendant's further liabilities for federal taxes, any additional money exaction is appropriately left for the state court.

gratitude to him for numerous acts of extraordinary generosity. (The court has also received a kind of petition, with fifty-odd signatures, in which the signers, based upon learning acquired as newspaper readers, denounce the defendant and urge a severe sentence. Unlike the pleas for mercy, which appear to reflect unquestioned facts inviting compassion, this document should and will be disregarded.) In addition to his good works, defendant has managed to amass considerable wealth in the ownership and operation of nursing homes, in real estate ventures, and in a course of substantial investments.

Beginning about two years ago, investigations of nursing homes in this area, including questions of fraudulent claims for Medicaid funds, drew to a focus upon this defendant among several others. The results that concern us were the present indictment and two state indictments. After extensive pretrial proceedings, defendant embarked upon elaborate plea negotiations with both state and federal prosecutors. A state guilty plea and the instant plea were entered in March of this year. (Another state indictment is expected to be dismissed after defendant is sentenced on those to which he has pled guilty.) As part of the detailed plea arrangements, it is expected that the prison sentence imposed by this court will comprise the total covering the state as well as the federal convictions.

For purposes of the sentence now imposed, the precise details of the charges, and of defendant's carefully phrased admissions of guilt, are not matters of prime importance. Suffice it to say that the plea on Count One (carrying a maximum of five years in prison and a $10,000 fine) confesses defendant's knowing and willful participation in a scheme to defraud the United States in various ways, including the presentation of wrongfully padded claims for payments under the Medicaid program to defendant's nursing homes. Count Three, for which the guilty plea carries a theoretical maximum of three more years in prison and another $5,000 fine, is a somewhat more "technical" charge. Here, defendant admits to having participated in the filing of a partnership return which was false and fraudulent in failing to list people who had bought partnership interests from him in one of his nursing homes, had paid for such interests, and had made certain capital withdrawals.

The conspiracy to defraud, as defendant has admitted it, is by no means the worst of its kind; it is by no means as flagrant or extensive as has been portrayed in the press; it is evidently less grave than other nursing-home wrongs for which others have been convicted or publicized. At the same time, the sentence, as defendant has acknowledged, is imposed for two federal felonies including, as the more important, a knowing and purposeful conspiracy to mislead and defraud the Federal Government.

II. *The Guiding Principles of Sentencing*

Proceeding through the short list of the supposed justifications for criminal sanctions, defense counsel urge that no licit purpose could be served by defendant's incarceration. Some of these arguments are plainly sound; others are not.

The court agrees that this defendant should not be sent to prison for "rehabilitation." Apart from the patent inappositeness of the concept to this individual, this court shares the growing understanding that no one should ever be sent to prison *for rehabilitation.* That is to say, nobody who would not otherwise be locked up should suffer that fate on the incongruous premise that it will be good for him or her. Imprisonment is punishment. Facing the simple reality should help us to be civilized. It is less agreeable to confine someone when we deem it an affliction rather than a benefaction. If someone must be imprisoned—for other, valid reasons—we should seek to make rehabilitative resources available to him or her. But the goal of rehabilitation cannot fairly serve in itself as grounds for the sentence to confinement.

Equally clearly, this defendant should not be confined to incapacitate him. He is not dangerous. It is most improbable that he will commit similar, or any, offenses in the future. There is no need for "specific deterrence."

Contrary to counsel's submissions, however, two sentencing considerations demand a prison sentence in this case:

> *First,* the aim of *general deterrence,* the effort to discourage similar wrongdoing by others through a reminder that the law's warnings are real and that the grim consequence of imprisonment is likely to follow from crimes of deception for gain like those defendant has admitted.

> *Second,* the related, but not identical, concern that any lesser penalty would, in the words of the Model Penal Code, § 7.01(1)(c), "depreciate the seriousness of the defendant's crime."

Resisting the first of these propositions, defense counsel invoke Immanuel Kant's axiom that "one man ought never to be dealt with merely as a means subservient to the purposes of another."[4] * * *

As for Dr. Kant, * * * we take the widely accepted stance that a criminal punished in the interest of general deterrence is not being employed "*merely* as a means * * *." Reading Kant to mean that every man must be deemed *more* than the instrument of others, and must "always be treated as an end in himself," the humane principle is not offended here. Each of us is served by the enforcement of the law—not least a person like

---

[4]   Quoting from I. Kant, *Philosophy of Law* 1986 (Hastie Trans.1887).

the defendant in this case, whose wealth and privileges, so long enjoyed, are so much founded upon law. * * *

But the whole business, defendant argues further, is guesswork; we are by no means certain that deterrence "works." The position is somewhat overstated; there is, in fact, some reasonably "scientific" evidence for the efficacy of criminal sanctions as deterrents, at least as against some kinds of crimes. Moreover, the time is not yet here when all we can "know" must be quantifiable and digestible by computers. The shared wisdom of generations teaches meaningfully, if somewhat amorphously, that the utilitarians have a point; we do, indeed, lapse often into rationality and act to seek pleasure and avoid pain. It would be better, to be sure, if we had more certainty and precision. Lacking these comforts, we continue to include among our working hypotheses a belief (with some concrete evidence in its support) that crimes like those in this case—deliberate, purposeful, continuing, non-impulsive, and committed for profit—are among those most likely to be generally deterrable by sanctions most shunned by those exposed to temptation.

The idea of avoiding depreciation of the seriousness of the offense implicates two or three thoughts, not always perfectly clear or universally agreed upon, beyond the idea of deterrence. It should be proclaimed by the court's judgment that the offenses are grave, not minor or purely technical. Some attention must be paid to the demand for equal justice; it will not do to leave the penalty of imprisonment a dead letter as against "privileged" violators while it is employed regularly, and with vigor, against others. There probably is in these conceptions an element of retributiveness, as counsel urge. And retribution, so denominated, is in some disfavor as a reason for punishment. It remains a factor, however, * * * as is known to anyone who talks to judges, lawyers, defendants, or people generally. It may become more palatable, and probably more humanely understood, under the rubric of "deserts" or "just deserts." However the concept is formulated, we have not yet reached a state, supposing we ever should, in which the infliction of punishments for crime may be divorced generally from ideas of blameworthiness, recompense, and proportionality.

III. An Alternative, "Behavioral Sanction"

Resisting prison above all else, defense counsel included in their thorough memorandum on sentencing two proposals for what they call a "constructive," and therefore a "preferable" form of "behavioral sanction." One is a plan for Dr. Bergman to create and run a program of Jewish vocational and religious high school training. The other is for him to take charge of a "Committee on Holocaust Studies," again concerned with education at the secondary school level.

A third suggestion was made orally at yesterday's sentencing hearing. It was proposed that Dr. Bergman might be ordered to work as a volunteer in some established agency as a visitor and aide to the sick and the otherwise incapacitated. The proposal was that he could read, provide various forms of physical assistance, and otherwise give comfort to afflicted people.

No one can doubt either the worthiness of these proposals or Dr. Bergman's ability to make successes of them. But both of the carefully formulated "sanctions" in the memorandum involve work of an honorific nature, not unlike that done in other projects to which the defendant has devoted himself in the past. It is difficult to conceive of them as "punishments" at all. The more recent proposal is somewhat more suitable in character, but it is still an insufficient penalty. The seriousness of the crimes to which Dr. Bergman has pled guilty demands something more than "requiring" him to lend his talents and efforts to further philanthropic enterprises. It remains open to him, of course, to pursue the interesting suggestions later on as a matter of unforced personal choice.

IV. "Measuring" the Sentence

In cases like this one, the decision of greatest moment is whether to imprison or not. As reflected in the eloquent submissions for defendant, the prospect of the closing prison doors is the most appalling concern; the feeling is that the length of the sojourn is a lesser question once that threshold is passed. Nevertheless, the setting of a term remains to be accomplished. And in some respects it is a subject even more perplexing, unregulated, and unprincipled.

Days and months and years are countable with a sound of exactitude. But there can be no exactitude in the deliberations from which a number emerges. Without pretending to a nonexistent precision, the court notes at least the major factors.

The criminal behavior, as has been noted, is blatant in character and unmitigated by any suggestion of necessitous circumstance or other pressures difficult to resist. However metaphysicians may conjure with issues about free will, it is a fundamental premise of our efforts to do criminal justice that competent people, possessed of their faculties, make choices and are accountable for them. In this sometimes harsh light, the case of the present defendant is among the clearest and least relieved. Viewed against the maxima Congress ordained, and against the run of sentences in other federal criminal cases, it calls for more than a token sentence.[14]

On the other side are factors that take longer to enumerate. Defendant's illustrious public life and works are in his favor, though

---

[14] Despite Biblical teachings concerning what is expected from those to whom much is given, the court has not, as his counsel feared might happen, held Dr. Bergman to a higher standard of responsibility because of his position in the community. But he has not been judged under a lower standard either.

diminished, of course, by what this case discloses. This is a first, probably a last, conviction. Defendant is 64 years old and in imperfect health, though by no means so ill, from what the court is told, that he could be expected to suffer inordinately more than many others of advanced years who go to prison.

Defendant invokes an understandable, but somewhat unworkable, notion of "disparity." He says others involved in recent nursing home fraud cases have received relatively light sentences for behavior more culpable than his. He lays special emphasis upon one defendant whose frauds appear indeed to have involved larger amounts and who was sentenced to a maximum of six months' incarceration, to be confined for that time only on week nights, not on week days or weekends. This court has examined the minutes of that sentencing proceeding and finds the case distinguishable in material respects. But even if there were a threat of such disparity as defendant warns against, it could not be a major weight on the scales.

Our sentencing system, deeply flawed, is characterized by disparity. We are to seek to "individualize" sentences, but no clear or clearly agreed standards govern the individualization. The lack of meaningful criteria does indeed leave sentencing judges far too much at large. But the result, with its nagging burdens on conscience, cannot be meaningfully alleviated by allowing any handful of sentences in a short series to fetter later judgments. The point is easy, of course, where Sentence No. 1 or Sentences 1–5 are notably harsh. It cannot be that a later judge, disposed to more leniency, should feel in any degree "bound." The converse is not identical, but it is not totally different. The net of this is that this court has considered and has given some weight to the trend of the other cited sentences (though strict logic might call for none), but without treating them as forceful "precedents" in any familiar sense.

How, then, the particular sentence adjudged in this case? As has been mentioned, the case calls for a sentence that is more than nominal. Given the other circumstances, however—including that this is a first offense, by a man no longer young and not perfectly well, where danger of recidivism is not a concern—it verges on cruelty to think of confinement for a term of years. We sit, to be sure, in a nation where prison sentences of extravagant length are more common than they are almost anywhere else. By that light, the term imposed today is not notably long. For this sentencing court, however, for a nonviolent first offense involving no direct assaults or invasions of others' security (as in bank robbery, narcotics, etc.), it is a stern sentence. For people like Dr. Bergman, who might be disposed to engage in similar wrongdoing, it should be sufficiently frightening to serve the major end of general deterrence. For all but the profoundly vengeful, it should not depreciate the seriousness of his offenses.

V. *Punishment in or for the Media*

Much of defendant's sentencing memorandum is devoted to the extensive barrage of hostile publicity to which he has been subjected during the years before and since his indictment. He argues, and it appears to be undisputed, that the media (and people desiring to be featured in the media) have vilified him for many kinds of evildoing of which he has in fact been innocent. Two main points are made on this score with respect to the problem of sentencing.

First, as has been mentioned, counsel express the concern that the court may be pressured toward severity by the force of the seeming public outcry. That the court should not allow itself to be affected in this way is clear beyond discussion. Nevertheless, it is not merely permissible, but entirely wholesome and responsible, for counsel to bring the expressed concern out in the open. Whatever our ideals and mixed images about judges, it would be naive to doubt that judges have sometimes been swept by a sense of popular demand toward draconian sentencing decisions. It cannot hurt for the sentencing judge to be reminded of this and cautioned about it. There can be no guarantees. The sentencer must confront and regulate himself. But it bears reaffirmance that the court must seek to discount utterly the fact of notoriety in passing its judgment upon the defendant.

* * *

Defendant's second point about his public humiliation is the frequently heard contention that he should not be incarcerated because he "has been punished enough." The thought is not without some initial appeal. If punishment were wholly or mainly retributive, it might be a weighty factor. In the end, however, it must be a matter of little or no force. Defendant's notoriety should not in the last analysis serve to lighten, any more than it may be permitted to aggravate, his sentence. The fact that he has been pilloried by journalists is essentially a consequence of the prestige and privileges he enjoyed before he was exposed as a wrongdoer. The long fall from grace was possible only because of the height he had reached. The suffering from loss of public esteem reflects a body of opinion that the esteem had been, in at least some measure, wrongly bestowed and enjoyed. It is not possible to justify the notion that this mode of nonjudicial punishment should be an occasion for leniency not given to a defendant who never basked in such an admiring light at all. The quest for both the appearance and the substance of equal justice prompts the court to discount the thought that the public humiliation serves the function of imprisonment.

Writing, as judges rarely do, about a particular sentence concentrates the mind with possibly special force upon the experience of the sentencer as well as the person sentenced. Consigning someone to prison, this defendant or any other, "is a sad necessity." There are impulses of avoidance from time to time—toward a personally gratifying leniency or toward an opposite extreme. But there is, obviously, no place for private impulse in the judgment of the court. The course of justice must be sought with such objective rationality as we can muster, tempered with mercy, but obedient to the law, which, we do well to remember, is all that empowers a judge to make other people suffer.

* * *

QUESTIONS AND POINTS FOR DISCUSSION

1.   Do you agree with the sentence imposed by the court in *Bergman*? Why or why not?

2.   If you were the sentencing judge, what sentence would you impose in the following four cases? Explain your conclusions in light of what you consider the appropriate purpose or purposes of sentences.

    a.   When driving while intoxicated, the defendant ran through two red lights, hit a car, and killed two passengers in the car. Before getting into his car, the defendant had been warned by a police officer not to drive, because of his apparent drunkenness. At the time of the accident, the defendant was twenty years old and was employed as a delivery driver. He had no prior felony convictions or any convictions for reckless driving or driving while intoxicated. However, he had received seven traffic tickets in the past three years, one of which was for leaving the scene of an accident after running into a car in a parking lot.

    The defendant was willing to plead guilty to voluntary manslaughter, but refused to plead guilty to second-degree murder as the prosecutor insisted. A state statute defined second-degree murder to include "intentionally perform[ing] an act that results in the death of another person under circumstances manifesting an extreme indifference to the value of human life." A jury found the defendant guilty of two counts of second-degree murder and one count of assault.

    b.   During a three-month period, the defendant, a former college and professional football player, a member of the state legislature, and an alcoholic, wrote seventy-six checks on a closed account to pay for $8,000 worth of goods and services. He pled guilty to one count of theft over $250. By the time of the sentencing hearing, he had paid back the money owed for the bad checks.

    c.   A jury found the defendant guilty on all counts of an indictment charging him with defrauding investors of millions of dollars. The convictions were the defendant's first, and he never had expressed any remorse for his crimes.

After the defendant's trial, he had a stroke, which left him unable to speak and the right side of his body paralyzed. After participating in an intensive therapy program conducted both in Colorado and New York, he regained much of his ability to speak. He still, however, had curtailed use of his right arm and leg and had difficulty thinking clearly. He also continued to periodically suffer what were described as small strokes.

At the sentencing hearing, five defense witnesses—three neurologists and two rehabilitation specialists—described the defendant's physical progress since the stroke. They also testified that this progress might be halted or reversed if the defendant's physical-therapy program was stopped or its quality reduced and that subsequent therapy might not be able to undo this damage.

d.   The defendant pled guilty to conspiracy to distribute and possess with intent to distribute cocaine base after police officers found 191.8 grams of cocaine base in a bag she was carrying. The defendant had no prior criminal record and no history of substance abuse. She was a single mother with three children ages three, thirteen months, and three months, and she was breastfeeding the infant.

3.   The deterrent objective of criminal sanctions has met with controversy in recent years. Of particular concern has been the failure of the prison experience to deter many people from committing further crimes after they have been released from prison. One recidivism study, for example, revealed that 68% of the people released from prison were rearrested within three years and 50% were reimprisoned. Bureau of Justice Statistics, U.S. Dep't of Justice, Recidivism of Prisoners Released in 30 States in 2005: Patterns from 2005 to 2010, at 1, 15 (2014). The individuals returned to prison during this time frame were closely divided between those reincarcerated after a new criminal conviction and those reincarcerated for having violated a condition of their community supervision. Id. at 15.

One of the postulated reasons why the possibility of incarceration or reincarceration often has no or limited deterrent effect is that many people are under the influence of drugs, alcohol, or both at the time of their crimes, making it unlikely that they can and will coolly assess the costs and benefits of a crime before its commission. See Nat'l Ctr. on Addiction & Substance Abuse at Columbia Univ., Behind Bars II: Substance Abuse and America's Prison Population 11 (2010) (43% of prison and jail inmates were under the influence of alcohol or drugs at the time of their crimes). In addition, many crimes are committed impulsively or when in the grip of a strong emotion, like anger, without any reflection about the potential consequences of the criminal behavior. Michael Tonry, Learning from the Limitations of Deterrence Research, 37 Crime and Justice: A Review of Research 179, 282 (Michael Tonry ed., 2008). What other factors can you identify that might limit the deterrent impact of incarceration?

4.   Some people cite incapacitation as the principal reason for incarcerating more people for their crimes. These incapacitation proponents argue that by incarcerating more people convicted of crimes, public safety will be enhanced as they are physically disabled from preying on the public. Set forth below are excerpts from three sources—a report of the Sentencing Project, an overview of research findings compiled by the Centre for Criminology & Sociolegal Studies at the University of Toronto, and a policy essay written by Dr. Todd Clear, a criminologist—offering a different perspective and citing what are believed to be some overlooked limits of, and complexities about, incapacitation.

————

a.   Sentencing Project, Incarceration and Crime: A Complex Relationship 6, 8 (2005)

Limits of Incarceration's Impact on Criminal Behavior

* * * Among the reasons for incarceration's limited impact on crime rates are:

Diminishing Returns—Expanding the use of imprisonment inevitably results in diminishing returns in crime control. This is because high-rate and serious or violent offenders will generally be incarcerated even at modest levels of imprisonment, but as prison systems expand, new admissions will increasingly draw in lower-rate offenders. This growth in lower-rate and lower-level offenders shifts the cost-to-benefit ratio, as an equal amount of resources are spent per offender, but the state receives less return on its investment in terms of declining crime rates. * * *

Limited Drug Offender Effects—* * * Compared to other offenses, the effect of sentencing and incarceration on drug offenses is quite limited since drug selling is subject to a "replacement effect." For example, if an armed robber is convicted and sentenced to prison, the effect of incapacitation removes that person's crime potential during the period of imprisonment. But street-level drug sellers are often replaced quickly by other sellers seeking to make profits from the drug market. As criminologist Alfred Blumstein has noted, ". . . drug markets are inherently demand driven. As long as the demand is there, a supply network will emerge to satisfy that demand. While efforts to assault the supply-side may have some disruptive effects in the short term, the ultimate need is to reduce the demand in order to have an effect on drug abuse in the society."

* * *

Impact of Incarceration Compared to Other Interventions

* * * A variety of research demonstrates that investments in drug treatment, interventions with at-risk families, and school completion programs are more cost-effective than expanded incarceration as crime control measures. Regarding drug use, a RAND analysis concluded that the expenditure of $1 million to expand mandatory minimum sentencing would result in a national decrease in drug consumption of 13 kilograms, while dedicating those funds to drug treatment would reduce consumption by 100 kilograms.[24] * * *

In terms of prevention, an analysis of a wide range of national programs aimed at school completion and addressing the needs of at-risk youth found similar returns on taxpayer investments, in terms of increased productivity and decreased crime * * *.[27] * * *

b. Anthony N. Doob et al., Centre for Criminology & Sociolegal Studies, University of Toronto, Issues Related to Harsh Sentences and Mandatory Minimum Sentences: General Deterrence and Incapacitation A-10 to A-11 (2014)

One seemingly incontrovertible fact about harsh penalties involving imprisonment is that when people are in prison, they are not committing offenses in the community. By this argument, high imprisonment rates might be seen as almost automatically leading to crime reduction.

This simple hypothesis is, however, challenged by the findings * * * demonstrating that imprisonment can make people *more* likely to reoffend once the sentence is complete. Said differently, people may not commit offenses while incarcerated, but this "savings" in public safety could be nullified (if not outweighed) if they are more likely to commit offenses when released.

* * *

The empirical findings on the impact of incapacitation are not encouraging. For example, there are serious problems in determining who is likely, in the future, to be a "high rate" offender. * * *

---

[24] Caulkins, J.P., Rydell, C.P., Scwabe, W.L., Chiesa, J. (1997). *Mandatory Minimum Drug Sentences: Throwing Away The Key or The Taxpayers' Money?* Santa Monica, CA: RAND. (pp. xvii–xviii).

[27] Aos, S., Phipps, P., Barnoski, R., & Lieb, R. (2001). *The Comparative Costs and Benefits of Programs to Reduce Crime.* Olympia, WA: Washington State Institute for Public Policy.

The problem is simple: Most of those predicted to be high rate offenders turn out not to be.[b] More generally, it has been suggested that *any* crime control strategy based on intervening in the lives of those who are predicted to be "at risk" for serious offending is likely to be ineffective. There is an understandable criminological reason for this: as people get older they are increasingly less likely to offend. Thus, precisely at the time when people are identified—from past behavior—to have been high rate offenders, their offending rate declines.

c. Todd R. Clear, "A Thug in Prison Can't Shoot Your Sister," 15(2) Criminology & Public Policy 343, 345 (2016)

There has long been good reason to doubt the simple, push-button idea that putting people behind bars automatically prevents crime. * * *

[T]here has been a realization that because prison concentrates in communities of disadvantage, and among men of color, it constitutes a problematic intervention into those places and groups. Various studies have shown that prison has a negative impact on family formation, family functioning, children's life chances, community health, economic well-being, informal social control, and community respect for legitimate authority. Prison, as we know, is not really good for people. It turns out that in heavy doses, it is not good for communities either. There is evidence that when the concentrations of incarceration get high enough, crime rates even go up. * * *

In some ways, the community-level consequences of incarceration expose the most pernicious aspect of incapacitation theory. It is one thing to say that, on average, prisons make the people who go there worse. * * * However, it is another to say that prisons damage the very communities of people who are most likely to suffer the consequences of crime. * * *

––––––

5. Researchers have identified additional limits on the cost-effectiveness of incarceration. A report of the National Academy of Sciences, for example, spotlights another fact that curtails the capacity of incarceration to curb crime, whether through incapacitation or deterrence: Most crimes are not solved, so many people never will be apprehended or expect to be apprehended for any crimes they commit, much less charged and convicted. Comm. On Causes & Consequences of High Rates of Incarceration, Nat'l Research Council, The Growth of Incarceration in the United States: Exploring

––––––––––

[b] People incorrectly identified as posing high risks to the community are often called "false positives."

Causes and Consequences 133 (Jeremy Travis et al. eds., 2014) [hereinafter National Research Council Study]. About half of crimes are never even reported to police. Id. See also Bureau of Justice Statistics, U.S. Dep't of Justice, Criminal Victimization, 2016, at 7 (2017) (only 42% of violent crimes reported to police in 2016). And even when they are reported, most reported crimes do not culminate in an arrest. There is an arrest, for example, for approximately only one of every four reported robberies and one of every five reported burglaries. National Research Council Study, at 133.

6. Research on the association between the crime rate and the rate of incarceration provides further evidence that increased incarceration will not lead to a proportionate increase in the public's safety. While the nation's incarceration rate climbed steadily, beginning in the early 1970s, for approximately forty years, the national crime rate fluctuated greatly, sometimes rising and sometimes falling. James Austin, Reducing America's Correctional Populations: A Strategic Plan, 12 Just. Res. & Pol'y 9, 11–14 (2010). Statistics at the state level further confirm two complexities about crime and incarceration rates. First, the correlation between the incarceration rate and the crime rate varies greatly from state to state. See Dr. Oliver Roeder et al., Brennan Center for Justice, What Caused the Crime Decline? 27–29 (2015) (reporting that the crime rate rose in some states and dropped in others in which the imprisonment rate increased between 2000 and 2013 while 14 states experienced a drop in both their imprisonment and crime rates). And second, a multitude of factors other than incarceration, such as the rate of unemployment, wage levels, high-school graduation rate, and number of young people in the population, affect the crime rate more than incarceration. Don Stemen, Vera Inst. of Justice, The Prison Paradox: More Incarceration Will Not Make Us Safer 2 (2017).

7. The federal sentencing system reflects the view espoused by Judge Frankel in *United States v. Bergman* that a defendant should not be sent to prison in order to be rehabilitated. Title 18 U.S.C. § 3582(a) states that "imprisonment is not an appropriate means of promoting correction and rehabilitation," foreclosing judges from sentencing a defendant to prison or increasing the length of a prison sentence because of perceived benefits of a prison-based treatment or training program. Tapia v. United States, 564 U.S. 319, 131 S.Ct. 2382 (2011). But a federal court can still consider the goal of rehabilitation when sentencing a defendant. When deciding, for example, whether to impose probation or when contouring the conditions of a sentence to be served in the community, the court can assess whether the defendant would benefit from a community-based treatment or training program and can require participation in such a program. Id. at 330, 131 S.Ct. at 2390.

8. The retributive theory of punishment is not new. The Bible verse importuning that "life *shall go* for life, eye for eye, tooth for tooth, hand for hand, foot for foot" is widely known. *Deuteronomy* 19:21 (King James) (emphasis in the original). Do you subscribe to the retributive theory? If so, how do we determine what punishment is "deserved" for a crime, and how can a consensus be reached on this question?

9.   The American Bar Association has called for the integration of what is known as the "least-restrictive-alternative principle" or "parsimony principle" into sentencing systems and decisions: "Sentences authorized and imposed, taking into account the gravity of the offenses, should be no more severe than necessary to achieve the societal purposes for which they are authorized." ABA Standards for Criminal Justice: Sentencing, Standard 18–2.4 (3d ed. 1994). The Model Penal Code also embraces the least-restrictive-alternative principle as a bedrock of sentencing. Model Penal Code: Sentencing § 1.02(2)(a)(iii) (American Law Inst. 2017) (sentences should be "no more severe than necessary" to achieve the delineated purposes). The least-restrictive-alternative principle has been described as both "utilitarian and humanitarian." Norval Morris, The Future of Imprisonment 61 (1974). Do you agree? If so, how can this general principle be given practical effect when drafting sentencing statutes and guidelines and making sentencing decisions?

C. A LOOK TOWARDS THE FUTURE

1.   AN EMERGING NEW PARADIGM: RESTORATIVE JUSTICE AND PRACTICES

Dissatisfaction with present criminal-justice systems that are premised on retributive and utilitarian theories, like deterrence and incapacitation, has spurred calls for a new criminal-justice model, one that is founded on the restorative justice to which Professor LaFave referred in his discussion of sentencing purposes. See pages 6–7. Restorative justice, which functions in response to crimes and other conduct causing harm, is part of what is known as "restorative practices." Restorative practices can also be used proactively to prevent conflict and the infliction of harm. The following portion of a local task force's report calling for the integration of restorative justice and restorative practices throughout a county's criminal-justice system provides a closer look at restorative justice and practices. As you read this overview, consider how restorative justice and practices could and should affect sentencing structures and decisions.

CHAMPAIGN COUNTY RACIAL JUSTICE TASK FORCE, REPORT AND RECOMMENDATIONS DEVELOPED TO REDUCE RACIAL DISPARITIES IN THE CHAMPAIGN COUNTY CRIMINAL-JUSTICE SYSTEM
October 2017.

Overview of Restorative Justice and Practices

The premise of restorative practices is that people are more cooperative, productive, happier, and more likely to change their behavior in positive ways when we work *with* them rather than doing things *to* or *for* them. The focus of restorative practices is on:

- building and strengthening community and relationships,
- restoring and repairing relationships when there is conflict or harm,
- averting and remedying harm caused by a person's actions, and
- holding people accountable in a meaningful way when their actions cause harm.

Three examples of restorative practices found in both the criminal-justice and juvenile-justice contexts include:

1.   *Restorative-Justice Conferences (RJCs).* Restorative-justice conferences "involve the community of people most affected by the offense—the harmed, the harmer, and the family, friends, and key supporters of both . . . . These affected parties are brought together by a trained facilitator to discuss how they and others have been harmed and how that harm might be repaired." Before the restorative-justice conference, the facilitator prepares the participants for it, ensuring that they know, for example, questions they will be asked during the RJC. The facilitated dialogue results in an agreement setting forth what the person responsible for the harm will do to repair the harm, restore relationships damaged by the offense, and otherwise "make things right." The agreement might include apologies, community service, restitution, skill building, educational or employment commitments, or other creative and personalized actions to meet obligations and needs discussed during the restorative dialogue. Participation by all involved in an RJC is voluntary.

2.   *Circles.* A variety of types of circles can be employed to prevent and respond to harmful actions and delinquency and for other purposes * * * [Two examples of circles described in the Task Force's report are set forth below.]

   a.   *Peacemaking Circles.* Peacemaking Circles are grounded in the shared values of those in the circle, such as respect for others and a recognition of our interconnectedness. Peacemaking Circles create a safe place for fostering an understanding of others, building and repairing relationships, solving problems, and resolving conflict and disputes. The circles' participants may include those who have been harmed, those who have harmed others, their support people, neighborhood or community representatives, and, at times, justice officials (such as police officers). The "keeper" of the circle, unlike the facilitator in a restorative-justice conference, is an equal participant in the circle discussions, though the keeper ensures that each participant can be heard. Unlike RJCs, which are in response to a specific harm/incident, Peacemaking Circles are convened for a variety of reasons. They can be utilized, for example, when an incident involving conflict or harm has deeper and wider roots and implications. Examples include ongoing related incidents between groups (e.g., gangs or families), such as retaliation, violence within a neighborhood or the whole community, and hate crimes.

b. *Circles of Support and Accountability (COSAs).* Circles of Support and Accountability can be used for people who are at high risk of committing a serious crime. While there are different ways of structuring COSAs, one classic model entails three to six trained volunteers meeting regularly, in a circle, with the "core member"—the person at risk of recidivating. COSAs have multiple goals, including (1) to ensure the core member understands that the circle members accept him or her as a person even though they reject the core member's past crime; (2) to develop strong, positive relationships with the core member, which is a protective factor against crime; (3) to alter cognitive distortions, such as a core member's attempt to diminish the seriousness of the crime; and (4) to help link the core member with resources, such as a job, that help avert repeat criminal behavior. In addition to COSAs, other kinds of circles, including Peacemaking Circles and "Welcome and Reentry Circles," can be used when a confined person is returning to his or her community.

* * *

3. *Family Group Decision Making (FGDM).* Family group decision making can be used for an array of reasons, such as to develop a reentry plan for an imprisoned person returning to the community, help an individual on probation lead a law-abiding life and be a productive citizen, or provide needed structure and support to a youth who is a chronic truant. During FGDM, family members and the person for whom a plan is being developed meet. The "family" is loosely defined, often including other people, such as a best friend or mentor, who are close to the person on whom the plan is focused. At the beginning of the meeting, service providers and other treatment professionals share information about support services and treatment available within the community. The professionals then leave the room, and the family members develop the plan. The plan typically outlines key responsibilities that the person for whom the plan is being developed and family members will assume under the plan.

Restorative practices give a voice to people affected by crime or delinquency who typically are shunted to the sidelines of the criminal-justice and juvenile-justice systems. A restorative-justice conference, for example, affords the victim of a crime the opportunity to ask the person who committed the act questions to which the victim wants or needs answers and to play a role in determining how the harm the act caused can be remedied. Researchers are confirming the positive outcomes that ensue when restorative practices are integrated into a criminal-justice system. For example, in both cases involving violent crimes as well as those involving nonviolent crimes, restorative-justice conferences are more effective than traditional, non-restorative court processing of cases in reducing recidivism. [Strang, H., Sherman, L., Mayo-Wilson, E., Woods, D., & Ariel, B. (2013). Restorative justice conferencing (RJC) using face-to-face meetings of offenders and victims: Effects on offender recidivism and victim satisfaction. A systematic review. *Campbell Systematic Reviews, 2013*(12), 1–63; Sherman, L., Strang, H., Mayo-Wilson, E., Woods, D., & Ariel, B. (2015). Are restorative justice conferences effective in reducing repeat offending? *Journal of Quantitative Criminology, 31*(1), 1–24.] Restorative-justice conferences are also more effective in producing victim satisfaction, decreasing victims' fear that they will be victimized again, and reducing post-traumatic stress symptoms. [Angel, C., Sherman L., Strang H., Ariel, B., Inkpen N., Keane, A., & Richmond, T. (2014). Short-term effects of restorative justice conferences on post-traumatic stress symptoms among robbery and burglary victims: A randomized controlled trial. *Journal of Experimental Criminology*, 10(3), 291–307.] Restorative-justice conferences also yield significant cost savings, in part through reduction in reoffending. * * *

* * *

QUESTIONS AND POINTS FOR DISCUSSION

1.   What is known as "victim-offender mediation" was the precursor to restorative-justice conferences. Victim-offender mediation has been criticized for not being "fully restorative," in part because it excludes a third stakeholder, one referred to as "communities of care." Ted Wachtel, Int'l Inst. for Restorative Just., Defining Restorative 2–4 (2016). Family members, friends, or others who can provide support to the victim and the person who harmed the victim typically comprise this community. Including several of these individuals in the restorative process, it is felt, not only helps to more fully illumine the harmful impact of a crime but can be helpful in identifying how that harm can be repaired.

2.   During a restorative-justice conference, the facilitator will ask the person who caused the harm such questions as:

- "What happened?"
- "What were you thinking of at the time?"
- "What have you thought about since?"
- "Who has been affected by what you have done?"
- "What do you think you need to do to make things right?"

Questions that may be posed to the person harmed include:

- "What did you think when you realized what happened?"
- "What impact has this incident had on you and others?"
- "What has been the hardest thing for you?"
- "What do you think needs to happen to make things right?"

As mentioned earlier, the answers to questions asked of other RJC participants further unveil a crime's harmful effects as well as possible reparative steps to be considered when the discussion turns to the subject of how to remedy that harm. For additional information about restorative-justice conferences, including a script from which the above questions were drawn that can be utilized by facilitators during the conferences, see Ted Wachtel et al., Restorative Justice Conferencing (2010).

3. The above Racial Justice Task Force report mentioned benefits to be reaped if restorative justice and practices were to permeate the criminal-justice system, from the front end to the back. Do you discern any other uncited benefits or potential benefits from this integration of restorative justice and practices into criminal-justice systems? What concerns, on the other hand, might restorative justice and practices raise? If the following program requirements promulgated by the American Bar Association for victim-offender mediation were extended to restorative-justice conferences, would they adequately address any of these concerns?

1. Participation in a program by both the offender and victim must be voluntary.

2. Program goals are specified in writing and procedures are established to meet those goals.

3. A plan exists for ongoing evaluation and review of goals and the steps taken to reach such goals.

4. Before participating in such programs, victims and offenders are appropriately screened on a case-by-case basis, are fully informed orally and in writing about the mediation-dialogue process, procedures and goals, and are specifically told that their participation in the process is voluntary.

5. Refusal to participate in a program in no way adversely affects an offender, and procedural safeguards are established to ensure that there are no systemic negative repercussions because of an offender's refusal to participate in the program.

6. A face-to-face meeting is encouraged.

7. When agreements are reached between victims and offenders, which may include restitution, a process is established to monitor and follow up on the agreements reached.

8. The statements made by victims and offenders and documents and other materials produced during the mediation/dialogue process are inadmissible in criminal or civil court proceedings.

9. Properly trained mediator-facilitators are used in the mediation/dialogue process.

10. The programs are adequately funded and staffed.

11. Mediator-facilitators are selected from a cross-section of the community to ensure that they reflect the diversity of their community in terms of race, ethnicity, and gender.

12. Criminal justice professionals and the public are educated about these programs, and these programs are fully integrated with other components of the criminal justice system.

13. Participation in a program that occurs prior to an adjudication of guilt takes place only with the consent of the prosecutor and with the victim's and offender's informed consent, obtained in writing, or orally in court. If the offender is represented by an attorney, the offender's consent should be given only after the offender has had the chance to discuss with the attorney the advisability of participating in the victim-offender mediation/dialogue program. Participation in a program that occurs after an adjudication of guilt takes place only after notification to the prosecutor and defense attorney, if any.

Am. Bar Ass'n, Victim-Offender Mediation/Dialogue Program Requirements, Appendix to Rep. 101B, Summary of Action of the House of Delegates, 1994 Annual Meeting.

4. Some states and communities have begun to integrate restorative justice into their criminal-justice systems. A Colorado statute, for example, has established a state-level Restorative Justice Coordinating Council to foster the importation of restorative practices into criminal-justice systems throughout the state. Colo. Rev. Stat. § 19–2–213. And in 2017, a "restorative justice community court" commenced operating in Chicago. See Amanda Svachula, First community court in Illinois to open next month in North Lawndale, Chi. Sun-Times, July 20, 2017.

Restorative practices can be incorporated into all levels of a criminal-justice system. For example, in some cases, police and prosecutors may refer individuals to a restorative-justice program in lieu of processing their cases through the criminal-justice system. In other cases, restorative-justice conferences can occur after a conviction but before sentencing, with their outcomes perhaps helping to inform the sentencing decision. And sometimes, such as when the person who caused the harm or the person who was harmed does not feel ready to participate in a restorative-justice conference, the conference will occur post-sentencing. Such post-sentencing restorative-justice conferences have been held, for example, in prisons.

5. Dr. Howard Zehr has outlined several key distinctions between restorative justice and currently prevailing views about criminal justice:

Criminal Justice

- Crime is a violation of the law and the state.

- Violations create guilt.

- Justice requires the state to determine blame (guilt) and impose pain (punishment).

- *Central focus: offenders getting what they deserve.*

Restorative Justice

- Crime is a violation of people and relationships.

- Violations create obligations.

- Justice involves victims, offenders, and community members in an effort to repair the harm, to "put things right."

- *Central focus: victim needs and offender responsibility for repairing harm.*

Howard Zehr, The Little Book of Restorative Justice 30 (2015). Reprinted by permission of Good Books, an imprint of Skyhorse Publishing, Inc.

Do you subscribe to the precepts of restorative justice? How do you believe the criminal-justice system would change if restorative justice became the centerpiece of the system?

2.   QUESTIONS FOR THE FUTURE

Set forth below are four questions bearing on the future of sentencing in the United States. These questions emanate from proposals of criminal-justice experts and others for changes in the status quo. As you contemplate these questions, consider what complexities they raise.

Question 1: Would you favor or oppose placing a limit on the per-capita imprisonment rate in a state?

A statute implementing such a cap might say, in effect: "The imprisonment rate for prisoners under this state's jurisdiction shall not exceed "x" number of prisoners per every 100,000 residents (or adults)." If a jurisdiction were to decide to adopt such a cap, it would also need to determine the level of the cap, how to come into compliance with it, the prescribed timetable for doing so, and other implementation details. For one criminologist's assessment of a viable per-capita rate towards which to aim (an approximately 50% drop in the national rate), steps that would lead to this reduction, and a feasible implementation timetable, see James Austin, Reducing America's Correctional Populations: A Strategic Plan, 12 Just. Res. & Pol'y 9, 26–37 (2010).

Question 2: Should drug offenses be decriminalized, and if not, what are the most appropriate sentences for drug crimes?

Many people confined in prison are there for drug-related crimes. See Bureau of Justice Statistics, U.S. Dep't of Justice, Prisoners in 2016, at 13, 18, 20 (2018) (15% of state prisoners and almost half of all federal prisoners were serving sentences for drug crimes in 2016). The Global Commission on Drug Policy has called for the decriminalization of the use of drugs and the development of sentences other than incarceration for "small-scale" and "first-time" drug dealers. War on Drugs: Report of the Global Commission on Drug Policy (2011). (The members of this nineteen-member Commission included Kofi Annan, a former Secretary General of the United Nations; George Shultz, who served as Secretary of State of the United States; and Paul Volcker, who once chaired the Federal Reserve Board.) What arguments would you advance in support of, and in opposition to, the Commission's recommendations?

Question 3: Should the length of prison sentences be reduced, and if so, by how much?

In 2006, people in the United States were sentenced to state prison for an average of four years and eleven months. Bureau of Justice Statistics, U.S. Dep't of Justice, Felony Sentences in State Courts, 2006–Statistical Tables 6 (2010). Prison sentences in the United States are for much longer periods of time than in a number of other countries in the Western world. See Justice Policy Inst., Finding Direction: Expanding Criminal Justice Options by Considering Policies of Other Nations 22 (2011) (reporting higher average sentences in the United States than in comparison countries for similar crimes). Germany, for example, offers a stark contrast to the United States. Most prison sentences in Germany (75%) are under a year, and fully 93% are under two years. Jörg-Martin Jehle, Fed. Ministry of Justice & Consumer Prot., Criminal Justice in Germany 35–36 (2015). It also bears noting that a majority of these prison sentences that are two years or less in length are suspended, with the defendant then placed on probation. Id.

Question 4: What steps can and should be taken, and by whom, to reduce racial and ethnic disparity in the persons subject to correctional supervision?

One of the distinguishing features of sentencing and correctional systems in the United States is the disproportionate involvement of racial and ethnic minorities in them. The imprisonment rate is emblematic of that disparity. In 2016, the imprisonment rate was 274 per every 100,000 white adults, 856 per every 100,000 Hispanic adults, and 1,608 per every 100,000 African-American adults, the latter rate over five and a half times higher than the rate for white adults. Bureau of Justice, U.S. Dep't of Justice, Prisoners in 2016, at 10 (2018). Evidence of this disparity persists when other forms of correctional supervision are added to the mix. In 2007, one of every eleven African-American adult males and one of every twenty-seven Hispanic adult males was in prison or jail or on probation or parole compared to one of every forty-five white adult males. The Pew Ctr. on the States, One in 31: The Long Reach of Corrections 5, 7 (2009).

Researchers have identified multiple factors contributing to this disparity. Three examples include:

- *Pretrial detention when people with low or no incomes are unable to post bail or meet other financial conditions for pretrial release.* Research has revealed that people detained in jail pretrial due to a lack of funds to pay for their release are more likely to later be sentenced to prison or jail and to receive longer prison or jail sentences than similar individuals released pretrial. See, e.g., Christopher T. Lowenkamp et al., Investigating the Impact of Pretrial Detention on Sentencing Outcomes 10–19 (2013). A disproportionate number of African Americans and people who are Hispanic live below the poverty level. Jessica L. Semega et al., U.S. Census Bureau, Income and Poverty in the United States: 2016, at 12–13 (2017).

- *Prosecutorial charging decisions.* One study found, for example, that prosecutors in federal cases were twice as likely to charge African Americans with a crime carrying a mandatory-minimum sentence than white people who had been arrested for the same crime and had comparable criminal histories. Sonja B. Starr & M. Marit Rehavi, Racial Disparity in Federal Criminal Charging and Its Sentencing Consequences (Univ. of Mich. Program in Law & Econ., Working Paper No. 12–002, 2012).

- *Offense differences.* Researchers have cited differences in the types of crimes committed as a factor contributing to racial disparity in imprisonment. Distilling this research, Dr. Marie Gottschalk observed that African Americans "disproportionately commit the types of crimes that usually draw a long prison sentence." Marie Gottschalk, Caught: The Prison State and the Lockdown of American Politics 125–26 (2015) (pointing to studies on the commission of homicides, robberies, and several other "serious crimes"). In 2006, 51% of the people convicted of murder or non-negligent manslaughter and 57% of those convicted of robbery were, for example, African Americans. Bureau of Justice Statistics, U.S. Dep't of Justice, Felony Sentences in State Courts,

2006—Statistical Tables 17 (2010). In that year, African Americans constituted 12% of the adult population. Id. at 15.

What other factors might account for the racial and ethnic disparity in imprisonment and other sentences being served? For examples of other factors or potential factors contributing to this disparity, see Richard Frase, What Explains Persistent Racial Disproportionality in Minnesota's Prison and Jail Populations?, 38 Crime & Just. 201 (2009). For several articles spotlighting research that could lead to a better understanding of certain complexities about these causal factors, see Eric P. Baumer, Reassessing and Redirecting Research on Race and Sentencing, 30 Just. Q. 231 (2013) and Richard S. Frase, Research on Race and Sentencing: Goals, Methods, and Topics (2013).

————

In the succeeding chapters of this book, you will learn about sentencing policies in this country, the sentencing process, and the rights of people during and after sentencing. As you read these materials, consider what changes need to be made in sentencing and other governmental policies and procedures to ensure that sentences and other responses to the commission of a crime are effective, humane, nondiscriminatory, affordable, and sensitive to the needs of those harmed by a crime.

CHAPTER 2

GUILTY PLEAS AND PLEA BARGAINING

■ ■ ■

An individual charged with a crime can enter one of several different pleas to the charge. The individual can plead guilty or not guilty. In some jurisdictions, a third alternative exists: a plea of *nolo contendere,* which means "no contest." See, e.g., Fed.R.Crim.P. 11(a)(1) (defendant can, with the court's consent, enter a plea of *nolo contendere*). With one exception, such a plea generally has the same consequences as entering a plea of guilty. The person who pleads "no contest" can be sentenced as if he or she had pled guilty to the crime, even to a period of incarceration. The principal distinction between a plea of *nolo contendere* and a guilty plea is that evidence of the former type of plea is inadmissible in civil lawsuits, such as those brought by victims of the crime in question.

The vast majority of criminal convictions are obtained through guilty pleas. In 2006, for example, 94% of the individuals convicted of felonies in the state courts pled guilty. Bureau of Justice Statistics, U.S. Dep't of Justice, Felony Sentences in State Courts, 2006—Statistical Tables 24–25 (2009). This statistic underscores the central role that guilty pleas presently play in the operation of the criminal-justice system.

There are two main types of guilty pleas—what are called "blind" pleas and negotiated pleas. A blind plea is a plea that is uninduced by any commitment made by a prosecutor or judge. The defendant simply acknowledges his or her guilt and awaits the imposition of a sentence by the court. By contrast, when a defendant enters a negotiated plea, the defendant has been promised a benefit in return for the guilty plea. That benefit may come in many forms. The defendant, for example, may be permitted to plead guilty to a crime that is less serious than the crime with which he or she was originally charged. Even if the defendant does not plead guilty to a reduced charge, other criminal charges may be dismissed or not filed in return for the plea of guilty. Or the defendant may plead guilty upon the condition that the prosecutor recommends, or the court imposes, a particular sentence.

The practice of plea bargaining has been sharply attacked. Chief among the criticisms of plea bargaining include: (1) that favorable plea offers induce innocent defendants to plead guilty; (2) that because of plea agreements, the unconstitutional actions of law-enforcement officials are often concealed; (3) that plea bargaining results in more favorable dispositions for defendants who forgo their constitutional right to trial, in effect punishing other defendants who invoke this constitutional right; (4) that plea bargaining results in dispositions that compromise public safety and fail to meet the objectives of criminal sentences; and (5) that behind-the-scenes negotiations invite abuse by the participants in the negotiation process, who labor under conflicts of interest. The latter criticism is prompted in part by the fact that in order to maintain a high conviction rate, some prosecutors are more willing to enter into a plea agreement when their case against a defendant is weak, thereby enhancing the risk of an innocent person being convicted. Albert W. Alschuler, The Prosecutor's Role in Plea Bargaining, 36 U. Chi. L.Rev. 50, 58–60 (1968). Public defenders, who are often overburdened with very heavy caseloads, also have a strong incentive to resolve cases through plea bargaining rather than trials. Stephanos Bibas, Plea Bargaining Outside the Shadow of Trial, 117 Harv. L.Rev. 2463, 2479 (2004). In addition, some private defense attorneys maximize their profits on a case by simply "copping a plea" and then collecting their fee, without fully exploring whether entry of a guilty plea and the terms of a plea agreement are in their client's best interests. See, e.g., Albert W. Alschuler, *Lafler* and *Frye*: Two Small Band-Aids for a Festering Wound, 51 Duq. L.Rev. 673, 682 (2013).

Plea bargaining, however, has many defenders. Many of these plea-bargaining proponents candidly acknowledge the abuses that can attend plea bargaining. Yet they contend that these abuses can be limited and that the retention of plea bargaining is good for, and in fact essential to, the effective operation of the criminal-justice system.

Some of the primary argued benefits of plea bargaining include the following: (1) that without plea bargaining, the criminal-justice system would simply break down, particularly in the urban areas of this country, since the system lacks the resources to provide trials for many more criminal defendants; (2) that plea bargains can relieve victims, other witnesses, defendants, and the families of victims and defendants from the uncertainty and financial and psychological burdens that attend litigation; (3) that plea bargains reduce the costs to taxpayers of prosecuting criminal cases; (4) that plea bargains can forestall the imposition of unduly harsh sentences, particularly under mandatory-minimum sentencing laws; (5) that plea bargaining can facilitate law enforcement, since in exchange for leniency, defendants can be persuaded to provide officials with information needed to apprehend and convict other criminals; and (6) that because of plea bargains, the amount of time that defendants who cannot post bail must spend in jail while awaiting trial can be reduced, to the benefit not only of them and their families, but also the public that must pay for the costs of their confinement.

The defenders of plea bargaining also charge its opponents with exaggerating its drawbacks, including the risk it purportedly creates of convicting innocent persons. Some of these plea-bargaining proponents argue that the abolition of plea bargaining would decrease the time available for trials and trial preparation, leading to truncated trials that actually enhance the risk of innocent persons being convicted. See Robert E. Scott & William J. Stuntz, Plea Bargaining as Contract, 101 Yale L.J. 1909, 1950 (1992). Others argue that plea bargaining is at least as effective, and possibly more effective, than trials in differentiating innocent and guilty people, in part because prosecutors are more adept than jurors in assessing the probative value of evidence, particularly eyewitness testimony. See Frank H. Easterbrook, Plea Bargaining as Compromise, 101 Yale L.J. 1969, 1970–72 (1992).

Many of the cases and materials set forth below focus on the extent to which the Constitution places constraints on plea bargaining. However, even though the Constitution may permit plea bargaining and some plea-bargaining practices that have been contested by defendants, fundamental policy questions about plea bargaining, as well as the process for entering guilty pleas, remain. While some of these policy questions are interspersed throughout the chapter, you will be asked to address several of them at the end of the chapter: whether plea bargaining should be abolished and if not, the extent to which and ways in which it should be controlled. As you read about the constitutional constraints that apply to guilty pleas and plea negotiations, you are encouraged to keep these questions in mind.

A. THE DUE PROCESS REQUIREMENT OF AN INTELLIGENT AND VOLUNTARY PLEA

1. "INTELLIGENT" GUILTY PLEAS AND CLAIMS RELINQUISHED THROUGH THE ENTRY OF GUILTY PLEAS

BOYKIN V. ALABAMA
Supreme Court of the United States, 1969.
395 U.S. 238, 89 S.Ct. 1709, 23 L.Ed.2d 274.

MR. JUSTICE DOUGLAS delivered the opinion of the Court.

[In 1966, the petitioner was charged with, and pled guilty to, committing five armed robberies. At the time, these crimes were punishable by death. The record did not reflect that the judge asked the petitioner any questions when he entered his guilty pleas, nor did the petitioner apparently address the court when his pleas were entered.

The petitioner was sentenced to death for each of the robberies to which he had pled guilty. On appeal, the Alabama Supreme Court affirmed, and the United States Supreme Court then granted certiorari.]

It was error, plain on the face of the record, for the trial judge to accept petitioner's guilty plea without an affirmative showing that it was intelligent and voluntary. * * *

* * * The requirement that the prosecution spread on the record the prerequisites of a valid waiver is no constitutional innovation. In *Carnley v. Cochran,* 369 U.S. 506, 516, we dealt with a problem of waiver of the right to counsel, a Sixth Amendment right. We held: "Presuming waiver from a silent record is impermissible. The record must show, or there must be an allegation and evidence which show, that an accused was offered counsel but intelligently and understandingly rejected the offer. Anything less is not waiver."

We think that the same standard must be applied to determining whether a guilty plea is voluntarily made. For, as we have said, a plea of guilty is more than an admission of conduct; it is a conviction.[4] * * *

Several federal constitutional rights are involved in a waiver that takes place when a plea of guilty is entered in a state criminal trial. First, is the privilege against compulsory self-incrimination guaranteed by the Fifth Amendment and applicable to the States by reason of the Fourteenth. Second, is the right to trial by jury. Third, is the right to confront one's accusers. We cannot presume a waiver of these three important federal rights from a silent record.

What is at stake for an accused facing death or imprisonment demands the utmost solicitude of which courts are capable in canvassing the matter with the accused to make sure he has a full understanding of what the plea connotes and of its consequence. When the judge discharges that function, he leaves a record adequate for any review that may be later sought and forestalls the spin-off of collateral proceedings that seek to probe murky memories.[7]

* * *

MR. JUSTICE HARLAN, whom MR. JUSTICE BLACK joins, dissenting. [Opinion omitted.]

QUESTIONS AND POINTS FOR DISCUSSION

1. The Supreme Court distinguished *Boykin v. Alabama* in Parke v. Raley, 506 U.S. 20, 113 S.Ct. 517 (1992). In *Parke,* the petitioner in a federal

---

[4] "A plea of guilty is more than a voluntary confession made in open court. It also serves as a stipulation that no proof by the prosecution need be advanced. . . . It supplies both evidence and verdict, ending controversy." *Woodard v. State,* 171 So.2d 462, 469.

[7] "A majority of criminal convictions are obtained after a plea of guilty. If these convictions are to be insulated from attack, the trial court is best advised to conduct an on the record examination of the defendant which should include, inter alia, an attempt to satisfy itself that the defendant understands the nature of the charges, his right to a jury trial, the acts sufficient to constitute the offenses for which he is charged and the permissible range of sentences." *Commonwealth ex rel. West v. Rundle,* 237 A.2d 196, 197–198 (1968).

habeas corpus action had been sentenced as a "persistent felony offender" under a Kentucky statute because he had two previous convictions for burglary in addition to his current conviction for robbery. He contended that his two previous burglary convictions, obtained through guilty pleas, were invalid under *Boykin* since there were no transcripts of the plea proceedings that confirmed that the guilty pleas were knowing and voluntary. Under the law in Kentucky, however, a presumption existed that prior convictions were valid, and the person challenging them had the burden of producing evidence that rebutted this presumption. Only after producing some evidence that a right was infringed during a prior proceeding culminating in a conviction did the burden shift to the government to prove by a preponderance of the evidence that the conviction was obtained in conformance with the law.

One of the questions before the Supreme Court was whether the presumption that a prior conviction was valid violated due process. In the course of holding that this presumption of regularity was constitutional, the Court distinguished *Boykin*. In *Boykin,* the Court noted, the defendant was challenging his conviction on appeal, while in this case, the petitioner was challenging his prior convictions in a collateral proceeding. (A collateral proceeding is one that follows the exhaustion or relinquishment of the right to appeal a conviction.) The Court held that in such a collateral proceeding, it is constitutional to apply a presumption of regularity, at least to the extent that the burden of production on the issue of a prior conviction's validity is placed on the person convicted. The Supreme Court furthermore held that it was constitutional for Kentucky to allow the government to prove the validity of a prior conviction by only a preponderance of the evidence. The Court did not resolve, because it did not need to, the question whether it would be constitutional to place the entire burden of proof in a collateral proceeding on the person contesting the validity of a prior conviction.

2. The Supreme Court has elaborated on the constitutional requirements for a valid guilty plea, holding that a defendant must be apprised of the elements of the crime to which the defendant is pleading guilty. Bradshaw v. Stumpf, 545 U.S. 175, 183, 125 S.Ct. 2398, 2405 (2005). See also Henderson v. Morgan, 426 U.S. 637, 96 S.Ct. 2253 (1976) (guilty plea to second-degree murder vacated because defendant was not aware that intent to kill was an element of the crime). Providing the defendant with a copy of the indictment creates a presumption, though a rebuttable one, that the defendant has received the requisite notice. Bousley v. United States, 523 U.S. 614, 618, 118 S.Ct. 1604, 1609 (1998). But according to the Supreme Court, a judge need not explain the elements of the crime to the defendant on the record. The requirements of due process are met as long as the record reflects that the defendant's attorney informed the defendant of the nature of the charge and the elements of the crime to which the defendant is pleading guilty. In addition, the record generally does not have to include the details of the information relayed by defense counsel to the defendant. In *Bradshaw*, the Supreme Court stated that "[w]here a defendant is represented by competent counsel, the court usually may rely on that counsel's assurance that the defendant has been

properly informed of the nature and elements of the charge to which he is pleading guilty." Id. at 183, 125 S.Ct. at 2406.

Do you agree that defense counsel's statement on the record that she has apprised her client of the nature of the charge and the elements of the crime generally satisfies due process? See Julian A. Cook, III, Crumbs from the Master's Table: The Supreme Court, Pro Se Defendants and the Federal Guilty Plea Process, 81 Notre Dame L.Rev. 1895, 1910 (2006) (criticizing *Bradshaw* for allowing "blanket and largely unsubstantiated assertions of extra-judicial explanations" of the nature and elements of the crime).

3.   Ismael Ramirez was a permanent legal resident from Mexico living in the United States. He had married a woman who was a United States citizen, and their four children, three-year-old twins and two siblings, ages five and six, were also U.S. citizens. Under a plea agreement, Ramirez pled guilty to the crime of possessing a controlled substance with intent to deliver. He received a suspended prison sentence of ten years and was placed on probation. Only after he entered his plea and was sentenced did Ramirez discover that his conviction would result in his mandatory deportation from the United States. Should the court's failure to ensure that Ramirez was aware of the deportation consequences of entering his plea invalidate the guilty plea? Why or why not?

In State v. Ramirez, 636 N.W.2d 740, 743 (Iowa 2001), the Iowa Supreme Court held that due process does not require a court to apprise a defendant that a guilty plea will result in his mandatory deportation. A majority of the courts concur with this view. See People v. Guzman, 43 N.E.3d 954, 960 (Ill. 2015) (listing cases). Consider this question anew after reading the Supreme Court's decision in Padilla v. Kentucky, 559 U.S. 356, 130 S.Ct. 1473 (2010) on page 57. *Padilla* involved, not the steps that a court must take to comply with the requirements of due process, but the scope of a different right—a defendant's Sixth Amendment right to the effective assistance of counsel when deciding whether to plead guilty to a crime.

4.   Apart from the constitutional requirements that must be met in order for a guilty plea to be valid are the requirements which must be met under federal and state statutes and court rules. Rule 11 of the Federal Rules of Criminal Procedure, which governs the rendering and acceptance of guilty pleas in federal courts, is an example of one such court rule. That rule, which is set forth below, requires that before accepting a guilty or *nolo contendere* plea, a court apprise a defendant who is not a citizen of the United States that a criminal conviction may result in removal from the United States, denial of citizenship, or denied admission into the United States should the defendant later leave the country.

Rule 11. Pleas

    (a) Entering a Plea.

        (1) In General. A defendant may plead not guilty, guilty, or (with the court's consent) nolo contendere.

(2) Conditional Plea. With the consent of the court and the government, a defendant may enter a conditional plea of guilty or nolo contendere, reserving in writing the right to have an appellate court review an adverse determination of a specified pretrial motion. A defendant who prevails on appeal may then withdraw the plea.

(3) Nolo Contendere Plea. Before accepting a plea of nolo contendere, the court must consider the parties' views and the public interest in the effective administration of justice.

(4) Failure to Enter a Plea. If a defendant refuses to enter a plea or if a defendant organization fails to appear, the court must enter a plea of not guilty.

(b) Considering and Accepting a Guilty or Nolo Contendere Plea.

(1) Advising and Questioning the Defendant. Before the court accepts a plea of guilty or nolo contendere, the defendant may be placed under oath, and the court must address the defendant personally in open court. During this address, the court must inform the defendant of, and determine that the defendant understands, the following:

(A) the government's right, in a prosecution for perjury or false statement, to use against the defendant any statement that the defendant gives under oath;

(B) the right to plead not guilty, or having already so pleaded, to persist in that plea;

(C) the right to a jury trial;

(D) the right to be represented by counsel—and if necessary have the court appoint counsel—at trial and at every other stage of the proceeding;

(E) the right at trial to confront and cross-examine adverse witnesses, to be protected from compelled self-incrimination, to testify and present evidence, and to compel the attendance of witnesses;

(F) the defendant's waiver of these trial rights if the court accepts a plea of guilty or nolo contendere;

(G) the nature of each charge to which the defendant is pleading;

(H) any maximum possible penalty, including imprisonment, fine, and term of supervised release;

(I) any mandatory minimum penalty;

(J) any applicable forfeiture;

(K) the court's authority to order restitution;

(L) the court's obligation to impose a special assessment;

(M) in determining a sentence, the court's obligation to calculate the applicable sentencing-guideline range and to consider that range, possible departures under the Sentencing Guidelines, and other sentencing factors under 18 U.S.C. § 3553(a);

(N) the terms of any plea-agreement provision waiving the right to appeal or to collaterally attack the sentence; and

(O) that, if convicted, a defendant who is not a United States citizen may be removed from the United States, denied citizenship, and denied admission to the United States in the future.

(2) Ensuring That a Plea Is Voluntary. Before accepting a plea of guilty or nolo contendere, the court must address the defendant personally in open court and determine that the plea is voluntary and did not result from force, threats, or promises (other than promises in a plea agreement).

(3) Determining the Factual Basis for a Plea. Before entering judgment on a guilty plea, the court must determine that there is a factual basis for the plea.

(c) Plea Agreement Procedure.

(1) In General. An attorney for the government and the defendant's attorney, or the defendant when proceeding pro se, may discuss and reach a plea agreement. The court must not participate in these discussions. If the defendant pleads guilty or nolo contendere to either a charged offense or a lesser or related offense, the plea agreement may specify that an attorney for the government will:

(A) not bring, or will move to dismiss, other charges;

(B) recommend, or agree not to oppose the defendant's request, that a particular sentence or sentencing range is appropriate or that a particular provision of the Sentencing Guidelines, or policy statement, or sentencing factor does or does not apply (such a recommendation or request does not bind the court); or

(C) agree that a specific sentence or sentencing range is the appropriate disposition of the case, or that a particular provision of the Sentencing Guidelines, or policy statement, or sentencing factor does or does not apply (such a recommendation or request binds the court once the court accepts the plea agreement).

(2) Disclosing a Plea Agreement. The parties must disclose the plea agreement in open court when the plea is offered, unless the court for good cause allows the parties to disclose the plea agreement in camera.

(3) Judicial Consideration of a Plea Agreement.

(A) To the extent the plea agreement is of the type specified in Rule 11(c)(1)(A) or (C), the court may accept the agreement, reject it, or defer a decision until the court has reviewed the presentence report.

(B) To the extent the plea agreement is of the type specified in Rule 11(c)(1)(B), the court must advise the defendant that the defendant has no right to withdraw the plea if the court does not follow the recommendation or request.

(4) Accepting a Plea Agreement. If the court accepts the plea agreement, it must inform the defendant that to the extent the plea agreement is of the type specified in Rule 11(c)(1)(A) or (C), the agreed disposition will be included in the judgment.

(5) Rejecting a Plea Agreement. If the court rejects a plea agreement containing provisions of the type specified in Rule 11(c)(1)(A) or (C), the court must do the following on the record and in open court (or, for good cause, in camera):

(A) inform the parties that the court rejects the plea agreement;

(B) advise the defendant personally that the court is not required to follow the plea agreement and give the defendant an opportunity to withdraw the plea; and

(C) advise the defendant personally that if the plea is not withdrawn, the court may dispose of the case less favorably toward the defendant than the plea agreement contemplated.

(d) Withdrawing a Guilty or Nolo Contendere Plea. A defendant may withdraw a plea of guilty or nolo contendere:

(1) before the court accepts the plea, for any reason or no reason; or

(2) after the court accepts the plea, but before it imposes sentence if:

(A) the court rejects a plea agreement under Rule 11(c)(5); or

(B) the defendant can show a fair and just reason for requesting the withdrawal.

(e) Finality of a Guilty or Nolo Contendere Plea. After the court imposes sentence, the defendant may not withdraw a plea of guilty or nolo contendere, and the plea may be set aside only on direct appeal or collateral attack.

(f) Admissibility or Inadmissibility of a Plea, Plea Discussions, and Related Statements. The admissibility or inadmissibility of a plea, a plea discussion, and any related statement is governed by Federal Rule of Evidence 410.

(g) Recording the Proceedings. The proceedings during which the defendant enters a plea must be recorded by a court reporter or by a suitable recording device. If there is a guilty plea or a nolo contendere plea, the record must include the inquiries and advice to the defendant required under Rule 11(b) and (c).

(h) Harmless Error. A variance from the requirements of this rule is harmless error if it does not affect substantial rights.

Of the requirements that must be met in order for a guilty plea to be valid under Rule 11, which do you believe are also required by the Constitution? How, if at all, should Rule 11 be modified? Contrast some of the consequences of a conviction of which a defendant pleading guilty or *nolo contendere* must be informed under Rule 11(b)(1) with the information that Standard 14–1.4(c) of the ABA Standards for Criminal Justice: Pleas of Guilty (3d ed. 1999) prescribes be relayed:

Standard 14–1.4. Defendant to be advised

(c) Before accepting a plea of guilty or nolo contendere, the court should also advise the defendant that by entering the plea, the defendant may face additional consequences including but not limited to the forfeiture of property, the loss of certain civil rights, disqualification from certain governmental benefits, enhanced punishment if the defendant is convicted of another crime in the future, and, if the defendant is not a United States citizen, a change in the defendant's immigration status. The court should advise the defendant to consult with defense counsel if the defendant needs additional information concerning the potential consequences of the plea.

BRADY v. UNITED STATES

Supreme Court of the United States, 1970.
397 U.S. 742, 90 S.Ct. 1463, 25 L.Ed.2d 747.

MR. JUSTICE WHITE delivered the opinion of the Court.

In 1959, petitioner was charged with kidnaping in violation of 18 U.S.C. § 1201(a).[1] Since the indictment charged that the victim of the kidnaping was not liberated unharmed, petitioner faced a maximum penalty of death if the verdict of the jury should so recommend. Petitioner,

---

[1] "Whoever knowingly transports in interstate or foreign commerce, any person who has been unlawfully seized, confined, inveigled, decoyed, kidnapped, abducted, or carried away and held for ransom or reward or otherwise, except, in the case of a minor, by a parent thereof, shall be punished (1) by death if the kidnapped person has not been liberated unharmed, and if the verdict of the jury shall so recommend, or (2) by imprisonment for any term of years or for life, if the death penalty is not imposed."

represented by competent counsel throughout, first elected to plead not guilty. * * * Upon learning that his codefendant, who had confessed to the authorities, would plead guilty and be available to testify against him, petitioner changed his plea to guilty. * * * [He was sentenced to prison for fifty years, though this sentence was later reduced to thirty years. The petitioner claimed that his guilty plea was neither intelligently rendered nor voluntary, as required by due process. The Supreme Court's analysis of his first claim follows. Excerpts from the Court's opinion analyzing the voluntariness of the petitioner's guilty plea can be found on page 46.]

* * *

In *United States v. Jackson*[, 390 U.S. 570 (1968)], the defendants were indicted under § 1201(a). The District Court dismissed the § 1201(a) count of the indictment, holding the statute unconstitutional because it permitted imposition of the death sentence only upon a jury's recommendation and thereby made the risk of death the price of a jury trial. This Court held the statute valid, except for the death penalty provision; with respect to the latter, the Court agreed with the trial court "that the death penalty provision . . . imposes an impermissible burden upon the exercise of a constitutional right. . . ." * * *

* * *

The record before us * * * supports the conclusion that Brady's plea was intelligently made. He was advised by competent counsel, he was made aware of the nature of the charge against him, and there was nothing to indicate that he was incompetent or otherwise not in control of his mental faculties; once his confederate had pleaded guilty and became available to testify, he chose to plead guilty, perhaps to ensure that he would face no more than life imprisonment or a term of years. * * *

It is true that Brady's counsel advised him that § 1201(a) empowered the jury to impose the death penalty and that nine years later in *United States v. Jackson,* the Court held that the jury had no such power as long as the judge could impose only a lesser penalty if trial was to the court or there was a plea of guilty. But these facts do not require us to set aside Brady's conviction.

Often the decision to plead guilty is heavily influenced by the defendant's appraisal of the prosecution's case against him and by the apparent likelihood of securing leniency should a guilty plea be offered and accepted. Considerations like these frequently present imponderable questions for which there are no certain answers; judgments may be made that in the light of later events seem improvident, although they were perfectly sensible at the time. The rule that a plea must be intelligently made to be valid does not require that a plea be vulnerable to later attack if the defendant did not correctly assess every relevant factor entering into his decision. * * * More particularly, absent misrepresentation or other impermissible conduct by state agents, a voluntary plea of guilty intelligently made in the light of the then applicable law does not become vulnerable because later judicial decisions indicate that the plea rested on a faulty premise. A plea of guilty triggered by the expectations of a competently counseled defendant that the State will have a strong case against him is not subject to later attack because the defendant's lawyer correctly advised him with respect to the then existing law as to possible penalties but later pronouncements of the courts, as in this case, hold that the maximum penalty for the crime in question was less than was reasonably assumed at the time the plea was entered.

The fact that Brady did not anticipate *United States v. Jackson* does not impugn the truth or reliability of his plea. We find no requirement in the Constitution that a defendant must be permitted to disown his solemn admissions in open court that he committed the act with which he is charged simply because it later develops that the State would have had a weaker case than the defendant had thought or that the maximum penalty then assumed applicable has been held inapplicable in subsequent judicial decisions.

This is not to say that guilty plea convictions hold no hazards for the innocent * * *. This mode of conviction is no more foolproof than full trials to the court or to the jury. * * * We would have serious doubts about this case if the encouragement of guilty pleas by offers of leniency substantially increased the likelihood that defendants, advised by competent counsel, would falsely condemn themselves. But our view is to the contrary and is based on our expectations that courts will satisfy themselves that pleas of guilty are voluntarily and intelligently made by competent defendants with adequate advice of counsel and that there is nothing to question the accuracy and reliability of the defendants' admissions that they committed the crimes with which they are charged. * * *

* * *

QUESTIONS AND POINTS FOR DISCUSSION

1. In McMann v. Richardson, 397 U.S. 759, 90 S.Ct. 1441 (1970), several defendants claimed that the constitutional requirement that their guilty pleas be "intelligent" was not satisfied because their attorneys had failed to recognize that their confessions were involuntary and could not have been introduced in evidence had they gone to trial. The Supreme Court rejected this argument for the reasons set forth below:

> That a guilty plea must be intelligently made is not a requirement that all advice offered by the defendant's lawyer withstand retrospective examination in a post-conviction hearing. Courts continue to have serious differences among themselves on the

admissibility of evidence, both with respect to the proper standard by which the facts are to be judged and with respect to the application of that standard to particular facts. That this Court might hold a defendant's confession inadmissible in evidence, possibly by a divided vote, hardly justifies a conclusion that the defendant's attorney was incompetent or ineffective when he thought the admissibility of the confession sufficiently probable to advise a plea of guilty.

In our view a defendant's plea of guilty based on reasonably competent advice is an intelligent plea not open to attack on the ground that counsel may have misjudged the admissibility of the defendant's confession. Whether a plea of guilty is unintelligent and therefore vulnerable when motivated by a confession erroneously thought admissible in evidence depends as an initial matter, not on whether a court would retrospectively consider counsel's advice to be right or wrong, but on whether that advice was within the range of competence demanded of attorneys in criminal cases.

Id. at 770–71, 90 S.Ct. at 1448–49.

Tracking *McMann*, the Supreme Court in Tollett v. Henderson, 411 U.S. 258, 93 S.Ct. 1602 (1973) rejected the defendant's claim that his lack of knowledge of an earlier violation of his constitutional rights—the exclusion of African Americans from the grand jury that had indicted him—automatically invalidated his guilty plea. The Court explained: "When a criminal defendant has solemnly admitted in open court that he is in fact guilty of the offense with which he is charged, he may not thereafter raise independent claims relating to the deprivation of constitutional rights that occurred prior to the entry of the guilty plea." Id. at 267, 93 S.Ct. at 1608. The Court indicated that only if counsel's failure to apprise the defendant of the unconstitutional grand-jury selection methods itself rose to the level of a constitutional violation would the defendant's guilty plea be invalid.

2. The Supreme Court distinguished its decision in *Tollett* in the succeeding case of Menna v. New York, 423 U.S. 61, 96 S.Ct. 241 (1975) (per curiam). In that case, the defendant was held in criminal contempt of court and sentenced to thirty days in jail after he refused to answer questions posed by a grand jury. He also was indicted for his refusal to cooperate with the grand jury. After unsuccessfully moving to dismiss the indictment on double-jeopardy grounds, the defendant pled guilty to the indictment, but then appealed, claiming his conviction was barred by the Fifth Amendment's Double Jeopardy Clause. The state responded that the defendant had waived this claim by pleading guilty.

The Supreme Court sided with the defendant, holding that "[w]here the State is precluded by the United States Constitution from haling a defendant into court on a charge, federal law requires that a conviction on that charge be set aside even if the conviction was entered pursuant to a counseled plea of guilty." Id. at 62, 96 S.Ct. at 242. In a footnote, the Court explained the distinction between the case before it and *Tollett*:

Neither *Tollett v. Henderson* nor our earlier cases on which it relied, e.g., *Brady v. United States* and *McMann v. Richardson,* stand for the proposition that counseled guilty pleas inevitably "waive" all antecedent constitutional violations. * * * The point of these cases is that a counseled plea of guilty is an admission of factual guilt so reliable that, where voluntary and intelligent, it *quite validly* removes the issue of factual guilt from the case. In most cases, factual guilt is a sufficient basis for the State's imposition of punishment. A guilty plea, therefore, simply renders irrelevant those constitutional violations not logically inconsistent with the valid establishment of factual guilt and which do not stand in the way of conviction, if factual guilt is validly established. Here, however, the claim is that the State may not convict petitioner no matter how validly his factual guilt is established. The guilty plea, therefore, does not bar the claim.

We do not hold that a double jeopardy claim may never be waived. We simply hold that a plea of guilty to a charge does not waive a claim that—judged on its face—the charge is one which the State may not constitutionally prosecute.

Id. at 62–63 n.2, 96 S.Ct. at 242 n.2.

In United States v. Broce, 488 U.S. 563, 109 S.Ct. 757 (1989), the Supreme Court confirmed that not all double-jeopardy claims can be asserted by a defendant following entry of a guilty plea. The defendants in that case had pled guilty to two counts of conspiracy. They later sought to vacate their sentence on one of the two counts on the grounds that they had really participated in only one overarching conspiracy and that to punish them for two contravened the Double Jeopardy Clause.

The Supreme Court responded by invoking the general rule that attacks on guilty pleas due to non-plea-related violations of constitutional rights that preceded their entry are barred. The exception to that rule discussed in *Menna v. New York* was inapplicable here, according to the Court, because that exception was limited to those instances where "on the face of the record the court had no power to enter the conviction or impose the sentence." Id. at 569, 109 S.Ct. at 762. Since a reviewing court would have to go beyond the record to determine whether the defendants had been involved in one or two conspiracies and since they did not allege they had received ineffective assistance of counsel, their guilty pleas to, and sentences for, two separate conspiracies would remain in effect.

3.   Assume that a defendant was indicted under a federal statute that bars individuals from possessing firearms on the grounds of the United States Capitol in Washington, D.C. The defendant's firearms were in a locked jeep in a parking lot on those grounds. The defendant moved to dismiss the indictment, arguing, in part, that the statute under which he was charged abridged the Second Amendment. After the district court denied his motion, he pleaded guilty to one of the charges leveled against him. The government dropped the other charges. The defendant then appealed his conviction,

contending that the statute under which he was convicted was unconstitutional. By entering a guilty plea, did the defendant waive this constitutional claim? Why or why not? For the Supreme Court's analysis and resolution of this question, see Class v. United States, 138 S.Ct. 798 (2018).

4. Although a defendant may not have a constitutional right to assert certain constitutional claims following the entry of a guilty plea, a state retains the prerogative to permit a defendant to later assert these claims on appeal. See, e.g., N.Y.Crim.Proc.Law § 710.70(2) (defendant who has pled guilty can, on appeal, still challenge denial of a motion to suppress evidence). In addition, many jurisdictions allow a defendant to enter a conditional guilty plea, preserving the right to appeal an adverse ruling of the trial court and then withdraw the guilty plea if the ruling is reversed on appeal. See, e.g., Rule 11(a)(2) of the Federal Rules of Criminal Procedure, on page 37, which allows for the entry of such a conditional plea provided that both the court and the prosecutor consent.

5. Defendants who go to trial have a constitutional right, grounded in due process, to be informed by the prosecutor of any material evidence that points to the defendant's innocence or would mitigate the defendant's punishment. Brady v. Maryland, 373 U.S. 83, 87, 83 S.Ct. 1194, 1197 (1963). This right to be apprised of exculpatory evidence before trial includes certain impeachment evidence—evidence that discredits the credibility of a prosecution witness. Giglio v. United States, 405 U.S. 150, 154, 92 S.Ct. 763, 766 (1972). In United States v. Ruiz, 536 U.S. 622, 122 S.Ct. 2450 (2002), the Supreme Court rejected the argument that the refusal to disclose impeachment evidence or evidence supporting an affirmative defense to a defendant invalidates a guilty plea. While the Court acknowledged that the disclosure of this information would make the defendant's plea decision "wiser," it emphasized that "the Constitution does not require the prosecutor to share all useful information with the defendant." Id. at 629, 122 S.Ct. at 2455. The Court also cited the adverse consequences that might ensue from the disclosure of the exculpatory evidence in question: the revelation of informants' identities might interfere with ongoing criminal investigations and jeopardize witnesses' safety. In addition, requiring the government to ferret out impeachment evidence and evidence supporting affirmative defenses would place a burden on the government, substantially diminishing one of plea bargaining's principal advantages—the conservation of government resources.

The Supreme Court in *Ruiz* did not resolve whether the failure to disclose other kinds of *Brady* material, such as the fact that someone else had admitted committing the crime or that DNA evidence pointed to someone else's guilt, can invalidate a guilty plea. How would you resolve this question and why? See Buffey v. Ballard, 782 S.E.2d 204, 212–16 (W. Va.2015) (noting that while divided on the question, a majority of courts have held due process requires the government to disclose material evidence of a defendant's factual innocence before entry of a guilty plea).

2. VOLUNTARY GUILTY PLEAS AND THE FACTUAL BASIS FOR A PLEA

In the following two cases, the Supreme Court addressed, among other issues, some of the implications of the due-process requirement that a guilty plea be voluntary.

BRADY v. UNITED STATES

Supreme Court of the United States, 1970.
397 U.S. 742, 90 S.Ct. 1463, 25 L.Ed.2d 747.

MR. JUSTICE WHITE delivered the opinion of the Court.

[As you will recall from the excerpt of this case on page 40, the petitioner was charged with kidnapping under a statute, 18 U.S.C. § 1201(a), that authorized a maximum penalty of death only when a person elected to have a jury trial and the jury recommended a death sentence. When the petitioner learned that his codefendant was going to plead guilty and therefore become available to testify against him, the petitioner pled guilty.] His plea was accepted after the trial judge twice questioned him as to the voluntariness of his plea.[2] Petitioner was sentenced to 50 years' imprisonment, later reduced to 30.

In 1967, petitioner sought relief under 28 U.S.C. § 2255, claiming that his plea of guilty was not voluntarily given because § 1201(a) operated to coerce his plea * * *.

After a hearing, the District Court for the District of New Mexico denied relief. * * * The court * * * found that petitioner decided to plead guilty when he learned that his codefendant was going to plead guilty: petitioner pleaded guilty "by reason of other matters and not by reason of the statute" or because of any acts of the trial judge. The court concluded that "the plea was voluntarily and knowingly made."

The Court of Appeals for the Tenth Circuit affirmed * * *. * * *

---

[2]   Eight days after petitioner pleaded guilty, he was brought before the court for sentencing. At that time, the court questioned petitioner for a second time about the voluntariness of his plea:

"THE COURT: . . . Having read the presentence report and the statement you made to the probation officer, I want to be certain that you know what you are doing and you did know when you entered a plea of guilty the other day. Do you want to let that plea of guilty stand, or do you want to withdraw it and plead not guilty?

"DEFENDANT BRADY: I want to let that plea stand, sir.

"THE COURT: You understand that in doing that you are admitting and confessing the truth of the charge contained in the indictment and that you enter a plea of guilty voluntarily, without persuasion, coercion of any kind? Is that right?

"DEFENDANT BRADY: Yes, your Honor.

"THE COURT: And you do do that?

"DEFENDANT BRADY: Yes, I do.

"THE COURT: You plead guilty to the charge?

"DEFENDANT BRADY: Yes, I do."

* * *

Since the "inevitable effect" of the death penalty provision of § 1201(a) was said by the Court [in *United States v. Jackson*, 390 U.S. 570 (1968)] to be the needless encouragement of pleas of guilty and waivers of jury trial, Brady contends that *Jackson* requires the invalidation of every plea of guilty entered under that section, at least when the fear of death is shown to have been a factor in the plea. Petitioner, however, has read far too much into the *Jackson* opinion.

* * *

Plainly, it seems to us, *Jackson* ruled neither that all pleas of guilty encouraged by the fear of a possible death sentence are involuntary pleas nor that such encouraged pleas are invalid whether involuntary or not. *Jackson* prohibits the imposition of the death penalty under § 1201(a), but that decision neither fashioned a new standard for judging the validity of guilty pleas nor mandated a new application of the test theretofore fashioned by courts and since reiterated that guilty pleas are valid if both "voluntary" and "intelligent."

* * *

The voluntariness of Brady's plea can be determined only by considering all of the relevant circumstances surrounding it. One of these circumstances was the possibility of a heavier sentence following a guilty verdict after a trial. It may be that Brady, faced with a strong case against him and recognizing that his chances for acquittal were slight, preferred to plead guilty and thus limit the penalty to life imprisonment rather than to elect a jury trial which could result in a death penalty. But even if we assume that Brady would not have pleaded guilty except for the death penalty provision of § 1201(a), this assumption merely identifies the penalty provision as a "but for" cause of his plea. That the statute caused the plea in this sense does not necessarily prove that the plea was coerced and invalid as an involuntary act.

* * *

Of course, the agents of the State may not produce a plea by actual or threatened physical harm or by mental coercion overbearing the will of the defendant. But nothing of the sort is claimed in this case; nor is there evidence that Brady was so gripped by fear of the death penalty or hope of leniency that he did not or could not, with the help of counsel, rationally weigh the advantages of going to trial against the advantages of pleading guilty. * * *

Insofar as the voluntariness of his plea is concerned, there is little to differentiate Brady from (1) the defendant, in a jurisdiction where the judge and jury have the same range of sentencing power, who pleads guilty because his lawyer advises him that the judge will very probably be more lenient than the jury; (2) the defendant, in a jurisdiction where the judge alone has sentencing power, who is advised by counsel that the judge is normally more lenient with defendants who plead guilty than with those who go to trial; (3) the defendant who is permitted by prosecutor and judge to plead guilty to a lesser offense included in the offense charged; and (4) the defendant who pleads guilty to certain counts with the understanding that other charges will be dropped. In each of these situations,[8] as in Brady's case, the defendant might never plead guilty absent the possibility or certainty that the plea will result in a lesser penalty than the sentence that could be imposed after a trial and a verdict of guilty. * * *

* * *

[W]e cannot hold that it is unconstitutional for the State to extend a benefit to a defendant who in turn extends a substantial benefit to the State and who demonstrates by his plea that he is ready and willing to admit his crime and to enter the correctional system in a frame of mind that affords hope for success in rehabilitation over a shorter period of time than might otherwise be necessary.

A contrary holding would require the States and Federal Government to forbid guilty pleas altogether, to provide a single invariable penalty for each crime defined by the statutes, or to place the sentencing function in a separate authority having no knowledge of the manner in which the conviction in each case was obtained. In any event, it would be necessary to forbid prosecutors and judges to accept guilty pleas to selected counts, to lesser included offenses, or to reduced charges. The Fifth Amendment does not reach so far.

* * *

* * * Brady first pleaded not guilty; prior to changing his plea to guilty he was subjected to no threats or promises in face-to-face encounters with the authorities. He had competent counsel and full opportunity to assess the advantages and disadvantages of a trial as compared with those attending a plea of guilty; there was no hazard of an impulsive and improvident response to a seeming but unreal advantage. His plea of guilty was entered in open court and before a judge obviously sensitive to the requirements of the law with respect to guilty pleas. Brady's plea * * * was voluntary.

---

[8] We here make no reference to the situation where the prosecutor or judge, or both, deliberately employ their charging and sentencing powers to induce a particular defendant to tender a plea of guilty. In Brady's case there is no claim that the prosecutor threatened prosecution on a charge not justified by the evidence or that the trial judge threatened Brady with a harsher sentence if convicted after trial in order to induce him to plead guilty.

The standard as to the voluntariness of guilty pleas must be essentially that defined by Judge Tuttle of the Court of Appeals for the Fifth Circuit:

> " '[A] plea of guilty entered by one fully aware of the direct consequences, including the actual value of any commitments made to him by the court, prosecutor, or his own counsel, must stand unless induced by threats (or promises to discontinue improper harassment), misrepresentation (including unfulfilled or unfulfillable promises), or perhaps by promises that are by their nature improper as having no proper relationship to the prosecutor's business (e.g. bribes).' 242 F.2d at page 115."

Under this standard, a plea of guilty is not invalid merely because entered to avoid the possibility of a death penalty.

* * *

Although Brady's plea of guilty may well have been motivated in part by a desire to avoid a possible death penalty, we are convinced that his plea was voluntarily and intelligently made and we have no reason to doubt that his solemn admission of guilt was truthful.

MR. JUSTICE BRENNAN, with whom MR. JUSTICE DOUGLAS and MR. JUSTICE MARSHALL join, concurring in the result.

* * *

An independent examination of the record in the instant case convinces me that the conclusions of the lower courts are not clearly erroneous. Although Brady was aware that he faced a possible death sentence, there is no evidence that this factor alone played a significant role in his decision to enter a guilty plea. Rather, there is considerable evidence, which the District Court credited, that Brady's plea was triggered by the confession and plea decision of his codefendant and not by any substantial fear of the death penalty. * * * Furthermore, Brady's plea was accepted by a trial judge who manifested some sensitivity to the seriousness of a guilty plea and questioned Brady at length concerning his guilt and the voluntariness of the plea before it was finally accepted.

In view of the foregoing, I concur in the result reached by the Court in the *Brady* case.

NORTH CAROLINA V. ALFORD
Supreme Court of the United States, 1970.
400 U.S. 25, 91 S.Ct. 160, 27 L.Ed.2d 162.

MR. JUSTICE WHITE delivered the opinion of the Court.

On December 2, 1963, Alford was indicted for first-degree murder, a capital offense under North Carolina law. The court appointed an attorney to represent him, and this attorney questioned all but one of the various witnesses who appellee said would substantiate his claim of innocence. The witnesses, however, did not support Alford's story but gave statements that strongly indicated his guilt. Faced with strong evidence of guilt and no substantial evidentiary support for the claim of innocence, Alford's attorney recommended that he plead guilty, but left the ultimate decision to Alford himself. The prosecutor agreed to accept a plea of guilty to a charge of second-degree murder, and on December 10, 1963, Alford pleaded guilty to the reduced charge.

Before the plea was finally accepted by the trial court, the court heard the sworn testimony of a police officer who summarized the State's case. Two other witnesses besides Alford were also heard. Although there was no eyewitness to the crime, the testimony indicated that shortly before the killing Alford took his gun from his house, stated his intention to kill the victim, and returned home with the declaration that he had carried out the killing. After the summary presentation of the State's case, Alford took the stand and testified that he had not committed the murder but that he was pleading guilty because he faced the threat of the death penalty if he did not do so.[2] In response to the questions of his counsel, he acknowledged that his counsel had informed him of the difference between second- and first-degree murder and of his rights in case he chose to go to trial. The trial court then asked appellee if, in light of his denial of guilt, he still desired to plead guilty to second-degree murder and appellee answered, "Yes, sir. I plead guilty on—from the circumstances that he [Alford's attorney] told me." After eliciting information about Alford's prior criminal

---

[2] After giving his version of the events of the night of the murder, Alford stated:

"I pleaded guilty on second degree murder because they said there is too much evidence, but I ain't shot no man, but I take the fault for the other man. We never had an argument in our life and I just pleaded guilty because they said if I didn't they would gas me for it, and that is all."

In response to questions from his attorney, Alford affirmed that he had consulted several times with his attorney and with members of his family and had been informed of his rights if he chose to plead not guilty. Alford then reaffirmed his decision to plead guilty to second-degree murder:

"Q. [by Alford's attorney]. And you authorized me to tender a plea of guilty to second degree murder before the court?

"A. Yes, sir.

"Q. And in doing that, that you have again affirmed your decision on that point?

"A. Well, I'm still pleading that you all got me to plead guilty. I plead the other way, circumstantial evidence; that the jury will prosecute me on—on the second. You told me to plead guilty, right. I don't—I'm not guilty but I plead guilty."

record, which was a long one, the trial court sentenced him to 30 years' imprisonment, the maximum penalty for second-degree murder.

* * *

If Alford's statements were to be credited as sincere assertions of his innocence, there obviously existed a factual and legal dispute between him and the State. Without more, it might be argued that the conviction entered on his guilty plea was invalid, since his assertion of innocence negatived any admission of guilt, which * * * is normally "[c]entral to the plea and the foundation for entering judgment against the defendant. . . ."

In addition to Alford's statement, however, the court had heard an account of the events on the night of the murder, including information from Alford's acquaintances that he had departed from his home with his gun stating his intention to kill and that he had later declared that he had carried out his intention. Nor had Alford wavered in his desire to have the trial court determine his guilt without a jury trial. * * *

* * * Some courts * * * have concluded that they should not "force any defense on a defendant in a criminal case," particularly when advancement of the defense might "end in disaster. . . ." They have argued that, since "guilt, or the degree of guilt, is at times uncertain and elusive," "[a]n accused, though believing in or entertaining doubts respecting his innocence, might reasonably conclude a jury would be convinced of his guilt and that he would fare better in the sentence by pleading guilty. . . ." As one state court observed nearly a century ago, "[r]easons other than the fact that he is guilty may induce a defendant to so plead, . . . [and] [h]e must be permitted to judge for himself in this respect."

This Court has not confronted this precise issue, but prior decisions do yield relevant principles. * * *

The issue in *Hudson v. United States,* 272 U.S. 451 (1926), was whether a federal court has power to impose a prison sentence after accepting a plea of *nolo contendere,* a plea by which a defendant does not expressly admit his guilt, but nonetheless waives his right to a trial and authorizes the court for purposes of the case to treat him as if he were guilty. The Court held that a trial court does have such power * * *. Implicit in the *nolo contendere* cases is a recognition that the Constitution does not bar imposition of a prison sentence upon an accused who is unwilling expressly to admit his guilt but who, faced with grim alternatives, is willing to waive his trial and accept the sentence.

* * *

Nor can we perceive any material difference between a plea that refuses to admit commission of the criminal act and a plea containing a protestation of innocence when, as in the instant case, a defendant intelligently concludes that his interests require entry of a guilty plea and the record before the judge contains strong evidence of actual guilt. Here the State had a strong case of first-degree murder against Alford. * * * Because of the overwhelming evidence against him, a trial was precisely what neither Alford nor his attorney desired. Confronted with the choice between a trial for first-degree murder, on the one hand, and a plea of guilty to second-degree murder, on the other, Alford quite reasonably chose the latter and thereby limited the maximum penalty to a 30-year term. When his plea is viewed in light of the evidence against him, which substantially negated his claim of innocence and which further provided a means by which the judge could test whether the plea was being intelligently entered,[10] its validity cannot be seriously questioned. In view of the strong factual basis for the plea demonstrated by the State and Alford's clearly expressed desire to enter it despite his professed belief in his innocence, we hold that the trial judge did not commit constitutional error in accepting it.[11]

MR. JUSTICE BRENNAN, with whom MR. JUSTICE DOUGLAS and MR. JUSTICE MARSHALL join, dissenting.

* * *[W]ithout reaching the question whether due process permits the entry of judgment upon a plea of guilty accompanied by a contemporaneous denial of acts constituting the crime, I believe that at the very least such a denial of guilt is also a relevant factor in determining whether the plea was voluntarily and intelligently made. With these factors in mind, it is sufficient in my view to state that the facts set out in the majority opinion demonstrate that Alford was "so gripped by fear of the death penalty" that his decision to plead guilty was not voluntary but was "the product of duress as much so as choice reflecting physical constraint." * * *

QUESTIONS AND POINTS FOR DISCUSSION

1.   At least two purposes are served by requiring a factual basis for a guilty plea. First, the existence of a factual basis helps to ensure that the defendant is not unknowingly pleading guilty to a crime that he or she did not commit. McCarthy v. United States, 394 U.S. 459, 467, 89 S.Ct. 1166, 1171 (1969). Second, the factual basis for the plea helps to ensure that the defendant's plea is in fact voluntary and not the result of impermissible

---

[10] Because of the importance of protecting the innocent and of insuring that guilty pleas are a product of free and intelligent choice, various state and federal court decisions properly caution that pleas coupled with claims of innocence should not be accepted unless there is a factual basis for the plea, and until the judge taking the plea has inquired into and sought to resolve the conflict between the waiver of trial and the claim of innocence.

[11] Our holding does not mean that a trial judge must accept every constitutionally valid guilty plea merely because a defendant wishes so to plead. A criminal defendant does not have an absolute right under the Constitution to have his guilty plea accepted by the court, although the States may by statute or otherwise confer such a right. Likewise, the States may bar their courts from accepting guilty pleas from any defendants who assert their innocence. We need not now delineate the scope of that discretion.

threats, promises, or other pressures. *Libretti v. United States*, 516 U.S. 29, 42, 116 S.Ct. 356, 364 (1995).

A number of courts have deduced from *North Carolina v. Alford* that a factual basis for a guilty plea must be established when the defendant claims to be innocent of the charge to which a guilty plea is being entered. *Loftis v. Almager*, 704 F.3d 645, 650 (9th Cir.2012). But most courts have concluded that in the absence of such a protestation of innocence or some other "special circumstances," due process does not require that a factual basis for a guilty plea be established before the plea is accepted. *Id.* at 648. Consequently, in states with no statutes or court rules requiring factual bases for guilty pleas, a court generally may accept a guilty plea without any evidence or information being tendered to the court that would support the conclusion that the defendant is culpable of the offense to which he or she is pleading guilty. The absence of a factual basis or strong factual basis for the guilty plea simply is one of a number of factors bearing on the question whether the defendant's guilty plea is intelligent and voluntary.

In your opinion, when, if ever, is a factual basis for a guilty plea constitutionally required?

2. The Notes of the Advisory Committee on Rules, which drafted Rule 11 of the Federal Rules of Criminal Procedure, state that the factual basis for a guilty plea can be established in a variety of ways. A defendant may, when entering the plea, make inculpatory admissions in court which establish the defendant's guilt of the crime to which a guilty plea is being entered. Alternatively, the prosecutor or defense attorney may recite details about the defendant's crime on the record as a way of establishing the factual basis. The Advisory Committee Notes also suggest that the factual-basis requirement might be satisfied by a presentence report or by other undefined means.

3. If a court accepts a defendant's guilty plea, the defendant's statements, including incriminating admissions, made at the Rule 11 hearing are admissible against the defendant at later proceedings, such as a sentencing hearing. *Mitchell v. United States*, 526 U.S. 314, 324, 119 S.Ct. 1307, 1313 (1999) (*dictum*). But invoking the Fifth Amendment privilege against self-incrimination at a Rule 11 hearing poses a risk to a defendant: the court may then decide not to accept the plea because the factual basis for it has not, at least sometimes, been adequately established. *Id.*

4. Most jurisdictions remit the decisions whether to accept a guilty plea or a plea agreement to the court's discretion. While most courts have underscored the breadth of the trial judge's discretion to accept or reject a guilty plea, some federal courts have held that the trial judge has no authority to reject an unconditional guilty plea if the plea meets the requirements of Rule 11(b). See *In re Vasquez-Ramirez*, 443 F.3d 692, 695–96 (9th Cir.2006).

Defendants sometimes challenge a trial judge's decision to reject a guilty plea or plea agreement on the grounds that the rejection constituted an abuse of discretion. After the rejection of their guilty pleas, these defendants generally have gone to trial, been found guilty, and received a more severe sentence than would have been imposed under a proffered plea agreement. Courts usually have found no abuse of discretion when a guilty plea was rejected because the defendant professed innocence or there was an inadequate factual basis to support the plea. See, e.g., France v. Artuz, 1999 WL 1251817, at *7 (E.D.N.Y.1999) (no abuse of discretion to reject guilty plea to manslaughter when the defendant, whom the jury later convicted of murder, contended he was innocent); Elsten v. State, 698 N.E.2d 292, 295 (Ind.1998) (no abuse of discretion in rejecting plea of "guilty but mentally ill" of defendant, who was later convicted of murder, when two court-ordered psychological evaluations found no evidence that the defendant was mentally ill when he shot his wife). Examples of other decisions in which no abuse of discretion was found in the trial court's rejection of a guilty plea or plea agreement include: Hoskins v. Maricle, 150 S.W.3d 1, 25 (Ky.2004) (no abuse of discretion to reject, because unduly lenient, plea agreement under which defendants charged with capital murder would have received a ten-year prison sentence for manslaughter); Newsome v. State, 797 N.E.2d 293, 298 (Ind.Ct.App.2003) (no abuse of discretion in rejecting guilty plea to two counts of molestation and incest when the court believed the plea was tendered to avert the introduction of evidence in the defendant's trial for rape that he had fathered the child of the victim he had molested and later raped); United States v. Severino, 800 F.2d 42, 46–47 (2d Cir.1986) (no abuse of discretion where the judge thought the defendant had lied during his plea allocution); United States v. Escobar Noble, 653 F.2d 34, 36–37 (1st Cir.1981) (no abuse of discretion where judge rejected plea to a misdemeanor so that prerogative to impose a more severe sentence upon conviction of a felony could be preserved); United States v. David E. Thompson, Inc., 621 F.2d 1147, 1150–51 (1st Cir.1980) (no abuse of discretion to reject *nolo contendere* plea that would have denied victims bringing civil actions against the defendant of the benefit of the government's prosecutorial efforts).

On occasion, but infrequently, an appellate court will find that a trial court abused its discretion in rejecting a guilty plea or plea agreement. See, e.g., State v. Justice, 361 P.3d 39, 45 (Or.Ct.App.2015) (abuse of discretion to reject guilty plea, tendered under a plea agreement, solely due to court policy not to allow defendants charged with misdemeanors to plead guilty to violations); United States v. Washington, 969 F.2d 1073, 1077–79 (D.C.Cir.1992) (improper to reject guilty plea because defendant would not inculpate his codefendant). The courts are split on whether the refusal to accept a plea agreement solely because it was tendered after a court-imposed deadline constitutes an abuse of discretion. See State v. Brown, 689 N.W.2d 347, 351–52 (Neb.2004) (listing cases). For example, in United States v. Gamboa, 166 F.3d 1327, 1331 (11th Cir.1999), the Eleventh Circuit Court of Appeals found no abuse of discretion when the trial judge refused to accept plea agreements submitted forty minutes after the court's deadline, while in State v. Hager, 630 N.W.2d 828, 837 (Iowa 2001), the Iowa Supreme Court held that the trial court had abused its discretion when it automatically rejected a plea agreement because it was tendered the morning of the trial. What competing policy considerations underlie this disagreement amongst the courts, and how would you balance them?

B. THE SIXTH AMENDMENT RIGHT TO COUNSEL

When an uncounselled defendant is entering a guilty plea, the court must take steps to ensure not only that the guilty plea is otherwise voluntary and intelligent but that the defendant is validly waiving his or her right to counsel. In order for the waiver of the Sixth Amendment right to counsel at a plea hearing to be valid, a defendant needs to be apprised of the "nature" of the pending charges, the right to have counsel provide advice regarding the tendering of a plea, and the range of penalties that might be imposed if the defendant enters a plea of guilty. Iowa v. Tovar, 541 U.S. 77, 81, 124 S.Ct. 1379, 1383 (2004). The judge need not elaborate further and highlight the potential adverse consequences of forgoing counsel's assistance, such as the risk that the defendant will unwittingly relinquish a viable defense to the criminal charges. Id. at 91–92, 124 S.Ct. at 1389.

Arguing in an amicus brief in *Iowa v. Tovar* that additional warnings are needed in order for the waiver of the constitutional right to counsel to be knowing, intelligent, and voluntary, the National Association of Criminal Defense Lawyers cited several examples of the impact a lawyer's advice can have on a defendant's decision whether, and to what, to plead guilty:

> The defendant pleads guilty to driving while intoxicated without realizing that the results of his breathalyzer test are suppressible. An innocent defendant pleads guilty without realizing that he has an entrapment defense, a duress defense, or that his intoxication negates the specific intent required by the crime. The defendant pleads guilty to what he thinks is a nonserious theft without realizing that the consideration of his relevant conduct, including uncharged or acquitted conduct, will likely lead to a sentence at the high end of the statutory range. The defendant pleads guilty to a minor felony to resolve the case quickly and get on with his life without realizing that the conviction will lead to his deportation.

Brief for National Ass'n of Criminal Defense Lawyers as Amici Curiae Supporting Respondent at 7, *Tovar* (No. 02–1541), 2003 WL 23051967. In your opinion, are the warnings specified by the Supreme Court in *Iowa v. Tovar* adequate to safeguard a defendant's Sixth Amendment right to counsel at a plea hearing? If not, how should the warnings be augmented to meet the requirements of the Constitution?

The constitutional right to counsel includes the right to the effective assistance of counsel. In Hill v. Lockhart, 474 U.S. 52, 106 S.Ct. 366 (1985), the Supreme Court expanded upon its holding in McMann v. Richardson, 397 U.S. 759, 90 S.Ct. 1441 (1970), which was discussed in note 1 on page 42, ruling that even if an attorney's advice given to a defendant deciding whether to plead guilty is palpably deficient, the defendant's guilty plea is not necessarily invalid. The Court in *Hill* held that a two-part test previously adopted by the Court in Strickland v. Washington, 466 U.S. 668, 104 S.Ct. 2052 (1984) should be applied when determining whether a defendant received ineffective assistance of counsel during the plea process, rendering the guilty plea invalid. Under the first part of this test, a defendant must establish that the attorney acted unreasonably under "prevailing professional norms" when advising the defendant and acting on his or her behalf. Id. at 688, 104 S.Ct. at 2065. To satisfy this part of the test, the defendant must rebut a "strong presumption" that the attorney acted within "the wide range of reasonable professional assistance." Id. at 689, 104 S.Ct. at 2065. Even if the attorney acted unreasonably, however, the defendant must still establish that he or she was prejudiced by counsel's deficient performance. When a defendant has entered a guilty plea, the defendant must demonstrate that there is a "reasonable probability" that had the attorney rendered reasonable professional assistance, the defendant would not have pled guilty and would instead have gone to trial. *Hill,* 474 U.S. at 59, 106 S.Ct. at 370. To establish prejudice in this context, the defendant does not also have to prove that the trial would have resulted in a more favorable outcome. Lee v. United States, 137 S.Ct. 1958, 1965 (2017).

In *Hill* itself, the defendant alleged that he had received ineffective assistance of counsel, in violation of his Sixth Amendment right to counsel, when he decided to plead guilty after his attorney apprised him that he would have to serve only one-third of his sentence before becoming eligible for parole. He later learned that he would actually have to serve one-half of his sentence before becoming eligible for parole. The Supreme Court held that the defendant had failed to establish that he had received ineffective assistance of counsel; he had not satisfied the second prong of the *Strickland* test because he had failed to allege that he would have gone to trial had he received accurate advice about his eligibility for parole.

By contrast, in Meyers v. Gillis, 142 F.3d 664, 667–70 (3d Cir.1998), the Third Circuit Court of Appeals held that the defendant had received ineffective assistance of counsel, thereby invalidating his guilty plea, when counsel had erroneously apprised him that he would be eligible for parole if he pleaded guilty to second-degree murder. In *Meyers*, unlike *Hill*, the defendant had asserted, in testimony that the district court found credible, that he would not have pleaded guilty if his attorney had accurately apprised him that his plea would subject him to a life sentence without the possibility of parole.

Consider again the facts of State v. Ramirez, 636 N.W.2d 740 (Iowa 2001) recounted in note 3 on page 36. Should an attorney's failure to advise a client of the deportation consequences of entering a guilty plea be considered the ineffective assistance of counsel that requires the vacating of the guilty plea if the defendant was prejudiced by this failure? The Supreme Court addressed this question in the case below.

PADILLA V. KENTUCKY

Supreme Court of the United States, 2010.
559 U.S. 356, 130 S.Ct. 1473, 176 L.Ed.2d 284.

JUSTICE STEVENS delivered the opinion of the Court.

Petitioner Jose Padilla, a native of Honduras, has been a lawful permanent resident of the United States for more than 40 years. Padilla served this Nation with honor as a member of the U.S. Armed Forces during the Vietnam War. He now faces deportation after pleading guilty to the transportation of a large amount of marijuana in his tractor-trailer in the Commonwealth of Kentucky.

In this postconviction proceeding, Padilla claims that his counsel not only failed to advise him of this consequence prior to his entering the plea, but also told him that he " 'did not have to worry about immigration status since he had been in the country so long.' " Padilla relied on his counsel's erroneous advice when he pleaded guilty to the drug charges that made his deportation virtually mandatory. He alleges that he would have insisted on going to trial if he had not received incorrect advice from his attorney.

* * *

* * * Under contemporary law, if a noncitizen has committed a removable offense * * *, his removal is practically inevitable but for the possible exercise of limited remnants of equitable discretion vested in the Attorney General to cancel removal for noncitizens convicted of particular classes of offenses. See 8 U.S.C. § 1229b. Subject to limited exceptions, this discretionary relief is not available for an offense related to trafficking in a controlled substance. See § 1101(a)(43)(B); § 1228.

These changes to our immigration law * * * confirm our view that, as a matter of federal law, deportation is an integral part—indeed, sometimes the most important part—of the penalty that may be imposed on noncitizen defendants who plead guilty to specified crimes.

* * * The Supreme Court of Kentucky rejected Padilla's ineffectiveness claim on the ground that the advice he sought about the risk of deportation concerned only collateral matters, i.e., those matters not within the sentencing authority of the state trial court. * * *

We, however, have never applied a distinction between direct and collateral consequences to define the scope of constitutionally "reasonable professional assistance" required under *Strickland*. Whether that distinction is appropriate is a question we need not consider in this case because of the unique nature of deportation.

We have long recognized that deportation is a particularly severe "penalty" * * *. Although removal proceedings are civil in nature, deportation is nevertheless intimately related to the criminal process. Our law has enmeshed criminal convictions and the penalty of deportation for nearly a century. And, importantly, recent changes in our immigration law have made removal nearly an automatic result for a broad class of noncitizen offenders. * * *

* * * The collateral versus direct distinction is thus ill suited to evaluating a *Strickland* claim concerning the specific risk of deportation. We conclude that advice regarding deportation is not categorically removed from the ambit of the Sixth Amendment right to counsel. * * *

* * *

The weight of prevailing professional norms supports the view that counsel must advise her client regarding the risk of deportation. "[A]uthorities of every stripe—including the American Bar Association, criminal defense and public defender organizations, authoritative treatises, and state and city bar publications—universally require defense attorneys to advise as to the risk of deportation consequences for non-citizen clients . . . ."

* * *

In the instant case, the terms of the relevant immigration statute are succinct, clear, and explicit in defining the removal consequence for Padilla's conviction. Padilla's counsel could have easily determined that his plea would make him eligible for deportation simply from reading the text of the statute, which addresses not some broad classification of crimes but specifically commands removal for all controlled substances convictions except for the most trivial of marijuana possession offenses. Instead, Padilla's counsel provided him false assurance that his conviction would not result in his removal from this country. This is not a hard case in which to find deficiency. * * *

Immigration law can be complex, and it is a legal specialty of its own. * * * The duty of the private practitioner in such cases is more limited. When the law is not succinct and straightforward * * *, a criminal defense attorney need do no more than advise a noncitizen client that pending criminal charges may carry a risk of adverse immigration consequences. But when the deportation consequence is truly clear, as it was in this case, the duty to give correct advice is equally clear.

* * *

The Solicitor General has urged us to conclude that *Strickland* applies to Padilla's claim only to the extent that he has alleged affirmative misadvice. * * *

* * *

A holding limited to affirmative misadvice would invite two absurd results. First, it would give counsel an incentive to remain silent on matters of great importance, even when answers are readily available. * * * Second, it would deny a class of clients least able to represent themselves the most rudimentary advice on deportation even when it is readily available. * * *

* * *

Taking as true the basis for his motion for postconviction relief, we have little difficulty concluding that Padilla has sufficiently alleged that his counsel was constitutionally deficient. Whether Padilla is entitled to relief will depend on whether he can demonstrate prejudice as a result thereof, a question we do not reach because it was not passed on below.

* * *

JUSTICE ALITO, with whom THE CHIEF JUSTICE joins, concurring in the judgment.

I concur in the judgment because a criminal defense attorney fails to provide effective assistance within the meaning of *Strickland v. Washington* if the attorney misleads a noncitizen client regarding the removal consequences of a conviction. In my view, such an attorney must (1) refrain from unreasonably providing incorrect advice and (2) advise the defendant that a criminal conviction may have adverse immigration consequences and that, if the alien wants advice on this issue, the alien should consult an immigration attorney. * * *

* * *

* * * But the Court's opinion would not just require defense counsel to warn the client of a general *risk* of removal; it would also require counsel in at least some cases, to specify what the removal *consequences* of a conviction would be.

* * *

The Court tries to downplay the severity of the burden it imposes on defense counsel by suggesting that the scope of counsel's duty to offer advice concerning deportation consequences may turn on how hard it is to determine those consequences. Where "the terms of the relevant immigration statute are succinct, clear, and explicit in defining the removal consequence[s]" of a conviction, the Court says, counsel has an affirmative duty to advise the client that he will be subject to deportation as a result of the plea. But "[w]hen the law is not succinct and straightforward . . . , a criminal defense attorney need do no more than advise a noncitizen client that pending criminal charges may carry a risk of adverse immigration consequences." This approach is problematic * * *.

First, it will not always be easy to tell whether a particular statutory provision is "succinct, clear, and explicit." How can an attorney who lacks general immigration law expertise be sure that a seemingly clear statutory provision actually means what it seems to say when read in isolation? What if the application of the provision to a particular case is not clear but a cursory examination of case law or administrative decisions would provide a definitive answer?

Second, if defense counsel must provide advice regarding only one of the many collateral consequences of a criminal conviction, many defendants are likely to be misled. To take just one example, a conviction for a particular offense may render an alien excludable but not removable. If an alien charged with such an offense is advised only that pleading guilty to such an offense will not result in removal, the alien may be induced to enter a guilty plea without realizing that a consequence of the plea is that the alien will be unable to reenter the United States if the alien returns to his or her home country for any reason, such as to visit an elderly parent or to attend a funeral. Incomplete legal advice may be worse than no advice at all because it may mislead and may dissuade the client from seeking advice from a more knowledgeable source.

* * *

In sum, * * * unreasonable and incorrect information concerning the risk of removal can give rise to an ineffectiveness claim. In addition, silence alone is not enough to satisfy counsel's duty to assist the client. Instead, an alien defendant's Sixth Amendment right to counsel is satisfied if defense counsel advises the client that a conviction may have immigration consequences, that immigration law is a specialized field, that the attorney is not an immigration lawyer, and that the client should consult an immigration specialist if the client wants advice on that subject.

JUSTICE SCALIA, with whom JUSTICE THOMAS joins, dissenting.

In the best of all possible worlds, criminal defendants contemplating a guilty plea ought to be advised of all serious collateral consequences of conviction, and surely ought not to be misadvised. The Constitution, however, is not an all-purpose tool for judicial construction of a perfect world * * *.

The Sixth Amendment guarantees the accused a lawyer "for his defence" against a "criminal prosecutio[n]"—not for sound advice about the collateral consequences of conviction. * * * I do not believe that affirmative misadvice about those consequences renders an attorney's assistance in defending against the prosecution constitutionally inadequate; or that the Sixth Amendment requires counsel to warn immigrant defendants that a conviction may render them removable. * * *

* * *

Adding to counsel's duties an obligation to advise about a conviction's collateral consequences has no logical stopping-point. As the concurrence observes,

> "[A] criminal convictio[n] can carry a wide variety of consequences other than conviction and sentencing, including civil commitment, civil forfeiture, the loss of the right to vote, disqualification from public benefits, ineligibility to possess firearms, dishonorable discharge from the Armed Forces, and loss of business or professional licenses. . . . All of those consequences are 'serious' . . . ."

* * * [T]he concurrence's suggestion that counsel must warn defendants of potential removal consequences—what would come to be known as the "*Padilla* warning"—cannot be limited to those consequences except by judicial caprice. * * *

* * *

QUESTIONS AND POINTS FOR DISCUSSION

1.   *Padilla* has left a host of unanswered questions in its wake, to one of which Justice Scalia alluded: Of what other consequences of a conviction, if any, that are not part of the sentence imposed by the court does the Sixth Amendment require a defense attorney to apprise the defendant? How would you resolve this question? If, for example, a defense attorney did not tell the defendant that a guilty plea to a particular sex crime would subject the defendant to sex-offender registration and community-notification provisions and if the defendant would not have pleaded guilty if aware of these automatic repercussions of the conviction, was the defendant deprived of the constitutional right to the effective assistance of counsel? (See pages 483–486 for a discussion of sex-offender registration and notification laws.) What if a defendant is not told that a guilty plea may result in the defendant's eviction from public housing? Consider these questions again after reading in Chapter 10 about the range of enmeshed penalties—often referred to as "collateral consequences"—that can ensue from a criminal conviction.

2.   Defense attorneys generally have a duty to communicate to their clients any formal plea offer tendered by the prosecution. Missouri v. Frye, 566 U.S. 133, 145, 132 S.Ct. 1399, 1408 (2012). If the failure to meet this duty prejudiced the defendant, the failure constitutes the ineffective assistance of counsel proscribed by the Sixth Amendment. To prove prejudice in this context, a defendant must establish that there is a reasonable probability that: (1) she

would have accepted the offer; (2) the prosecutor would not have withdrawn the offer; and (3) the trial court would have accepted the plea agreement, resulting in a guilty plea to a less serious criminal charge or a less harsh sentence. Id. at 147, 132 S.Ct. at 1409.

In his dissenting opinion in *Missouri v. Frye*, Justice Scalia criticized this test for prejudice. Terming it "retrospective crystal-ball gazing posing as legal analysis," Justice Scalia observed that the prejudice inquiry would require after-the-fact "mind-readings" in an effort to determine how the prosecutor and judge would have exercised—not did exercise—their discretion. Id. at 154, 132 S.Ct. at 1413 (Scalia, J., dissenting). How, if at all, would you modify the Court's test for prejudice when a defense attorney failed to communicate a formal plea offer to his or her client?

3. In Lafler v. Cooper, 566 U.S. 156, 132 S.Ct. 1376 (2012), the Supreme Court addressed the questions of whether and when a defense attorney's deficient advice to a defendant to reject a proposed plea agreement causes prejudice, in the constitutional sense. In that case, the prosecutor twice offered to dismiss two pending criminal charges and recommend a prison sentence of 51 to 85 months if the defendant pled guilty to the remaining two charges. Instead, acting on what the parties before the Supreme Court agreed was the inadequate advice of counsel, the defendant rejected the plea offer and, after being convicted of all the criminal charges, received a mandatory minimum prison sentence of 185 to 360 months.

The Supreme Court described the test for prejudice to be applied when counsel's inadequate advice leads, not to the acceptance of a plea offer, but to its rejection:

> In these circumstances a defendant must show that but for the ineffective advice of counsel there is a reasonable probability that the plea offer would have been presented to the court (*i.e.*, that the defendant would have accepted the plea and the prosecution would not have withdrawn it in light of intervening circumstances), that the court would have accepted its terms, and that the conviction or sentence, or both, under the offer's terms would have been less severe than under the judgment and sentence that in fact were imposed.

Id. at 164, 132 S.Ct. at 1385.

The Court then tackled the question of what is an appropriate remedy when a defense attorney's advice to reject a plea offer represents the ineffective assistance of counsel. The Supreme Court noted, in general terms, that the remedy falls within the trial court's discretion. For example, if the ill-advised rejection of the plea offer denied the defendant the opportunity to receive a less stringent sentence, a court has the discretion to impose the sentence set forth in the plea offer, the sentence imposed after trial, or some intermediate sentence. And if counsel's defective advice deprived the defendant of the opportunity of being sentenced on fewer criminal counts or less serious counts, the remedy might entail, according to the Court, requiring the prosecutor to retender the plea offer. The trial court would then have the discretion to either vacate the conviction and accept the plea agreement or leave in place the judgment of conviction entered after the trial.

Professor Albert Alschuler has criticized *Lafler* for leaving the remedy for the violation of the constitutional right to the effective assistance of counsel in this context to the court's discretion: The judge "may restore you to the position you would have occupied if your lawyer had been competent, or he may not." *Lafler* and *Frye*: Two Small Band-Aids for a Festering Wound, 51 Duq. L.Rev. 673, 677 (2013). What arguments would you make for and against this remedy-related decision of the Court?

4.   In Roe v. Flores-Ortega, 528 U.S. 470, 120 S.Ct. 1029 (2000), the Supreme Court considered when a defense attorney's failure to file a notice of appeal following the entry of a guilty plea constitutes ineffective assistance of counsel. The Court noted that the threshold query is whether the defense attorney consulted with the defendant about taking an appeal, apprising the defendant of the advantages and disadvantages of appealing and then determining whether the defendant wanted to do so. If this consultation occurred and the defendant asked the attorney to file an appeal, the failure to do so constituted unconstitutional ineffectiveness. On the other hand, if the defendant indicated, after this consultation, that he did not want to pursue an appeal, the failure to file a notice of appeal did not abridge the defendant's Sixth Amendment right to the effective assistance of counsel.

But what if a defense attorney failed to even consult with a defendant about taking an appeal? The Supreme Court acknowledged in *Roe* that in the "vast majority of cases," an attorney's failure to consult with a client about the prospect of taking an appeal would be unreasonable in the constitutional sense. Id. at 481, 120 S.Ct. at 1037. But the Court refused to hold that such a failure should always be considered deficient performance under the first prong of the *Strickland* test for constitutional ineffectiveness, instead requiring that courts engage in a "circumstance-specific reasonableness inquiry":

> For example, suppose that a defendant consults with counsel; counsel advises the defendant that a guilty plea probably will lead to a 2 year sentence; the defendant expresses satisfaction and pleads guilty; the court sentences the defendant to 2 years' imprisonment as expected and informs the defendant of his appeal rights; the defendant does not express any interest in appealing, and counsel concludes that there are no nonfrivolous grounds for appeal. Under these circumstances, it would be difficult to say that counsel is "professionally unreasonable," as a constitutional matter, in not consulting with such a defendant regarding an appeal. Or, for example, suppose a sentencing court's instructions to a defendant about his appeal rights in a particular case are so clear and informative as to substitute for counsel's duty to consult. In some cases, counsel might then reasonably decide that he need not repeat

that information. We therefore reject a bright-line rule that counsel must always consult with the defendant regarding an appeal.

We instead hold that counsel has a constitutionally-imposed duty to consult with the defendant about an appeal when there is reason to think either (1) that a rational defendant would want to appeal (for example, because there are nonfrivolous grounds for appeal), or (2) that this particular defendant reasonably demonstrated to counsel that he was interested in appealing. In making this determination, courts must take into account all the information counsel knew or should have known. Although not determinative, a highly relevant factor in this inquiry will be whether the conviction follows a trial or a guilty plea, both because a guilty plea reduces the scope of potentially appealable issues and because such a plea may indicate that the defendant seeks an end to judicial proceedings. Even in cases when the defendant pleads guilty, the court must consider such factors as whether the defendant received the sentence bargained for as part of the plea and whether the plea expressly reserved or waived some or all appeal rights. Only by considering all relevant factors in a given case can a court properly determine whether a rational defendant would have desired an appeal or that the particular defendant sufficiently demonstrated to counsel an interest in an appeal.

Id. at 479–80, 120 S.Ct. at 1036.

The Supreme Court underscored that a finding that counsel's failure to consult with the defendant about an appeal was unreasonable does not necessarily mean the defendant's right to the effective assistance of counsel was violated, entitling the defendant to now take an appeal. To prevail on the ineffectiveness claim, the defendant also has to establish that there is a reasonable probability that an appeal would have been timely filed had that consultation occurred. Two particularly relevant factors to consider when determining whether the defendant has met this burden are whether the defendant had nonfrivolous grounds for appealing and whether the defendant had "promptly" expressed an interest in filing an appeal. Id. at 485, 120 S.Ct. at 1039.

The Supreme Court emphasized in *Roe* that while the defendant's showing that there were nonfrivolous grounds for an appeal would give credence to the argument that an appeal would have been filed had the attorney properly consulted with the defendant, a defendant does not have to demonstrate that he or she would have prevailed on the appeal to successfully assert a claim of ineffective assistance of counsel. The Court noted that it would be "unfair" to require a defendant, often proceeding without the assistance of counsel, to identify the claims that would have been asserted on appeal and to prove their legal merit. Id. at 486, 120 S.Ct. at 1040.

C. BREACHES OF PLEA AGREEMENTS

SANTOBELLO v. NEW YORK

Supreme Court of the United States, 1971.
404 U.S. 257, 92 S.Ct. 495, 30 L.Ed.2d 427.

MR. CHIEF JUSTICE BURGER delivered the opinion of the Court.

We granted certiorari in this case to determine whether the State's failure to keep a commitment concerning the sentence recommendation on a guilty plea required a new trial.

The facts are not in dispute. The State of New York indicted petitioner in 1969 on two felony counts, Promoting Gambling in the First Degree, and Possession of Gambling Records in the First Degree. Petitioner first entered a plea of not guilty to both counts. After negotiations, the Assistant District Attorney in charge of the case agreed to permit petitioner to plead guilty to a lesser-included offense, Possession of Gambling Records in the Second Degree, conviction of which would carry a maximum prison sentence of one year. The prosecutor agreed to make no recommendation as to the sentence.

On June 16, 1969, petitioner accordingly withdrew his plea of not guilty and entered a plea of guilty to the lesser charge. * * * The court accepted the plea and set a date for sentencing. * * *

* * *

At this appearance, another prosecutor had replaced the prosecutor who had negotiated the plea. The new prosecutor recommended the maximum one-year sentence. In making this recommendation, he cited petitioner's criminal record and alleged links with organized crime. Defense counsel immediately objected on the ground that the State had promised petitioner before the plea was entered that there would be no sentence recommendation by the prosecution. * * * The second prosecutor, apparently ignorant of his colleague's commitment, argued that there was nothing in the record to support petitioner's claim of a promise, but the State, in subsequent proceedings, has not contested that such a promise was made.

The sentencing judge ended discussion, with the following statement, quoting extensively from the presentence report:

* * * I am not at all influenced by what the District Attorney says * * *. It doesn't make a particle of difference what the District Attorney says he will do, or what he doesn't do.

"I have here * * * a probation report. I have here a history of a long, long serious criminal record. I have here a picture of the life history of this man. . . .

" 'He is unamenable to supervision in the community. He is a professional criminal.' This is in quotes. 'And a recidivist. Institutionalization?'; that means, in plain language, just putting him away, 'is the only means of halting his anti-social activities,' and protecting you, your family, me, my family, protecting society. 'Institutionalization.' Plain language, put him behind bars.

"Under the plea, I can only send him to the New York City Correctional Institution for men for one year, which I am hereby doing."

The judge then imposed the maximum sentence of one year.

* * *

Disposition of charges after plea discussions is not only an essential part of the process but a highly desirable part for many reasons. It leads to prompt and largely final disposition of most criminal cases; it avoids much of the corrosive impact of enforced idleness during pretrial confinement for those who are denied release pending trial; it protects the public from those accused persons who are prone to continue criminal conduct even while on pretrial release; and, by shortening the time between charge and disposition, it enhances whatever may be the rehabilitative prospects of the guilty when they are ultimately imprisoned.

However, all of these considerations presuppose fairness in securing agreement between an accused and a prosecutor. * * *

* * * [W]hen a plea rests in any significant degree on a promise or agreement of the prosecutor, so that it can be said to be part of the inducement or consideration, such promise must be fulfilled.

On this record, petitioner "bargained" and negotiated for a particular plea in order to secure dismissal of more serious charges, but also on condition that no sentence recommendation would be made by the prosecutor. It is now conceded that the promise to abstain from a recommendation was made, and at this stage the prosecution is not in a good position to argue that its inadvertent breach of agreement is immaterial. The staff lawyers in a prosecutor's office have the burden of "letting the left hand know what the right hand is doing" or has done. That the breach of agreement was inadvertent does not lessen its impact.

We need not reach the question whether the sentencing judge would or would not have been influenced had he known all the details of the negotiations for the plea. He stated that the prosecutor's recommendation did not influence him and we have no reason to doubt that. Nevertheless, we conclude that the interests of justice and appropriate recognition of the duties of the prosecution in relation to promises made in the negotiation of pleas of guilty will be best served by remanding the case to the state courts for further consideration. The ultimate relief to which petitioner is entitled we leave to the discretion of the state court, which is in a better position to decide whether the circumstances of this case require only that there be specific performance of the agreement on the plea, in which case petitioner should be resentenced by a different judge, or whether, in the view of the state court, the circumstances require granting the relief sought by petitioner, *i.e.,* the opportunity to withdraw his plea of guilty.[2] * * *

* * *

MR. JUSTICE DOUGLAS, concurring.

* * *

I join the opinion of the Court and favor a constitutional rule for this as well as for other pending or oncoming cases. Where the "plea bargain" is not kept by the prosecutor, the sentence must be vacated and the state court will decide in light of the circumstances of each case whether due process requires (a) that there be specific performance of the plea bargain or (b) that the defendant be given the option to go to trial on the original charges. One alternative may do justice in one case, and the other in a different case. In choosing a remedy, however, a court ought to accord a defendant's preference considerable, if not controlling, weight inasmuch as the fundamental rights flouted by a prosecutor's breach of a plea bargain are those of the defendant, not of the State.

MR. JUSTICE MARSHALL, with whom MR. JUSTICE BRENNAN and MR. JUSTICE STEWART join, concurring in part and dissenting in part.

I agree with much of the majority's opinion, but conclude that petitioner must be permitted to withdraw his guilty plea. This is the relief petitioner requested, and, on the facts set out by the majority, it is a form of relief to which he is entitled.

* * *

QUESTIONS AND POINTS FOR DISCUSSION

1.   While the prosecutor in *Santobello* had agreed as part of the plea bargain to refrain from making a sentencing recommendation, prosecutors often agree to make a particular sentencing recommendation as part of a plea agreement. In United States v. Benchimol, 471 U.S. 453, 105 S.Ct. 2103 (1985), for example, the parties had agreed that the prosecutor would recommend probation in return for the defendant's guilty plea. The court nonetheless sentenced the defendant to prison for six years.

The defendant later moved to vacate his guilty plea or to be resentenced because the prosecutor, according to the defendant, had not enthusiastically recommended a sentence of probation to the court at the sentencing hearing

---

[2]   If the state court decides to allow withdrawal of the plea, the petitioner will, of course, plead anew to the original charge on two felony counts.

and had not explained the government's reasons for recommending probation. The Supreme Court held that a defendant may bargain for a commitment by the prosecutor to enthusiastically make a particular recommendation to the court or to explain the reasons for the government's recommendation. No such agreements were made between the parties in this case, however, and the Court refused to imply the existence of such terms into their agreement.

2.   Assume that a defendant, who was charged with first-degree murder, entered into a plea agreement under which he agreed to plead guilty to second-degree murder in return for the prosecutor's promise not to recommend a life sentence. At the defendant's sentencing hearing, the prosecutor recommended a prison sentence of seventy to one hundred years, and the court sentenced the defendant to prison for thirty-five to fifty-five years. Did the prosecutor breach the plea agreement in violation of due process? See Smith v. Stegall, 385 F.3d 993 (6th Cir.2004).

3.   The Supreme Court distinguished *Santobello* in Mabry v. Johnson, 467 U.S. 504, 104 S.Ct. 2543 (1984). In *Mabry,* the defendant, who was already serving concurrent sentences of twenty-one and twelve years for burglary and assault, was facing a murder charge. The prosecutor offered to recommend a twenty-one-year sentence, to be served concurrently with the defendant's other sentences, if he agreed to plead guilty to being an accessory after a felony murder. The defendant's attorney then called the prosecutor, accepting the offer. The prosecutor, however, said that he had made a mistake in making the offer to the defendant and retracted the offer. The prosecutor instead offered to recommend a twenty-one-year sentence, to be served consecutively with the defendant's other sentences, if he pled guilty. The defendant eventually accepted this offer and received a twenty-one-year consecutive sentence.

The defendant then filed a habeas corpus petition, contending that his due-process rights were violated when the prosecutor refused to abide by the terms of his original plea offer. The Supreme Court unanimously disagreed. Noting that at the time the defendant pled guilty he knew fully well that the prosecutor would recommend a consecutive sentence, the Court concluded that the defendant's plea simply was not induced by the prosecutor's original plea offer. Consequently, the original plea offer, even though "accepted" by the defendant, was "without constitutional significance." Id. at 510, 104 S.Ct. at 2548.

4.   Plea agreements may be breached, of course, not only by prosecutors, but by defendants. The Supreme Court case of Ricketts v. Adamson, 483 U.S. 1, 107 S.Ct. 2680 (1987) reveals the potentially severe consequences that can ensue from such a breach by a defendant. That case involved a defendant who was charged with first-degree murder. The prosecutor and the defendant entered into a plea agreement under which the defendant agreed to plead guilty to second-degree murder and to testify "when requested" against two other people involved in the murder. In return, the defendant would receive a prison sentence of forty-eight to forty-nine years. The trial court accepted this plea agreement.

The defendant then testified in the trials of his two codefendants, as he had agreed to do, and they were convicted of first-degree murder. Their convictions, however, were reversed on appeal and their cases remanded for retrial. At this point, the defendant, believing that he had fulfilled the terms of the plea agreement, balked at testifying again on the government's behalf unless the government agreed to release him from prison after the retrials. The state informed the defendant that he was in breach of the plea agreement and once again charged him with first-degree murder. Following a trial, the defendant was convicted of first-degree murder and sentenced to death.

The defendant contended that his right not to be subjected to double jeopardy barred his prosecution for first-degree murder, but the Supreme Court held that the terms of the plea agreement foreclosed that claim. The agreement specifically provided that " '[s]hould the defendant refuse to testify or should he at any time testify untruthfully * * * then this entire agreement is null and void and the original charge will be automatically reinstated.' " According to the Court, when the defendant decided to unilaterally pursue his own interpretation of the meaning of the plea agreement, he assumed the risk that he would be found in breach of it and subject to a first-degree murder prosecution. Even if he had acted in good faith, the defendant had taken a calculated gamble, exposing himself to the risk of a death sentence.

The defendant, in the end, did not lose his life as the price for his miscalculation. On remand from the Supreme Court, the Ninth Circuit Court of Appeals reversed the defendant's conviction for other reasons. Adamson v. Ricketts, 865 F.2d 1011, 1017–19 (9th Cir.1988). The prosecutor and the defendant then eventually agreed to reinstate the original plea agreement requiring the defendant to testify against his two codefendants. State v. Dunlap, 930 P.2d 518, 525 (Ariz.Ct.App.1996).

D. CONSTRAINTS ON PLEA NEGOTIATIONS AND INCENTIVES TO PLEAD GUILTY

BORDENKIRCHER V. HAYES

Supreme Court of the United States, 1978.
434 U.S. 357, 98 S.Ct. 663, 54 L.Ed.2d 604.

MR. JUSTICE STEWART delivered the opinion of the Court.

The question in this case is whether the Due Process Clause of the Fourteenth Amendment is violated when a state prosecutor carries out a threat made during plea negotiations to reindict the accused on more serious charges if he does not plead guilty to the offense with which he was originally charged.

The respondent, Paul Lewis Hayes, was indicted by a Fayette County, Ky., grand jury on a charge of uttering a forged instrument in the amount of $88.30, an offense then punishable by a term of 2 to 10 years in prison.

After arraignment, Hayes, his retained counsel, and the Commonwealth's Attorney met in the presence of the Clerk of the Court to discuss a possible plea agreement. During these conferences the prosecutor offered to recommend a sentence of five years in prison if Hayes would plead guilty to the indictment. He also said that if Hayes did not plead guilty and "save the court the inconvenience and necessity of a trial," he would return to the grand jury to seek an indictment under the Kentucky Habitual Criminal Act, which would subject Hayes to a mandatory sentence of life imprisonment by reason of his two prior felony convictions. Hayes chose not to plead guilty, and the prosecutor did obtain an indictment charging him under the Habitual Criminal Act. It is not disputed that the recidivist charge was fully justified by the evidence, that the prosecutor was in possession of this evidence at the time of the original indictment, and that Hayes' refusal to plead guilty to the original charge was what led to his indictment under the habitual criminal statute.

A jury found Hayes guilty on the principal charge of uttering a forged instrument and, in a separate proceeding, further found that he had twice before been convicted of felonies. As required by the habitual offender statute, he was sentenced to a life term in the penitentiary. * * *

* * *

* * * While the prosecutor did not actually obtain the recidivist indictment until after the plea conferences had ended, his intention to do so was clearly expressed at the outset of the plea negotiations. Hayes was thus fully informed of the true terms of the offer when he made his decision to plead not guilty. This is not a situation, therefore, where the prosecutor without notice brought an additional and more serious charge after plea negotiations relating only to the original indictment had ended with the defendant's insistence on pleading not guilty. As a practical matter, in short, this case would be no different if the grand jury had indicted Hayes as a recidivist from the outset, and the prosecutor had offered to drop that charge as part of the plea bargain.

The Court of Appeals nonetheless drew a distinction between "concessions relating to prosecution under an existing indictment," and threats to bring more severe charges not contained in the original indictment—a line it thought necessary in order to establish a prophylactic rule to guard against the evil of prosecutorial vindictiveness.[6] Quite apart

---

[6] "Although a prosecutor may in the course of plea negotiations offer a defendant concessions relating to prosecution under an existing indictment . . . he may not threaten a defendant with the consequence that more severe charges may be brought if he insists on going to trial. When a prosecutor obtains an indictment less severe than the facts known to him at the time might permit, he makes a discretionary determination that the interests of the state are served by not seeking more serious charges. . . . Accordingly, if after plea negotiations fail, he then procures an indictment charging a more serious crime, a strong inference is created that the only reason for the more serious charges is vindictiveness. Under these circumstances, the prosecutor should be required to justify his action." 547 F.2d, at 44–45.

from this chronological distinction, however, the Court of Appeals found that the prosecutor had acted vindictively in the present case since he had conceded that the indictment was influenced by his desire to induce a guilty plea. * * *

* * *

This Court held in *North Carolina v. Pearce,* 395 U.S. 711, 725, that the Due Process Clause of the Fourteenth Amendment "requires that vindictiveness against a defendant for having successfully attacked his first conviction must play no part in the sentence he receives after a new trial."[a] The same principle was later applied to prohibit a prosecutor from reindicting a convicted misdemeanant on a felony charge after the defendant had invoked an appellate remedy, since in this situation there was also a "realistic likelihood of 'vindictiveness.' " *Blackledge v. Perry,* 417 U.S., at 27.[b]

In those cases the Court was dealing with the State's unilateral imposition of a penalty upon a defendant who had chosen to exercise a legal right to attack his original conviction—a situation "very different from the give-and-take negotiation common in plea bargaining between the prosecution and defense, which arguably possess relatively equal bargaining power." The Court has emphasized that the due process violation in cases such as *Pearce* and *Perry* lay not in the possibility that a defendant might be deterred from the exercise of a legal right, but rather in the danger that the State might be retaliating against the accused for lawfully attacking his conviction.

To punish a person because he has done what the law plainly allows him to do is a due process violation of the most basic sort, and for an agent of the State to pursue a course of action whose objective is to penalize a person's reliance on his legal rights is "patently unconstitutional." But in the "give-and-take" of plea bargaining, there is no such element of punishment or retaliation so long as the accused is free to accept or reject the prosecution's offer.

---

[a] In *North Carolina v. Pearce,* the defendant successfully appealed his conviction for assault with intent to commit rape. He then was retried, convicted again, and sentenced to prison for an amount of time that exceeded his original sentence. The Court held that to impose a greater sentence on the defendant to retaliate against him for having taken an appeal violated due process of law, and that under the circumstances, there was a presumption that the increased sentence was due to proscribed judicial vindictiveness. This presumption could be rebutted by the prosecution, but in *Pearce,* was not.

[b] In *Blackledge,* the defendant was charged with, and convicted of, the misdemeanor of assault with a deadly weapon in a district court in North Carolina. He received a six-month prison sentence. As he was entitled to do under a state statute, he then filed a notice of appeal, seeking a trial *de novo* in a superior court. Following the filing of this notice of appeal, the prosecutor obtained an indictment charging the defendant with felony assault. The defendant pled guilty to this charge and was sentenced to prison for five to seven years. The Court held that, under the circumstances, there was a presumption that the enhanced charge was the product of prosecutorial vindictiveness and hence violative of the defendant's due-process rights.

Plea bargaining flows from "the mutuality of advantage" to defendants and prosecutors, each with his own reasons for wanting to avoid trial. Defendants advised by competent counsel and protected by other procedural safeguards are presumptively capable of intelligent choice in response to prosecutorial persuasion, and unlikely to be driven to false self-condemnation. * * *

While confronting a defendant with the risk of more severe punishment clearly may have a "discouraging effect on the defendant's assertion of his trial rights, the imposition of these difficult choices [is] an inevitable"—and permissible—"attribute of any legitimate system which tolerates and encourages the negotiation of pleas." It follows that, by tolerating and encouraging the negotiation of pleas, this Court has necessarily accepted as constitutionally legitimate the simple reality that the prosecutor's interest at the bargaining table is to persuade the defendant to forgo his right to plead not guilty.

It is not disputed here that Hayes was properly chargeable under the recidivist statute, since he had in fact been convicted of two previous felonies. In our system, so long as the prosecutor has probable cause to believe that the accused committed an offense defined by statute, the decision whether or not to prosecute, and what charge to file or bring before a grand jury, generally rests entirely in his discretion.[8] * * * To hold that the prosecutor's desire to induce a guilty plea is an "unjustifiable standard," which, like race or religion, may play no part in his charging decision, would contradict the very premises that underlie the concept of plea bargaining itself. Moreover, a rigid constitutional rule that would prohibit a prosecutor from acting forthrightly in his dealings with the defense could only invite unhealthy subterfuge that would drive the practice of plea bargaining back into the shadows from which it has so recently emerged.

There is no doubt that the breadth of discretion that our country's legal system vests in prosecuting attorneys carries with it the potential for both individual and institutional abuse. And broad though that discretion may be, there are undoubtedly constitutional limits upon its exercise. We hold only that the course of conduct engaged in by the prosecutor in this case, which no more than openly presented the defendant with the unpleasant alternatives of forgoing trial or facing charges on which he was plainly subject to prosecution, did not violate the Due Process Clause of the Fourteenth Amendment.

* * *

---

[8]   This case does not involve the constitutional implications of a prosecutor's offer during plea bargaining of adverse or lenient treatment for some person *other* than the accused, which might pose a greater danger of inducing a false guilty plea by skewing the assessment of the risks a defendant must consider.

MR. JUSTICE BLACKMUN, with whom MR. JUSTICE BRENNAN and MR. JUSTICE MARSHALL join, dissenting.

I feel that the Court * * * is departing from, or at least restricting, the principles established in *North Carolina v. Pearce,* 395 U.S. 711 (1969), and in *Blackledge v. Perry,* 417 U.S. 21 (1974). * * *

* * *

* * * In this case vindictiveness is present to the same extent as it was thought to be in *Pearce* and in *Perry;* the prosecutor here admitted that the sole reason for the new indictment was to discourage the respondent from exercising his right to a trial. Even had such an admission not been made, when plea negotiations, conducted in the face of the less serious charge under the first indictment, fail, charging by a second indictment a more serious crime for the same conduct creates "a strong inference" of vindictiveness. * * *

Prosecutorial vindictiveness, it seems to me, in the present narrow context, is the fact against which the Due Process Clause ought to protect. I perceive little difference between vindictiveness after what the Court describes as the exercise of a "legal right to attack his original conviction," and vindictiveness in the " 'give-and-take negotiation common in plea bargaining.' " Prosecutorial vindictiveness in any context is still prosecutorial vindictiveness. * * *

It might be argued that it really makes little difference how this case, now that it is here, is decided. The Court's holding gives plea bargaining full sway despite vindictiveness. A contrary result, however, merely would prompt the aggressive prosecutor to bring the greater charge initially in every case, and only thereafter to bargain. The consequences to the accused would still be adverse, for then he would bargain against a greater charge, face the likelihood of increased bail, and run the risk that the court would be less inclined to accept a bargained plea. Nonetheless, it is far preferable to hold the prosecution to the charge it was originally content to bring and to justify in the eyes of its public.[2]

---

[2] That prosecutors, without saying so, may sometimes bring charges more serious than they think appropriate for the ultimate disposition of a case, in order to gain bargaining leverage with a defendant, does not add support to today's decision, for this Court, in its approval of the advantages to be gained from plea negotiations, has never openly sanctioned such deliberate overcharging or taken such a cynical view of the bargaining process. Normally, of course, it is impossible to show that this is what the prosecutor is doing, and the courts necessarily have deferred to the prosecutor's exercise of discretion in initial charging decisions.

Even if overcharging is to be sanctioned, there are strong reasons of fairness why the charges should be presented at the beginning of the bargaining process, rather than as a filliped threat at the end. First, it means that a prosecutor is required to reach a charging decision without any knowledge of the particular defendant's willingness to plead guilty; hence the defendant who truly believes himself to be innocent, and wishes for that reason to go to trial, is not likely to be subject to quite such a devastating gamble since the prosecutor has fixed the incentives for the average case.

MR. JUSTICE POWELL, dissenting. [Opinion omitted.]

QUESTIONS AND POINTS FOR DISCUSSION

1.   In United States v. Goodwin, 457 U.S. 368, 102 S.Ct. 2485 (1982), the Supreme Court addressed a question left open in *Bordenkircher*—whether due process is violated when unsuccessful plea negotiations are followed by the bringing, without notice, of additional and more serious charges by the prosecutor. *Goodwin* involved a defendant who had been stopped for speeding and then fled in his car after the police officer noticed a plastic bag under the armrest of the car and asked the defendant to lift up the armrest. While trying to flee, the defendant struck the police officer with his car.

The defendant was charged with multiple misdemeanor and petty offenses. Although the defendant and the prosecutor initially engaged in plea negotiations, the defendant ultimately decided that he wanted a jury trial. A few weeks later, he was indicted for the felony of forcibly assaulting a federal officer and three other crimes stemming from the incident at the scene of the traffic stop. He was convicted of the felony as well as one misdemeanor.

The defendant moved to set aside the jury's verdict on the grounds that the prosecutor, in violation of due process of law, had charged the defendant with a felony to retaliate against him for having invoked his right to a jury trial. The prosecutor responded by citing a number of reasons why he had sought the felony indictment, including his belief that the defendant was trafficking in drugs when his car was stopped, the number of violent crimes committed by the defendant in the past, and the fact that the defendant had fled from the jurisdiction for three years following his initial arrest and arraignment.

The Supreme Court considered whether a presumption of vindictiveness is warranted when new and more serious charges are brought before trial following a defendant's decision to stand trial. According to the Court, for such a presumption to exist, there would have to be a "reasonable likelihood" that in such circumstances, the government's actions are due to proscribed vindictiveness. Id. at 373, 102 S.Ct. at 2488. The Court noted that such a presumption was warranted in Blackledge v. Perry, 417 U.S. 21, 94 S.Ct. 2098 (1974), where the new charge was brought after the defendant was convicted in one court but then exercised his statutory right to a trial *de novo* in a different court. The Court, however, distinguished the pretrial setting in which the new charges were brought in this case:

> There is good reason to be cautious before adopting an inflexible presumption of prosecutorial vindictiveness in a pretrial setting. In the course of preparing a case for trial, the prosecutor may uncover

---

Second, it is healthful to keep charging practices visible to the general public, so that political bodies can judge whether the policy being followed is a fair one. Visibility is enhanced if the prosecutor is required to lay his cards on the table with an indictment of public record at the beginning of the bargaining process, rather than making use of unrecorded verbal warnings of more serious indictments yet to come.

additional information that suggests a basis for further prosecution or he simply may come to realize that information possessed by the State has a broader significance. At this stage of the proceedings, the prosecutor's assessment of the proper extent of prosecution may not have crystallized. In contrast, once a trial begins—and certainly by the time a conviction has been obtained—it is much more likely that the State has discovered and assessed all of the information against an accused and has made a determination, on the basis of that information, of the extent to which he should be prosecuted. Thus, a change in the charging decision made after an initial trial is completed is much more likely to be improperly motivated than is a pretrial decision.

* * *

Thus, the timing of the prosecutor's action in this case suggests that a presumption of vindictiveness is not warranted. A prosecutor should remain free before trial to exercise the broad discretion entrusted to him to determine the extent of the societal interest in prosecution. An initial decision should not freeze future conduct. * * *

* * *

* * * Moreover, unlike the trial judge in *Pearce,* no party is asked "to do over what it thought it had already done correctly." A prosecutor has no "personal stake" in a bench trial and thus no reason to engage in "self-vindication" upon a defendant's request for a jury trial. Perhaps most importantly, the institutional bias against the retrial of a decided question that supported the decisions in *Pearce* and *Blackledge* simply has no counterpart in this case.

457 U.S. at 381–83, 102 S.Ct. at 2493–94.

Although defendants charged before trial with additional and more serious charges following their insistence on going to trial cannot avail themselves of the benefits of a presumption of vindictiveness, the Supreme Court in *Goodwin* did leave open the possibility that a defendant could prevail on a due-process claim by showing that the prosecutor's charging decision was actually prompted by vindictiveness. Can you reconcile this statement with the decision in *Bordenkircher,* where the Court acknowledged that the prosecutor had charged the defendant with being a habitual offender because of his decision to plead not guilty but found no due-process violation?

Concurring in the judgment in *Goodwin,* Justice Blackmun stated that when a defendant elects to go to trial and the prosecutor then files additional and more serious charges, there should be a presumption of vindictiveness, whether or not the new charges are filed before or after trial. He found, however, that the prosecutor had rebutted the presumption of vindictiveness in this case. Justice Brennan, joined by Justice Marshall, dissented, noting that the evidence of a due-process violation was even more compelling in this case, where the increased punishment followed the defendant's exercise of his constitutional right to a jury trial, than in *Blackledge*, where the increased punishment followed the defendant's invocation of his statutory right to a trial *de novo*.

2. In Alabama v. Smith, 490 U.S. 794, 109 S.Ct. 2201 (1989), the Supreme Court once again refused to permit a defendant to invoke a presumption of vindictiveness. In that case, the defendant pled guilty to burglary and rape in return for the state's dismissal of a sodomy charge. The trial court then sentenced the defendant to thirty years in prison for each conviction, with his sentences to be served concurrently.

The defendant successfully appealed his convictions on the grounds that his guilty pleas were invalid because he had not been sufficiently apprised of the penalties that could be imposed if he pled guilty. The government then reinstated the sodomy charge, and the case went to trial before a jury. The same judge who had initially sentenced the defendant presided at the trial.

Following the defendant's conviction on all three counts, the judge sentenced him to life imprisonment for the burglary, a concurrent life term for the sodomy, and 150 years in prison for the rape, with the latter sentence to be served consecutively with the other two sentences. In imposing these sentences, the trial judge noted that the trial had revealed additional facts about the defendant's crimes of which the judge was previously unaware, including that the defendant had raped the victim five times, forced her to have oral sex with him, and threatened her with a knife.

The defendant contended that the increased sentences were imposed by the judge in order to retaliate against him for getting his guilty plea set aside. The question before the Supreme Court was whether the defendant could avail himself of a presumption of vindictiveness or whether he would instead have to prove actual vindictiveness to prevail on his due-process claim.

Answering this question, according to the Court, required an assessment of whether there was a "reasonable likelihood" that sentences imposed after trial that are greater than those imposed following guilty pleas are the product of judicial vindictiveness. The Court answered this question in the negative:

> [W]hen a greater penalty is imposed after trial than was imposed after a prior guilty plea, the increase in sentence is not more likely than not attributable to the vindictiveness on the part of the sentencing judge. Even when the same judge imposes both sentences, the relevant sentencing information available to the judge after the plea will usually be considerably less than that available after a trial.

* * *

As this case demonstrates, in the course of the proof at trial the judge may gather a fuller appreciation of the nature and extent of the crimes charged. The defendant's conduct during trial may give the judge insights into his moral character and suitability for rehabilitation. See United States v. Grayson, 438 U.S. 41, 53 (1978) (sentencing authority's perception of the truthfulness of a defendant testifying on his own behalf may be considered in sentencing). Finally, after trial, the factors that may have indicated leniency as consideration for the guilty plea are no longer present. Here, too, although the same Judge who sentenced following the guilty plea also imposes sentence following trial, in conducting the trial the court is not simply "do[ing] over what it thought it had already done correctly."

Id. at 801–02, 109 S.Ct. at 2205–06. What might be the likely effect of the Court's decision on defendants' willingness to challenge the validity of their guilty pleas?

3.   Consider the facts of the following case. The defendant was charged with a number of crimes, including murder and multiple counts of rape. His mother, father, brother, two sisters, and sister-in-law were charged with a number of crimes stemming from their alleged attempts to cover up the defendant's crimes. The first trial, that of the defendant's brother, resulted in criminal convictions for which the brother was sentenced to prison for four and a half years. The prosecutor then promised the defendant that if he pled no contest to the murder charge and two counts of first-degree criminal sexual penetration, his brother would be released from prison, criminal charges against his sisters and sister-in-law would be dropped, and his parents would be permitted to plead no contest to a conspiracy charge and placed on probation. In addition, thirty other felony charges pending against the defendant would be dropped. The defendant agreed to this proposal. Was his guilty plea valid? Why or why not? See Miles v. Dorsey, 61 F.3d 1459, 1468–69 (10th Cir.1995).

4.   Federal Rule of Evidence 410(a)(4) provides that a defendant's statements made during plea negotiations are generally inadmissible at trial if the negotiations do not culminate in a guilty plea or the guilty plea is later withdrawn. In United States v. Mezzanatto, 513 U.S. 196, 115 S.Ct. 797 (1995), the Supreme Court held that a defendant can waive the protection afforded by this rule. The waiver at issue in *Mezzanatto*, which was extracted from the defendant before the prosecutor would enter into what proved to be unsuccessful plea negotiations, permitted the defendant's statements during the negotiations to be admitted for impeachment purposes—in other words, to contradict his testimony at trial. Three of the Justices who joined the seven-person majority in the case—Justices Ginsburg, O'Connor, and Breyer— emphasized in a concurring opinion that the case did not involve or resolve the question whether a waiver of the exclusionary rule can encompass statements of the defendant introduced in the prosecution's case-in-chief to prove the defendant's guilt.

Since *Mezzanatto*, federal prosecutors frequently have refused to enter into plea negotiations unless defendants agree that any statements they make during plea discussions can be used to impeach their contradictory testimony at trial. Many "proffer letters," the documents which spell out the government's conditions for entering into plea discussions, go even further, providing that the defendant's statements during plea negotiations can be used to rebut any evidence offered or elicited at any stage of the criminal prosecution or any factual assertions made on the defendant's behalf. See, e.g., United States v. Hardwick, 544 F.3d 565, 570–71 (3d Cir.2008) (holding that proffer agreement was triggered and enforceable when defense counsel, through the cross-examination of government witnesses during the prosecution's case-in-chief, inferred that others were responsible for two killings for which the defendant had admitted culpability in his proffer statement); United States v. Barrow, 400 F.3d 109, 120–122 (2d Cir.2005) (interpreting and enforcing proffer agreement to allow government to introduce defendant's admissions of drug dealing, made during plea negotiations, after defense counsel argued in his opening statement at trial that someone else perpetrated the drug crimes). And some proffer letters require a defendant to waive objections to the introduction of plea-related statements at any point during a trial, including during the prosecution's case-in-chief. See, e.g., United States v. Mitchell, 633 F.3d 997, 1004–06 (10th Cir.2011) (upholding Rule 410 case-in-chief waivers).

As a policy matter, should court rules permit the use, for impeachment purposes, of a defendant's statements made during plea negotiations? What are the competing arguments for and against enforcing a waiver when the defendant's statements are used, not to impeach the defendant's testimony, but to rebut other contradictory evidence introduced by the defendant or to refute arguments made by defense counsel? Finally, should court rules allow, and does the Constitution permit, statements made by a defendant during plea negotiations to be admitted in the prosecution's case-in-chief to prove one or more elements of a crime? For tips on what defense attorneys can do to protect their clients' interests when a proffer letter has spelled out preconditions to plea negotiations, see David P. Leonard, Waiver of Protections Against the Use of Plea Bargains and Plea Bargaining Statements after *Mezzanatto*, 23 Crim. Just. 8 (Fall 2008).

5.   In Newton v. Rumery, 480 U.S. 386, 107 S.Ct. 1187 (1987), the Supreme Court considered the validity of what are called release-dismissal agreements. In that case, Bernard Rumery was charged with the felony of tampering with a witness. After his attorney threatened to file suit due to the bringing of unfounded charges against Rumery, the prosecutor agreed to dismiss the criminal charge in return for Rumery's agreement not to bring a civil suit against the town, local officials, and the witness. Rumery acquiesced, and the criminal charge was dismissed.

Ten months later, Rumery brought a § 1983 civil-rights suit against the town and various local officials, claiming, among other things, that his arrest was unlawful. In a motion to dismiss, the defendants argued that the release-dismissal agreement barred the lawsuit. Rumery responded that the agreement was contrary to public policy and consequently void.

In a 5–4 decision, the Supreme Court held that the release-dismissal agreement at issue in the case was valid and enforceable. The Court acknowledged that the prospect of obtaining such agreements might induce prosecutors to file frivolous criminal charges as a way of pressuring individuals to forgo plans to sue government officials. In addition, such agreements might lead to the abandonment of criminal prosecutions when the interests of the public favor prosecution. Such agreements might also permit constitutional violations to go unremedied. Nonetheless, the Court concluded that such agreements are not *per se* invalid. The circumstances surrounding an agreement instead have to be examined to determine its validity and enforceability.

Justice O'Connor wrote a concurring opinion in *Newton* to emphasize that the burden is upon government officials sued under § 1983 to establish that a release-dismissal agreement was "voluntarily made, not the product of prosecutorial overreaching, and in the public interest." Id. at 401, 107 S.Ct. at 1197 (O'Connor, J., concurring). She identified some of the factors relevant to these questions:

> Many factors may bear on whether a release was voluntary and not the product of overreaching, some of which come readily to mind. The knowledge and experience of the criminal defendant and the circumstances of the execution of the release, including, importantly, whether the defendant was counseled, are clearly relevant. The nature of the criminal charges that are pending is also important, for the greater the charge, the greater the coercive effect. The existence of a legitimate criminal justice objective for obtaining the release will support its validity. And, importantly, the possibility of abuse is clearly mitigated if the release-dismissal agreement is executed under judicial supervision.

Id. at 401–02, 107 S.Ct. at 1197.

Even the four dissenters in this case—Justices Stevens, Brennan, Marshall, and Blackmun—acknowledged that in certain circumstances, release-dismissal agreements might be valid. The dissenters felt, however, that the government officials sued in this case had not established the validity of the release-dismissal agreement at issue in the case. By contrast, the majority of the Court felt that the release-dismissal agreement was valid, particularly because there was evidence that the prosecutor entered into the agreement largely to avoid trauma to the witness with whom Rumery had allegedly tampered and who might be called as a witness in the civil suit.

6.   Can a prosecutor condition a plea agreement on the defendant's agreement to refrain from interviewing a witness, such as the victim of a sex crime with which the defendant is charged? In State v. Draper, 784 P.2d 259, 264 (Ariz.1989), the Arizona Supreme Court held that conditioning a plea agreement on a defendant's surrender of his right to interview witnesses violates due process unless the record demonstrates a "special reason" that makes the condition reasonable. The court also held that such a condition violates the defendant's right to the effective assistance of counsel unless the

attorney has access to other information that would enable the attorney to represent the defendant effectively without interviewing the witness.

7.   Can and should a prosecutor be able to extract, as a condition of a plea agreement, a waiver by the defendant of his or her right to appeal? Is the waiver, for example, of the right to appeal a sentence enforceable when a sentencing court erroneously concluded that it could not impose concurrent sentences on the defendant but must impose consecutive sentences? See United States v. Hahn, 359 F.3d 1315, 1329 (10th Cir.2004) (holding a waiver enforceable in such circumstances).

A few courts have held that waivers in plea agreements of the right to appeal are unenforceable. See, e.g., State v. Ethington, 592 P.2d 768, 769–70 (Ariz.1979) (holding such waivers void as a matter of public policy). But the vast majority of the courts have held that conditioning a plea agreement on the defendant's waiver of the right to appeal is, as a general rule, permissible, provided the waiver is knowing and voluntary. See Kevin Bennardo, Post-Sentencing Appellate Waivers, 48 U. Mich. J.L. Reform 347, 351 n.28 (2015) (listing cases). Most of these courts have carved out exceptions to this rule. Some of the more common exceptions recognized by some, though not all, courts allow an appeal when a defendant claims that the sentence exceeded the statutory maximum, the defendant received ineffective assistance of counsel when negotiating the plea agreement, or the sentence was based on an unconstitutional criterion, such as race. United States v. Campbell, 813 F.3d 1016, 1018 (7th Cir.2016). For an article profiling the division in the courts regarding the enforceability of waivers barring later claims of plea-related ineffective assistance of counsel and analyzing this issue, see Nancy J. King, Plea Bargains that Waive Claims of Ineffective Assistance—Waiving *Padilla* and *Frye*, 51 Duq. L.Rev. 647 (2013).

Proponents of appeal waivers maintain that they have many benefits. Among the cited benefits are that they save the courts and the parties the time and money that would be expended on appeals, benefit defendants by giving them a bargaining chip, and help bring closure to victims, the defendant, and the government. Critics of these waivers, on the other hand, argue that they enable illegal sentences and convictions to remain in effect, insulate the misconduct of trial judges, defense attorneys, and prosecutors from judicial review, and exacerbate sentencing disparity. This latter argument is grounded in part on the premise that appellate review diminishes sentencing disparity. In addition, there may be significant differences within a jurisdiction in the frequency with which waiver-of-appeal clauses are inserted into plea agreements. See Nancy J. King & Michael E. O'Neill, Appeal Waivers and the Future of Sentencing Policy, 55 Duke L.J. 209, 231–32 (2005) (reporting that including a waiver clause in a plea agreement was, in the year on which the study focused, the norm in some federal circuits and the exception in others).

What additional arguments could be propounded in favor of and against enforcing waivers of the right to appeal incorporated into plea agreements? If, as a general rule, these appeal waivers are enforceable, what exceptions, if any, should apply to this rule?

8. Not only the Constitution, but statutes, court rules, and prosecution policies may limit what a prosecutor can do to induce a defendant to plead guilty. The National Advisory Commission on Criminal Justice Standards and Goals, Report on Courts (1973) recommended that the following limitations be placed on prosecutors during plea bargaining:

Standard 3.6. Prohibited Prosecutorial Inducements to Enter a Plea of Guilty

No prosecutor should, in connection with plea negotiations, engage in, perform, or condone any of the following:

1. Charging or threatening to charge the defendant with offenses for which the admissible evidence available to the prosecutor is insufficient to support a guilty verdict.

2. Charging or threatening to charge the defendant with a crime not ordinarily charged in the jurisdiction for the conduct allegedly engaged in by him.

3. Threatening the defendant that if he pleads not guilty, his sentence may be more severe than that which ordinarily is imposed in the jurisdiction in similar cases on defendants who plead not guilty.

4. Failing to grant full disclosure before the disposition negotiations of all exculpatory evidence material to guilt or punishment.

Are there any other prosecutorial inducements that you would consider improper, if not unconstitutional? See, e.g., Arizona v. Horning, 761 P.2d 728 (Ariz.Ct.App.1988) (plea involuntary when entered in return for prosecutor's agreement not to interfere with defendant's attempts to secure conjugal visits with his wife in jail).

9. The Supreme Court case of Corbitt v. New Jersey, 439 U.S. 212, 99 S.Ct. 492 (1978) dealt with the constitutionality, not of prosecutorial inducements to plead guilty, but of legislative inducements. The defendant in that case had been charged with first-degree murder. If convicted of first-degree murder following a jury trial, he faced a mandatory sentence of life imprisonment. If the jury instead found him guilty of second-degree murder, he could be sentenced to up to thirty years in prison. Although guilty pleas to murder were prohibited in New Jersey, a defendant could plead *nolo contendere* to a murder indictment. If a defendant entered such a plea, and the plea was accepted by the court, the judge could impose either a life sentence or the sentence for second-degree murder, *i.e.*, a maximum of thirty years.

The defendant in *Corbitt* opted to go to trial and was found guilty of first-degree murder by a jury. He was then sentenced to life in prison as required by the New Jersey statute. On appeal, he claimed that New Jersey unconstitutionally penalized defendants charged with first-degree murder who pursued their constitutional right to a jury trial. The Supreme Court disagreed:

[N]ot every burden on the exercise of a constitutional right, and not every pressure or encouragement to waive such a right, is invalid. Specifically, there is no *per se* rule against encouraging guilty pleas. We have squarely held that a State may encourage a guilty plea by offering substantial benefits in return for the plea. The plea may obtain for the defendant "the possibility or certainty . . . [not only of] a lesser penalty than the sentence that could be imposed after a trial and a verdict of guilty . . .," but also of a lesser penalty than that *required* to be imposed after a guilty verdict by a jury. [The Court here cited and discussed *Bordenkircher v. Hayes.*]

* * *

* * * There is no doubt that those homicide defendants who are willing to plead *non vult* may be treated more leniently than those who go to trial, but withholding the possibility of leniency from the latter cannot be equated with impermissible punishment as long as our cases sustaining plea bargaining remain undisturbed. Those cases, as we have said, unequivocally recognize the constitutional propriety of extending leniency in exchange for a plea of guilty and of not extending leniency to those who have not demonstrated those attributes on which leniency is based.

Id. at 218–20, 223–24, 99 S.Ct. at 497–98, 500.

In *Corbitt,* the Supreme Court distinguished United States v. Jackson, 390 U.S. 570, 88 S.Ct. 1209 (1968), discussed on page 41, a case where the Court had held the sentencing provisions of the Federal Kidnapping Act to be unconstitutional. Under that statute, a defendant found guilty by a jury of violating the Act could receive the death penalty. By contrast, the maximum penalty that could be imposed on a defendant tried in a bench trial or who pled guilty was life in prison. The Supreme Court in *Corbitt* highlighted the following distinctions between *Jackson* and the case before it:

The principal difference is that the pressures to forgo trial and to plead to the charge in this case are not what they were in *Jackson.* First, the death penalty, which is "unique in its severity and irrevocability," is not involved here. Although we need not agree with the New Jersey court that the *Jackson* rationale is limited to those cases where a plea avoids any possibility of the death penalty's being imposed, it is a material fact that under the New Jersey law the maximum penalty for murder is life imprisonment, not death. Furthermore, in *Jackson,* any risk of suffering the maximum penalty could be avoided by pleading guilty. Here, although the punishment when a jury finds a defendant guilty of first-degree murder is life imprisonment, the risk of that punishment is not completely avoided by pleading *non vult* because the judge accepting the plea has the authority to impose a life term. New Jersey does not reserve the maximum punishment for murder for those who insist on a jury trial.

439 U.S. at 217, 99 S.Ct. at 496.

10. In his concurring opinion in Brady v. United States, 397 U.S. 742, 90 S.Ct. 1463 (1970), Justice Marshall noted that threats or promises made by a trial judge to induce a guilty plea may render that plea involuntary. See, e.g., United States v. Anderson, 993 F.2d 1435, 1437–38 (9th Cir.1993) (guilty plea tendered after judge's statements at the arraignment that he would not accept a plea after that date to fewer than all thirty counts of the indictment was involuntary). Because of the risk that judicial participation in plea bargaining will place undue pressure on a defendant to plead guilty, a number of jurisdictions have barred the involvement of judges in plea discussions. See, e.g., Fed.R.Crim.P. 11(c)(1). The American Bar Association delineates, in a bit different way, the responsibilities of judges to avoid coercing guilty pleas or the terms of plea agreements:

Standard 14–3.3. Responsibilities of the Judge

* * *

(c) The judge should not through word or demeanor, either directly or indirectly, communicate to the defendant or defense counsel that a plea agreement should be accepted or that a guilty plea should be entered.

(d) A judge should not ordinarily participate in plea negotiation discussions among the parties. Upon the request of the parties, a judge may be presented with a proposed plea agreement negotiated by the parties and may indicate whether the court would accept the terms as proposed and if relevant, indicate what sentence would be imposed. * * *

* * *

ABA Standards for Criminal Justice: Pleas of Guilty, Standard 14–3.3 (3d ed. 1999). See also Nancy J. King & Ronald F. Wright, The Invisible Revolution in Plea Bargaining: Managerial Judging and Judicial Participation in Negotiations, 95 Tex. L.Rev. 325 (2016) (detailing how judges in ten states are, in varied ways, involved in settling criminal cases).

What constraints would you place on the participation of judges in plea negotiations? For examples of judges placing strong pressure on defendants to plead guilty, see Richard Klein, Due Process Denied: Judicial Coercion in the Plea Bargaining Process, 32 Hofstra L.Rev. 1349 (2004).

11. *Class Exercise*: Discuss and debate the following questions:

a. Should plea bargaining be abolished? If so, should the prohibition extend to some or all crimes? See, e.g., Fla. Stat. Ann. § 316.656(2)(a) (prohibiting judges from accepting a guilty plea to a lesser offense when a person charged with driving while under the influence of alcohol had a blood or breath alcohol content of .15 or more).

b. What restrictions should be placed on plea bargaining in jurisdictions that retain it? Should, for example, a cap be placed on the sentencing discount offered and afforded a defendant who pleads guilty? What would be the arguable advantages and disadvantages of such a cap? Can and should any other steps be taken to curtail plea-bargaining abuses and problems? For some of the ideas tendered to prevent or limit the problems that can attend plea bargaining, see Stephanos Bibas, Designing Plea Bargaining from the Ground Up: Accuracy and Fairness Without Trials as Backstops, 57 Wm. & Mary L.Rev. 1055, 1078–81 (2016); Nancy J. King & Ronald F. Wright, The Invisible Revolution in Plea Bargaining: Managerial Judging and Judicial Participation in Negotiations, 95 Tex. L.Rev. 325, 329, 392–96 (2016) (explaining why increased judicial participation in plea negotiations may be "a counterweight to intransigent prosecutors, a safeguard against overstretched defense counsel, and a source of more complete information for defendants during negotiations and for judges deciding sentences").

CHAPTER 3

SENTENCING STATUTES AND GUIDELINES

■ ■ ■

A. "PURE" SENTENCING MODELS

Two critical decisions must be made in the course of sentencing a person. First, what is known as the in-out decision must be made—the decision as to whether the defendant will be incarcerated. Once this decision has been made, the duration, amount, and terms of the sentence then must be determined—in other words, the length of any community-based or incarcerative sentence, the amount of any fine or restitution to be paid by the defendant, and other requirements to which the defendant will be subject, such as mandatory drug treatment. Set forth below is a description of three different ways of allocating the authority to make these important sentencing decisions.

ALAN M. DERSHOWITZ, BACKGROUND PAPER, IN FAIR AND CERTAIN PUNISHMENT: REPORT OF THE TWENTIETH CENTURY FUND TASK FORCE ON CRIMINAL SENTENCING
(1976). Reprinted with the permission of The Century Foundation.

* * *

The history of criminal sentencing in the United States has been a history of shift in institutional power and in the theories that have guided the exercise of such power. In each period, one of three sentencing models has predominated, either the legislative, judicial, or administrative model. These are so called in recognition of the institution or the group of policy makers [that] exercises the power to imprison and to determine the length of imprisonment. Although incarcerative powers usually are shared by several persons or agencies, it is nevertheless possible to postulate pure sentencing models.

In the *legislatively fixed model,* the legislature determines that conviction for a given crime warrants a given term of imprisonment. For example, a first offender convicted of armed robbery must be sentenced to five years' imprisonment. There is no judicial or administrative discretion under this model; the legislature has authorized but one sentence.

* * *

In the *judicially fixed model,* the legislature determines the general range of imprisonment for a given crime. For example, a first offender convicted of armed robbery shall be sentenced to no less than 1 and no more than 10 years' imprisonment. The sentencing judge must fix a determinate sentence within that range: "I sentence the defendant to five years' imprisonment." Once this sentence is fixed, it cannot be increased or reduced by any parole board or adult authority; the defendant must serve for five years. * * *

Under this model, discretion is vested in the sentencing judge; how much is vested depends on the range of imprisonment authorized by the legislature. On the day he is sentenced, however, the defendant knows precisely how long he will serve; there is no discretion vested in the parole board or prison authorities.

In the *administratively fixed model,* the legislature sets an extremely wide permissible range of imprisonment for a given crime. A first-offense armed robber, for example, shall be sentenced to a term of one day to life. The sentencing judge must—or may—impose the legislatively determined sentence: "You are sentenced to one day to life." The actual duration of the sentence is decided by an administrative agency while the prisoner is serving his sentence. For example, after five years of imprisonment, the adult authority decides that the prisoner is ready for release.

Under this model, vast discretion is vested in the administrative agency and in the prison authorities. On the day he is sentenced, the defendant does not know how long he will have to serve, although he probably can make an educated guess based on past practices.

* * *

QUESTIONS AND POINTS FOR DISCUSSION

1. What are the advantages and disadvantages of each of the three sentencing models described above? Can you construct a sentencing model that incorporates most or many of the advantages of the three "pure" sentencing models, but not their disadvantages?

2. The "pure" legislative sentencing model purports to eliminate judicial and administrative discretion in the sentencing process. Are there any reasons why this aim of eliminating the exercise of discretion as to the sentence to be served by a defendant might be frustrated in a jurisdiction adopting this model? See note 2 on page 96.

B. SENTENCING STATUTES

1. INDETERMINATE SENTENCING STATUTES

Most of the sentencing systems in this country are hybrids of the "pure" legislative, judicial, and administrative sentencing models described earlier. Sentencing statutes typically are divided into two general categories: indeterminate and determinate. When an indeterminate sentence is imposed, as its name suggests, the defendant does not know how much time he or she actually will spend in prison. The legislature, typically in conjunction with the sentencing judge, defines the minimum period of incarceration, if there is one, and the maximum term of confinement. A parole board, however, decides in the future when the person should be released from prison.

In practice, here is how an indeterminate sentencing structure might work. Assume that a legislature authorizes a sentence of from one to thirty years for a particular crime. The sentencing judge then imposes a sentence falling within this range, sentencing the defendant to a minimum of ten years in prison and a maximum of thirty. The parole board later decides when to actually release the defendant from prison, whether after ten years, thirty years, or some time in between.

The Iowa statutory provisions set forth below further exemplify the way in which an indeterminate sentencing system can operate:

IOWA CODE ANN. § 902.3 Indeterminate sentence

When a judgment of conviction of a felony other than a class "A" felony is entered against a person, the court, in imposing a sentence of confinement, shall commit the person into the custody of the director of the Iowa department of corrections for an indeterminate term, the maximum length of which shall not exceed the limits as fixed by section 902.9, unless otherwise prescribed by statute, nor shall the term be less than the minimum term imposed by law, if a minimum sentence is provided. * * *

IOWA CODE ANN. § 902.8 Minimum sentence—habitual offender

An habitual offender is any person convicted of a class "C" or a class "D" felony, who has twice before been convicted of any felony in a court of this or any other state, or of the United States. * * * A person sentenced as an habitual offender shall not be eligible for parole until the person has served the minimum sentence of confinement of three years.

IOWA CODE ANN. § 902.9 Maximum sentence for felons

1.   The maximum sentence for any person convicted of a felony shall be that prescribed by statute or, if not prescribed by statute, if other than a class "A" felony[a] shall be determined as follows:

* * *

b.   A class "B" felon shall be confined for no more than twenty-five years.

c.   An habitual offender shall be confined for no more than fifteen years.

d.   A class "C" felon, not an habitual offender, shall be confined for no more than ten years, and in addition shall be sentenced to a fine of at least one thousand dollars but not more than ten thousand dollars.

e.   A class "D" felon, not an habitual offender, shall be confined for no more than five years, and in addition shall be sentenced to a fine of at least seven hundred fifty dollars but not more than seven thousand five hundred dollars. * * *

QUESTIONS AND POINTS FOR DISCUSSION

1.   The provisions of indeterminate sentencing statutes vary widely from state to state. For example, statutes may differ as to whether a minimum period of incarceration is prescribed, what that minimum is, and what the maximum penalty is.

There are several ways in which a legislature can define the minimum prison sentence to be imposed or served for a crime. A state, for example, may do what Iowa does with habitual offenders, specifying a certain number of years that people must spend in prison before they can be considered for release on parole. Alternatively or in addition, a state can require that the minimum sentence be no more or no less than a certain percentage of the maximum sentence imposed on a defendant. See, e.g., N.Y. Penal Law § 70.00(3)(b) (McKinney) (minimum prison sentence for most felonies shall be no less than one year but no more than one-third of the maximum sentence imposed); Wyo.Stat. § 7–13–201 (minimum should be no greater than 90% of the maximum sentence). Why would a legislature limit a minimum sentence to a certain percentage of the maximum sentence?

2.   Professor Michael Tonry has summarized some of the chief criticisms of according judges broad sentencing discretion, as occurs with indeterminate sentencing:

---

[a]   Under Iowa Code Ann. § 902.1, a defendant convicted of a class "A" felony generally must be sentenced to life in prison and cannot be released on parole unless the governor commutes the sentence to a term of years.

Disparities. A principal criticism of indeterminate sentencing is that it too often results in stark differences in sentences for people who have committed similar crimes * * *. * * *

Bias and stereotypes. A second recurring criticism is that the broad discretion accorded judges and corrections officials gives too much rein to their conscious biases or unconscious stereotyping. * * *

Inadequate implementation. Some critics argue that corrections systems seldom if ever carry through on the implied promises of indeterminate sentencing. Vocational training is often not relevant to the job market. Psychiatric, psychological, and medical services often are of low quality. Funds are seldom sufficient to provide a rich array of services tailored to offenders' needs in prison or in the community. * * *

Deserved punishments. * * * The "deserved punishment" criticism holds that people should receive particular punishments and that anything less * * * "depreciates the seriousness of the crime." Put more colloquially, a "coddling criminals" complaint has regularly been lodged against indeterminate sentencing since its beginnings.

Public sentiment. Some critics contend that indeterminate sentencing allows the "behind-closed-doors" decisions of judges and others to frustrate realization of the public's (or elected officials') views. * * *

Michael Tonry, Reconsidering Indeterminate and Structured Sentencing, Sentencing & Corrections: Issues for the 21st Century 5–6 (1999).

Statistics gathered during a study of federal district courts conducted at a time, before adoption of the federal sentencing guidelines, when they imposed indeterminate sentences highlight the problem of sentencing disparity noted by Professor Tonry. These statistics revealed gross differences in the courts' sentencing decisions. For example, while 84% of the individuals convicted one year in the District of Minnesota of larceny or theft were sentenced to prison, only 8% of those convicted of these crimes in the District of Colorado were imprisoned. Legislation to Revise and Recodify Federal Criminal Laws: Hearings Before the Subcomm. on Criminal Justice of the House Comm. on the Judiciary, 95th Cong., 1st & 2d Sess. 2459 (1978) (statement of William J. Anderson). In addition to differences in the percentage of people incarcerated, the study revealed stark contrasts in the average length of prison sentences imposed by the courts. For example, in the Southern District of New York, the average sentence for bank robbery was seven years during the time of the study; in the District of South Carolina, by contrast, the average sentence was eighteen years. Id.

3. At least some of the disparity caused by indeterminate sentencing statutes can be alleviated through the use of parole guidelines. Parole guidelines identify what is the advised or, in some jurisdictions, presumptive release date for prisoners in "ordinary" cases based on specified factors, such

as the offense of conviction and criminal history. A person, however, can be released earlier or later than this date when the parole board explains in writing why he or she does not fit the prototypical case. While parole guidelines can help to reduce unwarranted disparity in the amount of time spent in prison, they have no effect on the disparity that can result when judges are making the in-out decision—the decision whether to imprison a person. Some people may be sentenced to prison while similar individuals serve their sentences in the community.

4. Concerns about parole have prompted a number, though not all, of the states with indeterminate sentencing systems to abolish discretionary parole release completely or eliminate it for prisoners convicted of violent or other specified crimes. A majority of states, though, still retain some form of indeterminate sentencing, and a few states that discarded parole have been reconsidering whether to restore this back-end release mechanism. Edward E. Rhine et al., The Future of Parole Release, 46 Crime & Just. 279, 279–80 (2017). If you were a policy maker, what data would help to inform your decision whether to preserve or restore indeterminate sentencing? Remember that the issue you are addressing is not whether released prisoners will be subject to supervision in the community for a period of time after their release from prison; the issue is who should decide how long an individual will be confined in prison.

5. Professor Steven Chanenson has proposed a blended sentencing structure to preserve the advantages of indeterminate sentencing while minimizing its drawbacks. Steven L. Chanenson, The Next Era of Sentencing Reform, 54 Emory Law Journal 377, 382, 432–35 (2005). This hybrid sentencing model, called "indeterminate structured sentencing," utilizes sentencing guidelines to guide and limit the discretion of judges when imposing a sentence that spells out a sentencing range, such as a minimum sentence of two years and a maximum of four. But parole release is preserved, with parole guidelines utilized to guide and limit the parole board's discretion as to when to release the sentenced individual during that designated time span. Pennsylvania is an example of a state in which one commission has been tasked with the responsibility of promulgating both sentencing guidelines and parole guidelines. Mark H. Bergstrom & Kristofer Bret Bucklen, Justice Reinvestment in Pennsylvania: Another Opportunity for Bold Action, 29 Fed. Sentencing Rep. 15, 16 (2016). After reading about sentencing guidelines later in this chapter, consider whether you favor indeterminate structured sentencing.

2. DETERMINATE SENTENCING STATUTES

As mentioned earlier, many states have abandoned their indeterminate sentencing systems, supplanting them with determinate sentencing laws. Determinate sentencing statutes differ from indeterminate sentencing statutes in that people receiving a determinate sentence generally know how much time they will spend in prison; they will be incarcerated for the amount of time designated in the sentencing order minus any good-time credits that they earn for their good behavior or participation in rehabilitative programs while in prison.

Determinate sentencing statutes can take many different forms. Three examples of determinate sentencing statutes are set forth below. The Illinois and Indiana statutes in subsection a exemplify two of the varied ways to structure what is known as a determinate-discretionary sentencing system. And the Michigan felony-firearm statute in subsection b is an example of a mandatory sentencing statute.

a.   Determinate-Discretionary Sentencing

730 ILL. COMP. STAT. 5/5–4.5–25. Class X Felonies; Sentence. For a Class X felony:

(a) The sentence of imprisonment shall be a determinate sentence of not less than 6 years and not more than 30 years. * * *

730 ILL. COMP. STAT. 5/5–4.5–30. Class 1 Felonies; Sentence. For a Class 1 felony:

(a) The sentence of imprisonment * * * shall be a determinate sentence of not less than 4 years and not more than 15 years. * * *

730 ILL. COMP. STAT. 5/5–4.5–35. Class 2 Felonies; Sentence. For a Class 2 felony:

(a) The sentence of imprisonment shall be a determinate sentence of not less than 3 years and not more than 7 years. * * *

730 ILL. COMP. STAT. 5/5–4.5–40. Class 3 Felonies; Sentence. For a Class 3 felony:

(a) The sentence of imprisonment shall be a determinate sentence of not less than 2 years and not more than 5 years. * * *

730 ILL. COMP. STAT. 5/5–4.5–45. Class 4 Felonies; Sentence. For a Class 4 felony:

(a) The sentence of imprisonment shall be a determinate sentence of not less than one year and not more than 3 years. * * *

730 ILL. COMP. STAT. 5/5–4.5–15(c). * * * Mandatory Supervised Release.

(c) Except when a term of natural life is imposed, every sentence includes a term in addition to the term of imprisonment. * * * For those sentenced on or after February 1, 1978, that term is a mandatory supervised release term.

730 ILL. COMP. STAT. 5/5–8–1(d). * * * Mandatory Supervised Release Terms.

(d) Subject to earlier termination under Section 3–3–8, the * * * mandatory supervised release term shall be written as part of the sentencing order and shall be as follows:

(1) for first degree murder or a Class X felony * * *, 3 years;

(2) for a Class 1 felony or a Class 2 felony * * *, 2 years;

(3) for a Class 3 felony or a Class 4 felony, 1 year;

* * *

IND. CODE ANN. § 35–50–2–3. Murder

(a) A person who commits murder shall be imprisoned for a fixed term of between forty-five (45) and sixty-five (65) years, with the advisory sentence being fifty-five (55) years. In addition, the person may be fined not more than ten thousand dollars ($10,000).

(b) Notwithstanding subsection (a), a person who was:

(1) at least eighteen (18) years of age at the time the murder was committed may be sentenced to:

(A) death; or

(B) life imprisonment without parole; and

(2) at least sixteen (16) years of age but less than eighteen (18) years of age at the time the murder was committed may be sentenced to life imprisonment without parole;

* * * unless a court determines under IC 35–36–9 that the person is an individual with mental retardation.

IND. CODE ANN. § 35–50–2–4(b). Level 1 felony

(b) * * * [A] person who commits a Level 1 felony * * * shall be imprisoned for a fixed term of between twenty (20) and forty (40) years, with the advisory sentence being thirty (30) years. In addition, the person may be fined not more than ten thousand dollars ($10,000).

IND. CODE ANN. § 35–50–2–4.5. Level 2 felony

A person who commits a Level 2 felony shall be imprisoned for a fixed term of between ten (10) and thirty (30) years, with the advisory sentence being seventeen and one-half (17 1/2) years. In addition, the person may be fined not more than ten thousand dollars ($10,000).

IND. CODE ANN. § 35–50–2–5(b). Level 3 felony

(b) A person who commits a Level 3 felony * * * shall be imprisoned for a fixed term of between three (3) and sixteen (16) years, with the advisory sentence being nine (9) years. In addition, the person may be fined not more than ten thousand dollars ($10,000).

IND. CODE ANN. § 35–50–2–5.5. Level 4 felony

A person who commits a Level 4 felony shall be imprisoned for a fixed term of between two (2) and twelve (12) years, with the advisory sentence being six (6) years. In addition, the person may be fined not more than ten thousand dollars ($10,000).

IND. CODE ANN. § 35–50–2–6(b). Level 5 felony

(b) A person who commits a Level 5 felony * * * shall be imprisoned for a fixed term of between one (1) and six (6) years, with the advisory sentence being three (3) years. In addition, the person may be fined not more than ten thousand dollars ($10,000).

IND. CODE ANN. § 35–50–2–7(b). Level 6 felony

(b) A person who commits a Level 6 felony * * * shall be imprisoned for a fixed term of between six (6) months and two and one-half (2 ½) years, with the advisory sentence being one (1) year. In addition, the person may be fined not more than ten thousand dollars ($10,000).

QUESTIONS AND POINTS FOR DISCUSSION

1. Determinate sentencing statutes, as well as indeterminate ones, that outline the possible prison sentences that can be imposed on convicted persons must be considered in conjunction with other statutes that often provide judges with the option of sentencing people to probation or imposing some other community sanction. An example of one such statute is set forth below:

730 ILL. COMP. STAT. 5/5–6–1. Sentences of Probation and of Conditional Discharge[b] and Disposition of Supervision

* * *

(a) Except where specifically prohibited by other provisions of this Code,[c] the court shall impose a sentence of probation or conditional discharge upon an offender unless, having regard to the nature and circumstance of the offense, and to the history, character and condition of the offender, the court is of the opinion that:

    (1) his imprisonment or periodic imprisonment is necessary for the protection of the public; or

---

    [b] 730 Ill. Comp. Stat. 5/5–1–4 defines conditional discharge as "a sentence or disposition of conditional and revocable release without probationary supervision but under such conditions as may be imposed by the court."

    [c] Examples of some of the crimes for which a sentence to probation or conditional discharge cannot be imposed include first-degree murder, some drug offenses, residential burglary, aggravated battery of a senior citizen, and a second or subsequent conviction for institutional vandalism when the property damage exceeded $300. 730 Ill. Comp. Stat. 5/5–5–3(c)(2).

(2) probation or conditional discharge would deprecate the seriousness of the offender's conduct and would be inconsistent with the ends of justice; or

(3) a combination of imprisonment with concurrent or consecutive probation when an offender has been admitted into a drug court program * * * is necessary for the protection of the public and for the rehabilitation of the offender.

* * *

(b) The court may impose a sentence of conditional discharge for an offense if the court is of the opinion that neither a sentence of imprisonment nor of periodic imprisonment nor of probation supervision is appropriate.

* * *

(c) The court may, upon a plea of guilty or a stipulation by the defendant of the facts supporting the charge or a finding of guilt, defer further proceedings and the imposition of a sentence, and enter an order for supervision[d] of the defendant, if the defendant is not charged with [certain specified Class A misdemeanors, such as domestic battery and resisting a police officer] or [a] felony. If the defendant is not barred from receiving an order for supervision as provided in this subsection, the court may enter an order for supervision after considering the circumstances of the offense, and the history, character and condition of the offender, if the court is of the opinion that:

(1) the offender is not likely to commit further crimes;

(2) the defendant and the public would be best served if the defendant were not to receive a criminal record; and

(3) in the best interests of justice an order of supervision is more appropriate than a sentence otherwise permitted under this Code.

* * *

2. As was mentioned earlier, even when a person receives a determinate prison sentence, the amount of time spent in prison may be reduced if he or she is awarded good-time credits for good behavior or participation in rehabilitative programs while in prison. An example of a good-time-credit statute is 730 Ill. Comp. Stat. 5/3–6–3. This statute provides for what is called day-for-day "sentence credits" for many, though not all, prisoners; for every day of good behavior while in prison, a sentence is reduced by one day. An individual who is sentenced to prison for six years and is eligible for day-for-

---

    [d]   In many ways, a sentence to court supervision is like a conditional-discharge sentence; the defendant is not subject to probationary supervision, but the court may impose various restrictions as conditions of the court-supervision sentence. The difference between the two types of sentences is that following successful completion of a period of court supervision, the charges against a defendant will be dismissed, which means that the defendant can avoid the onus of a criminal conviction. 730 Ill. Comp. Stat. 5/5–1–21.

day sentence credits therefore may be released in three years if, while incarcerated, he or she complies with all institutional rules and regulations. The amount of sentence credits awarded may be further increased when the prisoner successfully completes a full-time assignment to a correctional industry, an educational, behavior-modification, substance-abuse, or reentry-planning program, or life-skills training. Id. § 5/3–6–3(a)(4). And a prisoner who passes a high-school equivalency test and has not previously passed that test or received a high-school diploma is entitled to additional good-time credits. Id. § 5/3–6–3(a)(4.1).

3.   People are also often given credit on their sentences for time spent incarcerated while awaiting trial or sentencing. For example, 18 U.S.C. § 3585(b) provides that a person sentenced to prison for a federal crime must be given credit for time spent in "official detention" before the prison sentence began. In Reno v. Koray, 515 U.S. 50, 115 S.Ct. 2021 (1995), the Supreme Court held that 24-hour-a-day confinement in a community-treatment center while awaiting sentencing did not constitute the "official detention" for which credit must be given under § 3585(b). Because the imprisoned person in that case had been released on bail pending sentencing, although subject to the condition that he stay in the community-treatment center at all times of the day, he was not subject, according to the Court, to "official detention" within the meaning of the statute. In your opinion, should people ever receive credit for time spent awaiting trial or sentencing if they are not incarcerated in jail or prison during that time? If so, under what circumstances?

b. Mandatory Sentences

MICH. COMP. LAWS § 750.227b. Possession of firearm when committing or attempting to commit felony * * *

(1) A person who carries or has in his or her possession a firearm when he or she commits or attempts to commit a felony * * * is guilty of a felony, and shall be punished by imprisonment for 2 years. Upon a second conviction under this subsection, the person shall be punished by imprisonment for 5 years. Upon a third or subsequent conviction under this subsection, the person shall be punished by imprisonment for 10 years.

* * *

(3) A term of imprisonment prescribed by this section is in addition to the sentence imposed for the conviction of the felony or the attempt to commit the felony and shall be served consecutively with and preceding any term of imprisonment imposed for the conviction of the felony or attempt to commit the felony.

(4) A term of imprisonment imposed under this section shall not be suspended. The person subject to the sentence mandated by this section is not eligible for parole or probation during the mandatory term imposed under subsection (1) * * *.

* * *

QUESTIONS AND POINTS FOR DISCUSSION

1.   In response to public demands to "get tough on crime," legislatures across the country have enacted mandatory sentencing statutes, requiring that a designated prison or jail sentence be imposed for certain crimes regardless of any mitigating circumstances surrounding the crime or the person who committed it. Mandatory sentencing statutes typically extend to a range of crimes, including drug offenses, certain violent crimes, and felonies in which firearms were used, as well as to convicted individuals with specified prior felony convictions. Michael Tonry, The Mostly Unintended Effects of Mandatory Penalties: Two Centuries of Consistent Findings, 38 Crime & Just. 65, 66 (2009).

What arguments would you make if you were defending the utilization of mandatory-minimum penalties? What arguments would you make in opposition to their employment? What additional facts would you want to know to better inform your decision whether the use of mandatory minimums represents a sound policy choice? For a summary of some of the principal arguments asserted in favor of, and in opposition to, mandatory minimums, see U.S. Sentencing Comm'n, Report to the Congress: Mandatory Minimum Penalties in the Federal Criminal Justice System 85–102 (2011).

2.   Researchers have found that the purpose of mandatory sentencing laws—to ensure that a particular sentence is imposed for a particular crime—is often thwarted by police officers, prosecutors, and judges. Id. at 71–86. See also Barbara S. Vincent & Paul J. Hofer, Fed. Judicial Ctr., The Consequences of Mandatory Minimum Prison Terms: A Summary of Recent Findings 17–18 (1994) (studies conducted by the U.S. Sentencing Commission, Federal Judicial Center, and General Accounting Office found, respectively, that 40%, 46%, and 34% of defendants who had committed crimes subject to mandatory-minimum sentences received sentences lower than the statutory minimum). Police officers, for example, may not arrest an individual for a crime for which he or she, if convicted, would have to be incarcerated for a defined period of time. Or prosecutors, for the same reason, may refrain from filing charges, file charges for a related offense for which there is not a mandatory penalty, or, as part of a plea agreement, drop the charge that would trigger a mandatory-minimum sentence. Even judges may attempt to circumvent what they consider unduly harsh mandatory sentencing statutes by dismissing charges or finding defendants not guilty. In cases where a mandatory sentence is imposed because of particular conduct of the defendant during the course of a felony, such as using a firearm, a judge may also, in effect, nullify the mandatory penalty by decreasing the sentence for the underlying felony by the amount by which the sentence then will be increased under the mandatory sentencing statute.

3.   Studies also have found that the uneven application of mandatory-minimum sentences has disparate adverse effects on minorities. Non-Hispanic

Caucasians are able to avoid mandatory-minimum sentences more often than African Americans and Hispanics guilty of comparable conduct. U.S. Sentencing Comm'n, supra note 1, at 102 & n.545. The disproportionate arrest and prosecution of minorities for drug offenses, which frequently trigger mandatory minimums, compound, some argue, the unequal impact of mandatory minimums on certain racial and ethnic groups. Id. at 101 & n.541. Excerpts of an article in which Professor Stephen J. Schulhofer describes some additional effects of mandatory minimums are set forth below.

STEPHEN J. SCHULHOFER, RETHINKING MANDATORY MINIMUMS

28 Wake Forest Law Review 199 (1993).
Reprinted with the permission of the Wake Forest Law Review.

* * * Real-world mandatories may be truly mandatory or merely discretionary, and the great majority of mandatory minimum statutes fall squarely in the latter category. * * *

A. DISCRETIONARY MANDATORIES

Mandatories require the judge to impose a given minimum sentence upon conviction under a specified charge, but they do not necessarily obligate prosecutors to bring such a charge just because the facts support it. Therefore, the most important question in any mandatory minimum statute concerns the prosecutor's role: Does the statute entail a *mandate to prosecute* or merely an *option to bargain*? Legislatures rarely address this crucial threshold issue explicitly. Rather, they in effect delegate to prosecutors the power to decide whether the statute is really a mandate to impose a minimum sentence or instead is only a source of discretion. Prosecutors, in turn, often assume that the statute imposes no mandate *on them*. Mandatories then become little more than a bargaining chip, a "hammer" which the prosecutor can invoke at her option, to obtain more guilty pleas under more favorable terms. Bargaining-chip mandatories help avoid the high process costs of the additional trials that real mandatories can generate, and they may even *reduce* process costs because potentially severe penalties can induce pleas that would not otherwise be forthcoming. Bargaining-chip mandatories also have two important crime-control benefits. Though they do not constrain prosecutors, they do constrain judges, who are sometimes perceived as more likely than prosecutors to be "soft" on crime. Even when bargained away, the mandatories have crime-control value because they tend to increase the severity of sentences that guilty plea defendants will accept. Yet, the deterrence value of both severity effects is undercut by the uncertainty that mandatories will be applied and by the perception among offenders that the mandatory can be manipulated. Moreover, bargaining-chip mandatories tend to increase rather than reduce disparity because their application depends so much on low-visibility prosecutorial choices and because their most severe effects fall not on flagrantly guilty repeat offenders (who avoid the mandatory by their guilty pleas), but rather on first offenders in borderline situations (who may have plausible defenses and are more likely to insist upon trial).

These potential effects of the bargaining-chip approach are dramatically illustrated by recent experience in the Arizona state courts. Prosecutors there have treated mandatories primarily as a bargaining tool and have made clear their willingness, in return for a guilty plea, to drop counts carrying stiff minimum penalties. As a result, the trial rate in Arizona has fallen dramatically, from ten percent in the period just before introduction of mandatories to only four percent currently. Average sentences, prison populations, and, of course, the correctional budget have all risen substantially, but the deterrence pay-off from these effects remains speculative because of the perception that anyone willing to "cop a plea" can avoid the mandatory sentence. At the same time, mandatories have produced severe punishments for offenders of marginal culpability who showed the poor judgment to insist on trial.

* * *

C.   MANDATORY MANDATORIES

When mandatories are actually applied to all fact situations falling within their scope, predictable and severe sentences are achieved. The results are longer prison terms, increased correctional costs, and enhanced deterrence. Because mandatories prevent judges from awarding a discount for a guilty plea * * *, the percentage of defendants going to trial will rise sharply. Finally, mandatory-prosecution mandatories insure equal treatment of similarly situated offenders. However, this virtue of mandatories is also a central vice because equal treatment is achieved through inflexibility and deliberate inattention to context.

* * * [T]here are four common effects of inattention to context: cliffs, mistakes, misplaced equality, and the cooperation paradox. All four effects undermine the perceived fairness of mandatory minimum schemes. As a result, prosecutors and judges are less willing to apply mandatories with the consistency that the mandatory-prosecution model assumes. When that happens, bargaining-chip features tend to reappear.

1.   Cliffs

Cliffs result when an offender's conduct just barely brings him within the terms of a mandatory minimum. For example, a first offender who helps sell 495 grams of cocaine might be thought to deserve anywhere from two to four years of imprisonment. Under the sentencing guidelines, his presumptive sentence (after allowance for his acceptance of responsibility and minimal role in the offense) would fall in the range of twenty-seven to thirty-three months, or about two and one-half years. For an identical offender who sold just five grams more, the sentence would double, because the five-year mandatory minimum applicable to sales of 500 grams would kick in. Conversely, an offender facing the five-year minimum can obtain a dramatic decrease in his sentence if he can establish a very small reduction in the quantity for which he is held responsible. The cliff effect means that small drug quantities have enormous importance, while all other factors bearing on culpability and dangerousness have no importance at all.

* * *

2. Mistakes

Mistakes occur when mandatory provisions are badly drafted or poorly coordinated with other statutes. [The author then cites examples of what he considers "obvious bloopers," such as the required imposition for one drug-possession crime of a mandatory-minimum sentence that is higher than the maximum sentence for possessing a slightly smaller amount of the same drug.]

* * *

Of course, mistakes can be fixed. * * * But Congress can never foresee the full range of circumstances to which a mandatory might apply or the full scope of interconnections to other pertinent federal and state criminal statutes. *Mistakes are inevitable.* Anomalies and injustices will arise in any system that attempts to establish severe minimum sentences triggered by just one or two circumstances of a case.

3. Misplaced equality

Misplaced equality occurs even if all outright mistakes can be eliminated. Ensuring equal treatment of like offenders prevents one form of disparity, but the resulting equal treatment of *unlike* offenders creates another serious problem—*excessive uniformity.* Excessive uniformity is inevitable under mandatories because the statutes necessarily single out just one or a very small number of factors to determine the minimum sentence. Offenders who differ in a host of crucial respects receive inappropriately equal treatment.

For example, a common problem associated with mandatories is the equal treatment of offenders who played sharply different roles in the offense. The ringleader faces the same sentence as a moderately important underling, who in turn gets the same sentence as a young messenger or secretary who had little responsibility or control over the events. Parties who were pressured to provide minor assistance face the same sentence as the most violent and abusive leaders. Since mandatories are usually stated as minimums, they could, in theory, incorporate such factors by permitting an offender's role in the offense to aggravate the applicable sentence. However, this approach would require setting the mandatory penalty at the level appropriate for the least culpable offender, and such a statute would hardly "send a message" in the way that legislators intend. Instead, mandatories are invariably pegged at a level that the legislature considers appropriate for a highly culpable participant. In fact, in some of the federal mandatories, the "minimum" sentence is life imprisonment without parole. Just punishment for lesser roles is inevitably precluded.

A comparable problem is the absence of differentiation on the basis of a prior criminal record. Some mandatories do not consider an offender's prior record at all. Many of the federal mandatories do provide higher minimums for a subsequent offense, but the enhancement is invariably crude, failing to account for the recency of the prior offense or its similarity to the present misconduct. As with the variations in an offender's role, variations found in prior records are too complex to be captured in just one or a few factors. * * *

Other types of misplaced equality could be catalogued, but such a list would obscure the main point. Important differences among offenders are by nature difficult to anticipate and categorize. Hence, uniform treatment through mandatories invariably produces unfairness and generates systemic pressure for evasion. Mandatory-prosecution mandatories can be grossly unjust if faithfully applied, but (perhaps fortunately) they become difficult to sustain in practice because the misplaced equality such mandatories engender produces powerful resistance to their enforcement.

4.   The cooperation paradox

The cooperation paradox provides a final example of the serious distortions that result from inattention to context. One universally recognized exception to a mandatory minimum requirement is the situation in which a defendant offers to testify against confederates or to provide leads in other investigations. Informal mechanisms for avoiding mandatories, in federal courts and elsewhere, insure that sentence concessions will be available to those defendants who provide the most information at the earliest possible point in an investigation, thus guaranteeing that mandatories will not choke the flow of cooperation. Indeed, mandatories coupled with an exception for cooperation provide powerful inducements for assistance that might not otherwise be forthcoming. This practice is formalized in 18 U.S.C. § 3553(e), which renders all federal mandatories inoperable and authorizes the judge to impose a sentence below the mandatory minimum, if the government makes a motion for a lower sentence on the basis of a defendant's substantial assistance in the investigation or prosecution of others.

Yet, the escape hatch for cooperation creates a paradox. Defendants who are most in the know, and thus have the most "substantial assistance" to offer, are often those who are most centrally involved in conspiratorial crimes. The highly culpable offender may be the best placed to negotiate a big sentencing break. Minor players, peripherally involved and with little knowledge or responsibility, have little to offer and thus can wind up with far more severe sentences than the boss.[69]

Of course, sentence concessions for helping the government have always been part of American sentencing systems and always will be. The vice of an escape hatch for "substantial assistance" stems from its interaction with the unqualified rigidity that mandatories otherwise impose. The quantity-driven drug mandatories pose this problem in its most acute form. Normal principles holding defendants accountable for the acts of their co-conspirators, even if carefully applied, can leave low-level dealers, middlemen and more important distributors responsible for the same quantity of drugs flowing through the conspirational network. * * * Thus, the inflexibility of mandatories means that all participants tend to face the same high sentence, regardless of their limited role in the offense or any mitigating personal circumstances. The "big fish" and the "minnows" wind up in the same sentencing boat. Enter the statutory escape hatch, with sentence concessions that tend to increase with the knowledge and responsibility of the offender. The big fish get the big breaks, while the minnows are left to face severe and sometimes draconian penalties.

This result makes nonsense of the intuitively plausible scale of punishments that Congress and the ordinary person envisage when they think of sentences linked to drug quantity or other hallmarks of the most serious criminal responsibility. Instead of a pyramid of liability with long sentences for leaders at the top of the organizational ladder, the mandatory system can become an inverted pyramid with stiff sentences for minor players and modest punishments for knowledgeable insiders who can cut favorable deals.

D. SUMMARY

A mandatory minimum is not a discrete policy instrument; rather, it is a label for two different and partially opposed concepts. Mandatory mandatories constrain both judges and prosecutors. Discretionary mandatories are mandatory for judges, but not for prosecutors, and are largely used as bargaining chips for plea negotiation. * * *

Whichever element predominates in a particular statutory scheme brings with it drawbacks that undercut much of a mandatory minimum's expected benefits. Discretionary mandatories can enhance sentence severity for offenders convicted on the mandatory count, but the deterrent

---

[69] Thus, in United States v. Brigham, 977 F.2d 317 (7th Cir.1992), a low-level driver received a 120-month sentence, while the organization's kingpin received only an 84-month sentence because of his "substantial assistance." Reluctantly affirming the sentence, the court, per Easterbrook, J., wrote: "Mandatory minimum penalties, combined with a power to grant exemptions, create a prospect of inverted sentencing. The more serious the defendant's crimes, the lower the sentence—because the greater his wrongs, the more information and assistance he has to offer to a prosecutor." Id. at 318. See also United States v. Evans, 970 F.2d 663, 676–78 & n.19 (10th Cir.1992) (underlings received terms of 210 months, 292 months, 295 months and life, while more responsible organizers received sentences of mere probation or supervised release).

value of this effect is undermined by the uncertainty of its application to any particular case. At the same time, discretionary mandatories undermine the perceived fairness of the prescribed sentence as a just punishment because the penalty is haphazardly invoked and because the most culpable offenders can escape its impact by waiving their right to trial.

Truly mandatory mandatories avoid both of these difficulties while provoking new ones. Because real mandatories leave little room for plea incentives, trial rates and process costs are likely to rise sharply. At the same time, true mandatories present acute problems of inequitable punishment because of cliff effects, mistakes, misplaced equality and the cooperation paradox. These inequities, together with the process costs of true mandatories, make deterrence and "equal treatment" benefits costly to realize even when true mandatories are fully implemented in practice. Perhaps more important, these inequities and process costs generate powerful pressure for avoidance. Discretionary mandatories reemerge, though in less visible forms, and often with some of the acute process costs of true mandatories. The result, as with New York's Rockefeller drug law,[e] may be the worst of both worlds.

QUESTIONS AND POINTS FOR DISCUSSION

1.   What is known as the "safety-valve provision" in 18 U.S.C. § 3553(f) mitigates, at least somewhat, the effects of mandatory-minimum sentences for low-level perpetrators of certain federal drug crimes. This provision authorizes federal judges to impose sentences below the statutory minimum if the following conditions are met: (1) the defendant has no more than one criminal-history point under the federal sentencing guidelines; (2) the defendant did not use or threaten violence or possess a firearm or other dangerous weapon while committing the crime (or persuade a cohort to do so); (3) the crime did not lead to someone's death or serious bodily harm; (4) the defendant did not act as an organizer, leader, manager, or supervisor in committing the crime or engage in a "continuing criminal enterprise"; and (5) the defendant has provided the government with all the information and evidence the defendant has about the crime and other related crimes. In your opinion, is the safety-valve provision an effective means of redressing the problems of mandatory minimums highlighted by Professor Schulhofer and others? How, if at all, would you modify the safety-valve provision?

2.   The "three strikes and you're out" laws currently in effect in many states are an example of one type of mandatory sentencing statute. Under these laws, people with three convictions for certain felonies must be sentenced to prison for a very lengthy, statutorily prescribed period of time—under some

---

[e] This law restricted plea bargaining for certain drug crimes triggering severe mandatory minimums. After the law's enactment, the rate of indictment after arrest, the rate of conviction after indictment, and the number of arrests for the drug crimes declined, while trial rates and case-processing times increased dramatically See Professor Schulhofer's article at 207–08.

laws, to life in prison without possibility of parole. See, e.g., Wash.Rev.Code § 9.94A.570. Some states require a different number of "strikes" to impose these long sentences, with only two strikes needed in some states and four in others. See Paul H. Robinson et al., The Disutility of Injustice, 85 N.Y.U. L.Rev. 1940, 1950 n.27 (2010). The crimes that will trigger a strike also vary substantially from state to state. Id. at 1950–51. In some states, only violent felonies, like murder, rape, armed robbery, and kidnapping, can count as strikes. In other states, convictions for nonviolent felonies can constitute strikes.

If you were drafting a state's law governing the sentencing of people with multiple criminal convictions, what would be its key provisions? Would research findings that criminal activity peaks when individuals are in their late teens and early twenties and that most people refrain from committing crimes by the time they reach forty have any effect on the way in which you would draft such a law? Linda S. Beres & Thomas D. Griffith, Do Three Strikes Laws Make Sense? Habitual Offender Statutes and Criminal Incapacitation, 87 Georgetown L.J. 135–37 (1998). Would research findings revealing substantial differences, by county, in prosecutors' enforcement of a state's three-strikes law have a bearing on the statute you draft? See John Clark et al., U.S. Dep't of Justice, "Three Strikes and You're Out": A Review of State Legislation 4 (1997). Is there any other information you would want to obtain before making the final policy choices reflected in the statute?

3. Another offshoot of the get-tough-on-crime movement is what is called "truth in sentencing." Truth-in-sentencing laws generally require certain individuals sentenced to prison, such as those convicted of specified violent crimes, to serve most of their prison sentences—usually eighty-five percent of the sentence imposed—before becoming eligible for release. William J. Sabol et al., Influences of Truth-in-Sentencing Reforms on Changes in States' Sentencing Practices and Prison Populations 8–9 (2002). The laws were spawned, in part, by concerns that prisoners, as a whole, had been serving a fraction of the prison sentences imposed on them. See Bureau of Justice Statistics, U.S. Dep't of Justice, Truth in Sentencing in State Prisons 1 (1999) (prisoners released in 1996 had, on average, served 44% of their sentences). States have employed a variety of means to increase the time served in prison by the targeted individuals, such as restricting or eliminating the good-time credits they can accumulate and restricting their eligibility for parole. Federal legislation has supported these efforts by conditioning the awarding of grants to build or expand correctional facilities on the adoption of truth-in-sentencing laws for people convicted of certain violent crimes. See 34 U.S.C. §§ 12102–12104.

Would you advise a state legislature to incorporate "truth in sentencing" into its sentencing structure? If so, how? Consider these questions in light of the materials that follow.

C. SENTENCING GUIDELINES

Sentencing guidelines differ from sentencing statutes in that they generally are developed by a sentencing commission established by the legislature rather than by the legislature itself. Sentencing-guideline systems have been held constitutional despite arguments that they are the product of an excessive delegation of legislative power and violate separation-of-powers principles. See, e.g., Mistretta v. United States, 488 U.S. 361, 109 S.Ct. 647 (1989). In part, this is because the legislature still plays a role in a sentencing process governed by guidelines—defining the ranges of punishment within which the guidelines will operate and often approving the guidelines formulated by the sentencing commission. For example, a state statute might state that a person convicted of burglary can be sentenced to probation or anywhere from one to five years in prison. Sentencing guidelines then can provide further guidance as to whether a convicted burglar should be imprisoned and, if imprisoned, the length of the term of imprisonment.

Sentencing guidelines can be presumptive, which means that the sentence outlined in the guidelines must be imposed unless facts are established justifying a departure from the guidelines. Or guidelines may be advisory only, leaving individual judges with more leeway not to follow them, subject to limited appellate review for an abuse of sentencing discretion. Some examples of these two kinds of guidelines are discussed below.

1. PRESUMPTIVE GUIDELINES

Minnesota was the first state to establish a sentencing commission to draft presumptive sentencing guidelines. These guidelines were approved by the legislature in 1980 and have since often served as a starting point for other jurisdictions contemplating the adoption of sentencing guidelines. Portions of these guidelines and the commentary explaining them are set forth below.

MINNESOTA SENTENCING GUIDELINES AND COMMENTARY
Revised August 1, 2017.

1. Purpose and Definitions

A. Statement of Purpose and Principles

The purpose of the Sentencing Guidelines is to establish rational and consistent sentencing standards that reduce sentencing disparity and ensure that the sanctions imposed for felony convictions are proportional to the severity of the conviction offense and the offender's criminal history. Equity in sentencing requires that: (a) convicted felons with similar relevant sentencing criteria should receive similar sanctions; and (b) convicted felons with relevant sentencing criteria substantially different from a typical case should receive different sanctions.

The Sentencing Guidelines embody the following principles:

1. Sentencing should be neutral with respect to the race, gender, social, or economic status of convicted felons.

2. The severity of the sanction should increase in direct proportion to an increase in offense severity or the convicted felon's criminal history, or both. This promotes a rational and consistent sentencing policy.

3. Commitment to the Commissioner of Corrections is the most severe sanction that can be imposed for a felony conviction, but it is not the only significant sanction available to the court.

4. Because state and local correctional facility capacity is finite, confinement should be imposed only for offenders who are convicted of more serious offenses or who have longer criminal histories. To ensure such usage of finite resources, sanctions used in sentencing convicted felons should be the least restrictive necessary to achieve the purposes of the sentence.

5. Although the Sentencing Guidelines are advisory to the court, the presumptive sentences are deemed appropriate for the felonies covered by them. Therefore, departures from the presumptive sentences established in the Sentencing Guidelines should be made only when substantial and compelling circumstances can be identified and articulated.

* * *

2. Determining Presumptive Sentences

The presumptive sentence for any offender convicted of a felony * * * is found in the cell of the appropriate Grid located at the intersection of the criminal history score and the severity level.[f] The Grids represent the two dimensions most important in sentencing decisions.

A. Offense Severity

1. <u>General Rule</u>. The applicable offense severity level is determined by the conviction offense, not the charging offense. * * * The

---

[f] The grid that governs most felonies can be found on page 123. The guidelines also include separate guidelines grids for sex and drug offenses. Guidelines and commentary bearing on these latter two grids have been deleted, without denoting all deletions.

severity level for each felony offense is found in section 5A, Offense Severity Reference Table.

* * *

B. Criminal History

The horizontal axis on the Sentencing Guidelines Grids is the criminal history score. An offender's criminal history score is the sum of points from eligible:

- prior felonies;
- custody status at the time of the offense;
- prior misdemeanors and gross misdemeanors; and
- prior juvenile adjudications.

* * *

Comment

2.B.01. The Guidelines reduce the emphasis given to criminal history in sentencing decisions. Under past judicial practice, criminal history was the primary factor in dispositional decisions. Under the Guidelines, the conviction offense is the primary factor, and criminal history is a secondary factor in dispositional decisions. Prior to enactment of the Guidelines, there were no uniform standards regarding what should be included in an offender's criminal history, no weighting format for different types of offenses, and no systematic process to check the accuracy of the information on criminal history.

2.B.02. The Guidelines provide uniform standards for the inclusion and weighting of criminal history information. The sentencing hearing provides a process to assure the accuracy of the information in individual cases.

1. <u>Prior Felonies</u>. Assign a particular weight, as set forth [below], to each extended jurisdiction juvenile (EJJ) conviction and each felony conviction* * *.

   * * *

   a. <u>Current Offense on Standard Grid</u> * * *. If the current offense is **not** on the Sex Offender Grid, determine the weight assigned to each prior felony sentence according to its severity level, as follows:

	SEVERITY LEVEL	POINTS
Current Offense on Standard Grid	1 – 2	½
	3 – 5	1
	6 – 8	1 ½
	9 – 11	2
	Murder 1ˢᵗ Degree	2

* * *

c.   <u>Felony Decay Factor</u>. A prior felony sentence or stay of imposition following a felony conviction must not be used in computing the criminal history score if a period of fifteen years has elapsed since the date of discharge from or expiration of the sentence to the date of the current offense.

* * *

Comment

2.B.101. The basic rule for computing the number of prior felony points in the criminal history score is that the offender is assigned a particular weight for every felony conviction for which a felony sentence was stayed or imposed before the current sentencing or for which a stay of imposition of sentence was given for a felony level offense, no matter what period of probation is pronounced, before the current sentencing.[g]

2.B.102. No partial points are given—thus, an offender with less than a full point is not given that point. For example, an offender with a total weight of 2 ½ would have 2 felony points.

2.B.103. The Commission determined that it was important to establish a weighting scheme for prior felony sentences to assure a greater degree of proportionality in the current sentencing. Offenders who have a history of

---

[g] In Minnesota, there is a distinction between what is called a stay of imposition and a stay of execution. The distinction is explained in the definitional section of the guidelines as follows:

A "stayed sentence" may be accomplished by either a stay of imposition or a stay of execution. There are two steps in sentencing: the imposition of a sentence and the execution of the sentence imposed. The imposition of sentence consists of pronouncing the sentence to be served in prison (for example, three years imprisonment). The execution of an imposed sentence consists of transferring the felon to the custody of the Commissioner of Corrections to serve the prison sentence.

    a. <u>Stay of Imposition</u>. A "stay of imposition" occurs when the court accepts and records a finding or plea of guilty, but does not impose (or pronounce) a prison sentence. If the offender successfully completes the stay, the case is discharged, and the conviction is deemed a misdemeanor * * * but is still included in criminal history under section 2.B.

    b. <u>Stay of Execution</u>. A "stay of execution" occurs when the court accepts and records a finding or plea of guilty, and a prison sentence is pronounced, but is not executed. If the offender successfully completes the stay, the case is discharged, but the offender continues to have a record of a felony conviction, which is included in criminal history under section 2.B.

serious felonies are considered more culpable than those offenders whose prior felonies consist primarily of low severity, nonviolent offenses.

* * *

2.B.112. *The decision to stay execution of sentence rather than to stay imposition of sentence as a means to a probationary term following a felony conviction is discretionary with the court. Considerable disparity appears to exist in the use of these options. In the case of two similar offenders it is not uncommon for one to receive a stay of execution and another to receive the benefit of a stay of imposition. * * * As a result of the disparity that exists in the use of stays of imposition, the Commission determined to treat stays of execution and stays of imposition the same with respect to criminal history point accrual. * * **

* * *

2.B.115. *Under Minn. Stat. § 260B.130, a child alleged to have committed a felony offense under certain circumstances may be prosecuted as an extended jurisdiction juvenile (EJJ). * * * [T]he extended jurisdiction juvenile conviction must be treated the same as an adult felony sentence for purposes of calculating the prior felony record component of the criminal history score. * * **

* * *

2. <u>Custody Status at the Time of the Offense.</u>

    a. <u>One Custody Status Point.</u> Assign **one** custody status point when the conditions in paragraphs (1) through (3) are met:

       (1) The offender was under one of the following custody statuses:

         (i) probation;

         (ii) parole;

         (iii) supervised release;

         (iv) conditional release following release from an executed prison sentence * * *;

         (v) release pending sentencing;

         (vi) confinement in a jail, workhouse, or prison pending or after sentencing; or

         (vii) escape from confinement following an executed sentence.

       (2) The offender was under one of the custody statuses in paragraph (1) after entry of a guilty plea, guilty verdict, or conviction.* * *

(3) The offender was under one of the custody statuses in paragraph (1) for one of the following:

(i) a felony;

(ii) extended jurisdiction juvenile (EJJ) conviction;

(iii) non-traffic gross misdemeanor;

(iv) gross misdemeanor driving while impaired, refusal to submit to a chemical test, or reckless driving; or

(v) targeted misdemeanor.

* * *

Comment

2.B.201. *The basic rule assigns offenders one point if they were under some form of eligible criminal justice custody status when they committed the offense for which they are now being sentenced.*

* * *

2.B.205. *The custodial statuses covered by this policy are those occurring after conviction of a felony, non-traffic gross misdemeanor, gross misdemeanor driving while impaired or refusal to submit to a chemical test, gross misdemeanor reckless driving, or misdemeanor on the targeted misdemeanor list provided in Minn. Stat. § 299C.10, subd. 1(e). Thus, an offender who commits a new felony while on pre-trial diversion or pre-trial release on another charge does not get a custody status point.* * * *

* * *

3. <u>Prior Gross Misdemeanors and Misdemeanors</u>. Prior gross misdemeanor and misdemeanor convictions count as units comprising criminal history points. Four units equal one criminal history point; give no partial point for fewer than four units. * * *

a. <u>General Assignment of Units</u>. * * * [A]ssign the offender one unit for each prior conviction of the following offenses * * *:

(1) targeted misdemeanor, as defined in Minn. Stat. § 299C.10, subd. 1(e);

(2) non-traffic gross misdemeanor;

(3) gross misdemeanor driving while impaired;

(4) gross misdemeanor refusal to submit to a chemical test;

(5) gross misdemeanor reckless driving;

(6) a felony conviction resulting in a misdemeanor or gross misdemeanor sentence.

* * *

e. <u>Decay Factor</u>. A prior misdemeanor or gross misdemeanor sentence or stay of imposition following a misdemeanor or gross misdemeanor conviction must **not** be used in computing the criminal history score if ten years has elapsed between the date of discharge from or expiration of the sentence and the date of the current offense. * * *

f. <u>Maximum Assignment of Points</u>. [A]n offender cannot receive more than one point for prior misdemeanor or gross misdemeanor convictions.

* * *

Comment

2.B.301. *The Commission established a measurement procedure based on units for misdemeanor and gross misdemeanor sentences, which are totaled and then converted to a point value. The purpose of this procedure is to provide different weightings for convictions of felonies, gross misdemeanors, and misdemeanors. Under this procedure, misdemeanors and gross misdemeanors are assigned one unit. An offender must have a total of four units to receive one point in the criminal history score; thus an offender with three units is assigned no point value.*

* * *

2.B.303. *The Commission placed a limit of one point on the consideration of misdemeanors or gross misdemeanors in the criminal history score. This was done because, with no limit on point accrual, offenders with lengthy, but relatively minor, misdemeanor records could accrue high criminal history scores and thus be subject to inappropriately severe sentences upon their first felony conviction. The Commission limited consideration of misdemeanors to particularly relevant misdemeanors under existing state statute. Offenders whose criminal record includes at least four prior sentences for misdemeanors on the targeted misdemeanor list * * *, non-traffic gross misdemeanors, gross misdemeanor reckless driving, and gross misdemeanor driving while impaired or refusal to submit to a chemical test are considered more culpable and are given an additional criminal history point.*

* * *

4. <u>Prior Juvenile Adjudications</u>.

a. <u>Assignment of Points for Juvenile Adjudications</u>. Assign an offender one point for every two adjudications for felony offenses the offender committed, and for which the offender was prosecuted as a juvenile, provided that:

(1) each adjudication must have been for a separate offense or must have involved separate victims in a single course of conduct * * *; and

(2) the juvenile adjudications must have been for offenses committed after the offender's fourteenth birthday; and

(3) the offender was under the age of twenty-five when the offender committed the current felony.

b. Maximum Points for Juvenile Adjudications. An offender may receive only **one point** for juvenile adjudications as described in this section, except that the point limit does not apply to juvenile adjudications for offenses for which the Sentencing Guidelines would presume imprisonment if the offenses had been committed by an adult. Make this determination regardless of the criminal history score * * *.

* * *

Comment
* * *

2.B.406. *The Commission decided that it would take two juvenile adjudications to equal 1 point on the criminal history score, and generally, an offender may not receive more than 1 point on the basis of prior juvenile adjudications. This point limit does not apply to offenses committed and prosecuted as a juvenile for which the Guidelines would presume imprisonment, regardless of criminal history, if committed by an adult. * * * Again, no partial points are allowed, so an offender with only one juvenile adjudication meeting the above criteria would receive no point on the criminal history score.*

* * *

C. Presumptive Sentence

1. Finding the Presumptive Sentence. The presumptive sentence for a felony conviction is found in the appropriate cell on the applicable Grid located at the intersection of the criminal history score (horizontal axis) and the severity level (vertical axis). * * * For cases contained in cells within the shaded areas, the sentence should be stayed unless the conviction offense carries a mandatory minimum sentence.

Each cell on the Grids provides a fixed sentence duration. Minn. Stat. § 244.09 requires that the Guidelines provide a range for sentences that are presumptive commitments. For cells above the solid line, the Guidelines provide both a fixed presumptive duration and a range of time for that sentence * * *. The shaded areas of the grids do not display ranges. If the duration for a sentence that is a presumptive commitment is found in a shaded area, the standard range—15 percent lower and 20 percent higher than the fixed duration displayed—is permissible without departure, provided that the minimum sentence is not less than one year and one day, and the maximum sentence is not more than the statutory maximum.

* * *

Comment

2.C.01. The dispositional policy adopted by the Commission was designed so that scarce prison resources would primarily be used for serious person offenders and community resources would be used for most property offenders. The Commission believes that a rational sentencing policy requires such trade-offs to ensure the availability of correctional resources for the most serious offenders. * * *

2.C.02. In the cells outside the shaded areas of the grids, the Guidelines provide a fixed presumptive sentence length, and a range of time around that length. Presumptive sentence lengths are shown in months * * *. Any sentence length given that is within the range of sentence length shown in the appropriate cell on the applicable Grid is not a departure from the Guidelines, and any sentence length given that is outside the range is a departure from the Guidelines. In the cells in the shaded areas of the grids, the Guidelines provide a single fixed presumptive sentence length.

2.C.03. The presumptive duration listed on the grids, when executed, includes both the term of imprisonment and the period of supervised release. According to Minn. Stat. § 244.101, when the court sentences an offender to an executed sentence * * *, the sentence consists of two parts: a specified minimum term of imprisonment equal to two-thirds of the total executed sentence; and a specified maximum supervised release term equal to one-third of the total executed sentence. Separate tables following the Grids illustrate how executed sentences are broken down into their two components.

* * *

D. Departures from the Guidelines

1. <u>Departures in General</u>. The sentences provided in the Grids are presumed to be appropriate for the crimes to which they apply. The court must pronounce a sentence of the applicable disposition and within the applicable range unless there exist identifiable, substantial, and compelling circumstances to support a departure.

    The court may depart from the presumptive disposition or duration provided in the Guidelines, and stay or impose a sentence that is deemed to be more appropriate than the presumptive sentence. * * * A departure is not controlled by the Guidelines, but rather, is an exercise of judicial discretion constrained by statute or case law.

a. <u>Disposition and Duration</u>. Departures with respect to disposition and duration are separate decisions. A court may depart from the presumptive disposition without departing from the presumptive duration, and vice-versa. A court departing from the presumptive disposition as well as the presumptive duration has made two separate departure decisions, each requiring written departure reasons.

* * *

c. <u>Departure Report</u>. In exercising the discretion to depart from a presumptive sentence, the court must disclose in writing or on the record the particular substantial and compelling circumstances that make the departure more appropriate than the presumptive sentence. * * *

d. <u>Departure Reasons</u>. Because departures are by definition exceptions to the Guidelines, the departure factors in this section are advisory, except as otherwise established by case law.

Comment
* * *

2.D.102. *A defendant has the right to a jury trial to determine whether aggravating factors are proved beyond a reasonable doubt. See, e.g., Blakely v. Washington, 542 U.S. 296 (2004). If the departure facts are proved beyond a reasonable doubt, the court may exercise its discretion to depart from the presumptive sentence.*

* * *

2. <u>Factors that **should not** be used as Reasons for Departure</u>. The following factors should not be used as reasons for departing from the presumptive sentences provided in the appropriate cell on the applicable Grid:

a. Race

b. Sex

c. Employment factors, including:

(1) occupation or impact of sentence on profession or occupation;

(2) employment history;

    (3) employment at time of offense;

    (4) employment at time of sentencing.

  d. Social factors, including:

    (1) educational attainment;

    (2) living arrangements at time of offense or sentencing;

    (3) length of residence;

    (4) marital status.

  e. The defendant's exercise of constitutional rights during the adjudication process.

Comment

2.D.201. The Commission believes that sentencing should be neutral with respect to an offender's race, sex, and income level. Accordingly, the Commission has listed employment and social factors that should not be used as reasons for departure from the presumptive sentence, because these factors are highly correlated with sex, race, or income level. Employment is excluded as a reason for departure not only because of its correlation with race and income levels, but also because this factor is manipulable—e.g., offenders could lessen the severity of the sentence by obtaining employment between arrest and sentencing. While it may be desirable for offenders to obtain employment between arrest and sentencing, some groups (those with low income levels, low education levels, and racial minorities generally) find it more difficult to obtain employment than others. It is impossible to reward those employed without, in fact, penalizing those not employed at time of sentencing. * * *

* * *

2.D.203. It follows from the Commission's use of the conviction offense to determine offense severity that departures from the Guidelines should not be permitted for elements of alleged offender behavior not within the definition of the conviction offense. For example, if an offender is convicted of simple robbery, a departure from the Guidelines to increase the severity of the sentence should not be permitted because the offender possessed a firearm or used another dangerous weapon.

  3. <u>Factors that may be used as Reasons for Departure</u>. The following is a nonexclusive list of factors that may be used as reasons for departure:

  a. <u>Mitigating Factors</u>.

    (1) The victim was an aggressor in the incident.

(2) The offender played a minor or passive role in the crime or participated under circumstances of coercion or duress.

(3) The offender, because of physical or mental impairment, lacked substantial capacity for judgment when the offense was committed. The voluntary use of intoxicants (drugs or alcohol) does not fall within the purview of this factor.

(4) The offender's presumptive sentence is a commitment but not a mandatory minimum sentence, and either of the following exist:

   (a) The current conviction offense is at Severity Level 1 or Severity Level 2 and the offender received all of his or her prior felony sentences during fewer than three separate court appearances; or

   (b) The current conviction offense is at Severity Level 3 or Severity Level 4 and the offender received all of his or her prior felony sentences during one court appearance.

(5) Other substantial grounds exist that tend to excuse or mitigate the offender's culpability, although not amounting to a defense.

(6) The court is ordering an alternative placement under Minn. Stat. § 609.1055 for an offender with a serious and persistent mental illness.

(7) The offender is particularly amenable to probation. This factor may, but need not, be supported by the fact that the offender is particularly amenable to a relevant program of individualized treatment in a probationary setting.

* * *

b. <u>Aggravating Factors</u>.

(1) The victim was particularly vulnerable due to age, infirmity, or reduced physical or mental capacity, and the offender knew or should have known of this vulnerability.

(2) The victim was treated with particular cruelty for which the individual offender should be held responsible.

(3) The current conviction is for a criminal sexual conduct offense, or an offense in which the victim was otherwise

injured, and the offender has a prior felony conviction for a criminal sexual conduct offense or an offense in which the victim was otherwise injured.

(4)   The offense was a major economic offense, identified as an illegal act or series of illegal acts committed by other than physical means and by concealment or guile to obtain money or property, to avoid payment or loss of money or property, or to obtain business or professional advantage. The presence of two or more of the circumstances listed below are aggravating factors with respect to the offense:

   (a)   the offense involved multiple victims or multiple incidents per victim;

   (b)   the offense involved an attempted or actual monetary loss substantially greater than the usual offense or substantially greater than the minimum loss specified in the statutes;

   (c)   the offense involved a high degree of sophistication or planning or occurred over a lengthy period of time;

   (d)   the defendant used his or her position or status to facilitate the commission of the offense, including positions of trust, confidence, or fiduciary relationships; or

   (e)   the defendant has been involved in other conduct similar to the current offense as evidenced by the findings of civil or administrative law proceedings or the imposition of professional sanctions.

* * *

(6)   The offender committed, for hire, a crime against the person.

(7)   The offender is being sentenced as an "engrained offender" under Minn. Stat. § 609.3455, subd. 3a.

(8)   The offender is being sentenced as a "dangerous offender who commits a third violent crime" under Minn. Stat.§ 609.1095, subd. 2.

(9)   The offender is being sentenced as a "career offender" under Minn. Stat. § 609.1095, subd. 4.

(10) The offender committed the crime as part of a group of three or more offenders who all actively participated in the crime.

(11) The offender intentionally selected the victim or the property against which the offense was committed, in whole or in part, because of the victim's, the property owner's, or another's actual or perceived race, color, religion, sex, sexual orientation, disability, age, or national origin.

(12) The offender used another's identity without authorization to commit a crime. This aggravating factor may not be used when use of another's identity is an element of the offense.

(13) The offense was committed in the presence of a child.

(14) The offense was committed in a location in which the victim had an expectation of privacy.

Comment

2.D.301. The Commission provides a non-exclusive list of factors that may be used as departure reasons. The factors are intended to describe specific situations involving a small number of cases. The Commission rejects factors that are general in nature, and that could apply to large numbers of cases, such as intoxication at the time of the offense. * * * Some of these factors may be considered in establishing conditions of stayed sentences, even though they may not be used as reasons for departure. For example, whether an offender is employed at time of sentencing may be an important factor in deciding whether restitution should be used as a condition of probation, or in deciding the terms of restitution payment.

2.D.302. The Commission recognizes that the criminal history score does not differentiate between the crime spree offender who has been convicted of several offenses but has not been previously sanctioned by the criminal justice system, and the repeat offender who continues to commit new crimes despite receiving previous consequences from the criminal justice system. The Commission believes the nonviolent crime spree offender should perhaps be sanctioned in the community at least once or twice before a prison sentence is appropriate. The Commission believes that the court is best able to distinguish these offenders, and can depart from the Guidelines accordingly.

* * *

F.   Concurrent/Consecutive Sentences[h]

Generally, when an offender is convicted of multiple current offenses, or when there is a prior felony sentence that has not expired or been discharged, concurrent sentencing is presumptive. [The sentencing guidelines later describe when consecutive sentences are presumptive and when they are otherwise permitted—in other words, not considered a departure from the guidelines.]

* * *

3.   Related Policies

A.   Establishing Conditions of Stayed Sentences

1.   Method of Granting Stayed Sentences. When the appropriate cell on the applicable Grid specifies a stayed sentence, the court may pronounce a stay of execution or a stay of imposition. The court must pronounce the length of the stay, which may exceed the duration of the presumptive prison sentence, and may establish appropriate conditions.

   a.   Stay of Execution. When ordering a stay of execution, the court must pronounce the prison sentence duration, but its execution is stayed. The presumptive duration is shown in the appropriate cell.

   b.   Stay of Imposition. When ordering a stay of imposition, the court must not pronounce a sentence duration, and the imposition of the sentence is stayed.

   The Commission recommends that stays of imposition be used for offenders who are convicted of lower severity offenses and who have low criminal history scores. The Commission further recommends that convicted felons be given one stay of imposition, although for very low severity offenses, a second stay of imposition may be appropriate.

Comment

3.A.101. The use of either a stay of imposition or stay of execution is at the discretion of the court. The Commission has provided a non-presumptive recommendation regarding which categories of offenders should receive stays of imposition, and has recommended that convicted felons generally should receive only one stay of imposition. The Commission believes that stays of imposition are a less severe sanction, and should be used for those

---

[h]   When concurrent sentences are imposed, a person serves several sentences at the same time. When consecutive sentences are imposed, an individual first serves one sentence and then the other.

convicted of less serious offenses and those with short criminal histories.
* * *

3.A.102. *When a court grants a stayed sentence, the duration of the stayed sentence may exceed the presumptive sentence length indicated in the appropriate cell on the applicable Grid, and may be as long as the statutory maximum for the conviction offense. Thus, for an offender convicted of Theft over $5,000 (Severity Level 3), with a Criminal History Score of 1, the duration of the stay could be up to ten years. The 13-month sentence shown in the Guidelines is the presumptive sentence length and, if imposed, would be executed if: (a) the court departs from the dispositional recommendation and decides to execute the sentence; or (b) the stay is later revoked and the court decides to imprison the offender.*

2. Conditions of Stayed Sentences. While the Commission has chosen not to develop specific guidelines for the conditions of stayed sentences, it recognizes that there are several penal objectives to be considered in establishing conditions of stayed sentences, including:

   - deterrence;
   - public condemnation of criminal conduct;
   - public safety;
   - rehabilitation;
   - restitution;
   - retribution; and
   - risk reduction.

   The Commission also recognizes that the relative importance of these objectives may vary with both offense and offender characteristics and that multiple objectives may be present in any given sentence. The Commission urges courts to utilize the least restrictive conditions of stayed sentences that are consistent with the objectives of the sanction. The Commission further urges courts to consider the following principles in establishing the conditions of stayed sentences:

   (1) Retribution. If retribution is an important objective of the stayed sentence, the severity of the retributive sanction should be proportional to the severity of the offense and the prior criminal record of the offender. A period of confinement in a local jail or correctional facility may be appropriate.

   (2) Rehabilitation. If rehabilitation is an important objective of the stayed sentence, the court should make full use of

available local programs and resources. The absence of a rehabilitative resource, in general, should not be a basis for enhancing the retributive objective in sentencing and, in particular, should not be the basis for more extensive use of incarceration than is justified on other grounds.

(3) <u>Restitution</u>. The Commission urges courts to make expanded use of restitution and community work orders as conditions of a stayed sentence, especially for offenders with short criminal histories who are convicted of property crimes, although the use of these conditions in other cases may be appropriate.

(4) <u>Supervision</u>. Supervised probation should be a primary condition of stayed sentences.

(5) <u>Fines</u>. If fines are imposed, the Commission urges the expanded use of day fines,[i] which standardizes the financial impact of the sanction among offenders with different income levels.

Comment

3.A.201. *The court may attach any conditions to a stayed sentence that are permitted by law and that the court deems appropriate. * * * Minn. Stat. § 244.09, subd. 5 permits, but does not require, the Commission to establish guidelines covering conditions of stayed sentences. The Commission chose not to develop guidelines during its initial guideline development effort. The Commission has provided some language in the above section of the Guidelines that provides general direction in the use of conditions of stayed sentences.*

3.A.202. *While the Commission has resolved not to develop guidelines for nonimprisonment sanctions at this time, the Commission believes it is important for the sentencing courts to consider proportionality when pronouncing a period of local confinement as a condition of probation. * * * The period of local confinement should be proportional to the severity of the conviction offense and the criminal history score of the offender. * * **

B. Revocation of Stayed Sentences

The Commission views revocation of a stayed sentence and commitment to be justified when:

- The offender is convicted of a new felony for which the Guidelines recommend prison; or

- The offender continues to violate conditions of the stay despite the court's use of expanded and more onerous conditions.

---

[i]   Day fines are discussed on pages 245–248 of this casebook.

The decision to revoke an offender's stayed sentence should not be undertaken lightly. Great restraint should be exercised in imprisoning offenders who were originally convicted of low severity level offenses or who have short prior criminal histories. For these offenders, the Commission urges continuance of the stay and use of more restrictive and onerous conditions, such as periods of local confinement. Less judicial tolerance is urged for offenders who were convicted of a more severe offense or who had a longer criminal history. For both groups of offenders, however, the court should not reflexively order imprisonment for non-criminal violations of probationary conditions.

* * *

C.   Jail Credit

* * *

2.   <u>Applying Jail Credit</u>. To uphold the proportionality of sentencing, jail credit should be applied in the following manner:

   a.   The Commissioner of Corrections must deduct jail credit from the sentence imposed by subtracting the time from the specified minimum term of imprisonment. If there is any remaining time, it must be subtracted from the specified maximum period of supervised release.

* * *

Comment

3.C.01. * * * Granting jail credit to the time served in custody in connection with an offense ensures that a defendant who cannot post bail because of indigency will serve the same amount of time that an offender in identical circumstances who is able to post bail would serve. Also, the total amount of time a defendant is incarcerated should not turn on irrelevant concerns such as whether the defendant pleads guilty or insists on his right to trial.

* * *

3.C.03. The Commission also believes that jail credit should be awarded for time spent in custody as a condition of a stay of imposition or stay of execution when the stay is revoked and the offender is committed. The primary purpose of imprisonment is punishment, and the punishment imposed should be proportional to the severity of the conviction offense and the criminal history of the offender. If, for example, the presumptive duration in a case is 18 months, and the sentence was initially executed, the specified minimum term of imprisonment would be 12 months. If the execution of the sentence had initially been stayed and the offender had served four months in jail as a condition of the stay, and later the stay was revoked and the sentence executed, the offender would be confined for 16 months rather than 12 without awarding jail credit. By awarding jail credit for time spent in custody as a condition of a stay of imposition or execution, proportionality is maintained.

3.C.04. Credit for time spent in custody as a condition of a stay of imposition or stay of execution is appropriate for time spent in jails, workhouses, and regional correctional facilities. The Commission takes no position on the applicability of jail credit for time spent in other residential facilities, electronic monitoring, etc., and leaves it to the sentencing authority to determine whether jail credit should be granted in these situations.

3.C.05. In computing jail time credit, each day or portion of a day in jail should be counted as one full day of credit. For example, a defendant who spends part of a day in confinement on the day of arrest and part of a day in confinement on the day of release should receive a full day of credit for each day.

* * *

G. Modifications

1. <u>Policy Modifications</u>. Modifications to the Minnesota Sentencing Guidelines and associated commentary apply to offenders whose date of offense is on or after the specified modification effective date.

* * *

4.A. Sentencing Guidelines Grid

Presumptive sentence lengths are in months. Italicized numbers within the grid denote the discretionary range within which a court may sentence without the sentence being deemed a departure. Offenders with stayed felony sentences may be subject to local confinement.

SEVERITY LEVEL OF CONVICTION OFFENSE (Example offenses listed in italics)		CRIMINAL HISTORY SCORE						
		0	1	2	3	4	5	6 or more
Murder, 2nd Degree (intentional murder; drive-by shootings)	11	306 *261–367*	326 *278–391*	346 *295–415*	366 *312–439*	386 *329–463*	406 *346–480*	426 *363–480*
Murder, 3rd Degree; Murder, 2nd Degree (unintentional murder)	10	150 *128–180*	165 *141–198*	180 *153–216*	195 *166–234*	210 *179–252*	225 *192–270*	240 *204–288*
Assault, 1st Degree	9	86 *74–103*	98 *84–117*	110 *94–132*	122 *104–146*	134 *114–160*	146 *125–175*	158 *135–189*
Aggravated Robbery, 1st Degree; Burglary, 1st Degree (w/Weapon or Assault)	8	48 *41–57*	58 *50–69*	68 *58–81*	78 *67–93*	88 *75–105*	98 *84–117*	108 *92–129*
Felony DWI; Financial Exploitation of a Vulnerable Adult	7	36	42	48	54 *46–64*	60 *51–72*	66 *57–79*	72 *62–84*
Assault, 2nd Degree; Burglary, 1st Degree (Occupied Dwelling)	6	21	27	33	39 *34–46*	45 *39–54*	51 *44–61*	57 *49–68*
Residential Burglary; Simple Robbery	5	18	23	28	33 *29–39*	38 *33–45*	43 *37–51*	48 *41–57*
Nonresidential Burglary	4	12[1]	15	18	21	24 *21–28*	27 *23–32*	30 *26–36*
Theft Crimes (Over $5,000)	3	12[1]	13	15	17	19 *17–22*	21 *18–25*	23 *20–27*
Theft Crimes ($5,000 or less); Check Forgery ($251–$2,500)	2	12[1]	12[1]	13	15	17	19	21 *18–25*
Assault, 4th Degree; Fleeing a Peace Officer	1	12[1]	12[1]	12[1]	13	15	17	19 *17–22*

▢   Presumptive commitment to state imprisonment. First-degree murder has a mandatory life sentence and is excluded from the Guidelines * * *.

▨   Presumptive stayed sentence; at the discretion of the court, up to one year of confinement and other non-jail sanctions can be imposed as conditions of probation. * * *

[1] 12[1] = One year and one day.

Effective August 1, 2017

Examples of Executed Sentences (Length in Months) Broken Down by: Term of Imprisonment and Supervised Release Term

*Under Minn. Stat. § 244.101, offenders committed to the Commissioner of Corrections * * * will receive an executed sentence pronounced by the court consisting of two parts: a specified minimum term of imprisonment equal to* *two-thirds of the total executed sentence and a supervised release term equal to the remaining one-third. The court is required to pronounce the total executed sentence and explain the amount of time the offender will serve in prison and the amount of time the offender will serve on supervised release, assuming the offender commits no disciplinary offense in prison that results in the imposition of a disciplinary confinement period. The court must also explain that the amount of time the offender actually serves in prison may be extended by the Commissioner if the offender violates disciplinary rules while in prison or violates conditions of supervised release. This extension period could result in the offender's serving the entire executed sentence in prison.*

Executed Sentence	Term of Imprisonment	Supervised Release Term	Executed Sentence	Term of Imprisonment	Supervised Release Term
12 and 1 day	8 and 1 day	4	78	52	26
13	8 2/3	4 1/3	86	57 1/3	28 2/3
15	10	5	88	58 2/3	29 1/3
17	11 1/3	5 2/3	98	65 1/3	32 2/3
18	12	6	108	72	36
19	12 2/3	6 1/3	110	73 1/3	36 2/3
21	14	7	122	81 1/3	40 2/3
23	15 1/3	7 2/3	134	89 1/3	44 2/3
24	16	8	146	97 1/3	48 2/3
27	18	9	150	100	50
28	18 2/3	9 1/3	158	105 1/3	52 2/3
30	20	10	165	110	55
33	22	11	180	120	60
36	24	12	190	126 2/3	63 1/3
38	25 1/3	12 2/3	195	130	65
39	26	13	200	133 1/3	66 2/3
42	28	14	210	140	70
43	28 2/3	14 1/3	220	146 2/3	73 1/3
45	30	15	225	150	75
48	32	16	230	153 1/3	76 2/3
51	34	17	240	160	80
54	36	18	306	204	102
57	38	19	326	217 1/3	108 2/3
58	38 2/3	19 1/3	346	230 2/3	115 1/3
60	40	20	366	244	122
66	44	22	386	257 1/3	128 2/3
68	45 1/3	22 2/3	406	270 2/3	135 1/3
72	48	24	426	284	142

[Additional grids, tables, and lists, including the table identifying the offense severity level for numerous felonies and the list of "targeted misdemeanors" used to compute units in the criminal-history score, have been omitted.]

QUESTIONS AND POINTS FOR DISCUSSION

1. How, if at all, would you modify the Minnesota sentencing guidelines?

2. Some of the sentencing guidelines adopted in other states are more expansive in scope than Minnesota's. For example, North Carolina's "punishment charts" establish presumptive sentences for misdemeanors as well as felonies. The North Carolina guidelines also define presumptive sentencing ranges for aggravated and mitigated felony sentences as well as standard sentences. And these guidelines further structure the imposition of nonincarcerative penalties, identifying when an "intermediate punishment" and when a "community punishment" is the presumptive sentence. An "intermediate punishment" is a sentence to supervised probation that can be combined with, among other conditions, participation in a drug-court program or a period of confinement for a defined period of time followed by probation (what is known as a "split sentence"). A "community punishment," by contrast, cannot include a split sentence or assignment to a drug court, although the sentence may include a number of other conditions. The felony and misdemeanor punishment charts and additional details about North Carolina's approach to what is called "structured sentencing" can be found in N.C. Sentencing & Policy Advisory Comm'n, A Citizen's Guide to Structured Sentencing (2014). For detailed information on the ways in which other states and the federal government have structured their sentencing guidelines, see the website of the Robina Institute of Criminal Law and Criminal Justice's Sentencing Guidelines Resource Center at http://sentencing.umn.edu.

3. Assume the Minnesota sentencing guidelines apply in each of the following cases. Before referring to the guidelines, consider what sentence you believe would be appropriate in each case and why. Is there any additional information you would want to know in order to identify the appropriate sentence? Now apply the guidelines to these cases. Do you need any additional information to properly apply the guidelines? How did the presumptive sentences under the guidelines differ from your initial views about the appropriate penalty? Upon reflection, which penalty is most appropriate?

Case #1

The defendant has been convicted of aggravated robbery. In Minnesota, aggravated robbery is defined as a robbery committed while armed with a dangerous weapon or during which the perpetrator inflicts bodily harm upon another. The defendant is twenty-one. He is unmarried and has no children, limited work skills, and a bad employment record. He also has a severe drug problem. The defendant was a juvenile when he committed two burglaries for each of which he received probation. He also has a prior adult conviction for robbery that resulted in a prison sentence. In the robbery for which the defendant is awaiting sentencing, the victim was assaulted and received a laceration on his skull which required stitches.

Case #2

Defendant Patty Hearst has been convicted of aggravated robbery. She is in her early twenties, comes from a wealthy family, is well-educated, and has no prior convictions. The defendant was kidnapped by a group of self-proclaimed revolutionaries and later participated with them in the bank robbery, while armed with a gun, for which she was convicted. Her defense was that she committed the crime out of fear for her safety since she was under the control of the kidnappers. The jury did not believe her.

Case #3

The defendant has been convicted of embezzlement of $5,000 from a bank where he had been employed for eight years. The defendant took the money to pay off gambling debts. He is in his early thirties, is married, and has two young children. He is also a college graduate, has secured a new record-keeping job, for which he is fairly well paid, at a local hospital, and has no prior criminal record.

4.   Under the Minnesota sentencing guidelines, a judge generally cannot impose a sentence that departs upwards from the presumptive sentence unless a jury has found beyond a reasonable doubt the facts on which the aggravated departure rests and the judge has explained in writing or on the record the reasons why the departure is justified. When applying the guidelines to the three cases described above, did the extra steps that need to be taken in order to depart upwards from the guidelines affect what sentence you imposed under the guidelines? Should the need to take those procedural steps factor, in your opinion, into the judge's sentencing decision?

5.   The Minnesota sentencing guidelines have had success in advancing two of their objectives—reducing sentencing disparity and ensuring that the punishment meted out in a particular case is proportionate to the severity of the crime committed and the defendant's criminal history. Judges adhere to both the guidelines' dispositional prescriptions, which govern the "in-out decision," and the durational prescriptions in the majority of cases. Minnesota Sentencing Guidelines Comm'n, Report to the Legislature 22–23, 27 (2017). In addition, the probability of being sentenced to prison in Minnesota increases, in accordance with the guidelines' goals, as the seriousness of a defendant's conviction offense or criminal history increases. Nat'l Ctr. for State Courts, Assessing Consistency and Fairness in Sentencing: A Comparative Study in Three States 13 (2008).

North Carolina also witnessed changes in the profile of persons receiving prison sentences after the enactment of its sentencing "guidelines." (North Carolina did not call its punishment charts "guidelines" in an attempt to distance itself from the widely criticized federal sentencing guidelines. Michael Tonry, Sentencing Matters 11–12 (1996)). For example, the percentage of people convicted of property crimes who were sentenced to prison dropped from 45% in 1993–94 to 28% in 1999–2000. Ronald F. Wright, Counting the Cost of Sentencing in North Carolina, 1980–2000, 29 Crime & Just. 39, 87 (2002).

During the same time period, the average length of the prison sentences served by people convicted of violent crimes increased from twenty-one to sixty-seven months. Id. at 88.

6.   The circumvention of sentencing guidelines through charging decisions and plea negotiations can undermine the effectuation of the goals of sentencing guidelines. Minnesota is a case in point. Displeasure with what many prosecutors considered the too lenient treatment of individuals for property crimes under the state's new guidelines led them to file more charges against them and to require guilty pleas to more such charges than in the past. Michael H. Tonry, U.S. Dep't of Justice, Sentencing Reform Impacts 71–73 (1987). For example, while in pre-guidelines days prosecutors might agree to entry of a plea of guilty to one count of theft by a defendant charged with several thefts, after adoption of the guidelines prosecutors often insisted on a plea of guilty to several of the thefts in order to increase the defendant's criminal-history score. Prosecutors also took steps to skirt guidelines sentences that they considered too severe. For example, because the offense-severity level is based on the offense of conviction, charge reductions were used to avoid what was considered too stringent a penalty.

The Minnesota Sentencing Guidelines Commission monitors the implementation of the guidelines and has continually made modifications to them to modulate the effects of charging and negotiation decisions on the realization of the guidelines' goals. For example, while the guidelines originally assigned one point to the criminal-history score for each prior felony conviction, the Sentencing Commission moved to weighing felony convictions based on their severity, with more serious felony convictions assigned a higher score. This change was designed to dissipate the effects of the stacking of criminal-history convictions by prosecutors, which in turn was resulting in the increased incarceration of people convicted of property crimes and a reduction in the resources available to punish those who had committed crimes of violence.

The prosecutorial discretion employed to skirt sentencing guidelines could, it has been argued, be further channeled if sentencing commissions required prosecutors to draft prosecutorial guidelines to guide their charging and plea-bargaining decisions and then monitored their implementation. See Ronald F. Wright, Sentencing Commissions as Provocateurs of Prosecutorial Self-Regulation, 105 Colum. L.Rev. 1010, 1027–37 (2005). The taking of other steps has been prescribed to ensure that prosecutors adhere to their own prosecutorial guidelines. These steps include requiring prosecutors to explain on the record the reason for a departure from their own guidelines and empowering judges to review, in an individual case, whether a prosecutor's departure decision reflects an "abuse of discretion." Id. at 1038. Do you concur or disagree with these proposals?

7.   The federal sentencing guidelines have taken a different approach to limit, to a certain extent, the effects of plea bargaining on the operation of the guidelines, adopting a modified version of what is called "real-offense" sentencing. Under the federal guidelines, for example, the offense level for

certain crimes, such as those involving an amount of drugs or money, is based not only on the offense of conviction but on other "relevant conduct." U.S. Sentencing Comm'n, Federal Sentencing Guidelines Manual, § 1B1.3 (2016). Thus, if a defendant was charged with, and convicted of, distributing five grams of cocaine but the judge determined that the defendant had sold five kilograms as part of the "same course of conduct" or "common scheme or plan," the judge would adjust the defendant's offense level to reflect this higher amount. Under the federal guidelines, however, the sentence imposed on the defendant could not exceed the maximum penalty that could be imposed under the applicable statute for the crime of which the defendant was actually convicted. Id. § 5G1.1(a), (c)(1). In addition, after United States v. Booker, 543 U.S. 220, 125 S.Ct. 738 (2005), discussed in note 1 on page 183, the sentencing adjustments prescribed by the federal guidelines to reflect the defendant's "real offense" are advisory rather than mandatory.

8.   Real-offense sentencing has sparked heated controversy, and that controversy has not been mooted by United States v. Booker, 543 U.S. 220, 125 S.Ct. 738 (2005). For example, in an indeterminate sentencing system, a judge might be accorded the discretion to sentence a defendant based on the defendant's "real offense," with the caveat that the sentence not exceed the maximum sentence for the crime of which the defendant was convicted. Alternatively, as can occur in certain federal cases, a defendant's "real offense" might be a factor when sentencing the defendant under a set of advisory sentencing guidelines. Or, in a jurisdiction with presumptive sentencing guidelines, a judge might be authorized to consider the defendant's "real offense" when selecting a sentence from within the sentencing range that reflects the facts established by the jury's verdict or admitted in the defendant's guilty plea. Consequently, the soundness, from a policy perspective, of real-offense sentencing needs to be considered.

In an article, excerpts of which are set forth below, Professor Julie R. O'Sullivan defended real-offense sentencing:

> The use of this subset of relevant nonconviction conduct reflects sentencers' longstanding belief that "few things could be so relevant [to sentence] as other criminal activity of the defendant." Reference to just deserts and crime control considerations underscores the reasonableness of this historical estimation. Thus, for example, assume that a defendant is convicted on a single count of possessing a quantity of cocaine with the intent to distribute that drug. Assume further that the defendant in fact acted as the leader of a sophisticated and large-scale drug cartel and that the count of conviction was simply one act in furtherance of the defendant's ongoing business.

> Information about the true scope of the defendant's and his accomplices' related criminal activity informs our assessment of the defendant's just deserts for the offense of conviction in so far as it illuminates the defendant's motivation and purposefulness in

engaging in this criminal act. Certainly the "real" facts regarding the extent of the defendant's related criminal activity are essential to meaningful crime control judgments regarding the real danger the defendant's act poses to society, his likelihood of recidivism, and the likely deterrent effect of any particular sanction. In short, we may not be able to determine with certainty the precise sentence that would further the goals of sentencing in light of this information, but we certainly know that its exclusion must compromise the sentencing judge's ability to impose a sentence that will reflect the true seriousness of the offense of conviction, the defendant's danger to the community, and the deterrent effect that a significant sanction may have upon the defendant's and his co-conspirator's ongoing appetite for drug smuggling.

* * *

If consideration of nonconviction offense conduct were eliminated and a charge-offense sentencing scheme adopted, the prosecutor would essentially select the sentence by choosing the applicable charge. The system itself would not require uniform treatment of offenders based upon penologically relevant offense and offender characteristics. Rather, it would defer to prosecutorial decisions as to who should be treated alike and who should not. To illustrate, suppose that Congress created grades of fraud distinguished by elements relating to the amount of monetary loss flowing from the offense, the degree of planning that went into the fraud, and the number of victims affected by it. Under existing law and practice, a prosecutor who had evidence that a particular crime satisfied the highest grade of fraud would have the discretion to charge that grade or any grade beneath it. In a pure charge-offense system, the prosecutor's choice of the charge would determine the sentence. A defendant whose conduct is worthy of more severe punishment, then, would at the prosecutor's election be treated for sentencing purposes the same as a defendant of lesser culpability.

Such a system would necessarily create unwarranted sentencing disparities * * *.

Julie R. O'Sullivan, In Defense of the U.S. Sentencing Guidelines' Modified Real-Offense System, 91 Nw. U.L.Rev. 1342, 1369–70, 1401 (1997) (Reprinted by special permission of Northwestern University School of Law, *Law Review*). See also Frank O. Bowman, III, The Quality of Mercy Must Be Restrained, and Other Lessons in Learning to Love the Federal Sentencing Guidelines, 1996 Wis. L.Rev. 679, 702–04 (1996).

Critics of real-offense sentencing have charged that it is "incompatible with the basic values of our legal system" and "antithetical to basic notions of individual worth and liberty." Michael H. Tonry, Real Offense Sentencing: The Model Sentencing and Corrections Act, 72 J.Crim.L. & Criminology 1550, 1564

(1981). Professor Kevin R. Reitz has explained the underpinnings of this charge and expressed other concerns about real-offense sentencing:

> [A]ssume that defendant Smith has been convicted of one count of armed robbery, for which the maximum statutory penalty is ten years in prison. Smith is a first offender and, under normal circumstances, the sentencing judge would select a sentence of two years. In this case, however, the judge has been persuaded during sentencing proceedings (perhaps by hearsay in the presentence report) that Smith probably committed a second armed robbery for which he has not been tried. Based on this conclusion, the judge imposes a term of four years rather than two, which is the same sentence she would have chosen if Smith had been convicted of both robberies.
>
> * * * [T]he sentencing court has acted improperly in imposing an extra two years for the second robbery. The increment of punishment for the nonconviction offense bypasses all trial safeguards that should precede an independent guilt determination. Indeed, the judge has done something just as unwarranted as sending Smith to prison for the initial two-year term in the absence of any conviction at all, based only on an informal judicial finding that Smith "probably" committed the first robbery.
>
> A real-offense advocate might find this case too hastily made. If it is likely that Smith was a two-time armed robber, why should the state be foreclosed from responding to this probable reality? The answer is that the state is not foreclosed. Implementation of a conviction-offense system places a burden on prosecutors to file and prove, or bargain for, conviction charges that reflect the seriousness of an offenders' criminal behavior. If, with respect to certain nonconviction crimes, this is an obligation they cannot discharge, then we should have grave doubts that the imposition of punishment is justified.
>
> * * * In a slight alteration of the illustration above, suppose that a jury has acquitted Smith of one robbery while convicting him of the other. The sentencing judge, however, disagrees with the jury's verdict of acquittal or, more precisely, finds that she can reach a contrary factual conclusion when freed of the reasonable doubt standard and other trial constraints. Accordingly, the judge's sentence reflects two crimes.
>
> In this scenario, the judge effectively has entered a judgment of guilt notwithstanding the verdict, which she would not be permitted to do explicitly. Indeed, the procedural anomaly goes further. Presumably, if we were to abolish the jury-trial guarantee to allow judgments n.o.v. of guilt, we would still require judges to find that no reasonable jury could have discerned reasonable doubt as to the nonconviction charge. Moreover, we would insist that such a conclusion be based on evidence admitted at trial, under the rules of

evidence and other applicable safeguards. Real-offense practice, in contrast, allows courts to override the jury without satisfying such imposing requirements and, in most jurisdictions, without entering findings or an explanation on the record. Thus, at sentencing, an acquittal is overturned quite easily in comparison with the forbidden judgment n.o.v., and is subject to little or no appellate review.

The consideration of acquittal offenses is unique among real-offense practices because it involves the redetermination of factual disputes fully litigated at trial. On a symbolic level, this carries at least two effects. It would be excusable for members of the jury to conclude that their hard work, and careful parsing of the allegations, was for naught. From the perspective of the public, the message conveyed is that criminal trials, expensive as they are, determine little more than raw guilt or innocence. Beyond symbolism, the relitigation of acquittal counts at sentencing adds a substantial burden on defendants convicted of some charges and acquitted of others. Acquittal charges must be defended twice, and the defense must be more vigorous the second time around because the available procedures are more spare. On policy grounds, we should question the wisdom of requiring those accused of crime to "run the gauntlet" of successive proceedings, apart from the unseemliness of ignoring the jury's decision.

* * *

* * * There may also be special reason to bar the real-offense use of dismissed charges, or charges not brought, under the terms of plea bargains, as a basis for increased sentences. This practice, when anticipated by offenders, can discourage settlement. Aside from affecting incentives to plea bargain, real-offense consideration of dismissed charges raises ethical questions of permitting the government to strike meaningless bargains. * * * [D]efendants may be deceived into thinking that a sizable charge concession will have a meaningful impact on sentence. The waiver of important trial rights, supposedly allowed only when "intelligent and voluntary," should not be premised on such a misunderstanding.

* * *

* * * Some have argued that real-offense sentencing diminishes prosecutors' abilities to influence sentencing through the selection of charges. This claim centers on the distorting effect of the charging decision as one filter between factual and legal guilt. It contends that sentence decisions will bear closer resemblance to "reality," and will be less marked by the prosecutor's stamp, if the boundaries of formal conviction can be overlooked.

* * *

[I]t is exceedingly strange to cast real-offense sentencing as a brake on prosecutorial power when the great force of its impact is in the opposite direction. Real-offense practice gives the government two opportunities to establish criminal conduct: once at trial or by plea, and again at sentencing. Indeed, the second bite at the apple is a dramatic addition to the state's arsenal because so many trial protections have fallen by the wayside. This creates the temptation, if not the practice, of undercharging or underbargaining on the part of prosecutors, who can wait for sentencing to make out their full case. Also, in tried cases that are not fully successful for the government, real-offense rules allow the state to recoup its losses.

Kevin R. Reitz, Sentencing Facts: Travesties of Real-Offense Sentencing, 45 Stan. L.Rev. 523, 550–53, 563–64 (1993) (Republished with the permission of the Stanford Law Review).

What do you believe is the appropriate focus when determining the offense-severity level when sentencing a defendant—the offense of conviction or the "real offense"?

2. ADVISORY GUIDELINES

a. The Federal Sentencing Guidelines: Several Key Distinctions

As a result of the Supreme Court's decision in United States v. Booker, 543 U.S. 220, 125 S.Ct. 738 (2005), which is discussed in note 1 on page 183, the federal sentencing guidelines are advisory only, not presumptive like those in Minnesota. The federal guidelines differ from the Minnesota guidelines in a number of other ways. The federal guidelines, for example, contain forty-three offense levels, as compared to the eleven offense levels in Minnesota, and include detailed rules for the raising and lowering of sentences by prescribed increments. The complexity of the federal sentencing guidelines has provoked complaints from many federal judges and practitioners frustrated with what Second Circuit Judge Jose A. Cabranes has described as "a byzantine system of rules." Frank O. Bowman, III, The Quality of Mercy Must Be Restrained, and Other Lessons in Learning to Love the Federal Sentencing Guidelines, 1996 Wis. L.Rev. 679, 705 n.104 (1996). See also Albert W. Alschuler, The Failure of Sentencing Guidelines: A Plea for Less Aggregation, 58 U. Chi. L.Rev. 901, 950 (1991) ("The 258-box federal sentencing grid * * * should be relegated to a place near the Edsel in a museum of twentieth-century bad ideas.").

Many of the differences between the Minnesota guidelines and the federal guidelines are attributable to the sentencing commissions' differing views about the appropriate kinds and amount of punishment for certain types of crimes. Of particular importance are the different opinions as to what constitutes a proportionate penalty for nonviolent crimes and what is an appropriate use of prison resources. The Minnesota sentencing guidelines reflect the belief that most people convicted of nonviolent crimes can be punished effectively in the community and that prisons generally should be reserved for people who commit violent crimes and individuals with particularly serious criminal histories. The vast majority of people convicted of felonies in Minnesota are presumptively subject to community sanctions under the guidelines, although judges have the option of imposing a jail term as a condition of probation. See Minnesota Sentencing Guidelines Comm'n, Report to the Legislature 1–2 (2017) (reporting that since the sentencing guidelines went into effect in 1980, Minnesota almost every year has had one of the three lowest imprisonment rates in the country, with the imprisonment rate in 2015 less than half the state imprisonment rate nationally).

By contrast, the vast majority of people sentenced under the federal sentencing guidelines are subject to some period of confinement, either in prison or elsewhere. Only under the first eight, out of a total of forty-three, offense levels is a person with no prior criminal convictions eligible for probation without any attending confinement or detention. Id. at § 5B1.1(a). See also U.S. Sentencing Comm'n, 2016 Sourcebook of Federal Sentencing Statistics S-28 fig. D (2017) (during fiscal year 2016, 87.5% of defendants sentenced under the federal guidelines received a "prison only" sentence, with 7.3% receiving a "probation only" sentence).

To what extent do your views correspond with those of the United States Sentencing Commission? To what extent do they mirror those of the Minnesota Sentencing Guidelines Commission? For additional information about the federal sentencing guidelines, see U.S. Sentencing Comm'n, Federal Sentencing: The Basics (2015) for a general overview of them and Roger W. Haines, Jr. et al., Federal Sentencing Guidelines Handbook (2016–17 ed.) for in-depth guidance on how to apply them.

b. Application of the Advisory Federal Guidelines at Sentencing

The Supreme Court and other federal courts have struggled with the import of the Supreme Court's holding in *Booker* that the federal sentencing guidelines are advisory only. One question is how the federal guidelines can and should factor into sentencing decisions. In Gall v. United States, 552 U.S. 38, 49, 128 S.Ct. 586, 596 (2007), the Supreme Court said that the guidelines are the "starting point"—the "initial benchmark"—for the sentencing judge. But the judge cannot presume that a sentence within the guidelines range is reasonable. Instead, in determining the appropriate sentence, the judge must consider the sentencing factors outlined in 18 U.S.C. § 3553(a), such as the need to protect the public from future crimes committed by the defendant and the need to provide the defendant with necessary educational services, vocational training, medical care, and other treatment in the "most effective manner." (See footnote c on page 264 of the casebook for a list of the sentencing factors set forth in § 3553(a).) If the judge then decides that a sentence outside the guidelines is warranted, the judge must make sure the reason for this variance from the guidelines is "sufficiently compelling" to justify a variance of that amount. Id. at 50, 128 S.Ct. at 597. And the sentencing judge must provide a "more significant justification" for a "major" deviation from the guidelines than for a "minor" one. Id.

Gall illustrates the wider variation in sentences for a crime that can potentially ensue when sentencing guidelines are advisory rather than presumptive. The lowest sentence under the guidelines range for the crime to which the defendant pled guilty in that case—conspiracy to distribute several controlled substances—was thirty months in prison. Citing the defendant's voluntary withdrawal from the conspiracy over four years before his indictment, his subsequent securing of a college degree and employment, and other facts, the district judge sentenced the defendant to probation for thirty-six months. Giving "due deference" to this decision, the Supreme Court found that the district judge had not abused his discretion in rendering this sentence. Id. at 59–60, 128 S.Ct. at 602. See also Kimbrough v. United States, 552 U.S. 85, 128 S.Ct. 558 (2007) (upholding a sentence for drug-related crimes that was over four years lower than the bottom sentence in the guidelines range). Is this greater variation in sentences for a crime, in your opinion, a positive or negative repercussion of the Supreme Court's holding that the federal sentencing guidelines are no longer mandatory?

c.   Appellate Review of Federal Sentences

In *Booker*, the Supreme Court held that when a federal sentence is challenged on appeal the appellate court should determine whether the sentence was "unreasonable." 543 U.S. at 261, 125 S.Ct. at 765. When making this determination, the appellate court is to apply a "deferential abuse-of-discretion standard." Gall v. United States, 552 U.S. at 41, 128 S.Ct. at 591.

Federal appellate courts can apply, but are not required to apply, a presumption that a sentence falling within the range set forth in the federal sentencing guidelines is reasonable. The Supreme Court reasoned in Rita v. United States, 551 U.S. 338, 127 S.Ct. 2456 (2007) that such a presumption is permissible since both the Sentencing Commission, through the crafting of the guideline range within whose parameters the sentence fell, and the district court, through the imposition of a sentence in line with the guidelines, have concurred that the within-the-guidelines sentence comports with the sentencing factors set forth in 18 U.S.C. § 3553(a).

The Supreme Court emphasized in *Rita* that the rebuttable presumption that a within-the-guidelines sentence is reasonable is an *"appellate* court presumption"; the sentencing judge, as noted earlier, cannot invoke such a presumption. Id. at 351, 127 S.Ct. at 2465. But the Court conceded that an appellate presumption that a within-the-guidelines sentence is reasonable might exert what Justice Souter, in dissent, described as a "gravitational pull" on federal district judges to adhere to the guidelines when imposing sentences. Id. at 390, 127 S.Ct. at 2487 (Souter, J., dissenting).

While a federal appellate court can apply a presumption of reasonableness when reviewing a sentence that fell within the guidelines range, the court cannot apply a presumption of unreasonableness when reviewing a sentence falling outside that range. According to the Supreme Court in *Gall*, a presumption of unreasonableness would give too much weight to the federal sentencing guidelines, conflicting with the Court's attempt in *Booker* to remedy a Sixth Amendment problem with the guidelines by treating them as advisory in nature. To avoid undermining *Booker*, an appellate court also cannot require that there be "extraordinary circumstances" to justify a substantial variance from the guidelines. Gall, 552 U.S. at 47, 128 S.Ct. at 595. But the extent to which the sentence imposed varies from the recommended sentence under the guidelines is, according to the Supreme Court, a relevant factor to be considered by an appellate court deciding whether the sentence was unreasonable and an abuse of the sentencing judge's discretion.

D. THE RETROACTIVE EFFECTS OF CHANGES IN SENTENCING STATUTES AND GUIDELINES

1. *EX POST FACTO* LIMITATIONS

Guideline 3.G.1. of the Minnesota sentencing guidelines, which limits the application of guideline modifications to defendants who committed their crimes on or after the date a modification went into effect, is designed to avoid *ex post facto* problems with the guidelines. Article I, § 10 of the United States Constitution prohibits the states from enacting any *ex post facto* laws, and Article I, § 9 prohibits Congress from enacting such laws. A law which increases the punishment for a crime after the crime has been committed falls within this *ex post facto* prohibition. Lindsey v. Washington, 301 U.S. 397, 401, 57 S.Ct. 797, 799 (1937).

The Supreme Court has interpreted the *Ex Post Facto* Clause as prohibiting the imposition of the presumptive sentence set forth in sentencing guidelines in effect at the time of sentencing that was higher than the presumptive sentence under the guidelines in effect at the time of the defendant's crime. Miller v. Florida, 482 U.S. 423, 107 S.Ct. 2446

(1987). An *ex post facto* violation may ensue even when the heightened penalty is set forth in sentencing guidelines that are considered only advisory. Peugh v. United States, 569 U.S. 530, 543, 133 S.Ct. 2072, 2084 (2013) (applying amended federal sentencing guidelines when calculating the guidelines range created a "sufficient risk" of a higher sentence to abridge the Ex Post Facto Clause). Reducing the good-time or other sentencing credits that could be earned under the law in effect at the time of the crime also violates the *ex post facto* prohibition. See Lynce v. Mathis, 519 U.S. 433, 117 S.Ct. 891 (1997) (statute revoking sentencing credits to which the prisoner was entitled under a statute in effect at the time of his crime, which provided for the awarding of such credits when the state's prison system reached a certain level of crowding, violated the Constitution's *ex post facto* prohibition); Weaver v. Graham, 450 U.S. 24, 101 S.Ct. 960 (1981) (law enacted after the date of the defendant's crime and sentencing, which decreased the rate that good-time credits accumulate, is an unconstitutional *ex post facto* law).

In California Department of Corrections v. Morales, 514 U.S. 499, 115 S.Ct. 1597 (1995), however, the Supreme Court held that a state statute that increased the length of time between parole-suitability hearings for certain prisoners did not constitute an *ex post facto* law. The statute in question authorized the parole board to defer the parole-suitability hearing of a prisoner with two or more homicide convictions for up to three years if the board found that it was "not reasonable to expect" parole would be granted during the intervening years and explained the reason for this conclusion. The statute in effect at the time of the murder for which the prisoner in this case was imprisoned had provided, by contrast, for annual parole-suitability hearings. The prisoner argued that the new statute unconstitutionally increased the punishment to which he was subjected since it eliminated the possibility that he might be released on parole during the three-year period between his parole-suitability hearings. The Supreme Court responded that the risk that the statute enhanced his punishment was too remote and speculative to give rise to a constitutional violation. The Court emphasized both that the statute applied to a category of prisoners whose release on parole was extremely unlikely and that the board had to follow certain procedures to ensure that parole-suitability hearings were deferred only in appropriate cases, such as explain the bases for a finding that deferral would not prolong the length of a person's confinement.

In Garner v. Jones, 529 U.S. 244, 120 S.Ct. 1362 (2000), the Supreme Court went even further than *Morales*, holding that a change in a parole board's rules lengthening the period of time before parole reconsideration from three years to up to eight years for prisoners serving life sentences did not necessarily violate the constitutional prohibition on *ex post facto* laws. The Court concluded that the new rules, on their face, did not create a "significant risk" of prolonged confinement for prisoners with life sentences because, under the board's procedures, a prisoner could be afforded expedited reconsideration for parole based on a "change in circumstances." Id. at 251, 255, 120 S.Ct. at 1368, 1370. The Court added, though, that while the new rules were not unconstitutional on their face, an individual prisoner must be afforded the opportunity to show that the way in which the rules actually have been applied to him or her has created a significant risk of increased punishment.

In a separate opinion concurring, in part, in the judgment, Justice Scalia objected to giving a prisoner the chance to demonstrate that the board's new procedures have significantly increased the risk, to that particular prisoner, of prolonged incarceration. Underscoring that parole is "a matter of grace" and not an entitlement—an opportunity for "mercy" remitted to the parole board's discretion, Justice Scalia contended:

> It makes no more sense to freeze in time the Board's discretion as to procedures than it does to freeze in time the Board's discretion as to substance. Just as the *Ex Post Facto* Clause gives respondent no cause to complain that the Board in place at the time of his offense has been replaced by a new, tough-on-crime Board that is much more parsimonious with parole, it gives him no cause to complain that it has been replaced by a new, big-on-efficiency Board that cuts back on reconsiderations without cause.

Id. at 259, 120 S.Ct. at 1372 (Scalia, J., concurring in part in judgment). In your opinion, under what circumstances, if any, does a change in the time interval before parole consideration or reconsideration violate the *Ex Post Facto* Clause?

2. REDUCTIONS IN AUTHORIZED SENTENCES

After a defendant has been sentenced, the legislature sometimes reduces the authorized penalty for the crime of which the defendant was convicted, or a sentencing commission lowers the prescribed or recommended sentence or the sentencing range for the crime. In your opinion, when, if ever, should such changes lead to a modification of the defendant's prison sentence or a decrease in the time served under that sentence? Should a reduction in the punishment for a crime be given no retroactive effect? Or should a defendant be eligible for a sentence reduction? If so, when? For one example of the scale of sentence reductions that can occur following the retroactive application of amended sentencing guidelines, see U.S. Sentencing Comm'n, 2014 Drug Guidelines Amendment Retroactivity Data Report (2017) (reporting that federal district courts reduced the sentences of over 30,000 people convicted of drug trafficking before an amendment went into effect).

CHAPTER 4

PROCEDURAL RIGHTS DURING SENTENCING

■ ■ ■

Defendants who are charged with crimes are protected by an array of constitutional rights if their cases proceed to trial. They have the right, for example, to the assistance of an attorney, a right bestowed by the Sixth Amendment, and if they are indigent, they have the right, in certain circumstances, to appointed counsel. Gideon v. Wainwright, 372 U.S. 335, 344, 83 S.Ct. 792, 796 (1963). They have the right to a jury trial when charged with a non-petty offense. Duncan v. Louisiana, 391 U.S. 145, 158–59, 88 S.Ct. 1444, 1452 (1968). They have the right to present witnesses who will testify on their behalf, Washington v. Texas, 388 U.S. 14, 18–19, 87 S.Ct. 1920, 1923 (1967), and the right to confront and cross-examine adverse witnesses. Coy v. Iowa, 487 U.S. 1012, 1019–20, 108 S.Ct. 2798, 2802 (1988). Defendants are also presumed innocent unless and until the government rebuts this presumption and establishes their guilt beyond a reasonable doubt. In re Winship, 397 U.S. 358, 364, 90 S.Ct. 1068, 1072 (1970).

The procedural safeguards that must attend the guilt-innocence stage of a criminal prosecution stand in contrast to the more limited rights that, according to the courts, attend the sentencing stage of criminal prosecutions. The succeeding subsections discuss some of the rights defendants have claimed they have during the sentencing process and courts' responses to those claims.

A. RIGHTS TO CONFRONTATION, CROSS-EXAMINATION, AND REBUTTAL

The Sixth Amendment provides that "[i]n all criminal prosecutions, the accused shall enjoy the right . . . to be confronted with the witnesses against him." As mentioned earlier, defendants have the related right to cross-examine adverse witnesses at trial. In the case that follows, the Supreme Court considered whether the rights to confront and cross-examine witnesses extend to sentencing proceedings.

WILLIAMS V. NEW YORK

Supreme Court of the United States, 1949.
337 U.S. 241, 69 S.Ct. 1079, 93 L.Ed. 1337.

MR. JUSTICE BLACK delivered the opinion of the Court.

A jury in a New York state court found appellant guilty of murder in the first degree. The jury recommended life imprisonment, but the trial judge imposed [a] sentence of death. In giving his reasons for imposing the death sentence the judge discussed in open court the evidence upon which the jury had convicted stating that this evidence had been considered in the light of additional information obtained through the court's "Probation Department, and through other sources." * * *

* * * The evidence proved a wholly indefensible murder committed by a person engaged in a burglary. * * *

About five weeks after the verdict of guilty with recommendation of life imprisonment, and after a statutory pre-sentence investigation report to the judge, the defendant was brought to court to be sentenced. Asked what he had to say, appellant protested his innocence. After each of his three lawyers had appealed to the court to accept the jury's recommendation of a life sentence, the judge gave reasons why he felt that the death sentence should be imposed. He narrated the shocking details of the crime as shown by the trial evidence, expressing his own complete belief in appellant's guilt. He stated that the pre-sentence investigation revealed many material facts concerning appellant's background which though relevant to the question of punishment could not properly have been brought to the attention of the jury in its consideration of the question of guilt. He referred to the experience appellant "had had on thirty other burglaries in and about the same vicinity" where the murder had been committed. The appellant had not been convicted of these burglaries although the judge had information that he had confessed to some and had been identified as the perpetrator of some of the others. The judge also referred to certain activities of appellant as shown by the probation report that indicated appellant possessed "a morbid sexuality" and classified him as a "menace to society." The accuracy of the statements made by the judge as to appellant's background and past practices was not challenged by appellant or his counsel, nor was the judge asked to disregard any of them or to afford appellant a chance to refute or discredit any of them by cross-examination or otherwise.

* * * Within limits fixed by statutes, New York judges are given a broad discretion to decide the type and extent of punishment for convicted defendants. Here, for example, the judge's discretion was to sentence to life imprisonment or death. To aid a judge in exercising this discretion intelligently the New York procedural policy encourages him to consider information about the convicted person's past life, health, habits, conduct,

and mental and moral propensities. The sentencing judge may consider such information even though obtained outside the courtroom from persons whom a defendant has not been permitted to confront or cross-examine. * * *

Appellant urges that the New York statutory policy is in irreconcilable conflict with the underlying philosophy of a second procedural policy grounded in the due process of law clause of the Fourteenth Amendment. That policy * * * is in part that no person shall be tried and convicted of an offense unless he is given reasonable notice of the charges against him and is afforded an opportunity to examine adverse witnesses. * * *

* * * [B]oth before and since the American colonies became a nation, courts in this country and in England practiced a policy under which a sentencing judge could exercise a wide discretion in the sources and types of evidence used to assist him in determining the kind and extent of punishment to be imposed within limits fixed by law. Out-of-court affidavits have been used frequently, and of course in the smaller communities sentencing judges naturally have in mind their knowledge of the personalities and backgrounds of convicted offenders. * * *

In addition to the historical basis for different evidentiary rules governing trial and sentencing procedures there are sound practical reasons for the distinction. * * * A sentencing judge * * * is not confined to the narrow issue of guilt. His task within fixed statutory or constitutional limits is to determine the type and extent of punishment after the issue of guilt has been determined. Highly relevant—if not essential—to his selection of an appropriate sentence is the possession of the fullest information possible concerning the defendant's life and characteristics. * * *

* * *

* * * We must recognize that most of the information now relied upon by judges to guide them in the intelligent imposition of sentences would be unavailable if information were restricted to that given in open court by witnesses subject to cross-examination. And the modern probation report draws on information concerning every aspect of a defendant's life. The type and extent of this information make totally impractical if not impossible open court testimony with cross-examination. Such a procedure could endlessly delay criminal administration in a retrial of collateral issues.

The considerations we have set out admonish us against treating the due process clause as a uniform command that courts throughout the Nation abandon their age-old practice of seeking information from out-of-court sources to guide their judgment toward a more enlightened and just sentence. New York criminal statutes set wide limits for maximum and minimum sentences. * * * In determining whether a defendant shall receive a one-year minimum or a twenty-year maximum sentence, we do not think the Federal Constitution restricts the view of the sentencing judge to the information received in open court. * * *

* * *

MR. JUSTICE RUTLEDGE dissents. [Opinion omitted.]

MR. JUSTICE MURPHY, dissenting. [Opinion omitted.]

———

QUESTIONS AND POINTS FOR DISCUSSION

1.   *Williams v. New York* involved the scope of protection afforded by due process. But since the Supreme Court's decision in that case, most courts have rejected defendants' claims that they have a right under either the Sixth Amendment's Confrontation Clause or due process to cross-examine witnesses at sentencing hearings. United States v. Umaña, 750 F.3d 320, 346 (4th Cir.2014).

If you were representing a defendant in a case raising the question whether defendants have a constitutional right to confront and cross-examine witnesses at a sentencing hearing, how would you distinguish *Williams v. New York*? What additional arguments would you make in support of your position that defendants have a constitutional right to confront and cross-examine witnesses at sentencing hearings? After reading Gardner v. Florida, 430 U.S. 349, 97 S.Ct. 1197 (1977) on page 152 and the line of cases discussed in § E. of this chapter on the scope of the Sixth Amendment right to a jury trial, consider once again the arguments you might make on your client's behalf. For arguments that might be made in support of the position that the Sixth Amendment's Confrontation Clause applies in federal sentencing proceedings, see Sopen B. Shah, Guidelines for Guidelines: Implications of the Confrontation Clause's Revival for Federal Sentencing, 48 John Marshall L.Rev. 2039 (2015).

2.   The adoption of the federal sentencing guidelines highlighted the significance of the question whether the Constitution affords a defendant the right to confront and cross-examine adverse witnesses at sentencing hearings. Under these guidelines, the sentence imposed under the often broad sentencing range established by statute depends in part on the offense of which the defendant was convicted. Federal Sentencing Guidelines Manual § 1B1.2(a) (2016). The "base offense level" for this crime then is frequently raised to reflect other "relevant conduct," including other crimes with which the defendant has not been charged that have a defined connection to the offense of conviction. Id. §§ 1B1.2(b), 1B1.3. Although, as discussed in Chapter 3 and later in this chapter, the Supreme Court has ruled that the federal sentencing guidelines are only advisory, they still are factored into a court's

sentencing decision. See pages 133–134 and the discussion of United States v. Booker, 543 U.S. 220, 125 S.Ct. 738 (2005) in note 1 on page 183.

United States v. Silverman, 976 F.2d 1502 (6th Cir.1992) illustrates the potential significance of "relevant conduct" to a defendant's sentence. In that case, the defendant pled guilty to one count of possession with intent to distribute drugs after he was arrested for selling a quarter of an ounce of cocaine to a confidential government informant. The base offense level for this crime, coupled with his criminal-history level, would have yielded a maximum prison sentence of two years and three months. At the sentencing hearing, however, the probation officer who had prepared the presentence investigation report and a Drug Enforcement Agency (DEA) agent testified that several individuals had reported that the defendant had sold a kilogram of cocaine the previous year. The defendant was not told the names of these individuals or given an opportunity to cross-examine them. Based on the "relevant conduct" disclosed in these hearsay statements, the district court imposed a sentence more than five years higher than the base offense level. On appeal, the Sixth Circuit Court of Appeals concluded that the defendant had no right to confront and cross-examine the witnesses whose statements had led to the increase in his sentence. Do you agree with this holding?

3. To assist you in your analysis of the question whether the Constitution accords a defendant the right to confront and cross-examine adverse witnesses during the sentencing stage of a criminal prosecution, an example of a presentence investigation report is set forth on the next page. The report, written about a defendant who pled guilty to criminal sexual conduct in the first degree, is reprinted here with the permission of the Probation Office of the Ingham County Circuit Court, Ingham County, Michigan. Names and other identifying information in the report have been changed or deleted.

MICHIGAN DEPARTMENT OF CORRECTIONS
PRESENTENCE INVESTIGATION REPORT

Honorable <u>Andrew Lopez</u>   County <u>Ingham</u>   Sentence Date <u>7-24-95</u>

Docket <u>54154</u>   Attorney <u>Ann Witt</u>   Appt. _____   Retained <u>xx</u>

Defendant <u>Fred Jones</u>   Age <u>46</u>   D.O.B <u>9-19-48</u>

CURRENT CONVICTION(S) $50,000 Surety

Final Charge(s)	Max.	Jail Credit	Bond
1. CT. II. CSC 1st Degree	LIFE	2 days	yes
2.		days	
3.		days	

Convicted by: Plea <u>x</u> Jury ___ Judge ___ Plea Under Advisement ___ Nolo Contendere .
Conviction Date <u>6-26-95</u>   Plea Agreement <u>nolle pross Cts. I. II. & IV</u>
Pending Charges <u>none</u>   Where _____

PRIOR RECORD

Convictions: Felonies <u>1</u>   Misdemeanors <u>1</u>   Juvenile Record: Yes ___ No <u>x</u>
Probation: Active ___   Former <u>yes</u>   Pending Violation _____
Parole: Active ___   Former ___   Pending Violation _____
Current Michigan Prisoner: Yes ___ No <u>x</u>   Number _____
Currently Under Sentence: Offense _____   Sentence _____

PERSONAL HISTORY

(Self-employed)
Education <u>12th</u>   Employed <u>yes</u> Where <u>Fred's Automotive Diagnostics, Inc.</u>
Psychiatric History: Yes ___ No <u>x</u>   Physical Handicaps: Yes ___ No <u>x</u>   Marital Status <u>divorced</u>
Substance Abuse History: Yes <u>x</u> No ___ What <u>alcohol</u>   How Long _____

RECOMMENDATION

1. 30 to 45 years with the Michigan Corrections Commission.
2. Mental Health therapy for sex offenders.

Agent <u>Marie Franklin</u>   Date <u>7-22-95</u>
Signature _____   Supervisor's Approval _____

EVALUATION AND PLAN:

Fred Jones age 46 is before the court for his second felony conviction. His other felony conviction occurred in 1979 and it was Accosting Children for Immoral Purposes. He was given three days in jail and two years' probation.

The defendant has resided in Lansing almost all of his life. After graduating from Eastern High School in 1967 he entered the United States Army. He was honorably discharged after serving three years.

The defendant is self-employed. He owns and operates Fred's
Automotive Diagnostics Inc., 2308 Curry Street. He began operating
this business on the date of his arrest for this offense, May 10, 1995.
Respondent has worked in the automotive field four years, and he
previously owned his own shop between 88 and 93. It was then
located at 400 Northampton Street.

Mr. Jones is also the State Commissioner for the American Bicycle
Association's BMX Racing Program. * * * As commissioner, the
defendant traveled to various tracks in the state, set up promotional
activities, and got tracks going as well as directed the local BMX Race
Program.

Right after leaving the military the defendant was employed by
Spartan Oil, and managed a station before opening his mechanic shop
in 1988.

Respondent admits to a history of heavy drinking. He said that after
the breakup of his first marriage he, "Got into drinking constantly. I
was drinking all day. I filed bankruptcy. I finally woke up and started
seeing Jane (second wife)." He said he then went back to drinking
heavily in 1988 or 1989 when his business was going bad. He said, "I
started drinking heavy again around 1992 or 93. I had gotten into
hanging out all night and running with people who were smoking
pot." Mr. Jones has never participated in an alcohol or drug program.
He denies selling marijuana to children in his former neighborhood,
contrary to the statements given to police by some of the youngsters.
Jones does admit to "occasionally" arranging for adults to purchase
marijuana.

The defendant reports no physical problems. He does indicate that
his left leg and foot are smaller than the right. He believes this is the
result of a mild case of polio.

Since his arrest for the instant offense the defendant has gone into
mental health therapy with Dr. Gilbert Riler of the Community
Mental Health Program. Respondent is seeing Dr. Riler once per
week. Dr. Riler said that he would provide an evaluation to the court,
prior to the defendant's sentencing. When I spoke with the Doctor on
July 8, 1995, he said the defendant's MMPI test shows subject is
essentially a personality disorder, characterized by "Hedonistic" and
"Pleasure Oriented" manifestation. Dr. Riler states the defendant's
positive qualities are the fact that he is acknowledging his guilt in
the instant offense. Also, he has been open and candid with the
doctor, advising the doctor that he has been involved with 40 to 50
different boys. Also, Mr. Jones has displayed no indication of
psychopathic or manipulative behavior in therapy.

Mr. Jones notes the following liabilities: Ingham County Friend of the
Court $1500 in arrearages (at $40 per month); Mr. Donald Smith

(Holder of defendant's land contract) $135,000 at $1700 per month; Ronald Gorman (Business associate) $9000 at $400 per month; Bank of Lansing $1900 (executive credit) at $100 per month; Master Charge/VISA $200 at $40 per month; American Express $500 at $150 per month; June Wiler (ex-wife) $2000; Attorney fees $1300.

He reports the following assets: Fred's Automotive Diagnostics Inc. $150,000 ($15,000 equity); 1983 Chrysler $600; 1986 Cadillac $3000.

In summation, before the court is an intelligent individual with marketable skills, who has functioned as a productive member of society. He has, however, been plagued with substance abuse for many years. Also, Mr. Jones has displayed a propensity toward sexual involvement with pre-adolescent boys for well over a decade. His tendency toward pedophilic behavior has left emotional scars not only on the instant offense victim, but the uncharged victims as well as their families. The community deserves to be protected from Mr. Jones. In the defendant's favor, he does acknowledge his guilt, but also acknowledges that his behavior is something over which he has little in the way of control.

Placement in a structured setting where he will not have access to pre-adolescent teenage boys is strongly recommended. Mr. Jones should be provided treatment in an effort to help him overcome his illness. However, the main issue in sentencing, in my opinion, is protecting other potential victims from the defendant.

INVESTIGATOR'S VERSION OF OFFENSE:

According to Lansing Police Department complaint #95–05592: On or about April 12 or 19th, 1995, the defendant Fred Jones engaged in sexual penetration with Greg Daley, dob: 5–23–82, a person under 13 years of age. Daley told investigating officers that on that occasion he had spent the night at Fred Jones's residence in Lansing, Michigan. Daley was asleep on a couch in the living room. He awoke to find Jones crawling underneath the sheet and pulling Daley's undershorts off. When asked by officers what Jones did next, Daley said, "He gave me a blow job." Upon further questioning, Daley revealed the defendant had given him a glass of beer earlier in the evening. Daley also told officers that this same type of incident had happened, "Maybe five or six times."

Daley upon further questioning told officers that on one occasion Fred Jones was performing oral sex upon him, while two other adult males were also in the room performing fellatio on each other.

Lansing Police Officers became aware of Daley's situation as well as the assault upon numerous other early adolescent boys via an anonymous tip that was phoned into the police department on May 7, 1995. The tipster told officers that Jones was involving himself sexually with a number of children at the Jones residence. Four names were provided by the tipster. Investigating officers James Martin and Alex Finch went to the schools that the various boys attended and after getting permission from their parents, interviewed several of them. All of the boys acknowledged that they had been to Jones's home and they were aware that he was sexually involved with numerous young boys. Some of the boys interviewed said they were not sexually involved with Jones, while others admitted to the officers that Jones had been engaging in sexual activities with them. They also told the officers Jones had been providing beer, as well as marijuana, to the boys while at his home. The boys also told the officers that Jones had been showing them numerous pornographic movies, most of which involved homosexual activity between males. The boys had also been shown numerous items of sexual paraphernalia including magazines, pictures, and various other sexual paraphernalia.

Based on the information gathered through interviewing the boys, a search warrant was requested and granted by Judge Claude R. Thomas of Lansing District Court, on May 10, 1995.

At approximately 4:15 p.m. May 10, 1995, the defendant was arrested at his place of work. He was served with a four count felony warrant for Criminal Sexual Conduct. Fifteen minutes later four officers of the Lansing Police Department Criminal Intelligence Unit executed a search warrant at the defendant's residence. A large quantity of evidence was seized and transported to the Police Department Evidence Room. Attached to this report is the list of items seized during the search. The items include numerous pictures of some of his victims in sexually provocative poses. I viewed the photographs at the Lansing Police Department. There were photographs of the victims performing and having oral sex performed upon them. There were photographs of boys sitting on the defendant's lap, kissing him on the mouth; there was a photograph of the defendant in bed with one of the victims, engaging in anal intercourse; there were a number of photographs taken at a "Birthday Party" where there were a number of joints placed on the cake so as to resemble candles.

As noted above, the defendant was arrested on May 10, 1995, and was released on bond the following day. He remains free awaiting sentence. Officers James Martin and Alex Finch, who investigated this case and interviewed the victims, both recommend life imprisonment. Martin pointed out that there was a total of 19 counts against the defendant. The officers spoke with 13 different children who acknowledged they had been sexually involved with the defendant, and who were willing to press charges. Further, Martin and Finch stressed the devastating emotional effect Jones has had on the children in arriving at their recommendation for sentencing. Daley, for instance, was a straight 'A' student at Otto Junior High School, but dropped out of school after the instant offense became publicized for fear of being ridiculed by his fellow students. Another young man, Gordon Taylor, a student at Waverly West Junior High said he felt like a monster, and he also said he would commit suicide if his fellow students were to find out about his involvement with Jones. Finally, the officers said a number of the children involved had started to display acting out behavior; they had started dropping out of school and were getting involved with drinking and drugs, all of which the officers feel is related to their experiences with the defendant.

I spoke to the mother of Greg Daley (the victim that the defendant has pled guilty to assaulting), on July 12, 1995. Mrs. Daley is very bitter about the whole incident. She said that she and her family have known the defendant approximately seven years. She said he always presented himself as a "nice neighbor" who was always interested in the kids' well-being. She said the defendant often said, "Let's do things for the kids." She went on to say that he professed to wanting to get the kids involved in BMX Racing as a way of, "Keeping them off the street."

Mrs. Daley said her child's experience with the defendant has changed his personality. She said previously Greg, "Was usually a quiet easy-going person, but now he is very closed. He just doesn't want to talk about the incident. He gets very angry. He used to be very easy-going, but now he flies off the handle. I feel this has really screwed him up." Mrs. Daley said Jones had also been involved with Greg's older brother Mark, though Mark refuses to discuss his involvement with the defendant. Mark is learning disabled and has always been involved in special education.

When asked for a recommendation for sentencing, Mrs. Daley responded, "I think he should go natural life. No parole. Don't let him get to no one else. I am not a person with a lot of hate, but I know that if he were to walk and I saw him on the street, I wouldn't hesitate to run him down."

I spoke with Gordon Taylor's mother on July 18, 1995. Mrs. Taylor said, "We trusted Fred. Fred had become a real good friend of ours. He was in our home. We had him in our home for dinner. If I had a chance, I would have killed Fred. I just wanted to kill him. My husband feels the same way. My son Gordon does too. I am very hostile."

Mrs. Taylor went on to explain to me just how devastated her entire family is as the result of learning that the defendant was engaging in sexual activity with Gordon. She said that both she and her husband are in counseling with Gordon. She also said immediately after they were told of what was going on between Fred Jones and their son, her husband went to Jones's home with a gun. He was sitting outside of Jones's home. Mrs. Taylor called Lansing Police because she was afraid there would be trouble. The police officers arrived and told Mr. Taylor to go home, and at that point he broke down and cried because he was so devastated.

Mrs. Taylor continued, "Fred bought Gordon a $160 bow for a birthday present. Fred was buying Gordon everything. He was going on vacation with him, going fishing and on vacation. It was like Fred was a big brother. I just don't know why I didn't see through it."

When asked how her son had been affected, Mrs. Taylor said, "Gordon is a straight 'A' student in school. When this happened he didn't go to school, see his friends, or go outside." Mrs. Taylor said during the summer of 1994, Gordon has now related to her, on one occasion Fred chased a young man out of his (Fred's) residence with a gun. Gordon was present. Fred told Gordon if Gordon told anyone about what was going on he would kill him. It was at that point that Gordon developed an ulcer. Gordon is 14 years of age.

Mrs. Taylor continued, "I blame myself for not being able to see it. I will never trust anybody again, I don't care if it is a baseball coach, or a teacher. Whenever an adult is friends with my kid I won't have it." I asked Mrs. Taylor her recommendation for sentencing. She said, "I want him to pay for what he did to my son. I want him to hurt like we hurt. I want him to think about this for a long, long time. This hurt is the most hurt we have ever had. . . . I just pray to God Fred doesn't come around us any time again. I hope the law can make us happy by putting him away and not letting him out. Fred is a sick man and he needs lots of help."

OFFENDER'S VERSION OF OFFENSE:

"Greg Daley and I have known each other for about five years. We have basically been good friends. He has stayed with me and come with me on many occasions over the five years. Greg's been a boy that always wanted fatherly attention. He has climbed in bed with me and cuddled and everything. Over the last six months he started sexually maturing and things happen."

The defendant admits to having sexual relations with Greg Daley dob: 5–23–82, Gordon Taylor dob: 4–30–81, Allen Freeman dob: 1–18–80, and Michael Cook dob: 11–16–80. Mr. Jones admits to being sexually involved with boys he has met through BMX, over the past four to five years. He went on to say he would sometimes feel "guilty" after going "all the way" with the boys. He stated, "I would discuss personal problems with the boys, when they were having them." He said he discussed the dangers of becoming involved in drugs with them.

Jones continued, "I think it started out as a kind of father/son and I let it go too far. I wouldn't always have sex with them. We spent a lot of time together fishing, bowling and spending time on the BMX track. But I would feel guilty afterwards. I don't feel like I took advantage of them, but I did let it go too far. But, the boys were aggressive in the sex acts and I feel they kept coming back because they enjoyed visiting."

Over the past four years Jones estimates he has worked with "about 400 youngsters," "but there has not always been the sexual activity." Finally, Jones stated, "I have gotten back involved with my own sons and I am trying to get my business back together. It was not my intention to hurt anybody. At that time I felt I was doing something I hadn't ought to be doing. I hadn't any intention of doing any harm or hurting anybody. I tried to help them, by helping with their home life and school problems. We discussed lives and I was trying to help them. I know I went too far, but what's the old saying hindsight is better than foresight. I guess sometimes when you are alone and lonely, and the aggressiveness is there and everything and especially if you are getting high you let everything go to the wind."

PREVIOUS CRIMINAL HISTORY:

Juvenile: None

Adult:

1–2–67—Lansing—Larc/Bldg.—final charge: Larc/$100—sentenced 1–3–67—3 months' probation—$30 fine.

6–27–79—Lansing—Indecent Liberties with a Child—final charge: Accosting Children for Immoral Purposes—sentenced 9–19–79—2 yrs. probation 3 days jail—$200 costs.

PERSONAL HISTORY:

Lorraine Jones—Mother—age 65—Daytona Beach, Florida.

Willis Jones—Stepfather—age 68—Daytona Beach, Florida.

Oliver Cartwright—Father—deceased (defendant knows nothing about him).

Richard Jones—Brother—age 48—Lansing.

Donald Jones—Brother—age 43—Daytona Beach, Florida.

James Jones—Son—age 23—attends Western Michigan University.

David Jones—Son—age 20—attends MSU.

The defendant was born and raised in Lansing. Until age 11 he resided with his mother and grandparents. Subject's mother married Willis Jones when the defendant was 11 years of age.

Mr. Jones adopted the defendant and his siblings. The elder Jones was employed by the United States Postal Service while the defendant's mother was pretty much a dental office receptionist. As a teenager, respondent reports a very poor relationship with his stepfather. He describes it as, "He (stepfather) was a Navy man. He [would] strike first and maybe ask questions later." At about age 16 the defendant ran away from home and lived above a store in downtown Lansing. He said he supported himself by managing a bowling alley on South Washington. After living on his own at the apartment, and briefly at the YMCA he "begged" the principal at Eastern High School to let him return. He said he did return and graduated in 1967.

Respondent reports becoming involved in homosexual activities in his late teens.

Jones reports a good relationship with his mother, and a satisfactory relationship with his stepfather. He said he and his brothers have never been close. Jones goes on to say he attempted to talk with his mother as well as his minister about his homosexual inclinations in his teens, but Jones said, "They just kind of said it would go away; they didn't want to deal with it."

MARITAL HISTORY:

The defendant married the former June Takahisha in 1970 while serving with the United States Army in Tokyo, Japan. She returned to his country with him, and two sons were born to their union. They were married 8 or 9 years, but he said his long work hours and the strain of having children caused the breakdown in their relationship. He said after a while, "It seemed like I was just a paycheck to her."

Respondent states that he and his former wife rarely communicate, however, she did loan him $2000 of the necessary money to post bond.

The defendant married the former Jane Francis in 1980. The marriage lasted five years. There were no children born to the union. This was Jones's second marriage. Respondent said, "I turned into a workaholic, alcoholic and dopeaholic, and conflicts with our children and then my gay activities started flaring up," leading to the demise of this marriage.

———

As is apparent from the presentence investigation report set forth above, presentence investigation reports, upon which sentencing courts frequently rely when imposing sentences, often are filled with references to the hearsay statements of witnesses. Whether defendants have a constitutional right to have access to these reports and to respond to information contained within them were issues in the following case.

GARDNER V. FLORIDA

Supreme Court of the United States, 1977.
430 U.S. 349, 97 S.Ct. 1197, 51 L.Ed.2d 393.

MR. JUSTICE STEVENS announced the judgment of the Court and delivered an opinion, in which MR. JUSTICE STEWART and MR. JUSTICE POWELL joined.

Petitioner was convicted of first-degree murder and sentenced to death. When the trial judge imposed the death sentence he stated that he was relying in part on information in a presentence investigation report.[a] Portions of the report were not disclosed to counsel for the parties. Without reviewing the confidential portion of the presentence report, the Supreme Court of Florida, over the dissent of two justices, affirmed the death sentence. We conclude that this procedure does not satisfy the constitutional command that no person shall be deprived of life without due process of law.

* * *

* * * [W]e consider the justifications offered by the State for a capital-sentencing procedure which permits a trial judge to impose the death sentence on the basis of confidential information which is not disclosed to the defendant or his counsel.

The State first argues that an assurance of confidentiality to potential sources of information is essential to enable investigators to obtain relevant but sensitive disclosures from persons unwilling to comment publicly about a defendant's background or character. The availability of such information, it is argued, provides the person who prepares the report with greater detail on which to base a sentencing recommendation and, in turn, provides the judge with a better basis for his sentencing decision. But consideration must be given to the quality, as well as the quantity, of the information on which the sentencing judge may rely. Assurances of secrecy are conducive to the transmission of confidences which may bear no closer relation to fact than the average rumor or item of gossip, and may imply a pledge not to attempt independent verification of the information received. The risk that some of the information accepted in confidence may be erroneous, or may be misinterpreted, by the investigator or by the sentencing judge, is manifest.

If, as the State argues, it is important to use such information in the sentencing process, we must assume that in some cases it will be decisive in the judge's choice between a life sentence and a death sentence. * * * [I]f it is the basis for a death sentence, the interest in reliability plainly

---

a   In imposing the death sentence, the trial judge rejected a jury recommendation that the defendant be sentenced to life in prison. The jury had no access to the presentence investigation report that was prepared after the jury had returned its advisory verdict.

outweighs the State's interest in preserving the availability of comparable information in other cases.

The State also suggests that full disclosure of the presentence report will unnecessarily delay the proceeding. We think the likelihood of significant delay is overstated because we must presume that reports prepared by professional probation officers * * * are generally reliable.[10] In those cases in which the accuracy of a report is contested, the trial judge can avoid delay by disregarding the disputed material. Or if the disputed matter is of critical importance, the time invested in ascertaining the truth would surely be well spent if it makes the difference between life and death.

The State further urges that full disclosure of presentence reports, which often include psychiatric and psychological evaluations, will occasionally disrupt the process of rehabilitation. The argument, if valid, would hardly justify withholding the report from defense counsel. Moreover, whatever force that argument may have in noncapital cases, it has absolutely no merit in a case in which the judge has decided to sentence the defendant to death. * * *

Finally, Florida argues that trial judges can be trusted to exercise their discretion in a responsible manner, even though they may base their decisions on secret information. * * * The argument rests on the erroneous premise that the participation of counsel is superfluous to the process of evaluating the relevance and significance of aggravating and mitigating facts. Our belief that debate between adversaries is often essential to the truth-seeking function of trials requires us also to recognize the importance of giving counsel an opportunity to comment on facts which may influence the sentencing decision in capital cases.

Even if it were permissible to withhold a portion of the report from a defendant, and even from defense counsel, pursuant to an express finding of good cause for nondisclosure, it would nevertheless be necessary to make the full report a part of the record to be reviewed on appeal. Since the State must administer its capital-sentencing procedures with an even hand, it is important that the record on appeal disclose to the reviewing court the considerations which motivated the death sentence in every case in which it is imposed. * * *

* * *

We conclude that petitioner was denied due process of law when the death sentence was imposed, at least in part, on the basis of information which he had no opportunity to deny or explain.

---

[10] Our presumption that the reports are normally reliable is, of course, not inconsistent with our concern about the possibility that critical unverified information may be inaccurate and determinative in a particular case.

* * *

THE CHIEF JUSTICE concurs in the judgment.

MR. JUSTICE WHITE, concurring in the judgment.

* * *

* * * Here the sentencing judge indicated that he selected petitioner Gardner for the death penalty in part because of information contained in a presentence report which information was not disclosed to petitioner or to his counsel and to which petitioner had no opportunity to respond. A procedure for selecting people for the death penalty which permits consideration of such secret information relevant to the "character and record of the individual offender" fails to meet the "need for reliability in the determination that death is the appropriate punishment" * * *. This conclusion stems solely from the Eighth Amendment's ban on cruel and unusual punishments and my conclusion is limited to cases in which the death penalty is imposed. I thus see no reason to address in this case the possible application to sentencing proceedings—in death or other cases—of the Due Process Clause, other than as the vehicle by which the strictures of the Eighth Amendment are triggered in this case. For these reasons, I do not join the plurality opinion but concur in the judgment.

MR. JUSTICE BLACKMUN, concurring in the judgment. [Opinion omitted.]

MR. JUSTICE BRENNAN.

[JUSTICE BRENNAN concurred that due process is violated when a defendant in a capital case is not apprised of the contents of the presentence investigation report provided to the sentencing judge.]

MR. JUSTICE MARSHALL, dissenting. [Opinion omitted.]

MR. JUSTICE REHNQUIST, dissenting. [Opinion omitted.]

QUESTIONS AND POINTS FOR DISCUSSION

1.   *Gardner* concerned the constitutional rights of a defendant in a capital case to have access to a presentence investigation report and to explain or rebut information in it before sentencing. The Supreme Court has yet to definitively resolve whether these rights extend to defendants in noncapital cases. The Sixth Circuit Court of Appeals has capsulized the law's uncertainty: "The upshot is this: while a defendant may not have the constitutional right to *confront* the witnesses against him at sentencing, it remains unclear under modern sentencing practices what due process right he has to *know* who these witnesses are and what they have said, to *respond* meaningfully to the accusations or otherwise to *ensure* that the accusations are accurate." United States v. Hamad, 495 F.3d 241, 247 (6th Cir.2007).

As is discussed in the next chapter, basing a sentence on materially false information can abridge a defendant's due-process rights. See page 217. Does this constitutional limitation on the information on which a sentence can be grounded have a bearing on the question whether the constitutional rights recognized in *Gardner* extend to defendants in noncapital cases? The Sixth Circuit has queried, "'How can a due process guarantee against a sentence predicated on misinformation be viable, and not rendered meaningless, if the defendant has no way of determining that the sentencing judge was misadvised?'" Stewart v. Erwin, 503 F.3d 488, 498 (6th Cir.2007) (quoting Baker v. United States, 388 F.2d 931, 935 n.1 (4th Cir.1968) (Winter, J., concurring)).

2.   When determining whether due process accords a right to a particular procedural safeguard, the Supreme Court typically applies what has come to be known as the *Mathews* balancing test. Mathews v. Eldridge, 424 U.S. 319, 335, 96 S.Ct. 893, 903 (1976). Three factors are balanced under this test. The first factor is the "private interest" at stake. The more weighty the interest the more likely it is that the procedural safeguard in question is constitutionally mandated. The second factor focuses on the risk that the individual will be deprived erroneously of this private interest under current procedures and the "probable value" of the additional safeguard in averting this erroneous deprivation. The greater the benefits of the procedural safeguard in preventing erroneous deprivations of the private interest the more likely it is that there is a due-process right to this procedural safeguard. The third and final factor is the impact on governmental interests if the safeguard were required. To the extent that the safeguard would advance a governmental interest this factor points towards finding the procedural safeguard to be part of due process. On the other hand, if providing the safeguard would adversely affect a governmental interest, this factor points against finding the safeguard subsumed within due process.

Under the *Mathews* balancing test, do defendants convicted of noncapital crimes have the constitutional rights, in your opinion, to have access to information in a presentence investigation report and the opportunity to deny or explain that information? Explain your reasoning.

B. THE RIGHT TO COUNSEL

1. RETAINED AND APPOINTED COUNSEL

In Mempa v. Rhay, 389 U.S. 128, 88 S.Ct. 254 (1967), the Supreme Court concluded that the Sixth Amendment right to counsel extends to sentencing hearings. Underscoring the "critical nature of sentencing in a criminal case," the Court observed that an attorney can assist "in marshaling the facts, introducing evidence of mitigating circumstances and in general aiding and assisting the defendant to present his case as to sentence." Id. at 134–35, 88 S.Ct. at 256–57.

The holding of the Supreme Court in *Mempa* must be read against the backdrop of the Court's subsequent decision in Scott v. Illinois, 440 U.S. 367, 99 S.Ct. 1158 (1979), a misdemeanor case that concerned the right to be represented by appointed counsel at trial. In *Scott,* the Court held, in a 5–4 decision, that whether an indigent defendant has the right to appointed counsel at trial depends on the sanction ultimately imposed on the defendant. (The defendant in that case had been fined fifty dollars after being convicted of misdemeanor theft.) The Court noted that an indigent defendant has no such right to appointed counsel unless the sanction imposed includes some period of incarceration. However, in a subsequent case, Nichols v. United States, 511 U.S. 738, 743 n.9, 114 S.Ct. 1921, 1925 n.9 (1994), the Supreme Court indicated that this actual-incarceration standard does not apply in a felony case, observing: "In felony cases, in contrast to misdemeanor charges, the Constitution requires that an indigent defendant be offered appointed counsel unless that right is intelligently and competently waived."

In Alabama v. Shelton, 535 U.S. 654, 122 S.Ct. 1764 (2002), the Supreme Court added another limitation to the actual-incarceration standard. In that case, the Court, in another 5–4 decision, held that the right to appointed counsel in a misdemeanor case exists even if a court suspends a prison or jail sentence and places the defendant on probation. A question left open by the Court in *Shelton* was whether a defendant has a right to appointed counsel in a misdemeanor case that results in a stand-alone sentence to probation—one not coupled with an actual or suspended term of incarceration. Some courts have concluded that the right to appointed counsel does not apply in that situation, while acknowledging that the failure to appoint counsel might foreclose incarceration of a defendant whose probation is later revoked. See, e.g., United States v. Pollard, 389 F.3d 101, 104–06 (4th Cir.2004); United States v. Perez-Macias, 335 F.3d 421, 426–28 (5th Cir.2003).

If the Sixth Amendment right to appointed counsel at a sentencing hearing tracks the scope of the right to appointed counsel at trial, then all indigent defendants convicted of felonies have the right to assistance from an appointed attorney during the sentencing process. In addition, indigent defendants convicted of misdemeanors have a Sixth Amendment right to the assistance of appointed counsel at a sentencing hearing when the penalty imposed involved some period of incarceration, whether suspended or not. Do you agree with this method of differentiating between misdemeanants who do and do not have the right to the assistance of appointed counsel at sentencing?

Separate and apart from questions concerning the right to the assistance of counsel at sentencing hearings is the question whether the defendant has the Sixth Amendment right to the assistance of counsel at certain interviews during which information is gathered from the defendant that will be considered at the sentencing hearing. The Supreme Court addressed this question in Estelle v. Smith, 451 U.S. 454, 101 S.Ct. 1866 (1981). In that case, the defendant was charged with murder. When the state disclosed that it intended to seek imposition of the death penalty, the trial judge directed that the defendant be examined by a psychiatrist to determine his competency to stand trial. After the defendant was convicted of murder, the state called the psychiatrist as a witness at the sentencing hearing. The psychiatrist testified that the defendant was a sociopath for whom treatment would be unavailing. This testimony bore on the question of the defendant's future dangerousness, an issue which, if resolved against the defendant, could, and in this case did, lead to the imposition of the death penalty.

The Supreme Court unanimously concluded that the interviewing of the defendant by the psychiatrist without prior notification to the defendant's attorney that the interview would cover the subject of future dangerousness, as well as competency to stand trial, violated the defendant's Sixth Amendment right to counsel. Without such notice, the defendant was deprived of the opportunity to make a knowing decision as to whether to participate in the interview. The Supreme Court, however, added a caveat to its opinion, emphasizing that the defendant did not claim he had the right to have his attorney actually present during the interview with the psychiatrist; he only claimed that his attorney should have received advance notice of the scope of topics that would be considered during the psychiatric examination. With seeming approval, the Court then quoted from the opinion of the court of appeals, which had stated that "an attorney present during the psychiatric interview could contribute little and might seriously disrupt the examination." Id. at 470 n.14, 101 S.Ct. at 1877 n.14.

When faced with the question whether a defendant has a Sixth Amendment right to have counsel present when being interviewed by a probation officer conducting a presentence investigation, most courts have distinguished *Estelle v. Smith*. State v. Garreau, 864 N.W.2d 771, 778 (S.D. 2015). United States v. Jackson, 886 F.2d 838 (7th Cir.1989) is a case in point. In that case, the Seventh Circuit Court of Appeals observed:

> A district judge's use of a defendant's statement to a probation officer in applying the Sentencing Guidelines is markedly unlike the *prosecutor's* adversarial use of a defendant's pretrial statement to a psychiatrist to carry the state's burden of proof before a jury. A federal probation officer is an extension of the court and not an agent of the government. The probation officer does not have an adversarial role in the sentencing proceedings. In interviewing a defendant as part of the

presentence investigation, the probation officer serves as a neutral information gatherer for the sentencing judge.

Id. at 844.

Do you find the reasoning of the court in *Jackson* persuasive? Consider the facts of In re Carter, 848 A.2d 281 (Vt.2004). The defendant in that case had been convicted of aggravated sexual assault of a former girlfriend. When two probation officers preparing his presentence investigation report approached the defendant to interview him, he said that he did not want to talk to them without his attorney present. The two probation officers, however, proceeded with the interview.

During the interview, the defendant talked about his hatred of the victim and his unwillingness to participate in sex-offender treatment:

> I've got a lot of hate for this girl. She didn't say no, she put the rubber on me and everything. . . . She knows she lied. I didn't do anything. I'm not doing no sex offender shit. I'll max my sentence. I'll do violent offender, but no sex shit. I have a lot of hate for her and frustrated anger. I could have killed her and been looking at the same amount of time I'm facing now.

These statements were quoted in the presentence report and cited in support of the recommendation in the report that the defendant be sentenced to thirty years to life. The sentencing judge referred to and relied upon these statements when imposing a prison sentence of forty-five years to life. Pointing to the defendant's lack of remorse for his actions and his denial of criminal responsibility, the judge explained that such a long sentence was necessary because the defendant posed a serious threat to the victim and others.

In concluding that a presentence interview by a probation officer is a critical stage of the prosecution to which the Sixth Amendment right to counsel attaches, the Supreme Court of Vermont proffered a different perspective that that shared by the majority of the courts:

> "The presentence interview plays a crucial role in determining the probation officer's recommended sentence. . . . [A] single finding by the probation officer can significantly affect the ultimate sentencing range." At a presentence interview, a defendant is likely to address matters that were not raised at trial and that will likely have a significant impact on sentencing. Moreover, a defendant's statements during a presentence interview can even have an impact on later prosecutions—of both the defendant and others. * * *

> The facts of this case are a clear example of the importance of the presentence investigation and a criminal defendant's participation in the development of the report. It is not an

overstatement to say that petitioner committed sentencing suicide in his PSI interview. His criminal conduct warranted a long sentence of incarceration, but in a single paragraph he ensured that he would spend virtually all of his adult life in jail. * * *

* * *

* * * [A] criminal defendant, who testifies that he is innocent of the charged conduct, is unlikely to understand the need to admit responsibility for that conduct to improve his prospects at sentencing. On the other hand, admission of responsibility will constitute a waiver of defendant's self-incrimination right and could be the basis for a perjury prosecution.* * *

* * * [N]o Supreme Court decision supports the rationale of *Jackson* and other circuit court decisions that conclude that the right to counsel is limited to proceedings with an "adversary character." Further, this assertion is contrary to the long line of Supreme Court cases holding that a defendant's right to counsel under the Sixth Amendment depends primarily on the possibility of prejudice and unfairness in the proceedings and the ability of the presence of counsel to protect against such prejudice and unfairness.

Id. at 296–97, 299–300.

Do you believe that a probation officer's interview with a defendant during a presentence investigation is a critical stage of the prosecution to which the Sixth Amendment right to counsel attaches? Does your answer hinge on whether the presentence interview is conducted in a capital or a noncapital case? See Hoffman v. Arave, 236 F.3d 523, 540 (9th Cir.2001) (defendant, who received a death sentence, had a Sixth Amendment right to have counsel present at the presentence interview during which the defendant admitted being present at two other murders and doing nothing to stop them).

2. RIGHT TO THE EFFECTIVE ASSISTANCE OF COUNSEL

The Sixth Amendment right to the assistance of counsel at a sentencing hearing includes the right to the effective assistance of counsel. Strickland v. Washington, 466 U.S. 668, 104 S.Ct. 2052 (1984). In *Strickland,* the Supreme Court outlined the test to be applied when determining whether a defendant at a sentencing hearing for a capital crime received the effective assistance of counsel. To prevail on an ineffectiveness claim under the *Strickland* test, the defendant must prove two things: first, that his or her attorney acted unreasonably, in contravention of "prevailing professional norms," and second, that the defendant was prejudiced by this deficient performance. Id. at 687–88, 104 S.Ct. at 2064–65. To establish prejudice, the defendant must prove that there is a "reasonable probability" that the death penalty would not have been imposed if the defense attorney had performed competently. Id. at 694, 104 S.Ct. at 2068. Even when the defendant meets this burden, however, the prejudice requirement will, on occasion, not be satisfied, as Lockhart v. Fretwell, 506 U.S. 364, 113 S.Ct. 838 (1993) makes clear.

In *Lockhart,* the defendant's attorney had failed at the sentencing hearing to make an objection that, based on the case law in existence at the time of the hearing, was meritorious and would have prevented imposition of a death sentence. The case upon which an objection could have been founded, however, was later overruled. While the Supreme Court seemed to recognize that the defendant would not have received the death sentence had his attorney made the appropriate objection at the sentencing hearing, the Court noted that the probable effect of counsel's deficient performance on the outcome of the sentencing process was not the end of the prejudice inquiry. A court also had to determine whether the deficient performance had led to a result that was "fundamentally unfair or unreliable." Id. at 369, 113 S.Ct. at 842. And in this case, the Court noted, the result was neither unfair nor unreliable because counsel's mistake only had deprived the defendant of "the chance to have the state court make an error in his favor." Id. at 371, 113 S.Ct. at 843.

In Williams v. Taylor, 529 U.S. 362, 120 S.Ct. 1495 (2000), the Supreme Court clarified that *Lockhart* did not supplant the two-part *Strickland* test for ineffective assistance of counsel with a three-pronged test. The Court noted that the *Strickland* test applies to "virtually all" claims of ineffective assistance of counsel. Id. at 391, 120 S.Ct. at 1512. Only in "unusual" cases—when it would be "unjust" to treat the difference in outcome as "prejudice"—will the inept performance of counsel that likely affected the outcome of the proceeding not lead to a finding of unconstitutional ineffectiveness. Id. at 391–92, 393 n.18, 120 S.Ct. at 1512, 1513 n.18). Put in other words, "prejudice" under the *Strickland* test exists when counsel's deficient representation deprived the defendant of a "substantive or procedural right to which the law entitles him." Id. at 392–93 & n.17, 120 S.Ct. at 1513 & n.17.

In Glover v. United States, 531 U.S. 198, 121 S.Ct. 696 (2001), a noncapital case, the Supreme Court further defined the contours of the prejudice prong of the *Strickland* test. In that case, the defendant's attorneys failed, both at the sentencing hearing and on appeal, to contest an alleged error in the sentencing court's calculation of the defendant's sentence under the federal sentencing guidelines. That error led to an increase in the defendant's sentence by six to twenty-one months.

The lower courts held that this increase in the sentence length was not long enough to constitute the requisite "prejudice" under the *Strickland* test. The Supreme Court disagreed, noting that any increase in the length of incarceration due to counsel's deficient performance can constitute the prejudice needed to sustain a claim of ineffective assistance of counsel. The Court's decision was driven in part by pragmatic considerations, with the Court observing that there is no "obvious dividing line" between sentence increases that cause "substantial" prejudice and those that do not. Id. at 204, 121 S.Ct. at 700.

C. THE RIGHTS TO PRESENT EVIDENCE AND MAKE A STATEMENT TO THE SENTENCER

Defendants have claimed that they not only have a right to speak to the court through their attorneys on the subject of their sentence but that they also have a constitutional right to address the court themselves. The right the defendants are invoking is known as the right of allocution.

Most courts have held that defendants have no constitutionally-based right of allocution. State v. Abdullah, 348 P.3d 1, 93 (Idaho 2015). The courts concluding that there is no constitutional right of allocution have relied heavily on the Supreme Court's decision in Hill v. United States, 368 U.S. 424, 82 S.Ct. 468 (1962). In *Hill,* however, the Court emphasized some special facts about the case. First, the Court noted that the sentencing court simply had failed to ask the defendant if he had anything to say before the court imposed sentence; the court had not forbidden a defendant who expressed his desire to address the court from doing so. Second, the Court underscored that the defendant had not claimed that the sentencing judge misunderstood, or was unaware of, relevant facts in sentencing the defendant. And finally, the Court emphasized that the defendant in *Hill* was represented by an attorney at the sentencing hearing.

Should this latter fact have any bearing on the question whether a defendant has a constitutional right of allocution? See Green v. United States, 365 U.S. 301, 304, 81 S.Ct. 653, 655 (1961), a case in which the Supreme Court, when discussing the right of allocution under Rule 32 of the Federal Rules of Criminal Procedure, stated: "The most persuasive counsel may not be able to speak for a defendant as the defendant might, with halting eloquence, speak for himself." Does it matter, in your opinion, whether the sentencing hearing is in a capital or a noncapital case? See United States v. Lawrence, 735 F.3d 385, 407 (6th Cir.2014) (citing, and agreeing with, decisions of other federal courts of appeals that defendants have no constitutional right to make an unsworn statement to a capital sentencing jury). Is it relevant to the constitutional question whether the defendant will be sentenced by a judge or a jury? See United States v. Hall,

152 F.3d 381, 393 (5th Cir.1998) (noting that a jury, unlike a judge, may not recognize that a defendant's unsworn statements may be less credible).

Though a defendant may or may not have a constitutional right of allocution, it is clear that at least in some circumstances, the defendant has a constitutional right to present evidence at a sentencing hearing. For example, in Green v. Georgia, 442 U.S. 95, 99 S.Ct. 2150 (1979) (per curiam), the Supreme Court held that the defendant's due-process rights were violated when he was not permitted to call a witness to testify at a sentencing hearing in a capital case because the witness's testimony, under the state's evidentiary rules, would be hearsay. The witness apparently would have testified that a codefendant had admitted to the witness that he was the one who had actually shot the victim whom the defendant was convicted of murdering. In concluding that the defendant's due-process rights were violated when he was not allowed to call the witness to testify at the sentencing hearing, the Court emphasized both that the witness's testimony was "highly relevant" to a "critical issue" in the sentencing hearing and that there were "substantial reasons" for believing the testimony was reliable. The reasons mentioned by the Court included the following: the codefendant was a close friend of the witness; the codefendant had made a declaration against penal interest; there was evidence that corroborated the codefendant's admission; and the state had considered the admission reliable enough to use against the codefendant during his own trial for capital murder. See also Ake v. Oklahoma, 470 U.S. 68, 83–84, 86–87, 105 S.Ct. 1087, 1096–98 (1985) (indigent defendant convicted of capital murders had a due-process right to be afforded access to a psychiatrist to help the defendant prepare and present evidence on the question of his future dangerousness, a question that was a "significant factor" at his sentencing hearing).

The Supreme Court distinguished *Green v. Georgia* in Oregon v. Guzek, 546 U.S. 517, 126 S.Ct. 1226 (2006). In *Guzek*, the Court held that the defendant in that case had no constitutional right to present evidence at his capital sentencing hearing that he was innocent of the crime of which he had been convicted. The Court cited three factors that underlay its conclusion that the Eighth and Fourteenth Amendments afforded the defendant no such right: one, sentencing hearings traditionally have focused on how, not whether, the defendant committed the crime; two, the parties already had litigated the question of the defendant's guilt; and three, a state statute permitted the defendant to introduce at the sentencing hearing any evidence of his innocence adduced at the original trial, mitigating the adverse effects of the bar on the introduction at the sentencing hearing of new evidence of innocence, such as new evidence supporting an alibi defense.

In Morrissey v. Brewer, 408 U.S. 471, 92 S.Ct. 2593 (1972), which can be found on page 416, the Supreme Court outlined a number of procedural safeguards to which due process entitles a person at a parole-revocation hearing. Two include the right to call witnesses and to present documentary evidence. How might you argue, under the *Mathews* balancing test, that the case for finding these rights embedded in due process is even stronger in the sentencing, as opposed to parole-revocation, context? How would you respond to these arguments?

D. RIGHT TO A STATEMENT OF REASONS FOR THE SENTENCE IMPOSED

According to the courts, defendants generally do not have a constitutional right to be apprised, whether orally or in writing, of the reasons why a particular sentence was imposed by a sentencer. United States v. Golomb, 754 F.2d 86, 90 (2d Cir.1985). Do you concur with this conclusion? Does the *Mathews* balancing test point towards or against the existence of a constitutional right to this statement of reasons?

In some exceptional circumstances, courts have found a statement of reasons required by, or linked to, the Constitution. For example, in North Carolina v. Pearce, 395 U.S. 711, 726, 89 S.Ct. 2072, 2081 (1969), the Supreme Court held that the reasons for a higher sentence imposed on a defendant who successfully had appealed his first conviction and been convicted again after a second trial had to "affirmatively appear" on the record. The Court's rationale was that in these circumstances, there was too high a risk that the increased sentence was imposed, in violation of due process, to retaliate against the defendant for having exercised his right to appeal his conviction.

In subsequent cases, the Supreme Court has described the *Pearce* rule as a "judicially created means" of effectuating a constitutional right, in this case the right not to have a sentence increased for vindictive reasons. Texas v. McCullough, 475 U.S. 134, 138, 106 S.Ct. 976, 978 (1986)). Consequently, the Court has limited the application of the *Pearce* rule to circumstances where the risk of an increased sentence being imposed is sufficiently high to create a presumption of vindictiveness. Thus, in *Texas v. McCullough*, the Court ruled that the risk of vindictiveness is not great enough when the sentence was imposed by a "different sentencer" the second time around. 475 U.S. at 140, 106 S.Ct. at 979. Nor does a presumption of vindictiveness necessitating a statement of reasons for an increased sentence exist when the second sentence was imposed even by the same sentencer, but following the granting of a motion for a new trial. Id. at 138–39, 106 S.Ct. at 979. In these circumstances, according to the Court, the fact that the trial judge acknowledged the need for a new trial, instead of being ordered by the appellate court to hold one, sufficiently reduces the risk that the increased sentence was due to proscribed vindictiveness. Finally, as was discussed in Chapter 2, no presumption of vindictiveness exists when a defendant's guilty plea was set aside on appeal and the increased sentence was imposed following the defendant's trial on the reinstated charges. See the discussion of Alabama v. Smith, 490 U.S. 794, 109 S.Ct. 2201 (1989) in note 2 on pages 76–77.

E. STANDARD OF PROOF/RIGHT TO JURY TRIAL

1. DISTINGUISHING AGGRAVATING SENTENCING FACTORS AND ELEMENTS OF A CRIME

When deciding what sentence to impose on a defendant, a court typically will consider a number of facts, including facts about the defendant, the defendant's crime, and the impact of a particular sentence on others. The constitutional rights that apply during sentencing proceedings hinge in part on whether a fact affecting a sentencing outcome is a sentencing factor or is, in actuality, an element of the crime. The Supreme Court has wrestled with the distinction between sentencing factors and elements of a crime, as the cases in this subsection confirm.

In Almendarez-Torres v. United States, 523 U.S. 224, 118 S.Ct. 1219 (1998), the Supreme Court confronted the question whether a statutory provision described an element of a crime or a sentencing factor. Under the statute before the Court, a person deported for being in the country illegally and who later illegally returned to the United States was subject to a maximum prison sentence of two years. But if the deportation had followed a conviction for an "aggravated felony," a prison sentence of up to twenty years could be imposed.

The Fifth Amendment requires that a federal indictment spell out the elements of a felony with which a defendant has been charged. But in a 5–4 decision in *Almendarez-Torres*, the Supreme Court held that the defendant's prior conviction was a sentencing factor, not an element. As a result, the prior conviction did not have to be alleged in the indictment. The Court explained that traditionally recidivism has been treated as a sentencing factor.

Justice Scalia, in a dissenting opinion joined by Justices Stevens, Souter, and Ginsburg, argued that there is " 'serious doubt' whether the Constitution permits a defendant's sentencing exposure to be increased tenfold on the basis of a fact that is not charged, tried to a jury, and found beyond a reasonable doubt." Id. at 260, 118 S.Ct. at 1238. In order to avoid resolving what he described as a "difficult constitutional issue," Justice Scalia therefore construed the statute as setting forth an element of the crime rather than a sentencing factor.

In Monge v. California, 524 U.S. 721, 118 S.Ct. 2246 (1998), the Supreme Court considered another issue stemming from the imposition of a sentencing enhancement. The defendant in that case was convicted of using a minor to sell marijuana. Under California law, a defendant's sentence had to be doubled when the defendant had been convicted previously of a "serious felony." An assault conviction was considered a serious felony if the defendant had inflicted great bodily harm or had used a dangerous or deadly weapon during the assault. After the prosecutor produced a prison record at trial indicating that the defendant had been convicted previously of assault with a deadly weapon, the sentencing judge doubled the defendant's prison sentence from five to ten years.

On appeal, the state admitted that it had not, as required by the state statute, proven beyond a reasonable doubt that the defendant either had inflicted great bodily injury or used a deadly weapon during the prior assault of which he had been convicted. The state therefore requested that the case be remanded so that the state could attempt to meet its burden of proof by introducing evidence regarding the circumstances surrounding the assault.

The defendant responded that a retrial would violate his constitutional right not to be subjected to double jeopardy. The defendant based his double-jeopardy argument on the Supreme Court's decision in Bullington v. Missouri, 451 U.S. 430, 101 S.Ct. 1852 (1981). In that case, which involved a capital crime, the defendant was sentenced to life in prison by the original sentencing jury. After his conviction was reversed on appeal, the state announced that it, once again, would seek the death penalty.

The Supreme Court held in *Bullington* that the Fifth Amendment's double-jeopardy prohibition foreclosed further pursuit of the death penalty. The Court cited the longstanding rule that a state cannot reprosecute a person for a crime of which he or she was acquitted. The Court concluded that this rule should be extended to cases where the original sentencing jury had decided not to impose the death penalty after a trial-like sentencing proceeding in which the state had had to prove beyond a reasonable doubt the aggravating factors warranting imposition of the death penalty.

The defendant in *Monge* pointed out that his prior conviction of a "serious felony" had been considered during a trial in which he, like the defendant in *Bullington*, had a number of rights. Under California law, he had the right to a jury trial on the prior-conviction issue, the right to confront witnesses, and the privilege against self-incrimination. In addition, the state had to prove the prior conviction beyond a reasonable doubt.

Emphasizing the uniqueness of the death penalty, the Supreme Court, however, refused to extend the ruling in *Bullington* to a noncapital case. Thus, when a state fails to introduce enough evidence in the original sentencing proceeding to support an enhanced sentence, the state may be given, as far as double jeopardy is concerned, "another bite at the apple" in a noncapital case. The only constraint double jeopardy places on sentencing in a noncapital case is that a defendant resentenced for a crime must be given credit for time served on the initial sentence. North Carolina v. Pearce, 395 U.S. 711, 718–21, 89 S.Ct. 2072, 2077–79 (1969).

While Justice Scalia agreed, in a dissenting opinion in *Monge* in which Justices Souter and Ginsburg joined, that the Double Jeopardy Clause does not apply to noncapital sentencing proceedings, he disagreed that this case involved only sentencing. Resolving the question that he had discussed, but not decided, a few months earlier in *Almendarez-Torres v. United States*, Justice Scalia concluded that so-called sentencing enhancements that increase the maximum sentence for a crime are actually elements of that crime. Therefore, according to Justice Scalia, because insufficient evidence was originally introduced regarding the defendant's prior conviction, the state could not constitutionally be given a second chance to prove the aggravated crime of which the defendant, in effect, had been acquitted.

Consider whether the Supreme Court's decisions in *Almendarez-Torres* and *Monge* can be reconciled with the case that follows.

APPRENDI V. NEW JERSEY
Supreme Court of the United States, 2000.
530 U.S. 466, 120 S.Ct. 2348, 147 L.Ed.2d 435.

JUSTICE STEVENS delivered the opinion of the Court.

A New Jersey statute classifies the possession of a firearm for an unlawful purpose as a "second-degree" offense. Such an offense is punishable by imprisonment for "between five years and 10 years." A separate statute, described by that State's Supreme Court as a "hate crime" law, provides for an "extended term" of imprisonment if the trial judge finds, by a preponderance of the evidence, that "[t]he defendant in committing the crime acted with a purpose to intimidate an individual or group of individuals because of race, color, gender, handicap, religion, sexual orientation or ethnicity." The extended term authorized by the hate crime law for second-degree offenses is imprisonment for "between 10 and 20 years."

The question presented is whether the Due Process Clause of the Fourteenth Amendment requires that a factual determination authorizing an increase in the maximum prison sentence for an offense from 10 to 20 years be made by a jury on the basis of proof beyond a reasonable doubt.

I

At 2:04 a.m. on December 22, 1994, petitioner Charles C. Apprendi, Jr., fired several .22-caliber bullets into the home of an African-American family that had recently moved into a previously all-white neighborhood in Vineland, New Jersey. Apprendi was promptly arrested and, at 3:05 a.m., admitted that he was the shooter. After further questioning, at 6:04 a.m., he made a statement—which he later retracted—that even though he did not know the occupants of the house personally, "because they are black in color he does not want them in the neighborhood."

A New Jersey grand jury returned a 23-count indictment charging Apprendi with four first-degree, eight second-degree, six third-degree, and five fourth-degree offenses. The charges alleged shootings on four different dates, as well as the unlawful possession of various weapons. None of the counts referred to the hate crime statute, and none alleged that Apprendi acted with a racially biased purpose.

The parties entered into a plea agreement, pursuant to which Apprendi pleaded guilty to two counts (3 and 18) of second-degree possession of a firearm for an unlawful purpose and one count (22) of the third-degree offense of unlawful possession of an antipersonnel bomb. * * * As part of the plea agreement, however, the State reserved the right to request the court to impose a higher "enhanced" sentence on count 18 (which was based on the December 22 shooting) on the ground that that offense was committed with a biased purpose * * *. Apprendi, correspondingly, reserved the right to challenge the hate crime sentence enhancement on the ground that it violates the United States Constitution.

* * * Because the plea agreement provided that the sentence on the sole third-degree offense (count 22) would run concurrently with the other sentences, the potential sentences on the two second-degree counts were critical. If the judge found no basis for the biased purpose enhancement, the maximum consecutive sentences on those counts would amount to 20 years in aggregate; if, however, the judge enhanced the sentence on count 18, the maximum on that count alone would be 20 years and the maximum for the two counts in aggregate would be 30 years, with a 15-year period of parole ineligibility.

After the trial judge accepted the three guilty pleas, the prosecutor filed a formal motion for an extended term. The trial judge thereafter held an evidentiary hearing on the issue of Apprendi's "purpose" for the shooting on December 22. Apprendi adduced evidence from a psychologist and from seven character witnesses who testified that he did not have a reputation for racial bias. He also took the stand himself, explaining that the incident was an unintended consequence of overindulgence in alcohol, denying that he was in any way biased against African-Americans, and denying that his statement to the police had been accurately described. The judge, however, found the police officer's testimony credible, and concluded that the evidence supported a finding "that the crime was motivated by racial bias." Having found "by a preponderance of the evidence" that Apprendi's actions were taken "with a purpose to intimidate" as provided by the statute, the trial judge held that the hate crime enhancement applied. Rejecting

Apprendi's constitutional challenge to the statute, the judge sentenced him to a 12-year term of imprisonment on count 18, and to shorter concurrent sentences on the other two counts.

* * *

III

* * *

At stake in this case are constitutional protections of surpassing importance: the proscription of any deprivation of liberty without "due process of law" and the guarantee that "[i]n all criminal prosecutions, the accused shall enjoy the right to a speedy and public trial, by an impartial jury."[3] Taken together, these rights indisputably entitle a criminal defendant to "a jury determination that [he] is guilty of every element of the crime with which he is charged, beyond a reasonable doubt."

[The Court then described common-law sentencing practices, spanning hundreds of years, through which a defendant could ascertain the maximum punishment he faced from the face of the indictment.]

* * *

We should be clear that nothing in this history suggests that it is impermissible for judges to exercise discretion—taking into consideration various factors relating both to offense and offender—in imposing a judgment *within the range* prescribed by statute. * * *[10]

[P]ractice must at least adhere to the basic principles undergirding the requirements of trying to a jury all facts necessary to constitute a statutory offense, and proving those facts beyond reasonable doubt. As we made clear in *Winship*, the "reasonable doubt" requirement "has a vital role in our criminal procedure for cogent reasons." Prosecution subjects the criminal defendant both to "the possibility that he may lose his liberty upon conviction and . . . the certainty that he would be stigmatized by the conviction." We thus require this, among other, procedural protections in order to "provid[e] concrete substance for the presumption of innocence," and to reduce the risk of imposing such deprivations erroneously. If a defendant faces punishment beyond that provided by statute when an

---

[3] Apprendi has not here asserted a constitutional claim based on the omission of any reference to sentence enhancement or racial bias in the indictment. He relies entirely on the fact that the "due process of law" that the Fourteenth Amendment requires the States to provide to persons accused of crime encompasses the right to a trial by jury, *Duncan v. Louisiana*, 391 U.S. 145 (1968), and the right to have every element of the offense proved beyond a reasonable doubt, *In re Winship*, 397 U.S. 358 (1970). That Amendment has not, however, been construed to include the Fifth Amendment right to "presentment or indictment of a Grand Jury" that was implicated in our recent decision in *Almendarez-Torres v. United States*, 523 U.S. 224 (1998). * * *

[10] * * * The [historical] evidence * * * point[s] to a single, consistent conclusion: The judge's role in sentencing is constrained at its outer limits by the facts alleged in the indictment and found by the jury. Put simply, facts that expose a defendant to a punishment greater than that otherwise legally prescribed were by definition "elements" of a separate legal offense.

offense is committed under certain circumstances but not others, it is obvious that both the loss of liberty and the stigma attaching to the offense are heightened; it necessarily follows that the defendant should not—at the moment the State is put to proof of those circumstances—be deprived of protections that have, until that point, unquestionably attached.

* * *

* * * *Almendarez-Torres v. United States*, 523 U.S. 224 (1998), represents at best an exceptional departure from the historic practice that we have described. In that case, we considered a federal grand jury indictment, which charged the petitioner with "having been 'found in the United States . . . after being deported,'" in violation of 8 U.S.C. § 1326(a)—an offense carrying a maximum sentence of two years. Almendarez-Torres pleaded guilty to the indictment, admitting at the plea hearing that he had been deported, that he had unlawfully reentered this country, and that "the earlier deportation had taken place 'pursuant to' three earlier 'convictions' for aggravated felonies." The Government then filed a presentence report indicating that Almendarez-Torres' offense fell within the bounds of § 1326(b) because, as specified in that provision, his original deportation had been subsequent to an aggravated felony conviction; accordingly, Almendarez-Torres could be subject to a sentence of up to 20 years. Almendarez-Torres objected, contending that because the indictment "had not mentioned his earlier aggravated felony convictions," he could be sentenced to no more than two years in prison.

Rejecting Almendarez-Torres' objection, we concluded that sentencing him to a term higher than that attached to the offense alleged in the indictment did not violate the strictures of *Winship* in that case. Because Almendarez-Torres had *admitted* the three earlier convictions for aggravated felonies—all of which had been entered pursuant to proceedings with substantial procedural safeguards of their own—no question concerning the right to a jury trial or the standard of proof that would apply to a contested issue of fact was before the Court. * * * Both the certainty that procedural safeguards attached to any "fact" of prior conviction, and the reality that Almendarez-Torres did not challenge the accuracy of that "fact" in his case, mitigated the due process and Sixth Amendment concerns otherwise implicated in allowing a judge to determine a "fact" increasing punishment beyond the maximum of the statutory range.[14]

---

[14] The principal dissent's contention that our decision in *Monge v. California*, 524 U.S. 721 (1998), "demonstrates that *Almendarez-Torres* was" something other than a limited exception to the jury trial rule is both inaccurate and misleading. *Monge* was another recidivism case in which the question presented and the bulk of the Court's analysis related to the scope of double jeopardy protections in sentencing. * * * Most telling of *Monge*'s distance from the issue at stake in this case is that the double jeopardy question in *Monge* arose because the State had failed to satisfy its own statutory burden of proving beyond a reasonable doubt that the defendant had committed a prior offense (and was therefore subject to an enhanced, recidivism-based sentence). 524 U.S., at 725

Even though it is arguable that *Almendarez-Torres* was incorrectly decided and that a logical application of our reasoning today should apply if the recidivist issue were contested, Apprendi does not contest the decision's validity and we need not revisit it for purposes of our decision today to treat the case as a narrow exception to the general rule we recalled at the outset. Given its unique facts, it surely does not warrant rejection of the otherwise uniform course of decision during the entire history of our jurisprudence.

* * * Other than the fact of a prior conviction, any fact that increases the penalty for a crime beyond the prescribed statutory maximum must be submitted to a jury, and proved beyond a reasonable doubt. * * *[16]

V

The New Jersey statutory scheme that Apprendi asks us to invalidate allows a jury to convict a defendant of a second-degree offense based on its finding beyond a reasonable doubt that he unlawfully possessed a prohibited weapon; after a subsequent and separate proceeding, it then allows a judge to impose punishment identical to that New Jersey provides for crimes of the first degree based upon the judge's finding, by a preponderance of the evidence, that the defendant's "purpose" for unlawfully possessing the weapon was "to intimidate" his victim on the basis of a particular characteristic the victim possessed. In light of the

---

("According to California law, a number of procedural safeguards surround the assessment of prior conviction allegations: Defendants may invoke the right to a jury trial . . .; the prosecution must prove the allegation beyond a reasonable doubt; and the rules of evidence apply"). The Court thus itself warned against a contrary double jeopardy rule that could "create disincentives that would diminish these important procedural protections."

[16] The principal dissent would reject the Court's rule as a "meaningless formalism," because it can conceive of hypothetical statutes that would comply with the rule and achieve the same result as the New Jersey statute. While a State could, hypothetically, undertake to revise its entire criminal code in the manner the dissent suggests, extending all statutory maximum sentences to, for example, 50 years and giving judges guided discretion as to a few specially selected factors within that range—this possibility seems remote. Among other reasons, structural democratic constraints exist to discourage legislatures from enacting penal statutes that expose every defendant convicted of, for example, weapons possession, to a maximum sentence exceeding that which is, in the legislature's judgment, generally proportional to the crime. * * *

In all events, if such an extensive revision of the State's entire criminal code were enacted for the purpose the dissent suggests, or if New Jersey simply reversed the burden of the hate crime finding (effectively assuming a crime was performed with a purpose to intimidate and then requiring a defendant to prove that it was not), we would be required to question whether the revision was constitutional under this Court's prior decisions.

Finally, the principal dissent ignores the distinction the Court has often recognized between facts in aggravation of punishment and facts in mitigation. If facts found by a jury support a guilty verdict of murder, the judge is authorized by that jury verdict to sentence the defendant to the maximum sentence provided by the murder statute. If the defendant can escape the statutory maximum by showing, for example, that he is a war veteran, then a judge that finds the fact of veteran status is neither exposing the defendant to a deprivation of liberty greater than that authorized by the verdict according to statute, nor is the judge imposing upon the defendant a greater stigma than that accompanying the jury verdict alone. Core concerns animating the jury and burden-of-proof requirements are thus absent from such a scheme.

constitutional rule explained above, and all of the cases supporting it, this practice cannot stand.

* * *

* * * Despite what appears to us the clear "elemental" nature of the factor here, the relevant inquiry is one not of form, but of effect—does the required finding expose the defendant to a greater punishment than that authorized by the jury's guilty verdict?[19]

* * *

JUSTICE SCALIA, concurring.

I feel the need to say a few words in response to Justice Breyer's dissent. * * *

* * * I think it not unfair to tell a prospective felon that if he commits his contemplated crime he is exposing himself to a jail sentence of 30 years—and that if, upon conviction, he gets anything less than that he may thank the mercy of a tenderhearted judge (just as he may thank the mercy of a tenderhearted parole commission if he is let out inordinately early, or the mercy of a tenderhearted governor if his sentence is commuted). Will there be disparities? Of course. But the criminal will never get *more* punishment than he bargained for when he did the crime, and his guilt of the crime (and hence the length of the sentence to which he is exposed) will be determined *beyond a reasonable doubt by the unanimous vote of 12 of his fellow citizens.*

* * *

JUSTICE THOMAS, with whom JUSTICE SCALIA joins as to Parts I and II, concurring.

I join the opinion of the Court in full. I write separately to explain my view that the Constitution requires a broader rule than the Court adopts.

* * *

* * * [O]ne of the chief errors of *Almendarez-Torres*—an error to which I succumbed—was to attempt to discern whether a particular fact is traditionally (or typically) a basis for a sentencing court to increase an offender's sentence. * * * What matters is the way by which a fact enters into the sentence. If a fact is by law the basis for imposing or increasing

---

[19] This is not to suggest that the term "sentencing factor" is devoid of meaning. The term appropriately describes a circumstance, which may be either aggravating or mitigating in character, that supports a specific sentence *within the range* authorized by the jury's finding that the defendant is guilty of a particular offense. On the other hand, when the term "sentence enhancement" is used to describe an increase beyond the maximum authorized statutory sentence, it is the functional equivalent of an element of a greater offense than the one covered by the jury's guilty verdict. * * *

punishment—for establishing or increasing the prosecution's entitlement—it is an element. * * *

* * *

JUSTICE O'CONNOR, with whom THE CHIEF JUSTICE, JUSTICE KENNEDY, and JUSTICE BREYER join, dissenting.

* * *

Our Court has long recognized that not every fact that bears on a defendant's punishment need be charged in an indictment, submitted to a jury, and proved by the government beyond a reasonable doubt. Rather, we have held that the "legislature's definition of the elements of the offense is usually dispositive." * * *

In one bold stroke the Court today casts aside our traditional cautious approach and instead embraces a universal and seemingly bright-line rule limiting the power of Congress and state legislatures to define criminal offenses and the sentences that follow from convictions thereunder. The Court states: "Other than the fact of a prior conviction, any fact that increases the penalty for a crime beyond the prescribed statutory maximum must be submitted to a jury, and proved beyond a reasonable doubt." * * *

* * *

* * * *Almendarez-Torres* constituted a clear repudiation of the rule the Court adopts today. My understanding is bolstered by *Monge v. California*, a decision relegated to a footnote by the Court today. In *Monge*, in reasoning essential to our holding, we reiterated that "the Court has rejected an absolute rule that an enhancement constitutes an element of the offense any time that it increases the maximum sentence to which a defendant is exposed." At the very least, *Monge* demonstrates that *Almendarez-Torres* was not an "exceptional departure" from "historic practice."

* * *

* * * [A]pparently New Jersey could cure its sentencing scheme, and achieve virtually the same results, by drafting its weapons possession statute in the following manner: * * *

* * *

* * * First, New Jersey could prescribe, in the weapons possession statute itself, a range of 5 to 20 years' imprisonment for one who commits that criminal offense. Second, New Jersey could provide that a defendant convicted under the statute whom a judge finds, by a preponderance of the evidence, *not* to have acted with a purpose to intimidate an individual on

the basis of race may receive a sentence no greater than 10 years' imprisonment.

* * *

JUSTICE BREYER, with whom CHIEF JUSTICE REHNQUIST joins, dissenting. [Opinion omitted.]

QUESTIONS AND POINTS FOR DISCUSSION

1.   In Walton v. Arizona, 497 U.S. 639, 110 S.Ct. 3047 (1990), a case decided before *Apprendi*, the Supreme Court had held that the sentencing structure for imposing the death penalty in Arizona was constitutional. Under an Arizona statute, a judge decided whether to sentence a defendant to death after a jury had found a defendant guilty of first-degree murder. A death sentence required a finding by the judge of at least one aggravating factor enumerated in the statute. In Ring v. Arizona, 536 U.S. 584, 122 S.Ct. 2428 (2002), the Supreme Court concluded that *Apprendi* and *Walton* were irreconcilable. In overruling *Walton*, the Court observed: "The right to trial by jury guaranteed by the Sixth Amendment would be senselessly diminished if it encompassed the factfinding necessary to increase a defendant's sentence by two years, but not the factfinding necessary to put him to death." Id. at 609, 122 S.Ct. at 2443.

2.   The "*Apprendi* rule" also extends to the imposition of fines. Southern Union Co. v. United States, 567 U.S. 343, 132 S.Ct. 2344 (2012). In other words, if the existence of a fact, such as the amount of a victim's loss or the number of days a defendant violated the law, would increase the size of a fine beyond the maximum level authorized by the jury's verdict, a defendant has a constitutional right to have a jury determine whether the government has proven that additional fact beyond a reasonable doubt.

Set forth below is a closely divided decision in which the Supreme Court once again addressed the implications of *Apprendi*.

BLAKELY V. WASHINGTON
Supreme Court of the United States, 2004.
542 U.S. 296, 124 S.Ct. 2531, 159 L.Ed.2d 403.

JUSTICE SCALIA delivered the opinion of the Court.

* * *

Petitioner married his wife Yolanda in 1973. He was evidently a difficult man to live with, having been diagnosed at various times with psychological and personality disorders including paranoid schizophrenia. His wife ultimately filed for divorce. In 1998, he abducted her from their orchard home in Grant County, Washington, binding her with duct tape and forcing her at knifepoint into a wooden box in the bed of his pickup truck. In the process, he implored her to dismiss the divorce suit and related trust proceedings.

When the couple's 13-year-old son Ralphy returned home from school, petitioner ordered him to follow in another car, threatening to harm Yolanda with a shotgun if he did not do so. Ralphy escaped and sought help when they stopped at a gas station, but petitioner continued on with Yolanda to a friend's house in Montana. He was finally arrested after the friend called the police.

The State charged petitioner with first-degree kidnapping. Upon reaching a plea agreement, however, it reduced the charge to second-degree kidnapping involving domestic violence and use of a firearm. Petitioner entered a guilty plea admitting the elements of second-degree kidnapping and the domestic-violence and firearm allegations, but no other relevant facts.

The case then proceeded to sentencing. In Washington, second-degree kidnapping is a class B felony. State law provides that "[n]o person convicted of a [class B] felony shall be punished by confinement . . . exceeding . . . a term of ten years." Other provisions of state law, however, further limit the range of sentences a judge may impose. Washington's Sentencing Reform Act specifies, for petitioner's offense of second-degree kidnapping with a firearm, a "standard range" of 49 to 53 months. A judge may impose a sentence above the standard range if he finds "substantial and compelling reasons justifying an exceptional sentence." The Act lists aggravating factors that justify such a departure, which it recites to be illustrative rather than exhaustive. Nevertheless, "[a] reason offered to justify an exceptional sentence can be considered only if it takes into account factors other than those which are used in computing the standard range sentence for the offense." When a judge imposes an exceptional sentence, he must set forth findings of fact and conclusions of law supporting it. A reviewing court will reverse the sentence if it finds that "under a clearly erroneous standard there is insufficient evidence in the record to support the reasons for imposing an exceptional sentence."

Pursuant to the plea agreement, the State recommended a sentence within the standard range of 49 to 53 months. After hearing Yolanda's description of the kidnapping, however, the judge rejected the State's recommendation and imposed an exceptional sentence of 90 months—37 months beyond the standard maximum. He justified the sentence on the ground that petitioner had acted with "deliberate cruelty," a statutorily enumerated ground for departure in domestic-violence cases.

Faced with an unexpected increase of more than three years in his sentence, petitioner objected. The judge accordingly conducted a 3-day bench hearing featuring testimony from petitioner, Yolanda, Ralphy, a police officer, and medical experts. After the hearing, he issued 32 findings of fact * * *. The judge adhered to his initial determination of deliberate cruelty.

Petitioner appealed, arguing that this sentencing procedure deprived him of his federal constitutional right to have a jury determine beyond a reasonable doubt all facts legally essential to his sentence. The State Court of Appeals affirmed * * *. * * *

This case requires us to apply the rule we expressed in *Apprendi v. New Jersey,* 530 U.S. 466, 490 (2000): "Other than the fact of a prior conviction, any fact that increases the penalty for a crime beyond the prescribed statutory maximum must be submitted to a jury, and proved beyond a reasonable doubt." * * *6

* * *

In this case, petitioner was sentenced to more than three years above the 53-month statutory maximum of the standard range because he had acted with "deliberate cruelty." The facts supporting that finding were neither admitted by petitioner nor found by a jury. The State nevertheless contends that there was no *Apprendi* violation because the relevant "statutory maximum" is not 53 months, but the 10-year maximum for class B felonies * * *. Our precedents make clear, however, that the "statutory maximum" for *Apprendi* purposes is the maximum sentence a judge may impose *solely on the basis of the facts reflected in the jury verdict or admitted by the defendant.* See *Ring* [*v. Arizona,* 536 U.S. 584,] 602 [(2002)]. In other words, the relevant "statutory maximum" is not the maximum sentence a judge may impose after finding additional facts, but the maximum he may impose *without* any additional findings. * * *

The judge in this case could not have imposed the exceptional 90-month sentence solely on the basis of the facts admitted in the guilty plea. * * * Had the judge imposed the 90-month sentence solely on the basis of the plea, he would have been reversed. * * *

The State defends the sentence by drawing an analogy to * * * *Williams v. New York,* 337 U.S. 241 (1949). * * * *Williams* involved an indeterminate-sentencing regime that allowed a judge (but did not compel him) to rely on facts outside the trial record in determining whether to sentence a defendant to death. The judge could have "sentenced [the defendant] to death giving no reason at all." Thus, [*Williams* did not involve] a sentence greater than what state law authorized on the basis of the verdict alone.

---

6   * * * It bears repeating that the issue between us is not *whether* the Constitution limits States' authority to reclassify elements as sentencing factors (we all agree that it does); it is only which line * * * the Constitution draws. * * * Justice O'Connor does not even provide a coherent alternative meaning for the jury-trial guarantee, unless one considers "whatever the legislature chooses to leave to the jury, so long as it does not go too far" coherent.

* * *

Because the State's sentencing procedure did not comply with the Sixth Amendment, petitioner's sentence is invalid.

Our commitment to *Apprendi* in this context reflects not just respect for longstanding precedent, but the need to give intelligible content to the right of jury trial. That right is no mere procedural formality, but a fundamental reservation of power in our constitutional structure. Just as suffrage ensures the people's ultimate control in the legislative and executive branches, jury trial is meant to ensure their control in the judiciary. *Apprendi* carries out this design by ensuring that the judge's authority to sentence derives wholly from the jury's verdict. Without that restriction, the jury would not exercise the control that the Framers intended.

Those who would reject *Apprendi* are resigned to one of two alternatives. The first is that the jury need only find whatever facts the legislature chooses to label elements of the crime, and that those it labels sentencing factors—no matter how much they may increase the punishment—may be found by the judge. This would mean, for example, that a judge could sentence a man for committing murder even if the jury convicted him only of illegally possessing the firearm used to commit it— or of making an illegal lane change while fleeing the death scene. Not even *Apprendi*'s critics would advocate this absurd result. The jury could not function as circuitbreaker in the State's machinery of justice if it were relegated to making a determination that the defendant at some point did something wrong, a mere preliminary to a judicial inquisition into the facts of the crime the State *actually* seeks to punish.[10]

The second alternative is that legislatures may establish legally essential sentencing factors *within limits*—limits crossed when, perhaps, the sentencing factor is a "tail which wags the dog of the substantive offense." What this means in operation is that the law must not go *too far*— it must not exceed the judicial estimation of the proper role of the judge.

The subjectivity of this standard is obvious. Petitioner argued below that second-degree kidnapping with deliberate cruelty was essentially the same as first-degree kidnapping, the very charge he had avoided by pleading to a lesser offense. The court conceded this might be so but held it irrelevant. Petitioner's 90-month sentence exceeded the 53-month standard maximum by almost 70%; the Washington Supreme Court in other cases has upheld exceptional sentences 15 times the standard

---

[10] Justice O'Connor believes that a "built-in political check" will prevent lawmakers from manipulating offense elements in this fashion. But the many immediate practical advantages of judicial factfinding suggest that political forces would, if anything, pull in the opposite direction. In any case, the Framers' decision to entrench the jury-trial right in the Constitution shows that they did not trust government to make political decisions in this area.

maximum. See *State v. Oxborrow*, 723 P.2d 1123, 1125, 1128 (1986) (15-year exceptional sentence; 1-year standard maximum sentence); *State v. Branch*, 919 P.2d 1228, 1235 (1996) (4-year exceptional sentence; 3-month standard maximum sentence). Did the court go *too far* in any of these cases? There is no answer that legal analysis can provide. With *too far* as the yardstick, it is always possible to disagree with such judgments and never to refute them.

Whether the Sixth Amendment incorporates this manipulable standard rather than *Apprendi*'s bright-line rule depends on the plausibility of the claim that the Framers would have left definition of the scope of jury power up to judges' intuitive sense of how far is *too far*. We think that claim not plausible at all, because the very reason the Framers put a jury-trial guarantee in the Constitution is that they were unwilling to trust government to mark out the role of the jury.

By reversing the judgment below, we are not, as the State would have it, "find[ing] determinate sentencing schemes unconstitutional." This case is not about whether determinate sentencing is constitutional, only about how it can be implemented in a way that respects the Sixth Amendment. * * *

* * * [T]he Sixth Amendment by its terms is not a limitation on judicial power, but a reservation of jury power. It limits judicial power only to the extent that the claimed judicial power infringes on the province of the jury. Indeterminate sentencing does not do so. * * * Of course indeterminate schemes involve judicial factfinding, in that a judge (like a parole board) may implicitly rule on those facts he deems important to the exercise of his sentencing discretion. But the facts do not pertain to whether the defendant has a legal *right* to a lesser sentence—and that makes all the difference insofar as judicial impingement upon the traditional role of the jury is concerned. In a system that says the judge may punish burglary with 10 to 40 years, every burglar knows he is risking 40 years in jail. In a system that punishes burglary with a 10-year sentence, with another 30 added for use of a gun, the burglar who enters a home unarmed is *entitled* to no more than a 10-year sentence—and by reason of the Sixth Amendment the facts bearing upon that entitlement must be found by a jury.

But even assuming that restraint of judicial power unrelated to the jury's role is a Sixth Amendment objective, it is far from clear that *Apprendi* disserves that goal. Determinate judicial-factfinding schemes entail less judicial power than indeterminate schemes, but more judicial power than determinate *jury*-factfinding schemes. Whether *Apprendi* increases judicial power overall depends on what States with determinate judicial-factfinding schemes would do, given the choice between the two alternatives. * * * When the Kansas Supreme Court found *Apprendi* infirmities in that State's determinate-sentencing regime * * *, the legislature responded not by reestablishing indeterminate sentencing but by applying *Apprendi*'s requirements to its current regime. See Kan. Stat. Ann. § 21–4718.[b] The result was less, not more, judicial power.

Justice Breyer argues that *Apprendi* works to the detriment of criminal defendants who plead guilty by depriving them of the opportunity to argue sentencing factors to a judge. But nothing prevents a defendant from waiving his *Apprendi* rights. When a defendant pleads guilty, the State is free to seek judicial sentence enhancements so long as the defendant either stipulates to the relevant facts or consents to judicial factfinding. If appropriate waivers are procured, States may continue to offer judicial factfinding as a matter of course to all defendants who plead guilty. Even a defendant who stands trial may consent to judicial factfinding as to sentence enhancements, which may well be in his interest if relevant evidence would prejudice him at trial. * * *[12]

* * *

Ultimately, our decision cannot turn on whether or to what degree trial by jury impairs the efficiency or fairness of criminal justice. One can certainly argue that both these values would be better served by leaving justice entirely in the hands of professionals; many nations of the world, particularly those following civil-law traditions, take just that course. There is not one shred of doubt, however, about the Framers' paradigm for criminal justice: not the civil-law ideal of administrative perfection, but the common-law ideal of limited state power accomplished by strict division of authority between judge and jury. * * *

* * *

Petitioner was sentenced to prison for more than three years beyond what the law allowed for the crime to which he confessed, on the basis of a disputed finding that he had acted with "deliberate cruelty." The Framers would not have thought it too much to demand that, before depriving a man of three more years of his liberty, the State should suffer the modest

---

     [b]   This Kansas statute requires a prosecutor seeking an upward durational departure in a defendant's sentence to file a pretrial motion, generally thirty days before trial. The court then decides whether the facts supporting the departure will be presented at trial or, alternatively, to the jury following the adjudication of the defendant's guilt or innocence. Absent a waiver of the jury-trial right, a jury must find beyond a reasonable doubt the fact or facts (other than facts regarding the defendant's prior convictions) justifying an upward departure.

     [12]   Justice Breyer responds that States are not *required* to give defendants the option of waiving jury trial on some elements but not others. True enough. But why would the States that he asserts we are coercing into hard-heartedness—that is, States that *want* judge-pronounced determinate sentencing to be the norm but we won't let them—want to prevent a defendant from *choosing* that regime? Justice Breyer claims this alternative may prove "too expensive and unwieldy for States to provide," but there is no obvious reason why forcing defendants to choose between contesting all elements of his hypothetical 17-element robbery crime and contesting none of them is less expensive than also giving them the third option of pleading guilty to some elements and submitting the rest to judicial factfinding. * * *

inconvenience of submitting its accusation to "the unanimous suffrage of twelve of his equals and neighbors."

* * *

JUSTICE O'CONNOR, with whom JUSTICE BREYER joins, and with whom THE CHIEF JUSTICE and JUSTICE KENNEDY join as to all but Part IV–B, dissenting.

The legacy of today's opinion, whether intended or not, will be the consolidation of sentencing power in the State and Federal Judiciaries. The Court says to Congress and state legislatures: If you want to constrain the sentencing discretion of judges and bring some uniformity to sentencing, it will cost you—dearly. * * *

One need look no further than the history leading up to and following the enactment of Washington's guidelines scheme to appreciate the damage that today's decision will cause. Prior to 1981, Washington, like most other States and the Federal Government, employed an indeterminate sentencing scheme. Washington's criminal code separated all felonies into three broad categories: "class A," carrying a sentence of 20 years to life; "class B," carrying a sentence of 0 to 10 years; and "class C," carrying a sentence of 0 to 5 years. Sentencing judges, in conjunction with parole boards, had virtually unfettered discretion to sentence defendants to prison terms falling anywhere within the statutory range, including probation—i.e., no jail sentence at all.

This system of unguided discretion inevitably resulted in severe disparities in sentences received and served by defendants committing the same offense and having similar criminal histories. Indeed, rather than reflect legally relevant criteria, these disparities too often were correlated with constitutionally suspect variables such as race.

To counteract these trends, the state legislature passed the Sentencing Reform Act of 1981. * * * The Act * * * placed meaningful constraints on discretion to sentence offenders within the statutory ranges, and eliminated parole. * * *

Far from disregarding principles of due process and the jury trial right, as the majority today suggests, Washington's reform has served them. Before passage of the Act, a defendant charged with second degree kidnapping, like petitioner, had no idea whether he would receive a 10-year sentence or probation. The ultimate sentencing determination could turn as much on the idiosyncrasies of a particular judge as on the specifics of the defendant's crime or background. A defendant did not know what facts, if any, about his offense or his history would be considered relevant by the sentencing judge or by the parole board. After passage of the Act, a defendant charged with second degree kidnapping knows what his presumptive sentence will be; he has a good idea of the types of factors that a sentencing judge can and will consider when deciding whether to sentence him outside that range; he is guaranteed meaningful appellate review to protect against an arbitrary sentence. Criminal defendants still face the same statutory maximum sentences, but they now at least know, much more than before, the real consequences of their actions.

Washington's move to a system of guided discretion has served equal protection principles as well. Over the past 20 years, there has been a substantial reduction in racial disparity in sentencing across the State. * * *

* * * While not a constitutional prohibition on guidelines schemes, the majority's decision today exacts a substantial constitutional tax.

The costs are substantial and real. Under the majority's approach, any fact that increases the upper bound on a judge's sentencing discretion is an element of the offense. Thus, facts that historically have been taken into account by sentencing judges to assess a sentence within a broad range—such as drug quantity, role in the offense, risk of bodily harm—all must now be charged in an indictment and submitted to a jury, simply because it is the legislature, rather than the judge, that constrains the extent to which such facts may be used to impose a sentence within a pre-existing statutory range.

While that alone is enough to threaten the continued use of sentencing guidelines schemes, there are additional costs. For example, a legislature might rightly think that some factors bearing on sentencing, such as prior bad acts or criminal history, should not be considered in a jury's determination of a defendant's guilt—such "character evidence" has traditionally been off limits during the guilt phase of criminal proceedings because of its tendency to inflame the passions of the jury. If a legislature desires uniform consideration of such factors at sentencing, but does not want them to impact a jury's initial determination of guilt, the State may have to bear the additional expense of a separate, full-blown jury trial during the penalty phase proceeding.

* * *

* * * A rule of deferring to legislative labels * * * would be easier to administer than the majority's rule, inasmuch as courts would not be forced to look behind statutes and regulations to determine whether a particular fact does or does not increase the penalty to which a defendant was exposed.

The majority is correct that rigid adherence to such an approach *could conceivably* produce absurd results * * *. The pre-*Apprendi* rule of deference to the legislature retains a built-in political check to prevent lawmakers from shifting the prosecution for crimes to the penalty phase proceedings of lesser included and easier-to-prove offenses—*e.g.*, the majority's hypothesized prosecution of murder in the guise of a traffic offense sentencing proceeding. * * *

* * *

The consequences of today's decision will be as far reaching as they are disturbing. Washington's sentencing system is by no means unique. Numerous other States have enacted guidelines systems, as has the Federal Government. Today's decision casts constitutional doubt over them all * * *.

* * *

JUSTICE KENNEDY, with whom JUSTICE BREYER joins, dissenting. [Opinion omitted.]

JUSTICE BREYER, with whom JUSTICE O'CONNOR joins, dissenting.

* * *

* * * As a result of the majority's rule, sentencing must now take one of three forms, each of which risks either impracticality, unfairness, or harm to the jury trial right the majority purports to strengthen. This circumstance shows that the majority's Sixth Amendment interpretation cannot be right.

A

A first option for legislators is to create a simple, pure or nearly pure "charge offense" or "determinate" sentencing system. In such a system, an indictment would charge a few facts which, taken together, constitute a crime, such as robbery. Robbery would carry a single sentence, say, five years' imprisonment. And every person convicted of robbery would receive that sentence * * *.

Such a system assures uniformity, but at intolerable costs. First, simple determinate sentencing systems impose identical punishments on people who committed their crimes in very different ways. When dramatically different conduct ends up being punished the same way, an injustice has taken place. * * *

Second, in a world of statutorily fixed mandatory sentences for many crimes, determinate sentencing gives tremendous power to prosecutors to manipulate sentences through their choice of charges. * * *

B

A second option for legislators is to return to a system of indeterminate sentencing * * *.

* * *

Returning to such a system * * * would do little to "ensur[e] [the] control" of what the majority calls "the peopl[e,]" *i.e.,* the jury, "in the judiciary," since "the peopl[e]" would only decide the defendant's guilt, a finding with no effect on the duration of the sentence. While "the judge's authority to sentence" would formally derive from the jury's verdict, the jury would exercise little or no control over the sentence itself. * * *

C

A third option is that which the Court seems to believe legislators will in fact take. That is the option of retaining structured schemes that attempt to punish similar conduct similarly and different conduct differently, but modifying them to conform to *Apprendi*'s dictates. Judges would be able to depart *downward* from presumptive sentences upon finding that mitigating factors were present, but would not be able to depart *upward* unless the prosecutor charged the aggravating fact to a jury and proved it beyond a reasonable doubt. * * *

This option can be implemented in one of two ways. The first way would be for legislatures to subdivide each crime into a list of complex crimes, each of which would be defined to include commonly found sentencing factors such as drug quantity, type of victim, presence of violence, degree of injury, use of gun, and so on. * * *

* * * The prosecutor, through control of the precise charge, controls the punishment, thereby marching the sentencing system directly away from, not toward, one important guideline goal: rough uniformity of punishment for those who engage in roughly the same *real* criminal conduct. The artificial (and consequently unfair) nature of the resulting sentence is aggravated by the fact that prosecutors must charge all relevant facts about the way the crime was committed before a presentence investigation examines the criminal conduct, perhaps before the trial itself, *i.e.,* before many of the facts relevant to punishment are known.

This "complex charge offense" system also prejudices defendants who seek trial, for it can put them in the untenable position of contesting material aggravating facts in the guilt phases of their trials. Consider a defendant who is charged, not with mere possession of cocaine, but with the specific offense of possession of more than 500 grams of cocaine. Or consider a defendant charged, not with murder, but with the new crime of murder using a machete. Or consider a defendant whom the prosecution wants to claim was a "supervisor," rather than an ordinary gang member. How can a Constitution that guarantees due process put these defendants, as a matter of course, in the position of arguing, "I did not sell drugs, and if I did, I did not sell more than 500 grams" or, "I did not kill him, and if I did, I did not use a machete," or "I did not engage in gang activity, and certainly not as a supervisor" to a single jury? * * *

* * * States may very well decide that they will *not* permit defendants to carve subsets of facts out of the new, *Apprendi*-required 17-element robbery crime, seeking a judicial determination as to some of those facts and a jury determination as to others. Instead, States may simply require defendants to plead guilty to all 17 elements or proceed with a (likely prejudicial) trial on all 17 elements.

* * *

The second way to make sentencing guidelines *Apprendi*-compliant would be to require at least two juries for each defendant whenever aggravating facts are present: one jury to determine guilt of the crime charged, and an additional jury to try the disputed facts that, if found, would aggravate the sentence. Our experience with bifurcated trials in the capital punishment context suggests that requiring them for run-of-the-mill sentences would be costly, both in money and in judicial time and resources. * * *

* * *

D

* * * The simple fact is that the design of any fair sentencing system must involve efforts to make practical compromises among competing goals. The majority's reading of the Sixth Amendment makes the effort to find those compromises—already difficult—virtually impossible.

* * *

[O]ur modern, pre-*Apprendi* cases made clear that legislatures could, within broad limits, distinguish between "sentencing facts" and "elements of crimes." * * *

Is there a risk of unfairness involved in permitting Congress to make this labeling decision? Of course. As we have recognized, the "tail" of the sentencing fact might "wa[g] the dog of the substantive offense." Congress might permit a judge to sentence an individual for murder though convicted only of making an illegal lane change. But that is the kind of problem that the Due Process Clause is well suited to cure. * * *

* * *

QUESTIONS AND POINTS FOR DISCUSSION

1.   In United States v. Booker, 543 U.S. 220, 125 S.Ct. 738 (2005), the Supreme Court held that there was "no distinction of constitutional significance" between the federal sentencing guidelines and the sentencing structure in the state of Washington deemed unconstitutional in *Blakely*. Id. at 733, 125 S.Ct. at 749. The defendant in *Booker* was charged with a drug offense punishable by up to life in prison. The jury found that the defendant had possessed 92.5 grams of crack cocaine. In the absence of any additional

factual findings, the jury's verdict would have required the judge to impose a prison sentence under the federal sentencing guidelines falling between 210 and 262 months. However, the sentencing judge found by a preponderance of the evidence that the defendant had possessed an additional 566 grams of crack cocaine and had obstructed justice. The guidelines therefore required the judge to choose a sentence from a higher sentencing range: 360 months to life imprisonment. The judge imposed a thirty-year sentence on the defendant.

Because the defendant's sentence exceeded the maximum sentence authorized by the facts reflected in the jury's verdict, the Supreme Court held that the sentence violated the defendant's Sixth Amendment right to a jury trial. Turning to the question of how to remedy the Sixth Amendment problem with the federal guidelines, the Court concluded that the guidelines would remain in effect but be advisory, rather than mandatory. In other words, federal judges would consult the guidelines when deciding what sentence to impose on a defendant but would not be bound by them.

The Court furthermore found that this modified sentencing structure necessitated changes in the standards applied by federal appellate courts when reviewing sentences on appeal. In 2003, Congress had enacted legislation requiring appellate courts to conduct a *de novo* review of a sentence when a sentencing judge had departed from the presumptive sentencing range set forth in the sentencing guidelines. The purpose of this legislation was to curtail judicial discretion when sentencing federal defendants, a purpose that the Court in *Booker* considered at odds with what were now advisory guidelines. Consequently, the Court announced that federal sentences henceforth would be reviewed on appeal for "unreasonable[ness]." Id. at 261, 125 S.Ct. at 765.

2.   Justice Thomas has charged that the Supreme Court's decision to remedy the Sixth Amendment problem with the federal sentencing guidelines by treating them as advisory has forced the Court to perform the "legislative role" of creating a new sentencing structure. Kimbrough v. United States, 552 U.S. 85, 115, 128 S.Ct. 558, 578 (2007) (Thomas, J., dissenting). After reading again the discussion on pages 133–135 of Supreme Court cases explaining how to apply the federal sentencing guidelines at the time of sentencing and on appeal, consider whether you agree with this criticism. If so, should the Court, as Justice Thomas suggested, have continued to view the guidelines as mandatory but require a jury to resolve factual questions bearing on a sentence when the Sixth Amendment so dictates? Or should the Court simply have left to Congress the question of how to remediate the Sixth Amendment problem with the guidelines?

3.   If the federal sentencing guidelines had remained mandatory, would judicial factfinding when applying the guidelines necessarily have violated the Sixth Amendment right to a jury trial and the due-process right to have an element of a crime established beyond a reasonable doubt? After answering this question, consider the following comments of Justice Stevens in *Booker*:

> * * * To be clear, our holding * * * that *Blakely* applies to the Guidelines does not establish the "impermissibility of judicial

factfinding." Instead, judicial factfinding to support an offense level determination or an enhancement is *only unconstitutional when that finding raises the sentence beyond the sentence that could have lawfully been imposed by reference to facts found by the jury or admitted by the defendant.* This distinction is crucial to a proper understanding of why the Guidelines could easily function as they are currently written.

Consider, for instance, a case in which the defendant's initial sentencing range under the Guidelines is 130-to-162 months, calculated by combining a base offense level of 28 and a criminal history category of V. Depending upon the particular offense, the sentencing judge may use her discretion to select any sentence within this range, even if her selection relies upon factual determinations beyond the facts found by the jury. If the defendant described above also possessed a firearm, the Guidelines would direct the judge to apply a two-level enhancement * * *, which would raise the defendant's total offense level from 28 to 30. That, in turn, would raise the defendant's eligible sentencing range to 151-to-188 months. That act of judicial factfinding would comply with the Guidelines and the Sixth Amendment so long as the sentencing judge then selected a sentence between 151-to-162 months—the lower number (151) being the bottom of offense level 30 and the higher number (162) being the maximum sentence under level 28, which is the upper limit of the range supported by the jury findings alone. This type of overlap between sentencing ranges is the rule, not the exception, in the Guidelines as currently constituted. * * * The interaction of these various Guidelines provisions demonstrates the fallacy in the assumption that judicial factfinding can never be constitutional under the Guidelines.

Id. at 278–79, 125 S.Ct. at 775–76 (Stevens, J., dissenting in part).

4. In Cunningham v. California, 549 U.S. 270, 127 S.Ct. 856 (2007), the Supreme Court ruled that California's determinate-sentencing law violated the constitutional right to have a jury find a fact beyond a reasonable doubt when it will subject a defendant to an elevated sentence—one beyond that authorized by the jury's verdict at trial or the defendant's factual admissions to the court. That law had directed the sentencing judge to impose the middle of three potential imprisonment terms unless the court identified aggravating circumstances warranting imposition of the elevated sentence (or mitigating circumstances justifying imposition of the "lower term").

5. In both McMillan v. Pennsylvania, 477 U.S. 79, 106 S.Ct. 2411 (1986) and Harris v. United States, 536 U.S. 545, 122 S.Ct. 2406 (2008), the Supreme Court considered and rejected the claim that the judicial fact-finding that led to the imposition of a mandatory-minimum sentence abridged the Constitution. Writing for a plurality of the Court in *Harris*, Justice Kennedy noted: "That a fact affects the defendant's sentence, even dramatically so, does

not by itself make it an element." Id. at 566, 122 S.Ct. at 2419. Interestingly, a majority of the Court in *Harris*—the four dissenters (Justices Thomas, Stevens, Souter, and Ginsburg) and Justice Breyer, who wrote a concurring opinion—found the logic of *Apprendi* difficult to distinguish from the fact-finding triggering a mandatory-minimum sentence. But because Justice Breyer disagreed with *Apprendi*, he refused to extend its scope even further.

In the case below, the Supreme Court once again revisited the implications of *Apprendi* to mandatory-minimum sentences.

ALLEYNE V. UNITED STATES

Supreme Court of the United States, 2013.
570 U.S. 99, 133 S.Ct. 2151, 186 L.Ed.2d 314.

JUSTICE THOMAS announced the judgment of the Court and delivered the opinion of the Court with respect to Parts I, III-B, III-C, and IV, and an opinion with respect to Parts II and III-A, in which JUSTICE GINSBURG, JUSTICE SOTOMAYOR, and JUSTICE KAGAN join.

* * *

I

Petitioner Allen Ryan Alleyne and an accomplice devised a plan to rob a store manager as he drove the store's daily deposits to a local bank. By feigning car trouble, they tricked the manager to stop. Alleyne's accomplice approached the manager with a gun and demanded the store's deposits, which the manager surrendered. Alleyne was later charged with multiple federal offenses, including robbery affecting interstate commerce, 18 U.S.C. § 1951(a), and using or carrying a firearm in relation to a crime of violence, § 924(c)(1)(A). Section 924(c)(1)(A) provides, in relevant part, that anyone who "uses or carries a firearm" in relation to a "crime of violence" shall:

"(i) be sentenced to a term of imprisonment of not less than 5 years;

"(ii) if the firearm is brandished, be sentenced to a term of imprisonment of not less than 7 years * * *."

The jury convicted Alleyne. The jury indicated on the verdict form that Alleyne had "[u]sed or carried a firearm during and in relation to a crime of violence," but did not indicate a finding that the firearm was "[b]randished."

The presentence report recommended a 7-year sentence on the § 924(c) count, which reflected the mandatory minimum sentence for cases in which a firearm has been "brandished." Alleyne objected to this recommendation. He argued that it was clear from the verdict form that the jury did not find brandishing beyond a reasonable doubt and that he was subject only to the

5-year minimum for "us[ing] or carr[ying] a firearm." Alleyne contended that raising his mandatory minimum sentence based on a sentencing judge's finding that he brandished a firearm would violate his Sixth Amendment right to a jury trial.

The District Court overruled Alleyne's objection. * * * It found that the evidence supported a finding of brandishing, and sentenced Alleyne to seven years' imprisonment on the § 924(c) count. The Court of Appeals affirmed * * *.

* * *

[III] B

* * *

* * * *Apprendi* concluded that any "facts that increase the prescribed range of penalties to which a criminal defendant is exposed" are elements of the crime. * * *

It is indisputable that a fact triggering a mandatory minimum alters the prescribed range of sentences to which a criminal defendant is exposed. But for a finding of brandishing, the penalty is five years to life in prison; with a finding of brandishing, the penalty becomes seven years to life. Just as the maximum of life marks the outer boundary of the range, so seven years marks its floor. And because the legally prescribed range *is* the penalty affixed to the crime, it follows that a fact increasing either end of the range produces a new penalty and constitutes an ingredient of the offense.

* * * [C]riminal statutes have long specified both the floor and ceiling of sentence ranges, which is evidence that both define the legally prescribed penalty. This historical practice allowed those who violated the law to know, *ex ante,* the contours of the penalty that the legislature affixed to the crime—and comports with the obvious truth that the floor of a mandatory range is as relevant to wrongdoers as the ceiling. A fact that increases a sentencing floor, thus, forms an essential ingredient of the offense.

Moreover, it is impossible to dispute that facts increasing the legally prescribed floor *aggravate* the punishment. Elevating the low-end of a sentencing range heightens the loss of liberty associated with the crime: the defendant's "expected punishment has increased as a result of the narrowed range" and "the prosecution is empowered, by invoking the mandatory minimum, to require the judge to impose a higher punishment than he might wish." * * * This reality demonstrates that the core crime and the fact triggering the mandatory minimum sentence together constitute a new, aggravated crime, each element of which must be submitted to the jury.[2]

* * *

* * * It is no answer to say that the defendant could have received the same sentence with or without that fact. * * *

[B]ecause the fact of brandishing aggravates the legally prescribed range of allowable sentences, it constitutes an element of a separate, aggravated offense that must be found by the jury, regardless of what sentence the defendant *might* have received if a different range had been applicable. Indeed, if a judge were to find a fact that increased the statutory maximum sentence, such a finding would violate the Sixth Amendment, even if the defendant ultimately received a sentence falling within the original sentencing range (*i.e.,* the range applicable without that aggravating fact). * * *

* * *

C

In holding that facts that increase mandatory minimum sentences must be submitted to the jury, we take care to note what our holding does not entail. Our ruling today does not mean that any fact that influences judicial discretion must be found by a jury. * * * Our decision today is wholly consistent with the broad discretion of judges to select a sentence within the range authorized by law.

IV

Here, the sentencing range supported by the jury's verdict was five years' imprisonment to life. The District Court imposed the 7-year mandatory minimum sentence based on its finding by a preponderance of evidence that the firearm was "brandished." Because the finding of brandishing increased the penalty to which the defendant was subjected, it was an element, which had to be found by the jury beyond a reasonable doubt. * * *

* * *

JUSTICE SOTOMAYOR, with whom JUSTICE GINSBURG and JUSTICE KAGAN join, concurring. [Opinion omitted.]

---

[2] Juries must find any facts that increase either the statutory maximum or minimum because the Sixth Amendment applies where a finding of fact both alters the legally prescribed range *and* does so in a way that aggravates the penalty. Importantly, this is distinct from factfinding used to guide judicial discretion in selecting a punishment "within limits fixed by law." While such findings of fact may lead judges to select sentences that are more severe than the ones they would have selected without those facts, the Sixth Amendment does not govern that element of sentencing.

JUSTICE BREYER, concurring in part and concurring in the judgment.

* * * I continue to disagree with *Apprendi*. * * * But *Apprendi* has now defined the relevant legal regime for an additional decade. * * *

* * *

[I]t seems to me highly anomalous to read *Apprendi* as insisting that juries find sentencing facts that *permit* a judge to impose a higher sentence while not insisting that juries find sentencing facts that *require* a judge to impose a higher sentence.

[T]o apply *Apprendi*'s basic jury-determination rule to mandatory minimum sentences would erase that anomaly. Where a *maximum* sentence is at issue, *Apprendi* means that a judge who *wishes* to impose a higher sentence cannot do so unless a jury finds the requisite statutory factual predicate. Where a *mandatory minimum* sentence is at issue, application of *Apprendi* would mean that the government cannot force a judge who *does not wish* to impose a higher sentence to do so unless a jury finds the requisite statutory factual predicate. In both instances the matter concerns higher sentences; in both instances factfinding must trigger the increase; in both instances jury-based factfinding would act as a check: in the first instance, against a sentencing judge wrongly imposing the higher sentence that the judge believes is appropriate, and in the second instance, against a sentencing judge wrongly being required to impose the higher sentence that the judge believes is inappropriate.

* * *

CHIEF JUSTICE ROBERTS, with whom JUSTICE SCALIA and JUSTICE KENNEDY join, dissenting.

Suppose a jury convicts a defendant of a crime carrying a sentence of five to ten years. And suppose the judge says he would sentence the defendant to five years, but because he finds that the defendant used a gun during the crime, he is going to add two years and sentence him to seven. No one thinks that this violates the defendant's right to a jury trial in any way.

Now suppose the legislature says that two years should be added to the five year minimum, if the judge finds that the defendant used a gun during the crime. Such a provision affects the role of the judge—limiting his discretion—but has no effect on the role of the jury. And because it does not affect the jury's role, it does not violate the jury trial guarantee of the Sixth Amendment.

The Framers envisioned the Sixth Amendment as a protection for defendants from the power of the Government. The Court transforms it into a protection for judges from the power of the legislature. * * *

* * *

* * * Our holdings that a judge may not sentence a defendant to more than the jury has authorized properly preserve the jury right as a guard against judicial overreaching.

There is no such risk of judicial overreaching here. * * *

* * *

In my view, that is enough to resolve this case. The jury's verdict authorized the judge to impose the precise sentence he imposed for the precise factual reason he imposed it. * * *

* * *

I find this new rule impossible to square with the historical understanding of the jury right as a defense *from* judges, not a defense *of* judges. * * *

* * *

* * * [T]he fact that statutes have long specified both floor and ceiling is evidence of nothing more than that statutes have long specified both the floor and the ceiling. Nor does it help to say that "the floor of a mandatory range is as relevant to wrongdoers as the ceiling." The meaning of the Sixth Amendment does not turn on what wrongdoers care about most.

* * *

[T]he majority offers that "it is impossible to dispute that facts increasing the legally prescribed floor *aggravate* the punishment." This argument proves too much, for it would apply with equal force to any fact which leads the judge, in the exercise of his own discretion, to choose a penalty higher than he otherwise would have chosen. The majority nowhere explains what it is about the jury right that bars a determination by Congress that brandishing (or any other fact) makes an offense worth two extra years, but not an identical determination by a judge. Simply calling one "aggravation" and the other "discretion" does not do the trick.

JUSTICE ALITO, dissenting. [Opinion omitted.]

QUESTIONS AND POINTS FOR DISCUSSION

1.   In your opinion, does it matter, for constitutional purposes, whether a fact raises the floor or the ceiling of the punishment to which a defendant may be subject? Why or why not?

2.   When a defendant is convicted of multiple crimes, the sentences will be served either consecutively or concurrently. If the judge imposes consecutive sentences, the defendant will serve the first sentence and then the second. For example, if the defendant receives two ten-year sentences to be served consecutively, the defendant will be imprisoned for twenty years. By contrast,

if the ten-year sentences are concurrent, the defendant will serve them at the same time and be confined for ten years.

Assume a state statute prohibits the imposition of consecutive sentences for crimes committed in a "single course of conduct" unless one of the crimes was a Class X or Class 1 felony and the defendant caused "severe bodily injury" to someone during the crime. Assume also that a defendant was convicted of armed robbery and aggravated battery. At the sentencing hearing, the judge found that the defendant had inflicted severe bodily injury during the armed robbery, a Class X felony. Consequently, the judge imposed a 29-year sentence for the armed robbery and a ten-year sentence for the aggravated battery, with the sentences to run consecutively. In your opinion, were the defendant's constitutional rights abridged by this judicial fact-finding?

In Oregon v. Ice, 555 U.S. 160, 129 S.Ct. 711 (2009), the Supreme Court held, in a 5–4 decision, that there is no Sixth Amendment right to have a jury find beyond a reasonable doubt a fact necessary for the imposition of consecutive sentences. The Court underscored that historically judges have had full discretion to impose either concurrent or consecutive sentences. The Court further observed: "All agree that a scheme making consecutive sentences the rule, and concurrent sentences the exception, encounters no Sixth Amendment shoal. To hem in States by holding that they may not equally choose to make concurrent sentences the rule, and consecutive sentences the exception, would make scant sense." Id. at 171, 129 S.Ct. at 719.

Because the defendant in *Oregon v. Ice* received consecutive, not concurrent, sentences, he was sentenced to prison for 340 months, as opposed to ninety. If you had been charged with writing the dissenting opinion in that case, what arguments would you have made? Compare your arguments with those of Justice Scalia, who wrote the dissenting opinion in *Ice*.

3. How would you differentiate between sentencing factors and elements of a crime? Under your approach, would the outcomes in *Almendarez-Torres, Apprendi, Blakely, Booker, Alleyne,* or *Oregon v. Ice* have been different?

2. AGGRAVATING SENTENCING FACTORS

Facts considered aggravating sentencing factors, not elements of the crime, continue to play a significant role in sentencing. For example, when sentencing guidelines establish a presumption that a sentence will fall within a prescribed range, such as two to four years, the existence of a particular aggravating factor may lead a judge to impose a sentence on the higher end of that range. Aggravating factors may influence the selection of a sentence under advisory sentencing guidelines as well. And in a jurisdiction with indeterminate sentencing or determinate-discretionary sentencing, a finding of an aggravating factor may lead a judge to impose a higher sentence within the statutory sentencing range than the judge otherwise would have imposed.

In McMillan v. Pennsylvania, 477 U.S. 79, 106 S.Ct. 2411 (1986), the Supreme Court held that the prosecution does not have to prove the existence of an aggravating factor by clear and convincing evidence. The clear-and-convincing-evidence standard of proof is higher than the preponderance-of-the-evidence standard, which requires proof that a fact is more likely than not to exist, though lower than the standard of proof beyond a reasonable doubt. Noting that "sentencing courts have always operated without constitutionally imposed burdens of proof," the Court stated that requiring aggravating factors to be established by clear and convincing evidence would "significantly alter criminal sentencing." Id. at 92 n.8, 106 S.Ct. at 2419 n.8.

Because the statute whose constitutionality was at issue in *McMillan* required a court to find, by a preponderance of the evidence, that what the Supreme Court deemed an aggravating factor existed, the Court did not need to resolve whether due process requires the government to prove an aggravating factor by a preponderance of the evidence. How would you answer this question?

3.　MITIGATING SENTENCING FACTORS

While prosecutors often cite aggravating factors to support the imposition of a more stringent sentence on a defendant, defendants often argue that mitigating factors warrant imposition of a more lenient sentence. Whatever the government's burden of proof with respect to aggravating facts that do not constitute elements of the crime, due process is not violated when the burden of proving mitigating circumstances by a preponderance of the evidence is placed on a defendant, even in a death-penalty case. Walton v. Arizona, 497 U.S. 639, 650, 110 S.Ct. 3047, 3055 (1990). Courts have reasoned that it is fundamentally fair to place the burden on a defendant of proving the facts about such things as family stability, educational background, and employment history of which the defendant, but not the government, is readily aware.

F.　NONCONSTITUTIONAL SOURCES OF SENTENCING RIGHTS

Apart from the procedural safeguards required by the United States Constitution during the sentencing process, additional rights may be bestowed by state constitutions, statutes, court rules, and sentencing guidelines. An example of one such source of additional rights is Rule 32 of the Federal Rules of Criminal Procedure, which governs sentencing proceedings in the federal courts. Pertinent excerpts from Rule 32 are set forth below. As you review the rule, consider how, if at all, you would revise it.

Rule 32. Sentencing and Judgment

* * *

(b) Time of Sentencing.

(1) In General. The court must impose sentence without unnecessary delay.

(2) Changing Time Limits. The court may, for good cause, change any time limits prescribed in this rule.

(c) Presentence Investigation.

(1) Required Investigation.

(A) In General. The probation officer must conduct a presentence investigation and submit a report to the court before it imposes sentence unless:

(i) 18 U.S.C. § 3593(c) or another statute requires otherwise; or

(ii) the court finds that the information in the record enables it to meaningfully exercise its sentencing authority under 18 U.S.C. § 3553, and the court explains its finding on the record.

(B) Restitution. If the law requires restitution, the probation officer must conduct an investigation and submit a report that contains sufficient information for the court to order restitution.

(2) Interviewing the Defendant. The probation officer who interviews a defendant as part of a presentence investigation must, on request, give the defendant's attorney notice and a reasonable opportunity to attend the interview.

(d) Presentence Report.

(1) Applying the Advisory Sentencing Guidelines. The presentence report must:

(A) identify all applicable guidelines and policy statements of the Sentencing Commission;

(B) calculate the defendant's offense level and criminal history category;

(C) state the resulting sentencing range and kinds of sentences available;

(D) identify any factor relevant to:

(i) the appropriate kind of sentence, or

(ii) the appropriate sentence within the applicable sentencing range; and

(E) identify any basis for departing from the applicable sentencing range.

(2) Additional Information. The presentence report must also contain the following:

(A) the defendant's history and characteristics, including:

(i) any prior criminal record;

(ii) the defendant's financial condition; and

(iii) any circumstances affecting the defendant's behavior that may be helpful in imposing sentence or in correctional treatment;

(B) information that assesses any financial, social, psychological, and medical impact on any victim;

(C) when appropriate, the nature and extent of nonprison programs and resources available to the defendant;

(D) when the law provides for restitution, information sufficient for a restitution order;

(E) if the court orders a study under 18 U.S.C. § 3552(b),[c] any resulting report and recommendation;

(F) a statement of whether the government seeks forfeiture under Rule 32.2 and any other law; and

(G) any other information that the court requires, including information relevant to the factors under 18 U.S.C. § 3553(a).

(3) Exclusions. The presentence report must exclude the following:

(A) any diagnoses that, if disclosed, might seriously disrupt a rehabilitation program;

(B) any sources of information obtained upon a promise of confidentiality; and

(C) any other information that, if disclosed, might result in physical or other harm to the defendant or others.

---

[c] 18 U.S.C. § 3552(b) authorizes a sentencing judge who wants more information about a defendant before imposing sentence to order a study of the defendant by "qualified consultants" within the community or, where there is a "compelling reason" or inadequate professional resources to conduct the study in the community, by the Bureau of Prisons.

(e) Disclosing the Report and Recommendation.

(1) Time to Disclose. Unless the defendant has consented in writing, the probation officer must not submit a presentence report to the court or disclose its contents to anyone until the defendant has pleaded guilty or nolo contendere, or has been found guilty.

(2) Minimum Required Notice. The probation officer must give the presentence report to the defendant, the defendant's attorney, and an attorney for the government at least 35 days before sentencing unless the defendant waives this minimum period.

(3) Sentence Recommendation. By local rule or by order in a case, the court may direct the probation officer not to disclose to anyone other than the court the officer's recommendation on the sentence.

(f) Objecting to the Report.

(1) Time to Object. Within 14 days after receiving the presentence report, the parties must state in writing any objections, including objections to material information, sentencing guideline ranges, and policy statements contained in or omitted from the report.

(2) Serving Objections. An objecting party must provide a copy of its objections to the opposing party and to the probation officer.

(3) Action on Objections. After receiving objections, the probation officer may meet with the parties to discuss the objections. The probation officer may then investigate further and revise the presentence report as appropriate.

(g) Submitting the Report. At least 7 days before sentencing, the probation officer must submit to the court and to the parties the presentence report and an addendum containing any unresolved objections, the grounds for those objections, and the probation officer's comments on them.

(h) Notice of Possible Departure from Sentencing Guidelines. Before the court may depart from the applicable sentencing range on a ground not identified for departure either in the presentence report or in a party's prehearing submission, the court must give the parties reasonable notice that it is contemplating such a departure. The notice must specify any ground on which the court is contemplating a departure.

(i) Sentencing.

(1) In General. At sentencing, the court:

(A) must verify that the defendant and the defendant's attorney have read and discussed the presentence report and any addendum to the report;

(B) must give to the defendant and an attorney for the government a written summary of—or summarize in camera—any information excluded from the presentence report under Rule 32(d)(3) on which the court will rely in sentencing, and give them a reasonable opportunity to comment on that information;

(C) must allow the parties' attorneys to comment on the probation officer's determinations and other matters relating to an appropriate sentence; and

(D) may, for good cause, allow a party to make a new objection at any time before sentence is imposed.

(2) Introducing Evidence; Producing a Statement. The court may permit the parties to introduce evidence on the objections. If a witness testifies at sentencing, Rule 26.2(a)–(d) and (f) applies.[d] If a party fails to comply with a Rule 26.2 order to produce a witness's statement, the court must not consider that witness's testimony.

(3) Court Determinations. At sentencing, the court:

(A) may accept any undisputed portion of the presentence report as a finding of fact;

(B) must—for any disputed portion of the presentence report or other controverted matter—rule on the dispute or determine that a ruling is unnecessary either because the matter will not affect sentencing, or because the court will not consider the matter in sentencing; and

(C) must append a copy of the court's determinations under this rule to any copy of the presentence report made available to the Bureau of Prisons.

(4) Opportunity to Speak.

(A) By a Party. Before imposing sentence, the court must:

(i) provide the defendant's attorney an opportunity to speak on the defendant's behalf;

(ii) address the defendant personally in order to permit the defendant to speak or present any information to mitigate the sentence; and

(iii) provide an attorney for the government an opportunity to speak equivalent to that of the defendant's attorney.

---

d   Rule 26.2(a) of the Federal Rules of Criminal Procedure requires the court to direct a party who has called a witness, other than the defendant, to testify to provide the other party, upon motion, with any statements of that witness bearing on the witness's testimony. Other sections of the rule further delineate the scope of this requirement.

(B) By a Victim. Before imposing sentence, the court must address any victim of the crime who is present at sentencing and must permit the victim to be reasonably heard.

(C) In Camera Proceedings. Upon a party's motion and for good cause, the court may hear in camera any statement made under Rule 32(i)(4).

(j) Defendant's Right to Appeal.

(1) Advice of a Right to Appeal.

(A) Appealing a Conviction. If the defendant pleaded not guilty and was convicted, after sentencing the court must advise the defendant of the right to appeal the conviction.

(B) Appealing a Sentence. After sentencing—regardless of the defendant's plea—the court must advise the defendant of any right to appeal the sentence.

(C) Appeal Costs. The court must advise a defendant who is unable to pay appeal costs of the right to ask for permission to appeal in forma pauperis.

(2) Clerk's Filing of Notice. If the defendant so requests, the clerk must immediately prepare and file a notice of appeal on the defendant's behalf.

* * *

CHAPTER 5

SENTENCING EVIDENCE

■ ■ ■

A. AGGRAVATING AND MITIGATING FACTORS

Separate and apart from the question on which the preceding chapter focused of the procedural rights a defendant has during the sentencing process is the question of what evidence or information can be considered when selecting a sentence. As the Supreme Court noted in Williams v. New York, 337 U.S. 241, 69 S.Ct. 1079 (1949), which is on page 140, courts have traditionally considered a wide range of facts about the defendant and the defendant's crime to inform the sentencing decision. Statutes and sentencing guidelines often delineate the factors to be considered by a judge when sentencing a defendant. The mitigating and aggravating factors outlined in the Illinois statutes set forth below exemplify the variety of factors that may enter into the sentencing decision.

730 ILL. COMP. STAT. 5/5–5–3.1 Factors in Mitigation

(a) The following grounds shall be accorded weight in favor of withholding or minimizing a sentence of imprisonment:

(1) The defendant's criminal conduct neither caused nor threatened serious physical harm to another.

(2) The defendant did not contemplate that his criminal conduct would cause or threaten serious physical harm to another.

(3) The defendant acted under a strong provocation.

(4) There were substantial grounds tending to excuse or justify the defendant's criminal conduct, though failing to establish a defense.

(5) The defendant's criminal conduct was induced or facilitated by someone other than the defendant.

(6) The defendant has compensated or will compensate the victim of his criminal conduct for the damage or injury that he sustained.

(7) The defendant has no history of prior delinquency or criminal activity or has led a law-abiding life for a substantial period of time before the commission of the present crime.

(8) The defendant's criminal conduct was the result of circumstances unlikely to recur.

(9)   The character and attitudes of the defendant indicate that he is unlikely to commit another crime.

(10) The defendant is particularly likely to comply with the terms of a period of probation.

(11) The imprisonment of the defendant would entail excessive hardship to his dependents.

(12) The imprisonment of the defendant would endanger his or her medical condition.

(13) The defendant was a person with an intellectual disability * * *.

(14) The defendant sought or obtained emergency medical assistance for an overdose and was convicted of a Class 3 felony or higher possession, manufacture, or delivery of a controlled, counterfeit, or look-alike substance or a controlled substance analog under the Illinois Controlled Substances Act or a Class 2 felony or higher possession, manufacture or delivery of methamphetamine under the Methamphetamine Control and Community Protection Act.

(15) At the time of the offense, the defendant is or had been the victim of domestic violence and the effects of the domestic violence tended to excuse or justify the defendant's criminal conduct. * * *.

(16) At the time of the offense, the defendant was suffering from a serious mental illness which, though insufficient to establish the defense of insanity, substantially affected his or her ability to understand the nature of his or her acts or to conform his or her conduct to the requirements of the law.

(b)   If the court, having due regard for the character of the offender, the nature and circumstances of the offense and the public interest finds that a sentence of imprisonment is the most appropriate disposition of the offender, or where other provisions of this Code mandate the imprisonment of the offender, the grounds listed in paragraph (a) of this subsection shall be considered as factors in mitigation of the term imposed.

730 ILL. COMP. STAT. 5/5–5–3.2 Factors in Aggravation * * *

(a)   The following factors shall be accorded weight in favor of imposing a term of imprisonment or may be considered by the court as reasons to impose a more severe sentence * * *:

(1)   the defendant's conduct caused or threatened serious harm;

(2)   the defendant received compensation for committing the offense;

(3)   the defendant has a history of prior delinquency or criminal activity;

(4) the defendant, by the duties of his office or by his position, was obliged to prevent the particular offense committed or to bring the offenders committing it to justice;

(5) the defendant held public office at the time of the offense, and the offense related to the conduct of that office;

(6) the defendant utilized his professional reputation or position in the community to commit the offense, or to afford him an easier means of committing it;

(7) the sentence is necessary to deter others from committing the same crime;

(8) the defendant committed the offense against a person 60 years of age or older or such person's property;

(9) the defendant committed the offense against a person who has a physical disability or such person's property;

(10) by reason of another individual's actual or perceived race, color, creed, religion, ancestry, gender, sexual orientation, physical or mental disability, or national origin, the defendant committed the offense against (i) the person or property of that individual; (ii) the person or property of a person who has an association with, is married to, or has a friendship with the other individual; or (iii) the person or property of a relative (by blood or marriage) of a person described in clause (i) or (ii). * * *;

(11) the offense took place in a place of worship or on the grounds of a place of worship, immediately prior to, during or immediately following worship services. * * *;

(12) the defendant was convicted of a felony committed while he was released on bail or his own recognizance pending trial for a prior felony and was convicted of such prior felony, or the defendant was convicted of a felony committed while he was serving a period of probation, conditional discharge, or mandatory supervised release * * * for a prior felony;

(13) the defendant committed or attempted to commit a felony while he was wearing a bulletproof vest. * * *;

(14) the defendant held a position of trust or supervision such as, but not limited to, family member as defined in Section 12–12 of the Criminal Code of 1961, teacher, scout leader, baby sitter, or day care worker, in relation to a victim under 18 years of age, and the defendant committed [one of several specified sexual crimes] * * * against that victim;

(15) the defendant committed an offense related to the activities of an organized gang. * * *;

(16) the defendant committed an offense in violation of [certain specified statutory provisions that prohibit an array of crimes, including sexual abuse and assault, kidnapping, aggravated assaults and batteries, juvenile prostitution, armed robbery, armed violence, and "compelled organization membership"] while in a school, regardless of the time of day or time of year; on any conveyance owned, leased, or contracted by a school to transport students to or from school or a school-related activity; on the real property of a school; or on a public way within 1,000 feet of the real property comprising any school * * *;

(16.5) the defendant committed an offense in violation of one of [the specified statutory provisions proscribing certain sex crimes] while in a day care center, regardless of the time of day or time of year; on the real property of a day care center, regardless of the time of day or time of year; or on a public way within 1,000 feet of the real property comprising any day care center, regardless of the time of day or time of year * * *;

(17) the defendant committed the offense by reason of any person's activity as a community policing volunteer or to prevent any person from engaging in activity as a community policing volunteer. * * *;

(18) the defendant committed the offense in a nursing home or on the real property comprising a nursing home. * * *;

(19) the defendant was a federally licensed firearm dealer and was previously convicted of a violation of subsection (a) of Section 3 of the Firearm Owners Identification Card Act and has now committed either a felony violation of the Firearm Owners Identification Card Act or an act of armed violence while armed with a firearm;

(20) the defendant (i) committed the offense of reckless homicide * * * or the offense of driving under the influence of alcohol, other drug or drugs, intoxicating compound or compounds or any combination thereof * * * and (ii) was operating a motor vehicle in excess of 20 miles per hour over the posted speed limit * * *;

(21) the defendant (i) committed the offense of reckless driving or aggravated reckless driving * * * and (ii) was operating a motor vehicle in excess of 20 miles per hour over the posted speed limit * * *;

(22) the defendant committed the offense against a person that the defendant knew, or reasonably should have known, was a member of the Armed Forces of the United States serving on active duty. * * *;

(23) the defendant committed the offense against a person who was elderly or infirm or who was a person with a disability by taking advantage of a family or fiduciary relationship with the elderly or infirm person or person with a disability;

(24) the defendant committed [the crime of child pornography] and possessed 100 or more images;

(25) the defendant committed the offense while the defendant or the victim was in a train, bus, or other vehicle used for public transportation;

(26) the defendant committed the offense of child pornography or aggravated child pornography * * * where a child engaged in, solicited for, depicted in, or posed in [certain described sexual acts and abuse];

(27) the defendant committed the offense of first-degree murder, assault, aggravated assault, battery, aggravated battery, robbery, armed robbery, or aggravated robbery against a person who was a veteran and the defendant knew, or reasonably should have known, that the person was a veteran performing duties as a representative of a veterans' organization. * * * ;

(28) the defendant committed the offense of assault, aggravated assault, battery, aggravated battery, robbery, armed robbery, or aggravated robbery against a person that the defendant knew or reasonably should have known was a letter carrier or postal worker while that person was performing his or her duties delivering mail for the United States Postal Service;

(29) the defendant committed the offense of criminal sexual assault, aggravated criminal sexual assault, criminal sexual abuse, or aggravated criminal sexual abuse against a victim with an intellectual disability, and the defendant holds a position of trust, authority, or supervision in relation to the victim; or

(30) the defendant committed the offense of promoting juvenile prostitution, patronizing a prostitute, or patronizing a minor engaged in prostitution and at the time of the commission of the offense knew that the prostitute or minor engaged in prostitution was in the custody or guardianship of the Department of Children and Family Services.

QUESTIONS AND POINTS FOR DISCUSSION

1.   Are there any additional aggravating or mitigating factors that should be added to the above lists? Are there any, in your opinion, that should be deleted?

2.   Assume that a defendant's initial prison sentence for a drug-related crime was set aside on appeal, and the case was remanded for resentencing. During the time between the two sentencing hearings, the defendant had taken significant steps to revamp his life. He had, for example, completed a 500-hour drug-treatment program and no longer used drugs. He was attending college and garnering high grades. And he had secured employment and commenced supporting his wife and child financially. In your opinion, should evidence of the defendant's post-sentence rehabilitation be a factor considered

when he is resentenced? How would you respond to the argument that the consideration of post-sentence rehabilitation will lead to disparity between those defendants who were first sentenced in error (and therefore had the opportunity to compile evidence of post-sentence rehabilitation) and those who were not? For one jurisdiction's response to these questions, see Pepper v. United States, 562 U.S. 476, 131 S.Ct. 1229 (2011) (holding that a federal court, at resentencing, can consider evidence of a defendant's post-sentence rehabilitation).

     3.   Section 2.D.2 of the Minnesota Sentencing Guidelines, on pages 113–114, lists facts, such as the defendant's educational level and employment status, that cannot be the basis for departing from the presumptive sentence spelled out in the guidelines. Do you agree that these facts should neither elevate nor decrease a sentence? Are there any other facts that you would bar a judge from considering when deciding a sentence's severity level?

B. OTHER CRIMINAL CONDUCT AND CONVICTIONS

UNITED STATES V. GRAYSON

Supreme Court of the United States, 1978.
438 U.S. 41, 98 S.Ct. 2610, 57 L.Ed.2d 582.

MR. CHIEF JUSTICE BURGER delivered the opinion of the Court.

We granted certiorari to review a holding of the Court of Appeals that it was improper for a sentencing judge, in fixing the sentence within the statutory limits, to give consideration to the defendant's false testimony observed by the judge during the trial.

I

In August 1975, respondent Grayson was confined in a federal prison camp under a conviction for distributing a controlled substance. In October, he escaped but was apprehended two days later by FBI agents in New York City. He was indicted for prison escape * * *.

* * *

Grayson testified in his own defense. He admitted leaving the camp but asserted that he did so out of fear: "I had just been threatened with a large stick with a nail protruding through it by an inmate that was serving time at Allenwood, and I was scared, and I just ran." He testified that the threat was made in the presence of many inmates by prisoner Barnes who sought to enforce collection of a gambling debt and followed other threats and physical assaults made for the same purpose. Grayson called one inmate, who testified: "I heard [Barnes] talk to Grayson in a loud voice one day, but that's all. I never seen no harm, no hands or no shuffling whatsoever."

Grayson's version of the facts was contradicted by the Government's rebuttal evidence and by cross-examination on crucial aspects of his story. For example, Grayson stated that after crossing the prison fence he left his prison jacket by the side of the road. On recross, he stated that he also left his prison shirt but not his trousers. Government testimony showed that on the morning after the escape, a shirt marked with Grayson's number, a jacket, and a pair of prison trousers were found outside a hole in the prison fence.[1] Grayson also testified on cross-examination: "I do believe that I phrased the rhetorical question to Captain Kurd, who was in charge of [the prison], and I think I said something if an inmate was being threatened by somebody, what would . . . he do? First of all he said he would want to know who it was." On further cross-examination, however, Grayson modified his description of the conversation. Captain Kurd testified that Grayson had never mentioned in any fashion threats from other inmates. Finally, the alleged assailant, Barnes, by then no longer an inmate, testified that Grayson had never owed him any money and that he had never threatened or physically assaulted Grayson.

The jury returned a guilty verdict * * *. At the sentencing hearing, the judge stated:

"I'm going to give my reasons for sentencing in this case with clarity, because one of the reasons may well be considered by a Court of Appeals to be impermissible; and although I could come into this Court Room and sentence this Defendant to a five-year prison term without any explanation at all, I think it is fair that I give the reasons so that if the Court of Appeals feels that one of the reasons which I am about to enunciate is an improper consideration for a trial judge, then the Court will be in a position to reverse this Court and send the case back for re-sentencing.

"In my view a prison sentence is indicated, and the sentence that the Court is going to impose is to deter you, Mr. Grayson, and others who are similarly situated. Secondly, *it is my view that your defense was a complete fabrication without the slightest merit whatsoever. I feel it is proper for me to consider that fact in the sentencing, and I will do so.*" (Emphasis added.)

He then sentenced Grayson to a term of two years' imprisonment, consecutive to his unexpired sentence.

---

[1] The testimony regarding the prison clothing was important for reasons in addition to the light it shed on quality of recollection. Grayson stated that after unpremeditatedly fleeing the prison with no possessions and crossing the fence, he hitchhiked to New York City—a difficult task for a man with no trousers. The United States suggested that by prearrangement Grayson met someone, possibly a woman friend, on the highway near the break in the fence and that this accomplice provided civilian clothes. It introduced evidence that the friend visited Grayson often at prison, including each of the three days immediately prior to his penultimate day in the camp.

On appeal, a divided panel of the Court of Appeals for the Third Circuit directed that Grayson's sentence be vacated and that he be resentenced by the District Court without consideration of false testimony. * * *

* * *

II

In *Williams v. New York,* 337 U.S. 241, 247 (1949), Mr. Justice Black observed that the "prevalent modern philosophy of penology [is] that the punishment should fit the offender and not merely the crime," and that, accordingly, sentences should be determined with an eye toward the "[r]eformation and rehabilitation of offenders." * * *

* * *

A defendant's truthfulness or mendacity while testifying on his own behalf, almost without exception, has been deemed probative of his attitudes toward society and prospects for rehabilitation and hence relevant to sentencing. Soon after *Williams* was decided, the Tenth Circuit concluded that "the attitude of a convicted defendant with respect to his willingness to commit a serious crime [perjury] . . . is a proper matter to consider in determining what sentence shall be imposed within the limitations fixed by statute." *Humes v. United States,* 186 F.2d 875, 878 (1951). * * *

Only one Circuit has directly rejected the probative value of the defendant's false testimony in his own defense. In *Scott v. United States,* 135 U.S.App.D.C. 377, 382, 419 F.2d 264, 269 (1969), the court argued that

> "the peculiar pressures placed upon a defendant threatened with jail and the stigma of conviction make his willingness to deny the crime an unpromising test of his prospects for rehabilitation if guilty. It is indeed unlikely that many men who commit serious offenses would balk on principle from lying in their own defense. The guilty man may quite sincerely repent his crime but yet, driven by the urge to remain free, may protest his innocence in a court of law."

The *Scott* rationale rests not only on the realism of the psychological pressures on a defendant in the dock—which we can grant—but also on a deterministic view of human conduct that is inconsistent with the underlying precepts of our criminal justice system. A "universal and persistent" foundation stone in our system of law, and particularly in our approach to punishment, sentencing, and incarceration, is the "belief in freedom of the human will and a consequent ability and duty of the normal individual to choose between good and evil." Given that long-accepted view of the "ability and duty of the normal individual to choose," we must conclude that the defendant's readiness to lie under oath—especially when, as here, the trial court finds the lie to be flagrant—may be deemed probative of his prospects for rehabilitation.

III

Against this background we evaluate Grayson's constitutional argument that the District Court's sentence constitutes punishment for the crime of perjury for which he has not been indicted, tried, or convicted by due process. A second argument is that permitting consideration of perjury will "chill" defendants from exercising their right to testify on their own behalf.

A

In his due process argument, Grayson does not contend directly that the District Court had an impermissible purpose in considering his perjury and selecting the sentence. Rather, he argues that this Court, in order to preserve due process rights, not only must prohibit the impermissible sentencing practice of incarcerating for the purpose of saving the Government the burden of bringing a separate and subsequent perjury prosecution but also must prohibit the otherwise *permissible* practice of considering a defendant's untruthfulness for the purpose of illuminating his need for rehabilitation and society's need for protection. He presents two interrelated reasons. The effect of both permissible and impermissible sentencing practices may be the same: additional time in prison. Further, it is virtually impossible, he contends, to identify and establish the impermissible practice. We find these reasons insufficient * * *.

First, the evolutionary history of sentencing * * * demonstrates that it is proper—indeed, even necessary for the rational exercise of discretion— to consider the defendant's whole person and personality, as manifested by his conduct at trial and his testimony under oath, for whatever light those may shed on the sentencing decision. The "parlous" effort to appraise "character" degenerates into a game of chance to the extent that a sentencing judge is deprived of relevant information concerning "every aspect of a defendant's life." The Government's interest, as well as the offender's, in avoiding irrationality is of the highest order. That interest more than justifies the risk that Grayson asserts is present when a sentencing judge considers a defendant's untruthfulness under oath.

Second, in our view, *Williams* fully supports consideration of such conduct in sentencing. There the Court permitted the sentencing judge to consider the offender's history of prior antisocial conduct, including burglaries for which he had not been duly convicted. This it did despite the risk that the judge might use his knowledge of the offender's prior crimes for an improper purpose.

Third, the efficacy of Grayson's suggested "exclusionary rule" is open to serious doubt. No rule of law, even one garbed in constitutional terms, can prevent improper use of firsthand observations of perjury. The integrity of the judges, and their fidelity to their oaths of office, necessarily provide the only, and in our view adequate, assurance against that.

B

Grayson's argument that judicial consideration of his conduct at trial impermissibly "chills" a defendant's statutory right, 18 U.S.C. § 3481 (1976 ed.), and perhaps a constitutional right to testify on his own behalf is without basis. The right guaranteed by law to a defendant is narrowly the right to testify truthfully in accordance with the oath. * * * Assuming, *arguendo,* that the sentencing judge's consideration of defendants' untruthfulness in testifying has any chilling effect on a defendant's decision to testify falsely, that effect is entirely permissible. There is no protected right to commit perjury.

Grayson's further argument that the sentencing practice challenged here will inhibit exercise of the right to testify truthfully is entirely frivolous. That argument misapprehends the nature and scope of the practice we find permissible. Nothing we say today requires a sentencing judge to enhance, in some wooden or reflex fashion, the sentences of all defendants whose testimony is deemed false. Rather, we are reaffirming the authority of a sentencing judge to evaluate carefully a defendant's testimony on the stand, determine—with a consciousness of the frailty of human judgment—whether that testimony contained willful and material falsehoods, and, if so, assess in light of all the other knowledge gained about the defendant the meaning of that conduct with respect to his prospects for rehabilitation and restoration to a useful place in society. Awareness of such a process realistically cannot be deemed to affect the decision of an accused but unconvicted defendant to testify truthfully in his own behalf.

* * *

MR. JUSTICE STEWART, with whom MR. JUSTICE BRENNAN and MR. JUSTICE MARSHALL join, dissenting.

The Court begins its consideration of this case with the assumption that the respondent gave false testimony at his trial. But there has been no determination that his testimony was false. This respondent was given a greater sentence than he would otherwise have received—how much greater we have no way of knowing—solely because a single judge *thought* that he had not testified truthfully. In essence, the Court holds today that *whenever* a defendant testifies in his own behalf and is found guilty, he opens himself to the possibility of an enhanced sentence. Such a sentence is nothing more or less than a penalty imposed on the defendant's exercise of his constitutional and statutory rights to plead not guilty and to testify in his own behalf.

It does not change matters to say that the enhanced sentence merely reflects the defendant's "prospects for rehabilitation" rather than an additional punishment for testifying falsely. The fact remains that all defendants who choose to testify, and only those who do so, face the very real prospect of a greater sentence based upon the trial judge's unreviewable perception that the testimony was untruthful. The Court prescribes no limitations or safeguards to minimize a defendant's rational fear that his truthful testimony will be perceived as false.[4] Indeed, encumbrance of the sentencing process with the collateral inquiries necessary to provide such assurance would be both pragmatically unworkable and theoretically inconsistent with the assumption that the trial judge is merely considering one more piece of information in his overall evaluation of the defendant's prospects for rehabilitation. But without such safeguards I fail to see how the Court can dismiss as "frivolous" the argument that this sentencing practice will "inhibit exercise of the right to testify truthfully."

* * * Other witnesses risk punishment for perjury only upon indictment and conviction in accord with the full protections of the Constitution. Only the defendant himself, whose testimony is likely to be of critical importance to his defense, faces the additional risk that the disbelief of a single listener will itself result in time in prison.

The minimal contribution that the defendant's possibly untruthful testimony might make to an overall assessment of his potential for rehabilitation cannot justify imposing this additional burden on his right to testify in his own behalf. I do not believe that a sentencing judge's discretion to consider a wide range of information in arriving at an appropriate sentence allows him to mete out additional punishment to the defendant simply because of his personal belief that the defendant did not testify truthfully at the trial.

* * *

QUESTIONS AND POINTS FOR DISCUSSION

1.   In Witte v. United States, 515 U.S. 389, 115 S.Ct. 2199 (1995), the Supreme Court held that a defendant's Fifth Amendment right not to be subjected to double jeopardy was not violated when uncharged criminal conduct was used to increase the defendant's offense level and the defendant

---

[4]   For example, the dissenting judge in the Court of Appeals in this case suggested that a sentencing judge "should consider his independent evaluation of the testimony and behavior of the defendant only when he is convinced beyond a reasonable doubt that the defendant intentionally lied on material issues of fact . . . [and] the falsity of the defendant's testimony [is] necessarily established by the finding of guilt." * * * I do not believe that the latter requirement was met in this case. The jury could have believed Grayson's entire story but concluded, in the words of the trial judge's instructions on the defense of duress, that "an ordinary man" would *not* "have felt it necessary to leave the Allenwood Prison Camp when faced with the same degree of compulsion, coercion or duress as the Defendant was faced with in this case."

later was convicted of a crime based on the same conduct. In that case, the defendant pled guilty to one count of attempting to possess marijuana with intent to distribute it. While the indictment charged the defendant with being involved in a drug transaction that occurred in early 1991, the judge considered the defendant's alleged involvement in the importation of large quantities of cocaine and marijuana into the country in 1990 as "relevant conduct" bearing on the defendant's offense level under the federal sentencing guidelines. Consideration of these uncharged crimes increased the defendant's offense level under the guidelines, raising the low end of the sentencing range by over seventeen years.

When the defendant subsequently was charged with, and convicted of, crimes stemming from the 1990 drug transactions, he argued that he unconstitutionally was being punished twice for the same crimes. The Supreme Court rejected that claim, noting that the defendant previously had been punished only for the 1991 crime. The 1990 conduct had been considered solely to determine what would be an appropriate penalty for that crime. Do you agree with the Court's reasoning?

2.   United States v. Watts, 519 U.S. 148, 117 S.Ct. 633 (1997) perhaps best illustrates the breadth of information that can be considered by courts when sentencing someone. In that case, after police found cocaine base, two loaded guns, and ammunition in the defendant's house, he was charged with two crimes—possession of cocaine base with intent to distribute and use of a firearm in relation to a drug offense. A jury found the defendant guilty of the first crime but not guilty of the second. When sentencing the defendant, though, the judge found, by a preponderance of the evidence, that the guns related to the drug crime, a finding that raised the offense level under the federal sentencing guidelines used to calculate the defendant's sentence. As a result, the defendant received a longer prison sentence, though one that still fell within the statutory maximum for the drug crime. In a *per curiam* opinion (one rendered without briefing and arguments by the parties), the Supreme Court held that the Double Jeopardy Clause does not prohibit the consideration during the sentencing process of conduct underlying charges of which a defendant has been acquitted "so long as that conduct has been proved by a preponderance of the evidence." Id. at 156, 117 S.Ct. at 638. From a policy perspective, do you support or oppose the consideration of such conduct during the sentencing process?

3.   United States v. Tucker, 404 U.S. 443, 92 S.Ct. 589 (1972) involved the validity of a sentence imposed on a defendant who had been found guilty of an armed bank robbery. Having been apprised that the defendant had three prior felony convictions, the sentencing judge imposed the maximum sentence for the armed robbery—25 years. Only later was it determined that two of the defendant's three prior convictions had been obtained unconstitutionally, in violation of his Sixth Amendment right to counsel.

While acknowledging the breadth of the information that can be considered by a sentencing court when imposing sentence, the Supreme Court held that the defendant's sentence in this case was invalid because it was based "at least in part upon misinformation of constitutional magnitude." Id. at 447, 92 S.Ct. at 591–92. The defendant therefore had to be resentenced since his original sentence "might have been different" had the sentencing judge been aware that the defendant already had spent ten years of his life unconstitutionally locked up in prison. Id. at 448, 92 S.Ct. at 592.

In the case which follows, the Supreme Court considered whether *Tucker* means that defendants generally have a constitutional right at a sentencing hearing to challenge the constitutionality of prior convictions about which evidence is introduced to increase their sentences.

CUSTIS V. UNITED STATES

Supreme Court of the United States, 1994.
511 U.S. 485, 114 S.Ct. 1732, 128 L.Ed.2d 517.

CHIEF JUSTICE REHNQUIST delivered the opinion of the Court.

The Armed Career Criminal Act, 18 U.S.C. § 924(e) (ACCA), raises the penalty for possession of a firearm by a felon from a maximum of 10 years in prison to a mandatory minimum sentence of 15 years and a maximum of life in prison without parole if the defendant "has three previous convictions . . . for a violent felony or a serious drug offense." [After a jury convicted Daniel Custis in 1991 of possession of a firearm and possession of cocaine, a federal prosecutor moved to have Custis's sentence enhanced under § 924(e) based on three prior felony convictions—state convictions in 1985 for robbery and burglary and a state conviction in 1989 for attempted burglary. Custis claimed that two of those convictions had been obtained in violation of his constitutional rights—his Sixth Amendment right to the effective assistance of counsel and his due-process right to have judgment entered on a guilty plea only when it is knowing and intelligent. The federal district court concluded that Custis had no statutory or constitutional right to challenge, at the time of sentencing, the constitutionality of prior convictions supporting an enhanced sentence under § 924(e), and the Fourth Circuit Court of Appeals affirmed. The Supreme Court agreed with these courts that there was no statutory right under § 924(e) to mount a collateral attack on the constitutionality of prior convictions upon which an enhanced sentence might otherwise be based. The Court then turned to the question whether Custis had a constitutional right to challenge the constitutionality of the predicate convictions during the sentencing proceeding under § 924(e).]

Custis argues that regardless of whether § 924(e) permits collateral challenges to prior convictions, the Constitution requires that they be allowed. He relies upon our decisions in *Burgett v. Texas*, 389 U.S. 109 (1967), and *United States v. Tucker*, 404 U.S. 443 (1972), in support of this argument. Both of these decisions relied upon our earlier decision in *Gideon v. Wainwright*, 372 U.S. 335 (1963), holding that the Sixth

Amendment of the United States Constitution required that an indigent defendant in state court proceedings have counsel appointed for him. * * *

Following our decision in *Gideon,* the Court decided *Burgett v. Texas.* There the defendant was charged under a Texas recidivist statute with having been the subject of four previous felony convictions. The prosecutor introduced certified records of one of the defendant's earlier convictions in Tennessee. The defendant objected to the admission of this conviction on the ground that he had not been represented by counsel and had not waived his right to counsel, but his objection was overruled by the trial court. This Court reversed, finding that the certified records of the Tennessee conviction on their face raised a "presumption that petitioner was denied his right to counsel . . ., and therefore that his conviction was void." The Court held that the admission of a prior criminal conviction which is constitutionally infirm under the standards of *Gideon* is inherently prejudicial and to permit use of such a tainted prior conviction for sentence enhancement would undermine the principle of *Gideon.*

* * *

Custis invites us to extend the right to attack collaterally prior convictions used for sentence enhancement beyond the right to have appointed counsel established in *Gideon.* We decline to do so. We think that * * * running through our decisions in *Burgett* and *Tucker,* there has been a theme that failure to appoint counsel for an indigent defendant was a unique constitutional defect. Custis attacks his previous convictions claiming the denial of the effective assistance of counsel, that his guilty plea was not knowing and intelligent, and that he had not been adequately advised of his rights in opting for a "stipulated facts" trial. None of these alleged constitutional violations rises to the level of a jurisdictional defect resulting from the failure to appoint counsel at all.

Ease of administration also supports the distinction. * * * [F]ailure to appoint counsel at all will generally appear from the judgment roll itself, or from an accompanying minute order. But determination of claims of ineffective assistance of counsel, and failure to assure that a guilty plea was voluntary, would require sentencing courts to rummage through frequently nonexistent or difficult to obtain state court transcripts or records that may date from another era, and may come from any one of the 50 States.

The interest in promoting the finality of judgments provides additional support for our constitutional conclusion. As we have explained, "[i]nroads on the concept of finality tend to undermine confidence in the integrity of our procedures" and inevitably delay and impair the orderly administration of justice. * * * By challenging the previous conviction, the defendant is asking a district court "to deprive [the] [state court judgment] of [its] normal force and effect in a proceeding that ha[s] an independent purpose other than to overturn the prior judgmen[t]." These principles bear extra weight in cases in which the prior convictions, such as one challenged by Custis, are based on guilty pleas, because when a guilty plea is at issue, "the concern with finality served by the limitation on collateral attack has special force."

We therefore hold that § 924(e) does not permit Custis to use the federal sentencing forum to gain review of his state convictions. Congress did not prescribe and the Constitution does not require such delay and protraction of the federal sentencing process. We recognize, however, * * * that Custis, who was still "in custody" for purposes of his state convictions at the time of his federal sentencing under § 924(e), may attack his state sentences in Maryland or through federal habeas review. If Custis is successful in attacking these state sentences, he may then apply for reopening of any federal sentence enhanced by the state sentences. We express no opinion on the appropriate disposition of such an application.

* * *

JUSTICE SOUTER, with whom JUSTICE BLACKMUN and JUSTICE STEVENS join, dissenting.

[Justice Souter concluded that Congress had accorded defendants a statutory right to challenge, at a sentencing hearing, the constitutionality of prior convictions offered in support of an enhanced sentence under § 924(e). He therefore criticized the majority for unnecessarily deciding what he termed "a difficult constitutional question."]

This is a difficult question, for one thing, because the language and logic of *Burgett* and *Tucker* are hard to limit to claimed violations of the right, recognized in *Gideon v. Wainwright,* to have a lawyer appointed if necessary. * * * *Tucker* made it clear that "the real question" before the Court was whether the defendant's sentence might have been different if the sentencing judge had known that the defendant's "previous convictions had been unconstitutionally obtained."

Even if, consistently with principles of *stare decisis, Burgett* and *Tucker* could be read as applying only to some class of cases defined to exclude claimed violations of *Strickland* or *Boykin,* the question whether to confine them so is not easily answered. *Burgett* and *Tucker* deal directly with claimed violations of *Gideon,* and distinguishing for these purposes between violations of *Gideon* and *Strickland* would describe a very fine line. To establish a violation of the Sixth Amendment under *Strickland,* a defendant must show that "counsel's performance was deficient," and that "the deficient performance prejudiced the defense" in that "counsel's errors were so serious as to deprive the defendant of a fair trial, a trial whose result is reliable." It is hard to see how such a defendant is any better off than one who has been denied counsel altogether, and why the conviction of such a defendant may be used for sentence enhancement if the conviction of one who has been denied counsel altogether may not. The Sixth Amendment guarantees no mere formality of appointment, but the "assistance" of counsel, and whether the violation is of *Gideon* or *Strickland,* the defendant has been denied that constitutional right.

It is also difficult to see why a sentencing court that must entertain a defendant's claim that a prior conviction was obtained in violation of the Sixth Amendment's right to counsel need not entertain a defendant's claim that a prior conviction was based on an unknowing or involuntary guilty plea. That claim, if meritorious, would mean that the defendant was convicted despite invalid waivers of at least one of two Sixth Amendment rights (to trial by jury and to confront adverse witnesses) or of a Fifth Amendment right (against compulsory self-incrimination). It is, to be sure, no simple task to prove that a guilty plea was the result of "[i]gnorance, incomprehension, coercion, terror, inducements, [or] subtle or blatant threats," but it is certainly at least a difficult question whether a defendant who can make such a showing ought to receive less favorable treatment than the defendants in *Burgett* and *Tucker.*

* * *

The Court invokes "[e]ase of administration" to support its constitutional holding. * * * [T]he burden argument here is not a strong one. * * *

* * * [T]he Court sees administrative burdens arising because "sentencing courts [would be required] to rummage through frequently nonexistent or difficult to obtain state-court transcripts or records that may date from another era, and may come from any of the 50 States." It would not be sentencing courts that would have to do this rummaging, however, but defendants seeking to avoid enhancement, for no one disagrees that the burden of showing the invalidity of prior convictions would rest on the defendants.

Whatever administrative benefits may flow from insulating sentencing courts from challenges to prior convictions will likely be offset by the administrative costs of the alternative means of raising the same claims. The Court acknowledges that an individual still in custody for a state conviction relied upon for enhancement may attack that conviction through state or federal habeas review and, if successful, "may . . . apply for reopening any federal sentence enhanced by the state sentence." * * * From the perspective of administrability, it strikes me as entirely sensible to resolve any challenges to the lawfulness of a predicate conviction in the single sentencing proceeding, especially since defendants there will normally be represented by counsel, who bring efficiency to the litigation (as well as equitable benefits).

* * *

QUESTIONS AND POINTS FOR DISCUSSION

1.   Federal prisoners in custody under a sentence imposed in violation of the Constitution or federal laws can file a petition under 28 U.S.C. § 2255 to have the sentence vacated or corrected. In Daniels v. United States, 532 U.S. 374, 121 S.Ct. 1578 (2001), the Supreme Court considered whether someone imprisoned under the Armed Career Criminal Act could challenge the federal sentence under § 2255 on the grounds that the sentence was enhanced because of a prior unconstitutional conviction. In a 5–4 decision, the Supreme Court answered that question in the negative. Writing for the majority, Justice O'Connor explained that the same factors that propelled the Court's decision in *Custis v. United States*—the difficulty of unearthing state records needed to adjudicate the constitutional claim and the interest in preserving the finality of state-court judgments—at least generally foreclose collateral attacks on prior convictions in § 2255 proceedings.

The Court in *Daniels* emphasized that individuals have many opportunities to challenge the constitutionality of their state convictions—on appeal, in state postconviction proceedings, and in federal habeas corpus actions brought under 28 U.S.C. § 2254. If they fail, however, to avail themselves of these opportunities or do so unsuccessfully, they generally have no right to "another bite at the apple" simply because an allegedly unconstitutional conviction augmented their federal sentence. Id. at 383, 121 S.Ct. at 1584.

In a dissenting opinion, Justice Souter countered that oftentimes people do not appeal a conviction because the light penalty imposed does not warrant the bringing of an appeal. In addition, they may refrain from challenging the conviction in a state postconviction proceeding because they have no attorney to assist them in collaterally attacking the conviction. To the argument that individuals may have little or no reason to challenge a conviction until it results in the imposition of an enhanced sentence, the majority responded:

> [T]he fact remains that avenues of redress are generally available if sought in a timely manner. If a person chooses not to pursue those remedies, he does so with the knowledge that the conviction will stay on his record. This knowledge should serve as an incentive not to commit a subsequent crime and risk having the sentence for that crime enhanced under a recidivist sentencing statute.

Id. at 381 n.1, 121 S.Ct. at 1583 n.1.

The Supreme Court in *Daniels* did carve out what Justice Souter described as "a textually untethered exception to its own rule." Id. at 390, 121 S.Ct. at 1588 (Souter, J., dissenting). According to the Court, a § 2255 petition can be a vehicle for challenging a prior conviction that resulted in an enhanced federal sentence if the prior conviction was the by-product of an unconstitutional failure to appoint counsel to represent the petitioner, at least if the *Gideon* challenge was raised at the time the court imposed the enhanced federal sentence. In addition, a plurality of the Court (Justice Scalia did not join this portion of Justice O'Connor's opinion) alluded to the possibility that there might be other "rare cases" when a constitutional challenge to a prior conviction can be mounted in a § 2255 proceeding. Id. at 383, 121 S.Ct. at 1584. In a companion case decided the same day as *Daniels*, Lackawanna County Dist. Attorney v. Coss, 532 U.S. 394, 121 S.Ct. 1567 (2001), the same plurality described two situations when a person might be able to challenge a prior conviction in such a proceeding. First, the petitioner might introduce "compelling evidence" that could not have been timely discovered and that demonstrates the petitioner's innocence of the crime of which he or she previously was convicted. Id. at 405, 121 S.Ct. at 1575. Second, the failure to obtain an earlier review of the validity of the prior conviction might have been the government's, not the petitioner's, fault. According to the plurality, the second scenario might arise, for example, when a state court had previously refused, for no reason, to adjudicate the constitutional claim.

2.   State prisoners in custody in violation of the Constitution or federal laws can seek release from their illegal confinement by filing a petition in federal court under 28 U.S.C. § 2254 for a writ of habeas corpus. In *Lackawanna County Dist. Attorney v. Coss*, the companion case to *Daniels* discussed above, the Supreme Court extended its holding in *Daniels* to state prisoners attempting to challenge in a habeas corpus proceeding the constitutionality of prior convictions that resulted in the imposition of an augmented sentence. Holding that prior state convictions are "conclusively valid" once those convictions can no longer be directly or collaterally attacked, id. at 403, 121 S.Ct. at 1574, the Court once again recognized a *Gideon* exception to this rule. In addition, a plurality of the Court observed, but did not decide, that the general rule might not apply in the two situations described earlier: when, as a practical matter, the habeas corpus proceeding might be "the first and only forum" for challenging the constitutionality of the prior conviction. Id. at 406, 121 S.Ct. at 1575.

3.   Johnson v. Mississippi, 486 U.S. 578, 108 S.Ct. 1981 (1988) involved a defendant who was sentenced to death for murder in Mississippi. One of the aggravating circumstances relied upon in imposing the death penalty was the defendant's prior conviction in New York for assault with intent to commit rape. That conviction, however, was set aside by a New York court after the death-penalty hearing in Mississippi. The Supreme Court concluded that since the defendant's death sentence was predicated on an invalid conviction, it violated the Eighth Amendment's prohibition of cruel and unusual punishments.

4.   As discussed in Chapter 4, the Supreme Court has held that an indigent defendant who was unrepresented by counsel at trial cannot, if convicted, be sentenced to any period of incarceration for a misdemeanor of which he or she was convicted. See page 156. But according to the Court, a misdemeanor conviction obtained when the defendant was not represented by counsel can be used to increase the prison sentence imposed for a subsequent

crime. In Nichols v. United States, 511 U.S. 738, 114 S.Ct. 1921 (1994), factoring an uncounseled misdemeanor conviction into the computation of the defendant's criminal-history score had increased his prison sentence by over two years. However, the Supreme Court reasoned that a conviction that is initially valid does not suddenly become invalid when used for enhancement purposes. In a dissenting opinion, Justice Blackmun, joined by Justices Stevens and Ginsburg, objected that a conviction which is too unreliable, because it was obtained without the assistance of counsel, to permit incarceration in the first place is too unreliable to be used subsequently to increase the amount of time that a defendant will be incarcerated.

C. FALSE AND UNRELIABLE INFORMATION

The Federal Rules of Evidence are inapplicable in sentencing hearings. Fed.R.Evid. 1101(d)(3). Thus, although hearsay statements are generally inadmissible in federal trials, the rules do not preclude judges from considering them at the time of sentencing. An example of such a statement would be a presentence investigation report's reference to the remark of a witness that the defendant had committed a certain crime in the past for which he was neither arrested nor convicted.

Hearsay statements are generally inadmissible at trial because of the risk that they are untruthful or inaccurate. But while hearsay statements may be admissible at sentencing hearings, courts have held that there is a due-process right for the information on which a sentence is grounded, including a hearsay statement, to have "sufficient indicia of reliability to support its probable accuracy." United States v. Tankson, 836 F.3d 873, 881 (7th Cir.2016). The existence of corroborating evidence can be one such indicator of reliability that surmounts what the Sixth Circuit Court of Appeals has described as the "relatively low hurdle" of the "minimum-indicia-of-reliability standard." United States v. Johnson, 732 F.3d 577, 583 (6th Cir.2013).

The notion, for purposes of sentencing, of "reliable hearsay" that would be inadmissible at trial under prevailing evidentiary rules has been derided by some commentators as an "oxymoron." See, e.g., Deborah Young, Fact-Finding at Federal Sentencing: Why the Guidelines Should Meet the Rules, 79 Cornell L.Rev. 299, 342, 362 (1994) (advocating the extension of the Federal Rules of Evidence to federal sentencing hearings). In your view, should evidence considered too unreliable to be introduced in evidence at trial be admissible for sentencing purposes?

In Townsend v. Burke, 334 U.S. 736, 68 S.Ct. 1252 (1948), the Supreme Court was confronted with questions about when a judge's reliance on false information when sentencing a defendant violates due process of law. In that case, a defendant, who was unrepresented by counsel, was sentenced to prison for ten to twenty years for burglary and robbery. At the sentencing hearing, the judge recited the defendant's criminal record. In fact, however, the defendant had been acquitted, or the criminal charges dismissed, in three of the cited cases. On these facts, the Supreme Court concluded that the defendant's right to due process of law had been violated:

> It is not the duration or severity of this sentence that renders it constitutionally invalid; it is the careless or designed pronouncement of sentence on a foundation so extensively and materially false, which the prisoner had no opportunity to correct by the services which counsel would provide, that renders the proceedings lacking in due process.

> Nor do we mean that mere error in resolving a question of fact on a plea of guilty by an uncounseled defendant in a non-capital case would necessarily indicate a want of due process of law. Fair prosecutors and conscientious judges sometimes are misinformed or draw inferences from conflicting evidence with which we would not agree. But even an erroneous judgment, based on a scrupulous and diligent search for truth, may be due process of law.

Id. at 741, 68 S.Ct. at 1255.

As *Townsend v. Burke* makes clear, due process is violated only when the sentencing judge actually relies on certain false information when imposing a sentence. Consequently, Federal Rule of Criminal Procedure 32(i)(3)(B), which can be found on page 196, provides a judge with two options when faced with a defendant's challenge to the accuracy of information included in a presentence investigation report. The judge either must resolve the factual dispute or confirm that the disputed information was not considered when sentencing the defendant or did not otherwise affect the sentence.

Even when a judge considers demonstrably false information when sentencing a defendant, the defendant's due-process rights are not necessarily violated. Due process, for example, is not violated if the mistake involved an immaterial fact. See, e.g., United States v. Addonizio, 442 U.S. 178, 99 S.Ct. 2235 (1979) (sentencing judge's expectations about the defendant's parole-release date were not enforceable against the parole board and therefore the judge's erroneous prediction when sentencing the defendant as to when the defendant would be released on parole did not involve "misinformation of constitutional magnitude" that would entitle the defendant to be resentenced).

D. FIRST AMENDMENT LIMITATIONS

The Supreme Court's decision in Dawson v. Delaware, 503 U.S. 159, 112 S.Ct. 1093 (1992) illustrates another limitation the Constitution places on the factors that may be taken into account at the time of sentencing. In that case, the Court considered whether the introduction of evidence in a capital sentencing hearing that the defendant was a member of a prison gang of white racists violated his rights under the First and Fourteenth Amendments. The Court first rejected the defendant's broad argument that all evidence regarding a defendant's beliefs or activities that are protected by the First Amendment must be excluded from consideration at sentencing. Sometimes, the Court observed, such beliefs or activities will be relevant to the issues considered at sentencing. For example, if a defendant were a member of a group that advocates killing certain individuals, evidence of that membership would help to show that the defendant could endanger the public in the future.

The Court proceeded to conclude, however, that introduction of the evidence of the defendant's gang membership at the sentencing hearing in this case violated his constitutional rights. This evidence was presented to the jury in the form of a stipulation that basically said that the Aryan Brotherhood, whose name was tattooed on the defendant's hand, was a "white prison gang" organized to respond to gangs comprised of racial minorities. According to the Court, this stipulation was too narrow to make evidence of the defendant's gang membership admissible. At most, the evidence revealed that the defendant was racist, which the Court said was irrelevant in this case since his murder victim was white. The Court intimated, however, that had the stipulation extended beyond the defendant's "abstract beliefs" and mentioned the Aryan Brotherhood's involvement in drugs, violent prison escapes, and advocacy of the murder of other inmates, introducing evidence of the defendant's membership in the gang would not have violated the Constitution.

The Supreme Court's decision in *Dawson* can be contrasted with its decision in Wisconsin v. Mitchell, 508 U.S. 476, 113 S.Ct. 2194 (1993). In *Mitchell,* the Court upheld a statute under which the penalty for battery was increased when the victim was selected because of his or her race. While the defendant contended that he was being punished for his beliefs and speech in violation of the First Amendment, the Court underscored that the statute was directed at conduct—a criminal battery—that was unprotected by the First Amendment. In holding that examination at the sentencing hearing of the motive behind that conduct was constitutionally permissible, the Court added that the motive for committing a crime traditionally has been a factor of central importance to the sentencing decision.

As a matter of policy, do you believe that penalties should be enhanced because a crime was motivated by the victim's race? If so, should crimes against any other categories of individuals trigger enhanced penalties under what are often referred to as "hate-crime laws"? For contrasting views on the advisability of enacting hate-crime laws, see Frederick M. Lawrence, Punishing Hate: Bias Crimes under American Law (1999) and

James B. Jacobs & Kimberly Potter, Hate Crimes: Criminal Law & Identity Politics (1998).

E. A DEFENDANT'S WILLINGNESS OR REFUSAL TO COOPERATE WITH AUTHORITIES OR MAKE INCRIMINATING STATEMENTS

ROBERTS V. UNITED STATES

Supreme Court of the United States, 1980.
445 U.S. 552, 100 S.Ct. 1358, 63 L.Ed.2d 622.

MR. JUSTICE POWELL delivered the opinion of the Court.

[When being questioned by investigators, the petitioner confessed to participating in the trafficking of heroin and discussing drug transactions on the telephone. He would not disclose, though, the identity of his drug suppliers. After the petitioner pleaded guilty, under a plea agreement, to two counts of using a telephone to facilitate the distribution of heroin, the district court imposed prison sentences of one to four years on each count, with the sentences to run consecutively. One of the reasons the court cited for this sentence was the defendant's failure to cooperate with the government in its investigation. The Court of Appeals for the District of Columbia Circuit upheld this decision.]

* * *

* * * There is no question that petitioner rebuffed repeated requests for his cooperation over a period of three years. Nor does petitioner contend that he was unable to provide the requested assistance. * * *

* * * Concealment of crime has been condemned throughout our history. * * * [G]ross indifference to the duty to report known criminal behavior remains a badge of irresponsible citizenship.

This deeply rooted social obligation is not diminished when the witness to crime is involved in illicit activities himself. * * * The petitioner, for example, was asked to expose the purveyors of heroin in his own community in exchange for a favorable disposition of his case. By declining to cooperate, petitioner rejected an "obligatio[n] of community life" that should be recognized before rehabilitation can begin. Moreover, petitioner's refusal to cooperate protected his former partners in crime, thereby preserving his ability to resume criminal activities upon release. * * *

Petitioner * * * contends that his failure to cooperate was justified by legitimate fears of physical retaliation and self-incrimination. In view of these concerns, petitioner asserts that his refusal to act as an informer has no bearing on his prospects for rehabilitation. He also believes that the

District Court punished him for exercising his Fifth Amendment privilege against self-incrimination.

These arguments would have merited serious consideration if they had been presented properly to the sentencing judge. But the mere possibility of unarticulated explanations or excuses for antisocial conduct does not make that conduct irrelevant to the sentencing decision. * * *

* * *

* * * Thus, if petitioner believed that his failure to cooperate was privileged, he should have said so at a time when the sentencing court could have determined whether his claim was legitimate.

* * *

* * * We conclude that the District Court committed no constitutional error. * * *

MR. JUSTICE BRENNAN, concurring. [Opinion omitted.]

MR. JUSTICE MARSHALL, dissenting.

* * * I do not believe that a defendant's failure to inform on others may properly be used to aggravate a sentence of imprisonment, and accordingly, I dissent.

* * *

[P]etitioner's refusal to provide the requested information was lawful and may have been motivated by the possibility of self-incrimination or a reasonable fear of reprisal. * * *

* * *

The enhancement of petitioner's sentence, then, was impermissible because it may have burdened petitioner's exercise of his constitutional rights or been based on a factor unrelated to the permissible goals of sentencing. In addition, it represented an improper involvement of the judicial office in the prosecutorial function * * *.

The usual method for obtaining testimony which may be self-incriminatory is through a grant of immunity from prosecution. Prosecutors would have little incentive to offer defendants immunity for their testimony if they could achieve the same result without giving up the option to prosecute. * * *

A second method available to the prosecutor for obtaining a defendant's testimony against others is the plea-bargaining process. * * * But if the judge can be counted on to increase the defendant's sentence if he fails to cooperate, the balance of bargaining power is tipped in favor of the prosecution. Not only is the prosecutor able to offer less in exchange for cooperation, but a defendant may agree for fear of incurring the displeasure of the sentencing judge. * * *

I find disturbing the majority's willingness to brush aside these serious objections to the propriety of petitioner's sentence on the strength of "the duty to report known criminal behavior." * * *

* * * [O]ur admiration of those who inform on others has never been as unambiguous as the majority suggests. The countervailing social values of loyalty and personal privacy have prevented us from imposing on the citizenry at large a duty to join in the business of crime detection. If the Court's view of social mores were accurate, it would be hard to understand how terms such as "stool pigeon," "snitch," "squealer," and "tattletale" have come to be the common description of those who engage in such behavior.

* * * I do not, of course, suggest that those who have engaged in criminal activity should refuse to cooperate with the authorities. The informer plays a vital role in the struggle to check crime, especially the narcotics trade. We could not do without him. In recognition of this role, it is fully appropriate to encourage such behavior by offering leniency in exchange for "cooperation." Cooperation of that sort may be a sign of repentance and the beginning of rehabilitation. But our Government has allowed its citizens to decide for themselves whether to enlist in the enterprise of enforcing the criminal laws; it has never imposed a duty to do so * * *. I find no justification for creating such a duty in this case and applying it only to persons about to be sentenced for a crime.

* * *

QUESTIONS AND POINTS FOR DISCUSSION

1.   Even when a defendant does not specifically invoke the privilege against self-incrimination at a sentencing hearing, the Fifth Amendment places at least some limits on the drawing of a negative inference from the defendant's failure to testify at that hearing. Mitchell v. United States, 526 U.S. 314, 119 S.Ct. 1307 (1999) involved a defendant who pled guilty to four federal drug crimes. When entering her plea, the defendant reserved her right to contest the amount of drugs involved in the conspiracy count to which she was pleading guilty, a factor that would affect the length of her sentence. The judge warned the defendant that by entering the plea, she was agreeing to relinquish a number of rights, including her right to remain silent at trial. The judge then described the factual basis for the plea and asked the defendant, "Did you do that?" "Some of it," the defendant replied.

At the sentencing hearing, the prosecution introduced evidence about the frequency with which the defendant sold drugs and the amount of drugs she sold. The defendant did not take the stand to rebut this testimony. The judge then found that the amount of drugs the defendant had conspired to sell exceeded the five kilograms needed to trigger a ten-year minimum term of imprisonment under the statute in question. The court acknowledged that this finding was predicated in part on the defendant's failure to testify and refute the government's evidence regarding the quantity of drugs.

The threshold question before the Supreme Court was whether a defendant who pleads guilty to a crime waives the protection of the privilege against self-incrimination at the sentencing hearing. The Court observed that by entering a plea of guilty, a defendant is expressing a willingness to forgo a trial and the rights that accompany a trial, including the privilege against self-incrimination. The Court held, though, that the entry of the guilty plea and the defendant's statements made during the plea colloquy do not constitute a relinquishment of the privilege at the sentencing hearing, typically the most important stage of the criminal prosecution for defendants who plead guilty.

The Supreme Court then turned to the question whether a court constitutionally can draw an adverse inference against a defendant because of his or her failure to testify at the sentencing hearing. The Court cited the general rule set forth in Griffin v. California, 380 U.S. 609, 614, 85 S.Ct. 1229, 1232–33 (1965) prohibiting the drawing of a negative inference from a defendant's failure to testify at trial. The Court held that this rule extends to sentencing hearings as well, at least to the extent of prohibiting a defendant's failure to testify regarding "the circumstances and details of the crime" to give rise to a negative inference about those circumstances, such as the amount of drugs involved in a drug crime. 526 U.S. at 328, 119 S.Ct. at 1315. The Court left open the question whether a court can take the defendant's silence into account when resolving other issues at the sentencing hearing, such as whether the defendant's sentence should be lowered for accepting responsibility for his or her crimes. Assuming, *arguendo*, that *Mitchell* was correctly decided, should the no-adverse-inference rule extend to other issues at sentencing, such as the defendant's future dangerousness and whether the defendant is remorseful for the crime?

2.   While protesting the extension of *Griffin*'s no-adverse-inference rule to the sentencing context, Justice Scalia referred to the question left open by the Court in *Mitchell v. United States*:

> If the Court ultimately decides—in the fullness of time and after a decent period of confusion in the lower courts—that the "no inference" rule is indeed *limited* to "determining facts of the offense," then we will have a system in which a state court *can* increase the sentence of a convicted drug possessor who refuses to say how many ounces he possessed—not because that suggests he possessed the larger amount (to make such an inference would be unconstitutional!) but because his refusal to cooperate suggests he is unrepentant. Apart from the fact that there is no logical basis for drawing such a line *within* the sentencing phase * * *, the result produced provides new support for Mr. Bumble's renowned evaluation of the law.[a] Its only sensible

---

[a]   In *Oliver Twist*, the classic written by Charles Dickens, Mr. Bumble rumbled that if the law assumes that his wife acts under his direction, "the law is a ass—a idiot."

feature is that it will almost always be unenforceable, since it will ordinarily be impossible to tell whether the sentencer has used the silence for either purpose or for neither.

If, on the other hand, the Court ultimately decides—in the fullness of time and after a decent period of confusion in the lower courts—that the extension of *Griffin* announced today is *not* limited to "determining facts of the offense," then it will have created a system in which we give the sentencing judge access to all sorts of out-of-court evidence, including the most remote hearsay, concerning the character of the defendant, his prior misdeeds, his acceptance of responsibility and determination to mend his ways, but declare taboo the most obvious piece of firsthand evidence standing in front of the judge: the defendant's refusal to cooperate with the court. Such a rule orders the judge to avert his eyes from the elephant in the courtroom when it is the judge's job to size up the elephant.

* * * Sooner or later the choice must be made, and the fact that both alternatives are unsatisfactory cries out that the Court's extension of *Griffin* is a mistake.

Id. at 340–41, 119 S.Ct. at 1320–21 (Scalia, J., dissenting).

3.   *Roberts v. United States* demonstrates that a defendant's refusal to cooperate in the investigation of crimes committed by others may at times lead to the imposition of a sentence higher than the one the judge would otherwise have imposed. Conversely, a defendant's cooperation in such an investigation may at times lead to a diminution in the sentence. For example, upon motion of a prosecutor, a federal court has the authority under 18 U.S.C. § 3553(e) to impose a sentence below the statutory mandatory minimum when the defendant has provided "substantial assistance" in the criminal investigation or prosecution of someone else. A substantial-assistance motion can also seek and support a downward departure from the federal sentencing guidelines that are factored into federal sentencing decisions. U.S. Sentencing Guidelines Manual § 5K1.1 (2016). And courts have held that even in the absence of a prosecutor's motion for such a downward departure, evidence of a defendant's cooperation can support a variance from the guidelines as judges exercise the more expansive sentencing discretion allotted by what are now considered advisory guidelines. See United States v. Robinson, 741 F.3d 588, 600 (5th Cir.2014) (listing cases). Finally, upon motion of a prosecutor, a defendant can be resentenced due to substantial assistance that occurred after the date of the original sentencing, with the assistance supporting a reduction of the sentence below the guideline range or an applicable mandatory minimum. Fed. R. Crim. P. 35(b). For tips on what a defense attorney can do to secure and maximize a reduction in a federal sentence due to a client's cooperation in the investigation or prosecution of another person, see Mark P. Rankin & Rachel R. May, The Key to Freedom, 31 Champion 12 (July 2007).

F. ILLEGALLY OBTAINED EVIDENCE

Just because evidence was obtained unconstitutionally and is inadmissible at trial does not necessarily mean the evidence is also inadmissible during a sentencing hearing. For example, assume that during a patently unconstitutional warrantless search of the home of a murder suspect, the police find a diary revealing the deliberateness with which the defendant had planned the murder. The diary will be inadmissible at trial because of the violation of the defendant's Fourth Amendment rights. However, if he is nonetheless convicted, most courts have held that such illegally seized evidence can be considered by the sentencing judge, at least when the purpose of the search was not to find evidence to enhance the defendant's sentence. See, e.g., United States v. Acosta, 303 F.3d 78, 84–85 (1st Cir.2002) (listing cases).

Seventh Circuit Judge Frank Easterbrook has sharply criticized both the prevailing rule that illegally seized evidence is admissible at sentencing and the exception some courts have carved out to that rule:

> [S]uch an exception is chimerical. Police do not mull over the potential uses of evidence, fix on *a* use, and then seize the evidence for that purpose. Officers have multiple purposes—they want to close down drug operations (even if no prosecution ensues), they want to get the goods that will help turn a dope peddler against his supplier, they want to facilitate convictions, they want to maximize sentences when convictions occur. It is inconceivable that any defendant will be able to show that the police had only one of these purposes in mind when making a seizure. * * *
>
> It is awfully hard to see why motive should matter on either prudential or doctrinal grounds. Is the seizure less offensive to the Constitution, or is deterrence less important, when the police drain their minds of the possibility that the seizure will contribute to a conviction? As for doctrine: the fourth amendment establishes an objective standard. *Graham v. Connor*, 490 U.S. 386, 397 (1989). I think it most unlikely that the Supreme Court will admit intent through the back door in deciding whether to apply the exclusionary rule. Application is categorical: the exclusionary rule applies, or it doesn't, to one or another juncture of litigation. * * *

* * *

* * * Today prosecutors often present at trial only a small fraction of the defendant's provable conduct. The rest is reserved for sentencing. * * * In drug cases the guidelines require the court to take into consideration all quantities sold or under negotiation as "part of the same course of conduct or common scheme or plan as the offense of conviction". U.S.S.G. § 1B1.3(a)(2). Our case is

the norm: the prosecutor charged the defendants with distributing slightly more than 5 kilograms of drugs but asked for a sentence based on more than 50 (and the court imposed a sentence based on more than 15). Where once courts sentenced the offender and not the conduct, now courts sentence for crimes that were the subject of neither charge nor conviction. In proving such additional crimes, illegally seized evidence may play a central role—the same sort of role it used to play in supporting convictions on additional counts.

* * * The crime of which Jewel and Jackson were convicted, selling more than 5 kilograms of a mixture containing a detectable amount of cocaine, carries a minimum of 10 years and a maximum of life. Parole has been abolished. If the police seize 5 kilograms legally and another 46 illegally, this statute, coupled with § 1B1.3(a)(2), allows the court to impose a sentence of life imprisonment, just as if all of the drugs had been seized in compliance with the Constitution. * * *

Judge Silberman recognized that to allow the use of unconstitutionally seized evidence in sentencing is to take "a big bite out of the exclusionary rule", [*United States v.*] *McCrory*, 930 F.2d at 72 [D.C. Cir. 1991]. * * * [I]f we do not apply the exclusionary rule in sentencing under the guidelines, the constitutional ban on unreasonable searches and seizures will become a parchment barrier.

United States v. Jewel, 947 F.2d 224, 238–40 (7th Cir.1991) (Easterbrook, J., concurring). Do you agree with Judge Easterbrook's comments?

According to the Supreme Court, when resolving questions concerning the applicability of the Fourth Amendment exclusionary rule, the benefits of excluding the evidence during the stage of the criminal prosecution in question must be weighed against the costs of such exclusion. United States v. Calandra, 414 U.S. 338, 349, 94 S.Ct. 613, 620 (1974) (Fourth Amendment exclusionary rule does not apply to grand-jury proceedings). How would you assess the costs and benefits of applying the Fourth Amendment exclusionary rule during sentencing hearings? For a Supreme Court decision on the applicability of the exclusionary rule in parole-revocation hearings, see Pennsylvania Bd. of Probation and Parole v. Scott, 524 U.S. 357, 118 S.Ct. 2014 (1998), which is discussed in note 5 on pages 448–449.

G. VICTIM-IMPACT EVIDENCE

Laws authorizing or requiring consideration of victim-impact statements during the sentencing stage of criminal prosecutions are now commonplace. See, e.g., Mich.Comp.Laws § 771.14(2)(b); Va.Code Ann.

§ 19.2–299.1. In the case which follows, the Supreme Court considered the constitutionality of introducing such statements at a sentencing hearing in a capital case.

PAYNE V. TENNESSEE

Supreme Court of the United States, 1991.
501 U.S. 808, 111 S.Ct. 2597, 115 L.Ed.2d 720.

CHIEF JUSTICE REHNQUIST delivered the opinion of the Court.

* * *

Petitioner, Pervis Tyrone Payne, was convicted by a jury on two counts of first-degree murder and one count of assault with intent to commit murder in the first degree. He was sentenced to death for each of the murders and to 30 years in prison for the assault.

The victims of Payne's offenses were 28-year-old Charisse Christopher, her 2-year-old daughter Lacie, and her 3-year-old son Nicholas. The three lived together in an apartment in Millington, Tennessee, across the hall from Payne's girlfriend, Bobbie Thomas. On Saturday, June 27, 1987, Payne visited Thomas' apartment several times in expectation of her return from her mother's house in Arkansas, but found no one at home. * * *

Payne passed the morning and early afternoon injecting cocaine and drinking beer. * * * Sometime around 3 p.m., Payne returned to the apartment complex, entered the Christophers' apartment, and began making sexual advances towards Charisse. Charisse resisted and Payne became violent. A neighbor who resided in the apartment directly beneath the Christophers heard Charisse screaming, " 'Get out, get out,' as if she were telling the children to leave." The noise briefly subsided and then began, " 'horribly loud.' " The neighbor called the police after she heard a "blood curdling scream" from the Christopher's apartment.

When the first police officer arrived at the scene, he immediately encountered Payne, who was leaving the apartment building, so covered with blood that he appeared to be " 'sweating blood.' " * * *

Inside the apartment, the police encountered a horrifying scene. Blood covered the walls and floor throughout the unit. Charisse and her children were lying on the floor in the kitchen. Nicholas, despite several wounds inflicted by a butcher knife that completely penetrated through his body from front to back, was still breathing. Miraculously, he survived, but not until after undergoing seven hours of surgery and a transfusion of 1,700 cc's of blood—400 to 500 cc's more than his estimated normal blood volume. Charisse and Lacie were dead.

Charisse's body was found on the kitchen floor on her back, her legs fully extended. She had sustained 42 direct knife wounds and 42 defensive wounds on her arms and hands. * * *

Lacie's body was on the kitchen floor near her mother. She had suffered stab wounds to the chest, abdomen, back, and head. The murder weapon, a butcher knife, was found at her feet. * * *

* * *

At trial, Payne took the stand and, despite the overwhelming and relatively uncontroverted evidence against him, testified that he had not harmed any of the Christophers. * * * The jury returned guilty verdicts against Payne on all counts.

During the sentencing phase of the trial, Payne presented the testimony of four witnesses: his mother and father, Bobbie Thomas, and Dr. John T. Hutson, a clinical psychologist specializing in criminal court evaluation work. * * *

* * *

The State presented the testimony of Charisse's mother, Mary Zvolanek. When asked how Nicholas had been affected by the murders of his mother and sister, she responded:

"He cries for his mom. He doesn't seem to understand why she doesn't come home. And he cries for his sister Lacie. He comes to me many times during the week and asks me, Grandmama, do you miss my Lacie. And I tell him yes. He says, I'm worried about my Lacie."

In arguing for the death penalty during closing argument, the prosecutor commented on the continuing effects of Nicholas' experience, stating:

"But we do know that Nicholas was alive. And Nicholas was in the same room. Nicholas was still conscious. His eyes were open. He responded to the paramedics. He was able to follow their directions. He was able to hold his intestines in as he was carried to the ambulance. So he knew what happened to his mother and baby sister."

* * *

"Somewhere down the road Nicholas is going to grow up, hopefully. He's going to want to know what happened. And he is going to know what happened to his baby sister and his mother. He is going to want to know what type of justice was done. He is going to want to know what happened. With your verdict, you will provide the answer."

In the rebuttal to Payne's closing argument, the prosecutor stated:

"You saw the videotape this morning. You saw what Nicholas Christopher will carry in his mind forever. When you talk about cruel, when you talk about atrocious, and when you talk about heinous, that picture will always come into your mind, probably throughout the rest of your lives. . . .

* * *

". . . No one will ever know about Lacie Jo because she never had the chance to grow up. Her life was taken from her at the age of two years old. So, no there won't be a high school principal to talk about Lacie Jo Christopher, and there won't be anybody to take her to her high school prom. And there won't be anybody there—there won't be her mother there or Nicholas' mother there to kiss him at night. His mother will never kiss him good night or pat him as he goes off to bed, or hold him and sing him a lullaby.

* * *

"[Petitioner's attorney] wants you to think about a good reputation, people who love the defendant and things about him. He doesn't want you to think about the people who love Charisse Christopher, her mother and daddy who loved her. The people who loved little Lacie Jo, the grandparents who are still here. The brother who mourns for her every single day and wants to know where his best little playmate is. He doesn't have anybody to watch cartoons with him, a little one. These are the things that go into why it is especially cruel, heinous, and atrocious, the burden that that child will carry forever."

The jury sentenced Payne to death on each of the murder counts.

The Supreme Court of Tennessee affirmed the conviction and sentence. * * *

* * *

We granted certiorari to reconsider our holdings in *Booth* [*v. Maryland,* 482 U.S. 496 (1987)] and [*South Carolina v.*] *Gathers*[, 490 U.S. 805 (1989)] that the Eighth Amendment prohibits a capital sentencing jury from considering "victim impact" evidence relating to the personal characteristics of the victim and the emotional impact of the crimes on the victim's family.

In *Booth,* the defendant robbed and murdered an elderly couple. As required by a state statute, a victim impact statement was prepared based on interviews with the victims' son, daughter, son-in-law, and granddaughter. The statement, which described the personal characteristics of the victims, the emotional impact of the crimes on the family, and set forth the family members' opinions and characterizations of the crimes and the defendant, was submitted to the jury at sentencing. The jury imposed the death penalty. * * *

This Court held by a 5-to-4 vote that the Eighth Amendment prohibits a jury from considering a victim impact statement at the sentencing phase of a capital trial. * * * In *Gathers,* decided two years later, the Court extended the rule announced in *Booth* to statements made by a prosecutor to the sentencing jury regarding the personal qualities of the victim.

* * *

Booth and *Gathers* were based on two premises: that evidence relating to a particular victim or to the harm that a capital defendant causes a victim's family do not in general reflect on the defendant's "blameworthiness," and that only evidence relating to "blameworthiness" is relevant to the capital sentencing decision. However, the assessment of harm caused by the defendant as a result of the crime charged has understandably been an important concern of the criminal law, both in determining the elements of the offense and in determining the appropriate punishment. Thus, two equally blameworthy criminal defendants may be guilty of different offenses solely because their acts cause differing amounts of harm. * * * The same is true with respect to two defendants, each of whom participates in a robbery, and each of whom acts with reckless disregard for human life; if the robbery in which the first defendant participated results in the death of a victim, he may be subjected to the death penalty, but if the robbery in which the second defendant participates does not result in the death of a victim, the death penalty may not be imposed.

* * *

We have held that a State cannot preclude the sentencer from considering "any relevant mitigating evidence" that the defendant proffers in support of a sentence less than death. * * * *Booth* has, we think, unfairly weighted the scales in a capital trial; while virtually no limits are placed on the relevant mitigating evidence a capital defendant may introduce concerning his own circumstances, the State is barred from either offering "a quick glimpse of the life" which a defendant "chose to extinguish" or demonstrating the loss to the victim's family and to society which has resulted from the defendant's homicide.

The *Booth* Court reasoned that victim impact evidence must be excluded because it would be difficult, if not impossible, for the defendant to rebut such evidence without shifting the focus of the sentencing hearing away from the defendant, thus creating a " 'mini-trial' on the victim's character." * * * [T]he mere fact that for tactical reasons it might not be prudent for the defense to rebut victim impact evidence makes the case no different than others in which a party is faced with this sort of a dilemma. * * *

Payne echoes the concern voiced in *Booth*'s case that the admission of victim impact evidence permits a jury to find that defendants whose victims were assets to their community are more deserving of punishment than those whose victims are perceived to be less worthy. As a general matter, however, victim impact evidence is not offered to encourage comparative judgments of this kind—for instance, that the killer of a hardworking, devoted parent deserves the death penalty, but that the murderer of a reprobate does not. It is designed to show instead *each* victim's "uniqueness as an individual human being," whatever the jury might think the loss to the community resulting from his death might be. The facts of *Gathers*[b] are an excellent illustration of this: The evidence showed that the victim was an out of work, mentally handicapped individual, perhaps not, in the eyes of most, a significant contributor to society, but nonetheless a murdered human being.

* * *

* * * In the majority of cases, and in this case, victim impact evidence serves entirely legitimate purposes. In the event that evidence is introduced that is so unduly prejudicial that it renders the trial fundamentally unfair, the Due Process Clause of the Fourteenth Amendment provides a mechanism for relief. * * *

We are now of the view that a State may properly conclude that for the jury to assess meaningfully the defendant's moral culpability and blameworthiness, it should have before it at the sentencing phase evidence of the specific harm caused by the defendant. "[T]he State has a legitimate interest in counteracting the mitigating evidence which the defendant is entitled to put in, by reminding the sentencer that just as the murderer should be considered as an individual, so too the victim is an individual whose death represents a unique loss to society and in particular to his family." By turning the victim into a "faceless stranger at the penalty phase of a capital trial," *Booth* deprives the State of the full moral force of its evidence and may prevent the jury from having before it all the information necessary to determine the proper punishment for a first-degree murder.

* * * The capital sentencing jury heard testimony from Payne's girlfriend that they met at church; that he was affectionate, caring, and kind to her children; that he was not an abuser of drugs or alcohol; and that it was inconsistent with his character to have committed the murders. Payne's parents testified that he was a good son, and a clinical psychologist

---

b During closing arguments to the jury in the death-penalty hearing in *Gathers,* the prosecutor had mentioned a Bible and voter's registration card that the victim was carrying when the defendant murdered him. The prosecutor then argued that these items revealed that the victim cared about God and the United States.

testified that Payne was an extremely polite prisoner and suffered from a low IQ. None of this testimony was related to the circumstances of Payne's brutal crimes. In contrast, the only evidence of the impact of Payne's offenses during the sentencing phase was Nicholas' grandmother's description—in response to a single question—that the child misses his mother and baby sister. * * * [T]he testimony illustrated quite poignantly some of the harm that Payne's killing had caused; there is nothing unfair about allowing the jury to bear in mind that harm at the same time as it considers the mitigating evidence introduced by the defendant. * * *

* * *

We thus hold that if the State chooses to permit the admission of victim impact evidence and prosecutorial argument on that subject, the Eighth Amendment erects no *per se* bar. * * *

* * *

[W]e conclude, for the reasons heretofore stated, that [*Booth* and *Gathers*] were wrongly decided and should be, and now are, overruled.[2]

JUSTICE O'CONNOR, with whom JUSTICE WHITE and JUSTICE KENNEDY join, concurring.

* * *

* * * "Murder is the ultimate act of depersonalization." It transforms a living person with hopes, dreams, and fears into a corpse, thereby taking away all that is special and unique about the person. The Constitution does not preclude a State from deciding to give some of that back.

* * *

JUSTICE SOUTER, with whom JUSTICE KENNEDY joins, concurring.

* * *

* * * Every defendant knows, if endowed with the mental competence for criminal responsibility, that the life he will take by his homicidal behavior is that of a unique person, like himself, and that the person to be killed probably has close associates, "survivors," who will suffer harms and deprivations from the victim's death. * * * Thus, when a defendant chooses to kill, or to raise the risk of a victim's death, this choice necessarily relates to a whole human being and threatens an association of others, who may be distinctly hurt. The fact that the defendant may not know the details of a victim's life and characteristics, or the exact identities and needs of those

---

2   Our holding today is limited to the holdings of *Booth v. Maryland* and *South Carolina v. Gathers* that evidence and argument relating to the victim and the impact of the victim's death on the victim's family are inadmissible at a capital sentencing hearing. *Booth* also held that the admission of a victim's family members' characterizations and opinions about the crime, the defendant, and the appropriate sentence violates the Eighth Amendment. No evidence of the latter sort was presented at the trial in this case.

who may survive, should not in any way obscure the further facts that death is always to a "unique" individual, and harm to some group of survivors is a consequence of a successful homicidal act so foreseeable as to be virtually inevitable.

That foreseeability of the killing's consequences imbues them with direct moral relevance, and evidence of the specific harm caused when a homicidal risk is realized is nothing more than evidence of the risk that the defendant originally chose to run despite the kinds of consequences that were obviously foreseeable. It is morally both defensible and appropriate to consider such evidence when penalizing a murderer * * *. * * *

* * *

I do not, however, rest my decision to overrule wholly on the constitutional error that I see in the cases in question. I must rely as well on my further view that *Booth* sets an unworkable standard of constitutional relevance * * *. * * *

A hypothetical case will illustrate these facts and raise what I view as the serious practical problems with application of the *Booth* standard. Assume that a minister, unidentified as such and wearing no clerical collar, walks down a street to his church office on a brief errand, while his wife and adolescent daughter wait for him in a parked car. He is robbed and killed by a stranger, and his survivors witness his death. * * * The defendant did not know his victim was a minister, or that he had a wife and child, let alone that they were watching. Under *Booth,* these facts were irrelevant to his decision to kill, and they should be barred from consideration at sentencing. Yet evidence of them will surely be admitted at the guilt phase of the trial. The widow will testify to what she saw, and, in so doing, she will not be asked to pretend that she was a mere bystander. She could not succeed at that if she tried. The daughter may well testify too. The jury will not be kept from knowing that the victim was a minister, with a wife and child, on an errand to his church. This is so not only because the widow will not try to deceive the jury about her relationship, but also because the usual standards of trial relevance afford factfinders enough information about surrounding circumstances to let them make sense of the narrowly material facts of the crime itself. No one claims that jurors in a capital case should be deprived of such common contextual evidence, even though the defendant knew nothing about the errand, the victim's occupation, or his family. And yet, if these facts are not kept from the jury at the guilt stage, they will be in the jurors' minds at the sentencing stage.

Booth thus raises a dilemma with very practical consequences. If we were to require the rules of guilt-phase evidence to be changed to guarantee the full effect of *Booth's* promise to exclude consideration of specific facts unknown to the defendant and thus supposedly without significance in morally evaluating his decision to kill, we would seriously reduce the comprehensibility of most trials by depriving jurors of those details of context that allow them to understand what is being described. If, on the other hand, we are to leave the rules of trial evidence alone, *Booth's* objective will not be attained without requiring a separate sentencing jury to be empaneled. This would be a major imposition on the States, however, and I suppose that no one would seriously consider adding such a further requirement.

But, even if *Booth* were extended one way or the other to exclude completely from the sentencing proceeding all facts about the crime's victims not known by the defendant, the case would be vulnerable to the further charge that it would lead to arbitrary sentencing results. In the preceding hypothetical, *Booth* would require that all evidence about the victim's family, including its very existence, be excluded from sentencing consideration because the defendant did not know of it when he killed the victim. Yet, if the victim's daughter had screamed "Daddy, look out," as the defendant approached the victim with drawn gun, then the evidence of at least the daughter's survivorship would be admissible even under a strict reading of *Booth,* because the defendant, prior to killing, had been made aware of the daughter's existence, which therefore became relevant in evaluating the defendant's decision to kill. Resting a decision about the admission of impact evidence on such a fortuity is arbitrary.

* * *

* * * Therefore, I join the Court in its partial overruling of *Booth* and *Gathers.*

JUSTICE MARSHALL, with whom JUSTICE BLACKMUN joins, dissenting.

Power, not reason, is the new currency of this Court's decisionmaking. Four Terms ago, a five-Justice majority of this Court held that "victim impact" evidence of the type at issue in this case could not constitutionally be introduced during the penalty phase of a capital trial. * * * Neither the law nor the facts supporting *Booth* and *Gathers* underwent any change in the last four years. Only the personnel of this Court did.

* * * Because I believe that this Court owes more to its constitutional precedents in general and to *Booth* and *Gathers* in particular, I dissent.

* * *

JUSTICE STEVENS, with whom JUSTICE BLACKMUN joins, dissenting.

* * *

Until today our capital punishment jurisprudence has required that any decision to impose the death penalty be based solely on evidence that tends to inform the jury about the character of the offense and the character of the defendant. Evidence that serves no purpose other than to appeal to the sympathies or emotions of the jurors has never been considered admissible. Thus, if a defendant, who had murdered a convenience store clerk in cold blood in the course of an armed robbery, offered evidence unknown to him at the time of the crime about the immoral character of his victim, all would recognize immediately that the evidence was irrelevant and inadmissible. Evenhanded justice requires that the same constraint be imposed on the advocate of the death penalty.

* * *

* * * The fact that each of us is unique is a proposition so obvious that it surely requires no evidentiary support. * * * Evidence offered to prove such differences can only be intended to identify some victims as more worthy of protection than others. Such proof risks decisions based on the same invidious motives as a prosecutor's decision to seek the death penalty if a victim is white but to accept a plea bargain if the victim is black.

* * *

QUESTIONS AND POINTS FOR DISCUSSION

1. Victim-impact information can be presented to a sentencing court in an array of ways. A victim might, for example, prepare a written statement for the court's review or make an oral statement at the sentencing hearing. Or the presentence investigation report prepared by a probation officer might include information reported by the victim about a crime's effects. Should victims, in your opinion, have a legal right to what has been called "victim allocution"— the right to give an oral impact statement at a sentencing hearing? Why or why not? For an overview of state laws governing victim impact statements, see Paul G. Cassell, Victim Impact Statements and Ancillary Harm: The American Perspective, 15 Can. Crim. L.Rev. 149, 175 app. (2011).

2. Apart from the questions of whether and when victims should have the right to address the court at a sentencing hearing is the question of what procedures should or must govern the tendering of such a verbal impact statement. One point of contention is whether a victim's oral statement made at a sentencing hearing should or must be under oath. Compare Uniform Victims of Crime Act, § 216(a) (1992) (oral statement should be under oath) with ABA Standards for Criminal Justice: Sentencing, Standard 18–5.12(a)–(b) (3d ed. 1993) (oral statement need not be under oath, but unsworn statement cannot serve as the basis for any findings of fact by the sentencing court). See also Buschauer v. Nevada, 804 P.2d 1046, 1048 (1990) (due process requires that victim testifying at sentencing hearing be under oath). How should this issue, in your opinion, be resolved?

3. The portion of the Supreme Court's ruling in *Booth v. Maryland* that the Eighth Amendment prohibits a victim's family members from submitting a sentencing recommendation or sharing opinions about the crime and the defendant in a capital case remains in effect. Bosse v. Oklahoma, 137 S.Ct. 1 (2016). The Model Penal Code bars any victim-impact statement, including

those delivered in noncapital cases, from including a recommendation about the sentence to be imposed on a defendant. Model Penal Code: Sentencing § 7.07C(7) (American Law Inst. 2017). What are the arguments for and against disallowing such a recommendation? After reading, at the link cited below, the written victim-impact statement read in court by a woman who was sexually assaulted by the defendant, consider whether she should have been permitted to tender this message: "The probation officer's recommendation of a year or less in county jail is a soft timeout, a mockery of the seriousness of his assaults, an insult to me and all women." Lindsey Bever, "You Took Away My Worth": A Sexual Assault Victim's Powerful Message to Her Stanford Attacker, Wash. Post: Early Lead (June 4, 2016), https://www.washingtonpost.com/news/early-lead/wp/2016/06/04/you-took-away-my-worth-a-rape-victim-delivers-powerful-message-to-a-former-stanford-swimmer.

4.   Courts have been grappling with the question whether they can and should permit a videotape about a murder victim's life, including video clips of the victim when he or she was alive, to be played at a sentencing hearing. See State v. Hess, 23 A.3d 373, 392–93 (N.J.2011) (listing cases permitting and forbidding the playing of a videotape about the victim). What arguments might be mounted for and against the showing of such videotapes? If victim-impact videos are allowed, what limitations should be placed on them? For example, should videos with music playing in the background be permitted? For a discussion of some of the facts courts have considered when prohibiting or allowing victim-impact videos during sentencing proceedings, see Emily Holland, Moving Pictures . . . Maintaining Justice? Clarifying the Right Role for Victim Impact Videos in the Capital Context, 173 Berkeley J. Crim. L. 147, 158–66 (2012). For the videotape at the center of People v. Kelly, 171 P.3d 548 (Cal.2007) that was narrated by the victim's mother and showed the victim interacting with her family and friends, riding a horse, and singing "You Light Up My Life," see http://www.supremecourt.gov/media/media.aspx.

CHAPTER 6

COMMUNITY-BASED SENTENCES

■ ■ ■

A. A CONTINUUM OF SENTENCING OPTIONS

Policymakers, criminal-justice experts, and others have increasingly espoused the view that, in the words of one state statute, "[r]ational and consistent sentencing policy requires a continuum of sanctions" of varying severity. Ark. Code Ann. § 16–90–801(c)(1). One of the arguments that has been propounded in support of the development of a continuum of community-based sentencing options is that if judges do not have a range of options from which to choose, they will sometimes be forced to violate the parsimony principle referred to in Chapter 1; they will have to impose a sentence that is more restrictive than necessary to achieve its purposes. What other arguments would you make in support of making a range of community-based sentencing options available to judges?

Set forth below is an overview of some of the more prevalent community-based sentences that courts currently impose. As you read these materials, consider what other community-based sentences should, in your opinion, be readily available sentencing options.

1. FINES

Requiring a person to pay a fine is one form of punishment for a crime. Constitutional questions have arisen, however, when indigent defendants sentenced to pay a fine have been jailed because of their failure to do so. In Williams v. Illinois, 399 U.S. 235, 90 S.Ct. 2018 (1970), the Supreme Court addressed one of these questions. In that case, the defendant, who had been convicted of petty theft, had been sentenced to one year in jail and to pay a $500 fine and five dollars in court costs. He was unable, however, to pay the fine and court costs because he was indigent and, due to his incarceration, unemployed. In this type of situation, a state statute authorized a person's continued detention in jail until he had "worked off" his overdue fine at the rate of five dollars a day. The end result was that the defendant was required to remain in jail 101 days longer than the maximum jail sentence authorized for the crime of which he had been convicted.

The Supreme Court concluded that keeping an indigent person unable to pay a fine in jail for a period exceeding the maximum sentence that could be imposed on a nonindigent person violated the indigent defendant's right under the Fourteenth Amendment to be afforded equal protection of the law. At the same time, the Court emphasized that indigent individuals are not exempt from punishment for their crimes if they fail to pay a fine:

> The State is not powerless to enforce judgments against those financially unable to pay a fine; indeed, a different result would amount to inverse discrimination since it would enable an indigent to avoid both the fine and imprisonment for nonpayment whereas other defendants must always suffer one or the other [penalty].

Id. at 244, 90 S.Ct. at 2024.

The Supreme Court found *Williams* to be controlling in the later case of Tate v. Short, 401 U.S. 395, 91 S.Ct. 668 (1971). That case involved a defendant who had been fined for a series of traffic offenses, none of which were punishable by incarceration. He too was unable to pay the fines because of his indigency, so he was sentenced to a prison farm to "work off" the fines at the rate of five dollars a day. The Court held that the defendant had been discriminated against, in violation of the Equal Protection Clause, when he received a sentence exceeding the maximum penalty for the traffic offenses and imposed on him "solely because of his indigency." Id. at 398, 91 S.Ct. at 670.

In Bearden v. Georgia, 461 U.S. 660, 103 S.Ct. 2064 (1983), the case which follows, the Supreme Court once again explored the effect that indigency constitutionally can have on the criminal sanction imposed on a defendant.

BEARDEN V. GEORGIA

Supreme Court of the United States, 1983.
461 U.S. 660, 103 S.Ct. 2064, 76 L.Ed.2d 221.

JUSTICE O'CONNOR delivered the opinion of the Court.

* * *

In September 1980, petitioner was indicted for the felonies of burglary and theft by receiving stolen property. He pleaded guilty, and was sentenced on October 8, 1980. Pursuant to the Georgia First Offender's Act, the trial court did not enter a judgment of guilt, but deferred further proceedings and sentenced petitioner to three years on probation for the burglary charge and a concurrent one year on probation for the theft charge. As a condition of probation, the trial court ordered petitioner to pay a $500 fine and $250 in restitution. Petitioner was to pay $100 that day, $100 the next day, and the $550 balance within four months.

Petitioner borrowed money from his parents and paid the first $200. About a month later, however, petitioner was laid off from his job. Petitioner, who has only a ninth-grade education and cannot read, tried repeatedly to find other work but was unable to do so. The record indicates that petitioner had no income or assets during this period.

Shortly before the balance of the fine and restitution came due in February 1981, petitioner notified the probation office he was going to be late with his payment because he could not find a job. In May 1981, the State filed a petition in the trial court to revoke petitioner's probation because he had not paid the balance. After an evidentiary hearing, the trial court revoked probation for failure to pay the balance of the fine and restitution, entered a conviction, and sentenced petitioner to serve the remaining portion of the probationary period in prison. * * *

* * *

The question presented here is whether a sentencing court can revoke a defendant's probation for failure to pay the imposed fine and restitution, absent evidence and findings that the defendant was somehow responsible for the failure or that alternative forms of punishment were inadequate. The parties, following the framework of *Williams* [*v. Illinois*] and *Tate* [*v. Short*], have argued the question primarily in terms of equal protection, and debate vigorously whether strict scrutiny or rational basis is the appropriate standard of review. There is no doubt that the State has treated the petitioner differently from a person who did not fail to pay the imposed fine and therefore did not violate probation. To determine whether this differential treatment violates the Equal Protection Clause, one must determine whether, and under what circumstances, a defendant's indigent status may be considered in the decision whether to revoke probation. This is substantially similar to asking directly the due process question of whether and when it is fundamentally unfair or arbitrary for the State to revoke probation when an indigent is unable to pay the fine. Whether analyzed in terms of equal protection or due process,[8] the issue cannot be resolved by resort to easy slogans or pigeonhole analysis, but rather requires a careful inquiry into such factors as "the nature of the individual interest affected, the extent to which it is affected, the rationality of the connection between legislative means and purpose, [and] the existence of alternative means for effectuating the purpose. . . ."

---

[8] A due process approach has the advantage in this context of directly confronting the intertwined question of the role that a defendant's financial background can play in determining an appropriate sentence. When the court is initially considering what sentence to impose, a defendant's level of financial resources is a point on a spectrum rather than a classification. Since indigency in this context is a relative term rather than a classification, fitting "the problem of this case into an equal protection framework is a task too Procrustean to be rationally accomplished." The more appropriate question is whether consideration of a defendant's financial background in setting or resetting a sentence is so arbitrary or unfair as to be a denial of due process.

* * *

The rule of *Williams* and *Tate* is that * * * if the State determines a fine or restitution to be the appropriate and adequate penalty for the crime, it may not thereafter imprison a person solely because he lacked the resources to pay it. Both *Williams* and *Tate* carefully distinguished this substantive limitation on the imprisonment of indigents from the situation where a defendant was at fault in failing to pay the fine. * * *

This distinction, based on the reasons for nonpayment, is of critical importance here. If the probationer has willfully refused to pay the fine or restitution when he has the means to pay, the State is perfectly justified in using imprisonment as a sanction to enforce collection. Similarly, a probationer's failure to make sufficient bona fide efforts to seek employment or borrow money in order to pay the fine or restitution may reflect an insufficient concern for paying the debt he owes to society for his crime. In such a situation, the State is likewise justified in revoking probation and using imprisonment as an appropriate penalty for the offense. But if the probationer has made all reasonable efforts to pay the fine or restitution, and yet cannot do so through no fault of his own, it is fundamentally unfair to revoke probation automatically without considering whether adequate alternative methods of punishing the defendant are available. * * *

The State, of course, has a fundamental interest in appropriately punishing persons—rich and poor—who violate its criminal laws. A defendant's poverty in no way immunizes him from punishment. * * *

The decision to place the defendant on probation, however, reflects a determination by the sentencing court that the State's penological interests do not require imprisonment. A probationer's failure to make reasonable efforts to repay his debt to society may indicate that this original determination needs reevaluation, and imprisonment may now be required to satisfy the State's interests. But a probationer who has made sufficient bona fide efforts to pay his fine and restitution, and who has complied with the other conditions of probation, has demonstrated a willingness to pay his debt to society and an ability to conform his conduct to social norms. The State nevertheless asserts three reasons why imprisonment is required to further its penal goals.

First, the State argues that revoking probation furthers its interest in ensuring that restitution be paid to the victims of crime. A rule that imprisonment may befall the probationer who fails to make sufficient bona fide efforts to pay restitution may indeed spur probationers to try hard to pay, thereby increasing the number of probationers who make restitution. Such a goal is fully served, however, by revoking probation only for persons who have not made sufficient bona fide efforts to pay. Revoking the probation of someone who through no fault of his own is unable to make restitution will not make restitution suddenly forthcoming. Indeed, such a policy may have the perverse effect of inducing the probationer to use illegal means to acquire funds to pay in order to avoid revocation.

Second, the State asserts that its interest in rehabilitating the probationer and protecting society requires it to remove him from the temptation of committing other crimes. This is no more than a naked assertion that a probationer's poverty by itself indicates he may commit crimes in the future and thus that society needs for him to be incapacitated. * * * This would be little more than punishing a person for his poverty.

Third, and most plausibly, the State argues that its interests in punishing the lawbreaker and deterring others from criminal behavior require it to revoke probation for failure to pay a fine or restitution. The State clearly has an interest in punishment and deterrence, but this interest can often be served fully by alternative means. * * * For example, the sentencing court could extend the time for making payments, or reduce the fine, or direct that the probationer perform some form of labor or public service in lieu of the fine. * * *

We hold, therefore, that in revocation proceedings for failure to pay a fine or restitution, a sentencing court must inquire into the reasons for the failure to pay. If the probationer willfully refused to pay or failed to make sufficient bona fide efforts legally to acquire the resources to pay, the court may revoke probation and sentence the defendant to imprisonment within the authorized range of its sentencing authority. If the probationer could not pay despite sufficient bona fide efforts to acquire the resources to do so, the court must consider alternative measures of punishment other than imprisonment. Only if alternative measures are not adequate to meet the State's interests in punishment and deterrence may the court imprison a probationer who has made sufficient bona fide efforts to pay. To do otherwise would deprive the probationer of his conditional freedom simply because, through no fault of his own, he cannot pay the fine. Such a deprivation would be contrary to the fundamental fairness required by the Fourteenth Amendment.[12]

* * *

---

[12] As our holding makes clear, we agree with Justice White that poverty does not insulate a criminal defendant from punishment or necessarily prevent revocation of his probation for inability to pay a fine. We reject as impractical, however, the approach suggested by Justice White. He would require a "good-faith effort" by the sentencing court to impose a term of imprisonment that is "roughly equivalent" to the fine and restitution that the defendant failed to pay. Even putting to one side the question of judicial "good faith," we perceive no meaningful standard by which a sentencing or reviewing court could assess whether a given prison sentence has an equivalent sting to the original fine.

JUSTICE WHITE, with whom THE CHIEF JUSTICE, JUSTICE POWELL, and JUSTICE REHNQUIST join, concurring in the judgment.

* * *

Poverty does not insulate those who break the law from punishment. When probation is revoked for failure to pay a fine, I find nothing in the Constitution to prevent the trial court from revoking probation and imposing a term of imprisonment if revocation does not automatically result in the imposition of a long jail term and if the sentencing court makes a good-faith effort to impose a jail sentence that in terms of the State's sentencing objectives will be roughly equivalent to the fine and restitution that the defendant failed to pay.

The Court holds, however, that if a probationer cannot pay the fine for reasons not of his own fault, the sentencing court must at least consider alternative measures of punishment other than imprisonment, and may imprison the probationer only if the alternative measures are deemed inadequate to meet the State's interests in punishment and deterrence. There is no support in our cases or, in my view, the Constitution, for this novel requirement.

* * *

In this case, in view of the long prison term imposed, the state court obviously did not find that the sentence was "a rational and necessary trade-off to punish the individual who possesse[d] no accumulated assets." Accordingly, I concur in the judgment.

QUESTIONS AND POINTS FOR DISCUSSION

1.   Assume that a judge would have imposed a $1000 fine for a crime if the defendant had the resources to pay it. Aware that the defendant was indigent and unable to pay the fine, the judge instead imposed a 5-day jail sentence. Is there any constitutional basis for challenging this sentence?

2.   In Black v. Romano, 471 U.S. 606, 105 S.Ct. 2254 (1985), the Supreme Court considered whether, in all cases in which a defendant's probation is revoked, the court must state on the record that there are no sentencing alternatives, other than incarceration, that would meet the government's penological objectives. The Court held that due process normally does not require such a statement. The Court explained its conclusion:

> We do not question the desirability of considering possible alternatives to imprisonment before probation is revoked. Nonetheless, incarceration for violation of a probation condition is not constitutionally limited to circumstances where that sanction represents the only means of promoting the State's interest in punishment and deterrence. The decision to revoke probation is generally predictive and subjective in nature, and the fairness

guaranteed by due process does not require a reviewing court to second-guess the factfinder's discretionary decision as to the appropriate sanction. * * * We believe that a general requirement that the factfinder elaborate upon the reasons for a course not taken would unduly burden the revocation proceeding without significantly advancing the interests of the probationer.

Id. at 613, 105 S.Ct. at 2258.

The Court in *Black* emphasized that one reason why probationers would not benefit that much from a specific statement that other sentencing alternatives had been found unsatisfactory is because of the number of procedural safeguards that already must attend probation-revocation proceedings. See Gagnon v. Scarpelli, 411 U.S. 778, 93 S.Ct. 1756 (1973), *infra* note 2 on pages 422–423. When probation is revoked, for example, probationers are entitled to a written statement outlining the evidence relied on in revoking their probation and the reasons for the revocation decision. This procedural safeguard as well as others, according to the Court, will adequately protect probationers from unfounded probation revocations.

Even if a finding that incarceration is the only appropriate response to a probation violation is not constitutionally required before a probationer can be confined in prison or jail for the violation, should a legislature require such a court finding? Should a legislature require such a court finding outside the probation-revocation context—before a court imposes, in the first instance, a sentence to a period of incarceration? Why or why not?

3.   For a discussion of the constraints the Eighth Amendment places on the imposition of fines and the forfeiture of property—a type of "in-kind fine," see note 4 on pages 388–389.

———

The following two reports, both of which were published by the National Institute of Justice, describe several different approaches utilized when calculating fines. The approaches chronicled in the first report, which contains the findings of a study on the use of fines in the United States, continue to prevail today in this country. Day-fine systems, which are the focus of the report written by Dr. Edwin Zedlewski, represent a stark contrast to these conventional approaches and are common in a number of countries in Europe and Latin America.

SALLY T. HILLSMAN, JOYCE L. SICHEL, & BARRY MAHONEY, FINES IN SENTENCING: A STUDY OF THE USE OF THE FINE AS A CRIMINAL SANCTION (EXECUTIVE SUMMARY)

National Institute of Justice (1984).

* * *

Most criminal court defendants are poor, but some are not. The heart of the problem, with respect to the use of the fine as a sanction, is how to set fine amounts at a level which will reflect the seriousness of an offense yet also be within the ability of the offender to pay. Courts vary widely in how they deal with this problem. One approach is to use a kind of "tariff" system. The judges who follow this approach make sentencing judgments more or less across the board for defendants convicted of particular offenses, after developing a presumption about their "typical" defendants' degree of poverty and the fine amount most are likely to be able to pay. Similar offenses result in fines of similar amounts and little or no inquiry is made into the financial situation of individual defendants. For instance, the presumption among many New York City judges seems to be that few defendants have money to pay fines and that almost no one will be able to pay a substantial fine. Therefore, they limit the amounts of most of the fines they impose in Criminal Court and seldom use fines at all in felony cases. In contrast, some courts visited in Georgia use fines extensively in felony cases. They tend to assume that defendants, however poor, will be able to pay substantial fines and to make restitution payments as well, if given the duration of a probation sentence to pay and pressure from probation officers to do so. Only when default occurs do they seem to consider seriously the offender's actual ability to pay.

At the other end of the spectrum, some judges inquire carefully into the economic situations of convicted defendants for whom a fine is a possible sentence. This approach is consistent with the ability-to-pay concept that has been incorporated into many state statutes. For example, New Jersey's statutes provide that:

> In determining the amount and method of payment of a fine, the court shall consider the financial resources of the defendant and the nature of the burden that its payment will impose.

This statutory directive is followed by judges who ask offenders questions about the reality of their day-to-day living. For example, one judge in the Newark Municipal Court typically asks defendants such questions as: "Do you have a car? Do you buy gas? Do you smoke?"

Many of the judges interviewed during this study, when asked how they determined whether a defendant would be likely to pay a fine, tended to talk about a "feel" for the individual defendant's financial condition based on whether he was working, his age, his personal appearance, and his address of residence. Some of them would ask the defendant what he could afford (sometimes directly and sometimes through the defense attorney) and would then tailor the fine to that amount. And when court papers showed that a defendant failed to raise even a low bail, judges sometimes used this information as a basis for setting a low fine. Especially if the offense was minor and the fine set was relatively small, judges appeared to be comfortable with these "soft data." When they were contemplating a high fine or restitution in a more major case, they would be more likely to rely on presentence reports prepared by probation staffs.

The principal problem with a tariff system is that its impacts upon defendants convicted of similar offenses can be grossly inequitable. Some poverty-stricken defendants are fined more than they can possibly pay, while some relatively affluent defendants are given fines that are meaningless as punishment. Both results undermine the fine's effectiveness as a sanction. But an approach centered on the defendant's ability to pay also has conceptual and practical difficulties. If poor defendants are given very low fines (and no other punishment), there is a risk that the public will perceive such sentences as unduly lenient. On the other hand, if a judge's inquiry into the defendant's ability to pay indicates that the defendant is seriously impoverished, the sentencing decision may be jail instead of a fine.

* * *

EDWIN W. ZEDLEWSKI, ALTERNATIVES TO CUSTODIAL SUPERVISION: THE DAY FINE

National Institute of Justice (2010).

* * *

* * * Day fines are monetary penalties imposed on an offender that take into consideration the offender's financial means. They are an outgrowth of traditional fining systems, which were seen as disproportionately punishing offenders with modest means while imposing no more than slaps on the wrist for well-to-do offenders.

* * *

Calculating Day Fines

Day fines take the financial circumstances of the offender into account. They are calculated using two factors:

- **Gravity of the offense.** The number of fine units (also called offense units) imposed is based on the gravity of the offense. Most jurisdictions have written guidelines that rank offenses by severity and then assign a fine unit to each. * * *

- **Offender's daily income.** Court officials determine the daily income of the offender. The daily income is the net amount an offender makes per day minus certain fixed expenses. * * *

Once these two factors have been determined, the officer calculates the amount of fine imposed by multiplying the fine units an offender receives by his or her daily income (adjusted for family and housing obligations).

* * *

Strengths of Day Fines

Day fines convey a number of advantages in terms of ease of use and containment of other system costs:

- **Day fines achieve equity and proportionality in sentencing.** One benefit of the day fine is that it achieves proportionality and equality in sentencing offenders with different financial means. It is equitable in its attempt to treat the rich offender and the poor offender the same. It is proportionate because in order to treat the rich and poor offender the same, it only fines an offender an amount that the offender is capable of paying.

- **Day fines are punitive.** Day fines can be just as punitive as imprisonment or other alternatives to incarceration because they attack the offender's pocketbook. * * *

- **The U.S. justice system already accepts fines as criminal sanctions.** * * *

- **Day fines impose fewer system costs.** Fining offenders instead of placing them under correctional supervision reduces costs to the criminal justice system. Costs associated with enforcing compliance with probation or parole conditions are reduced. These include costs to "prepare arrest warrants, the clerical time to record and prepare arrest warrants, law enforcement apprehension, booking and conveying prisoners, additional court appearances, and court personnel time for violators repeatedly brought back to court on warrant returns, and commitment to correctional facilities."

- **Day fines divert people from more expensive forms of custody.** Because day fines allow for a larger range in the amount of the fines imposed (no minimums and ideally no caps) they allow for a greater range of punishments (more severe offenses can be considered) and can be used in place of other intermediate sanctions such as probation, community service and boot camps. By imposing monetary fines on offenders instead of removing them from society, criminal justice systems avoid severing the social bonds and networks that offenders have with their communities and families. Day fines punish offenders monetarily without depriving them of social support. Offenders can still live in the community and earn an income while paying off their debts to victims and society.

Weaknesses of Day Fines

- **Day fine administration requires sound collection systems, which are not present in most jurisdictions.** European countries have developed collection and monitoring protocols that require minimal effort, but U.S. jurisdictions have not implemented such systems. * * *

* * *

One * * * recommendation would be to move the collection process out of the courts, which are ill-equipped to track payments and manage a fine-collection system. Responsibilities could be transferred to some other office of municipal government with capabilities for collecting revenues (e.g., a tax assessor). Alternatively, courts could contract with private collection services that routinely collect funds for a variety of loans. Either solution would remove a significant challenge to administration of the system.

Another suggestion that would help with day fine administration is to follow the example of Nordic countries, who try to collect the fine in a lump-sum payment (via credit card) at the point of levy. This vastly simplifies the administration of the system and reduces monitoring overhead.

Finally, enforcement of collections should follow the Swedish model: confiscate property to remedy nonpayment. If the primary reason for implementing day fines is to reduce corrections populations, it seems counterproductive to consume prison and jail resources as part of the process.

QUESTIONS AND POINTS FOR DISCUSSION

1.   What other benefits might a jurisdiction reap from the incorporation of day fines into its sentencing system? What other drawbacks of day fines or complications they raise should a jurisdiction consider when deciding whether to adopt a system of day fines? For additional information on day fines and how to implement them, see Bureau of Justice Assistance, U.S. Dep't of Justice, How to Use Structured Fines (Day Fines) as an Intermediate Sanction (1996).

2.   Germany is one of the countries that has instituted day fines. This decision was, in part, a response to research finding that individuals incarcerated for six months or less were becoming "hardened by the system," coming out of confinement more violent and dangerous than before. See page

4 of Dr. Zedlewski's report excerpted above. With the advent of day fines, custodial sentences shorter than six months dropped sharply—from 113,000 in 1968, the year before the enactment of the legislation to generally replace these custodial sentences with fines, to 11,000 in 1976. See page 17 of the 1984 study on fines excerpted above. Prison sentences are now a relative rarity in Germany. In 2013, for example, fines were the sentence of choice in over 82% of the criminal cases. Jörg-Martin Jehle, Fed. Ministry of Justice & Consumer Prot., Criminal Justice in Germany 34 (2015). Prison sentences that were not suspended represented only 5% of the total sentences. Id.

3.   Fines are the preferred criminal sanction in a number of other countries. For example, in the Netherlands, fines are presumed under the law to be the most appropriate penalty, and when judges impose a sentence to confinement, they must explain why they did not impose a fine. Ram Subramanian & Alison Shames, Vera Inst. of Justice, Sentencing and Prison Practices in Germany and the Netherlands: Implications for the United States 8 (2013). Do you believe the law should make a fine the presumptive penalty for a crime, with an explanation required if a judge imposes a prison or jail sentence? Why or why not?

2.   RESTITUTION

A restitution order, like a fine, imposes a financial burden on a person. The difference between the two sanctions is that restitution is paid to the victim of a crime, while a fine is paid to the government. Restitution is designed to compensate the victim for at least some of the losses sustained due to the crime.

Restitution, like a fine, may be the sole sanction imposed on a defendant. Or the defendant may be placed on probation with restitution ordered as one of the conditions of that probation. Restitution also may be ordered in conjunction with other sanctions, such as a prison sentence. Set forth below are portions of the Victim and Witness Protection Act (VWPA), 18 U.S.C. §§ 3663–64, which reflects one approach to implementing the restitution sanction.

18 U.S.C. § 3663. ORDER OF RESTITUTION

(a)(1)(A)   The court, when sentencing a defendant convicted of [certain specified crimes] may order, in addition to or, in the case of a misdemeanor, in lieu of any other penalty authorized by law, that the defendant make restitution to any victim of such offense, or if the victim is deceased, to the victim's estate. The court may also order, if agreed to by the parties in a plea agreement, restitution to persons other than the victim of the offense.

(B)(i)   The court, in determining whether to order restitution under this section, shall consider—

(I) the amount of the loss sustained by each victim as a result of the offense; and

(II) the financial resources of the defendant, the financial needs and earning ability of the defendant and the defendant's dependents, and such other factors as the court deems appropriate.

(ii) To the extent that the court determines that the complication and prolongation of the sentencing process resulting from the fashioning of an order of restitution under this section outweighs the need to provide restitution to any victims, the court may decline to make such an order.

(2) For the purposes of this section, the term "victim" means a person directly and proximately harmed as a result of the commission of an offense for which restitution may be ordered * * *.

(3) The court may also order restitution in any criminal case to the extent agreed to by the parties in a plea agreement.

(b) The order may require that such defendant—

(1) in the case of an offense resulting in damage to or loss or destruction of property of a victim of the offense—

(A) return the property to the owner of the property or someone designated by the owner; or

(B) if return of the property under subparagraph (A) is impossible, impractical, or inadequate, pay an amount equal to the greater of—

(i) the value of the property on the date of the damage, loss, or destruction, or

(ii) the value of the property on the date of sentencing, less the value (as of the date the property is returned) of any part of the property that is returned;

(2) in the case of an offense resulting in bodily injury to a victim * * *—

(A) pay an amount equal to the cost of necessary medical and related professional services and devices relating to physical, psychiatric, and psychological care * * *;

(B) pay an amount equal to the cost of necessary physical and occupational therapy and rehabilitation; and

(C) reimburse the victim for income lost by such victim as a result of such offense;

(3) in the case of an offense resulting in bodily injury [that] also results in the death of a victim, pay an amount equal to the cost of necessary funeral and related services;

(4) in any case, reimburse the victim for lost income and necessary child care, transportation, and other expenses related to participation in the investigation or prosecution of the offense or attendance at proceedings related to the offense;

(5) in any case, if the victim (or if the victim is deceased, the victim's estate) consents, make restitution in services in lieu of money, or make restitution to a person or organization designated by the victim or the estate; and

(6) in the case of an offense [involving specified forms of identity theft], pay an amount equal to the value of the time reasonably spent by the victim in an attempt to remediate the intended or actual harm incurred by the victim from the offense.

(c)(1) Notwithstanding any other provision of law (but subject to the provisions of subsections (a)(1)(B)(i)(II) and (ii)), when sentencing a defendant convicted of [certain drug offenses] in which there is no identifiable victim, the court may order that the defendant make restitution in accordance with this subsection.

(2)(A) An order of restitution under this subsection shall be based on the amount of public harm caused by the offense, as determined by the court in accordance with guidelines promulgated by the United States Sentencing Commission.

(B) In no case shall the amount of restitution ordered under this subsection exceed the amount of the fine which may be ordered for the offense charged in the case.

(3) Restitution under this subsection shall be distributed as follows:

(A) 65 percent of the total amount of restitution shall be paid to the State entity designated to administer crime victim assistance in the State in which the crime occurred.

(B) 35 percent of the total amount of restitution shall be paid to the State entity designated to receive Federal substance abuse block grant funds.

(4) The court shall not make an award under this subsection if it appears likely that such award would interfere with a forfeiture under [specified statutes].

(5) * * * [A] penalty assessment under section 3013 or a fine under subchapter C of chapter 227 shall take precedence over an order of restitution under this subsection.

* * *

18 U.S.C. § 3664. PROCEDURE FOR ISSUANCE AND ENFORCEMENT OF ORDER OF RESTITUTION

(a) For orders of restitution under this title, the court shall order the probation officer to obtain and include in its presentence report, or in a separate report, as the court may direct, information sufficient for the court to exercise its discretion in fashioning a restitution order. The report shall include, to the extent practicable, a complete accounting of the losses to each victim, any restitution owed pursuant to a plea agreement, and information relating to the economic circumstances of each defendant. If the number or identity of victims cannot be reasonably ascertained, or other circumstances exist that make this requirement clearly impracticable, the probation officer shall so inform the court.

(b) The court shall disclose to both the defendant and the attorney for the Government all portions of the presentence or other report pertaining to the matters described in subsection (a) of this section.

* * *

(d)(1) Upon the request of the probation officer, but not later than 60 days prior to the date initially set for sentencing, the attorney for the Government, after consulting, to the extent practicable, with all identified victims, shall promptly provide the probation officer with a listing of the amounts subject to restitution.

(2) The probation officer shall, prior to submitting the presentence report under subsection (a), to the extent practicable—

    (A) provide notice to all identified victims of—

        (i) the offense or offenses of which the defendant was convicted;

        (ii) the amounts subject to restitution submitted to the probation officer;

        (iii) the opportunity of the victim to submit information to the probation officer concerning the amount of the victim's losses;

        (iv) the scheduled date, time, and place of the sentencing hearing;

(v) the availability of a lien in favor of the victim * * *; and

(vi) the opportunity of the victim to file with the probation officer a separate affidavit relating to the amount of the victim's losses subject to restitution; and

(B) provide the victim with an affidavit form to submit pursuant to subparagraph (A)(vi).

(3) Each defendant shall prepare and file with the probation officer an affidavit fully describing the financial resources of the defendant, including a complete listing of all assets owned or controlled by the defendant as of the date on which the defendant was arrested, the financial needs and earning ability of the defendant and the defendant's dependents, and such other information that the court requires relating to such other factors as the court deems appropriate.

(4) After reviewing the report of the probation officer, the court may require additional documentation or hear testimony. The privacy of any records filed, or testimony heard, pursuant to this section shall be maintained to the greatest extent possible, and such records may be filed or testimony heard in camera.

(5) If the victim's losses are not ascertainable by the date that is 10 days prior to sentencing, the attorney for the Government or the probation officer shall so inform the court, and the court shall set a date for the final determination of the victim's losses, not to exceed 90 days after sentencing. If the victim subsequently discovers further losses, the victim shall have 60 days after discovery of those losses in which to petition the court for an amended restitution order. Such order may be granted only upon a showing of good cause for the failure to include such losses in the initial claim for restitutionary relief.

(6) The court may refer any issue arising in connection with a proposed order of restitution to a magistrate judge or special master for proposed findings of fact and recommendations as to disposition, subject to a de novo determination of the issue by the court.

(e) Any dispute as to the proper amount or type of restitution shall be resolved by the court by the preponderance of the evidence. The burden of demonstrating the amount of the loss sustained by a victim as a result of the offense shall be on the attorney for the Government. The burden of demonstrating the financial resources of the defendant and the financial needs of the defendant's dependents, shall be on the defendant. The burden of demonstrating such other matters as the court deems appropriate shall be upon the party designated by the court as justice requires.

(f)(1)(A)   In each order of restitution, the court shall order restitution to each victim in the full amount of each victim's losses as determined by the court and without consideration of the economic circumstances of the defendant.

(B) In no case shall the fact that a victim has received or is entitled to receive compensation with respect to a loss from insurance or any other source be considered in determining the amount of restitution.

(2) Upon determination of the amount of restitution owed to each victim, the court shall * * * specify in the restitution order the manner in which, and the schedule according to which, the restitution is to be paid, in consideration of—

(A) the financial resources and other assets of the defendant, including whether any of these assets are jointly controlled;

(B) projected earnings and other income of the defendant; and

(C) any financial obligations of the defendant, including obligations to dependents.

(3)(A) A restitution order may direct the defendant to make a single, lump-sum payment, partial payments at specified intervals, in-kind payments, or a combination of payments at specified intervals and in-kind payments.

(B) A restitution order may direct the defendant to make nominal periodic payments if the court finds from facts on the record that the economic circumstances of the defendant do not allow the payment of any amount of a restitution order, and do not allow for the payment of the full amount of a restitution order in the foreseeable future under any reasonable schedule of payments.

(4) An in-kind payment described in paragraph (3) may be in the form of—

(A) return of property;

(B) replacement of property; or

(C) if the victim agrees, services rendered to the victim or a person or organization other than the victim.

(g)(1) No victim shall be required to participate in any phase of a restitution order.

(2) A victim may at any time assign the victim's interest in restitution payments to the Crime Victims Fund in the Treasury without in any way impairing the obligation of the defendant to make such payments.

(h) If the court finds that more than 1 defendant has contributed to the loss of a victim, the court may make each defendant liable for payment of the full amount of restitution or may apportion liability among the defendants to reflect the level of contribution to the victim's loss and economic circumstances of each defendant.

(i) If the court finds that more than 1 victim has sustained a loss requiring restitution by a defendant, the court may provide for a different payment schedule for each victim based on the type and amount of each victim's loss and accounting for the economic circumstances of each victim. In any case in which the United States is a victim, the court shall ensure that all other victims receive full restitution before the United States receives any restitution.

(j)(1) If a victim has received compensation from insurance or any other source with respect to a loss, the court shall order that restitution be paid to the person who provided or is obligated to provide the compensation, but the restitution order shall provide that all restitution of victims required by the order be paid to the victims before any restitution is paid to such a provider of compensation.

(2) Any amount paid to a victim under an order of restitution shall be reduced by any amount later recovered as compensatory damages for the same loss by the victim in—

(A) any Federal civil proceeding; and

(B) any State civil proceeding, to the extent provided by the law of the State.

(k) A restitution order shall provide that the defendant shall notify the court and the Attorney General of any material change in the defendant's economic circumstances that might affect the defendant's ability to pay restitution. The court may also accept notification of a material change in the defendant's economic circumstances from the United States or from the victim. The Attorney General shall certify to the court that the victim or victims owed restitution by the defendant have been notified of the change in circumstances. Upon receipt of the notification, the court may, on its own motion, or the motion of any party, including the victim, adjust the payment schedule, or require immediate payment in full, as the interests of justice require.

(l) A conviction of a defendant for an offense involving the act giving rise to an order of restitution shall estop the defendant from denying the essential allegations of that offense in any subsequent Federal civil proceeding or State civil proceeding, to the extent consistent with State law, brought by the victim.

(m)(1)(A)(i) An order of restitution may be enforced by the United States in the manner provided for in subchapter C of chapter 227 and subchapter B of chapter 229 of this title; or

(ii) by all other available and reasonable means.

(B) At the request of a victim named in a restitution order, the clerk of the court shall issue an abstract of judgment certifying that a judgment has been entered in favor of such victim in the amount specified in the restitution order. Upon registering, recording, docketing, or indexing such abstract in accordance with the rules and requirements relating to judgments of the court of the State where the district court is located, the abstract of judgment shall be a lien on the property of the defendant located in such State in the same manner and to the same extent and under the same conditions as a judgment of a court of general jurisdiction in that State.

(2) An order of in-kind restitution in the form of services shall be enforced by the probation officer.

(n) If a person obligated to provide restitution, or pay a fine, receives substantial resources from any source, including inheritance, settlement, or other judgment, during a period of incarceration, such person shall be required to apply the value of such resources to any restitution or fine still owed.

* * *

QUESTIONS AND POINTS FOR DISCUSSION

1.   The Mandatory Victims Restitution Act (MVRA), 18 U.S.C. § 3663A, mandates the payment of restitution to victims of certain crimes, such as violent crimes. Do you favor mandatory restitution? Why or why not?

2.   Assume a defendant was convicted in a federal court of knowingly possessing child pornography. Two of the pornographic images found on his computer depicted a girl being sexually abused by her uncle when she was eight or nine years old. These images have been circulated and viewed by thousands of people in the United States and worldwide. In her victim-impact statement, the victim, now a young woman, stated that knowing these pictures are being disseminated on the Internet made her feel "like I am being abused over and over and over again." She sought a restitution order directing the defendant to pay her approximately 3.4 million dollars for the lost income and treatment costs ensuing from circulation on the Internet of images of her being

sexually victimized. A federal statute, 18 U.S.C. § 2259, states that a district court "shall order restitution" for the crime of possessing child pornography, that issuance of the restitution order is "mandatory," and that the restitution order "shall direct" the defendant to pay the victim "the full amount of the victim's losses." The statute furthermore provides that 18 U.S.C. § 3664, which is set forth above, governs the issuance and enforcement of these restitution orders. Section 3664(e), as you recall, places the burden on the government of proving, by a preponderance of the evidence, "the amount of the loss sustained by a victim as a result of the offense." How would you apply these restitution provisions in a case like this one in which the defendant was convicted of possessing pornographic images also viewed by thousands of other individuals? For three very differing constructions of how to apply § 3664(e) in this kind of case, see the majority and two dissenting opinions in Paroline v. United States, 134 S.Ct. 1710 (2014).

From a policy perspective, how would you craft a statute governing the ordering of restitution in a case like this one? Should a defendant be ordered to pay restitution covering all, some, or none of the victim's statutorily specified losses stemming from the viewing of pornographic images of the victim over the Internet? If you believe the defendant should be directed to pay a portion, but not all, of those losses, how would you calculate the proportion of the losses for which the defendant is responsible?

3.   The Seventh Amendment to the United States Constitution provides in part that "[i]n suits at common law, where the value in controversy shall exceed twenty dollars, the right of trial by jury shall be preserved." Some defendants have challenged the constitutionality of the federal restitution statutes on the grounds that they violate this right to a jury trial. The courts generally have rejected these claims, holding that the statutes exact a criminal penalty and not a civil one, even though the penalty is paid to the victim. See, e.g., United States v. Stanfill El, 713 F.3d 1150, 1155 (9th Cir.2013); United States v. Rochester, 898 F.2d 971, 982 (5th Cir.1990) (defendant ordered to pay over seven million dollars in restitution under the VWPA had no right to a jury trial on the amount of restitution owed). See also Kelly v. Robinson, 479 U.S. 36, 52–53, 107 S.Ct. 353, 362–63 (1986) (restitution obligation is penal and is ordered for the state's benefit rather than to provide "compensation for actual pecuniary loss" within the meaning of the bankruptcy statute, so the obligation is not dischargeable in a bankruptcy proceeding).

4.   Under many restitution statutes, the defendant's financial resources and financial obligations to others may reduce or forestall a restitution award. This reluctance to always order full restitution stems, in part, from a concern that such orders may impede convicted persons' rehabilitation, causing them to "rob Peter to pay Paul."

The American Bar Association's Standards for Criminal Justice: Sentencing (1994) reflect a different approach to this inability-to-pay problem. Courts are supposed to order restitution in the amount that will compensate the victim for the "losses suffered." Because of the defendant's financial constraints, though, the court may provide for the payment of the restitution in installments. Standard 18–3.15(a), (c).

5.   Sometimes defendants are ordered to pay more than one economic sanction, such as both a fine and restitution, and they may have difficulty paying all of them. One of the federal statutes set forth above, 18 U.S.C. § 3663(c)(5), states that the payment of a fine has priority over the payment of restitution. By contrast, the Model Penal Code makes the payment of restitution the overriding priority. See Model Penal Code: Sentencing § 6.04(10) (American Law Inst. 2017). What do you think should be the payment priorities established by the law?

3.   FEES AND DENIAL OF GOVERNMENT BENEFITS

Jurisdictions often levy fees and special assessments on people convicted of crimes to help defray the costs of certain criminal-justice operations and correctional programs. Some fees are included as part of the sentence for a crime. Others are imposed administratively. The types of fees that individuals are required to pay are varied. Examples include: booking fees for arrestees; bail administrative fees tacked on when a person posts bail to secure release pretrial; application fees for those seeking appointment of a public defender; fees to defray the costs when a public defender is appointed; DNA-collection fees; drug-testing and alcohol-monitoring fees; substance-abuse-treatment fees; probation- and parole-supervision fees; GPS-monitoring fees; community-services fees; fees to stay in a work-release center, other community correctional center, jail, or prison; and court costs. Laura Appleman, Nickel and Dimed into Incarceration: Cash-Register Justice in the Criminal System, 57 B.C. L.Rev. 1483, 1492–1504, 1506–11 (2016).

New York University School of Law's Brennan Center for Justice studied "user fees" imposed in fifteen states on people with criminal convictions, producing a report available at http://www.brennancenter.org/sites/default/files/legacy/Fees%20and%20Fines%20FINAL.pdf. Three of the study's principal findings about the effects of these fees are summarized below. Some observations of the Conference of State Court Administrators about these fees' effects then follow.

BRENNAN CENTER FOR JUSTICE, THE HIDDEN COSTS OF CRIMINAL JUSTICE DEBT

1–2 (2010). Reprinted with the permission of the Brennan Center for Justice, New York University School of Law.

Key Findings

- **Fees, while often small in isolation, regularly total hundreds and even thousands of dollars of debt.** All fifteen of the examined states charge a broad array of fees, which are often imposed without taking into account ability to pay. One person in Pennsylvania faced $2,464 in fees alone, approximately three times the amount imposed for fines and restitution. In some states, local government fees, on top of state-wide fees, add to fee burdens. Thirteen of the fifteen states also charge poor people public defender fees simply for exercising their constitutional right to counsel. This practice can push defendants to waive counsel, raising constitutional questions and leading to wrongful convictions, over-incarceration, and significant burdens on the operation of the courts.

- **Inability to pay leads to more fees and an endless cycle of debt.** Fourteen of the fifteen states also utilize "poverty penalties" —piling on additional late fees, payment plan fees, and interest when individuals are unable to pay their debts all at once * * *. Some of the collection fees are exorbitant * * *. For example, Alabama charges a 30 percent collection fee, while Florida permits private debt collectors to tack on a 40 percent surcharge to underlying debt.

* * *

- **Criminal justice debt significantly hobbles a person's chances to reenter society successfully after a conviction.** In all fifteen of the examined states, criminal justice debt and related collection practices create a significant barrier for individuals seeking to rebuild their lives after a criminal conviction. For example, eight of the fifteen states suspend driving privileges for missed debt payments, a practice that can make it impossible for people to work and that can lead to new convictions for driving with a suspended license. Seven states require individuals to pay off criminal justice debt before they can regain their eligibility to vote. And in all fifteen states, criminal justice debt and associated collection practices can damage credit and interfere with other commitments, such as child support obligations.

* * *

CONFERENCE OF STATE COURT ADMINISTRATORS, THE END OF DEBTORS' PRISONS: EFFECTIVE COURT POLICIES FOR SUCCESSFUL COMPLIANCE WITH LEGAL FINANCIAL OBLIGATIONS

2015–2016 Policy Paper, Conference of State Court Administrators,
National Center for State Courts, 2016.

* * *

In policy papers endorsed by the Conference of Chief Justices, the Conference of State Court Administrators (COSCA) has for a long time advocated reducing or eliminating court funding through fees. * * * COSCA found that "The proliferation of these fees and costs as chargeable fees and costs included in the judgment and sentence issued as part of the legal financial obligation of the defendant has recast the role of the court as a collection agency for executive branch services." In 2014, COSCA adopted the policy that a necessary component of judicial independence for courts of limited jurisdiction is segregation of court funding from fee generation, to avoid the perception of conflict of interest and provide for judicial independence.

* * *

In addition to the disparate impact LFOs [legal financial obligations] appear to have on the economically disadvantaged, they also appear to be inefficient as a means of producing revenue. * * * In Florida, clerk performance standards rely on the assumption that just 9% of fees imposed in felony cases can be expected to be collected. [The policy paper then recounts collection rates in several other states, ranging from a low of 25% to a high of 58%.]

The low collection rates on LFOs bring into question the viability of fees and cost assessments as a cost recoupment tool. "A true cost-benefit analysis of user fees would reveal that costs imposed on sheriffs' offices, local jails and prisons, prosecutors and defense attorneys, and the courts themselves surpass what the state takes in as revenue." * * *

* * *

In addition to the direct consequences of imposing high fees, there are collateral consequences. Penalties for failure to pay LFOs may include * * * issuance of arrest warrants, extensions of supervision/probation solely to collect debt, and garnishments that can be as high as 65% of wages.

A probation or parole violation resulting from missed or late payments on LFOs disqualifies an individual under federal law from receiving Temporary Assistance to Needy Families (TANF), Food Stamps, low income housing and housing assistance, and Supplemental Security

Income (SSI)[a] for the elderly and disabled.[20] State laws may further add to the list of collateral consequences. * * *

* * *

QUESTIONS AND POINTS FOR DISCUSSION

1. The Conference of Chief Justices and the Conference of State Court Administrators have established a National Task Force on Fines, Fees and Bail Practices. The Task Force's Resource Center includes a "50 State Criminal Justice Debt Reform Builder" created by Harvard Law School's Criminal Justice Program. This tool enables users to learn about the fees and surcharges authorized and imposed in each state as well as a wealth of other information about financial obligations in criminal cases across the country. See the Task Force's website at http://www.ncsc.org/Topics/Financial/Fines-Costs-and-Fees/Fines-and-Fees-Resource-Guide.aspx.

2. Explaining that "persons convicted of crimes should not be regarded as a special class of taxpayers called upon to make up for inadequate legislative appropriations for criminal-justice agencies and programming," the American Law Institute's Model Penal Code has endorsed the abolition of costs, fees, and assessments. Model Penal Code: Sentencing § 6.04D(1)(American Law Inst. 2017); id. cmt.b (Proposed Final Draft 2017). However, the ALI has also approved an alternative approach to these kinds of financial obligations, noting that there are substantial policy reasons for their retention. Alternative § 6.04D(3) requires the approval of the sentencing court before costs, fees, or assessments can be levied in a criminal case. Between these two approaches to the imposition of costs, fees, and assessments, which is preferable and why? What other steps could be taken to mitigate the adverse effects of costs, fees, and assessments? What are the advantages and disadvantages of these steps?

3. Under standards promulgated by the American Bar Association, assessed costs and fees, unlike fines and restitution, are not considered part of the criminal sentence. ABA Standards for Criminal Justice: Sentencing, Standard 18–3.22(a) (3d ed. 1994). The failure to pay these costs and fees therefore cannot lead to revocation proceedings. Instead, the court's assessment order must be enforced through other means, such as those utilized when enforcing a civil judgment.

4. Governments have crafted other criminal penalties that have financial repercussions on people, including the denial of certain government benefits. One federal statute, for example, authorizes, and in certain

---

[a] In some instances, a person may be exempted from this disqualification. For example, the Commissioner of Social Security "may, for good cause shown based on mitigating circumstances," treat a person who has violated a term of probation or parole as eligible to receive SSI benefits when the violation was nonviolent and not drug-related. 42 U.S.C. § 1382(e)(4)(C).

[20] * * * 42 U.S.C. section 608(a)(9)(A); 7 U.S.C. section 2015(k)(1); 42 U.S.C. section 1437d(l)(9); and 42 U.S.C. section 1382(e)(4)(A)(ii).

circumstances requires, the denial of benefits as part of the sentence for a drug crime. See 21 U.S.C. § 862. Some of the benefits that can be lost include student loans, small-business loans, academic grants, and federal contracts. The statute grants judges the discretion to include a ban on these benefits when sentencing individuals convicted of possessing or distributing a controlled substance, but the sentence must include such a ban when the defendant has been convicted of drug trafficking three or more times. The ineligibility period varies depending on whether the conviction was for trafficking or possession and whether, and how many times, the defendant has been previously convicted of that kind of drug crime. In addition, the ban on benefits cannot include certain benefits exempted by the statute, including retirement, welfare, Social Security, health, disability, public housing, and veterans' benefits.

People with criminal convictions can be barred from receiving certain government benefits even when the bar is not included as part of the sentence. These and other "enmeshed penalties" (also referred to as "collateral consequences" of a conviction) are discussed in Chapter 10.

4. COMMUNITY SERVICE

Requiring individuals to perform certain services for the community without pay is another criminal sentence. In a sense, community service is a form of restitution. But instead of paying their debts to crime victims, people performing community service are paying the community for the harm their crimes have caused.

Proponents of community-service sentences tout their many advantages. Rather than sitting idly as so many people incarcerated in prison or jail do, individuals sentenced to perform community service are involved in productive work—planting trees, picking up litter in parks and by roads, helping nonprofit organizations, and performing other services from which the public benefits. Community-service sentences also cost much less than incarceration and enable the criminogenic effects of prisons and jails to be avoided.

Despite these and other benefits, community service remains, in Professor Michael Tonry's words, "the most underused intermediate sanction in the United States." Michael Tonry, Sentencing Matters 121 (1996). One of the impediments that curbs the widespread use of this sanction is that there is no central agency in many jurisdictions that is responsible for ensuring both that community service is readily available as a sentencing option and that community-service sentences are meeting their objectives. Even when a sentence to community service could feasibly be imposed in a case, presentence investigators and defense attorneys often fail to apprise judges of the viability of this sentencing option. The community-service sentencing option also sometimes faces union opposition and raises concerns about liability for injuries that can occur when people are performing community-service work. See, e.g., Arriaga v. County of Alameda, 892 P.2d 150 (Cal.1995) (person injured when performing community-service work is entitled to workers' compensation benefits). For additional information on community-service programs, see Gordon Bazemore & David R. Karp, A Civic Justice Corps: Community Service as a Means of Reintegration, 1 Just. Pol'y J. 1 (2004); Michael Tonry, Sentencing Matters 121–24 (1996).

5. PROBATION

In the United States, probation is one of the most common sentences imposed in criminal cases. At the end of 2015, 3,789,800 adults were on probation, and another 870,500 were on parole or subject to some other form of post-prison supervision release. Bureau of Justice Statistics, U.S. Dep't of Justice, Probation and Parole in the United States, 2015, at 1 (2016). When added to the over 2.1 million adults incarcerated in prisons or jails in that year, almost 3% of the nation's adult population—one out of every thirty-seven adults—was under correctional supervision. Bureau of Justice Statistics, U.S. Dep't of Justice, Correctional Populations in the United States, 2015, at 1–2, 4 (2016).

Probation is a generic term used to describe a variety of ways of controlling, treating, and supervising people during their probationary period. In terms of the constraints placed on probationers, probation may consist of little more than a requirement that they refrain from criminal activity and talk with their probation officers, either in person or on the telephone, once a month or even more infrequently. Probationers may, on the other hand, be placed on what is called intensive supervision probation. These probationers may be required to meet with their probation officers several times a week or even every day and may be subject to a number of other conditions and constraints, such as curfews and frequent drug testing. For additional information on intensive supervision probation, see Christopher T. Lowenkamp et al., Intensive Supervision Programs: Does Program Philosophy and the Principles of Effective Intervention Matter?, 38 J. Crim. Just. 368 (2010).

Examples of some of the types of restrictions that may be placed on probationers can be found in 18 U.S.C. § 3563, which is set forth below.

18 U.S.C. § 3563. CONDITIONS OF PROBATION

(a) **Mandatory conditions.**—The court shall provide, as an explicit condition of a sentence of probation—

(1) for a felony, a misdemeanor, or an infraction, that the defendant not commit another Federal, State, or local crime during the term of probation;

(2) for a felony, that the defendant also abide by at least one condition set forth in subsection (b)(2) or (b)(12), unless the court has imposed a fine under this chapter, or unless the court finds on the record that extraordinary circumstances exist that would make such a condition plainly unreasonable, in which event the court shall impose one or more of the other conditions set forth under subsection (b);

(3) for a felony, a misdemeanor, or an infraction, that the defendant not unlawfully possess a controlled substance;

(4) for a domestic violence crime * * * by a defendant convicted of such an offense for the first time that the defendant attend a public, private, or private nonprofit offender rehabilitation program that has been approved by the court, in consultation with a State Coalition Against Domestic Violence or other appropriate experts, if an approved program is readily available within a 50-mile radius of the legal residence of the defendant; and

(5) for a felony, a misdemeanor, or an infraction, that the defendant refrain from any unlawful use of a controlled substance and submit to one drug test within 15 days of release on probation and at least 2 periodic drug tests thereafter (as determined by the court) for use of a controlled substance, but the condition stated in this paragraph may be ameliorated or suspended by the court for any individual defendant if the defendant's presentence report or other reliable sentencing information indicates a low risk of future substance abuse by the defendant;

(6) that the defendant—

(A) make restitution in accordance with sections 2248, 2259, 2264, 2327, 3663, 3663A, and 3664; and

(B) pay the assessment imposed in accordance with section 3013;[b]

(7) that the defendant will notify the court of any material change in the defendant's economic circumstances that might affect the defendant's ability to pay restitution, fines, or special assessments;

(8) for a person required to register under the Sex Offender Registration and Notification Act, that the person comply with the requirements of that Act; and

---

[b]   18 U.S.C. § 3013(a) requires a court to impose a "[s]pecial assessment" on each person convicted of a crime. The amount of the assessment imposed on an individual ranges from five dollars for an infraction or class C misdemeanor to one hundred dollars for a felony.

(9) that the defendant cooperate in the collection of a DNA sample from the defendant if the collection of such a sample is authorized pursuant to section 3 of the DNA Analysis Backlog Elimination Act of 2000.

If the court has imposed and ordered execution of a fine and placed the defendant on probation, payment of the fine or adherence to the court-established installment schedule shall be a condition of the probation.

(b) Discretionary conditions.—The court may provide, as further conditions of a sentence of probation, to the extent that such conditions are reasonably related to the factors set forth in section 3553(a)(1) and (a)(2)ᶜ and to the extent that such conditions involve only such deprivations of liberty or property as are reasonably necessary for the purposes indicated in section 3553(a)(2), that the defendant—

    (1) support his dependents and meet other family responsibilities;

    (2) make restitution to a victim of the offense under section 3556 * * *;

---

c   18 U.S.C. § 3553(a)(1)–(2) provides as follows:

(a) Factors to be considered in imposing a sentence.—The court shall impose a sentence sufficient, but not greater than necessary, to comply with the purposes set forth in paragraph (2) of this subsection. The court, in determining the particular sentence to be imposed, shall consider—

    (1) the nature and circumstances of the offense and the history and characteristics of the defendant;

    (2) the need for the sentence imposed—

        (A) to reflect the seriousness of the offense, to promote respect for the law, and to provide just punishment for the offense;

        (B) to afford adequate deterrence to criminal conduct;

        (C) to protect the public from further crimes of the defendant; and

        (D) to provide the defendant with needed educational or vocational training, medical care, or other correctional treatment in the most effective manner;

    (3) the kinds of sentences available;

    (4) the kinds of sentence and the sentencing range established for—

        (A) the applicable category of offense committed by the applicable category of defendant as set forth in the guidelines * * * issued by the Sentencing Commission * * *; or

        (B) in the case of a violation of probation or supervised release, the applicable guidelines or policy statements issued by the Sentencing Commission * * *;

    (5) any pertinent policy statement * * * issued by the Sentencing Commission * * *;

    (6) the need to avoid unwarranted sentence disparities among defendants with similar records who have been found guilty of similar conduct; and

    (7) the need to provide restitution to any victims of the offense.

(3) give to the victims of the offense the notice ordered pursuant to the provisions of section 3555;[d]

(4) work conscientiously at suitable employment or pursue conscientiously a course of study or vocational training that will equip him for suitable employment;

(5) refrain, in the case of an individual, from engaging in a specified occupation, business, or profession bearing a reasonably direct relationship to the conduct constituting the offense, or engage in such a specified occupation, business, or profession only to a stated degree or under stated circumstances;

(6) refrain from frequenting specified kinds of places or from associating unnecessarily with specified persons;

(7) refrain from excessive use of alcohol, or any use of a narcotic drug or other controlled substance * * * without a prescription by a licensed medical practitioner;

(8) refrain from possessing a firearm, destructive device, or other dangerous weapon;

(9) undergo available medical, psychiatric, or psychological treatment, including treatment for drug or alcohol dependency, as specified by the court, and remain in a specified institution if required for that purpose;

(10) remain in the custody of the Bureau of Prisons during nights, weekends, or other intervals of time, totaling no more than the lesser of one year or the term of imprisonment authorized for the offense, during the first year of the term of probation or supervised release;

(11) reside at, or participate in the program of, a community corrections facility * * * for all or part of the term of probation;

(12) work in community service as directed by the court;

(13) reside in a specified place or area, or refrain from residing in a specified place or area;

(14) remain within the jurisdiction of the court, unless granted permission to leave by the court or a probation officer;

(15) report to a probation officer as directed by the court or the probation officer;

(16) permit a probation officer to visit him at his home or elsewhere as specified by the court;

---

[d] 18 U.S.C. § 3555 authorizes a court to require a defendant convicted of fraud or "other intentionally deceptive practices" to notify victims of the crime of his or her conviction.

(17) answer inquiries by a probation officer and notify the probation officer promptly of any change in address or employment;

(18) notify the probation officer promptly if arrested or questioned by a law enforcement officer;

(19) remain at his place of residence during nonworking hours and, if the court finds it appropriate, that compliance with this condition be monitored by telephonic or electronic signaling devices, except that a condition under this paragraph may be imposed only as an alternative to incarceration;

(20) comply with the terms of any court order or order of an administrative process * * * requiring payments by the defendant for the support and maintenance of a child or of a child and the parent with whom the child is living;

(21) be ordered deported by a United States district court, or United States magistrate judge, pursuant to a stipulation entered into by the defendant and the United States * * *, except that, in the absence of a stipulation, the United States district court or a United States magistrate judge, may order deportation as a condition of probation, if, after notice and hearing * * *, the Attorney General demonstrates by clear and convincing evidence that the alien is deportable;

(22) satisfy such other conditions as the court may impose; or

(23) if required to register under the Sex Offender Registration and Notification Act, submit his person, and any property, house, residence, vehicle, papers, computer, other electronic communication or data storage devices or media, and effects to search at any time, with or without a warrant, by any law enforcement or probation officer with reasonable suspicion concerning a violation of a condition of probation or unlawful conduct by the person, and by any probation officer in the lawful discharge of the officer's supervision functions.

(c) Modifications of conditions.—The court may modify, reduce, or enlarge the conditions of a sentence of probation at any time prior to the expiration or termination of the term of probation, pursuant to the provisions of the Federal Rules of Criminal Procedure relating to the modification of probation and the provisions applicable to the initial setting of the conditions of probation.

* * *

QUESTIONS AND POINTS FOR DISCUSSION

1. The preceding sections of the Federal Probation Act exemplify the types of conditions that can be imposed as conditions of probation, supervised release, or parole. Judges traditionally have been accorded broad discretion when imposing probation and supervised-release conditions, as have parole boards when imposing parole conditions. As long as the conditions are reasonably related to one or more of the penological goals served by probation or other form of community supervision and meet any other statutory or constitutional requirements, the conditions generally have been upheld. See, e.g., People v. Olguin, 198 P.3d 1, 5–6 (Cal.2008) (probation condition requiring defendant to notify probation officer of any pets at defendant's residence facilitated unannounced searches of it and hence was reasonably related to the goal of deterring future crimes by the defendant); United States v. Jeremiah, 493 F.3d 1042, 1046 (9th Cir.2007) (condition requiring defendant, who "willfully" had failed to make restitution payments, to incur no credit charges without probation officer's prior approval was reasonably related to monitoring his ability to pay restitution).

Some courts have applied variants of this reasonable-relationship test. For example, in some states, a probation or parole condition must be reasonably related to the crime of which the person was convicted. See, e.g., Boyd v. State, 749 So.2d 536 (Fla.Dist.Ct.App.2000) (probation conditions prohibiting the defendant from possessing or consuming alcohol, frequenting bars, and associating with persons who consume alcohol were not reasonably related to the crime for which he was sentenced—solicitation or delivery of cocaine).

The application of the reasonable-relationship test or its variants often leads to the upholding of a probation or other community-supervision condition. See, e.g., United States v. Rodriguez, 558 F.3d 408, 413–14 (5th Cir.2009) (upholding supervised-release condition prohibiting defendant, who had been convicted of assaulting a federal officer and had a state charge for sexual assault of a minor pending against him, from "associating with" a child under the age of eighteen, including his own children, unless an adult designated in writing by the probation officer was present and supervising); Todd v. State, 911 S.W.2d 807, 817–18 (Tex.Ct.App.1995) (not an abuse of discretion to require defendant convicted of negligent homicide, as conditions of his probation, to perform one hundred hours of community service in a place where he would see the aftermath of automobile accidents and to write letters of apology to the victim's girlfriend and family on the first and second anniversaries of the crime and when his probation term ends). But sometimes an appellate court will find a probation, parole, or supervised-release condition to be unconstitutional or its imposition an abuse of discretion. See, e.g., State v. Herd, 87 P.3d 1017, 1022 (Mont.2004) (40-year driving ban, imposed on defendant who killed four people in a car accident while rushing to see her dying mother, was not reasonably related to defendant's rehabilitation or the protection of a victim or society); State v. Muhammad, 43 P.3d 318, 325 (Mont.2002) (probation condition requiring defendant convicted of a sex crime involving a fourteen-year-old to post a sign at every entrance of his residence stating, "CHILDREN UNDER THE AGE OF 18 ARE NOT ALLOWED BY COURT ORDER," not reasonably related to the goals of rehabilitating the defendant or protecting the victim and the public). For an in-depth analysis of whether a "shame sentence" imposed on a defendant was authorized by statute and was constitutional, see United States v. Gementera, 379 F.3d 596 (9th Cir.2004), on page 402.

2.   Courts have grappled with questions about the legality of community-supervision conditions restricting defendants' use of computers and access to the Internet. A number of appellate courts, though not all of them, have upheld conditions requiring the prior approval of a probation officer before a defendant convicted of using a computer to distribute child pornography can use the Internet or even use a computer with Internet access. See United States v. Accardi, 669 F.3d 340, 347–48 (D.C.Cir.2012) (listing cases). By contrast, in United States v. Crume, 422 F.3d 728, 733 (8th Cir.2005), the Eight Circuit Court of Appeals vacated a supervised-release condition that barred the defendant, who had been convicted of knowingly receiving and knowingly possessing child pornography, from accessing a computer and the Internet without first obtaining written consent from his probation officer. Concluding that this condition impinged on the defendant's First Amendment rights more than "reasonably necessary," the court mentioned a more narrow alternative: prohibiting the defendant from accessing certain websites and kinds of information on the Internet and monitoring compliance with this condition through a combination of software filters and random searches. In striking down the supervised-release condition, the court also emphasized that the defendant had used his computer and the Internet "merely" to possess child pornography and not, for example, to transmit pornographic images to others. Id. at 733.

What conditions do you believe should be placed on defendants' access to computers and to the Internet while they are serving or completing sentences within the community for crimes involving child pornography? Does it matter, in your opinion, whether a defendant has been convicted of possessing, as opposed to distributing, child pornography?

3.   As 18 U.S.C. § 3563 demonstrates, legislatures can mandate or authorize courts to impose certain probation conditions. Legislatures also can prohibit the imposition of certain probation conditions. In your opinion, should legislatures prohibit a court from ever requiring a defendant, as a condition of probation, to utilize birth control? See 730 Ill. Comp. Stat. 5/5–4.5–50(g) (prohibiting courts from requiring defendants "to be implanted or injected with or to use any form of birth control"). Or should legislatures specifically authorize imposition of such a probation condition in certain circumstances? If so, what are those circumstances? After reading the ensuing note, consider how, if at all, your opinions on these questions have changed.

4.   State v. Kline, 963 P.2d 697 (Or.Ct.App.1998) involved a defendant whose parental rights were terminated after he abused his son, breaking his

arm. Several years later, the defendant and his wife had a daughter, whom he also abused, both physically and emotionally, when he was high on methamphetamine. Holding the baby up to his face, the defendant would scream obscenities at her. He also would sometimes leave the baby in her crib all day and not let his wife check on her. And when his wife and her parents discovered bruises on the baby's chest and back, the defendant threatened to kill anyone who called the Children's Services Division.

One day, when the defendant went to retrieve the baby from her crib, she began screaming. Although the defendant's wife noticed a few minutes later that the baby appeared to have a leg injury, the defendant would not let her take the baby to a doctor for three days. When she did, X-rays revealed that the baby's leg had been fractured.

The defendant was convicted of criminal mistreatment in the first degree and placed on probation for thirty-six months. As a condition of probation, he was prohibited from "fathering a child" unless he first obtained the court's written approval and successfully completed a drug-treatment and anger-management program. If you were on the appellate court, would you uphold this probation condition? Would you uphold a condition, imposed on a defendant convicted of intentionally refusing to pay child support for the nine children he had had with four different women, prohibiting him from having another child unless he demonstrated that he would support the child and his other nine children? See State v. Oakley, 629 N.W.2d 200 (Wis.2001).

5.   As a condition of probation or parole or as a condition of being eligible for certain privileges in prison, individuals with substance-abuse problems have been required to attend Alcoholics Anonymous (AA) or Narcotics Anonymous (NA) meetings. The twelve steps to recovery prescribed by AA and NA and recited at their meetings include numerous references to God. For example, meeting attendees acknowledge that they have "made a decision to turn our will and our lives over to the care of God as we understood Him." Most courts have held that requiring convicted individuals to attend AA or NA meetings violates the First Amendment's proscription of governmental "establishment of religion." Inouye v. Kemna, 504 F.3d 705, 715 (9th Cir.2007) (listing cases). To avoid an Establishment Clause problem, they must be advised of, and if they wish afforded, a "meaningful" secular alternative to AA or NA. Bausch v. Sumiec, 139 F.Supp.2d 1029, 1033 n.4, 1036 (E.D.Wis.2001). The location, cost, and frequency of a secular alternative's meetings may bear on whether the choice offered is, in truth, a meaningful one. See Michael G. Honeymar, Jr., Note, Alcoholics Anonymous as a Condition of Drunk Driving Probation: When Does It Amount to Establishment of Religion, 97 Colum. L.Rev. 437, 465–67 (1997) (listing factors that may lead to "de facto compulsory Alcoholics Anonymous").

6.   Some probation and parole conditions prohibit entering or remaining in a particular geographical area. See, e.g., State v. Cornell, 146 A.3d 895, 904–05 (Vt.2016) (upholding probation condition barring defendant, who had been convicted of lewd and lascivious behavior with a 12-year-old boy, from "places

where children are known to congregate," including parks, playgrounds, and elementary and high-school grounds, without the prior approval of his probation officer or designee). Most courts have invalidated conditions banishing a person from the state, finding them to be unconstitutional abridgements on the right to interstate travel and not reasonably related to sentencing goals. Commonwealth v. Pike, 701 N.E.2d 951, 960 (Mass.1998). In striking down such a probation condition, the Supreme Judicial Court of Massachusetts observed that making other states a "dumping ground for our criminals" would contravene public policy and invite retaliation from other states. Id.

Courts, on the other hand, sometimes have upheld, and other times have stricken, more limited geographical restrictions. Compare Terry v. Hamrick, 663 S.E.2d 256, 258–60 (Ga.2008) (probation condition banishing defendant, who had been convicted of aggravated stalking of his wife and other crimes, from 158 of the state's 159 counties was valid) and Parrish v. State, 355 S.E.2d 682, 683–84 (Ga.Ct.App.1987) (probation condition banning defendant, who had been convicted of assault, obstruction of officers, possession of marijuana, and tampering with evidence, from judicial circuit for six-year probation period upheld) with State v. Stewart, 713 N.W.2d 165, 170–71 (Wis.Ct.App.2006) (probation condition banning defendant, who had been convicted of felony bail jumping and felony fleeing, from township for five years was overbroad; since most of his criminal conduct, which included abuse of his wife and children and masturbating in public, was directed towards his family and neighbors, the court could have imposed a "more narrowly drawn condition," banning the defendant from his house and the immediate neighborhood) and People v. Beach, 195 Cal.Rptr. 381, 386–87 (Cal.Ct.App.1983) (probation condition requiring defendant, who had been found guilty of involuntary manslaughter, to leave the community where she had lived for twenty-four years unconstitutionally impinged on her right to intrastate travel and to possess and enjoy her personal property).

Assume that a defendant was convicted of the felony of "sexual intercourse without consent." The crime occurred at a party where the defendant, who was twenty-two, met the victim, who was fourteen. Describe the analysis you would undertake and the factors you would consider if the prosecutor asked you, the sentencing judge, to banish the defendant, as a condition of the defendant's six-year suspended prison sentence, from the county in which he and the victim live.

Set forth below is a proposal for what the authors describe as a "new paradigm" in the structuring and operations of probation. As you read this proposal, consider its feasibility and soundness and identify what other or different steps you would propose to enhance the cost-effectiveness of this criminal sanction. For a book containing additional details on this different probation model, see Lacey Schaefer, Francis T. Cullen, & John E. Eck,

Environmental Corrections: A New Paradigm for Supervising Offenders in the Community (2016).

FRANCIS T. CULLEN, JOHN E. ECK, & CHRISTOPHER T. LOWENKAMP, ENVIRONMENTAL CORRECTIONS— A NEW PARADIGM FOR EFFECTIVE PROBATION AND PAROLE SUPERVISION

66 Federal Probation 28 (Sept. 2002).
Reprinted with the permission of Federal Probation.

* * *

The Need to Reinvent Community Supervision

At present, American criminologists hold two incompatible views of probation and parole. First, most criminologists—representing a liberal or progressive position—see community supervision as the *lesser of two evils*: at least it is better than incarceration! There is no agenda as to how probation and parole might be accomplished more effectively. Rather, value inheres in community supervision only—or mainly—because it is *not* prison. In this scenario, prisons are depicted as costly and inhumane. They are seen as causing crime in two ways: by making those placed behind bars more criminogenic and by so disrupting communities—especially minority communities that lose high percentages of young males to incarceration—as to exacerbate crime's root causes (e.g., increase institutional disorganization). * * *

Second, a minority of criminologists—representing a conservative position—sees community supervision *as an evil.* * * * [P]robation and premature parole are dangerous policies that allow not only petty offenders but also chronic and potentially violent offenders to continue their criminality. * * *

* * *

Where, then, do these various considerations leave us? First, in contrast to the desires of conservative commentators, the stubborn reality is that most offenders will not be incarcerated but will be placed under community supervision. And among those who are locked up, a high proportion will reenter society in a reasonably short period of time—and perhaps more criminogenic than they were before being imprisoned. Second, in contrast to the implicitly rosy portrait that liberals often paint of the criminally wayward, many of these offenders placed in the community will be occasional, if not high-rate, offenders. *In short, we are left with the inescapable necessity of supervising many potentially active, if not dangerous, offenders in the community.*

In this light, it is odd how little liberal commentators have had to say about the "technology" of offender supervision—that is, how to do it more effectively. * * * In part, this silence represents a larger rejection of the social welfare role in corrections and the belief that the two sides of the probation/parole officer role—treatment and control—are in inherent conflict and render officers ineffective in their efforts to improve offenders. * * *

In contrast, beginning in the 1980s, conservative commentators had much to say about how to "reform" community supervision: purge it of its social welfare functions and increase its policing and deterrence functions. We will revisit this matter soon, but we will give advance notice that this prescription has been detrimental to the practice of community supervision. It is a failed model.

* * * [T]he purpose of the current paper *is to suggest a new paradigm or strategy for improving the community supervision of offenders.* * * *

The main premise of this enterprise is that effective correctional intervention must be based on *effective criminological research and theory.* * * *

* * *

Crime in the Making—Propensity and Opportunity

For a criminal event to occur, two ingredients must converge in time and space: first, there must be a "motivated offender"—a person who has the propensity to commit the criminal act. Second, the person harboring a criminal propensity must have the *opportunity* to commit a crime. This simple idea—that the recipe for making a criminal act is propensity and opportunity—holds potentially profound and complex implications for how to reduce crime. These implications have seldom been systematically or scientifically explored within corrections.

What Works with Propensity

* * * Research from available meta-analysis is now incontrovertible that correctional intervention programs—especially in the community—reduce recidivism. These programs are especially effective in reducing reoffending when they are consistent with certain principles of effective intervention. Such principles include: 1) using cognitive-behavioral interventions within the context of multi-modal programs; 2) targeting for change the known predictors of recidivism; 3) focusing on higher-risk offenders; 4) applying a sufficient dosage of treatment; and 5) providing appropriate aftercare.

* * *

What Does Not Work with Opportunity

From the beginning period in which community supervision was invented, it was understood that "supervision" involved both trying to change offenders for the better *and* acting as an external source of control that, backed up by the threat of revocation, tried to keep offenders away from "trouble." When placed in the community, offenders often were given lists of "conditions" that spelled out the kind of situations they must avoid, including, for example, not frequenting bars, not having contact with criminal associates, and not carrying a weapon. There were also prescriptions of what offenders could do, such as staying employed and attending school. Embedded within these probation and parole "conditions" was the assumption that "going straight" was facilitated by offenders avoiding situations where *opportunities for crime* were present and frequenting situations where opportunities for crime were absent. Unfortunately, this core insight was never fully developed to its logical conclusion: the idea that a fundamental goal of community supervision was to *plan systematically with each offender on how precisely to reduce his or her opportunities for wayward conduct.*

     * * * [O]pportunity reduction involves, among other factors, problem solving—that is, figuring out how to keep offenders away from situations in which trouble inheres. This approach requires, fundamentally, changing the *nature of supervision.* In contrast, efforts from the 1980s to the present to "intensively supervise" offenders—the deterrence-oriented "reform" advocated by conservatives—have sought mainly to change the *amount of supervision.* This strategy is akin to a police crackdown on crime in hopes of increasing the risk of detection or arrest as opposed to using police resources to solve the problems fostering neighborhood crime; even if the crackdown works for a specific period or for specific offenders, the effects tend to wear off over time because the underlying problems are not addressed. In any event, whether the literature involves narrative reviews, meta-analyses, or randomized experimental evaluations, the results are clear in showing that deterrence-oriented intensive supervision simply does not reduce recidivism. * * *

     The weakness in the intensive supervision approach—the "pee 'em and see 'em" model as some officers call it—is that it is based on a crude understanding of crime. Efforts to specifically deter offenders through uncertain and distant threats of punishment are notoriously ineffective. It may seem like good "common sense" that more intense monitoring would increase the deterrent capacity of community supervision. But its effects are diminished by two factors: it does not do much to change the underlying propensity to offend and it does not do much to change the structure of opportunities that induce "motivated offenders" to recidivate. In short, the two key ingredients to making crime—propensity and opportunity—are not transformed by increasing the amount of supervision. * * *

* * *

A New Paradigm for Correctional Supervision

Probation and Parole Officers as Problem Solvers

Recidivism is due to offenders' retaining criminogenic motivation or propensity and their having access to opportunities for crime. Thus, to reduce reoffending, an important task for a probation or parole agency is to provide or place offenders into treatment programs, based on the principles of effective rehabilitation, that diminish their propensity for crime. The other task, however, is for probation and parole officers to reduce offenders' access to *crime opportunities.* * * *

* * *

In this context, we are proposing that probation and parole officers reconceptualize their supervision function as involving not only watching and busting offenders but also problem solving. The key problem to solve, of course, is how to reduce offenders' access to criminal opportunities. * * *

* * *

Working with Offenders. * * * [O]fficers would focus on three tasks. First, with individual supervisees, they would try to *disrupt routine activities that increase crime opportunities.* As opposed to broad supervision conditions, such as "not associating with known felons," officers would seek to prohibit contact with specific people (e.g., past co-offenders), traveling on specific streets (e.g., outlined on a map given to offenders), and access to specific establishments (e.g., bars where trouble often ensues). Second, behavioral change involves not only extinguishing inappropriate conduct, but also replacing it with preferred alternatives. Officers thus might work with offenders to develop daily "activity calendars" scheduling prosocial activities. This process might involve officers "brokering" prosocial activities—that is, developing rosters of "things to do" in the community or at home to lead offenders away from crime opportunities. Third, officers would see themselves not exclusively as "enforcing supervision conditions" but as *handlers of offenders.* Although the threat of revocation—a formal sanction—would necessarily loom in the background, the goal would be to exercise *informal social control* over offenders. This would entail using positive reinforcements for prosocial routine activities and building a "bond" with offenders. * * *

Working with Family Members and the Community. Ideally, officers would also attempt to enlist an offender's family, prosocial friends, and community members (e.g., minister, teacher) to assist in designing an opportunity reduction plan. * * * One strategy would be to have a "problem-solving conference" in which offenders and those in their intimate circle would jointly identify problematic routines and places and decide how these might be avoided. * * *

* * *

[A] new paradigm—a new way of thinking—is needed to replace the failed paradigm that, in large part, has tried to use scare tactics to keep offenders away from crime opportunities. The purpose of this paper has been to sketch the components of this new approach to community supervision—a paradigm that we have called *environmental corrections*.

* * *

We recognize that translating theory into practice is fraught with a host of difficulties, not the least of which is that our ideas on reducing crime opportunities are likely to be labor intensive. In practical terms, this approach is likely to be cost effective primarily with high-risk offenders, who already often receive more intensive supervision. * * *

QUESTIONS AND POINTS FOR DISCUSSION

1. Note one of the central premises of the preceding article—that criminal sanctions should be structured and continually refined to reflect research findings on what does and doesn't work in corrections. As a practical matter, what steps can be taken so that the policymakers authorizing the imposition of particular criminal sanctions are well informed about their relative efficacy or inefficacy? What steps can be taken so that corrections professionals are well informed about the effectiveness of the varied ways in which to implement those sanctions and of different treatment modalities?

2. As 18 U.S.C. § 3563 demonstrates, many of the sanctions that are discussed in this chapter, such as fines, restitution, community service, and home confinement, can be included as conditions of probation. Probation also can be combined with an incarcerative sanction when a defendant is sentenced. When what is known as a "split sentence" is imposed, the defendant is sentenced to prison or jail for a specified period of time, to be followed by a period of probation.

Another hybrid sanction is known as "shock incarceration." In a shock-incarceration program, commonly referred to as "boot camp," a person is subjected to a short, but intensive, incarceration program. The program generally has military-type features—a highly structured regimen, strict discipline, physical exercise, hard labor, and drills and ceremonies. What has been described as the "in your face" approach that typifies boot-camp programs is reflected in the following introduction of boot-camp participants to one such program:

> You are nothing and nobody, fools, maggots, dummies, motherf____ s___, and you have just walked into the worst nightmare you ever dreamed. I don't like you. I have no use for you, and I don't give a f___ who you are on the street. This is my acre, hell's half acre, and it matters not one damn to me whether you make it here or get tossed out into the general prison population, where, I promise you, you won't last three minutes before you're somebody's wife. Do you know what that means, tough guys?

Doris Layton MacKenzie & Claire Souryal, A "Machiavellian" Perspective on the Development of Boot Camp Prisons: A Debate, 2 U.Chi.L. Sch. Roundtable 435, 447 (1995). If a person successfully completes a boot-camp program, which usually lasts three to six months, he or she will be resentenced to probation and avoid confinement in prison.

Most studies of boot camps have found that they do not result in lower recidivism compared to prison or jail. David B. Wilson et al., Effects of Correctional Boot Camps on Offending, 6 Campbell Systematic Reviews 16, 18 (2005). There is some evidence, though, that boot camps with a strong emphasis on therapeutic programming, such as counseling, substance-abuse treatment, and post-release aftercare, are more effective in reducing recidivism than traditional incarceration. Doris Layton MacKenzie et al., An experimental study of a therapeutic boot camp: Impact on impulses, attitudes and recidivism, 3 J. Experimental Criminology 221, 223–24 (2007). Even if boot camps, on average, have little, if any, recidivism-reducing effects, could you make any arguments in favor of their use? What arguments would you make in opposition to the utilization of boot camps?

6. DAY REPORTING CENTERS

As an independent sanction or as a condition of probation, people may be sentenced to a day reporting center (DRC). During the parts of the day that they are at a day reporting center, they may have to participate in programs designed to redress some of the problems that may have contributed to their criminal behavior. For example, individuals who dropped out of school may have to go to classes and work towards obtaining a high-school-equivalency degree. Alternatively or in addition, individuals sentenced to DRCs may have to undergo vocational training, participate in counseling or other treatment programs, and get tested for signs of drug or alcohol use. DRCs can also offer opportunities to participate in the restorative practices described in Chapter 1—restorative-justice conferences, various kinds of circles, and family group decision-making.

During designated parts of the day, individuals may leave the DRC to work, attend school, or participate in other treatment programs, or they may be sent into the community to perform public-service work. They usually must complete daily itineraries apprising DRC staff where they will be when they are not at the day reporting center. The staff members then periodically take steps to verify their whereabouts, whether through calls placed to or from them, unannounced drop-in visits, or other means. For examples of some of the many different ways day reporting centers can be structured, see Sudipto Roy & Jennifer N. Grimes, Adult Offenders in a Day Reporting Center—A Preliminary Study, 66 Fed. Probation 44, 44–45 (June 2002); 1 Dale G. Parent et al., U.S. Dep't of Justice, Day Reporting Centers (1995).

7. HOME CONFINEMENT AND ELECTRONIC MONITORING

In the search for intermediate sanctions falling between the extremes of standard probation and incarceration, government officials have increasingly turned to a sanction known as home confinement. As the name of the sanction suggests, people sentenced to home confinement must remain in their homes or apartments at certain times. The conditions of their home confinement, however, may vary. For example, they may be required to be in their homes only a few designated hours a day, or they may have to stay in their homes up to twenty-four hours a day. Probation officers, police officers, and other individuals may monitor individuals' compliance with their home-confinement sentences through visits or phone calls to their homes, or electronic monitoring devices (EMDs) can be used to ensure they are in their homes when they are supposed to be.

In developing standards to govern the use of home confinement, with or without electronic monitoring, as a criminal sanction, policymakers, judges, and others have had to grapple with a number of questions, including the following:

1. Who should be subject to these sanctions? Should only people who would otherwise be sentenced to prison or jail be confined in their homes? Should only individuals convicted of nonviolent crimes be sentenced to home confinement?

2. Under what circumstances should people sentenced to home confinement be permitted to leave their homes? Should the yard of a home be considered part of the home into which a person can venture? If so, what should be done about people who have no homes and are confined in their apartments?

3. How long should home-confinement sentences be?

How would you resolve these questions?

A variety of EMDs have been developed to assist in the enforcement of the home-confinement sanction, and new monitoring devices are constantly being placed on the market. Jurisdictions most commonly use Global Positioning System (GPS) satellite monitoring to track individuals' whereabouts twenty-four hours a day. The PEW Charitable Trusts, Use of Electronic Offender-Tracking Devices Expands Sharply 3 (2016), available at http://www.pewtrusts.org/en/research-and-analysis/issue-briefs/2016/09/use-of-electronic-offender-tracking-devices-expands-sharply. GPS technology can be used to monitor a person's presence in "inclusion zones," areas where he or she must be at prescribed times, or in "exclusion zones," areas into which the person is prohibited from entering. When a person being actively tracked by GPS leaves an inclusion zone or enters an exclusion zone, the

GPS can alert authorities and any victim on the notification list programmed into the system.

EMDs can also be utilized for purposes other than to confirm a person's presence in the home or elsewhere. Some devices, for example, can analyze an individual's breath or perspiration to determine whether he or she has, in violation of the conditions of a sentence, consumed any alcohol. The technology also exists that would enable live video feeds of a person to be funneled continuously or periodically to authorities. Another tool in the technological arsenal being developed to monitor people convicted of crimes more closely is a microchip that can be implanted in the body just under the skin, making it possible to know where a person is at all times and whether he or she has ingested drugs or alcohol in contravention of the court's sentencing order. Do you favor the incorporation of these emerging technologies into criminal sentences? If so, under what circumstances, and if not, why not? For additional information on electronic monitoring, see William Bales et al., A Quantitative and Qualitative Assessment of Electronic Monitoring (2010); Matthew DeMichele & Brian Payne, Am. Prob. & Parole Ass'n, Offender Supervision with Electronic Technology: Community Corrections Resource (2d ed. 2009).

8. OTHER SENTENCING OPTIONS AND DEFERRED ADJUDICATION

Well-contoured sentencing and corrections systems will offer judges other sentencing options from which to choose. For example, in many jurisdictions, a court may sentence a person to reside in a correctional residential facility within the community for a prescribed period of time. People who live in these group-home-like facilities can leave to go to work, school, or other approved places during the day. While living in a community correctional center, they also typically receive counseling, life-skills training, and other treatment and services to aid them become law-abiding and productive citizens.

Most states also authorize what is usually referred to as "deferred adjudication" for some or many crimes. Collateral Consequences Res. Ctr., Forgiving and Forgetting in American Justice: A 50-State Guide to Expungement and Restoration of Rights 13–14 (2017). Typically, a defendant must enter a guilty plea or at least admit guilt to be eligible for deferred adjudication. The court then enters a continuance in the case. During the continuance, the defendant may be subject to supervision or have to meet certain conditions similar to those imposed as conditions of probation. If the defendant successfully meets the terms of the deferred adjudication, the court then dismisses the charges, enabling the defendant to avoid the stigma of a criminal conviction and the enmeshed penalties ("collateral consequences") that ensue from a conviction.

In your opinion, for what kinds of crimes should deferred adjudication be an option? For information on the states' varied treatment of the crimes for which deferred adjudication is available, see id. at 12–14, 69–95.

9. IMPOSITION OF THE APPROPRIATE SENTENCE

United States District Judge John Kane expressed the views of many trial judges when he said, "I know of no more excruciating decision for a judge to make than whether to confine and, if so, for how long and under what terms and conditions." United States v. O'Driscoll, 586 F.Supp. 1486, 1486 (D.Colo.1984). Having reviewed information about some of the many sentencing options that may be available to a judge, what sentence would you impose in the two cases set forth below if you were the sentencing judge and all sentencing options were available to you?[e] In addition, reconsider what the appropriate penalty would be in the cases described in note 2 on pages 15–16.

1.   Samuel E. Cole has pled guilty to two counts of Distribution of a Controlled Substance—Cocaine. Cole is twenty-six. His father is a former Marine who is presently self-employed as an insurance agent. His mother is a homemaker.

Cole has been described as having been hyperactive when growing up, but he never received medication or counseling for his hyperactivity. His academic skills were above average, but he was not interested in school and eventually dropped out of high school six months before graduation. Over the next six years, Cole worked at a variety of different jobs—as a horse groomer, salesman, construction carpenter apprentice, van and moving assistant, aluminum siding installer, and a waiter. Few of these jobs, however, appealed to him, but he did receive his high-school-equivalency degree by attending night classes during this time period.

Six years ago, Cole was involved in a car accident. According to Cole, the occupants of the car came up to him after the accident and began hitting him. In self-defense, he struck back, slapping one of his assailants. He was later charged with assault and battery. Though he insisted he was not guilty, Cole followed his attorney's advice and pled guilty. The court then placed Cole on what is called "Probation Before Judgment."

Three years ago, Cole began working at a restaurant where he met people who regularly used cocaine. Cole also began to use

---

[e]   Information about the two cases was drawn from sentencing proposals prepared by the National Center on Institutions and Alternatives (NCIA). NCIA, a private, nonprofit agency, was founded in 1977 by Dr. Jerome Miller and Herbert J. Hoeltner to promote the use of safe and effective alternative sanctions to prisons and jails.

the drug two to three times a week. Eventually, his cocaine use escalated, and he began losing weight and working only sporadically. Within a few months, he was in financial trouble, and about this time, he was also arrested for drunk driving.

When a police informant contacted Cole and asked him if he knew of a cocaine dealer from whom the informant could buy cocaine, Cole bought some cocaine from a dealer and sold it to the informant three different times. One sale involved a half-ounce of cocaine, one involved one ounce, and one involved two ounces. Cole was arrested for these three drug transactions and released on his own recognizance. Since Cole's arrest ten months ago, he has worked full-time as a restaurant employee. His manager has described Cole as "one of the restaurant's best employees."

2.   Nathan Forester is a 32-year-old dentist who was raised by religious and hardworking parents. His father has worked for Ford Motor Company for the last twenty-seven years, but sometimes worked two or three jobs at a time to support his family. His mother is a salesclerk in a men's clothing store.

Nathan was an above-average student and extremely athletic. He lettered in basketball, baseball, and football while in high school and played on the college baseball team.

After taking graduate courses in biology for several years, Nathan decided to become a dentist, and he acquired his D.D.S. in three years. He then entered two post-doctoral programs, one of which was in orthodontics. He also began working in two dental clinics five days a week for half-days.

The consequences of Nathan's extensive commitments soon became evident. His grades dropped, he fell behind in his research, and he could not meet deadlines. He began to feel desperate, incompetent, and depressed. It was during this time that Nathan attended the annual convention of the American Association of Orthodontists. On the first day of the convention, he felt "inexplainable anxiety" and skipped the meetings. Instead, he went and sat on a knoll near a bank. When he saw a woman enter the bank to use the automatic teller machine, he went in after her, threatened her, and then sexually assaulted her. During the assault, which was recorded on film by the bank's security camera, he was unable to have an erection.

After the assault, Nathan, who was extremely distraught, went to find one of his professors, and she accompanied him to his room. She described him as disoriented, incoherent, and suicidal. While she was in the room, he was crying and tried several times to jump out of the tenth-floor window.

Nathan was convicted of second-degree forcible rape. His dental license has been suspended, and it appears as though it soon will be revoked.

B. COMPREHENSIVE AND INTEGRATED SENTENCING AND CORRECTIONS SYSTEMS

It would seem self-evident that public safety can best be protected and correctional goals met when corrections systems within a state offer a comprehensive set of sentencing options and work in close partnership to maximize, for example, the cost-effectiveness of sentences being served. In reality, however, most corrections systems in this country are fragmented, not only failing to collaborate in the treatment and sanctioning of people who have committed crimes, but often working at cross-purposes. The following subsections provide an overview of some of the proposals that have been tendered and steps taken in an effort to make corrections and sentencing systems within a state more comprehensive and integrated. As you review these steps and proposals, consider how, if at all, they should be modified and what other steps could be taken to integrate corrections systems and diversify and improve the sentencing and supervision options for people convicted of crimes.

1. COMMUNITY-CORRECTIONS ACTS

To help ensure that the most appropriate sentence is imposed on a person, the American Bar Association has called on each state and United States territory to adopt what is known as a community-corrections act. In 1992, the ABA disseminated the following "Model Adult Community Corrections Act" to provide guidance to the states and territories as they adopt their own acts. Since the drafting of this Model Act, additional sentencing and deferred-adjudication options have been developed for courts. In addition, much knowledge has been gained about how to make sentences and their implementation more restorative and evidence-based. But the Model Act is still instructive in its outlining of one possible framework for promoting coordination in the development, implementation, and evaluation of community-based sentencing options. As you review the Act, consider how you would modify it.

MODEL ADULT COMMUNITY CORRECTIONS ACT

Approved by the American Bar Association House of Delegates—February, 1992.
Reprinted with the permission of the American Bar Association.

I.   OVERVIEW

A.   Goals and Objectives

(1)   To enhance public safety and achieve economies by encouraging the development and implementation of community sanctions as a sentencing option;

(2)   To enhance the value of criminal sanctions and ensure that the criminal penalties imposed are the most appropriate ones by encouraging the development of a wider array of criminal sanctions;

(3)   To increase the community's awareness of, participation in, and responsibility for the administration of the corrections system;

(4)   To ensure that the offender is punished in the least restrictive setting consistent with public safety and the gravity of the crime;

(5)   To provide offenders with education, training and treatment to enable them to become fully functional members of the community upon release from criminal justice supervision;

(6)   To make offenders accountable to the community for their criminal behavior, through community service programs, restitution programs, and a range of locally developed sanctions; and

(7)   To foster the development of policies and funding for programs that encourage jurisdictions to minimize the use of incarceration where other sanctions are appropriate.

B.   Definitions

(1)   Community. Any local jurisdiction, or any combination of jurisdictions, the government(s) of which undertake(s) joint efforts and shared responsibilities for purposes of providing community corrections options in the jurisdiction(s) in accordance with the purposes and requirements of this Act.

(2)   Community Corrections. Any of a number of sanctions which are served by the offender within the community in which the offender committed the offense or in the community in which the offender resides.

(3)   _Incarceration_. Any sanction which involves placement of the offender in a prison, jail, boot camp, or other secure facility.

II. SANCTIONS

A.   This Model Community Corrections Act provides for local implementation of the following community-based sanctions (the list is not intended to be exclusive of other community-based sanctions):

    (1)   Standard probation;

    (2)   Intensive supervision probation;

    (3)   Community service;

    (4)   Home confinement with or without electronic monitoring;

    (5)   Electronic surveillance (including telephone monitoring);

    (6)   Community-based residential settings offering structure, supervision, surveillance, drug/alcohol treatment, employment counseling and/or other forms of treatment or counseling;

    (7)   Outpatient treatment;

    (8)   Requirement of employment and/or education/training;

    (9)   Day reporting centers;

    (10) Restitution; and

    (11) Means-based fines.

* * *

III. STATE CRIMINAL JUSTICE COUNCIL

A.   The Community Corrections Act shall be administered by a State Criminal Justice Council that has oversight responsibility for state criminal justice policies and programs. The Council shall be responsible for ensuring that policies and activities undertaken by state or local governmental units or other organizations in furtherance of the purposes of the Act are consistent with those purposes and with the statewide community corrections plan required under Section III(D)(1) of this Act.

B.   Not later than 90 days after the effective date of this Act, the governor shall appoint, and the legislature shall confirm, the 15 members of the Council as follows:

    (1)   One member shall be a county sheriff;

(2)   One member shall be a chief of a city police department;

(3)   One member shall be a judge of a general jurisdiction trial court;

(4)   One member shall be a judge from an appellate level court;

(5)   One member shall be a county commissioner or county board head;

(6)   One member shall be a city government official;

(7)   One member shall represent an existing community corrections program;

(8)   One member shall be the director of the department of corrections or his or her designee;

(9)   One member shall be a county prosecutor;

(10)   One member shall be a criminal defense attorney;

(11)   One member shall be the head of a probation department; and

(12)   Four members shall be representatives of the general public.

C.   The governor shall ensure that there is a fair geographic representation on the State board and that minorities and women are fairly represented.

D.   The Council shall:

(1)   Develop a plan for statewide implementation of the Act that incorporates the purposes and objectives of the Act; ensures consistency of community corrections programs and requirements with other applicable State laws and regulations; and establishes goals, criteria, timetables, and incentives for initiation of community corrections programs;

(2)   Establish standards and guidelines for community development of plans to implement the Act in local jurisdictions, as described in Section IV of this Act;

(3)   Review initial community plans, require revisions as necessary, and monitor implementation of approved plans to ensure consistency with the statewide plan;

(4)   Award, administer, and monitor grants, loans, or other State funding mechanisms that the State Legislature establishes for assisting communities in implementing their community corrections plans, as provided in Section VI of this Act;

(5) Review community plans and their implementation at least annually to ensure consistency with the statewide plan and require modification of plans as necessary to ensure compliance with the objectives of this Act;

(6) Evaluate annually the effectiveness of policies and programs carried out under the Act and report to the Legislature on evaluation findings;

(7) Monitor and evaluate the effect of the Act's implementation on offenders of different races;

(8) Take steps to ensure that the community corrections program is adequately funded by the Legislature;

(9) Provide technical assistance and training to provide community corrections services in local jurisdictions;

(10) Provide guidance to local Community Corrections Boards, as defined in Section IV(A) of the Act, in educating the public concerning the purposes of the Act, the types of programs and activities to be undertaken under the Act, the possible impacts of the Act on local jurisdictions, and other matters that may assist the local Boards in establishing and carrying out their community corrections programs;

(11) Maintain records on the number of offenders who met the eligibility criteria in Section V(A)(1)(a) through V(A)(1)(c) but who were incarcerated;

(12) Monitor the results of appeals of offenders who met the eligibility criteria in Section V(A)(1)(a) through V(A)(1)(c) but who were incarcerated;

(13) Assess user fees against communities that incarcerate eligible offenders based on the per-inmate incarceration cost formula described in Section VI(C)(1); and

(14) Hire an executive director, who shall serve at the pleasure of the Council.

E. The Legislature shall appropriate such funds as are necessary for the Council to carry out its responsibilities under the Act, including funds to hire an executive director and necessary staff to implement the program. Appropriations shall be provided in a way and an amount to ensure program continuity and stability.

IV. COMMUNITY CORRECTIONS BOARDS

A. Every city and county in the State shall establish a community corrections program by applying individually or as part of a grouping designated as a "community," as defined in Section I of this Act, to participate in programs and activities, including grant and other financial assistance programs, authorized by this Act and the statewide plan described in Section III(D)(1) of this Act.

B. Each community shall establish a local Community Corrections Board that shall be responsible for developing and implementing a community corrections plan for the community (including locating suitable sites for community correctional programs). Each Board shall be comprised, at minimum, of representatives of the following categories:

(1) Local prosecutor;

(2) Local public defender;

(3) Local member of the criminal defense bar;

(4) Local judges from limited and general jurisdiction courts including courts with jurisdiction over criminal matters;

(5) Local law enforcement official;

(6) Local corrections official;

(7) Local representative from the probation department;

(8) Local government representative;

(9) Local health, education, and human services representatives;

(10) Nonprofit community corrections services provider; and

(11) Three or more representatives of the general public.

C. Each community shall ensure that minorities and women are fairly represented on the Community Corrections Board.

D. In accordance with such rules, regulations, or other policies as the State Council establishes under Section III(D) of this Act, each Board shall develop a comprehensive community corrections plan that, consistent with the objectives and requirements of the Act:

(1) Offers programs for the placement of offenders in the community rather than in correctional institutions; specifies the type(s) and scope of community-based sentencing options to be offered and the type(s) of offenders to be included in the program; describes the community's capacity to carry out the specified community-based sanction; and identifies the means by which the Board intends to provide the sentencing option;

(2) Addresses projected program costs and identifies sources of funds, including grants, loans, or other financial assistance available through the Council, to meet those costs;

(3) Provides for monitoring and annual reporting of program results to the Council;

(4) Provides for annual review of the plan and for its revision, as necessary or desirable;

(5) Includes a commitment to carry out the plan in cooperation and coordination with other governmental entities and to conduct the program in a manner designed to ensure public safety and the program's efficacy;

(6) Addresses the need for involvement and education of the community regarding the purposes and objectives of the Act generally and the local community corrections program specifically; and

(7) Identifies the extent to which its plan will affect the number of individuals who are incarcerated.

E. Each Board shall submit its plan to the State Council for review. An approved plan shall serve as the basis for subsequent Board activity and for the Council's determination of the extent of funding assistance to be provided for community corrections in that Board's community.

V. PROGRAM CRITERIA

A. Offender Eligibility

(1) The following offender groups shall be eligible for sentencing to community-based sanctions:

(a) misdemeanants;

(b) nonviolent felony offenders, including drug abusers and other offenders with special treatment needs;

(c) parole, probation, and community corrections condition violators whose violation conduct is either non-criminal or would meet either criterion (a) or (b) above had it been charged as a criminal violation;

(d) offenders who, although not eligible under criteria (a) through (c) above, are found by the court to be the type of individuals for whom such a sentence would serve the goals of this Act. In making such a determination, the judge shall consider factors that bear on the danger posed and likelihood of recidivism by the offender, including but not limited to the following:

(i) that the offender has a sponsor in the community;

(ii) that the offender either has procured employment or has enrolled in an educational or rehabilitative program; and

(iii) that the offender has not demonstrated a pattern of violent behavior and does not have a criminal record that indicates a pattern of violent offenses.

VI. FUNDING MECHANISM

A. Eligibility: A community will apply for State funding by submitting a community corrections plan to the State Criminal Justice Council. The plan will provide information on a community's demonstrated need for community corrections. The plan also will establish program criteria consistent with this Act. Once the Council has approved a proposed corrections plan, that community will be eligible to receive a grant payment for part of the plan's cost.

B. Funding

(1) Communities will be allocated grant funds to ensure program continuity and stability.

(2) To allocate funds appropriated by the State to implement the Community Corrections Act, the Council will equitably apportion funds to communities.

(3) The Council will redetermine periodically each community's appropriate level of funding, taking into account the community's proven commitment to the implementation of this Act.

(4) The funds provided under this Act shall not supplant current spending by the local jurisdiction for any existing community corrections program.

[C. Chargeback Provision

(1) Commencing two years after the approval of a community's corrections plan, the Criminal Justice Council will charge each community a user fee equivalent to 75 percent of the per-inmate cost of incarceration for each offender who has met the eligibility criteria in

Sections V(A)(1)(a) through V(A)(1)(c) but who has been either:

(a) Committed to a State correctional facility by a sentencing authority in the community; or

(b) Committed by a sentencing authority in the community to a county or regional jail facility.

(2) The amount charged to a community under this Section shall not exceed the amount of financial aid received under Section VI(B).]

D. <u>Audit</u>: Every two years, the state's general auditor will audit all community financial reports related to Community Corrections Act projects.

E. <u>Continual Grant Funding</u>: To receive aid, communities must comply with the requirements established by this Act and the standards promulgated by the State Criminal Justice Council under it. A community corrections program will be evaluated two years after the approval of the community's correction plan and every year thereafter.

F. <u>Notice</u>: If a community fails to meet the standards of the Act, the Council shall notify the community that it has 60 days to comply or funding will be discontinued. The community shall have the opportunity to respond within 30 days after receipt of such notice.

COMMENTARY

* * *

The chargeback provisions of Section VI(C) are a means of encouraging the development and use of community-based sanctions and of further ensuring that an offender for whom a community-based sanction or sanctions is appropriate will be so sentenced. The figure of 75% of the cost of incarceration as a charge to a community that fails to use community-based sanctions for eligible offenders is high enough to provide communities with a substantial incentive to punish those offenders within the community. The actual amount of the fee would be calculated by multiplying 75% of the cost of incarcerating the inmate in a correctional institution by the length of the incarcerative sentence imposed. The fee would not be assessed against the community if, because of the results of an appeal, an offender sentenced to a period of incarceration is not actually incarcerated.

The chargeback provision provides communities with an incentive to develop and implement effective community corrections programs. The potentially harsh effect of the provision is ameliorated by the limit on the amount that may be charged back to the community under Section VI(C)(2). In addition, the chargeback provision does not apply until after communities have had time to develop their community corrections programs.

Some jurisdictions * * * have avoided the use of a chargeback provision by adopting sentencing guidelines to ensure that community-based sanctions are imposed on offenders who fall within the target population. Sentencing guidelines that govern the imposition of community-based sanctions can help ensure their appropriate use while avoiding the criticism often leveled at chargeback provisions that they penalize city and county governments for decisions made by judges over whom they have little or no control. * * * If those guidelines include community-based sanctions, as is recommended by Section VII(D)(1) of this Act, reliance on the chargeback provisions of Section VI(C) would be unnecessary, which is why that section has been placed in brackets.

VII.   SENTENCING DETERMINATIONS

A.   Presentence Report

(1)   All presentence reports shall be required to specifically address whether a community-based sanction is a viable sentencing option.

B.   Judicial Sentencing Statement

(1)   The sentencing judge must consider the community-based sanctions set out in this statute before sentencing any eligible offender as defined in Section V(A).

(2)   Where the judge has decided that a community-based sanction is inappropriate, the judge must state on the record at the time of sentencing that the court considered community correction sentencing options and must explain why such sentencing options were rejected.

C.   Appellate Review

(1)   All individuals sentenced under this State's criminal statutes shall have a right of review of their sentence for conformity with the provisions of this Act, provided that such grounds for appeal are raised on direct appeal of the conviction.

D.   Relationship Between Community Corrections Sanctions and Sentencing Guidelines in Jurisdictions with Sentencing Guidelines

(1)   The [State legislature] in those jurisdictions with sentencing guidelines shall appoint a committee for the purpose of fashioning sentencing guidelines that

incorporate community corrections sentences in a manner consistent with the provisions of this Act.

(2)   Under guidelines drafted pursuant to Section VII(D)(1), non-incarceration sanctions will be the presumptively appropriate sentence for offenders meeting the criteria of Section V(A)(1)(a)–V(A)(1)(c).

* * *

QUESTIONS AND POINTS FOR DISCUSSION

1.   One noteworthy feature of the Model Adult Community Corrections Act is its requirement that a broad array of criminal-justice officials and other stakeholders be involved, at both the state and local levels, in the development and implementation of comprehensive community-corrections plans. Researchers and criminal-justice officials have found that without such broad participation in the development of community-corrections policies, community-corrections programs are more likely to fail, in part because of a lack of buy-in. See, e.g., Bureau of Justice Assistance, U.S. Dep't of Justice, Critical Elements in the Planning, Development, and Implementation of Successful Correctional Options 5–6 (1998). The participation of diverse stakeholders in the planning body's work also promotes a systemic approach to criminal-justice issues and problems. This systemic perspective contrasts with the fragmentation that is the norm when criminal-justice officials, service providers, and others focus only on their individual spheres of activity, such as prosecution, the processing of cases, or jail operations.

An increasing number of communities now have what are called "Criminal Justice Coordinating Councils" (CJCCs) to address criminal-justice issues systemically. See Justice Mgmt. Inst., National Network of Criminal Justice Coordinating Councils, at http://www.jmijustice.org/network-coordination/national-network-criminal-justice-coordinating-councils/. CJCCs can be utilized for the community-corrections-related planning, oversight, and evaluation described in the Model Adult Community Corrections Act. For recommendations on the structuring and operations of CJCCs, see Nat'l Inst. of Corrs., U.S. Dep't of Justice, Guidelines for Developing a Criminal Justice Coordinating Committee (2002).

2.   One of the premises of the Model Adult Community Corrections Act is that community sanctions can be punishing, if that is the sentencing goal. This premise is supported by surveys of people serving various sentences in multiple states in which they ranked certain community sanctions as equally or more punishing than prison. See E. Lea Johnston, Modifying Unjust Sentences, 49 Ga. L.Rev. 433, 469 n.166 (2015) (citing studies). This premise is buttressed further by research revealing that some people, when given the choice between serving a prison sentence or being subjected to intensive supervision in the community, have opted for incarceration. See, e.g., Joan Petersilia, Reforming Probation and Parole in the 21st Century 71 (2002)

(approximately one third of the individuals involved in a study in Oregon and eligible for intensive supervision probation chose instead to go to prison); Joan Petersilia, When Probation Becomes More Dreaded Than Prison, 54 Fed. Probation 23 (March 1990) (15% of prisoners in New Jersey who applied for placement in the intensive-supervision program withdrew their applications when apprised of the demands of the program).

3.   Another premise of the Model Act is that a community-based sentence is in many cases the most cost-effective one. This premise is grounded in research. Researchers have, for example, concluded that due to the criminogenic effects of prison, the imprisonment of some people augments risks to the public safety by increasing the rate at which they reoffend. James Austin et al., Brennan Ctr. for Justice, How Many Americans Are Unnecessarily Incarcerated? 21–22 (2016) (citing studies). The question then arises: Since community-based sanctions are generally much cheaper than incarceration and can often be more effective than incarceration in their crime-reduction effects, why are so many people still being sentenced to prison in the United States? The following article proffers one answer to this question as well as several potential solutions to the structural and funding-related problem it spotlights.

FRANCIS T. CULLEN, CHERYL LERO JONSON, & DANIEL P. MEARS, REINVENTING COMMUNITY CORRECTIONS

46 Crime and Justice 27 (2017).
Michael Tonry & Daniel S. Nagin, Editors.
© 2017 by The University of Chicago.
Reprinted with the permission of The University of Chicago.

* * *

* * * [C]ounties * * * receive a "free lunch" by being able to incarcerate offenders in state prisons at no cost to themselves. A comprehensive approach to reducing unnecessary or inappropriate use of state prisons entails forcing counties to have "skin in the game" by requiring them to finance, at least in part, their use of prisons. If financial burdens are shifted from states to counties, local jurisdictions may appreciate more fully the fiscal implications of relying on prison rather than more cost-effective community sanctions. The central thesis is, if communities must pay for how much imprisonment they consume, they will use less and rely more on community-based interventions.

* * *

* * * What concrete policies can states enact to dissuade the use of state prisons and encourage the use of community corrections? Three options exist. * * *

Option 1: Capping Prison Usage (CPU). Under this option, states first determine the number of prison beds each county has been using. Next, the state determines the percentage decrease in prison populations to be achieved the following year. The state then sets the number of prison admissions that will achieve the desired decrease. This statewide cap is allocated across counties on a per capita basis, with larger counties receiving more prison space and smaller counties receiving less. If the cap is not exceeded, a county need not "pay to imprison" that year and can imprison any offender it chooses. When counties surpass their caps, they must pay for each subsequent individual sentenced to prison. * * *

Under the CPU system, * * * [p]rison beds would no longer be an unlimited resource; rather, prison would be transformed into a commodity that must be reserved for the most dangerous offenders who pose the greatest threats to public safety. * * * The price of imprisonment would become transparent, and judges and prosecutors would need to explain why they exceeded their caps and imposed additional costs on the community. A central benefit would be that counties would have to be explicit about the criteria and the cost-benefit calculus used for incarcerating individuals. * * *

Of course, punishments for some crimes are likely to be dictated by state law. Murder, for example, typically would necessitate a prison term. * * * Accordingly, when setting caps, states should include guidelines for "exemption crimes" for which local jurisdictions do not have to pay for prison beds.

* * *

Option 2: Cap-and-Trade System. The second option is cap-and-trade. * * *

County A may have reached its cap of 500 people but wants to sentence 50 more offenders to the state prison system. * * * County B may have a cap of 200 people but have sent 150 offenders to state facilities. County B could sell the unneeded 50 beds to county A. County B could use that money for community correctional programming, treatment facilities, or other local needs. County A could then incarcerate all offenders that it wanted and, if it bargained well, at a lower cost than the state would charge. * * * Under cap-and-trade, judges and prosecutors would remain accountable to the public because exceeding the cap would have financial consequences for the county; either the state or other counties would have to be paid.

* * *

Option 3: Rebating and Charge. Option 3 differs markedly from the first two: a rebating and charge approach does not set a state prison population cap. Instead, the state correctional budget, minus a small portion for the administration costs, is given—or "rebated"—to communities on a per capita basis. Counties would manage their shares of the state correctional budget. Counties would pay the entire cost of incarceration for each individual sentenced to a state prison. * * * If counties exceed the funds they receive from state coffers, they must pay the difference from local tax revenues.

If counties do not spend all of their allocated funds, they could retain the surplus. The state could direct use of retained funds in one of two ways. First, states could mandate their use for criminal justice-related purposes. Second, the state could allow the counties to use the surplus funds for any governmental service they chose. * * *

* * * [L]ocal jurisdictions * * * would have to pay the costs for each individual deemed appropriate for a prison term. This would encourage local officials to use prison only when absolutely necessary or when it constitutes the most cost-efficient approach to reduce recidivism.

* * *

* * * To the extent that making state imprisonment a free good has resulted in excessive or needless incarceration, that needs to be changed. Institutionalized structures for incentivizing "smart" sanctioning—that is, the imposition of cost-efficient punishments—are essential. * * * This focus will do much to provide an impetus for taking seriously the need to reinvent community corrections.

QUESTIONS AND POINTS FOR DISCUSSION

1.   How would you remedy the problem of the " 'correctional free lunch,' " which can skew sentencing decisions towards imprisonment? W. David Ball, Defunding State Prisons, 50 Crim. L.Bull. 1060, 1062 (2014) (quoting Franklin E. Zimring & Gordon Hawkins, The Scale of Imprisonment 140 (1991)). Do you favor capping prison usage, the cap-and-trade system, the rebating-and-charge approach, the implementation of chargebacks as outlined in the Model Adult Community Corrections Act, or some other alternative? What are the advantages and drawbacks of each of these alternatives?

2.   In their article, Drs. Cullen, Jonson, and Mears argue that requiring communities to have "skin in the game," from a financial standpoint, when a community member is sentenced to prison will not only lead to a decrease in unnecessary incarceration but to improvements in community corrections. There is now a growing body of research about "what works and what does not" in community corrections to aid in the making of those improvements. Wash. State Inst. for Pub. Policy, Prison, Police, and Programs: Evidence-Based Options that Reduce Crime and Save Money 2 (2013). To assist policymakers in the state of Washington in their corrections-related decisions, including funding choices, the Washington State Institute for Public Policy has canvassed the research and tabulated the benefits compared to costs of various correctional interventions in that state. See id. at 5. For example, investing in cognitive behavioral treatment for individuals at high or moderate risk of reoffending reaps a high return on investment while intensive supervision that

entails supervision only, unaccompanied by treatment, nets a negative return. In other words, the costs of that form of supervision outweigh any benefits.

3. The Model Adult Community Corrections Act addresses another potential reason, outside of the "correctional free lunch," for the overutilization of imprisonment in the United States—lack of public knowledge about community corrections. One of the primary responsibilities of the local community corrections boards established under the Model Act is to educate the public about community-based sanctions—about what they are; about their costs and benefits compared to those of incarceration; and about how incarcerating some people can jeopardize the safety of the public by increasing recidivism rates. Studies have shown that when members of the public are informed about community sanctions, their support for them shifts dramatically. For example, in a study in Alabama, 422 adults were told about twenty-three hypothetical individuals whose crimes ranged from shoplifting, selling drugs, drunk driving, burglary, and embezzlement to rape and armed robbery. When first given the choice of either sentencing them to prison or probation, the respondents opted to incarcerate in eighteen of the twenty-three cases. When later instructed about five other sentencing options—"strict probation," which entailed meeting with a probation officer up to five times a week for up to two years; strict probation plus restitution; strict probation combined with community service; house arrest for up to one year; and boot camp for three to six months—the respondents chose imprisonment in only four of the cases. Significantly, many of the individuals for whom the respondents preferred an alternative sanction had been convicted of quite serious crimes, including embezzling $250,000, dealing drugs for a third time, and committing an unarmed burglary for the second time. See John Doble & Josh Klein, Punishing Criminals: The Public's View—An Alabama Survey (1989). See also John Doble et al., Punishing Criminals: The People of Delaware Consider the Options (1991) (findings of the Alabama study essentially replicated). Obviously, the kinds of details shared with the public about various sentencing options, including their relative costs and impact on recidivism, may affect the public's level of support for the imposition of a particular community sanction in lieu of incarceration. Francis T. Cullen et al., Public Opinion About Punishment and Corrections, 27 Crime & Just. 1, 43–45 (2000).

2. PROBLEM-SOLVING AND RESTORATIVE COURTS

Problem-solving courts represent a different way to foster coordination between various facets of the criminal-justice system in the development of plans—in this case, in individual cases. Drug courts are the most prevalent type of problem-solving court. Bureau of Justice Statistics, U.S. Dep't of Justice, Census of Problem-Solving Courts, 2012, at 1 (2016). People with a substance-abuse problem that has contributed to their commission of a crime may be eligible to have their cases processed through a drug court, though a number of jurisdictions exclude those with a history of committing violent or sex crimes from participating. Id. at 6. Drug-court participants must meet the terms of a treatment plan developed by a multidisciplinary team typically comprised of a judge, prosecutor, defense attorney, probation official, treatment provider, and others, such as a social worker. The strict treatment regimen outlined in the plan often includes meetings every week or even every day with treatment providers, urinalysis tests at least once a week, and frequent status hearings. During a status hearing, the drug-court judge reviews a participant's progress and modulates the constraints to which he or she is subject based on that progress or, conversely, lack of progress. The successful completion of the treatment program results in the dismissal of criminal charges in many jurisdictions and a suspended sentence in others. Id. at 13.

Most evaluations of drug courts have found that they reduce recidivism and that their benefits, in terms of recidivism reduction, outweigh their costs. Edward J. Latessa & Angela K. Reitler, What Works in Reducing Recidivism and How Does It Relate to Drug Courts?, 41 Ohio N.U. L.Rev. 757, 773–81 (2015). Besides recidivism reduction, what other outcome measures would you consider when deciding whether to integrate drug courts into deferred-adjudication and sentencing systems? For additional information about drug courts and research about them, see the National Institute of Justice's website on drug courts at https://www.nij. gov/topics/courts/drug-courts/Pages/welcome.aspx.

Drawing upon the drug-court model, jurisdictions are establishing, with increasing frequency, other specialized courts with a treatment and problem-solving orientation. Mental-health courts, through which cases involving people with mental illnesses can be processed, are a notable example. The National Center for State Courts has compiled a number of resources on mental-health courts, which can be accessed at http://www.ncsc.org/Topics/Alternative-Dockets/Problem-Solving-Courts/Mental-Health-Courts/Resource-Guide.aspx. Problem-solving courts also include, among many others, domestic-violence courts, DWI (driving while impaired) courts, and veterans' courts, which are hybrid courts for veterans that blend the features of mental-health courts and drug courts. See West Huddleston & Douglas B. Marlowe, Nat'l Drug Court Inst., Painting the Current Picture: A National Report on Drug Courts and Other Problem-Solving Court Programs in the United States 43–47 (2011) (describing different kinds of problem-solving courts in the United States). Reentry courts, another kind of problem-solving court designed to promote the successful return of formerly incarcerated people into their communities, are discussed in Chapter 10 on pages 516–519.

The development of drug courts and other problem-solving courts has been met with applause as well as criticism. One of the chief concerns about drug courts is that they foster the continued treatment of substance abuse as a criminal-justice matter rather than a public-health issue. See Nat'l Ass'n of Criminal Def. Lawyers, America's Problem-Solving Courts: The

Criminal Costs of Treatment and the Case for Reform 20–21 (2009). Another charge leveled against problem-solving courts is that they inefficiently allocate public resources by "picking the low-hanging fruit," processing low-risk defendants in order to augment their reported success rate rather than concentrating on high-risk individuals who face potentially long incarcerative sentences. Id. at 46–48. What other concerns might be raised about problem-solving courts? What steps could be taken to avert or limit the problems or potential problems identified?

As mentioned in Chapter 1, another kind of court, known as a "restorative court" or "restorative community court," is also beginning to appear in the United States. Restorative courts are at an early stage of development. Decisions are being made and will continue to be made about how to structure them to best realize the aims of restorative justice, such as averting and addressing conflict and promoting accountability to redress harm one's crime has caused. If you were planning a restorative court, how would you structure it and what would be its key features?

3. INCORPORATING COMMUNITY SANCTIONS INTO SENTENCING GUIDELINES

The need for a continuum of sanctions—a wide range of criminal sanctions of differing severity—was discussed in the beginning of this chapter. But with community-based sanctions, as with penalties involving incarceration, there is a concern about inequitable treatment of people convicted of crimes—a concern that the ad hoc exercise of discretion by sentencing judges will lead to the imposition of much more onerous community-based sanctions on some individuals compared to others who are similarly situated. A monograph written by Professor Michael Tonry, excerpts of which are set forth below, discusses some ways of structuring a comprehensive sentencing system to address this concern and limit disparity in the imposition of community-based sanctions.

MICHAEL TONRY, INTERMEDIATE SANCTIONS IN SENTENCING GUIDELINES

National Institute of Justice (1997).

* * *

Zones of Discretion

Most guidelines commissions that have tried to expand their guidelines' coverage to include nonconfinement sentences have altered the traditional guidelines format to include more zones of discretion. The first guidelines in Minnesota, Pennsylvania, and Washington divided their grids into two zones. One contained confinement cells setting presumptive ranges for prison sentences, and the other contained nonconfinement cells that gave the judge unfettered discretion to impose any other sentence, often including an option of jail sentences of up to one year. Minnesota's guidelines, for example, contained a bold black line that separated the confinement and nonconfinement zones.

New North Carolina [and other] guidelines, by contrast, have four or more zones. The details vary but they follow a common pattern. Sentences other than those authorized by the applicable zone are departures for which reasons must be given which are subject to review on appeal. One zone contains cells in which only prison sentences are presumed appropriate. A second might contain cells in which judges may choose between restrictive intermediate sanctions, such as residential drug treatment, house arrest with electronic monitoring, and a day-reporting center, and a prison sentence up to a designated length. A third might contain cells in which judges may choose among restrictive intermediate punishments. A fourth might authorize judges to choose between restrictive intermediate sanctions and a less restrictive penalty like community service or standard probation. A fifth might authorize sentencing choices only among less restrictive community penalties.

Punishment Units

A second approach that Oregon adopted and several other States considered is to express punishment in generic "punishment units" into which all sanctions can be converted. A hypothetical system might provide, for example, for the following conversion values:

- One year's confinement   100   units
- One year's partial confinement   50   units
- One year's house arrest   50   units
- One year's standard probation   20   units
- 25 days' community service   50   units
- 30 days' intensive supervision   5   units
- 90 days' income (day fines)   100   units
- 30 days' electronic monitoring   5   units

That is by no means a complete list; such things as drug testing, treatment conditions, and restitution might or might not be added. The values could be divided or multiplied to obtain values for other periods (for example, 75 days' confinement equals 20 units).

If guidelines, for example, set "120 punishment units" as the presumptive sentence for a particular offender, a judge could impose any combination of sanctions that represented 120 units. One year's confinement (100 units) plus 60 subsequent days' intensive supervision (10 units) on electronic monitoring (10 units) would be appropriate. So would a 90-unit day fine (100 units) plus one year's standard probation (20 units). So would 25 days' community service (50 units) and six months' intensive supervision (30 units), followed by two years' standard probation (40 units).

In practice, the punishment unit approach has proven too complicated to be workable.

* * *

Exchange Rates

Another approach is simply to specify equivalent custodial and noncustodial penalties and to authorize judges to impose them in the alternative. Washington's commission did this in a modest way and later proposed a more extensive system, which the legislature did not adopt. Partial confinement and community service were initially authorized as substitutes for presumptive prison terms on the basis of 1 day's partial confinement or 3 days' community service for 1 day of confinement. The partial confinement/confinement exchange is probably workable (for short sentences; house arrest, assuming that to count as partial confinement, is seldom imposed for more than a few months), but the community service exchange rate is not.

* * *

The difficulty is that community service programs, to be credible, must be enforced, and experience in this country and elsewhere instructs that they must be short. That is why the best-known American program in New York set 70 hours as a standard, and the national policies in England and Wales, Scotland, and the Netherlands set 240 hours as the upper limit.

* * *

Exchange rates are limited in their potential uses for the same reason punishment units are. For so long as prevailing views require that imprisonment be considered the normal punishment and that substitutes for imprisonment be comparably burdensome and intrusive, exchange rates are unlikely to play a significant role in sentencing guidelines.

* * *

Future sentencing commissions will probably develop current ideas in new ways. * * * [A] zones-of-discretion approach, for example, * * * [could] provide guidance to judges on how to choose *among* authorized intermediate sanctions or community penalties or between intermediate sanctions and authorized confinement or community sanctions. This could easily be done by setting policies that particular kinds of sanctions are appropriate for particular kinds of offenders: an obvious example would be a policy that residential drug treatment be presumed appropriate for a drug-dependent chronic property offender. Depending on how convinced the commission was about the wisdom of the policy, it could be made presumptive (and thus require a "departure" with reasons given for any other sentence) or only advisory.

* * *

QUESTIONS AND POINTS FOR DISCUSSION

1.   Do you agree that punishment units and exchange rates are not viable ways to channel judges' discretion in the imposition of community sanctions? If you developed a sentencing system utilizing exchange rates for custodial and noncustodial penalties, what exchange rates would you adopt and why?

2.   For another thought-provoking discussion of sanction exchange rates, see Norval Morris & Michael Tonry, Between Prison and Probation: Intermediate Punishments in a Rational Sentencing System 37–108 (1990).

CHAPTER 7

THE DEATH PENALTY

∎ ∎ ∎

A. CONSTITUTIONALITY IN GENERAL: CHALLENGES TO DEATH-PENALTY STATUTES ON THEIR FACE AND AS APPLIED

Few criminal-justice issues have engendered as much controversy as the questions whether the death penalty can and should be imposed on people convicted of certain crimes. The divergent opinions on these subjects have been reflected in the decisions of the Supreme Court, which are often marked by 5–4 holdings and a confusing mix of plurality, concurring, and dissenting opinions.

Since 1972, when the Supreme Court decided the seminal case of Furman v. Georgia, 408 U.S. 238, 92 S.Ct. 2726 (1972), the Court has been grappling constantly with questions concerning the constitutionality of the death penalty. In *Furman,* the Court held that two death-penalty statutes that left the decision whether to impose the death penalty to the unconfined discretion of the judge or jury violated the Eighth Amendment's prohibition of cruel and unusual punishment. These statutes had resulted in such arbitrary and haphazard imposition of the death penalty that, in the words of Justice White, there was "no meaningful basis for distinguishing the few cases in which it is imposed from the many cases in which it is not." Id. at 313, 92 S.Ct. at 2764 (White, J., concurring).

It was evident from *Furman* that other death-penalty statutes across the country were also unconstitutional. A number of state legislatures responded by enacting new death-penalty statutes that they hoped would pass constitutional muster. In several cases decided in 1976, one of which is set forth below, and another of which can be found on page 317, the Supreme Court considered the constitutionality of some of these statutes.

GREGG V. GEORGIA
Supreme Court of the United States, 1976.
428 U.S. 153, 96 S.Ct. 2909, 49 L.Ed.2d 859.

Judgment of the Court, and opinion of MR. JUSTICE STEWART, MR. JUSTICE POWELL, and MR. JUSTICE STEVENS, announced by MR. JUSTICE STEWART.

The issue in this case is whether the imposition of the sentence of death for the crime of murder under the law of Georgia violates the Eighth and Fourteenth Amendments.

I

The petitioner, Troy Gregg, was charged with committing armed robbery and murder. In accordance with Georgia procedure in capital cases, the trial was in two stages, a guilt stage and a sentencing stage. The evidence at the guilt trial established that on November 21, 1973, the petitioner and a traveling companion, Floyd Allen, while hitchhiking north in Florida were picked up by Fred Simmons and Bob Moore. * * * A short time later the four men interrupted their journey for a rest stop along the highway. The next morning the bodies of Simmons and Moore were discovered in a ditch nearby.

* * * The next afternoon, the petitioner and Allen, while in Simmons' car, were arrested in Asheville, N.C. * * * Allen recounted the events leading to the slayings. His version of these events was as follows: After Simmons and Moore left the car, the petitioner stated that he intended to rob them. The petitioner then took his pistol in hand and positioned himself on the car to improve his aim. As Simmons and Moore came up an embankment toward the car, the petitioner fired three shots and the two men fell near a ditch. The petitioner, at close range, then fired a shot into the head of each. He robbed them of valuables and drove away with Allen.

* * * Although Allen did not testify, a police detective recounted the substance of Allen's statements about the slayings and indicated that directly after Allen had made these statements the petitioner had admitted that Allen's account was accurate. * * *

* * * The jury found the petitioner guilty of two counts of armed robbery and two counts of murder.

At the penalty stage, * * * [t]he trial judge instructed the jury that it could recommend either a death sentence or a life prison sentence on each count. The judge further charged the jury that in determining what sentence was appropriate the jury was free to consider the facts and circumstances, if any, presented by the parties in mitigation or aggravation.

Finally, the judge instructed the jury that it "would not be authorized to consider [imposing] the penalty of death" unless it first found beyond a reasonable doubt one of these aggravating circumstances:

"One—That the offense of murder was committed while the offender was engaged in the commission of two other capital felonies, to-wit the armed robbery of [Simmons and Moore].

"Two—That the offender committed the offense of murder for the purpose of receiving money and the automobile described in the indictment.

"Three—The offense of murder was outrageously and wantonly vile, horrible and inhuman, in that they [sic] involved the depravity of [the] mind of the defendant."

Finding the first and second of these circumstances, the jury returned verdicts of death on each count.

The Supreme Court of Georgia affirmed the convictions and the imposition of the death sentences for murder. * * *

* * *

III

We address initially the basic contention that the punishment of death for the crime of murder is, under all circumstances, "cruel and unusual" in violation of the Eighth and Fourteenth Amendments of the Constitution. * * *

* * *

A

* * *

[T]he Court has not confined the prohibition embodied in the Eighth Amendment to "barbarous" methods that were generally outlawed in the 18th century. Instead, the Amendment has been interpreted in a flexible and dynamic manner. * * * Thus the Clause forbidding "cruel and unusual" punishments "is not fastened to the obsolete but may acquire meaning as public opinion becomes enlightened by a humane justice."

* * *

* * * As Mr. Chief Justice Warren said, in an oft-quoted phrase, "[t]he Amendment must draw its meaning from the evolving standards of decency that mark the progress of a maturing society." Thus, an assessment of contemporary values concerning the infliction of a challenged sanction is relevant to the application of the Eighth Amendment. * * * [T]his assessment does not call for a subjective judgment. It requires, rather, that

we look to objective indicia that reflect the public attitude toward a given sanction.

But our cases also make clear that public perceptions of standards of decency with respect to criminal sanctions are not conclusive. A penalty also must accord with "the dignity of man," which is the "basic concept underlying the Eighth Amendment." This means, at least, that the punishment not be "excessive." When a form of punishment in the abstract (in this case, whether capital punishment may ever be imposed as a sanction for murder) rather than in the particular (the propriety of death as a penalty to be applied to a specific defendant for a specific crime) is under consideration, the inquiry into "excessiveness" has two aspects. First, the punishment must not involve the unnecessary and wanton infliction of pain. Second, the punishment must not be grossly out of proportion to the severity of the crime.

B

Of course, the requirements of the Eighth Amendment must be applied with an awareness of the limited role to be played by the courts. This does not mean that judges have no role to play, for the Eighth Amendment is a restraint upon the exercise of legislative power. * * *[19]

But, while we have an obligation to insure that constitutional bounds are not overreached, we may not act as judges as we might as legislators. * * *

Therefore, in assessing a punishment selected by a democratically elected legislature against the constitutional measure, we presume its validity. We may not require the legislature to select the least severe penalty possible so long as the penalty selected is not cruelly inhumane or disproportionate to the crime involved. And a heavy burden rests on those who would attack the judgment of the representatives of the people.

This is true in part because the constitutional test is intertwined with an assessment of contemporary standards and the legislative judgment weighs heavily in ascertaining such standards. "[I]n a democratic society legislatures, not courts, are constituted to respond to the will and consequently the moral values of the people." * * *

C

* * * We now consider specifically whether the sentence of death for the crime of murder is a *per se* violation of the Eighth and Fourteenth Amendments to the Constitution. * * *

---

[19] Although legislative measures adopted by the people's chosen representatives provide one important means of ascertaining contemporary values, it is evident that legislative judgments alone cannot be determinative of Eighth Amendment standards since that Amendment was intended to safeguard individuals from the abuse of legislative power. * * *

The imposition of the death penalty for the crime of murder has a long history of acceptance both in the United States and in England. The common-law rule imposed a mandatory death sentence on all convicted murderers. And the penalty continued to be used into the 20th century by most American States, although the breadth of the common-law rule was diminished, initially by narrowing the class of murders to be punished by death and subsequently by widespread adoption of laws expressly granting juries the discretion to recommend mercy.

It is apparent from the text of the Constitution itself that the existence of capital punishment was accepted by the Framers. * * * The Fifth Amendment, adopted at the same time as the Eighth, contemplated the continued existence of the capital sanction by imposing certain limits on the prosecution of capital cases:

> "No person shall be held to answer for a capital, or otherwise infamous crime, unless on a presentment or indictment of a Grand Jury . . .; nor shall any person be subject for the same offense to be twice put in jeopardy of life or limb; . . . nor be deprived of life, liberty, or property, without due process of law. . . ."

And the Fourteenth Amendment, adopted over three-quarters of a century later, similarly contemplates the existence of the capital sanction in providing that no State shall deprive any person of "life, liberty, or property" without due process of law.

* * *

* * * Despite the continuing debate, dating back to the 19th century, over the morality and utility of capital punishment, it is now evident that a large proportion of American society continues to regard it as an appropriate and necessary criminal sanction.

The most marked indication of society's endorsement of the death penalty for murder is the legislative response to *Furman*. The legislatures of at least 35 States have enacted new statutes that provide for the death penalty for at least some crimes that result in the death of another person. And the Congress of the United States, in 1974, enacted a statute providing the death penalty for aircraft piracy that results in death. * * *

In the only statewide referendum occurring since *Furman* and brought to our attention, the people of California adopted a constitutional amendment that authorized capital punishment, in effect negating a prior ruling by the Supreme Court of California * * * that the death penalty violated the California Constitution.[25]

---

[25] * * * A December 1972 Gallup poll indicated that 57% of the people favored the death penalty, while a June 1973 Harris survey showed support of 59%.

The jury also is a significant and reliable objective index of contemporary values because it is so directly involved. The Court has said that "one of the most important functions any jury can perform in making . . . a selection [between life imprisonment and death for a defendant convicted in a capital case] is to maintain a link between contemporary community values and the penal system." It may be true that evolving standards have influenced juries in recent decades to be more discriminating in imposing the sentence of death. But the relative infrequency of jury verdicts imposing the death sentence does not indicate rejection of capital punishment *per se*. Rather, the reluctance of juries in many cases to impose the sentence may well reflect the humane feeling that this most irrevocable of sanctions should be reserved for a small number of extreme cases. * * * At the close of 1974 at least 254 persons had been sentenced to death since *Furman,* and by the end of March 1976, more than 460 persons were subject to death sentences.

As we have seen, however, the Eighth Amendment demands more than that a challenged punishment be acceptable to contemporary society. The Court also must ask whether it comports with the basic concept of human dignity at the core of the Amendment. Although we cannot "invalidate a category of penalties because we deem less severe penalties adequate to serve the ends of penology," the sanction imposed cannot be so totally without penological justification that it results in the gratuitous infliction of suffering.

The death penalty is said to serve two principal social purposes: retribution and deterrence of capital crimes by prospective offenders.[28]

In part, capital punishment is an expression of society's moral outrage at particularly offensive conduct. This function may be unappealing to many, but it is essential in an ordered society that asks its citizens to rely on legal processes rather than self-help to vindicate their wrongs. * * * "Retribution is no longer the dominant objective of the criminal law," but neither is it a forbidden objective nor one inconsistent with our respect for the dignity of men.[30] * * *

---

[28] Another purpose that has been discussed is the incapacitation of dangerous criminals and the consequent prevention of crimes that they may otherwise commit in the future.

[30] Lord Justice Denning, Master of the Rolls of the Court of Appeal in England, spoke to this effect before the British Royal Commission on Capital Punishment:

"Punishment is the way in which society expresses its denunciation of wrong doing: and, in order to maintain respect for law, it is essential that the punishment inflicted for grave crimes should adequately reflect the revulsion felt by the great majority of citizens for them. It is a mistake to consider the objects of punishment as being deterrent or reformative or preventive and nothing else. . . . The truth is that some crimes are so outrageous that society insists on adequate punishment, because the wrong-doer deserves it, irrespective of whether it is a deterrent or not." Royal Commission on Capital Punishment, Minutes of Evidence, Dec. 1, 1949, p. 207 (1950).

Statistical attempts to evaluate the worth of the death penalty as a deterrent to crimes by potential offenders have occasioned a great deal of debate. The results simply have been inconclusive. * * *

Although some of the studies suggest that the death penalty may not function as a significantly greater deterrent than lesser penalties, there is no convincing empirical evidence either supporting or refuting this view. We may nevertheless assume safely that there are murderers, such as those who act in passion, for whom the threat of death has little or no deterrent effect. But for many others, the death penalty undoubtedly is a significant deterrent. There are carefully contemplated murders, such as murder for hire, where the possible penalty of death may well enter into the cold calculus that precedes the decision to act. And there are some categories of murder, such as murder by a life prisoner, where other sanctions may not be adequate.

The value of capital punishment as a deterrent of crime is a complex factual issue the resolution of which properly rests with the legislatures. * * *

In sum, we cannot say that the judgment of the Georgia Legislature that capital punishment may be necessary in some cases is clearly wrong. Considerations of federalism, as well as respect for the ability of a legislature to evaluate, in terms of its particular State, the moral consensus concerning the death penalty and its social utility as a sanction, require us to conclude, in the absence of more convincing evidence, that the infliction of death as a punishment for murder is not without justification and thus is not unconstitutionally severe.

Finally, we must consider whether the punishment of death is disproportionate in relation to the crime for which it is imposed. There is no question that death as a punishment is unique in its severity and irrevocability. * * * But we are concerned here only with the imposition of capital punishment for the crime of murder, and when a life has been taken deliberately by the offender, we cannot say that the punishment is invariably disproportionate to the crime. * * *

We hold that the death penalty is not a form of punishment that may never be imposed, regardless of the circumstances of the offense, regardless of the character of the offender, and regardless of the procedure followed in reaching the decision to impose it.

IV

* * *

Furman mandates that where discretion is afforded a sentencing body on a matter so grave as the determination of whether a human life should be taken or spared, that discretion must be suitably directed and limited so as to minimize the risk of wholly arbitrary and capricious action.

* * *

* * * [T]he concerns expressed in *Furman* that the penalty of death not be imposed in an arbitrary or capricious manner can be met by a carefully drafted statute that ensures that the sentencing authority is given adequate information and guidance.[46] * * *

* * *

We now turn to consideration of the constitutionality of Georgia's capital-sentencing procedures. In the wake of *Furman,* Georgia amended its capital punishment statute. * * *

Georgia did act * * * to narrow the class of murderers subject to capital punishment by specifying 10 statutory aggravating circumstances, one of which must be found by the jury to exist beyond a reasonable doubt before a death sentence can ever be imposed. In addition, the jury is authorized to consider any other appropriate aggravating or mitigating circumstances. The jury is not required to find any mitigating circumstance in order to make a recommendation of mercy that is binding on the trial court, but it must find a *statutory* aggravating circumstance before recommending a sentence of death.

These procedures require the jury to consider the circumstances of the crime and the criminal before it recommends sentence. No longer can a Georgia jury do as Furman's jury did: reach a finding of the defendant's guilt and then, without guidance or direction, decide whether he should live or die. Instead, the jury's attention is directed to the specific circumstances of the crime: Was it committed in the course of another capital felony? Was it committed for money? Was it committed upon a peace officer or judicial officer? Was it committed in a particularly heinous way or in a manner that endangered the lives of many persons? In addition, the jury's attention is focused on the characteristics of the person who committed the crime: Does he have a record of prior convictions for capital offenses? Are there any special facts about this defendant that mitigate against imposing capital punishment (*e.g.,* his youth, the extent of his cooperation with the police, his emotional state at the time of the crime). As a result, while some jury discretion still exists, "the discretion to be exercised is controlled by clear and objective standards so as to produce non-discriminatory application."

As an important additional safeguard against arbitrariness and caprice, the Georgia statutory scheme provides for automatic appeal of all death sentences to the State's Supreme Court. That court is required by statute to review each sentence of death and determine whether it was

---

[46] A system could have standards so vague that they would fail adequately to channel the sentencing decision patterns of juries with the result that a pattern of arbitrary and capricious sentencing like that found unconstitutional in *Furman* could occur.

imposed under the influence of passion or prejudice, whether the evidence supports the jury's finding of a statutory aggravating circumstance, and whether the sentence is disproportionate compared to those sentences imposed in similar cases.

* * * On their face these procedures seem to satisfy the concerns of *Furman*. No longer should there be "no meaningful basis for distinguishing the few cases in which [the death penalty] is imposed from the many cases in which it is not."

The petitioner contends, however, that the changes in the Georgia sentencing procedures are only cosmetic, that the arbitrariness and capriciousness condemned by *Furman* continue to exist in Georgia * * *.

First, the petitioner focuses on the opportunities for discretionary action that are inherent in the processing of any murder case under Georgia law. He notes that the state prosecutor has unfettered authority to select those persons whom he wishes to prosecute for a capital offense and to plea bargain with them. Further, at the trial the jury may choose to convict a defendant of a lesser included offense rather than find him guilty of a crime punishable by death, even if the evidence would support a capital verdict. And finally, a defendant who is convicted and sentenced to die may have his sentence commuted by the Governor of the State and the Georgia Board of Pardons and Paroles.

The existence of these discretionary stages is not determinative of the issues before us. At each of these stages an actor in the criminal justice system makes a decision which may remove a defendant from consideration as a candidate for the death penalty. *Furman,* in contrast, dealt with the decision to impose the death sentence on a specific individual who had been convicted of a capital offense. Nothing in any of our cases suggests that the decision to afford an individual defendant mercy violates the Constitution. *Furman* held only that, in order to minimize the risk that the death penalty would be imposed on a capriciously selected group of offenders, the decision to impose it had to be guided by standards so that the sentencing authority would focus on the particularized circumstances of the crime and the defendant.[50]

* * *

---

[50]   The petitioner's argument is nothing more than a veiled contention that *Furman* indirectly outlawed capital punishment by placing totally unrealistic conditions on its use. In order to repair the alleged defects pointed to by the petitioner, it would be necessary to require that prosecuting authorities charge a capital offense whenever arguably there had been a capital murder and that they refuse to plea bargain with the defendant. If a jury refused to convict even though the evidence supported the charge, its verdict would have to be reversed and a verdict of guilty entered or a new trial ordered, since the discretionary act of jury nullification would not be permitted. Finally, acts of executive clemency would have to be prohibited. Such a system, of course, would be totally alien to our notions of criminal justice.

The petitioner next argues that the requirements of *Furman* are not met here because the jury has the power to decline to impose the death penalty even if it finds that one or more statutory aggravating circumstances are present in the case. * * * Since the proportionality requirement on review is intended to prevent caprice in the decision to inflict the penalty, the isolated decision of a jury to afford mercy does not render unconstitutional death sentences imposed on defendants who were sentenced under a system that does not create a substantial risk of arbitrariness or caprice.

* * *

For the reasons expressed in this opinion, we hold that the statutory system under which Gregg was sentenced to death does not violate the Constitution. * * *

* * *

MR. JUSTICE WHITE, with whom THE CHIEF JUSTICE and MR. JUSTICE REHNQUIST join, concurring in the judgment.

* * *

Petitioner * * * argues that decisions made by the prosecutor—either in negotiating a plea to some lesser offense than capital murder or in simply declining to charge capital murder—are standardless and will inexorably result in the wanton and freakish imposition of the penalty condemned by the judgment in *Furman*. I address this point separately because the cases in which no capital offense is charged escape the view of the Georgia Supreme Court and are not considered by it in determining whether a particular sentence is excessive or disproportionate.

Petitioner's argument that prosecutors behave in a standardless fashion in deciding which cases to try as capital felonies is unsupported by any facts. Petitioner simply asserts that since prosecutors have the power not to charge capital felonies they will exercise that power in a standardless fashion. This is untenable. Absent facts to the contrary, it cannot be assumed that prosecutors will be motivated in their charging decision by factors other than the strength of their case and the likelihood that a jury would impose the death penalty if it convicts. * * * Thus defendants will escape the death penalty through prosecutorial charging decisions only because the offense is not sufficiently serious; or because the proof is insufficiently strong. This does not cause the system to be standardless any more than the jury's decision to impose life imprisonment on a defendant whose crime is deemed insufficiently serious or its decision to acquit someone who is probably guilty but whose guilt is not established beyond a reasonable doubt. * * *

Petitioner's argument that there is an unconstitutional amount of discretion in the system which separates those suspects who receive the death penalty from those who receive life imprisonment, a lesser penalty, or are acquitted or never charged, seems to be in [the] final analysis an indictment of our entire system of justice. * * * Mistakes will be made and discriminations will occur which will be difficult to explain. However, one of society's most basic tasks is that of protecting the lives of its citizens and one of the most basic ways in which it achieves the task is through criminal laws against murder. I decline to interfere with the manner in which Georgia has chosen to enforce such laws on what is simply an assertion of lack of faith in the ability of the system of justice to operate in a fundamentally fair manner.

* * *

MR. JUSTICE BLACKMUN, concurring in the judgment. [Opinion omitted.]

MR. JUSTICE BRENNAN, dissenting.

* * *

The fatal constitutional infirmity in the punishment of death is that it treats "members of the human race as nonhumans, as objects to be toyed with and discarded. [It is] thus inconsistent with the fundamental premise of the Clause that even the vilest criminal remains a human being possessed of common human dignity." As such it is a penalty that "subjects the individual to a fate forbidden by the principle of civilized treatment guaranteed by the [Clause]." I therefore would hold, on that ground alone, that death is today a cruel and unusual punishment prohibited by the Clause. "Justice of this kind is obviously no less shocking than the crime itself, and the new 'official' murder, far from offering redress for the offense committed against society, adds instead a second defilement to the first."

* * *

MR. JUSTICE MARSHALL, dissenting.

* * *

Since the decision in *Furman,* the legislatures of 35 States have enacted new statutes authorizing the imposition of the death sentence for certain crimes, and Congress has enacted a law providing the death penalty for air piracy resulting in death. I would be less than candid if I did not acknowledge that these developments have a significant bearing on a realistic assessment of the moral acceptability of the death penalty to the American people. But if the constitutionality of the death penalty turns, as I have urged, on the opinion of an *informed* citizenry, then even the enactment of new death statutes cannot be viewed as conclusive. In *Furman,* I observed that the American people are largely unaware of the information critical to a judgment on the morality of the death penalty, and concluded that if they were better informed they would consider it shocking, unjust, and unacceptable. A recent study, conducted after the enactment of the post-*Furman* statutes, has confirmed that the American people know little about the death penalty, and that the opinions of an informed public would differ significantly from those of a public unaware of the consequences and effects of the death penalty.[1]

Even assuming, however, that the post-*Furman* enactment of statutes authorizing the death penalty renders the prediction of the views of an informed citizenry an uncertain basis for a constitutional decision, the enactment of those statutes has no bearing whatsoever on the conclusion that the death penalty is unconstitutional because it is excessive. An excessive penalty is invalid under the Cruel and Unusual Punishments Clause "even though popular sentiment may favor" it. The inquiry here, then, is simply whether the death penalty is necessary to accomplish the legitimate legislative purposes in punishment, or whether a less severe penalty—life imprisonment—would do as well.

The two purposes that sustain the death penalty as nonexcessive in the Court's view are general deterrence and retribution. In *Furman,* I canvassed the relevant data on the deterrent effect of capital punishment. * * * The available evidence, I concluded in *Furman,* was convincing that "capital punishment is not necessary as a deterrent to crime in our society."

* * *

There remains for consideration, however, what might be termed the purely retributive justification for the death penalty—that the death penalty is appropriate, not because of its beneficial effect on society, but because the taking of the murderer's life is itself morally good. * * *

* * * It is this latter notion, in particular, that I consider to be fundamentally at odds with the Eighth Amendment. The mere fact that the community demands the murderer's life in return for the evil he has done cannot sustain the death penalty, for * * * "the Eighth Amendment demands more than that a challenged punishment be acceptable to contemporary society." To be sustained under the Eighth Amendment, the death penalty must "compor[t] with the basic concept of human dignity at the core of the Amendment" * * *. Under these standards, the taking of life "because the wrongdoer deserves it" surely must fall, for such a punishment has as its very basis the total denial of the wrongdoer's dignity and worth.

The death penalty, unnecessary to promote the goal of deterrence or to further any legitimate notion of retribution, is an excessive penalty

[1] Sarat & Vidmar, Public Opinion, The Death Penalty, and the Eighth Amendment: Testing the Marshall Hypothesis, 1976 Wis.L.Rev. 171.

forbidden by the Eighth and Fourteenth Amendments. I respectfully dissent from the Court's judgment * * *.

QUESTIONS AND POINTS FOR DISCUSSION

1.   Thirty-one states and the federal government authorize the death penalty in some circumstances. Death Penalty Information Center, Facts about the Death Penalty, at http://www.deathpenaltyinfo.org/documents/Fact Sheet.pdf (updated Feb. 2, 2018). Since 1976, when it became apparent that the Supreme Court considered the death penalty constitutional in some cases, and February 2, 2018, 1468 peoples sentenced to death were executed. There were 2817 people on death row on July 1, 2017. Id.

Approximately two-thirds of the executions since 1976 occurred in five states—Texas, Virginia, Oklahoma, Florida, and Missouri, with Texas accounting for more than a third of the total executions. Id. In your opinion, is the disproportionate execution of people in a few states in the country relevant to the question whether the death penalty violates the Eighth Amendment?

2.   The debate between social scientists regarding whether the death penalty deters murders continues to this day. Some studies have concluded that the death penalty deters homicides, others that it increases the homicide rate, and still others that it has no effect on the commission of homicides. See Comm. on Deterrence & the Death Penalty & Comm. on Law & Justice, Nat'l Research Council, Deterrence and the Death Penalty 1–7 (Daniel S. Nagin & John V. Pepper eds., 2012) (reporting that methodological flaws in these studies make them "too weak" to inform policy decisions about the use of the death penalty). Does the answer to the empirical question whether the death penalty deters homicides have a bearing on your own views regarding its constitutionality?

3.   In *Gregg v. Georgia,* the Supreme Court emphasized the role that the proportionality review conducted by the Georgia Supreme Court played in reducing the risk that the death penalty had been imposed arbitrarily. Since *Gregg* was decided, however, the Court has held that such a proportionality review, during which the death penalty imposed in the case before an appellate court is compared with the sanction imposed in other capital cases, is not necessarily required in order for a capital-punishment system to be constitutional. Pulley v. Harris, 465 U.S. 37, 104 S.Ct. 871 (1984). Whether a proportionality review ever would be constitutionally mandated would depend on what other checks against arbitrariness are included in the system adopted by a jurisdiction for imposing capital punishment. Id. at 51, 104 S.Ct. at 879. In *Pulley,* those checks, deemed adequate by the Court, included review by the trial judge and the state supreme court of a jury's verdict of death.

Virtually all of the states in which the death penalty is authorized provide for the automatic review of a death sentence, typically by the state's highest appellate court. Bureau of Justice Statistics, U.S. Dep't of Justice, Capital Punishment, 2005, at 3 (2006) (reporting that all but one of the states provide for the automatic review of death sentences). Even if the defendant is opposed to the review, states generally require that the review be conducted. Id.

4. When analyzing the Eighth Amendment's prohibition of cruel and unusual punishments in *Gregg v. Georgia*, the Supreme Court emphasized the role the jury plays as an indicator of "contemporary community values" when deciding whether to impose the death penalty. As was discussed in note 1 on page 173, the Court has also held that a defendant has a right, under the Sixth Amendment, to have a jury make the final factual findings regarding the existence of aggravating factors that are, under state law, a prerequisite to the imposition of the death penalty. See Hurst v. Florida, 136 S.Ct. 616 (2016); Ring v. Arizona, 536 U.S. 584, 122 S.Ct. 2428 (2002).

In your opinion, is there also a constitutional right to have a jury weigh the aggravating and mitigating factors and decide whether a defendant's crime warrants the penalty of death? See Rauf v. State, 145 A.3d 430 (Del. 2016) (concluding the Sixth Amendment accords the right to have a jury decide whether a defendant will live or die).

5. To guard against arbitrariness in the imposition of the death penalty, courts have scrutinized the language of death-penalty statutes to ensure that they are not unconstitutionally vague. In Maynard v. Cartwright, 486 U.S. 356, 108 S.Ct. 1853 (1988), for example, the Supreme Court struck down, on Eighth Amendment grounds, a provision of a death-penalty statute treating the fact that a murder was "especially heinous, atrocious, or cruel" as an aggravating circumstance. In concluding that this language was unconstitutionally vague, the Court noted that "an ordinary person could honestly believe that every unjustified, intentional taking of human life is 'especially heinous.'" Id. at 364, 108 S.Ct. at 1859. How might this statute be redrafted to pass constitutional muster?

The Supreme Court's decision in Walton v. Arizona, 497 U.S. 639, 110 S.Ct. 3047 (1990) provides some helpful insights in answering that question. In that case, the Court upheld an Arizona death-penalty statute couched in language much like the wording of the statute held unconstitutional in *Maynard*; the Arizona statute listed the fact that a murder was committed in "an especially heinous, cruel or depraved manner" as an aggravating circumstance supporting the imposition of the death penalty. Nonetheless, the Supreme Court held that the Arizona Supreme Court's limiting construction of the statute eradicated any unconstitutional vagueness. The state supreme court had said that "a crime is committed in an especially cruel manner when the perpetrator inflicts mental anguish or physical abuse before the victim's death" and that "[m]ental anguish includes a victim's uncertainty as to his ultimate fate." Id. at 646, 110 S.Ct. at 3053. The state court had also clarified that a murder is "especially depraved" when the murderer "relishes the murder, evidencing debasement or perversion," or "shows an indifference to the suffering of the victim and evidences a sense of pleasure" in the victim's death. Id.

The Arizona Supreme Court, incidentally, found that these standards were met in *Walton* and that imposition of the death penalty on the defendant was appropriate. Walton and his two codefendants had accosted the victim at gunpoint and forced him into his car. They then drove him out into the desert where Walton shot him in the head. Returning to the car, Walton commented to his codefendants that he had "never seen a man pee in his pants before." The victim's body was found a week later. An autopsy revealed that the victim had not died immediately after being shot. Instead, blinded by the shot, he struggled about in the desert for six days, dying from dehydration, starvation, and pneumonia the day before his body was found.

6. Despite the Supreme Court's holding in *Gregg v. Georgia* that Georgia's system for imposing the death penalty, on its face, provided enough procedural safeguards to diminish sufficiently the risk of arbitrariness in the imposition of the death penalty, the Supreme Court later was confronted in McCleskey v. Kemp, 481 U.S. 279, 107 S.Ct. 1756 (1987) with the claim that the statutory framework, as applied, did not meet constitutional standards— that the system for imposing the death penalty in Georgia was suffused with arbitrariness. The defendant in *McCleskey,* an African American sentenced to death for the killing of a white police officer, produced statistics demonstrating that defendants in Georgia charged with killing white victims were 4.3 times more likely to be sentenced to death than defendants whose victims were black. In addition, a black defendant who killed a white victim was much more likely to receive the death penalty than a white defendant who killed a white victim. While 22% of the murder cases studied involving black defendants and white victims resulted in imposition of the death penalty, the death penalty was imposed in only 8% of the cases in which both the defendant and the victim were white. In cases involving black victims, 3% of the white defendants were sentenced to death, while only 1% of the black defendants received the death penalty.

The Supreme Court assumed that these statistics, drawn from what was known as the "Baldus study," were reliable, but nonetheless, in a 5–4 decision, upheld the constitutionality of the capital-punishment system in Georgia. Responding to the defendant's argument that the system violated his Fourteenth Amendment right to be afforded the equal protection of the law, the Court noted that the defendant had failed to prove, as required by the Equal Protection Clause, that he had been discriminated against intentionally. The Court refused to assume that the jury that had sentenced the defendant to death had done so because of his race or the race of his victim. In addition, the Court observed that there was no evidence that the Georgia legislature had enacted the death-penalty statute in order to discriminate against African Americans.

The Supreme Court also rejected the defendant's claim that his death sentence constituted cruel and unusual punishment, emphasizing, once again, that the statistical evidence adduced by the defendant did not demonstrate that race was actually a factor in the imposition of the death penalty in his case. Nor was the Court willing to conclude that the death penalty in Georgia was applied arbitrarily, in violation of the Eighth Amendment, because of the risk that racial bias entered into capital-sentencing decisions. The Court observed:

> At most, the Baldus study indicates a discrepancy that appears to correlate with race. Apparent disparities in sentencing are an inevitable part of our criminal justice system. * * * As this Court has recognized, any mode for determining guilt or punishment "has its weaknesses and the potential for misuse." Specifically, "there can be 'no perfect procedure for deciding in which cases governmental authority should be used to impose death.'" Despite these imperfections, our consistent rule has been that constitutional guarantees are met when "the mode [for determining guilt or punishment] itself has been surrounded with safeguards to make it as fair as possible." Where the discretion that is fundamental to our criminal process is involved, we decline to assume that what is unexplained is invidious. In light of the safeguards designed to minimize racial bias in the process, the fundamental value of jury trial in our criminal justice system, and the benefits that discretion provides to criminal defendants, we hold that the Baldus study does not demonstrate a constitutionally significant risk of racial bias affecting the Georgia capital sentencing process.

Id. at 312–13, 107 S.Ct. at 1777–78.

In a dissenting opinion, Justice Brennan, joined by Justices Marshall, Blackmun, and Stevens, objected to the majority's observation that the risk of racial bias when defendants are sentenced to death in Georgia is not "constitutionally significant." Justice Brennan noted that for every eleven defendants sentenced to death in the state for killing a white person, six would not have received the death penalty if their victims had been black. "Surely," Justice Brennan observed, "we would not be willing to take a person's life if the chance that his death was irrationally imposed is *more* likely than not." Id. at 328, 107 S.Ct. at 1786 (Brennan, J., dissenting). Interestingly, Justice Powell, who wrote the majority opinion in *McCleskey*, later rued that decision, stating after he was no longer on the Court that he wished he had voted differently in the case. John C. Jeffries, Jr., Justice Lewis F. Powell, Jr. 451 (1994).

7.   Could a state substantially reduce the risk of racial prejudice affecting capital-sentencing decisions without abandoning the death penalty? In a separate dissenting opinion in *McCleskey v. Kemp*, Justice Stevens answered this question in the affirmative. Justice Stevens pointed to the results of the Baldus study, which revealed that there is a class of extremely egregious murders that result in the imposition of the death penalty regardless of the race of the victim or defendant. Justice Stevens suggested that constitutional problems stemming from racial bias in the imposition of the death penalty could be averted if the death penalty were reserved for this limited category of murders.

Would mandating imposition of the death penalty in certain circumstances eliminate the problem of racial bias in the application of death-penalty statutes? Would such a death-penalty structure be constitutional? The Supreme Court addressed this latter question in Woodson v. North Carolina, 428 U.S. 280, 96 S.Ct. 2978 (1976), the case which follows.

WOODSON V. NORTH CAROLINA

Supreme Court of the United States, 1976.
428 U.S. 280, 96 S.Ct. 2978, 49 L.Ed.2d 944.

Judgment of the Court, and opinion of MR. JUSTICE STEWART, MR. JUSTICE POWELL, and MR. JUSTICE STEVENS, announced by MR. JUSTICE STEWART.

* * *

The petitioners were convicted of first-degree murder as the result of their participation in an armed robbery of a convenience food store, in the course of which the cashier was killed and a customer was seriously wounded. There were four participants in the robbery: the petitioners James Tyrone Woodson and Luby Waxton and two others, Leonard Tucker and Johnnie Lee Carroll. * * *

The evidence for the prosecution established that the four men had been discussing a possible robbery for some time. On the fatal day Woodson had been drinking heavily. About 9:30 p.m., Waxton and Tucker came to the trailer where Woodson was staying. When Woodson came out of the trailer, Waxton struck him in the face and threatened to kill him in an effort to make him sober up and come along on the robbery. The three proceeded to Waxton's trailer where they met Carroll. Waxton armed himself with a nickel-plated derringer, and Tucker handed Woodson a rifle. The four then set out by automobile to rob the store. Upon arriving at their destination Tucker and Waxton went into the store while Carroll and Woodson remained in the car as lookouts. Once inside the store, Tucker purchased a package of cigarettes from the woman cashier. Waxton then also asked for a package of cigarettes, but as the cashier approached him he pulled the derringer out of his hip pocket and fatally shot her at point-blank range. Waxton then took the money tray from the cash register and gave it to Tucker, who carried it out of the store, pushing past an entering customer as he reached the door. After he was outside, Tucker heard a second shot from inside the store, and shortly thereafter Waxton emerged, carrying a handful of paper money. Tucker and Waxton got in the car and the four drove away.

* * *

The petitioners were found guilty on all charges, and, as was required by statute, sentenced to death. The Supreme Court of North Carolina affirmed. * * *

* * *

* * * In ruling on the constitutionality of the sentences imposed on the petitioners under this North Carolina statute, the Court now addresses for the first time the question whether a death sentence returned pursuant to a law imposing a mandatory death penalty for a broad category of homicidal offenses[7] constitutes cruel and unusual punishment within the meaning of the Eighth and Fourteenth Amendments. * * *

A

The Eighth Amendment stands to assure that the State's power to punish is "exercised within the limits of civilized standards." Central to the application of the Amendment is a determination of contemporary standards regarding the infliction of punishment. As discussed in *Gregg v. Georgia,* indicia of societal values identified in prior opinions include history and traditional usage, legislative enactments, and jury determinations.

* * * At the time the Eighth Amendment was adopted in 1791, the States uniformly followed the common-law practice of making death the exclusive and mandatory sentence for certain specified offenses. Although the range of capital offenses in the American Colonies was quite limited in comparison to the more than 200 offenses then punishable by death in England, the Colonies at the time of the Revolution imposed death sentences on all persons convicted of any of a considerable number of crimes, typically including at a minimum, murder, treason, piracy, arson, rape, robbery, burglary, and sodomy. * * * Almost from the outset jurors reacted unfavorably to the harshness of mandatory death sentences. The States initially responded to this expression of public dissatisfaction with mandatory statutes by limiting the classes of capital offenses.

This reform, however, left unresolved the problem posed by the not infrequent refusal of juries to convict murderers rather than subject them to automatic death sentences. In 1794, Pennsylvania attempted to alleviate the undue severity of the law by confining the mandatory death penalty to "murder of the first degree" encompassing all "willful, deliberate and premeditated" killings. * * * [W]ithin a generation the practice spread to most of the States.

---

[7]   This case does not involve a mandatory death penalty statute limited to an extremely narrow category of homicide, such as murder by a prisoner serving a life sentence, defined in large part in terms of the character or record of the offender. We thus express no opinion regarding the constitutionality of such a statute.

Despite the broad acceptance of the division of murder into degrees, the reform proved to be an unsatisfactory means of identifying persons appropriately punishable by death. * * * Juries continued to find the death penalty inappropriate in a significant number of first-degree murder cases and refused to return guilty verdicts for that crime.

The inadequacy of distinguishing between murderers solely on the basis of legislative criteria narrowing the definition of the capital offense led the States to grant juries sentencing discretion in capital cases. * * * This flexibility remedied the harshness of mandatory statutes by permitting the jury to respond to mitigating factors by withholding the death penalty. * * * [B]y the end of World War I, all but eight States, Hawaii, and the District of Columbia either had adopted discretionary death penalty schemes or abolished the death penalty altogether. By 1963, all of these remaining jurisdictions had replaced their automatic death penalty statutes with discretionary jury sentencing.

The history of mandatory death penalty statutes in the United States thus reveals that the practice of sentencing to death all persons convicted of a particular offense has been rejected as unduly harsh and unworkably rigid. The two crucial indicators of evolving standards of decency respecting the imposition of punishment in our society—jury determinations and legislative enactments—both point conclusively to the repudiation of automatic death sentences. * * *

* * *

Still further evidence of the incompatibility of mandatory death penalties with contemporary values is provided by the results of jury sentencing under discretionary statutes. * * * Various studies indicate that even in first-degree murder cases juries with sentencing discretion do not impose the death penalty "with any great frequency."[31] * * *

* * *

* * * [T]here remains the question whether the mandatory statutes adopted by North Carolina and a number of other States following *Furman* evince a sudden reversal of societal values regarding the imposition of capital punishment. In view of the persistent and unswerving legislative rejection of mandatory death penalty statutes * * * for more than 130 years until *Furman,* it seems evident that the post-*Furman* enactments reflect attempts by the States to retain the death penalty in a form consistent with the Constitution, rather than a renewed societal acceptance of mandatory death sentencing. * * *

* * *

---

[31] Data compiled on discretionary jury sentencing of persons convicted of capital murder reveal that the penalty of death is generally imposed in less than 20% of the cases.

* * * North Carolina's mandatory death penalty statute for first-degree murder departs markedly from contemporary standards respecting the imposition of the punishment of death and thus cannot be applied consistently with the Eighth and Fourteenth Amendments' requirement that the State's power to punish "be exercised within the limits of civilized standards."

B

A separate deficiency of North Carolina's mandatory death sentence statute is its failure to provide a constitutionally tolerable response to *Furman*'s rejection of unbridled jury discretion in the imposition of capital sentences. Central to the limited holding in *Furman* was the conviction that the vesting of standardless sentencing power in the jury violated the Eighth and Fourteenth Amendments. It is argued that North Carolina has remedied the inadequacies of the death penalty statutes held unconstitutional in *Furman* by withdrawing all sentencing discretion from juries in capital cases. But when one considers the long and consistent American experience with the death penalty in first-degree murder cases, it becomes evident that mandatory statutes enacted in response to *Furman* have simply papered over the problem of unguided and unchecked jury discretion.

* * * American juries have persistently refused to convict a significant portion of persons charged with first-degree murder of that offense under mandatory death penalty statutes. * * * North Carolina's mandatory death penalty statute provides no standards to guide the jury in its inevitable exercise of the power to determine which first-degree murderers shall live and which shall die. * * * Instead of rationalizing the sentencing process, a mandatory scheme may well exacerbate the problem identified in *Furman* by resting the penalty determination on the particular jury's willingness to act lawlessly. While a mandatory death penalty statute may reasonably be expected to increase the number of persons sentenced to death, it does not fulfill *Furman*'s basic requirement by replacing arbitrary and wanton jury discretion with objective standards to guide, regularize, and make rationally reviewable the process for imposing a sentence of death.

C

A third constitutional shortcoming of the North Carolina statute is its failure to allow the particularized consideration of relevant aspects of the character and record of each convicted defendant before the imposition upon him of a sentence of death. * * * It treats all persons convicted of a designated offense not as uniquely individual human beings, but as members of a faceless, undifferentiated mass to be subjected to the blind infliction of the penalty of death.

* * * While the prevailing practice of individualizing sentencing determinations generally reflects simply enlightened policy rather than a constitutional imperative, we believe that in capital cases the fundamental respect for humanity underlying the Eighth Amendment requires consideration of the character and record of the individual offender and the circumstances of the particular offense as a constitutionally indispensable part of the process of inflicting the penalty of death.

This conclusion rests squarely on the predicate that the penalty of death is qualitatively different from a sentence of imprisonment, however long. Death, in its finality, differs more from life imprisonment than a 100-year prison term differs from one of only a year or two. Because of that qualitative difference, there is a corresponding difference in the need for reliability in the determination that death is the appropriate punishment in a specific case.

For the reasons stated, we conclude that the death sentences imposed upon the petitioners under North Carolina's mandatory death sentence statute violated the Eighth and Fourteenth Amendments and therefore must be set aside. * * *

* * *

MR. JUSTICE BRENNAN, concurring in the judgment. [Opinion omitted.]

MR. JUSTICE MARSHALL, concurring in the judgment. [Opinion omitted.]

MR. JUSTICE WHITE, with whom THE CHIEF JUSTICE and MR. JUSTICE REHNQUIST join, dissenting. [Opinion omitted.]

MR. JUSTICE BLACKMUN, dissenting. [Opinion omitted.]

MR. JUSTICE REHNQUIST, dissenting.

* * *

There was undoubted dissatisfaction, from more than one sector of 19th century society, with the operation of mandatory death sentences. One segment of that society was totally opposed to capital punishment, and was apparently willing to accept the substitution of discretionary imposition of that penalty for its mandatory imposition as a halfway house on the road to total abolition. Another segment was equally unhappy with the operation of the mandatory system, but for an entirely different reason. As the plurality recognizes, this second segment of society was unhappy with the operation of the mandatory system, not because of the death sentences imposed under it, but because people obviously guilty of criminal offenses were *not* being convicted under it. Change to a discretionary system was accepted by these persons not because they thought mandatory imposition of the death penalty was cruel and unusual, but because they thought that if jurors were permitted to return a sentence other than death upon the conviction of a capital crime, fewer guilty defendants would be acquitted.

So far as the action of juries is concerned, the fact that in some cases juries operating under the mandatory system refused to convict obviously guilty defendants does not reflect any "turning away" from the death penalty, or the mandatory death penalty, supporting the proposition that it is "cruel and unusual." Given the requirement of unanimity with respect to jury verdicts in capital cases, * * * it is apparent that a single juror could prevent a jury from returning a verdict of conviction. * * * The fact that the presence of such jurors could prevent conviction in a given case, even though the majority of society, speaking through legislatures, had decreed that it should be imposed, certainly does not indicate that society as a whole rejected mandatory punishment for such offenders; it does not even indicate that those few members of society who serve on juries, as a whole, had done so.

* * *

The second constitutional flaw which the plurality finds in North Carolina's mandatory system is that it has simply "papered over" the problem of unchecked jury discretion. * * *

* * *

In Georgia juries are entitled to return a sentence of life, rather than death, for no reason whatever, simply based upon their own subjective notions of what is right and what is wrong.[a] * * * Why these types of discretion are regarded by the plurality as constitutionally permissible, while that which may occur in the North Carolina system is not, is not readily apparent. * * *

* * *

QUESTIONS AND POINTS FOR DISCUSSION

1. In Sumner v. Shuman, 483 U.S. 66, 107 S.Ct. 2716 (1987), the Supreme Court answered a question left open in *Woodson*—whether a statute that requires imposition of the death penalty when an inmate commits a murder while serving a life sentence without possibility of parole is constitutional. The Court held that such a mandatory death sentence violates the Eighth Amendment. The Court noted that even when a person serving a life sentence without possibility of parole commits a murder, there might be mitigating circumstances that contraindicate imposition of the death penalty. Circumstances surrounding the murder itself, for example, might diminish the person's culpability, even though those circumstances did not rise to the level of a legal defense to the charge of murder. Or there might have been

---

[a]   In Gregg v. Georgia, 428 U.S. 153, 96 S.Ct. 2909 (1976), supra page 302, the Supreme Court upheld the Georgia death-penalty scheme alluded to above.

circumstances surrounding the conduct underlying the conviction for which the defendant is serving a life sentence that might suggest to the sentencer that imposition of the death penalty is unwarranted. Finally, there might be facts about the defendant, such as a severe mental or emotional disturbance from which the defendant was suffering at the time of the murder, that point against imposition of a death sentence.

To the argument that a mandatory death sentence is necessary in order to deter murders by people serving life sentences with no possibility of parole and to provide a means of punishing them, the Court responded that these purposes could be effectuated by retaining the death penalty, though not a mandatory one. If not sentenced to die, already-imprisoned people still could be punished for a murder, according to the Court, by withdrawing privileges from them that they otherwise would enjoy in the prison. See also Roberts v. Louisiana, 431 U.S. 633, 97 S.Ct. 1993 (1977) (mandatory death sentence for murdering a police officer violates the Eighth Amendment).

2.   According to the Supreme Court, not every death-penalty statute that has a mandatory component in it violates constitutional strictures. In Blystone v. Pennsylvania, 494 U.S. 299, 110 S.Ct. 1078 (1990), the Court upheld the constitutionality of a death-penalty statute which required the jury to sentence a defendant to death if it found that aggravating circumstances in the case outweighed any mitigating circumstances. The Supreme Court distinguished *Woodson,* noting that in the case before it "[d]eath is not automatically imposed upon conviction for certain types of murder. It is imposed only after a determination that the aggravating circumstances outweigh the mitigating circumstances present in the particular crime committed by the particular defendant, or that there are no such mitigating circumstances." Id. at 305, 110 S.Ct. at 1082–83. The Eighth Amendment also permits statutes to mandate imposition of a death sentence when the jury finds that the aggravating and mitigating factors are "in equipoise"—in other words, evenly balanced. Kansas v. Marsh, 548 U.S. 163, 166, 126 S.Ct. 2516, 2520 (2006).

3.   In applying the Eighth Amendment requirement, to which *Woodson* alluded, that a defendant in a death-penalty case be afforded an individualized sentencing determination, the Supreme Court has concluded that a sentencer must not be precluded from considering any relevant mitigating circumstances when deciding whether to sentence a defendant to death. See, e.g., Hitchcock v. Dugger, 481 U.S. 393, 107 S.Ct. 1821 (1987) (defendant has a right to introduce, and have the sentencer consider, evidence of mitigating circumstances not mentioned in the death-penalty statute); Skipper v. South Carolina, 476 U.S. 1, 106 S.Ct. 1669 (1986) (defendant should have been permitted to introduce evidence about how well he had adjusted to jail while awaiting trial); Eddings v. Oklahoma, 455 U.S. 104, 102 S.Ct. 869 (1982) (sentencing judge acted unconstitutionally in refusing to consider evidence of defendant's troubled childhood and his emotional problems). The Court has acknowledged that there is "some tension" between this Eighth Amendment requirement and the need, emphasized in *Gregg v. Georgia,* to place limits on the sentencer's exercise of discretion when decisions are being made regarding

imposition of the death penalty. Tuilaepa v. California, 512 U.S. 967, 973, 114 S.Ct. 2630, 2635 (1994). Nonetheless, the Court has concluded that what the Eighth Amendment seeks to ensure, and can ensure, is that systems developed for imposing the death penalty are "at once consistent and principled but also humane and sensible to the uniqueness of the individual." Eddings v. Oklahoma, 455 U.S. at 110, 102 S.Ct. at 874.

Several Justices on the Supreme Court have lambasted this conclusion. Justice Scalia, for one, reported that he saw not only "tension" between the line of Supreme Court cases emphasizing the need for structured decision making in capital cases and the line of decisions underscoring the need for individualized sentencing in such cases, but found them totally irreconcilable. He explained his views in a concurring opinion in Walton v. Arizona, 497 U.S. 639, 110 S.Ct. 3047 (1990):

> Shortly after introducing our doctrine *requiring* constraints on the sentencer's discretion to "impose" the death penalty, the Court began developing a doctrine *forbidding* constraints on the sentencer's discretion to "*decline* to impose" it. This second doctrine— counterdoctrine would be a better word—has completely exploded whatever coherence the notion of "guided discretion" once had.

> * * *

> To acknowledge that "there perhaps is an inherent tension" between this line of cases and the line stemming from *Furman* is rather like saying that there was perhaps an inherent tension between the Allies and the Axis Powers in World War II. And to refer to the two lines as pursuing "twin objectives" is rather like referring to the twin objectives of good and evil. They cannot be reconciled. Pursuant to *Furman,* and in order "to achieve a more rational and equitable administration of the death penalty," we require that States "channel the sentencer's discretion by 'clear and objective standards' that provide 'specific and detailed guidance.'" In the next breath, however, we say that "the State *cannot* channel the sentencer's discretion . . . to consider any relevant [mitigating] information offered by the defendant" and that the sentencer must enjoy unconstrained discretion to decide whether any sympathetic factors bearing on the defendant or the crime indicate that he does not "deserve to be sentenced to death." The latter requirement quite obviously destroys whatever rationality and predictability the former requirement was designed to achieve.

> * * * [T]he question remains why the Constitution demands that the aggravating standards and mitigating standards be accorded opposite treatment. It is impossible to understand why. Since the individualized determination is a unitary one (does this defendant deserve death for this crime?) once one says each sentencer must be able to answer "no" for whatever reason it deems morally sufficient (and indeed, for whatever reason any one of 12 jurors deems morally

sufficient), it becomes impossible to claim that the Constitution requires consistency and rationality among sentencing determinations to be preserved by strictly limiting the reasons for which each sentencer can say "yes." * * *

* * *

* * * *Stare decisis* cannot command the impossible. Since I cannot possibly be guided by what seem to me incompatible principles, I must reject the one that is plainly in error.

* * *

* * * Accordingly, I will not, in this case or in the future, vote to uphold an Eighth Amendment claim that the sentencer's discretion has been unlawfully restricted.

Id. at 661, 664–66, 673, 110 S.Ct. at 3061, 3063–64, 3068.

In Callins v. Collins, 510 U.S. 1141, 114 S.Ct. 1127 (1994) (Blackmun, J., dissenting), Justice Blackmun agreed that the Eighth Amendment requirements expounded in the Supreme Court's opinions are in conflict:

Any statute or procedure that could effectively eliminate arbitrariness from the administration of death would also restrict the sentencer's discretion to such an extent that the sentencer would be unable to give full consideration to the unique characteristics of each defendant and the circumstances of the offense. By the same token, any statute or procedure that would provide the sentencer with sufficient discretion to consider fully and act upon the unique circumstances of each defendant would "thro[w] open the back door to arbitrary and irrational sentencing." All efforts to strike an appropriate balance between these conflicting constitutional commands are futile because there is a heightened need for both in the administration of death.

Id. at 1155, 114 S.Ct. at 1136. Justice Blackmun, however, balked at the idea of eliminating this conflict by reading the individualized-sentencing requirement out of the Eighth Amendment, as Justice Scalia proposed. Convinced that the need for individualized sentencing in capital cases is deeply embedded in American standards of decency, Justice Blackmun observed that "[t]he notion of prohibiting a sentencer from exercising its discretion 'to dispense mercy on the basis of factors too intangible to write into a statute,' is offensive to our sense of fundamental fairness and respect for the uniqueness of the individual." Id. at 1150, 114 S.Ct. at 1133. Concluding that it was simply impossible to administer a death-penalty system in which death sentences were imposed both fairly and consistently, Justice Blackmun announced that he would no longer "tinker with the machinery of death"—that he would henceforth vote to strike down, on constitutional grounds, all death sentences reviewed by the Court. Id. at 1145, 114 S.Ct. at 1130.

Although the acknowledged "tension" between the general rules adopted to ensure consistency in the imposition of the death penalty and the requirement that there be unconstrained consideration of mitigating circumstances in capital cases has not led to the invalidation of the death penalty, the Supreme Court has cited that "tension" as a reason to limit the death penalty's scope. See Kennedy v. Louisiana, 554 U.S. 407, 440, 128 S.Ct. 2641, 2661 (2008) on page 340. With which view do you agree? With that of a majority of the Supreme Court that the twin Eighth Amendment goals of ensuring that imposition of the death penalty is both "consistent and principled" and "humane and sensible to the uniqueness of the individual" can be met but that the conflict between these goals should limit the kinds of cases in which a death sentence can be imposed? With Justice Scalia's view that this conflict should be eradicated by abandoning the individualized-sentencing requirement? Or with Justice Blackmun's view that death-penalty statutes cannot be administered constitutionally because of this conflict?

4.   Precluding a defendant from introducing evidence in a capital-sentencing hearing that imposition of the death penalty is unwarranted may violate not only the Eighth Amendment but due process as well. Simmons v. South Carolina, 512 U.S. 154, 114 S.Ct. 2187 (1994) is a case in point. In that case, the prosecutor urged the jury to sentence the defendant to death because he would continue to pose a danger to others in the future. The defendant, however, was barred from informing the jury, either through the arguments of his attorney or a court instruction, that if the defendant was not sentenced to death, he would be sentenced to life in prison without the possibility of parole. The Supreme Court reaffirmed that due process forbids imposing the death penalty based on information that a defendant had " 'no opportunity to deny or explain.' " Id. at 161, 114 S.Ct. at 2192–93 (quoting Gardner v. Florida, 430 U.S. 349, 362, 97 S.Ct. 1197, 1207 (1977), supra page 152). When a defendant's future dangerousness is an issue in a capital-sentencing hearing, the defendant therefore has a due-process right to inform the sentencing jury that a life sentence forecloses release on parole. Accord Kelly v. South Carolina, 534 U.S. 246, 122 S.Ct. 726 (2002); Shafer v. South Carolina, 532 U.S. 36, 121 S.Ct. 1263 (2001).

5.   To counterbalance a defendant's argument in a capital case that a life sentence without the possibility of parole will adequately safeguard the public, a prosecutor may seek to have the jury instructed about the possibility that the exercise of executive clemency powers might lead to the defendant's release from prison in the future. In California v. Ramos, 463 U.S. 992, 103 S.Ct. 3446 (1983), the Supreme Court held, in a 5–4 decision, that there is no federal constitutional impediment to the submission of such an instruction to the jury. If you were going to oppose, on state constitutional or policy grounds, permitting such an instruction, what arguments would you make? See Blaine LeCesne, Tipping the Scales Toward Death: Instructing Capital Jurors on the Possibility of Executive Clemency, 65 U. Cin. L.Rev. 1051 (1997).

B. DEATH SENTENCES FOR PARTICULAR KINDS OF CRIMES AND CATEGORIES OF PEOPLE

The mitigating circumstances that may lead a sentencing judge or jury to refrain from imposing a death sentence typically fall into two categories: facts about the defendant and facts about the crime itself. The question arises as to whether there are any mitigating facts about a defendant that, rather than just being weighed in the sentencing calculus, erect a *per se* bar to the imposition of the death penalty.

In Penry v. Lynaugh, 492 U.S. 302, 109 S.Ct. 2934 (1989), the Supreme Court held that while a defendant's intellectual disability (then referred to by the Court as "mental retardation") is a mitigating circumstance that should be considered by the sentencer when deciding whether to sentence the defendant to death, the disability does not automatically preclude imposition of the death penalty. Thirteen years later, in Atkins v. Virginia, 536 U.S. 304, 122 S.Ct. 2242 (2002), the Court reversed its position, holding that executing a person with an intellectual disability constitutes cruel and unusual punishment. The Court noted that while only two states barred the imposition of a death sentence on an intellectually disabled person at the time *Penry* was decided, eighteen states now generally prohibited such death sentences. The Court explained that it was the "consistency of the direction of change," more than the numerical count, that provided "powerful evidence" of a consensus view that had emerged since *Penry* that individuals with an intellectual disability are less culpable for their crimes. Id. at 315–16, 122 S.Ct. at 2249. The Court also opined that these individuals are at "special risk of wrongful execution," in part because their disability limits their effectiveness as witnesses and their ability to assist their attorneys in preparing their defense. Id. at 321, 122 S.Ct. at 2252.

The Court in *Atkins* left to the states the task of determining how to differentiate between defendants who are intellectually disabled and those who are not. There are limits, though, on the discretion accorded jurisdictions in capital cases to define what is an intellectual disability. For example, requiring a person to have an IQ test score of 70 or below to be considered intellectually disabled is, according to the Supreme Court, unconstitutional. Hall v. Florida, 134 S.Ct. 1986 (2014). Due, in part, to the imprecision of IQ tests (what is called the "standard error of measurement") and the "unanimous professional consensus" of medical experts, defendants with an IQ score between 71 and 75 must be permitted to present other evidence, such as school records, that they have an intellectual disability that forecloses imposition of the death penalty. Id. at 2000.

The Supreme Court also has vacillated, as it did in the intellectual-disability context, on the question whether the execution of individuals who were younger than eighteen at the time of their crimes violates the Eighth

Amendment. The Supreme Court considered this question in the case that follows.

ROPER V. SIMMONS

Supreme Court of the United States, 2005.
543 U.S. 551, 125 S.Ct. 1183, 161 L.Ed.2d 1.

JUSTICE KENNEDY delivered the opinion of the Court.

* * *

At the age of 17, when he was still a junior in high school, Christopher Simmons, the respondent here, committed murder. * * * Before its commission Simmons said he wanted to murder someone. In chilling, callous terms he talked about his plan, discussing it for the most part with two friends, Charles Benjamin and John Tessmer, then aged 15 and 16 respectively. Simmons proposed to commit burglary and murder by breaking and entering, tying up a victim, and throwing the victim off a bridge. Simmons assured his friends they could "get away with it" because they were minors.

The three met at about 2 a.m. on the night of the murder, but Tessmer left before the other two set out. * * * Simmons and Benjamin entered the home of the victim, Shirley Crook, after reaching through an open window and unlocking the back door. * * *

Using duct tape to cover her eyes and mouth and bind her hands, the two perpetrators put Mrs. Crook in her minivan and drove to a state park. They reinforced the bindings, covered her head with a towel, and walked her to a railroad trestle spanning the Meramec River. There they tied her hands and feet together with electrical wire, wrapped her whole face in duct tape and threw her from the bridge, drowning her in the waters below.

[After his arrest, Simmons confessed to the murder. He was tried for murder as an adult, convicted, and sentenced to death. The Missouri Supreme Court eventually set the death sentence aside on the grounds that the Eighth Amendment prohibited the execution of a defendant who was younger than eighteen when the crime was committed. The Supreme Court then granted certiorari.]

* * *

In *Thompson v. Oklahoma,* 487 U.S. 815 (1988), a plurality of the Court determined that our standards of decency do not permit the execution of any offender under the age of 16 at the time of the crime. * * *

* * * With Justice O'Connor concurring in the judgment on narrower grounds,[b] the Court set aside the death sentence that had been imposed on the 15-year-old offender.

The next year, in *Stanford v. Kentucky,* 492 U.S. 361 (1989), the Court, over a dissenting opinion joined by four Justices, referred to contemporary standards of decency in this country and concluded the Eighth and Fourteenth Amendments did not proscribe the execution of juvenile offenders over 15 but under 18. * * *

* * *

* * * [W]e now reconsider the issue decided in *Stanford.* The beginning point is a review of objective indicia of consensus, as expressed in particular by the enactments of legislatures that have addressed the question. * * * We then must determine, in the exercise of our own independent judgment, whether the death penalty is a disproportionate punishment for juveniles.

III

A

* * * [Thirty] States prohibit the juvenile death penalty, comprising 12 that have rejected the death penalty altogether and 18 that maintain it but, by express provision or judicial interpretation, exclude juveniles from its reach. * * * [E]ven in the 20 States without a formal prohibition on executing juveniles, the practice is infrequent. Since *Stanford,* six States have executed prisoners for crimes committed as juveniles. In the past 10 years, only three have done so * * *.

* * * Five States that allowed the juvenile death penalty at the time of *Stanford* have abandoned it in the intervening 15 years—four through legislative enactments and one through judicial decision.

Though less dramatic than the change from *Penry* [*v. Lynaugh,* 492 U.S. 302 (1989)] to *Atkins* [*v. Virginia,* 536 U.S. 304 (2002)] * * *, we still consider the change from *Stanford* to this case to be significant. * * * Since *Stanford,* no State that previously prohibited capital punishment for juveniles has reinstated it. * * * Any difference between this case and *Atkins* with respect to the pace of abolition is thus counterbalanced by the consistent direction of the change.

The slower pace of abolition of the juvenile death penalty over the past 15 years, moreover, may have a simple explanation. When we heard *Penry,* only two death penalty States had already prohibited the execution of the mentally retarded. When we heard *Stanford,* by contrast, 12 death penalty

---

b   In her concurring opinion in *Thompson,* Justice O'Connor noted that it was likely, though not entirely clear, that there was a national consensus against the death penalty for a crime committed when a defendant was fifteen years old or younger. She therefore considered imposition of the death penalty to be unconstitutional when a state, like Oklahoma, had not specifically authorized the execution of individuals who were younger than sixteen at the time of their crimes.

States had already prohibited the execution of any juvenile under 18, and 15 had prohibited the execution of any juvenile under 17. * * * "It would be the ultimate in irony if the very fact that the inappropriateness of the death penalty for juveniles was broadly recognized sooner than it was recognized for the mentally retarded were to become a reason to continue the execution of juveniles now that the execution of the mentally retarded has been barred."

* * *

As in *Atkins*, the objective indicia of consensus in this case—the rejection of the juvenile death penalty in the majority of States; the infrequency of its use even where it remains on the books; and the consistency in the trend toward abolition of the practice—provide sufficient evidence that today our society views juveniles * * * as "categorically less culpable than the average criminal."

B

* * *

Because the death penalty is the most severe punishment, the Eighth Amendment applies to it with special force. Capital punishment must be limited to those offenders who commit "a narrow category of the most serious crimes" and whose extreme culpability makes them "the most deserving of execution." * * *

Three general differences between juveniles under 18 and adults demonstrate that juvenile offenders cannot with reliability be classified among the worst offenders. First, as any parent knows and as the scientific and sociological studies respondent and his *amici* cite tend to confirm, "[a] lack of maturity and an underdeveloped sense of responsibility are found in youth more often than in adults and are more understandable among the young. These qualities often result in impetuous and ill-considered actions and decisions." * * * In recognition of the comparative immaturity and irresponsibility of juveniles, almost every State prohibits those under 18 years of age from voting, serving on juries, or marrying without parental consent.

The second area of difference is that juveniles are more vulnerable or susceptible to negative influences and outside pressures, including peer pressure. * * *

The third broad difference is that the character of a juvenile is not as well formed as that of an adult. * * *

These differences render suspect any conclusion that a juvenile falls among the worst offenders. The susceptibility of juveniles to immature and irresponsible behavior means "their irresponsible conduct is not as morally reprehensible as that of an adult." Their own vulnerability and comparative lack of control over their immediate surroundings mean juveniles have a greater claim than adults to be forgiven for failing to escape negative influences in their whole environment. The reality that juveniles still struggle to define their identity means it is less supportable to conclude that even a heinous crime committed by a juvenile is evidence of irretrievably depraved character. From a moral standpoint it would be misguided to equate the failings of a minor with those of an adult, for a greater possibility exists that a minor's character deficiencies will be reformed. * * *

* * *

Once the diminished culpability of juveniles is recognized, it is evident that the penological justifications for the death penalty apply to them with lesser force than to adults. * * * Whether viewed as an attempt to express the community's moral outrage or as an attempt to right the balance for the wrong to the victim, the case for retribution is not as strong with a minor as with an adult. Retribution is not proportional if the law's most severe penalty is imposed on one whose culpability or blameworthiness is diminished, to a substantial degree, by reason of youth and immaturity.

As for deterrence, it is unclear whether the death penalty has a significant or even measurable deterrent effect on juveniles * * *. * * * [T]he absence of evidence of deterrent effect is of special concern because the same characteristics that render juveniles less culpable than adults suggest as well that juveniles will be less susceptible to deterrence. In particular, * * * "[t]he likelihood that the teenage offender has made the kind of cost-benefit analysis that attaches any weight to the possibility of execution is so remote as to be virtually nonexistent." To the extent the juvenile death penalty might have residual deterrent effect, it is worth noting that the punishment of life imprisonment without the possibility of parole is itself a severe sanction, in particular for a young person.

* * * Certainly it can be argued, although we by no means concede the point, that a rare case might arise in which a juvenile offender has sufficient psychological maturity, and at the same time demonstrates sufficient depravity, to merit a sentence of death. Indeed, this possibility is the linchpin of one contention pressed by petitioner and his *amici*. They assert that even assuming the truth of the observations we have made about juveniles' diminished culpability in general, jurors nonetheless should be allowed to consider mitigating arguments related to youth on a case-by-case basis, and in some cases to impose the death penalty if justified. * * *

We disagree. The differences between juvenile and adult offenders are too marked and well understood to risk allowing a youthful person to receive the death penalty despite insufficient culpability. An unacceptable likelihood exists that the brutality or cold-blooded nature of any particular crime would overpower mitigating arguments based on youth as a matter of course, even where the juvenile offender's objective immaturity, vulnerability, and lack of true depravity should require a sentence less severe than death. * * *

* * *

IV

Our determination that the death penalty is disproportionate punishment for offenders under 18 finds confirmation in the stark reality that the United States is the only country in the world that continues to give official sanction to the juvenile death penalty. This reality does not become controlling, for the task of interpreting the Eighth Amendment remains our responsibility. Yet * * * the Court has referred to the laws of other countries and to international authorities as instructive for its interpretation of the Eighth Amendment's prohibition of "cruel and unusual punishments."

As respondent and a number of *amici* emphasize, Article 37 of the United Nations Convention on the Rights of the Child, which every country in the world has ratified save for the United States and Somalia, contains an express prohibition on capital punishment for crimes committed by juveniles under 18. * * *

Respondent and his *amici* have submitted, and petitioner does not contest, that only seven countries other than the United States have executed juvenile offenders since 1990: Iran, Pakistan, Saudi Arabia, Yemen, Nigeria, the Democratic Republic of Congo, and China. Since then each of these countries has either abolished capital punishment for juveniles or made public disavowal of the practice. In sum, it is fair to say that the United States now stands alone in a world that has turned its face against the juvenile death penalty.

* * *

* * * It does not lessen our fidelity to the Constitution or our pride in its origins to acknowledge that the express affirmation of certain fundamental rights by other nations and peoples simply underscores the centrality of those same rights within our own heritage of freedom.

* * *

The Eighth and Fourteenth Amendments forbid imposition of the death penalty on offenders who were under the age of 18 when their crimes were committed. * * *

* * *

JUSTICE STEVENS, with whom JUSTICE GINSBURG joins, concurring.

Perhaps even more important than our specific holding today is our reaffirmation of the basic principle that informs the Court's interpretation of the Eighth Amendment. If the meaning of that Amendment had been frozen when it was originally drafted, it would impose no impediment to the execution of 7-year-old children today. See *Stanford v. Kentucky,* 492 U.S. 361, 368 (1989) (describing the common law at the time of the Amendment's adoption). The evolving standards of decency that have driven our construction of this critically important part of the Bill of Rights foreclose any such reading of the Amendment. * * *

JUSTICE O'CONNOR, dissenting.

* * *

In determining whether the juvenile death penalty comports with contemporary standards of decency, our inquiry begins with the "clearest and most reliable objective evidence of contemporary values"—the actions of the Nation's legislatures. As the Court emphasizes, the overall number of jurisdictions that currently disallow the execution of under-18 offenders is the same as the number that forbade the execution of mentally retarded offenders when *Atkins* was decided. * * *

While the similarities between the two cases are undeniable, the objective evidence of national consensus is marginally weaker here. Most importantly, in *Atkins* there was significant evidence of *opposition* to the execution of the mentally retarded, but there was virtually no countervailing evidence of affirmative legislative *support* for this practice. The States that permitted such executions did so only because they had not enacted any prohibitory legislation. Here, by contrast, at least eight States have current statutes that specifically set 16 or 17 as the minimum age at which commission of a capital crime can expose the offender to the death penalty. * * *

Moreover, the Court in *Atkins* made clear that it was "not so much the number of [States forbidding execution of the mentally retarded] that [was] significant, but the consistency of the direction of change." In contrast to the trend in *Atkins,* the States have not moved uniformly towards abolishing the juvenile death penalty. Instead, since our decision in *Stanford,* two States have expressly reaffirmed their support for this practice by enacting statutes setting 16 as the minimum age for capital punishment. Furthermore, * * * the pace of legislative action in this context has been considerably slower than it was with regard to capital punishment of the mentally retarded. In the 13 years between our decisions in *Penry* and *Atkins,* no fewer than 16 States banned the execution of mentally retarded offenders. By comparison, since our decision 16 years ago in *Stanford,* only four States that previously permitted the execution of under-18 offenders, plus the Federal Government, have legislatively reversed course, and one additional State's high court has construed the State's death penalty statute not to apply to under-18 offenders. * * *

* * *

* * * Without a clearer showing that a genuine national consensus forbids the execution of such offenders, this Court should not substitute its own "inevitably subjective judgment" on how best to resolve this difficult moral question for the judgments of the Nation's democratically elected legislatures.

JUSTICE SCALIA, with whom THE CHIEF JUSTICE and JUSTICE THOMAS join, dissenting.

In urging approval of a constitution that gave life-tenured judges the power to nullify laws enacted by the people's representatives, Alexander Hamilton assured the citizens of New York that there was little risk in this, since "[t]he judiciary . . . ha[s] neither FORCE nor WILL but merely judgment." The Federalist No. 78, p. 465 (C. Rossiter ed.1961). But Hamilton had in mind a traditional judiciary, "bound down by strict rules and precedents which serve to define and point out their duty in every particular case that comes before them." Bound down, indeed. What a mockery today's opinion makes of Hamilton's expectation, announcing the Court's conclusion that the meaning of our Constitution has changed over the past 15 years—not, mind you, that this Court's decision 15 years ago was *wrong,* but that the Constitution *has changed.* The Court reaches this implausible result by purporting to advert, not to the original meaning of the Eighth Amendment, but to "the evolving standards of decency" of our national society. It then finds, on the flimsiest of grounds, that a national consensus which could not be perceived in our people's laws barely 15 years ago now solidly exists. * * *

* * *

* * * Now, the Court says a legislative change in four States is "significant" enough to trigger a constitutional prohibition.[4] It is amazing to think that this subtle shift in numbers can take the issue entirely off the table for legislative debate.

* * *

The Court's reliance on the infrequency of executions for under-18 murderers credits an argument that this Court considered and explicitly rejected in *Stanford.* That infrequency is explained, we accurately said, both by "the undisputed fact that a far smaller percentage of capital crimes

---

[4]   As the Court notes, Washington State's decision to prohibit executions of offenders under 18 was made by a judicial, not legislative, decision. * * * It is irrelevant to the question of changed national consensus.

are committed by persons under 18 than over 18" and by the fact that juries are required at sentencing to consider the offender's youth as a mitigating factor. Thus, "it is not only possible, but overwhelmingly probable, that the very considerations which induce [respondent] and [his] supporters to believe that death should *never* be imposed on offenders under 18 cause prosecutors and juries to believe that it should *rarely* be imposed."

* * *

Of course, the real force driving today's decision is not the actions of four state legislatures, but the Court's " ' "own judgment" ' " that murderers younger than 18 can never be as morally culpable as older counterparts. * * *

* * *

Today's opinion provides a perfect example of why judges are ill equipped to make the type of legislative judgments the Court insists on making here. To support its opinion that States should be prohibited from imposing the death penalty on anyone who committed murder before age 18, the Court looks to scientific and sociological studies, picking and choosing those that support its position. It never explains why those particular studies are methodologically sound; none was ever entered into evidence or tested in an adversarial proceeding. * * * In other words, all the Court has done today, to borrow from another context, is to look over the heads of the crowd and pick out its friends.

We need not look far to find studies contradicting the Court's conclusions. As petitioner points out, the American Psychological Association (APA), which claims in this case that scientific evidence shows persons under 18 lack the ability to take moral responsibility for their decisions, has previously taken precisely the opposite position before this very Court. In its brief in *Hodgson v. Minnesota*, 497 U.S. 417 (1990), the APA found a "rich body of research" showing that juveniles are mature enough to decide whether to obtain an abortion without parental involvement. The APA brief, citing psychology treatises and studies too numerous to list here, asserted: "[B]y middle adolescence (age 14–15) young people develop abilities similar to adults in reasoning about moral dilemmas, understanding social rules and laws, [and] reasoning about interpersonal relationships and interpersonal problems." Given the nuances of scientific methodology and conflicting views, courts—which can only consider the limited evidence on the record before them—are ill equipped to determine which view of science is the right one. Legislatures "are better qualified to weigh and 'evaluate the results of statistical studies in terms of their own local conditions and with a flexibility of approach that is not available to the courts.' "

Even putting aside questions of methodology, the studies cited by the Court offer scant support for a categorical prohibition of the death penalty for murderers under 18. At most, these studies conclude that, *on average,* or *in most cases,* persons under 18 are unable to take moral responsibility for their actions. Not one of the cited studies opines that all individuals under 18 are unable to appreciate the nature of their crimes.

* * *

That "almost every State prohibits those under 18 years of age from voting, serving on juries, or marrying without parental consent" is patently irrelevant * * *. * * * [I]t is "absurd to think that one must be mature enough to drive carefully, to drink responsibly, or to vote intelligently, in order to be mature enough to understand that murdering another human being is profoundly wrong, and to conform one's conduct to that most minimal of all civilized standards." Serving on a jury or entering into marriage also involve decisions far more sophisticated than the simple decision not to take another's life.

Moreover, the age statutes the Court lists "set the appropriate ages for the operation of a system that makes its determinations in gross, and that does not conduct individualized maturity tests." The criminal justice system, by contrast, provides for individualized consideration of each defendant. * * * In other contexts where individualized consideration is provided, we have recognized that at least some minors will be mature enough to make difficult decisions that involve moral considerations. For instance, we have struck down abortion statutes that do not allow minors deemed mature by courts to bypass parental notification provisions. See, *e.g., Bellotti v. Baird,* 443 U.S. 622, 643–644 (1979) (opinion of Powell, J.); *Planned Parenthood of Central Mo. v. Danforth,* 428 U.S. 52, 74–75 (1976). It is hard to see why this context should be any different. Whether to obtain an abortion is surely a much more complex decision for a young person than whether to kill an innocent person in cold blood.

The Court concludes, however, that juries cannot be trusted with the delicate task of weighing a defendant's youth along with the other mitigating and aggravating factors of his crime. * * * This assertion is based on no evidence; to the contrary, the Court itself acknowledges that the execution of under-18 offenders is "infrequent" even in the States "without a formal prohibition on executing juveniles," suggesting that juries take seriously their responsibility to weigh youth as a mitigating factor.

Nor does the Court suggest a stopping point for its reasoning. If juries cannot make appropriate determinations in cases involving murderers under 18, in what other kinds of cases will the Court find jurors deficient? * * *

The Court's contention that the goals of retribution and deterrence are not served by executing murderers under 18 is also transparently false. The argument that "[r]etribution is not proportional if the law's most severe penalty is imposed on one whose culpability or blameworthiness is diminished," is simply an extension of the earlier, false generalization that youth *always* defeats culpability. The Court claims that "juveniles will be less susceptible to deterrence," because " '[t]he likelihood that the teenage offender has made the kind of cost-benefit analysis that attaches any weight to the possibility of execution is so remote as to be virtually nonexistent.' " The Court unsurprisingly finds no support for this astounding proposition, save its own case law. The facts of this very case show the proposition to be false. Before committing the crime, Simmons encouraged his friends to join him by assuring them that they could "get away with it" because they were minors. * * *

* * *

Though the views of our own citizens are essentially irrelevant to the Court's decision today, the views of other countries and the so-called international community take center stage.

* * *

* * * Foreign sources are cited today, *not* to underscore our "fidelity" to the Constitution, our "pride in its origins," and "our own [American] heritage." To the contrary, they are cited *to set aside* the centuries-old American practice * * * of letting a jury of 12 citizens decide whether, in the particular case, youth should be the basis for withholding the death penalty. What these foreign sources "affirm," rather than repudiate, is the Justices' own notion of how the world ought to be, and their diktat that it shall be so henceforth in America. * * *

* * *

QUESTIONS AND POINTS FOR DISCUSSION

1. In your opinion, of what significance, if any, are the following factors to the question whether the death penalty, in certain or all circumstances, constitutes cruel and unusual punishment: public-opinion polls, the views of professional organizations, the practices of other countries, and the results of studies that bear on the question whether the death penalty effectuates penological goals?

2. The Supreme Court has identified another category of persons whose execution is barred by the Eighth Amendment: Prisoners who have been convicted of a capital crime and sentenced to death, but are now insane, cannot be executed unless and until their sanity is restored. In explaining why execution of an insane person would be cruel and unusual punishment, the Supreme Court in Ford v. Wainwright, 477 U.S. 399, 106 S.Ct. 2595 (1986)

noted that for a number of reasons, not one state in the country permits an insane person to be executed. One of these reasons is that many people doubt that the death penalty could serve its retributive aim when the person being executed is incapable of understanding why he is being put to death. The Court also mentioned the religious roots of such execution bans—the belief that it would be unconscionable to kill individuals who are incapable of first seeking God's forgiveness for their sins.

Courts still must resolve when a prisoner is "insane" in the constitutional sense that bars his or her execution. A mentally ill prisoner whose case was before the Supreme Court in Panetti v. Quarterman, 551 U.S. 930, 127 S.Ct. 2842 (2007) claimed that what he recognized was the state's asserted reason for executing him—his commission of two brutal murders—was a "sham" and that he really was being put to death by "forces of the darkness" to keep him from preaching. The Supreme Court noted that even though a prisoner with a psychotic disorder is aware that he is being executed for a crime, he still might be incompetent to be executed. Holding that the Eighth Amendment also requires that a prisoner have a "rational understanding" of the reason for his execution, the Court left to the courts on remand to decide whether the prisoner in this case met this requirement.

3.   A court's conclusion that a prisoner on death row, though mentally ill, is sane and therefore can be executed likely will be appealed. But by the time a round of appeals is completed, the prisoner's mental condition may have deteriorated to the point that the prisoner now is insane—to the point that the prisoner does not know, for example, why she is being executed or does not have a "rational understanding" of that reason. What, in your opinion, are the practical and constitutional implications, if any, of the fact that the gravity of a mental illness can fluctuate while courts adjudicate the question of the prisoner's sanity?

4.   In Washington v. Harper, 494 U.S. 210, 227, 110 S.Ct. 1028, 1039–40 (1990), the Supreme Court held that mentally ill prisoners can be forced to take antipsychotic drugs when they pose a danger to themselves or others and the administration of the medication is in their "medical interest." But the Supreme Court thus far has skirted the question whether the United States Constitution permits the government to force insane prisoners to take medication that will make them sane enough to be executed. Perry v. Louisiana, 498 U.S. 38, 111 S.Ct. 449 (1990). The Louisiana Supreme Court, on the other hand, has held that the compulsory administration of antipsychotic drugs for this purpose violates both the right to privacy and the right not to be subjected to cruel, excessive, or unusual punishments protected by the Louisiana Constitution. Louisiana v. Perry, 610 So.2d 746 (La.1992).

How would you resolve the federal constitutional question? As a constitutional matter, does it make any difference if the antipsychotic medication is administered involuntarily in order to protect the inmate or others from danger but has the collateral effect of making the prisoner competent for execution? See Singleton v. Norris, 319 F.3d 1018, 1026–27 (8th

Cir.2003) (involuntary administration of antipsychotic medication in conformance with the requirements of *Washington v. Harper* that had the side effect of making the prisoner competent to understand the nature of, and reason for, his execution did not violate due process or the Eighth Amendment).

5.   The constitutional ban on the execution of individuals who currently are insane leaves open another question: Is it cruel and unusual punishment to impose a death sentence on defendants who had a severe mental illness at the time of their crimes? Thus far, most courts have held that there is no categorical constitutional bar to death sentences in this context. See State v. Kleypas, 382 P.3d 373, 445–46 (Kan. 2016) (listing cases). Do you agree or disagree with these courts? Is there any additional information you would want or need before definitively resolving this constitutional question? For constitutional and policy arguments for categorically banning the death penalty's imposition on people who had a severe mental illness at the time of their crimes, see Death Penalty Due Process Review Project, ABA, Severe Mental Illness and the Death Penalty 25–38 (2016).

––––––––

Consider the following facts, which were drawn from a real case: The defendant's girlfriend left her one-year-old baby with the defendant for thirty minutes while she drove to her cousin's house. When she returned, she found the baby crying. The baby's underwear was soaked with blood. The defendant unsuccessfully tried to persuade his girlfriend not to take the baby to the hospital. The physical examination at the hospital revealed that the baby's rectum had been torn and was bleeding. Following his arrest, the defendant told the police that he had been sleeping on the bed with the baby when she rolled on top of him. He claimed that in the dark and in his drowsy state, he thought the baby was his girlfriend, so he penetrated her with his penis. He denied having an ejaculation, but semen matching the defendant's type was found in the baby's underwear. The defendant was convicted of aggravated rape.

What arguments would you make in support of the constitutionality of a statute authorizing imposition of the death penalty in this case? What arguments would you make against the statute's constitutionality? Is there any additional information you would want or need in order to complete your constitutional analysis? Compare your answers to these questions with the arguments and analysis in the following case.

KENNEDY V. LOUISIANA

Supreme Court of the United States, 2008.
554 U.S. 407, 128 S.Ct. 2641, 171 L.Ed.2d 525.

JUSTICE KENNEDY delivered the opinion of the Court.

* * * This case presents the question whether the Constitution bars respondent from imposing the death penalty for the rape of a child where the crime did not result, and was not intended to result, in death of the victim. * * *

I

* * * At 9:18 a.m. on March 2, 1998, petitioner called 911 to report that his stepdaughter, referred to here as L. H., had been raped. He told the 911 operator that L. H. had been in the garage while he readied his son for school. Upon hearing loud screaming, petitioner said, he ran outside and found L. H. in the side yard. Two neighborhood boys, petitioner told the operator, had dragged L. H. from the garage to the yard, pushed her down, and raped her. Petitioner claimed he saw one of the boys riding away on a blue 10-speed bicycle.

When police arrived at petitioner's home between 9:20 and 9:30 a.m., they found L. H. on her bed, wearing a T-shirt and wrapped in a bloody blanket. She was bleeding profusely from the vaginal area. Petitioner told police he had carried her from the yard to the bathtub and then to the bed. Consistent with this explanation, police found a thin line of blood drops in the garage on the way to the house and then up the stairs. Once in the bedroom, petitioner had used a basin of water and a cloth to wipe blood from the victim. This later prevented medical personnel from collecting a reliable DNA sample.

L. H. was transported to the Children's Hospital. An expert in pediatric forensic medicine testified that L. H.'s injuries were the most severe he had seen from a sexual assault in his four years of practice. A laceration to the left wall of the vagina had separated her cervix from the back of her vagina, causing her rectum to protrude into the vaginal structure. Her entire perineum was torn from the posterior fourchette to the anus. The injuries required emergency surgery.

At the scene of the crime, at the hospital, and in the first weeks that followed, both L. H. and petitioner maintained in their accounts to investigators that L. H. had been raped by two neighborhood boys. One of L. H.'s doctors testified at trial that L. H. told all hospital personnel the same version of the rape, although she reportedly told one family member that petitioner raped her. L. H. was interviewed several days after the rape by a psychologist. The interview was videotaped, lasted three hours over two days, and was introduced into evidence at trial. On the tape one can see that L. H. had difficulty discussing the subject of the rape. She spoke haltingly and with long pauses and frequent movement. Early in the interview, L. H. expressed reservations about the questions being asked:

"I'm going to tell the same story. They just want me to change it . . . They want me to say my Dad did it . . . I don't want to say it . . . I tell them the same, same story."

She told the psychologist that she had been playing in the garage when a boy came over and asked her about Girl Scout cookies she was selling; and that the boy "pulled [her by the legs to] the backyard," where he placed his hand over her mouth, "pulled down [her] shorts," and raped her.

Eight days after the crime, and despite L. H.'s insistence that petitioner was not the offender, petitioner was arrested for the rape. * * * [T]he case for the prosecution, credited by the jury, was based upon the following evidence: An inspection of the side yard immediately after the assault was inconsistent with a rape having occurred there, the grass having been found mostly undisturbed but for a small patch of coagulated blood. Petitioner said that one of the perpetrators fled the crime scene on a blue 10-speed bicycle but gave inconsistent descriptions of the bicycle's features, such as its handlebars. Investigators found a bicycle matching petitioner and L. H.'s description in tall grass behind a nearby apartment, and petitioner identified it as the bicycle one of the perpetrators was riding. Yet its tires were flat, it did not have gears, and it was covered in spider webs. In addition police found blood on the underside of L. H.'s mattress. This convinced them the rape took place in her bedroom, not outside the house.

Police also found that petitioner made two telephone calls on the morning of the rape. Sometime before 6:15 a.m., petitioner called his employer and left a message that he was unavailable to work that day. Petitioner called back between 6:30 and 7:30 a.m. to ask a colleague how to get blood out of a white carpet because his daughter had " 'just become a young lady.' " At 7:37 a.m., petitioner called B & B Carpet Cleaning and requested urgent assistance in removing bloodstains from a carpet. Petitioner did not call 911 until about an hour and a half later.

About a month after petitioner's arrest L. H. was removed from the custody of her mother, who had maintained until that point that petitioner was not involved in the rape. On June 22, 1998, L. H. was returned home and told her mother for the first time that petitioner had raped her. And on December 16, 1999, about 21 months after the rape, L. H. recorded her accusation in a videotaped interview with the Child Advocacy Center.

The state charged petitioner with aggravated rape of a child * * * and sought the death penalty. * * *

* * *

The trial began in August 2003. L. H. was then 13 years old. She testified that she " 'woke up one morning and Patrick was on top of [her].' " * * * L. H. acknowledged that she had accused two neighborhood boys but testified petitioner told her to say this and that it was untrue.

The jury having found petitioner guilty of aggravated rape, the penalty phase ensued. The State presented the testimony of S. L., who is the cousin and goddaughter of petitioner's ex-wife. S. L. testified that petitioner sexually abused her three times when she was eight years old and that the last time involved sexual intercourse. She did not tell anyone until two years later and did not pursue legal action.

The jury unanimously determined that petitioner should be sentenced to death. The Supreme Court of Louisiana affirmed. * * *

* * *

II

* * *

Evolving standards of decency must embrace and express respect for the dignity of the person, and the punishment of criminals must conform to that rule. * * * When the law punishes by death, it risks its own sudden descent into brutality, transgressing the constitutional commitment to decency and restraint.

* * *

III

A

* * *

In 1925, 18 States, the District of Columbia, and the Federal Government had statutes that authorized the death penalty for the rape of a child or an adult. Between 1930 and 1964, 455 people were executed for those crimes. * * *

In 1972, *Furman* invalidated most of the state statutes authorizing the death penalty for the crime of rape; and in *Furman*'s aftermath only six States reenacted their capital rape provisions. * * * All six statutes were later invalidated under state or federal law.

Louisiana reintroduced the death penalty for rape of a child in 1995. Under the current statute, any anal, vaginal, or oral intercourse with a child under the age of 13 constitutes aggravated rape and is punishable by death. Mistake of age is not a defense, so the statute imposes strict liability in this regard. Five States have since followed Louisiana's lead * * *. Four of these States' statutes are more narrow than Louisiana's in that only offenders with a previous rape conviction are death eligible. Georgia's statute makes child rape a capital offense only when aggravating circumstances are present, including but not limited to a prior conviction.

* * *

The evidence of a national consensus with respect to the death penalty for child rapists * * * shows divided opinion but, on balance, an opinion against it. Thirty-seven jurisdictions—36 States plus the Federal Government—have the death penalty. As mentioned above, only six of those jurisdictions authorize the death penalty for rape of a child. Though our review of national consensus is not confined to tallying the number of States with applicable death penalty legislation, it is of significance that, in 45 jurisdictions, petitioner could not be executed for child rape of any kind. * * *

B

* * *

* * * In *Coker* [*v. Georgia*, 433 U.S. 584 (1977)], a four-Member plurality of the Court, plus Justice Brennan and Justice Marshall in concurrence, held that a sentence of death for the rape of a 16-year-old woman, who was a minor under Georgia law yet was characterized by the Court as an adult, was disproportionate and excessive under the Eighth Amendment. (The Court did not explain why the 16-year-old victim qualified as an adult, but it may be of some significance that she was married, had a home of her own, and had given birth to a son three weeks prior to the rape.)

* * *

* * * The *Coker* plurality framed the question as whether, "with respect to rape of an adult woman," the death penalty is disproportionate punishment. The opinion does not speak to the constitutionality of the death penalty for child rape, an issue not then before the Court. * * *

* * *

We conclude * * * that there is no clear indication that state legislatures have misinterpreted *Coker* to hold that the death penalty for child rape is unconstitutional. The small number of States that have enacted this penalty, then, is relevant to determining whether there is a consensus against capital punishment for this crime.

C

Respondent insists that the six States where child rape is a capital offense, along with the States that have proposed but not yet enacted applicable death penalty legislation, reflect a consistent direction of change in support of the death penalty for child rape. Consistent change might counterbalance an otherwise weak demonstration of consensus. But whatever the significance of consistent change where it is cited to show emerging support for expanding the scope of the death penalty, no showing of consistent change has been made in this case.

Respondent and its *amici* identify five States where, in their view, legislation authorizing capital punishment for child rape is pending. It is not our practice, nor is it sound, to find contemporary norms based upon state legislation that has been proposed but not yet enacted. * * *

Aside from pending legislation, it is true that in the last 13 years there has been change towards making child rape a capital offense. This is evidenced by six new death penalty statutes, three enacted in the last two years.* * * Respondent argues the instant case is like *Roper* because, there, only five States had shifted their positions between 1989 and 2005, one less State than here. But in *Roper*, we emphasized that, though the pace of abolition was not as great as in *Atkins*, it was counterbalanced by the total number of States that had recognized the impropriety of executing juvenile offenders. * * * Here, the total number of States to have made child rape a capital offense after *Furman* is six. This is not an indication of a trend or change in direction comparable to the one supported by data in *Roper*.

D

There are measures of consensus other than legislation. Statistics about the number of executions may inform the consideration whether capital punishment for the crime of child rape is regarded as unacceptable in our society. These statistics confirm our determination from our review of state statutes that there is a social consensus against the death penalty for the crime of child rape.

Nine States * * * have permitted capital punishment for adult or child rape for some length of time between the Court's 1972 decision in *Furman* and today. Yet no individual has been executed for the rape of an adult or child since 1964, and no execution for any other nonhomicide offense has been conducted since 1963.

Louisiana is the only State since 1964 that has sentenced an individual to death for the crime of child rape; and petitioner and Richard Davis, who was convicted and sentenced to death for the aggravated rape of a 5-year-old child by a Louisiana jury, * * * are the only two individuals now on death row in the United States for a nonhomicide offense.

* * * [W]e conclude there is a national consensus against capital punishment for the crime of child rape.

IV

A

As we have said in other Eighth Amendment cases, objective evidence of contemporary values as it relates to punishment for child rape is entitled to great weight, but it does not end our inquiry. "[T]he Constitution contemplates that in the end our own judgment will be brought to bear on the question of the acceptability of the death penalty under the Eighth Amendment." * * *

* * *

Our concern here is limited to crimes against individual persons. We do not address, for example, crimes defining and punishing treason, espionage, terrorism, and drug kingpin activity, which are offenses against the State. As it relates to crimes against individuals, though, the death penalty should not be expanded to instances where the victim's life was not taken. * * *

* * *

Consistent with evolving standards of decency and the teachings of our precedents we conclude that, in determining whether the death penalty is excessive, there is a distinction between intentional first-degree murder on the one hand and nonhomicide crimes against individual persons, even including child rape, on the other. The latter crimes may be devastating in their harm, as here, but "in terms of moral depravity and of the injury to the person and to the public," they cannot be compared to murder in their "severity and irrevocability."

In reaching our conclusion we find significant the number of executions that would be allowed under respondent's approach. The crime of child rape, considering its reported incidents, occurs more often than first-degree murder. Approximately 5,702 incidents of vaginal, anal, or oral rape of a child under the age of 12 were reported nationwide in 2005; this is almost twice the total incidents of intentional murder for victims of all ages (3,405) reported during the same period. * * *

It might be said that narrowing aggravators could be used in this context, as with murder offenses, to ensure the death penalty's restrained application. We find it difficult to identify standards that would guide the decisionmaker so the penalty is reserved for the most severe cases of child rape and yet not imposed in an arbitrary way. Even were we to forbid, say, the execution of first-time child rapists or require as an aggravating factor a finding that the perpetrator's instant rape offense involved multiple victims, the jury still must balance, in its discretion, those aggravating factors against mitigating circumstances. In this context, which involves a crime that in many cases will overwhelm a decent person's judgment, we have no confidence that the imposition of the death penalty would not be so arbitrary as to be "freakis[h]." * * *

* * *

* * * [I]mprecision and the tension between evaluating the individual circumstances and consistency of treatment have been tolerated where the victim dies. It should not be introduced into our justice system, though, where death has not occurred.

* * *

B

* * *

The goal of retribution, which reflects society's and the victim's interests in seeing that the offender is repaid for the hurt he caused, does not justify the harshness of the death penalty here. * * *

* * *

There are, moreover, serious systemic concerns in prosecuting the crime of child rape that are relevant to the constitutionality of making it a capital offense. The problem of unreliable, induced, and even imagined child testimony means there is a "special risk of wrongful execution" in some child rape cases. * * *

* * *

With respect to deterrence, if the death penalty adds to the risk of non-reporting, that, too, diminishes the penalty's objectives. Underreporting is a common problem with respect to child sexual abuse. * * * [O]ne of the most commonly cited reasons for nondisclosure is fear of negative consequences for the perpetrator, a concern that has special force where the abuser is a family member. The experience of the *amici* who work with child victims indicates that, when the punishment is death, both the victim and the victim's family members may be more likely to shield the perpetrator from discovery, thus increasing underreporting. As a result, punishment by death may not result in more deterrence or more effective enforcement.

In addition, by in effect making the punishment for child rape and murder equivalent, a State that punishes child rape by death may remove a strong incentive for the rapist not to kill the victim. Assuming the offender behaves in a rational way, as one must to justify the penalty on grounds of deterrence, the penalty in some respects gives less protection, not more, to the victim, who is often the sole witness to the crime. * * *

Each of these propositions, standing alone, might not establish the unconstitutionality of the death penalty for the crime of child rape. Taken in sum, however, they demonstrate the serious negative consequences of making child rape a capital offense. These considerations lead us to conclude, in our independent judgment, that the death penalty is not a proportional punishment for the rape of a child.

V

* * *

* * * In most cases justice is not better served by terminating the life of the perpetrator rather than confining him and preserving the possibility that he and the system will find ways to allow him to understand the enormity of his offense. Difficulties in administering the penalty to ensure against its arbitrary and capricious application require adherence to a rule reserving its use, at this stage of evolving standards and in cases of crimes against individuals, for crimes that take the life of the victim.

* * *

JUSTICE ALITO, with whom THE CHIEF JUSTICE, JUSTICE SCALIA, and JUSTICE THOMAS join, dissenting.

The Court today holds that the Eighth Amendment categorically prohibits the imposition of the death penalty for the crime of raping a child. This is so, according to the Court, no matter how young the child, no matter how many times the child is raped, no matter how many children the perpetrator rapes, no matter how sadistic the crime, no matter how much physical or psychological trauma is inflicted, and no matter how heinous the perpetrator's prior criminal record may be. * * *

* * *

I turn first to the Court's claim that there is "a national consensus" that it is never acceptable to impose the death penalty for the rape of a child. * * * In assessing current norms, the Court relies primarily on the fact that only 6 of the 50 States now have statutes that permit the death penalty for this offense. But this statistic is a highly unreliable indicator of the views of state lawmakers and their constituents. * * * [D]icta in this Court's decision in *Coker* v. *Georgia*, 433 U.S. 584 (1977) * * * gave state legislators and others good reason to fear that any law permitting the imposition of the death penalty for this crime would meet precisely the fate that has now befallen the Louisiana statute that is currently before us, and this threat strongly discouraged state legislators—regardless of their own values and those of their constituents—from supporting the enactment of such legislation.

* * *

I do not suggest that six new state laws necessarily establish a "national consensus" or even that they are sure evidence of an ineluctable trend. In terms of the Court's metaphor of moral evolution, these enactments might have turned out to be an evolutionary dead end. But they might also have been the beginning of a strong new evolutionary line. We will never know, because the Court today snuffs out the line in its incipient stage.

THE DEATH PENALTY

The Court is willing to block the potential emergence of a national consensus in favor of permitting the death penalty for child rape because, in the end, what matters is the Court's "own judgment" regarding "the acceptability of the death penalty." * * *

* * *

A major theme of the Court's opinion is that permitting the death penalty in child-rape cases is not in the best interests of the victims of these crimes and society at large. * * *

These policy arguments, whatever their merits, are simply not pertinent to the question whether the death penalty is "cruel and unusual" punishment. The Eighth Amendment protects the right of an accused. It does not authorize this Court to strike down federal or state criminal laws on the ground that they are not in the best interests of crime victims or the broader society. * * *

The Court also contends that laws permitting the death penalty for the rape of a child create serious procedural problems. Specifically, the Court maintains that it is not feasible to channel the exercise of sentencing discretion in child-rape cases, and that the unreliability of the testimony of child victims creates a danger that innocent defendants will be convicted and executed. * * *

The Court's argument regarding the structuring of sentencing discretion is hard to comprehend. * * * Even assuming that the age of a child is not alone a sufficient factor for limiting sentencing discretion, the Court need only examine the child rape laws recently enacted in Texas, Oklahoma, Montana, and South Carolina, all of which use a concrete factor to limit quite drastically the number of cases in which the death penalty may be imposed. In those States, a defendant convicted of the rape of a child may be sentenced to death only if the defendant has a prior conviction for a specified felony sex offense.

Moreover, it takes little imagination to envision other limiting factors that a State could use to structure sentencing discretion in child rape cases. Some of these might be: whether the victim was kidnapped, whether the defendant inflicted severe physical injury on the victim, whether the victim was raped multiple times, whether the rapes occurred over a specified extended period, and whether there were multiple victims.

* * * [C]oncerns about limiting sentencing discretion provide no support for the Court's blanket condemnation of all capital child-rape statutes.

That sweeping holding is also not justified by the Court's concerns about the reliability of the testimony of child victims. * * * [I]f the Court's evidentiary concerns have Eighth Amendment relevance, they could be addressed by allowing the death penalty in only those child rape cases in which the independent evidence is sufficient to prove all the elements needed for conviction and imposition of a death sentence. * * *

* * *

The Court's final—and, it appears, principal—justification for its holding is that murder * * * is unique in its moral depravity and in the severity of the injury that it inflicts on the victim and the public. * * *

* * *

* * * I have little doubt that, in the eyes of ordinary Americans, the very worst child rapists—predators who seek out and inflict serious physical and emotional injury on defenseless young children—are the epitome of moral depravity.

With respect to the question of the harm caused by the rape of [a] child in relation to the harm caused by murder, it is certainly true that the loss of human life represents a unique harm, but that does not explain why other grievous harms are insufficient to permit a death sentence. And the Court does not take the position that no harm other than the loss of life is sufficient. The Court takes pains to limit its holding to "crimes against individual persons" and to exclude "offenses against the State," a category that the Court stretches—without explanation—to include "drug kingpin activity." But the Court makes no effort to explain why the harm caused by such crimes is necessarily greater than the harm caused by the rape of young children. * * *

The rape of any victim inflicts great injury, and "[s]ome victims are so grievously injured physically or psychologically that life *is* beyond repair." "The immaturity and vulnerability of a child, both physically and psychologically, adds a devastating dimension to rape that is not present when an adult is raped." * * *

* * *

The deep problems that afflict child-rape victims often become society's problems as well. Commentators have noted correlations between childhood sexual abuse and later problems such as substance abuse, dangerous sexual behaviors or dysfunction, inability to relate to others on an interpersonal level, and psychiatric illness. Victims of child rape are nearly 5 times more likely than nonvictims to be arrested for sex crimes and nearly 30 times more likely to be arrested for prostitution.

The harm that is caused to the victims and to society at large by the worst child rapists is grave. It is the judgment of the Louisiana lawmakers and those in an increasing number of other States that these harms justify the death penalty. The Court provides no cogent explanation why this legislative judgment should be overridden. * * *

QUESTIONS AND POINTS FOR DISCUSSION

1. In Tison v. Arizona, 481 U.S. 137, 107 S.Ct. 1676 (1987), the Supreme Court concluded that it is not necessarily cruel and unusual punishment to impose the death penalty on a defendant who did not kill a murder victim and did not intend that the victim be killed. In that case, the defendants, who were brothers, smuggled guns into a prison and then used them to help their father and another prisoner, both convicted murderers, escape. (The defendants' father was serving a life sentence for murdering a correctional officer during a prior prison escape.) When they later had car trouble, one of the defendants flagged down a passing car whose passengers included a mother and father, their two-year-old son, and their fifteen-year-old niece. The defendants' father and the other escaped prisoner eventually shot and killed all four passengers. The defendants then were convicted of four counts of capital murder under the state's felony-murder statute and another statute holding certain felons responsible for crimes committed by their accomplices.

The Supreme Court, in a 5–4 decision, held that there is nothing cruel and unusual about executing a defendant whose participation in "the felony" was "major" and who had acted with "reckless indifference to human life." Id. at 158, 107 S.Ct. at 1691. The Court observed that a defendant's reckless disregard for human life can be inferred when a defendant "knowingly engag[es] in criminal activities known to carry a grave risk of death." Id. at 157, 107 S.Ct. at 1688.

Do you agree with the Court's holding in *Tison*? For a case holding, on state constitutional grounds, that a death sentence is a grossly disproportionate penalty when imposed on a defendant who had no intent to kill or knowledge that his actions would lead to someone's death, see Vernon Kills on Top v. State, 928 P.2d 182, 206 (Mont.1996).

2. In its opinion in *Tison,* the Supreme Court distinguished Enmund v. Florida, 458 U.S. 782, 102 S.Ct. 3368 (1982), a case in which the Court had ruled that it was unconstitutional to impose the death penalty on a defendant who had driven the getaway car in an armed robbery but had not killed the two murder victims. As the Court explained in *Tison,* the defendant's role in the armed robbery and murders in *Enmund* was "minor," and there was no finding that he either had the intent to kill the victims or had acted with reckless indifference to human life. What if there had been a finding in *Enmund* that the defendant had acted with reckless disregard of the risk that the armed robbery could culminate in the death of the victims? Would imposition of the death penalty have been constitutional in those circumstances?

C. MODES OF EXECUTION

Sometimes a challenge is mounted, not against the constitutionality of executing a person falling within a certain category of individuals, but against the method of execution. The Supreme Court has upheld, though long ago, both the use of a firing squad and electrocution to implement a death sentence. Wilkerson v. Utah, 99 U.S. 130 (1878) (firing squad); In re Kemmler, 136 U.S. 436, 10 S.Ct. 930 (1890) (electrocution). In addition, in one case in which an effort to electrocute a prisoner failed to kill him, apparently because of a mechanical problem, the Court held that a second attempt to electrocute him would not subject him to cruel and unusual punishment. Louisiana ex rel. Francis v. Resweber, 329 U.S. 459, 67 S.Ct. 374 (1947).

All the states with prisoners who have received death sentences and the federal government authorize lethal injection, and most executions that have occurred in the United States since 1977 have been via this method. Bureau of Justice Statistics, U.S. Dep't of Justice, Capital Punishment, 2013—Statistical Tables 4, 16 tbl.13 (2014). In Baze v. Rees, 553 U.S. 35, 128 S.Ct. 1520 (2008), the Supreme Court considered whether the way in which the state of Kentucky was implementing a three-drug protocol when executing prisoners violated the Eighth Amendment. The first drug sedated the prisoner and, when administered properly, put the prisoner in a comalike state. The second drug paralyzed the prisoner and, by paralyzing the diaphragm, prevented the prisoner from breathing. The third drug then stopped the prisoner's heart from beating, inducing a cardiac arrest.

The prisoners on death row who contested the constitutionality of this three-drug protocol conceded that if the three drugs were administered properly, the end result would be a "humane death" comporting with the Constitution. But the prisoners contended that the state had adopted inadequate safeguards to prevent prisoners from being subjected to unnecessary and, in the words of the dissenters, "excruciating" pain. Id. at 113, 128 S.Ct. at 1567 (Ginsburg, J., dissenting). One of the prisoners' chief concerns was that misadministration of the first drug, the sedative, could leave a prisoner conscious, though not visibly so. Due to the paralysis caused by the second drug, the prisoner then would have to endure what the dissent described as "the agony of conscious suffocation" and the "searing pain" caused by the third drug when it induced a cardiac arrest. Id. at 121, 128 S.Ct. at 1571.

A majority of the Court rejected the constitutional challenge to the way in which Kentucky was following the three-drug protocol. The Justices were divided, however, on the standard to apply when assessing the constitutionality of a mode of execution. The plurality opinion, written by Justice Roberts and in which Justices Kennedy and Alito joined, stated that a threshold requirement must be met before a court need delve further into the Eighth Amendment claim: The means of execution must create a "substantial risk of serious harm" apart from the pain that inevitably accompanies death. Id. at 50, 52 n.3, 128 S.Ct. at 1531, 1532 n.3 (plurality opinion). If this requirement is met, a prisoner then has to demonstrate that an alternative execution method is "feasible, readily implemented, and in fact significantly reduce[s] a substantial risk of severe pain." Id. at 52, 128 S.Ct. at 1532. And even if such an alternative exists, the execution method does not inflict cruel and unusual punishment if the state has a "legitimate penological justification" for not utilizing this alternative. Id.

In an opinion concurring in the judgment, Justice Thomas, joined by Justice Scalia, objected to this multi-pronged test. Justice Thomas argued that a method of execution violates the Eighth Amendment "only if it is deliberately designed to inflict pain"—when it is employed to cause "terror, pain, or disgrace," not just death. Id. at 94, 107, 128 S.Ct. at 1556, 1563 (Thomas, J., concurring in judgment). As support for this conclusion, Justice Thomas cited the kinds of penalties that had sparked the Eighth Amendment's adoption, such as burning at the stake, disemboweling people while they were still alive, and hanging them in places where the public could view their bodies decomposing.

Three other Justices on the Court—Justices Ginsburg, Souter, and Breyer—opined that the pertinent inquiry is whether the execution method creates "an untoward, readily avoidable risk of inflicting severe and unnecessary pain." Id. at 114, 128 S.Ct. at 1567 (Ginsburg, J., dissenting); id. at 107, 128 S.Ct. at 1563 (Breyer, J., concurring in judgment). Three factors are considered when applying this test—one, the degree to which the execution method poses a risk of causing significant pain; two, the severity of the pain it risks causing; and three, the existence of a "readily available" alternative that will "materially increase" the probability that the mode of execution will not cause pain. Id. at 117, 128 S.Ct. at 1569 (Ginsburg, J., dissenting). Unlike the plurality's approach, this "untoward risk" test does not require a threshold showing that an execution method creates a substantial risk of serious harm. Instead, all three factors are weighed, with a strong showing on one factor depreciating the significance of the other two.

The plurality maintained that this consideration at the outset of execution alternatives "would threaten to transform courts into boards of inquiry charged with determining 'best practices' for execution, with each ruling supplanted by another round of litigation touting a new and improved methodology." Id. at 51, 128 S.Ct. at 1531 (plurality opinion). But Justice Thomas charged that the plurality's multi-pronged test also would embroil the courts in litigation as they were asked to determine whether a risk of severe pain was "substantial," whether alternative procedures were "feasible," whether they could be "readily implemented," whether they would lead to a "significant" reduction in the risk, and whether a penological justification for adhering to a current execution protocol was "legitimate." Id. at 105, 128 S.Ct. at 1562 (Thomas, J., concurring in judgment).

QUESTIONS AND POINTS FOR DISCUSSION

1.   Which of the three Eighth Amendment tests propounded in *Baze* is, in your opinion, the most appropriate? Why? Is there a different test that you believe courts should apply when assessing the constitutionality of execution methods?

2.   A majority of the Supreme Court Justices have termed the plurality opinion in *Baze* the "controlling opinion." Glossip v. Gross, 135 S.Ct. 2726, 2737 (2015); id. at 2750 (Thomas, J., concurring). In other words, the Eighth Amendment test set forth in that opinion is the one courts are to apply when evaluating the constitutionality of an execution method.

In *Glossip*, four Justices, in a dissenting opinion written by Justice Sotomayor, decried requiring a prisoner on death row to prove the existence of a viable alternative method of execution. Due to this requirement, according to the dissent, "[a] method of execution that is intolerably painful—even to the point of being the chemical equivalent of burning alive—will ... be unconstitutional *if*, and only if, there is a 'known and available alternative' method of execution." Id. at 2793.

The debate about whether there is a "known-and-available-alternative requirement" in the Eighth Amendment has been fueled by the difficulty states have faced procuring some of the drugs administered during executions. Responding to pressures exerted by opponents of the death penalty, pharmaceutical companies have stopped manufacturing or distributing, for execution purposes, some of the drugs once most commonly employed to sedate prisoners undergoing lethal injection. During several post-*Baze* executions using a replacement sedative selected by the state, the sedated prisoners have woken up, writhing or gasping. See id. at 2782, 2790–91.

3.   It behooves us to remember that the question of the test to be applied when resolving a constitutional issue is different from the question of what is the proper result when a particular test is applied. When the plurality in *Baze* applied its multi-pronged test, it concluded that the three-drug protocol used in Kentucky was constitutional. The plurality found that the prisoners had failed to meet the threshold requirement of demonstrating that there was a substantial risk that an insufficient amount of the first drug, the sedative, would be administered during the execution process—that a prisoner would be conscious when he was asphyxiated and his heart was stopped.

The plurality also responded to concerns that the second drug, the one that paralyzes a prisoner, could mask signs that the prisoner was still conscious. The plurality asserted that this drug serves two legitimate purposes. First, it furthers the state's "interest in preserving the dignity of the procedure," since it suppresses involuntary movements that others might misconstrue as signs that the prisoner is conscious or distressed. Id. at 57, 128 S.Ct. at 1535. And second, it expedites a prisoner's death by halting his breathing. Therefore, according to the plurality, the inclusion of this drug in the execution protocol did not render it unconstitutional.

In a concurring opinion, Justice Stevens spurned these rationales. Noting that Kentucky barred use of the second drug when euthanizing animals, he found it "unseemly—to say the least—that Kentucky may well kill petitioners using a drug that it would not permit to be used on their pets." Id. at 72–73, 128 S.Ct. at 1543 (Stevens, J., concurring in judgment). But because Justice Stevens believed that inadequate facts were adduced at trial to support a finding that Kentucky's execution protocol was unconstitutional, he concurred, though reluctantly, in the judgment.

4.   Execution methods whose constitutionality the Supreme Court has upheld have been condemned by others. For example, citing electrocution's "specter of excruciating pain and its certainty of cooked brains and blistered bodies," the Supreme Court of Georgia has ruled that death by electrocution abridges the state constitution's prohibition of cruel and unusual punishment. Dawson v. State, 554 S.E.2d 137, 144 (Ga. 2001). For very different reasons, Judge Kozinski, when serving as Chief Judge of the Ninth Circuit Court of Appeals, criticized states for utilizing lethal injection to execute people:

> Using drugs meant for individuals with medical needs to carry out executions is a misguided effort to mask the brutality of executions by making them look serene and peaceful—like something any one of us might experience in our final moments. But executions are, in fact, nothing like that. They are brutal, savage events, and nothing the state tries to do can mask that reality. Nor should it. If we as a society want to carry out executions, we should be willing to face the fact that the state is committing a horrendous brutality on our behalf.

> If some states and the federal government wish to continue carrying out the death penalty, they must turn away from this misguided path and return to more primitive—and foolproof—methods of execution. The guillotine is probably best but seems inconsistent with our national ethos. And the electric chair, hanging and the gas chamber are each subject to occasional mishaps. The firing squad strikes me as the most promising. Eight or ten large-caliber rifle bullets fired at close range can inflict massive damage, causing instant death every time. There are plenty of people employed by the state who can pull the trigger and have the training to aim true. The weapons and ammunition are bought by the state in massive quantities for law enforcement purposes, so it would be impossible to interdict the supply. And nobody can argue that the weapons are put to a purpose for which they were not intended: firearms have no purpose *other* than destroying their targets. Sure, firing squads can be messy, but if we are willing to carry out executions, we should not shield ourselves from the reality that we are shedding human blood. If we, as a society, cannot stomach the splatter from an execution carried out by firing squad, then we shouldn't be carrying out executions at all.

Wood v. Ryan, 759 F.3d 1076, 1102–03 (9th Cir.2014) (Kozinski, C.J., dissenting from the denial of rehearing en banc).

If you were required to select one execution method for a state, which would you choose and why? Should the choice regarding the means of execution be left to the person who has been sentenced to death? Why or why not?

D. THE ONGOING CONSTITUTIONAL AND POLICY DEBATE

In recent years, the death penalty has been the subject of increasing scrutiny and debate, both its constitutionality and soundness from a policy perspective. In a dissenting opinion in Glossip v. Gross, 135 S.Ct. 2726, 2755–80 (2015), Justice Breyer, joined by Justice Ginsburg, called for a full briefing on the question whether the death penalty is unconstitutional. Excerpts from his opinion recounting reasons why he considered it "highly likely" that the death penalty constitutes cruel and unusual punishment and Justice Scalia's response are set forth below.

GLOSSIP V. GROSS
Supreme Court of the United States, 2015.
135 S.Ct. 2726, 192 L.Ed.2d 761.

JUSTICE BREYER, with whom JUSTICE GINSBURG joins, dissenting.

* * *

* * * The Court has recognized that a "claim that punishment is excessive is judged not by the standards that prevailed * * * when the Bill of Rights was adopted, but rather by those that currently prevail." Indeed, the Constitution prohibits various gruesome punishments that were common in Blackstone's day. See 4 W. Blackstone, Commentaries on the Laws of England 369–370 (1769) (listing mutilation and dismembering, among other punishments).

* * *

In 1976, the Court thought that the constitutional infirmities in the death penalty could be healed; the Court in effect delegated significant responsibility to the States to develop procedures that would protect against those constitutional problems. Almost 40 years of studies, surveys, and experience strongly indicate, however, that this effort has failed. Today's administration of the death penalty involves three fundamental constitutional defects: (1) serious unreliability, (2) arbitrariness in application, and (3) unconscionably long delays that undermine the death penalty's penological purpose. * * *

* * *

I

"Cruel"—Lack of Reliability

This Court has specified that the finality of death creates a "qualitative difference" between the death penalty and other punishments (including life in prison). That "qualitative difference" creates "a corresponding difference in the need for reliability in the determination that death is the appropriate punishment in a specific case." There is increasing evidence, however, that the death penalty as now applied lacks that requisite reliability.

For one thing, despite the difficulty of investigating the circumstances surrounding an execution for a crime that took place long ago, researchers have found convincing evidence that, in the past three decades, innocent people have been executed.

For another, the evidence that the death penalty has been wrongly *imposed* (whether or not it was carried out), is striking. * * * (I use "exoneration" to refer to relief from *all* legal consequences of a capital conviction through a decision by a prosecutor, a Governor or a court, after new evidence of the defendant's innocence was discovered.) Since 2002, the number of exonerations in capital cases has risen to 115. * * *

* * *

[R]esearchers estimate that about 4% of those sentenced to death are actually innocent. See Gross, O'Brien, Hu, & Kennedy, Rate of False Conviction of Criminal Defendants Who Are Sentenced to Death, 111 Proceeding of the National Academy of Sciences 7230 (2014) (full-scale study of all death sentences from 1973 through 2004 estimating that 4.1% of those sentenced to death are actually innocent).

Finally, if we expand our definition of "exoneration" (which we limited to errors suggesting the defendant was actually innocent) and thereby also categorize as "erroneous" instances in which courts failed to follow legally required procedures, the numbers soar. Between 1973 and 1995, courts identified prejudicial errors in 68% of the capital cases before them. * * *

* * * Unlike 40 years ago, we now have plausible *evidence* of unreliability that (perhaps due to DNA evidence) is stronger than the evidence we had before. In sum, there is significantly more research-based evidence today indicating that courts sentence to death individuals who may well be actually innocent or whose convictions (in the law's view) do not warrant the death penalty's application.

II

"Cruel"—Arbitrariness

* * *

When the death penalty was reinstated in 1976, this Court acknowledged that the death penalty is (and would be) unconstitutional if "inflicted in an arbitrary and capricious manner."

* * *

Despite the *Gregg* Court's hope for fair administration of the death penalty, 40 years of further experience make it increasingly clear that the death penalty is imposed arbitrarily, *i.e.*, without the "reasonable consistency" legally necessary to reconcile its use with the Constitution's commands.

Thorough studies of death penalty sentences support this conclusion. A recent study, for example, examined all death penalty sentences imposed between 1973 and 2007 in Connecticut * * *. Donohue, An Empirical Evaluation of the Connecticut Death Penalty System Since 1973: Are There Unlawful Racial, Gender, and Geographic Disparities? 11 J. Empirical Legal Studies 637 (2014). The study * * * compared the egregiousness of the conduct of the 9 defendants sentenced to death with the egregiousness of the conduct of defendants in the remaining 196 cases (those in which the defendant, though found guilty of a death-eligible offense, was ultimately not sentenced to death). Application of the studies' metrics made clear that only 1 of those 9 defendants was indeed the "worst of the worst" (or was, at least, within the 15% considered most "egregious"). The remaining eight were not. Their behavior was no worse than the behavior of at least 33 and as many as *170* other defendants (out of a total pool of 205) who had not been sentenced to death.

Such studies indicate that the factors that most clearly ought to affect application of the death penalty—namely, comparative egregiousness of the crime—often do not. Other studies show that circumstances that ought *not* to affect application of the death penalty, such as race, gender, or geography, often *do*.

Numerous studies, for example, have concluded that individuals accused of murdering white victims, as opposed to black or other minority victims, are more likely to receive the death penalty.

Fewer, but still many, studies have found that the gender of the defendant or the gender of the victim makes a not-otherwise-warranted difference.

Geography also plays an important role in determining who is sentenced to death. And that is not simply because some States permit the death penalty while others do not. Rather *within* a death penalty State, the imposition of the death penalty heavily depends on the county in which a defendant is tried. * * *

What accounts for this county-by-county disparity? Some studies indicate that the disparity reflects the decisionmaking authority, the legal discretion, and ultimately the power of the local prosecutor.

Others suggest that the availability of resources for defense counsel (or the lack thereof) helps explain geographical differences.

Still others indicate that the racial composition of and distribution within a county plays an important role. See, *e.g.,* Levinson, Smith, & Young, Devaluing Death: An Empirical Study of Implicit Bias on Jury-Eligible Citizens in Six Death Penalty States, 89 N.Y.U. L.Rev. 513, 533–536 (2014) (summarizing research on this point).

Finally, some studies suggest that political pressures, including pressures on judges who must stand for election, can make a difference.

* * *

* * * I see discrepancies for which I can find no rational explanations. Why does one defendant who committed a single-victim murder receive the death penalty (due to aggravators of a prior felony conviction and an after-the-fact robbery), while another defendant does not, despite having kidnapped, raped, and murdered a young mother while leaving her infant baby to die at the scene of the crime[?] Why does one defendant who committed a single-victim murder receive the death penalty (due to aggravators of a prior felony conviction and acting recklessly with a gun), while another defendant does not, despite having committed a "triple murder" by killing a young man and his pregnant wife? * * * In each instance, the sentences compared were imposed in the same State at about the same time.

* * * From a defendant's perspective, to receive that sentence, and certainly to find it implemented, is the equivalent of being struck by lightning. How then can we reconcile the death penalty with the demands of a Constitution that first and foremost insists upon a rule of law?

III

"Cruel"—Excessive Delays

The problems of reliability and unfairness almost inevitably lead to a third independent constitutional problem: excessively long periods of time that individuals typically spend on death row, alive but under sentence of death. * * *

* * *

* * * In 2014, 35 individuals were executed. Those executions occurred, on average, nearly 18 years after a court initially pronounced its sentence of death. * * *

* * *

These lengthy delays create two special constitutional difficulties. First, a lengthy delay in and of itself is especially cruel because it "subjects death row inmates to decades of especially severe, dehumanizing conditions of confinement." * * *

[N]early all death penalty States keep death row inmates in isolation for 22 or more hours per day. * * * [I]t is well documented that such prolonged solitary confinement produces numerous deleterious harms. See, e.g., Haney, Mental Health Issues in Long-Term Solitary and "Supermax" Confinement, 49 Crime & Delinquency 124, 130 (2003) (cataloguing studies finding that solitary confinement can cause prisoners to experience "anxiety, panic, rage, loss of control, paranoia, hallucinations, and self-mutilations," among many other symptoms).

* * *

The second constitutional difficulty resulting from lengthy delays is that those delays undermine the death penalty's penological rationale, perhaps irreparably so. * * *

[A]s the Court has recognized, the death penalty's penological rationale in fact rests almost exclusively upon a belief in its tendency to deter and upon its ability to satisfy a community's interest in retribution. * * *c

Recently, the National Research Council * * * reviewed 30 years of empirical evidence and concluded that it was insufficient to establish a deterrent effect and thus should "not be used to inform" discussion about the deterrent value of the death penalty.

* * * [A]dd to these studies the fact that, today, very few of those sentenced to death are actually executed, and that even those executions occur, on average, after nearly two decades on death row. Then, does it still seem likely that the death penalty has a significant deterrent effect?

* * *

But what about retribution? Retribution is a valid penological goal. * * * But see A. Sarat, Mercy on Trial: What It Means To Stop an Execution 130 (2005) (Illinois Governor George Ryan explained his decision to commute all death sentences on the ground that it was "cruel and unusual" for "family members to go through this . . . legal limbo for [20] years").

---

c   Justice Breyer noted that "the major alternative to capital punishment—namely, life in prison without possibility of parole—also incapacitates."

The relevant question here, however, is whether a "community's sense of retribution" can often find vindication in "a death that comes," if at all, "only several decades after the crime was committed." By then the community is a different group of people. The offenders and the victims' families have grown far older. Feelings of outrage may have subsided. The offender may have found himself a changed human being. And sometimes repentance and even forgiveness can restore meaning to lives once ruined. * * *

* * * [T]he delays and low probability of execution * * * may well attenuate the community's interest in retribution to the point where it cannot by itself amount to a significant justification for the death penalty. In any event, I believe that whatever interest in retribution might be served by the death penalty as currently administered, that interest can be served almost as well by a sentence of life in prison without parole * * *.

* * *

* * * [T]his Court has said that, if the death penalty does not fulfill the goals of deterrence or retribution, "it is nothing more than the purposeless and needless imposition of pain and suffering and hence an unconstitutional punishment."

* * *

One might ask, why can Congress or the States * * * not take steps to shorten the time between sentence and execution, and thereby mitigate the problems just raised? * * *

For one thing, delays have helped to make application of the death penalty more reliable. * * *

In addition to those who are exonerated on the ground that they are innocent, there are other individuals whose sentences or convictions have been overturned for other reasons (as discussed above, state and federal courts found error in 68% of the capital cases they reviewed between 1973 and 1995). * * *

* * *

[W]e can have a death penalty that at least arguably serves legitimate penological purposes *or* we can have a procedural system that at least arguably seeks reliability and fairness in the death penalty's application. We cannot have both. And that simple fact, demonstrated convincingly over the past 40 years, strongly supports the claim that the death penalty violates the Eighth Amendment. * * *

* * *

JUSTICE SCALIA, with whom JUSTICE THOMAS joins, concurring.

* * *

Welcome to Groundhog Day. The scene is familiar: Petitioners, sentenced to die for the crimes they committed (including, in the case of one petitioner since put to death, raping and murdering an 11-month-old baby), come before this Court asking us to nullify their sentences as "cruel and unusual" under the Eighth Amendment. * * *

The response is also familiar: A vocal minority of the Court, waving over their heads a ream of the most recent abolitionist studies (a superabundant genre) as though they have discovered the lost folios of Shakespeare, insist that *now*, at long last, the death penalty must be abolished for good. Mind you, not once in the history of the American Republic has this Court ever suggested the death penalty is categorically impermissible. The reason is obvious: It is impossible to hold unconstitutional that which the Constitution explicitly *contemplates*. The Fifth Amendment provides that "[n]o person shall be held to answer for a capital . . . crime, unless on a presentment or indictment of a Grand Jury," and that no person shall be "deprived of life . . . without due process of law." * * *

* * *

Even accepting Justice Breyer's rewriting of the Eighth Amendment, his argument is full of internal contradictions and (it must be said) gobbledy-gook. He says that the death penalty is cruel because it is unreliable * * *. * * * The reality is that any innocent defendant is infinitely better off appealing a death sentence than a sentence of life imprisonment. (* * * "[C]ourts (or State Governors) are 130 times more likely to exonerate a defendant where a death sentence is at issue.") The capital convict will obtain endless legal assistance from the abolition lobby (and legal favoritism from abolitionist judges), while the lifer languishes unnoticed behind bars.

Justice Breyer next says that the death penalty is cruel because it is arbitrary. To prove this point, he points to a study of 205 cases that "measured the 'egregiousness' of the murderer's conduct" with "a system of metrics," and then "compared the egregiousness of the conduct of the 9 defendants sentenced to death with the egregiousness of the conduct of defendants in the remaining 196 cases [who were not sentenced to death]." * * * Egregiousness is a moral judgment susceptible of few hard-and-fast rules. More importantly, egregiousness of the crime is only one of several factors that render a punishment condign—culpability, rehabilitative potential, and the need for deterrence also are relevant. That is why this Court has required an individualized consideration of all mitigating circumstances, rather than formulaic application of some egregiousness test.

It is because these questions are contextual and admit of no easy answers that we rely on juries to make judgments about the people and crimes before them. The fact that these judgments may vary across cases is an inevitable consequence of the jury trial, that cornerstone of Anglo-American judicial procedure. But when a punishment is authorized by law—if you kill you are subject to death—the fact that some defendants receive mercy from their jury no more renders the underlying punishment "cruel" than does the fact that some guilty individuals are never apprehended, are never tried, are acquitted, or are pardoned.

Justice Breyer's third reason that the death penalty is cruel is that it entails delay, thereby (1) subjecting inmates to long periods on death row and (2) undermining the penological justifications of the death penalty. The first point is nonsense. Life without parole is an even lengthier period than the wait on death row; and if the objection is that death row is a more confining environment, the solution should be modifying the environment rather than abolishing the death penalty. As for the argument that delay undermines the penological rationales for the death penalty: In insisting that "the major alternative to capital punishment—namely, life in prison without possibility of parole—also incapacitates," Justice Breyer apparently forgets that one of the plaintiffs *in this very case* was already in prison when he committed the murder that landed him on death row. Justice Breyer further asserts that "whatever interest in retribution might be served by the death penalty as currently administered, that interest can be served almost as well by a sentence of life in prison without parole." My goodness. * * * I would not presume to tell parents whose life has been forever altered by the brutal murder of a child that life imprisonment is punishment enough.

And finally, Justice Breyer speculates that it does not "seem likely" that the death penalty has a "significant" deterrent effect. * * * But we federal judges live in a world apart from the vast majority of Americans. After work, we retire to homes in placid suburbia or to high-rise co-ops with guards at the door. We are not confronted with the threat of violence that is ever present in many Americans' everyday lives. The suggestion that the incremental deterrent effect of capital punishment does not seem "significant" reflects, it seems to me, a let-them-eat-cake obliviousness to the needs of others. Let the People decide how much incremental deterrence is appropriate.

* * *

QUESTIONS AND POINTS FOR DISCUSSION

1. In 2000, George Ryan, the governor of Illinois, declared a moratorium on executions, citing what he described as a "shameful record of convicting innocent people and putting them on death row." James S. Liebman et al., A Broken System: Error Rates in Capital Cases, 1973–1995, at 124 n.10 (2000). This decision helped spawn what has been described as "a tectonic shift in the politics of the death penalty," prompting other states to initiate studies of their capital-punishment systems. Id. at 2. Between 2007 and 2016, six states, including Illinois, abolished the death penalty, and the state supreme court in a seventh state struck down its death-penalty statute, declaring it to be unconstitutional. During that time span, another four states instituted moratoriums on executions at the directive of their governors. Death Penalty Information Center, States With and Without the Death Penalty, at http://www.deathpenaltyinfo.org/states-and-without-death-penalty. On the other hand, in referendums in 2016, voters in Nebraska overturned a prior legislative ban on the death penalty and, in two other states (California and Oklahoma), indicated their continued support for the death penalty. Jon Herskovitz, Death penalty gains new support from voters in several U.S. states, Reuters, Nov. 9, 2016, available at https://www.reuters.com/article/us-usa-election-execution/death-penalty-gains-new-support-from-voters-in-several-u-s-states-idUSKBN1343C7.

2. Justice Scalia has cited the setting aside of erroneous convictions and death sentences of persons on death row, whether by courts or through the exercise of executive clemency, as evidence of the "success" of the criminal-justice system, not its "failure." Kansas v. Marsh, 548 U.S. 163, 193, 126 S.Ct. 2516, 2536 (2006) (Scalia, J., concurring). Do you agree?

3. In *Kansas v. Marsh*, the Supreme Court acknowledged that "the criminal-justice system does not operate perfectly" and stated that the death penalty would have to be abolished if its imposition had to be error-free. Id. at 181, 126 S.Ct. at 2529. In your opinion, does the possibility that an innocent person may be executed have a bearing on the death penalty's constitutionality? Can the errors made in imposing the death penalty be eliminated through measures short of abolishing capital punishment? If so, what are those measures? For thirty-nine recommendations designed to avert errors and problems in the imposition and execution of death sentences, see The Constitution Project, Irreversible Error: Recommended Reforms for Preventing and Correcting Errors in the Administration of Capital Punishment (2014).

4. One of the problems contributing to erroneous convictions and death sentences in capital cases is the failure of some attorneys to afford capital defendants their constitutional right to the effective assistance of counsel. The quality of the assistance received by the defendant in Williams v. Taylor, 529 U.S. 362, 120 S.Ct. 1495 (2000) exemplifies what Judge David Bazelon has called "walking violations of the Sixth Amendment." David Bazelon, The Defective Assistance of Counsel, 42 U. Cin. L.Rev. 1, 2 (1973). In *Williams*, the

defendant was sentenced to death after his attorney failed to introduce evidence of what the Supreme Court termed a "nightmarish childhood." Id. at 395, 120 S.Ct. at 1514. The jury was unaware, for example, that the defendant's parents had been imprisoned for child neglect after the defendant and his siblings were discovered living in the following conditions:

> The home was a complete wreck. . . . There were several places on the floor where someone had had a bowel movement. Urine was standing in several places in the bedrooms. There were dirty dishes scattered over the kitchen, and it was impossible to step any place on the kitchen floor where there was no trash. . . . The children were all dirty and none of them had on under-pants. Noah and Lula were so intoxicated, they could not find any clothes for the children, nor were they able to put the clothes on them. . . . The children had to be put in Winslow Hospital, as four of them, by that time, were definitely under the influence of whiskey.

Id. at 395 n.19, 120 S.Ct. at 1514 n.19. The defendant's attorney also failed to disclose to the jury that the defendant's father often beat him severely and that the defendant was subjected to further abuse when living in a foster home while his parents were incarcerated. Nor was the jury apprised of other mitigating facts, including that the defendant was "borderline mentally retarded." Id. at 396, 120 S.Ct. at 1514.

When serving as the director of the Southern Center for Human Rights, Stephen Bright further highlighted the gravity of the problem of incompetent counsel in capital cases, some examples of which are set forth below:

> In the last forty-five years, judges in Houston, Texas have repeatedly appointed Joe Frank Cannon, known for hurrying through trials like "greased lightning," to defend indigent defendants despite his tendency to doze off during trial. * * * While representing Calvin Burdine at a capital trial, Cannon "dozed and actually fell asleep" during trial, "in particular during the guilt-innocence phase when the State's solo prosecutor was questioning witnesses and presenting evidence." The clerk of the court testified that "defense counsel was asleep on several occasions on several days over the course of the proceedings." Cannon's file on the case contained only three pages of notes. A law professor who later represented Carl Johnson, a previous Cannon client, in post-conviction proceedings found that Cannon's "ineptitude . . . jumps off the printed page" and that Cannon slept during the proceedings. Nevertheless, the death sentences in both cases were upheld. Carl Johnson has been executed.

* * *

> Some of those condemned to die in Texas could not have done any worse had they represented themselves than they did with the lawyers assigned to them by the Texas Court of Criminal Appeals.
> * * *

* * *

The court assigned to Ricky Eugene Kerr an attorney who had been in practice for only two years, had never tried or appealed a capital case even as assistant counsel, and had suffered severe health problems that kept him out of his office in the months before he was to file a habeas corpus application on behalf of Kerr. The lawyer so misunderstood habeas corpus law that, as he later admitted, he thought he was precluded from challenging Kerr's conviction and sentence—the very purpose of a post-conviction petition. As a result, the lawyer filed a "perfunctory application" that failed to raise any issue attacking the conviction. After he and his family were unable to contact the lawyer, Kerr wrote a letter to the court complaining about the lawyer and asking the court to appoint another lawyer to prepare a habeas petition. Even though prosecutors did not object to a stay, the Court of Criminal Appeals denied Kerr's motion for a stay of execution and for the appointment of competent counsel. Judge Overstreet, warning that the court would have "blood on its hands" if Kerr was executed, dissented in order to "wash [his] hands of such repugnance" * * *.

* * *

Andrew Cantu finally resorted to representing himself after three different lawyers, appointed by the Criminal Court of Appeals to represent him over a period of eighteen months, failed even to file a petition. The first two lawyers withdrew, and the third never came to see him. At the hearing held five months after the third lawyer was appointed, that lawyer testified that he had not visited Cantu, claiming that he did not know where Cantu was housed in the prison system, had not contacted any investigator or expert witnesses, was not familiar with and had not read the Antiterrorism and Effective Death Penalty Act, which contains a one-year statute of limitations for filing a federal habeas petition, and was not aware of any ramifications of the Act for Cantu. Cantu had no state post-conviction review of his case and was barred from federal review of his case because the statute of limitations expired before any petition was filed. Cantu was executed on February 16, 1999.

Stephen B. Bright, Neither Equal Nor Just: The Rationing and Denial of Legal Services to the Poor When Life and Liberty Are at Stake, 1997 Ann. Surv. Am. L. 783, 789–90, 802, 804–06 (1999) (Reprinted with the permission of the Annual Survey of American Law).

5. In your opinion, does the length of the delay between the imposition of a death sentence and its execution bear on the constitutionality of the death penalty, whether in an individual case or categorically? See Valle v. Florida, 564 U.S. 1067, 132 S.Ct. 1 (2011) (Breyer, J., dissenting from denial of stay of execution in a case in which thirty-three years had elapsed since the prisoner

was first sentenced to death). Why or why not? Putting the constitutional question aside, how, if at all, should such lengthy delays affect the policy decisions regarding whether to retain the death penalty and, if so, how capital cases should be processed following the imposition of a death sentence?

6.   *Class Exercise:* Discuss and debate the following questions:

a.   Is the death penalty, in your opinion, constitutional?

b.   Assuming that, as the Supreme Court has concluded, the death penalty is not invariably unconstitutional, should it be abolished on policy grounds? What factors should be incorporated into a policy analysis of the death penalty? Should the financial costs of the death penalty compared to the costs of lifetime incarceration be considered? Why or why not? For a discussion of these comparative costs and their increasing role in contemporary policy debates about retention of the death penalty, see Carol S. Steiker & Jordan M. Steiker, Cost and Capital Punishment: A New Consideration Transforms an Old Debate, 2010 U. Chi. Legal F. 117 (2010).

Consider the question whether capital punishment is advisable from a policy perspective against the backdrop of a real case in which the boyfriend of the mother of a four-year-old boy became irritated with his high-pitched voice and began beating him with his fists and sticks. These beatings continued over a period of months during which the boyfriend also burned the boy with cigarettes and an iron, stuck him with sewing needles, put his legs in scalding water, and hung him upside down in a locked, dark closet for hours at a time. The boy's mother never tried to intervene and protect her son.

One night, the boyfriend stuck a rag in the little boy's mouth, taped potato peelings over his eyes, and hung him in the closet overnight. The mother did not bother to check on her son the next morning, watching television instead. When the boyfriend finally released the boy from the closet, he pleaded for a drink of water. The boyfriend told the boy to get it himself, but the boy was too weak to walk across the room. The boyfriend then got angry and hit the boy on the head, killing him.

A newspaper columnist later wrote about this case and asked, "What possible justification could there be for permitting these two people to continue living among human beings?" How would you answer this question if you are or were an opponent of the death penalty?

c.   Should executions be televised? Why or why not? For some of the arguments that have been propounded in favor of, and in opposition to, the televising of executions, see Zachary B. Shemtob & David Lat, Executions Should Be Televised, N.Y.

Times, July 29, 2011, at SR4, available at http://www.nytimes.com/2011/07/31/opinion/sunday/executions-should-be-televised.html.

CHAPTER 8

CRUEL AND UNUSUAL PUNISHMENT AND NONCAPITAL CASES

■ ■ ■

The previous chapter dealt with limitations the Eighth Amendment places on the imposition of a death sentence as a penalty for a crime. We turn now to a discussion of the application of the prohibition on cruel and unusual punishments in cases where some sentence other than the death penalty was imposed.

A. CHALLENGES REGARDING THE LENGTH OR AMOUNT OF A CRIMINAL SANCTION

1. CASE-SPECIFIC ANALYSIS OF GROSS DISPROPORTIONALITY

There are two types of cases in which courts have addressed whether a sentence is grossly disproportionate to a crime, in contravention of the Eighth Amendment. In the first, the focus of this subsection, a court evaluates the facts and circumstances of an individual case to determine whether, for example, a prison sentence is unconstitutional due to its length. Rummel v. Estelle, 445 U.S. 263, 100 S.Ct. 1133 (1980) is an example of this kind of case. *Rummel* concerned the constitutionality of a life sentence imposed under a habitual-offender statute mandating life imprisonment for a third-time felon who had been imprisoned twice before. The defendant in that case had received a three-year prison sentence in 1964 after obtaining $80 worth of goods or services through the fraudulent use of a credit card. In 1969, he was convicted of a second felony—passing a forged check for $28.36—and sentenced to prison for four years. He then was convicted in 1973 of obtaining $120.75 through false pretenses, the felony that triggered the habitual-offender statute. In a 5–4 decision, the Supreme Court held that the defendant's life sentence, which included the possibility of parole, did not inflict the cruel and unusual punishment prohibited by the Eighth Amendment. The Court also inserted this observation in its opinion: "[O]ne could argue * * * that for crimes concededly classified and classifiable as felonies, that is, as punishable by significant terms of imprisonment in a state penitentiary, the length of the sentence actually imposed is purely a matter of legislative prerogative." Id. at 274, 100 S.Ct. at 1139.

Two years later, in Hutto v. Davis, 454 U.S. 370, 102 S.Ct. 703 (1982) (per curiam), the Supreme Court held, in another 5–4 decision, that a 40-year prison sentence for possessing and distributing approximately nine ounces of marijuana that had a street value of about $200 did not constitute cruel and unusual punishment. Justice Powell, who had written the dissenting opinion in *Rummel*, in his words, "reluctantly" concurred in the Court's judgment in *Hutto* because in his opinion, *Rummel* was controlling. He noted that the defendant in *Rummel* had committed crimes "far less serious" than the crimes committed by this defendant and yet had suffered a much greater penalty than the 40-year sentence imposed in this case. Id. at 380, 102 S.Ct. at 708 (Powell, J., concurring).

The next year, the Supreme Court revisited, in the case below, the question whether a sentence was unconstitutionally disproportionate. This time, Justice Powell wrote the majority opinion for the Court.

SOLEM V. HELM

Supreme Court of the United States, 1983.
463 U.S. 277, 103 S.Ct. 3001, 77 L.Ed.2d 637.

JUSTICE POWELL delivered the opinion of the Court.

* * *

The issue presented is whether the Eighth Amendment proscribes a life sentence without possibility of parole for a seventh nonviolent felony.

I

By 1975 the State of South Dakota had convicted respondent Jerry Helm of six nonviolent felonies. In 1964, 1966, and 1969 Helm was convicted of third-degree burglary. In 1972 he was convicted of obtaining money under false pretenses. In 1973 he was convicted of grand larceny. And in 1975 he was convicted of third-offense driving while intoxicated. The record contains no details about the circumstances of any of these offenses, except that they were all nonviolent, none was a crime against a person, and alcohol was a contributing factor in each case.

In 1979 Helm was charged with uttering a "no account" check for $100. * * * Helm pleaded guilty.

Ordinarily the maximum punishment for uttering a "no account" check would have been five years' imprisonment in the state penitentiary and a $5,000 fine. As a result of his criminal record, however, Helm was subject to South Dakota's recidivist statute:

> "When a defendant has been convicted of at least three prior convictions [*sic*] in addition to the principal felony, the sentence for the principal felony shall be enhanced to the sentence for a

Class 1 felony." S.D.Codified Laws § 22–7–8 (1979) (amended 1981).

The maximum penalty for a "Class 1 felony" was life imprisonment in the state penitentiary and a $25,000 fine. Moreover, South Dakota law explicitly provides that parole is unavailable: "A person sentenced to life imprisonment is not eligible for parole by the board of pardons and paroles." The Governor is authorized to pardon prisoners, or to commute their sentences, but no other relief from sentence is available even to a rehabilitated prisoner.

Immediately after accepting Helm's guilty plea, the South Dakota Circuit Court sentenced Helm to life imprisonment under § 22–7–8. * * * The South Dakota Supreme Court, in a 3–2 decision, affirmed the sentence despite Helm's argument that it violated the Eighth Amendment.

After Helm had served two years in the state penitentiary, he requested the Governor to commute his sentence to a fixed term of years. Such a commutation would have had the effect of making Helm eligible to be considered for parole when he had served three-fourths of his new sentence. The Governor denied Helm's request in May 1981.

[Helm then filed a petition for a writ of habeas corpus contending that his sentence constituted cruel and unusual punishment. The district court rejected this claim, but on appeal, the Eighth Circuit Court of Appeals reversed.]

II

The Eighth Amendment declares: "Excessive bail shall not be required, nor excessive fines imposed, nor cruel and unusual punishments inflicted." The final clause prohibits not only barbaric punishments, but also sentences that are disproportionate to the crime committed.

* * *

There is no basis for the State's assertion that the general principle of proportionality does not apply to felony prison sentences. The constitutional language itself suggests no exception for imprisonment. We have recognized that the Eighth Amendment imposes "parallel limitations" on bail, fines, and other punishments, and the text is explicit that bail and fines may not be excessive. It would be anomalous indeed if the lesser punishment of a fine and the greater punishment of death were both subject to proportionality analysis, but the intermediate punishment of imprisonment were not. There is also no historical support for such an exception. * * *

* * * We agree * * * that, "[o]utside the context of capital punishment, *successful* challenges to the proportionality of particular sentences [will be]

exceedingly rare." This does not mean, however, that proportionality analysis is entirely inapplicable in noncapital cases.

In sum, we hold as a matter of principle that a criminal sentence must be proportionate to the crime for which the defendant has been convicted. Reviewing courts, of course, should grant substantial deference to the broad authority that legislatures necessarily possess in determining the types and limits of punishments for crimes, as well as to the discretion that trial courts possess in sentencing convicted criminals.[16] But no penalty is *per se* constitutional. * * *

III

A

When sentences are reviewed under the Eighth Amendment, courts should be guided by objective factors that our cases have recognized. First, we look to the gravity of the offense and the harshness of the penalty. * * *

Second, it may be helpful to compare the sentences imposed on other criminals in the same jurisdiction. If more serious crimes are subject to the same penalty, or to less serious penalties, that is some indication that the punishment at issue may be excessive. * * *

Third, courts may find it useful to compare the sentences imposed for commission of the same crime in other jurisdictions. * * *

* * *

B

Application of these factors assumes that courts are competent to judge the gravity of an offense, at least on a relative scale. In a broad sense this assumption is justified, and courts traditionally have made these judgments—just as legislatures must make them in the first instance. Comparisons can be made in light of the harm caused or threatened to the victim or society, and the culpability of the offender. * * * For example, as the criminal laws make clear, nonviolent crimes are less serious than crimes marked by violence or the threat of violence.

There are other accepted principles that courts may apply in measuring the harm caused or threatened to the victim or society. The absolute magnitude of the crime may be relevant. Stealing a million dollars is viewed as more serious than stealing a hundred dollars—a point recognized in statutes distinguishing petty theft from grand theft. Few

---

[16] Contrary to the dissent's suggestions, we do not adopt or imply approval of a general rule of appellate review of sentences. Absent specific authority, it is not the role of an appellate court to substitute its judgment for that of the sentencing court as to the appropriateness of a particular sentence; rather, in applying the Eighth Amendment the appellate court decides only whether the sentence under review is within constitutional limits. In view of the substantial deference that must be accorded legislatures and sentencing courts, a reviewing court rarely will be required to engage in extended analysis to determine that a sentence is not constitutionally disproportionate.

would dispute that a lesser included offense should not be punished more severely than the greater offense. Thus a court is justified in viewing assault with intent to murder as more serious than simple assault. It also is generally recognized that attempts are less serious than completed crimes. Similarly, an accessory after the fact should not be subject to a higher penalty than the principal.

Turning to the culpability of the offender, there are again clear distinctions that courts may recognize and apply. * * * Most would agree that negligent conduct is less serious than intentional conduct. South Dakota, for example, ranks criminal acts in ascending order of seriousness as follows: negligent acts, reckless acts, knowing acts, intentional acts, and malicious acts. A court, of course, is entitled to look at a defendant's motive in committing a crime. Thus a murder may be viewed as more serious when committed pursuant to a contract.

This list is by no means exhaustive. It simply illustrates that there are generally accepted criteria for comparing the severity of different crimes on a broad scale, despite the difficulties courts face in attempting to draw distinctions between similar crimes.

C

Application of the factors that we identify also assumes that courts are able to compare different sentences. This assumption, too, is justified. * * * For sentences of imprisonment, the problem is not so much one of ordering, but one of line-drawing. It is clear that a 25-year sentence generally is more severe than a 15-year sentence, but in most cases it would be difficult to decide that the former violates the Eighth Amendment while the latter does not. Decisions of this kind, although troubling, are not unique to this area. The courts are constantly called upon to draw similar lines in a variety of contexts.

* * *

IV

It remains to apply the analytical framework established by our prior decisions to the case before us. * * *

A

Helm's crime was "one of the most passive felonies a person could commit." It involved neither violence nor threat of violence to any person. The $100 face value of Helm's "no account" check was not trivial, but neither was it a large amount. One hundred dollars was less than half the amount South Dakota required for a felonious theft. It is easy to see why such a crime is viewed by society as among the less serious offenses.

Helm, of course, was not charged simply with uttering a "no account" check, but also with being a habitual offender. And a State is justified in punishing a recidivist more severely than it punishes a first offender. Helm's status, however, cannot be considered in the abstract. His prior offenses, although classified as felonies, were all relatively minor. All were nonviolent and none was a crime against a person. Indeed, there was no minimum amount in either the burglary or the false pretenses statutes, and the minimum amount covered by the grand larceny statute was fairly small.

Helm's present sentence is life imprisonment without possibility of parole. Barring executive clemency, Helm will spend the rest of his life in the state penitentiary. This sentence is far more severe than the life sentence we considered in *Rummel v. Estelle.* Rummel was likely to have been eligible for parole within 12 years of his initial confinement,[25] a fact on which the Court relied heavily. Helm's sentence is the most severe punishment that the State could have imposed on any criminal for any crime. Only capital punishment, a penalty not authorized in South Dakota when Helm was sentenced, exceeds it.

We next consider the sentences that could be imposed on other criminals in the same jurisdiction. When Helm was sentenced, a South Dakota court was required to impose a life sentence for murder and was authorized to impose a life sentence for treason, first-degree manslaughter, first-degree arson, and kidnaping. No other crime was punishable so severely on the first offense. Attempted murder, placing an explosive device on an aircraft, and first-degree rape were only Class 2 felonies. Aggravated riot was only a Class 3 felony. Distribution of heroin and aggravated assault were only Class 4 felonies.

Helm's habitual offender status complicates our analysis, but relevant comparisons are still possible. Under [S.D.Codified Laws] § 22–7–7, the penalty for a second or third felony is increased by one class. * * *

In sum, there were a handful of crimes that were necessarily punished by life imprisonment: murder, and, on a second or third offense, treason, first-degree manslaughter, first-degree arson, and kidnaping. There was a larger group for which life imprisonment was authorized in the discretion of the sentencing judge, including: treason, first-degree manslaughter, first-degree arson, and kidnaping; attempted murder, placing an explosive device on an aircraft, and first-degree rape on a second or third offense; and any felony after three prior offenses. Finally, there was a large group of very serious offenses for which life imprisonment was not authorized, including a third offense of heroin dealing or aggravated assault.

Criminals committing any of these offenses ordinarily would be thought more deserving of punishment than one uttering a "no account" check—even when the bad-check writer had already committed six minor

---

[25] We note that Rummel was, in fact, released within eight months of the Court's decision in his case.

felonies. * * *[26] In any event, Helm has been treated in the same manner as, or more severely than, criminals who have committed far more serious crimes.

Finally, we compare the sentences imposed for commission of the same crime in other jurisdictions. The Court of Appeals found that "Helm could have received a life sentence without parole for his offense in only one other state, Nevada," and we have no reason to doubt this finding. At the very least, therefore, it is clear that Helm could not have received such a severe sentence in 48 of the 50 States. But even under Nevada law, a life sentence without possibility of parole is merely authorized in these circumstances. We are not advised that any defendant such as Helm, whose prior offenses were so minor, actually has received the maximum penalty in Nevada. It appears that Helm was treated more severely than he would have been in any other State.

B

The State argues that the present case is essentially the same as *Rummel v. Estelle,* for the possibility of parole in that case is matched by the possibility of executive clemency here. The State reasons that the Governor could commute Helm's sentence to a term of years. We conclude, however, that the South Dakota commutation system is fundamentally different from the parole system that was before us in *Rummel.*

As a matter of law, parole and commutation are different concepts, despite some surface similarities. Parole is a regular part of the rehabilitative process. Assuming good behavior, it is the normal expectation in the vast majority of cases. The law generally specifies when a prisoner will be eligible to be considered for parole, and details the standards and procedures applicable at that time. Thus it is possible to predict, at least to some extent, when parole might be granted. Commutation, on the other hand, is an ad hoc exercise of executive clemency. A Governor may commute a sentence at any time for any reason without reference to any standards.

* * *

The Texas and South Dakota systems in particular are very different. * * * A Texas prisoner became eligible for parole when his calendar time served plus "good conduct" time equaled one-third of the maximum sentence imposed or 20 years, whichever is less. An entering prisoner earned 20 days good-time per 30 days served, and this could be increased to 30 days good-time per 30 days served. Thus Rummel could have been

---

[26] The State contends that § 22–7–8 is more lenient than the Texas habitual offender statute in *Rummel,* for life imprisonment under § 22–7–8 is discretionary rather than mandatory. Helm, however, has challenged only his own sentence. No one suggests that § 22–7–8 may not be applied constitutionally to fourth-time heroin dealers or other violent criminals. * * *

eligible for parole in as few as 10 years, and could have expected to become eligible, in the normal course of events, in only 12 years.

In South Dakota commutation is more difficult to obtain than parole. For example, the Board of Pardons and Paroles is authorized to make commutation recommendations to the Governor, but § 24–13–4 provides that "no recommendation for the commutation of . . . a life sentence, or for a pardon . . ., shall be made by less than the unanimous vote of all members of the board." In fact, no life sentence has been commuted in over eight years * * *. Furthermore, even if Helm's sentence were commuted, he merely would be eligible to be considered for parole. Not only is there no guarantee that he would be paroled, but the South Dakota parole system is far more stringent than the one before us in *Rummel*. Helm would have to serve three-fourths of his revised sentence before he would be eligible for parole, and the provision for good-time credits is less generous.

The possibility of commutation is nothing more than a hope for "an *ad hoc* exercise of clemency." It is little different from the possibility of executive clemency that exists in every case in which a defendant challenges his sentence under the Eighth Amendment. Recognition of such a bare possibility would make judicial review under the Eighth Amendment meaningless.

V

The Constitution requires us to examine Helm's sentence to determine if it is proportionate to his crime. Applying objective criteria, we find that Helm has received the penultimate sentence for relatively minor criminal conduct. He has been treated more harshly than other criminals in the State who have committed more serious crimes. He has been treated more harshly than he would have been in any other jurisdiction, with the possible exception of a single State. We conclude that his sentence is significantly disproportionate to his crime, and is therefore prohibited by the Eighth Amendment.[32] * * *

CHIEF JUSTICE BURGER, with whom JUSTICE WHITE, JUSTICE REHNQUIST, and JUSTICE O'CONNOR join, dissenting.

* * * Only three Terms ago, we held in *Rummel v. Estelle* that a life sentence imposed after only a *third* nonviolent felony conviction did not constitute cruel and unusual punishment under the Eighth Amendment. Today, the Court ignores its recent precedent and holds that a life sentence

---

[32] Contrary to the suggestion in the dissent, our conclusion today is not inconsistent with *Rummel v. Estelle*. The *Rummel* Court recognized—as does the dissent—that some sentences of imprisonment are so disproportionate that they violate the Eighth Amendment. * * * *Rummel* did reject a proportionality challenge to a particular sentence. But since the *Rummel* Court—like the dissent today—offered no standards for determining when an Eighth Amendment violation has occurred, it is controlling only in a similar factual situation. Here the facts are clearly distinguishable. Whereas Rummel was eligible for a reasonably early parole, Helm, at age 36, was sentenced to life with no possibility of parole.

imposed after a *seventh* felony conviction constitutes cruel and unusual punishment under the Eighth Amendment.[3] Moreover, I reject the fiction that all Helm's crimes were innocuous or nonviolent. Among his felonies were three burglaries and a third conviction for drunken driving. By comparison Rummel was a relatively "model citizen." Although today's holding cannot rationally be reconciled with *Rummel,* the Court does not purport to overrule *Rummel.* I therefore dissent.

* * *

The *Rummel* Court categorically rejected the very analysis adopted by the Court today. * * *

First, it rejected the distinctions Rummel tried to draw between violent and nonviolent offenses, noting that "the absence of violence does not always affect the strength of society's interest in deterring a particular crime or in punishing a particular criminal."[a] Similarly, distinctions based on the amount of money stolen are purely "subjective" matters of line drawing.[b]

Second, the Court squarely rejected Rummel's attempt to compare his sentence with the sentence he would have received in other States—an argument that the Court today accepts. * * * [S]uch comparisons trample on fundamental concepts of federalism. Different states surely may view particular crimes as more or less severe than other states. Stealing a horse in Texas may have different consequences and warrant different punishment than stealing a horse in Rhode Island or Washington, D.C. Thus, even if the punishment accorded Rummel in Texas were to exceed that which he would have received in any other state,

---

[3] Both *Rummel* and *Hutto v. Davis* leave open the possibility that in extraordinary cases—such as a life sentence for overtime parking—it might be permissible for a court to decide whether the sentence is grossly disproportionate to the crime. I agree that the Cruel and Unusual Punishments Clause might apply to those rare cases where reasonable men cannot differ as to the inappropriateness of a punishment. In all other cases, we should defer to the legislature's line-drawing. However, the Court does not contend that this is such an extraordinary case that reasonable men could not differ about the appropriateness of this punishment.

[a] In disputing that the violent or nonviolent nature of a crime is necessarily an indicator of its gravity, the Court in *Rummel* added: "A high official in a large corporation can commit undeniably serious crimes in the area of antitrust, bribery, or clean air or water standards without coming close to engaging in any 'violent' or short-term 'life-threatening' behavior." 445 U.S. at 275, 100 S.Ct. at 1140.

[b] In rebuffing Rummel's argument that the amount of money stolen could be an "objective" criterion applied to assess whether a prison sentence of a certain length is tantamount to cruel and unusual punishment, the Court in *Rummel* noted:

> Rummel cites the "small" amount of money taken in each of his crimes. But to recognize that the State of Texas could have imprisoned Rummel for life if he had stolen $5,000, $50,000, or $500,000, rather than the $120.75 that a jury convicted him of stealing, is virtually to concede that the lines to be drawn are indeed "subjective," and therefore properly within the province of legislatures, not courts.

Id.

"that severity hardly would render Rummel's punishment 'grossly disproportionate' to his offenses or to the punishment he would have received in the other States. . . . *Absent a constitutionally imposed uniformity inimical to traditional notions of federalism, some State will always bear the distinction of treating particular offenders more severely than any other State.*"

Finally, we flatly rejected Rummel's suggestion that we measure his sentence against the sentences imposed by Texas for other crimes:

"Other crimes, of course, implicate other societal interests, making any such comparison inherently speculative. * * * "c

In short, *Rummel* held that the length of a sentence of imprisonment is a matter of legislative discretion * * *. * * *

* * *

———

In Harmelin v. Michigan, 501 U.S. 957, 111 S.Ct. 2680 (1991), the case which follows, the Supreme Court once again considered a claim that a sentence was cruel and unusual because it was disproportionate to the severity of the crime committed.

HARMELIN V. MICHIGAN

Supreme Court of the United States, 1991.
501 U.S. 957, 111 S.Ct. 2680, 115 L.Ed.2d 836.

JUSTICE SCALIA announced the judgment of the Court and delivered * * * an opinion with respect to Parts I, II, and III, in which THE CHIEF JUSTICE joins.d

Petitioner was convicted of possessing 672 grams of cocaine and sentenced to a mandatory term of life in prison without possibility of parole. * * *

Petitioner claims that his sentence is unconstitutionally "cruel and unusual" * * * because it is "significantly disproportionate" to the crime he committed * * *.

———

c   Amplifying this point, the Supreme Court in *Rummel* said:

The highly placed executive who embezzles huge sums from a state savings and loan association, causing many shareholders of limited means to lose substantial parts of their savings, has committed a crime very different from a man who takes a smaller amount of money from the same savings and loan at the point of a gun. Yet rational people could disagree as to which criminal merits harsher punishment.

Id. at 282–83 n.27, 100 S.Ct. at 1143–44 n.27.

d   Only Chief Justice Rehnquist joined this portion of the opinion written by Justice Scalia. The majority opinion on another issue before the Supreme Court in *Harmelin* can be found on page 399.

I

* * *

* * * *Solem* was simply wrong; the Eighth Amendment contains no proportionality guarantee.

* * *

* * * [A] disproportionate punishment can perhaps always be considered "cruel," but it will not always be (as the text also requires) "unusual." * * *

* * *

* * * [T]o use the phrase "cruel and unusual punishment" to describe a requirement of proportionality would have been an exceedingly vague and oblique way of saying what Americans were well accustomed to saying more directly. * * * Proportionality provisions had been included in several State Constitutions. See, e.g., Pa. Const., § 38 (1776) (punishments should be "in general more proportionate to the crimes"). * * * Both the New Hampshire Constitution, adopted 8 years before ratification of the Eighth Amendment, and the Ohio Constitution, adopted 12 years after, contain, in separate provisions, a prohibition of "cruel and unusual punishments" ("cruel *or* unusual," in New Hampshire's case) *and* a requirement that "all penalties ought to be proportioned to the nature of the offence."

* * *

The actions of the First Congress, which are of course persuasive evidence of what the Constitution means, belie any doctrine of proportionality. * * * Shortly after proposing the Bill of Rights, the First Congress * * * punished forgery of United States securities, "running away with [a] ship or vessel, or any goods or merchandise to the value of fifty dollars," treason, and murder on the high seas with the same penalty: death by hanging. * * *

II

We think it enough that those who framed and approved the Federal Constitution chose, for whatever reason, not to include within it the guarantee against disproportionate sentences that some State Constitutions contained. It is worth noting, however, that there was good reason for that choice—a reason that reinforces the necessity of overruling *Solem*. While there are relatively clear historical guidelines and accepted practices that enable judges to determine which *modes* of punishment are "cruel and unusual," *proportionality* does not lend itself to such analysis. * * * This is not to say that there are no absolutes; one can imagine extreme examples that no rational person, in no time or place, could accept. But for the same reason these examples are easy to decide, they are certain never to occur.[11] The real function of a constitutional proportionality principle, if it exists, is to enable judges to evaluate a penalty that *some* assemblage of men and women has considered proportionate—and to say that it is not. For that real-world enterprise, the standards seem so inadequate that the proportionality principle becomes an invitation to imposition of subjective values.

This becomes clear, we think, from a consideration of the three factors that *Solem* found relevant to the proportionality determination: (1) the inherent gravity of the offense, (2) the sentences imposed for similarly grave offenses in the same jurisdiction, and (3) sentences imposed for the same crime in other jurisdictions. As to the first factor: Of course some offenses, involving violent harm to human beings, will always and everywhere be regarded as serious, but that is only half the equation. The issue is *what else* should be regarded to be *as serious* as these offenses, or even to be *more serious* than some of them. * * *

The difficulty of assessing gravity is demonstrated in the very context of the present case: Petitioner acknowledges that a mandatory life sentence might not be "grossly excessive" for possession of cocaine with intent to distribute, see *Hutto v. Davis*, 454 U.S. 370 (1982). But surely whether it is a "grave" offense merely to possess a significant quantity of drugs—thereby facilitating distribution, subjecting the holder to the temptation of distribution, and raising the possibility of theft by others who might distribute—depends entirely upon how odious and socially threatening one believes drug use to be. Would it be "grossly excessive" to provide life imprisonment for "mere possession" of a certain quantity of heavy weaponry? If not, then the only issue is whether the possible dissemination of drugs can be as "grave" as the possible dissemination of heavy weapons. Who are we to say no? The members of the Michigan Legislature, and not we, know the situation on the streets of Detroit.

The second factor suggested in *Solem* fails for the same reason. One cannot compare the sentences imposed by the jurisdiction for "similarly grave" offenses if there is no objective standard of gravity. Judges will be comparing what *they* consider comparable. Or, to put the same point differently: When it happens that two offenses judicially determined to be "similarly grave" receive significantly *dis*similar penalties, what follows is not that the harsher penalty is unconstitutional, but merely that the legislature does not share the judges' view that the offenses are similarly grave. Moreover, even if "similarly grave" crimes could be identified, the

---

11 Justice White argues that the Eighth Amendment must contain a proportionality principle because otherwise legislatures could "mak[e] overtime parking a felony punishable by life imprisonment." * * * Justice White's argument has force only for those who believe that the Constitution prohibited everything that is intensely undesirable—which is an obvious fallacy, see Art. I, § 9 (implicitly permitting slavery). Nor is it likely that the horrible example imagined would ever in fact occur, unless, of course, overtime parking should one day become an arguably major threat to the common good, and the need to deter it arguably critical * * *.

penalties for them would not necessarily be comparable, since there are many other justifications for a difference. For example, since deterrent effect depends not only upon the amount of the penalty but upon its certainty, crimes that are less grave but significantly more difficult to detect may warrant substantially higher penalties. * * * In fact, it becomes difficult, even to speak intelligently of "proportionality," once deterrence and rehabilitation are given significant weight. Proportionality is inherently a retributive concept * * *.

As for the third factor mentioned by *Solem*—the character of the sentences imposed by other States for the same crime—it must be acknowledged that that can be applied with clarity and ease. The only difficulty is that it has no conceivable relevance to the Eighth Amendment. That a State is entitled to treat with stern disapproval an act that other States punish with the mildest of sanctions follows *a fortiori* from the undoubted fact that a State may criminalize an act that other States do not criminalize *at all*. * * * Though the different needs and concerns of other States may induce them to treat simple possession of 672 grams of cocaine as a relatively minor offense, see Wyo. Stat. § 35–7–1031(c) (1988) (6 months); W.Va. Code § 60A–4–401(c) (1989) (6 months), nothing in the Constitution requires Michigan to follow suit. * * *

III

* * *

* * * In *Coker v. Georgia*, [433 U.S. 584 (1977)], the Court held that, because of the disproportionality, it was a violation of the Cruel and Unusual Punishments Clause to impose capital punishment for rape of an adult woman. * * * Proportionality review is one of several respects in which we have held that "death is different," and have imposed protections that the Constitution nowhere else provides. We would leave it there, but will not extend it further.

* * *

JUSTICE KENNEDY, with whom JUSTICE O'CONNOR and JUSTICE SOUTER join, concurring in part and concurring in the judgment.

* * * I write this separate opinion because my approach to the Eighth Amendment proportionality analysis differs from Justice Scalia's. * * * [S]tare decisis counsels our adherence to the narrow proportionality principle that has existed in our Eighth Amendment jurisprudence for 80 years. * * *

I

* * *

* * * [C]lose analysis of our decisions yields some common principles that give content to the uses and limits of proportionality review.

The first of these principles is that the fixing of prison terms for specific crimes involves a substantive penological judgment that, as a general matter, is "properly within the province of legislatures, not courts." * * *

The second principle is that the Eighth Amendment does not mandate adoption of any one penological theory. * * * The federal and state criminal systems have accorded different weights at different times to the penological goals of retribution, deterrence, incapacitation, and rehabilitation. * * *

Third, marked divergences both in underlying theories of sentencing and in the length of prescribed prison terms are the inevitable, often beneficial, result of the federal structure. * * *

The fourth principle at work in our cases is that proportionality review by federal courts should be informed by " 'objective factors to the maximum possible extent.' " * * * Although "no penalty is per se constitutional," the relative lack of objective standards concerning terms of imprisonment has meant that " '[o]utside the context of capital punishment, successful challenges to the proportionality of particular sentences [are] exceedingly rare.' "

All of these principles—the primacy of the legislature, the variety of legitimate penological schemes, the nature of our federal system, and the requirement that proportionality review be guided by objective factors—inform the final one: The Eighth Amendment does not require strict proportionality between crime and sentence. Rather, it forbids only extreme sentences that are "grossly disproportionate" to the crime.

II

* * *

Petitioner's life sentence without parole is the second most severe penalty permitted by law. It is the same sentence received by the petitioner in *Solem*. Petitioner's crime, however, was far more grave than the crime at issue in *Solem*.

* * *

Petitioner was convicted of possession of more than 650 grams (over 1.5 pounds) of cocaine. This amount of pure cocaine has a potential yield of between 32,500 and 65,000 doses. * * * Petitioner's suggestion that his crime was nonviolent and victimless, echoed by the dissent, is false to the point of absurdity. To the contrary, petitioner's crime threatened to cause grave harm to society.

Quite apart from the pernicious effects on the individual who consumes illegal drugs, such drugs relate to crime in at least three ways: (1) A drug user may commit crime because of drug-induced changes in physiological functions, cognitive ability, and mood; (2) A drug user may commit crime in order to obtain money to buy drugs; and (3) A violent crime may occur as part of the drug business or culture. Studies bear out these possibilities and demonstrate a direct nexus between illegal drugs and crimes of violence. To mention but a few examples, 57 percent of a national sample of males arrested in 1989 for homicide tested positive for illegal drugs. The comparable statistics for assault, robbery, and weapons arrests were 55, 73, and 63 percent, respectively. * * *

* * *

The severity of petitioner's crime brings his sentence within the constitutional boundaries established by our prior decisions. In *Hutto v. Davis*, 454 U.S. 370 (1982), we upheld against proportionality attack a sentence of 40 years' imprisonment for possession with intent to distribute nine ounces of marijuana. Here Michigan could with good reason conclude that petitioner's crime is more serious than the crime in *Davis*. * * *

Petitioner and *amici* contend that our proportionality decisions require a comparative analysis between petitioner's sentence and sentences imposed for other crimes in Michigan and sentences imposed for the same crime in other jurisdictions. Given the serious nature of petitioner's crime, no such comparative analysis is necessary. Although *Solem* considered these comparative factors after analyzing "the gravity of the offense and the harshness of the penalty," it did not announce a rigid three-part test. In fact, *Solem* stated that in determining unconstitutional disproportionality, "no one factor will be dispositive in a given case."

On the other hand, one factor may be sufficient to determine the constitutionality of a particular sentence. Consistent with its admonition that "a reviewing court rarely will be required to engage in extended analysis to determine that a sentence is not constitutionally disproportionate," *Solem* is best understood as holding that comparative analysis within and between jurisdictions is not always relevant to proportionality review. The Court stated that "it *may* be helpful to compare sentences imposed on other criminals in the same jurisdiction," and that "courts *may* find it useful to compare the sentences imposed for commission of the same crime in other jurisdictions." It did not mandate such inquiries.

A better reading of our cases leads to the conclusion that intrajurisdictional and interjurisdictional analyses are appropriate only in the rare case in which a threshold comparison of the crime committed and the sentence imposed leads to an inference of gross disproportionality. * * *

* * *

III

* * * Reasonable minds may differ about the efficacy of Michigan's sentencing scheme, and it is far from certain that Michigan's bold

experiment will succeed. The accounts of pickpockets at Tyburn hangings[e] are a reminder of the limits of the law's deterrent force, but we cannot say the law before us has no chance of success and is on that account so disproportionate as to be cruel and unusual punishment. * * *

JUSTICE WHITE, with whom JUSTICE BLACKMUN and JUSTICE STEVENS join, dissenting.

The Eighth Amendment provides that "[e]xcessive bail shall not be required, nor excessive fines imposed, nor cruel and unusual punishments inflicted." * * *

The language of the Amendment does not refer to proportionality in so many words, but it does forbid "excessive" fines, a restraint that suggests that a determination of excessiveness should be based at least in part on whether the fine imposed is disproportionate to the crime committed. Nor would it be unreasonable to conclude that it would be both cruel and unusual to punish overtime parking by life imprisonment or, more generally, to impose any punishment that is grossly disproportionate to the offense for which the defendant has been convicted. * * *

Justice Scalia * * * asserts that if proportionality was an aspect of the restraint, it could have been said more clearly—as plain-talking Americans would have expressed themselves (as for instance, I suppose, in the Fifth Amendment's Due Process Clause or the Fourth Amendment's prohibition against unreasonable searches and seizures).

* * *

* * * Later in his opinion, however, Justice Scalia backtracks and appears to accept that the Amendment does indeed insist on proportional punishments in a particular class of cases, those that involve sentences of death. His fallback position * * * fails to explain why the words "cruel and unusual" include a proportionality requirement in some cases but not in others. * * *

* * *

While Justice Scalia seeks to deliver a swift death sentence to *Solem*, Justice Kennedy prefers to eviscerate it, leaving only an empty shell. * * *

* * *

Justice Kennedy's abandonment of the second and third factors set forth in *Solem* makes an attempt at an objective proportionality analysis futile. The first prong of *Solem* requires a court to consider two discrete factors—the gravity of the offense and the severity of the punishment. A court is not expected to consider the interaction of these two elements and

---

[e]   Tyburn Hill was the site in England where raucous crowds used to gather in medieval times to watch executions. The Oxford History of the Prison 35, 58 (Norval Morris & David J. Rothman eds., 1995).

determine whether "the sentence imposed was grossly excessive punishment for the crime committed." Were a court to attempt such an assessment, it would have no basis for its determination that a sentence was—or was not—disproportionate, other than the "subjective views of individual [judges]," which is the very sort of analysis our Eighth Amendment jurisprudence has shunned. * * * Indeed, only when a comparison is made with penalties for other crimes and in other jurisdictions can a court begin to make an objective assessment about a given sentence's constitutional proportionality, giving due deference to "public attitudes concerning a particular sentence."

Because there is no justification for overruling or limiting *Solem*, it remains to apply that case's proportionality analysis to the sentence imposed on petitioner. * * *

* * *

The first *Solem* factor requires a reviewing court to assess the gravity of the offense and the harshness of the penalty. The mandatory sentence of life imprisonment without possibility of parole "is the most severe punishment that the State could have imposed on any criminal for any crime," for Michigan has no death penalty.

Although these factors are "by no means exhaustive," in evaluating the gravity of the offense, it is appropriate to consider "the harm caused or threatened to the victim or society," based on such things as the degree of violence involved in the crime and "[t]he absolute magnitude of the crime," and "the culpability of the offender," including the degree of requisite intent and the offender's motive in committing the crime.

Drugs are without doubt a serious societal problem. To justify such a harsh mandatory penalty as that imposed here, however, the offense should be one which will *always* warrant that punishment. Mere possession of drugs—even in such a large quantity—is not so serious an offense that it will always warrant, much less mandate, life imprisonment without possibility of parole. * * *

To be constitutionally proportionate, punishment must be tailored to a defendant's personal responsibility and moral guilt. Justice Kennedy attempts to justify the harsh mandatory sentence imposed on petitioner by focusing on the subsidiary effects of drug use, and thereby ignores this aspect of our Eighth Amendment jurisprudence. While the collateral consequences of drugs such as cocaine are indisputably severe, they are not unlike those which flow from the misuse of other, legal substances. * * *

The "absolute magnitude" of petitioner's crime is not exceptionally serious. Because possession is necessarily a lesser included offense of possession with intent to distribute, it is odd to punish the former as severely as the latter. Nor is the requisite intent for the crime sufficient to render it particularly grave. To convict someone under the possession statute, it is only necessary to prove that the defendant knowingly possessed a mixture containing narcotics which weighs at least 650 grams. There is no *mens rea* requirement of intent to distribute the drugs, as there is in the parallel statute. * * * Finally, this statute applies equally to first-time offenders, such as petitioner, and recidivists. * * *

* * *

The second prong of the *Solem* analysis is an examination of "the sentences imposed on other criminals in the same jurisdiction." As noted above, there is no death penalty in Michigan; consequently, life without parole, the punishment mandated here, is the harshest penalty available. It is reserved for three crimes: first-degree murder; manufacture, distribution, or possession with intent to manufacture or distribute 650 grams or more of narcotics; and possession of 650 grams or more of narcotics. Crimes directed against the persons and property of others—such as second-degree murder, rape, and armed robbery, do not carry such a harsh mandatory sentence, although they do provide for the possibility of a life sentence in the exercise of judicial discretion. It is clear that petitioner "has been treated in the same manner as, or more severely than, criminals who have committed far more serious crimes."

The third factor set forth in *Solem* examines "the sentences imposed for commission of the same crime in other jurisdictions." No other jurisdiction imposes a punishment nearly as severe as Michigan's for possession of the amount of drugs at issue here. Of the remaining 49 States, only Alabama provides for a mandatory sentence of life imprisonment without possibility of parole for a first-time drug offender, and then only when a defendant possesses *10 kilograms* or more of cocaine. * * *

Application of *Solem*'s proportionality analysis leaves no doubt that the Michigan statute at issue fails constitutional muster. The statutorily mandated penalty of life without possibility of parole for possession of narcotics is unconstitutionally disproportionate in that it violates the Eighth Amendment's prohibition against cruel and unusual punishment. * * *

JUSTICE MARSHALL, dissenting. [Opinion omitted.]

JUSTICE STEVENS, with whom JUSTICE BLACKMUN joins, dissenting. [Opinion omitted.]

QUESTIONS AND POINTS FOR DISCUSSION

1. In People v. Bullock, 485 N.W.2d 866 (Mich.1992), the Michigan Supreme Court held that the statute under which the defendant in *Harmelin* had been sentenced violated the Michigan Constitution. The court noted that the prohibition in the state constitution of "cruel *or* unusual" punishments

encompassed more punishments than the more limited ban in the federal constitution of "cruel *and* unusual punishments." As a remedy, the court ordered that the no-parole provision in the Michigan statute be stricken, making defendants sentenced under the statute eligible for parole consideration after serving ten years of their sentences. To the argument that the court, by invalidating the statute, was encroaching undemocratically on the will of the people, as expressed through the enactments of the state legislature, the court responded: "The very purpose of a constitution is to subject the passing judgments of temporary legislative or political majorities to the deeper, more profound judgment of the people reflected in the constitution, the enforcement of which is entrusted to our judgment." Id. at 877.

2.   In his opinion concurring in the judgment in Ewing v. California, 538 U.S. 11, 123 S.Ct. 1179 (2003), which is discussed in note 6 on page 389, Justice Scalia once again skewered the idea, embraced by a majority of the Court, that a gross disproportionality principle applicable to prison sentences is embedded within the Eighth Amendment:

> Out of respect for the principle of *stare decisis*, I might nonetheless accept the contrary holding of *Solem v. Helm*—that the Eighth Amendment contains a narrow proportionality principle—if I felt I could intelligently apply it. This case demonstrates why I cannot.
>
> Proportionality—the notion that the punishment should fit the crime—is inherently a concept tied to the penological goal of retribution. "[I]t becomes difficult even to speak intelligently of 'proportionality,' once deterrence and rehabilitation are given significant weight," not to mention giving weight to the purpose of California's three strikes law: incapacitation. In the present case, the game is up once the plurality has acknowledged that "the Constitution does not mandate adoption of any one penological theory," and that a "sentence can have a variety of justifications, such as incapacitation, deterrence, retribution, or rehabilitation." That acknowledgment having been made, it no longer suffices merely to assess "the gravity of the offense compared to the harshness of the penalty"; that classic description of the proportionality principle (alone and in itself quite resistant to policy-free, legal analysis) now becomes merely the "first" step of the inquiry. Having completed that step (by a discussion which, in all fairness, does not convincingly establish that 25-years-to-life is a "proportionate" punishment for stealing three golf clubs), the plurality must then *add* an analysis to show that "Ewing's sentence is justified by the State's public-safety interest in incapacitating and deterring recidivist felons."
>
> Which indeed it is—though why that has anything to do with the principle of proportionality is a mystery. Perhaps the plurality should revise its terminology, so that what it reads into the Eighth Amendment is not the unstated proposition that all punishment

should be reasonably proportionate to the gravity of the offense, but rather the unstated proposition that all punishment should reasonably pursue the multiple purposes of the criminal law. That formulation would make it clearer than ever, of course, that the plurality is not applying law but evaluating policy.

Id. at 31–32, 123 S.Ct. at 1190–91 (Scalia, J., concurring). Do you concur with Justice Scalia's view that the Eighth Amendment does not contain a proportionality principle applicable to noncapital sentences? Would it violate the Eighth Amendment to punish the crime of aggravated robbery less severely than the lesser-included offense of robbery?

3.   Justice Stevens has found unpersuasive the argument that the difficulty of differentiating with exactitude between prison sentences that are grossly disproportionate and those that are not means that the Eighth Amendment contains no gross disproportionality principle applicable to prison sentences. In his rejoinder to Justice Scalia in *Ewing*, Justice Stevens noted that when construing the Constitution, "courts—faced with imprecise commands—must make difficult decisions." Id. at 34 n.2, 123 S.Ct. at 1192 n.2 (Stevens, J., dissenting). He cited the need for judges to determine, for example, whether an award of punitive damages in a civil case violated due process because the amount awarded was disproportionate to the defendant's wrongdoing; whether a defendant's Sixth Amendment right to a speedy trial in a criminal case was violated; whether a defendant's confession was coerced; whether the introduction at trial of illegally obtained evidence was a "harmless error"; and whether a defense attorney rendered unreasonable professional assistance and, if so, whether that deficiency prejudiced the defendant.

4.   The Eighth Amendment prohibits not only the infliction of cruel and unusual punishments, but also the imposition of "excessive fines." In United States v. Bajakajian, 524 U.S. 321, 118 S.Ct. 2028 (1998), the Supreme Court held that the same test applied when determining whether a punishment is cruel and unusual is to be applied when determining whether a fine is unconstitutionally "excessive." A court should assess whether the fine is "grossly disproportional to the gravity of a defendant's offense." Id. at 334, 118 S.Ct. at 2036.

Applying this test to the facts of the case before it, the Court concluded, in a 5–4 decision, that the forfeiture of $357,144 for failing to report, as required by law, that the defendant was transporting that amount of money out of the country would constitute an "excessive fine." The Court highlighted a number of factors in support of its conclusion: First, the defendant's only crime was failing to report certain information to the government. The actual transportation of the currency out of the country was legal. Second, the defendant's reporting crime was not related to any other crime. There was no evidence, for example, that the money had been obtained during illegal drug-dealing transactions. Third, the maximum sentence that could be imposed under the federal sentencing guidelines for the reporting crime—six months in prison and a $5,000 fine—confirmed that the defendant's criminal culpability was at the "minimal level." Id. at 339, 118 S.Ct. at 2038. And finally, the harm stemming from the defendant's crime was "minimal." Id., 118 S.Ct. at 2039. The government was the only party injured by the defendant's crime, and the harm was simply the loss of information about how much money was being taken out of the country.

Do you agree with the Court's analysis and conclusion? Do you discern any arguable inconsistency between *Bajakian* and *Harmelin*? See Pamela S. Karlan, "Pricking the Lines": The Due Process Clause, Punitive Damages, and Criminal Punishment, 88 Minn. L.Rev. 880, 900–02 (2004) (noting, for example, that while the Supreme Court in *Bajakian* focused solely on the harm caused by the defendant, Justice Kennedy factored into his analysis in *Harmelin* the harm caused generally by illegal drugs).

5. In Lockyer v. Andrade, 538 U.S. 63, 123 S.Ct. 1166 (2003), the defendant challenged the constitutionality of two lengthy prison sentences imposed under California's three-strikes law. At the time, that law mandated the imposition of a sentence of twenty-five years to life when a defendant had been convicted of a felony after previously having been convicted of two or more "serious" or "violent" felonies. (The since-changed law now generally requires that the third "strike" also be a "serious" or "violent" felony. Cal. Penal Code § 1170.12(c)(2)(C).) The law was invoked against the defendant after he was convicted of shoplifting, in two separate incidents, a total of nine videotapes worth $153.54. Because the defendant had a prior theft conviction, though a misdemeanor, the prosecutor had the option, of which he availed himself, of prosecuting the defendant's petty thefts as felonies. The defendant also had prior convictions for several nonviolent felonies; he had been convicted twice of transporting marijuana and had pled guilty to three counts of residential burglary in one consolidated court hearing. In accordance with the terms of the three-strikes law, the 37-year-old defendant was sentenced to prison for twenty-five years to life for each theft, with the sentences to be served consecutively and with no possibility of parole before he had served the minimum 25-year sentence on each count.

Since the defendant in *Lockyer* was contesting the constitutionality of his sentences in a habeas corpus action, the technical question before the Supreme Court was whether the state appellate court's decision upholding the defendant's sentences was "contrary to, or an unreasonable application of, clearly established federal law." Id. at 66, 123 S.Ct. at 1169. The Court answered that question in the negative, in part because its decisions applying the Eighth Amendment to prison sentences have not, in its words, been "a model of clarity." Id. at 72, 123 S.Ct. at 1173. In your opinion, was the defendant in this case more like the defendant in *Rummel*, *Solem*, or *Harmelin*?

6. In Ewing v. California, 538 U.S. 11, 123 S.Ct. 1179 (2003), a companion case to *Lockyer*, the 38-year-old defendant was sentenced to prison for twenty-five years to life under California's three-strikes law, a sentence that a majority of the Court found did not violate the Eighth Amendment. The

crime that triggered application of the three-strikes provision was the defendant's theft of three golf clubs priced at $399 apiece. The defendant also had an extensive criminal record, including prior convictions for several thefts, battery, possession of drug paraphernalia, possession of a firearm, four burglaries, and robbery.

What the Court in *Lockyer* aptly described as the Court-created "thicket of Eighth Amendment jurisprudence" was not eradicated in *Ewing*, another 5–4 decision. The plurality opinion, written by Justice O'Connor and in which Chief Justice Rehnquist and Justice Kennedy joined, followed the approach outlined in Justice Kennedy's concurring opinion in *Harmelin* in analyzing the defendant's Eighth Amendment claim. The concurring Justices, Scalia and Thomas, adhered to their position that there is no proportionality principle in the Eighth Amendment that constrains the length of prison sentences. Justice Stevens, in a dissenting opinion joined by Justices Souter, Ginsburg, and Breyer, stated that *Solem*'s three-part test was the most apropos, although Justice Breyer went ahead and applied the Kennedy test "for present purposes" in a separate dissenting opinion in which the other three dissenting Justices joined. Id. at 36, 123 S.Ct. at 1194 (Breyer, J., dissenting).

A majority of the Justices on the Supreme Court now describe Justice Kennedy's concurring opinion in *Harmelin* as the "controlling opinion." Graham v. Florida, 560 U.S. 48, 59–60, 130 S.Ct. 2011, 2021–22 (2010), and other courts typically apply the Kennedy test when analyzing a claim contesting the length of a prison sentence on Eighth Amendment grounds. See, e.g., In re Stevens, 90 A.3d 910, 913 (Vt.2014). If there were no prior Supreme Court cases on this subject, how would you analyze such a claim?

7.   Punitive damages are awarded in civil cases to punish and deter certain opprobrious illegal conduct. The Due Process Clause places constraints on these awards, prohibiting awards that are "grossly excessive" or "arbitrary." State Farm Mut. Automobile Ins. Co. v. Campbell, 538 U.S. 408, 416, 123 S.Ct. 1513, 1519–20 (2003). While the Supreme Court has generally been reluctant to set aside prison sentences on the grounds that they are unconstitutionally disproportionate, the Court has manifested no such hesitancy in vacating punitive-damages awards. See, e.g., id. (finding $145 million punitive-damages award unconstitutional in insurance-fraud case where plaintiff was awarded $1 million in compensatory damages); BMW of North America, Inc. v. Gore, 517 U.S. 559, 116 S.Ct. 1589 (1996) (vacating $2 million punitive-damages award in case in which plaintiff was awarded $4,000 in compensatory damages for defendant's fraud).

The Supreme Court also has applied a more exacting standard when assessing the constitutionality of punitive-damages awards in civil cases as opposed to prison sentences in criminal cases. Under this standard, three "guideposts" are factored into the analysis of whether a punitive-damages award is unconstitutionally excessive. A court first considers the reprehensibility of the defendant's conduct. Five facts bear on the extent to which the defendant's conduct is reprehensible: (1) whether the harm the defendant caused was physical or solely economic; (2) whether the defendant acted with indifference to the health or safety of others; (3) whether the victim was vulnerable financially; (4) whether the harmful conduct was recurrent or an "isolated incident"; and (5) whether the harm was caused accidentally or intentionally.

The second "guidepost" that a court considers when evaluating the constitutionality of a punitive-damages award is the ratio between the punitive damages and the harm caused by, and likely to ensue from, the defendant's illegal conduct. The Supreme Court has said that, as a general rule, a punitive-damages award that is ten or more times higher than the compensatory damages awarded in a case is unconstitutional. State Farm, 538 U.S. at 425, 123 S.Ct. at 1524.

The final "guidepost" in the constitutional analysis of a punitive-damages award focuses on the other penalties, both civil and criminal, that can be imposed for the kind of misconduct in which the defendant engaged. Notably, when discussing this "guidepost" in *BMW of North America, Inc. v. Gore*, the Supreme Court said that a punitive-damages award "cannot be justified on the ground that it was necessary to deter future misconduct without considering whether less drastic remedies could be expected to achieve that goal." 517 U.S. at 584, 116 S.Ct. at 1603.

Some commentators have criticized the Supreme Court for its laxity when evaluating the constitutionality of the length of a prison sentence compared to its greater scrutiny of punitive-damages awards. See, e.g., Erwin Chemerinsky, The Constitution and Punishment, 56 Stan. L.Rev. 1049, 1079 (2004) ("There is something just wrong with a Court that has no problem with putting a person in prison for life, with no possibility of parole for fifty years, for stealing $153 worth of videotapes, but is outraged when too much is taken from a company in punitive damages when it defrauds its customers.") Do you believe that the analytical approach in the punitive-damages context warrants changes in the way in which courts evaluate claims that prison sentences are unconstitutionally disproportionate? Why or why not?

8.   In your opinion, is a defendant's advanced age at the time of sentencing relevant to the question whether a prison sentence constitutes cruel and unusual punishment because of its length? Compare Lockyer v. Andrade, 538 U.S. 63, 74 n.1, 123 S.Ct. 1166, 1174 n.1 (2003) (plurality opinion) (rejecting the proposition that two different sentences—a life sentence without parole and a life sentence with the possibility of parole in ten years—can become "materially indistinguishable" because a defendant receiving the latter sentence is so old) with Crosby v. State, 824 A.2d 894, 910 (Del.2003) (considering defendant's 45-year sentence, which would result in his imprisonment until he was at least eighty-two and possibly as old as ninety-one, a life sentence "in the literal sense").

9.   Consider whether the sentence imposed in the following case violated the Eighth Amendment: The defendant, Grover Henderson, was convicted of delivering three "rocks" of crack cocaine weighing .238 grams, about a

hundredth of an ounce. The drug sale was initiated by a government informant, who paid Henderson twenty dollars for the crack. Henderson, who had no prior convictions, was sentenced to life in prison. Only if the government later commuted his sentence to a term of years would he become eligible for parole. According to the state's records, Henderson was apparently the only person with no prior convictions ever to receive a life sentence in the state for selling this quantity of a controlled substance. In addition, state sentencing guidelines promulgated after the crime's commission, and therefore not applicable to Henderson, prescribed a presumptive sentence of three and a half years imprisonment for a crime like Henderson's. Only three states authorized a life sentence for a person with no prior convictions convicted of delivering the amount of crack Henderson had sold, and in all but possibly one of those states, the convicted individual was eligible for parole. See Henderson v. Norris, 258 F.3d 706 (8th Cir.2001).

10. Since the Supreme Court's decision in *Harmelin*, few defendants have prevailed on a claim that their sentences were unconstitutionally disproportionate under the Eighth Amendment. One of the notable exceptions occurred in State v. Bartlett, 830 P.2d 823 (Ariz.1992). In that case, the defendant received two mandatory prison sentences totaling forty years, with no possibility of parole, for having had consensual sexual intercourse when he was twenty-three with two girls who were close to fifteen years old. In holding that the defendant's sentences violated the Eighth Amendment, the Arizona Supreme Court emphasized, among other factors, the defendant's lack of any criminal record, the nonviolent nature of the crimes, and the "realities of adolescent life," namely the fact that so many teenagers are sexually active. Id. at 829. The court also noted that the mandatory-minimum sentences for the defendant's crimes were the same as those to which he would have been subject if he had killed the girls and been convicted of second-degree murder. In your opinion, should the extent to which teenagers are sexually active have a bearing on the Eighth Amendment question?

The Ninth Circuit's decision in Gonzalez v. Duncan, 551 F.3d 875 (9th Cir.2008) represents another one of those rare instances when a sentence was deemed grossly disproportionate, in contravention of the Eighth Amendment. In that case, the defendant, who had two convictions for sex crimes occurring in a single incident, had failed to resubmit his sex-offender registration information within, as required by a California law, five working days of his birthday. He had, however, registered this information nine months before his birthday, and he provided it once again three months after his birthday. The information already in the sex-offender registry was still accurate at the time of the defendant's birthday.

Normally, any prison term imposed in the state for the crime in question—failure to reregister within the five-day time span—ranged from sixteen months to three years. However, the defendant had several prior criminal convictions—for cocaine possession, committing a lewd act with a child under the age of fourteen, attempted rape by force, and second-degree robbery. Consequently, the court applied the state's three-strikes law, imposing an indeterminate sentence of twenty-eight years to life in prison. The Ninth Circuit Court of Appeals held that this sentence violated the Eighth Amendment, finding it grossly disproportionate for an "entirely passive, harmless, and technical violation of the registration law." Id. at 889.

11. Even if a sentence is not unconstitutionally disproportionate, a defendant may argue that the court erred in imposing such a high prison sentence or fine for a specific crime. Although defendants sometimes prevail on claims that a sentence is excessive in length or amount, appellate courts generally accord great deference to a trial court's sentencing decision. A standard commonly applied when determining whether a sentence that fell within statutory limits should be set aside because of its length or amount is whether it reflects a "clear abuse of discretion." See, e.g., State v. McIntosh, 368 P.3d 621, 628 (Idaho 2016). For additional discussion on the appeal and reversal of sentences for abuse of sentencing discretion, see pages 134–135.

12. Prosecutors are at times concerned that a sentence is too lenient, not adequately reflecting the seriousness of the crime committed or the culpability of the defendant. Some legislatures have responded to this concern by enacting statutes under which prosecutors can, in limited circumstances, contest the leniency of a sentence on appeal. See, e.g., 18 U.S.C. § 3742(b) (providing for government appeals of sentences that (1) are imposed "in violation of law"; (2) are the product of an "incorrect application of the sentencing guidelines"; (3) are less than that specified in the guideline range; or (4) where no guidelines apply, are "plainly unreasonable").

In United States v. DiFrancesco, 449 U.S. 117, 101 S.Ct. 426 (1980), the Supreme Court held that imposing a greater sentence after a prosecutor successfully appeals a sentence under a statute authorizing such appeals does not violate the Double Jeopardy Clause of the Fifth Amendment. The Court reasoned that the government had, in effect, simply established a permissible "two-stage sentencing procedure." Id. at 140 n.16, 101 S.Ct. at 439 n.16.

13. The American Bar Association has flip-flopped on the question whether prosecutors should be allowed to appeal sentences they consider too lenient. For years, the ABA opposed such appeals, in part because of the concern that prosecutors might in effect force defendants to forgo certain rights, such as the right to trial, by threatening to seek higher sentences on appeal if they were convicted after a trial. See ABA Standards for Criminal Justice: Appellate Review of Sentences, Standard 20–1.1(d) (2d ed. 1980). This concern, however, was later overridden by the belief that fairness and equity demand that prosecutors be afforded the same opportunity as defendants to challenge a sentence. See ABA Standards for Criminal Justice: Sentencing, Standard 18–8.3 (3d ed. 1994). What is your view on this question?

2. CATEGORICAL BANS ON CERTAIN SENTENCES

In the cases discussed in the preceding subsection, courts evaluated the gross disproportionality of sentences on a case-by-case basis. Courts also sometimes consider whether a whole category of individuals are constitutionally exempt from a certain criminal penalty. The Supreme Court typically has enunciated such "categorical rules" in the capital context. It has held, for example, that the death penalty cannot be imposed on someone who was under the age of eighteen when committing a homicide or on any person for a nonhomicide crime committed against an individual. In the following case, the Supreme Court for the first time adopted a categorical rule in a case not involving the death penalty.

GRAHAM V. FLORIDA

Supreme Court of the United States, 2010.
560 U.S. 48, 130 S.Ct. 2011, 176 L.Ed.2d 825.

JUSTICE KENNEDY delivered the opinion of the Court.

[The question before the Supreme Court in this case was whether a life sentence without parole for a nonhomicide offense committed when the defendant was under eighteen abridged the Eighth Amendment. In answering this question, the Court first examined whether two "objective" indicators of societal standards—statutes and state practices—reveal that there is a "national consensus" against this criminal penalty. The Court acknowledged that the majority of jurisdictions in the United States— thirty-seven states, the District of Columbia, and the federal government— authorized a life-without-parole sentence for some nonhomicide crimes committed by juveniles. But the Court noted that in practice, few jurisdictions imposed such a sentence. A total of 129 prisoners in twelve jurisdictions were serving life sentences without parole for nonhomicide offenses they committed when they were younger than eighteen, and more than half of those prisoners (seventy-seven) had received the sentence in just one state—Florida. The rarity of such a sentence led the Court to conclude that a national consensus had developed against it.

As in other Eighth Amendment cases, the Supreme Court then observed that while the national consensus regarding the penalty in question was entitled to significant weight in its constitutional calculus, that consensus was not determinative; the Court would still have to exercise its "independent judgment" as to whether the sentence violated the Eighth Amendment's prohibition of cruel and unusual punishments. When doing so in this case, the Court first compared defendants' culpability in this context against the severity of a life sentence without parole. When assessing the defendants' culpability, the Court emphasized that a nonhomicide offense is not as serious as a crime that results in someone's death. The Court also reiterated what it had concluded in Roper v. Simmons, 543 U.S. 551, 125 S.Ct. 1183 (2005) (casebook page 328) when striking down the death penalty for convicted murderers who were under the age of eighteen at the time of their crimes: juveniles who commit crimes are not as culpable as adults. They are less mature and responsible, more susceptible to peer pressure and other external pressures, and have less fully formed characters.]

As for the punishment, life without parole is "the second most severe penalty permitted by law." It is true that a death sentence is "unique in its severity and irrevocability"; yet life without parole sentences share some characteristics with death sentences that are shared by no other sentences. The State does not execute the offender sentenced to life without parole, but the sentence alters the offender's life by a forfeiture that is irrevocable. It deprives the convict of the most basic liberties without giving hope of restoration, except perhaps by executive clemency—the remote possibility of which does not mitigate the harshness of the sentence. As one court observed in overturning a life without parole sentence for a juvenile defendant, this sentence "means denial of hope; it means that good behavior and character improvement are immaterial * * *."

* * *

Life without parole is an especially harsh punishment for a juvenile. Under this sentence a juvenile offender will on average serve more years and a greater percentage of his life in prison than an adult offender. A 16-year-old and a 75-year-old each sentenced to life without parole receive the same punishment in name only. * * *

The penological justifications for the sentencing practice are also relevant to the analysis. * * * A sentence lacking any legitimate penological justification is by its nature disproportionate to the offense. * * *

[A]s *Roper* observed, " * * * the case for retribution is not as strong with a minor as with an adult." The case becomes even weaker with respect to a juvenile who did not commit homicide. * * *

Deterrence does not suffice to justify the sentence either. * * * Because juveniles' "lack of maturity and underdeveloped sense of responsibility . . . often result in impetuous and ill-considered actions and decisions," they are less likely to take a possible punishment into consideration when making decisions. This is particularly so when that punishment is rarely imposed. * * * Even if the punishment has some connection to a valid penological goal, it must be shown that the punishment is not grossly disproportionate in light of the justification offered. Here, * * * any limited deterrent effect provided by life without parole is not enough to justify the sentence.

Incapacitation, a third legitimate reason for imprisonment, does not justify the life without parole sentence in question here. * * * [W]hile incapacitation may be a legitimate penological goal sufficient to justify life without parole in other contexts, it is inadequate to justify that punishment for juveniles who did not commit homicide. To justify life without parole on the assumption that the juvenile offender forever will be a danger to society requires the sentencer to make a judgment that the juvenile is incorrigible. The characteristics of juveniles make that judgment questionable. "It is difficult even for expert psychologists to differentiate between the juvenile offender whose crime reflects unfortunate yet transient immaturity, and the rare juvenile offender whose crime reflects irreparable corruption." * * *

* * *

A sentence of life imprisonment without parole * * * cannot be justified by the goal of rehabilitation. The penalty forswears altogether the rehabilitative ideal. By denying the defendant the right to reenter the community, the State makes an irrevocable judgment about that person's value and place in society. * * *

In sum, penological theory is not adequate to justify life without parole for juvenile nonhomicide offenders. This determination; the limited culpability of juvenile nonhomicide offenders; and the severity of life without parole sentences all lead to the conclusion that the sentencing practice under consideration is cruel and unusual. * * *

What the State must do * * * is give defendants like Graham some meaningful opportunity to obtain release based on demonstrated maturity and rehabilitation. It is for the State, in the first instance, to explore the means and mechanisms for compliance. * * * Those who commit truly horrifying crimes as juveniles may turn out to be irredeemable, and thus deserving of incarceration for the duration of their lives. The Eighth Amendment does not foreclose the possibility that persons convicted of nonhomicide crimes committed before adulthood will remain behind bars for life. It does prohibit States from making the judgment at the outset that those offenders never will be fit to reenter society.

* * *

* * * [T]he features that distinguish juveniles from adults also put them at a significant disadvantage in criminal proceedings. Juveniles mistrust adults and have limited understandings of the criminal justice system and the roles of the institutional actors within it. They are less likely than adults to work effectively with their lawyers to aid in their defense. Difficulty in weighing long-term consequences; a corresponding impulsiveness; and reluctance to trust defense counsel, seen as part of the adult world a rebellious youth rejects, all can lead to poor decisions by one charged with a juvenile offense. These factors are likely to impair the quality of a juvenile defendant's representation. A categorical rule avoids the risk that, as a result of these difficulties, a court or jury will erroneously conclude that a particular juvenile is sufficiently culpable to deserve life without parole for a nonhomicide.

Finally, a categorical rule gives all juvenile nonhomicide offenders a chance to demonstrate maturity and reform. * * * Life in prison without the possibility of parole gives no chance for fulfillment outside prison walls, no chance for reconciliation with society, no hope. * * *

* * *

[T]he United States is the only Nation that imposes life without parole sentences on juvenile nonhomicide offenders. * * *

* * *

* * * The Court has treated the laws and practices of other nations and international agreements as relevant to the Eighth Amendment not because those norms are binding or controlling but because the judgment of the world's nations that a particular sentencing practice is inconsistent with basic principles of decency demonstrates that the Court's rationale has respected reasoning to support it. * * *

* * *

The Constitution prohibits the imposition of a life without parole sentence on a juvenile offender who did not commit homicide. A State need not guarantee the offender eventual release, but if it imposes a sentence of life it must provide him or her with some realistic opportunity to obtain release before the end of that term. * * *

JUSTICE STEVENS, with whom JUSTICE GINSBURG and JUSTICE SOTOMAYOR join, concurring. [Opinion omitted.]

CHIEF JUSTICE ROBERTS, concurring in the judgment. [Opinion omitted.]

JUSTICE THOMAS, with whom JUSTICE SCALIA joins, and with whom JUSTICE ALITO joins as to Parts I and III, dissenting. [Opinion omitted.]

JUSTICE ALITO, dissenting. [Opinion omitted.]

QUESTIONS AND POINTS FOR DISCUSSION

1.   Do you agree with the Supreme Court's analysis and conclusion in *Graham*? In your opinion, does the Eighth Amendment also categorically ban a life sentence without parole when a person was under eighteen at the time of committing a homicide offense? Why or why not?

2.   In Miller v. Alabama, 567 U.S. 460, 132 S.Ct. 2455 (2012), the Supreme Court could have, but did not, resolve the question whether the Eighth Amendment also erects a categorical ban on life sentences without parole for homicide offenses committed by juveniles. As discussed in note 1 on page 401, the Court instead chose different grounds for striking down mandatory life sentences without parole in this context. But even if a life sentence without parole can sometimes be imposed for a homicide offense

committed when a defendant was under eighteen, the Supreme Court has indicated that it would be an unconstitutionally disproportionate penalty for "all but the rarest of children"—those whose crimes reflect "irreparable corruption." Montgomery v. Louisiana, 136 S.Ct. 718, 726 (2016). The Court has furthermore underscored how difficult it is, at the time of sentencing, to know whether a homicide stemmed from such rare "irreparable corruption" or, instead, the "transient immaturity" of youth. Miller, 567 U.S. at 479–80, 132 S.Ct. at 2469.

3.   A recurring theme throughout the Supreme Court's opinion in *Graham v. Florida* was that a life sentence without parole deprives a person of hope. In Vinter v. United Kingdom, 2013–III, Eur. Ct. H.R. 317, the European Court of Human Rights held that a life sentence violates Article 3 of the European Convention on Human Rights if no opportunity exists for later review of the sentence and potential release from prison. Article 3 prohibits torture and "inhuman or degrading treatment or punishment." The Court concluded that permanently depriving people of their freedom without affording them the chance to regain it conflicts with the "respect for human dignity" that lies at the heart of human rights. Id. at 347. A concurring opinion added:

> Article 3 encompasses what might be described as "the right to hope." * * * Those who commit the most abhorrent and egregious of acts and who inflict untold suffering upon others, nevertheless retain their fundamental humanity and carry within themselves the capacity to change. Long and deserved though their prison sentences may be, they retain the right to hope that, someday, they may have atoned for the wrongs which they have committed. * * * To deny them the experience of hope would be to deny a fundamental aspect of their humanity and, to do that, would be degrading.

Id. at 358 (Power-Forde, J., concurring).

In your view, does a life sentence without parole imposed on an adult for a nonhomicide crime constitute cruel and unusual punishment under the Eighth Amendment? For a homicide offense? Why or why not?

4.   Assume a defendant was sentenced to prison for 112 years for a nonhomicide crime committed when he was under eighteen and will not be eligible for potential release until he is ninety-two. Does *Graham* apply to this sentence? Why or why not?

In State v. Moore, 76 N.E.2d 1127, 1143 (Ohio 2016), the Ohio Supreme Court ruled that the Eighth Amendment's ban on life sentences without parole for nonhomicide offenses committed by juveniles extends to sentences to a specific term of years that are the "practical equivalent" of a life sentence. The court also held that *Graham* applies whether the de facto life sentence is for one or multiple crimes. By contrast, the Colorado Supreme Court held in Lucero v. People, 394 P.3d 1128 (Colo. 2017) that *Graham* does not extend to term-of-years sentences for multiple crimes, such as the aggregate 84-year sentence in that case. In your view, does the applicability of *Graham* to a de facto life sentence, such as the 112-year sentence mentioned above, depend on whether the defendant was sentenced for one crime or received consecutive sentences for multiple crimes?

5.   States that have retained life sentences for nonhomicide crimes committed when people were juveniles have instituted varied procedures for later reviewing that person's readiness for release. Some states allow these individuals, after a defined period of time, to petition a court to be resentenced. In other states, parole boards consider, after a set period of time, whether they should be released. See Beth Caldwell, Creating Meaningful Opportunities for Release: *Graham*, *Miller* and California's Youth Offender Parole Hearings, 40 N.Y.U. Rev. L. & Soc. Change 245, 260 (2016).

6.   The Supreme Court in *Graham* did not define what constitutes the required "meaningful" and "realistic" opportunity to secure release from prison based on "demonstrated maturity and rehabilitation." In your opinion, by when must the release review occur for this opportunity to be considered meaningful? Why did you select this point in time? See Sarah French Russell, Review for Release: Juvenile Offenders, State Parole Practices, and the Eighth Amendment, 89 Ind. L.J. 373, 409, 412 (2014) (noting that first reviewing a sentence within ten to fifteen years is "within constitutional limits," in part because juveniles' brains typically change so much by their early twenties).

Could the opportunity for release not be meaningful, in the constitutional sense, for reasons other than the timing of the release review? Does it matter, for example, whether release from prison after such a review is a rarity? See id. at 375–76 (for the release opportunity to be meaningful, there must be a "realistic likelihood" that rehabilitated individuals will be released). What if an imprisoned person has had no access to rehabilitative programming? Is the opportunity for release based on "demonstrated maturity and rehabilitation" meaningful? Why or why not?

3.   THE RIGHT TO INDIVIDUALIZED SENTENCING

HARMELIN V. MICHIGAN

Supreme Court of the United States, 1991.
501 U.S. 957, 111 S.Ct. 2680, 115 L.Ed.2d 836.

JUSTICE SCALIA announced the judgment of the Court and delivered the opinion of the Court with respect to Part IV [below].

[In the portion of its opinion found on page 378 of this casebook, the Supreme Court rejected the defendant's claim that his mandatory life sentence without parole for drug possession was grossly disproportionate, in violation of the Eighth Amendment. The Court then turned to the defendant's second basis for claiming that his sentence constituted cruel and unusual punishment.]

Petitioner claims that his sentence violates the Eighth Amendment for a reason in addition to its alleged disproportionality. He argues that it is "cruel and unusual" to impose a mandatory sentence of such severity, without any consideration of so-called mitigating factors such as, in his case, the fact that he had no prior felony convictions. He apparently contends that the Eighth Amendment requires Michigan to create a sentencing scheme whereby life in prison without possibility of parole is simply the most severe of a range of available penalties that the sentencer may impose after hearing evidence in mitigation and aggravation.

* * * [T]his claim has no support in the text and history of the Eighth Amendment. Severe, mandatory penalties may be cruel, but they are not unusual in the constitutional sense, having been employed in various forms throughout our Nation's history. * * *

Petitioner's "required mitigation" claim, like his proportionality claim, does find support in our death penalty jurisprudence. We have held that a capital sentence is cruel and unusual under the Eighth Amendment if it is imposed without an individualized determination that that punishment is "appropriate"—whether or not the sentence is "grossly disproportionate." See *Woodson v. North Carolina* [casebook page 317]. Petitioner asks us to extend this so-called "individualized capital-sentencing doctrine" to an "individualized mandatory life in prison without parole sentencing doctrine." We refuse to do so.

Our cases creating and clarifying the "individualized capital sentencing doctrine" have repeatedly suggested that there is no comparable requirement outside the capital context, because of the qualitative difference between death and all other penalties.

> "The penalty of death differs from all other forms of criminal punishment, not in degree but in kind. It is unique in its total irrevocability. It is unique in its rejection of rehabilitation of the convict as a basic purpose of criminal justice. And it is unique, finally, in its absolute renunciation of all that is embodied in our concept of humanity." *Furman v. Georgia*, 408 U.S., at 306 (Stewart, J., concurring).

* * * In some cases, moreover, there will be negligible difference between life without parole and other sentences of imprisonment—for example, a life sentence with eligibility for parole after 20 years, or even a lengthy term sentence without eligibility for parole, given to a 65-year-old man. But even where the difference is the greatest, it cannot be compared with death. We have drawn the line of required individualized sentencing at capital cases, and see no basis for extending it further.

QUESTIONS AND POINTS FOR DISCUSSION

1. In Miller v. Alabama, 567 U.S. 460, 132 S.Ct. 2455 (2012), the Supreme Court held, in a 5–4 decision, that the imposition of a mandatory life sentence without parole for a homicide offense committed when the defendant was younger than eighteen constitutes cruel and unusual punishment. The Court did not adjudicate the claim that the Eighth Amendment categorically bars life-without-parole sentences for juveniles convicted of homicide. Instead, the Court ruled that individuals who were under eighteen when they committed a homicide offense have a constitutional right to "individualized sentencing"—a right to have mitigating facts about their crimes or themselves considered by the sentencer—before the decision is made whether they should spend the rest of their lives in prison. See id. at 474 n.6, 132 S.Ct. at 2466 n.6 ("*Graham* established one rule (a flat ban) for nonhomicide offenses, while we set out a different one (individualized sentencing) for homicide offenses."). The Court observed:

> Mandatory life without parole for a juvenile precludes consideration of his chronological age and its hallmark features—among them, immaturity, impetuosity, and failure to appreciate risks and consequences. It prevents taking into account the family and home environment that surrounds him—and from which he cannot usually extricate himself—no matter how brutal or dysfunctional. It neglects the circumstances of the homicide offense, including the extent of his participation in the conduct and the way familial and peer pressures may have affected him. Indeed, it ignores that he might have been charged and convicted of a lesser offense if not for incompetencies associated with youth—for example, his inability to deal with police officers or prosecutors (including on a plea agreement) or his incapacity to assist his own attorneys. And finally, this mandatory punishment disregards the possibility of rehabilitation even when the circumstances most suggest it.

Id. at 477–78, 132 S.Ct. at 2468.

The Court in *Miller* did not find *Harmelin* controlling, noting "if (as *Harmelin* recognized) 'death is different,' children are different too." Id. at 481, 132 S.Ct. at 2470. Do you agree with the distinction the Supreme Court has drawn between adults and juveniles, with the latter, but not the former, constitutionally entitled to individualized sentencing in noncapital cases resulting in a life sentence without parole? Why or why not?

2. The Supreme Court of Iowa has held that all mandatory-minimum prison sentences, of whatever length, constitute cruel and unusual punishment under the state's constitution when imposed on someone who was under eighteen at the time of the crime. State v. Lyle, 854 N.W.2d 378 (Iowa 2014) (vacating mandatory-minimum term of seven years for second-degree robbery). What arguments would you make in support of the position that such sentences also violate the Eighth Amendment? How would you refute those arguments?

B. CHALLENGES REGARDING THE NATURE OF A CRIMINAL SANCTION

Some Eighth Amendment claims challenge the kind, rather than the length or amount, of a criminal sanction. These claims typically center on two types of sentences—what are called "shame sentences" and medical interventions.

1. SHAME SENTENCES

"Scarlet letter" or shame sentences provoke legal challenges on several different grounds. The following case addressed two of the claims most frequently asserted against these kinds of sentences—that the judge had no statutory authority to impose this kind of penalty and that the sentence violated the Eighth Amendment's prohibition of cruel and unusual punishments.

UNITED STATES V. GEMENTERA
Court of Appeals, Ninth Circuit, 2004.
379 F.3d 596.

O'SCANNLAIN, CIRCUIT JUDGE:

* * *

I

Shawn Gementera pilfered letters from several mailboxes along San Francisco's Fulton Street on May 21, 2001. * * * After indictment, Gementera entered a plea agreement pursuant to which he pled guilty to mail theft, and the government dismissed a second count of receiving a stolen U.S. Treasury check.

The offense was not Gementera's first encounter with the law. Though only twenty-four years old at the time, Gementera's criminal history was lengthy for a man of his relative youth, and it was growing steadily more serious. At age nineteen, he was convicted of misdemeanor criminal mischief. He was twice convicted at age twenty of driving with a suspended license. At age twenty-two, a domestic dispute led to convictions for driving with a suspended license and for failing to provide proof of financial responsibility. By twenty-four, the conviction was misdemeanor battery. Other arrests and citations listed in the Presentence Investigation Report included possession of drug paraphernalia, additional driving offenses (most of which involved driving on a license suspended for his failure to take chemical tests), and, soon after his twenty-fifth birthday, taking a vehicle without the owner's consent.

On February 25, 2003, Judge Vaughn Walker of the United States District Court for the Northern District of California sentenced Gementera.

The U.S. Sentencing Guidelines range was two to eight months incarceration; Judge Walker sentenced Gementera to the lower bound of the range, imposing two months incarceration and three years supervised release. He also imposed conditions of supervised release.

One such condition required Gementera to "perform 100 hours of community service," to consist of "standing in front of a postal facility in the city and county of San Francisco with a sandwich board which in large letters declares: 'I stole mail. This is my punishment.'" Gementera later filed a motion to correct the sentence by removing the sandwich board condition. *See* Fed.R.Crim.P. 35(a).

Judge Walker modified the sentence after inviting both parties to present "an alternative form or forms of public service that would better comport with the aims of the court." In lieu of the 100-hour signboard requirement, the district court imposed a four-part special condition in its stead. Three new terms, proposed jointly by counsel, mandated that the defendant observe postal patrons visiting the "lost or missing mail" window, write letters of apology to any identifiable victims of his crime, and deliver several lectures at a local school. It also included a scaled-down version of the signboard requirement:

> The defendant shall perform 1 day of 8 total hours of community service during which time he shall either (i) wear a two-sided sandwich board-style sign or (ii) carry a large two-sided sign stating, "I stole mail; this is my punishment," in front of a San Francisco postal facility identified by the probation officer. For the safety of defendant and general public, the postal facility designated shall be one that employs one or more security guards. Upon showing by defendant that this condition would likely impose upon defendant psychological harm or effect or result in unwarranted risk of harm to defendant, the public or postal employees, the probation officer may withdraw or modify this condition or apply to the court to withdraw or modify this condition. * * *4

II

We first address Gementera's argument that the eight-hour sandwich board condition violates the Sentencing Reform Act.

The Sentencing Reform Act affords district courts broad discretion in fashioning appropriate conditions of supervised release, while mandating that such conditions serve legitimate objectives. In addition to "any condition set forth as a discretionary condition of probation * * *," the statute explicitly authorizes the court to impose "*any other condition it*

---

4 Gementera was ordered to surrender on March 31, 2003. On March 12, 2003, prior to his surrender, Gementera was arrested for possession of stolen mail, for which he was convicted and received a twenty-four month sentence.

considers to be appropriate." 18 U.S.C. § 3583(d)(emphasis added). Such special * * * condition must be "reasonably related" to "the nature and circumstances of the offense and the history and characteristics of the defendant." *See* 18 U.S.C. 3553(a)(1). Moreover, it must be both "reasonably related" to and "involve no greater deprivation of liberty than is reasonably necessary" to "afford adequate deterrence to criminal conduct," *see id.* at 3553(a)(2)(B), "protect the public from further crimes of the defendant," *see id.* at 3553(a)(2)(C), and "provide the defendant with needed educational or vocational training, medical care, or other correctional treatment in the most effective manner." *See id.* at 3553(a)(2)(D). Accordingly, the three legitimate statutory purposes of deterrence, protection of the public, and rehabilitation frame our analysis.

* * *

[T]he district court's discretion, while broad, is limited—most significantly here, by the statute's requirement that any condition reasonably relate to a legitimate statutory purpose. "This test is applied in a two-step process; first, this court must determine whether the sentencing judge imposed the conditions for permissible purposes, and then it must determine whether the conditions are reasonably related to the purposes." * * *

A

Gementera first urges that the condition was imposed for an impermissible purpose of humiliation. He points to certain remarks of the district court at the first sentencing hearing:

> [H]e needs to understand the disapproval that society has for this kind of conduct, and that's the idea behind the humiliation. And it should be humiliation of having to stand and be labeled in front of people coming and going from a post office as somebody who has stolen the mail.

According to Gementera, these remarks, among others, indicate that the district court viewed humiliation as an end in itself and the condition's purpose.

* * *

The court expressed particular concern that the defendant did not fully understand the gravity of his offense. Mail theft is an anonymous crime and, by "bring[ing] home to defendant that his conduct has palpable significance to real people within his community," the court aimed to break the defendant of the illusion that his theft was victimless or not serious. In short, it explained:

> While humiliation may well be—indeed likely will be—a feature of defendant's experience in standing before a post office with such

a sign, the humiliation or shame he experiences should serve the salutary purpose of bringing defendant in close touch with the real significance of the crime he has acknowledged committing. Such an experience should have a specific rehabilitative effect on defendant that could not be accomplished by other means, certainly not by a more extended term of imprisonment.

Moreover, "[i]t will also have a deterrent effect on both this defendant and others who might not otherwise have been made aware of the real legal consequences of engaging in mail theft."

Read in its entirety, the record unambiguously establishes that the district court imposed the condition for the stated and legitimate statutory purpose of rehabilitation and, to a lesser extent, for general deterrence and for the protection of the public. We find no error in the condition's purpose.

B

Assuming the court articulated a legitimate purpose, Gementera asserts, under the second prong of our test, that humiliation or so-called "shaming" conditions are not "reasonably related" to rehabilitation. In support, he cites * * * several state court decisions[9] * * *.

---

[9] In *People v. Hackler*, 16 Cal.Rptr.2d 681 (Cal.Ct.App.1993), a California court vacated a condition requiring a defendant during his first year of probation to wear a t-shirt whenever he was outside his home. The t-shirt read, "My record plus two-six packs equal four years," and on the back, "I am on felony probation for theft." Noting with disapproval the trial court's stated intention of "going back to some extent to the era of stocks" and transforming the defendant into "a Hester Prin [sic]," the court held that the t-shirt could not serve the rehabilitative purpose because it would render the defendant unemployable. By contrast, Gementera's condition was sharply limited temporally (eight hours) and spatially (one post office in a large city), eliminating any risk that its effects would similarly spill over into all aspects of the defendant's life. Indeed, the district court's imposition of the condition in lieu of lengthier incarceration enables Gementera to enter the private labor market.

People v. Johnson, 528 N.E.2d 1360 (1988), involved a condition that a DWI offender publish a newspaper advertisement with apology and mug shot. Interpreting the state supervision law as intended "to aid the defendant in rehabilitation and in avoiding future violations," and for no other purpose, the court held that the publication requirement "possibly, adds public ridicule as a condition" of supervision and could inflict psychological harm that disserves the goal of rehabilitation. *Id.* at 1362 (noting that the Illinois statute does not "refer to deterrent to others"). Relying on the fact that defendant was a young lady and a good student with no prior criminal record, had injured no one, and otherwise had no alcohol or drug problem, it found the condition impermissible, given the perceived mental health risk. By contrast, we have specifically held that mandatory public apology may be rehabilitative. Moreover, the condition specifically provided that the signboard requirement would be withdrawn if the defendant showed that the condition would inflict psychological harm.

The defendant's third case, *People v. Letterlough*, 655 N.E.2d 146 (1995), also involved a probation condition imposed upon a DWI offender. If he regained driving privileges, the offender was required to affix a fluorescent sign to his license plate, stating "CONVICTED DWI". The court imposed the condition under a catch-all provision of the New York law authorizing "any other conditions reasonably related to his [or her] rehabilitation." * * * Because the condition's "true design was not to advance defendant's rehabilitation, but rather to 'warn the public' of the threat presented by his presence behind the wheel," the court voided the condition. In contrast to the New York scheme, the district court made plain the rehabilitative purpose of the condition. We also note that in the federal system, unlike the New York system, rehabilitation is not the sole legitimate objective.

In evaluating probation and supervised release conditions, we have emphasized that the "reasonable relation" test is necessarily a "very flexible standard," and that such flexibility is necessary because of "our uncertainty about how rehabilitation is accomplished." * * *

* * *

* * * [T]he district court concluded that public acknowledgment of one's offense—beyond the formal yet sterile plea in a cloistered courtroom—was necessary to his rehabilitation.

* * *

Gementera and amicus contend that shaming conditions cannot be rehabilitative because such conditions necessarily cause the offender to withdraw from society or otherwise inflict psychological damage, and they would erect a per se bar against such conditions.[11] * * *

Criminal offenses, and the penalties that accompany them, nearly always cause shame and embarrassment. Indeed, the mere fact of conviction, without which state-sponsored rehabilitation efforts do not commence, is stigmatic. The fact that a condition causes shame or embarrassment does not automatically render a condition objectionable; rather, such feelings generally signal the defendant's acknowledgment of his wrongdoing. * * *

While the district court's sandwich board condition was somewhat crude, and by itself could entail risk of social withdrawal and stigmatization, it was coupled with more socially useful provisions, including lecturing at a high school and writing apologies, that might loosely be understood to promote the offender's social reintegration. *See* John Braithwaite, *Crime, Shame and Reintegration* 55 (1989) ("The crucial distinction is between shaming that is reintegrative and shaming that is disintegrative (stigmatization). Reintegrative shaming means that expressions of community disapproval, which may range from mild rebuke to degradation ceremonies, are followed by gestures of reacceptance into the community of law-abiding citizens."). We see this factor as highly significant. In short, here we consider not a stand-alone condition intended solely to humiliate, but rather a comprehensive set of provisions that expose the defendant to social disapprobation, but that also then provide an opportunity for Gementera to repair his relationship with society—first

---

[11] Even if shaming conditions were sometimes rehabilitative, Gementera also urges that the condition would be psychologically damaging in his specific case * * *. * * * [T]he district court * * * inserted a provision into the condition providing an avenue for Gementera to present more reliable evidence of psychological harm:

> Upon showing by defendant that this condition would likely impose upon defendant psychological harm or effect or result in unwarranted risk of harm to defendant, the public or postal employees, the probation officer may withdraw or modify this condition or apply to the court to withdraw or modify this condition.

No such substantiation was presented. * * *

by seeking its forgiveness and then by making, as a member of the community, an independent contribution to the moral formation of its youth.[13] These provisions,[14] tailored to the specific needs of the offender,[15] counsel in favor of concluding that the condition passes the threshold of being reasonably related to rehabilitation.

Finally, we are aware that lengthier imprisonment was an alternative available to the court. * * * The judge's reasoning that rehabilitation would better be served by means other than extended incarceration and punishment is plainly reasonable.

Accordingly, we hold that the condition imposed upon Gementera reasonably related to the legitimate statutory objective of rehabilitation.[16] * * *

III

* * *

We turn then to the Eighth Amendment, which forbids the infliction of "cruel and unusual punishments." "The basic concept underlying the Eighth Amendment was nothing less than the dignity of man." *Trop v. Dulles,* 356 U.S. 86, 100 (1958).

A particular punishment violates the Eighth Amendment if it constitutes one of "those modes or acts of punishment that had been considered cruel and unusual at the time that the Bill of Rights was adopted." Shaming sanctions of far greater severity were common in the colonial era, and the parties do not quarrel on this point.

The Amendment's prohibition extends beyond those practices deemed barbarous in the 18th century, however. "[T]he words of the Amendment are not precise, and their scope is not static. The Amendment must draw its meaning from the evolving standards of decency that mark the progress of a maturing society." * * *

---

[13] The dissent faults our analysis for looking beyond the signboard clause to other provisions of the four-part condition. * * * By acting in concert with others, a provision may reasonably relate to rehabilitation, even though the relation existed primarily by virtue of its interaction with complementary provisions in an integrated program. A boot camp, for example, that operates by "breaking participants down" before "building them up again" is not rendered impermissible merely because the first step, standing alone, might be impermissible. Similarly, a program that emphasizes an offenders' separation from the community of law-abiding citizens, in order to generate contrition and an authentic desire to rejoin that community, need not be evaluated without reference to the program's affirmative provisions to reconcile the offender with the community and eventually to reintegrate him into it.

[14] We do not pass here on the more difficult case of the district court's original 100-hour condition, which lacked significant reintegrative aspects.

[15] We do acknowledge that one purpose of the Sentencing Guidelines was to promote greater uniformity in federal sentencing, and that permitting certain conditions of supervised release, as imposed here, may lead to less regularized sentences. * * *

[16] In view of this holding, we do not reach the separate issue of whether the condition reasonably relates to the objectives of deterrence and protection of the public.

The parties have offered no evidence whatsoever, aside from bare assertion, that shaming sanctions violate contemporary standards of decency. * * * Aside from a single case presenting concerns not at issue here,[17] we are aware of no case holding that contemporary shaming sanctions violate our Constitution's prohibition against cruel and unusual punishment.[18]

We do, however, note that *Blanton v. N. Las Vegas,* 489 U.S. 538 (1989), is instructive, if only indirectly. In *Blanton,* the Court considered whether a Nevada DUI defendant was entitled to a jury trial pursuant to the Sixth Amendment. The inquiry into whether the offense constituted a petty crime not subject to the Sixth Amendment trial provision required the Court to evaluate the severity of the maximum authorized penalty. The statute provided a maximum sentence of six months or, alternatively, forty-eight hours of community service while dressed in distinctive garb identifying the defendant as a DUI offender, payment of a $200–$1000 fine, loss of driving license, and attendance at an alcohol abuse course. The Court wrote:

> We are also unpersuaded by the fact that, instead of a prison sentence, a DUI offender may be ordered to perform 48 hours of community service dressed in clothing identifying him as a DUI offender. Even assuming the outfit is the source of some embarrassment during the 48-hour period, such a penalty will be less embarrassing and less onerous than six months in jail.

Id. at 544; *but see id.* at 544 n.10 ("We are hampered in our review of the clothing requirement because the record from the state courts contains

---

[17] Gementera points to *Williams v. State,* 505 S.E.2d 816 (1998), in which a defendant convicted of soliciting sodomy was ordered to walk for ten days, between 7 p.m. and 11 p.m. each day, along that portion of the street where the solicitation occurred, holding a large sign stating, "BEWARE HIGH CRIME AREA." The police were to be notified in advance in order to monitor his performance and provide an appropriate level of safety. While the court commended the trial judge for his "initiative" in developing a "new and creative form of sentencing which might very well have a positive effect on [the defendant] and be beneficial to the public," and explained that shaming punishments are not forbidden, it nonetheless found that the condition exposed the defendant to a constitutionally impermissible danger.

* * * The condition in *Gementera* does not expose the defendant to any significant risk of danger. By contrast with *Williams,* the *Gementera* signboard is worn during eight hours of daylight during the business day, not at night; in front of a United States Post Office, not a "high crime" neighborhood where criminal solicitation occurs; and the sign's message does not provoke violence by threatening the criminal livelihood of those who illegally trade sex in a red light district, as the *Williams* sign might. Moreover, the district court in *Gementera* explicitly included a provision allowing for withdrawal of the condition upon a showing that the condition would impose a safety risk upon the defendant. Gementera made no such showing.

[18] Numerous state courts have rejected Eighth Amendment challenges to shaming sanctions. *See, e.g., People v. Letterlough,* 613 N.Y.S.2d 687 (N.Y.App.Div.1994) ("CONVICTED DWI" sign on license plate); *Ballenger v. State,* 436 S.E.2d 793 ([Ga.App.]1993) (fluorescent pink DUI bracelet); *Lindsay v. State,* 606 So.2d 652, 656–57 (Fla.App.1992) (DUI advertisement in newspaper); *Goldschmitt v. State,* 490 So.2d 123, 125 (Fla.App.1986) ("Convicted DUI—Restricted License" bumper sticker); cf. *People v. McDowell,* 130 Cal.Rptr. 839 (Cal.App.1976) (tap shoes for purse thief who used tennis shoes to approach his victims quietly and flee swiftly).

neither a description of the clothing nor any details as to where and when it must be worn."). Just as the Court concluded that 48 hours of service dressed in distinctive DUI garb was less onerous than six months imprisonment, it would stretch reason to conclude that eight hours with a signboard, in lieu of incarceration, constitutes constitutionally cruel and unusual punishment.

* * *

HAWKINS, CIRCUIT JUDGE, dissenting:

Conditions of supervised release must be reasonably related to and "involve no greater deprivation of liberty than is reasonably necessary" to deter criminal conduct, protect the public, and rehabilitate the offender. Clearly, the shaming punishment at issue in this case was intended to humiliate Gementera. And that is all it will do. Any attempt to classify the goal of the punishment as anything other than humiliation would be disingenuous. Because humiliation is not one of the three proper goals under the Sentencing Reform Act, I would hold that the district court abused its discretion in imposing the condition.

* * *

* * * Admitting that the condition was "crude" and "could entail risk of social withdrawal and stigmatization," the majority nonetheless finds the condition acceptable because it was "coupled with more socially useful provisions." * * * The majority's position seems to be that even if one condition of a sentence manifestly violates the Sentencing Act, it can be cured by coupling the provision with other, proper ones. When such a novel proposition is put forward and no case law is cited to support it, there is usually a reason. At the end of the day, we *are* charged with evaluating a condition whose primary purpose is to humiliate, and that condition should simply not be upheld.

* * *

I would vacate the sentence and remand for re-sentencing, instructing the district court that public humiliation or shaming has no proper place in our system of justice.

QUESTIONS AND POINTS FOR DISCUSSION

1. If you were on the court of appeals deciding this case, how, if at all, would your analysis and resolution of the two claims in the case be affected if the district court had retained the original requirement that the defendant display the sign attesting to his guilt for one hundred hours? What if the display time was limited to eight hours but the sentencing court did not order the defendant to write letters of apology to victims of his crime and to give speeches at high schools recounting his remorse for his crime? Would that change in the facts alter your disposition of the appeal?

2. Courts have imposed an array of different shame sentences. Examples of such sentences, in addition to those recounted in *Gementera*, include: requiring a man convicted of sexual abuse to place signs outside his home and on his car that said, "Dangerous Sex Offender—No Children Allowed," State v. Bateman, 771 P.2d 314 (Or.Ct.App.1989); displaying on "John TV," a local television channel, the names and pictures of men convicted of soliciting prostitutes; and requiring a woman convicted of welfare fraud to wear a sign announcing, "I stole food from poor people." Dan Markel, Are Shaming Punishments Beautifully Retributive? Retributivism and the Implications for the Alternative Sanctions Debate, 54 Vand.L.Rev. 2157, 2171, 2175 (2001). (The latter defendant, incidentally, opted to go to jail rather than wear the sign.) Other shame sentences have ordered people to get on their hands and knees and apologize to their victims, directed a defendant who killed two people when he drove while intoxicated to hang a picture of his victims in his prison cell, and required a man convicted of assaulting his ex-wife to let her spit in his face. Henry J. Reske, Scarlet Letter Sentences, 82 A.B.A. J. 16, 17 (Jan. 1996). And as part of their sentences for stealing the baby Jesus figure from a nativity scene, two people had to lead a donkey through their hometown while carrying a sign reading "Sorry for the jackass offense." Alicia N. Harden, Rethinking the Shame: The Intersection of Shaming Punishments and American Juvenile Justice, 16 U.C. Davis J. Juv. L. & Pol'y 93, 120 (2012).

In your opinion, are any or all of the above sentences or those discussed in *Gementera* "cruel and unusual" within the meaning of the Eighth Amendment? Why or why not? Some courts have avoided this constitutional question, finding that the imposition of a particular shame punishment was not authorized by the state's sentencing statute. See, e.g., Commonwealth v. Melvin, 103 A.3d 1, 56–57 (Pa. Super. Ct. 2014) (while trial judge had statutory authority to order defendant, a former judge, to write letters of apology to other Pennsylvania judges, the court lacked the authority to direct that the letters be written on photographs of the defendant in handcuffs).

3. Apart from questions regarding courts' authority to impose shame punishments and their constitutionality is the question of their efficacy. While there is little empirical evidence regarding the effects of shame punishments on crime, Professor Toni Massaro has outlined five conditions that shame punishments need to meet in order to be "effective and meaningful":

> First, the potential offenders must be members of an identifiable group, such as a close-knit religious or ethnic community. Second, the legal sanctions must actually compromise potential offenders' group social standing. That is, the affected group must concur with the legal decisionmaker's estimation of what is, or should be, humiliating to group members. Third, the shaming must be communicated to the group and the group must withdraw from the offender—shun her— physically, emotionally, financially, or otherwise. Fourth, the shamed person must fear withdrawal by the group. Finally, the shamed person must be afforded some means of regaining community esteem,

unless the misdeed is so grave that the offender must be permanently exiled or demoted.

Toni M. Massaro, Shame, Culture, and American Criminal Law, 89 Mich. L.Rev. 1880, 1883 (1991). Do these conditions, assuming their validity, suggest that shame punishments would or would not be effectual in the United States? Are there any other considerations that should be factored into a decision whether to incorporate shame punishments into the country's sentencing structures?

4.   Which do you believe would be more effective in impressing upon defendants the significance and harm of their crimes—shame sentences or the restorative-justice conferences discussed in Chapter 1? (See page 22.) Why?

2.   MEDICAL INTERVENTIONS

Medical interventions can be incorporated into a defendant's sentence in ways that may give rise to claims of cruel and unusual punishment. For example, in State v. Brown, 326 S.E.2d 410 (S.C.1985), the trial judge sentenced the defendants, who had been convicted of first-degree criminal sexual conduct, to thirty years in prison. The judge, however, announced that if the defendants agreed to be surgically castrated, he would suspend their prison sentences and place them on probation for five years. The Supreme Court of South Carolina struck down this condition on the grounds that surgical castration, "a form of mutilation," was cruel and unusual punishment under the state's constitution. Id. at 411. Courts have also vacated sentences on statutory grounds when defendants elected to undergo surgical castration in lieu of incarceration or lengthier incarceration, finding that no state statute authorized surgical castration as a criminal penalty for the crime in question. See, e.g., Bruno v. State, 837 So.2d 521, 523 (Fla.Dist.Ct.App.2003).

Through medical research, drugs now have been developed that can "chemically castrate" a man. Some of the men to whom such drugs are administered still can have erections, but the drugs eliminate or dramatically reduce libido and sexual activity. Chemical castration can also have a number of adverse side effects. One of the most frequently administered drugs, medroxyprogesterone acetate, commonly known as Depo-Provera, can cause, among other effects, weight gain, high blood pressure, fatigue, nightmares, hot flashes, muscle aches, smaller testes, and a decrease in bone density. Other serious, though less common, side effects include blood clots, breathing difficulties, depression, and diverticulitis, an intestinal disorder.

The effects of chemical castration on recidivism have not been determined definitively. See Thomas Douglas et al., Coercion, Incarceration, and Chemical Castration: An Argument From Autonomy, 10 Bioethical Inquiry 393, 394–95 (2013). However, some researchers have reported that combining this form of pharmacological treatment with psychotherapy has a greater impact than psychotherapy alone in curbing repeat crimes against children by pedophiles. (Pedophiles fall within the category of people who commit sex crimes who are paraphiliacs—those whose compulsive sexual fantasies propel them to commit sex crimes.) See Ryan C.W. Hall & Richard C.W. Hall, A Profile of Pedophilia: Definition, Characteristics of Offenders, Recidivism, Treatment Outcomes, and Forensic Issues, 82 Mayo Clinic Proc. 457, 466 (April 2007).

Some state statutes authorize or require the chemical castration of certain people convicted of sex offenses. In California, for example, a court, in its discretion, may order that Depo-Provera or a similar drug be administered when persons convicted for the first time of specified sex crimes involving children under the age of thirteen are paroled. Cal. Penal Code § 645(a). Persons convicted for the second time of such crimes must receive Depo-Provera treatments when they are released on parole. Id. § 645(b). Depo-Provera treatments continue until the Board of Prison Terms determines that the treatments are no longer necessary, although a person can avoid the treatments by "voluntarily" undergoing surgical castration. Id. § 645(d)–(e). For one variant of the California statute, see Iowa Code Ann. § 903B.10(1) (also vesting the court with the authority to impose "hormonal intervention therapy" as a condition of release on probation).

QUESTIONS AND POINTS FOR DISCUSSION

1. In your opinion, is the California statute constitutional? Is it wise from a policy perspective? How, if at all, would you modify the statute?

2. The American Civil Liberties Union (ACLU) of Florida has outlined certain conditions that, in its opinion, should be met in order for a defendant to be subjected to chemical castration in lieu of incarceration. Those conditions include the following:

a. A psychiatrist or psychologist must attest that the drug can effectively treat the defendant's sexual problem.

b. The drug must not pose "significant health risks" to the defendant.

c. The drug must not be experimental.

d. The drug's effects must end once the drug is no longer being administered.

e. The defendant must be provided psychotherapy in addition to the drug treatment.

f. The defendant must consent to the drug treatment.

g. Before this consent is obtained, the defendant must consult with counsel and must also be informed by a medical professional of the drug's potential side effects and of the psychotherapy component of the treatment regimen.

h. The state must pay for the consultations if the defendant is indigent.

i. At the sentencing hearing, the judge must: (a) ensure that the defendant understands what the drug treatment entails and that he has been provided the information considered a predicate to informed consent; (b) must identify what sentence the court will impose if the defendant does not undergo treatment; and (c) must apprise the defendant that he can withdraw his consent to the treatment at any time.

j. If the defendant later rescinds his authorization for the drug treatment, the judge should not automatically impose an incarcerative sentence at the resentencing hearing but should instead consider the defendant's reasons for withdrawing from the treatment.

Larry Helm Spalding, Florida's 1997 Chemical Castration Law: A Return to the Dark Ages, 25 Fla. St. U.L.Rev. 117, 137–38 (1998).

CHAPTER 9

PAROLE RELEASE AND PROBATION AND PAROLE REVOCATION

■ ■ ■

Parole boards determine imprisoned persons' suitability for release from prison to serve the remainder of their sentences in the community. Despite the elimination of parole in a number of states, most states have retained discretionary parole release. See Edward Rhine et al., The Future of Parole Release, 46 Crime & Just. 279, 279–80 (2017) (reporting that at least twenty states no longer have parole). In states without it, sentences still often include a period of mandatory supervision in the community upon a person's release from prison. See, e.g., 730 Ill. Comp. Stat. 5/5–8–1(d) on page 92. Some jurisdictions utilize administrative bodies, though perhaps not denominated parole boards, to determine whether people have violated the conditions of their mandatory supervised-release term and should be required to serve some or all of the remainder of the supervision period in prison. See, e.g., 730 Ill. Comp. Stat. 5/3–3–9(a)(3).

In the sections that follow, the constitutional standards that must be adhered to when deciding whether to release people on parole and whether to revoke their parole are discussed. Because the Supreme Court's decision in Morrissey v. Brewer, 408 U.S. 471, 92 S.Ct. 2593 (1972), which concerned parole-revocation proceedings, informed its later decisions concerning parole-release hearings, we will focus first on the subject of parole revocation. References to parole revocation in the ensuing discussion include the revocation of supervised release since the courts have held that the due-process rights that exist in parole-revocation proceedings also extend to the revocation of supervised release. See, e.g., United States v. Jimison, 825 F.3d 260, 263 (5th Cir.2016).

A. PROBATION AND PAROLE REVOCATION

1. DUE PROCESS

MORRISSEY V. BREWER

Supreme Court of the United States, 1972.
408 U.S. 471, 92 S.Ct. 2593, 33 L.Ed.2d 484.

MR. CHIEF JUSTICE BURGER delivered the opinion of the Court.

We granted certiorari in this case to determine whether the Due Process Clause of the Fourteenth Amendment requires that a State afford an individual some opportunity to be heard prior to revoking his parole.

Petitioner Morrissey was convicted of false drawing or uttering of checks in 1967 pursuant to his guilty plea, and was sentenced to not more than seven years' confinement. He was paroled from the Iowa State Penitentiary in June 1968. Seven months later, at the direction of his parole officer, he was arrested in his home town as a parole violator and incarcerated in the county jail. One week later, after review of the parole officer's written report, the Iowa Board of Parole revoked Morrissey's parole, and he was returned to the penitentiary * * *. Petitioner asserts he received no hearing prior to revocation of his parole.

The parole officer's report on which the Board of Parole acted shows that petitioner's parole was revoked on the basis of information that he had violated the conditions of parole by buying a car under an assumed name and operating it without permission, giving false statements to police concerning his address and insurance company after a minor accident, obtaining credit under an assumed name, and failing to report his place of residence to his parole officer. * * *

* * *

I

* * *

During the past 60 years, the practice of releasing prisoners on parole before the end of their sentences has become an integral part of the penological system. Rather than being an *ad hoc* exercise of clemency, parole is an established variation on imprisonment of convicted criminals. Its purpose is to help individuals reintegrate into society as constructive individuals as soon as they are able, without being confined for the full term of the sentence imposed. It also serves to alleviate the costs to society of keeping an individual in prison. * * *

To accomplish the purpose of parole, those who are allowed to leave prison early are subjected to specified conditions for the duration of their terms. These conditions restrict their activities substantially beyond the ordinary restrictions imposed by law on an individual citizen. Typically, parolees are forbidden to use liquor or to have associations or correspondence with certain categories of undesirable persons. Typically, also they must seek permission from their parole officers before engaging in specified activities, such as changing employment or living quarters, marrying, acquiring or operating a motor vehicle, traveling outside the community, and incurring substantial indebtedness. Additionally, parolees must regularly report to the parole officer to whom they are assigned and sometimes they must make periodic written reports of their activities.

* * *

* * * In practice, not every violation of parole conditions automatically leads to revocation. Typically, a parolee will be counseled to abide by the conditions of parole, and the parole officer ordinarily does not take steps to have parole revoked unless he thinks that the violations are serious and continuing so as to indicate that the parolee is not adjusting properly and cannot be counted on to avoid antisocial activity. * * *

* * * The first step in a revocation decision thus involves a wholly retrospective factual question: whether the parolee has in fact acted in violation of one or more conditions of his parole. Only if it is determined that the parolee did violate the conditions does the second question arise: should the parolee be recommitted to prison or should other steps be taken to protect society and improve chances of rehabilitation? The first step is relatively simple; the second is more complex. The second question involves the application of expertise by the parole authority in making a prediction as to the ability of the individual to live in society without committing antisocial acts. This part of the decision, too, depends on facts, and therefore it is important for the board to know not only that some violation was committed but also to know accurately how many and how serious the violations were. Yet this second step, deciding what to do about the violation once it is identified, is not purely factual but also predictive and discretionary.

If a parolee is returned to prison, he usually receives no credit for the time "served" on parole. Thus, the returnee may face a potential of substantial imprisonment.

II

We begin with the proposition that the revocation of parole is not part of a criminal prosecution and thus the full panoply of rights due a defendant in such a proceeding does not apply to parole revocations. Parole arises after the end of the criminal prosecution, including imposition of sentence. * * * Revocation deprives an individual, not of the absolute liberty to which every citizen is entitled, but only of the conditional liberty properly dependent on observance of special parole restrictions.

We turn, therefore, to the question whether the requirements of due process in general apply to parole revocations. * * * Whether any procedural protections are due depends on the extent to which an individual will be "condemned to suffer grievous loss." The question is not merely the "weight" of the individual's interest, but whether the nature of the interest is one within the contemplation of the "liberty or property" language of the Fourteenth Amendment. * * *

We turn to an examination of the nature of the interest of the parolee in his continued liberty. The liberty of a parolee enables him to do a wide range of things open to persons who have never been convicted of any crime. * * * Subject to the conditions of his parole, he can be gainfully employed and is free to be with family and friends and to form the other enduring attachments of normal life. Though the State properly subjects him to many restrictions not applicable to other citizens, his condition is very different from that of confinement in a prison. He may have been on parole for a number of years and may be living a relatively normal life at the time he is faced with revocation.[9] The parolee has relied on at least an implicit promise that parole will be revoked only if he fails to live up to the parole conditions. In many cases, the parolee faces lengthy incarceration if his parole is revoked.

We see, therefore, that the liberty of a parolee, although indeterminate, includes many of the core values of unqualified liberty and its termination inflicts a "grievous loss" on the parolee and often on others. It is hardly useful any longer to try to deal with this problem in terms of whether the parolee's liberty is a "right" or a "privilege." By whatever name, the liberty is valuable and must be seen as within the protection of the Fourteenth Amendment. Its termination calls for some orderly process, however informal.

Turning to the question what process is due, we find that the State's interests are several. The State has found the parolee guilty of a crime against the people. That finding justifies imposing extensive restrictions on the individual's liberty. * * * Given the previous conviction and the proper imposition of conditions, the State has an overwhelming interest in being able to return the individual to imprisonment without the burden of a new adversary criminal trial if in fact he has failed to abide by the conditions of his parole.

Yet, the State has no interest in revoking parole without some informal procedural guarantees. * * *

* * * The parolee is not the only one who has a stake in his conditional liberty. Society has a stake in whatever may be the chance of restoring him to normal and useful life within the law. Society thus has an interest in not

---

9   See, e.g., *Murray v. Page*, 429 F.2d 1359 (C.A.10 1970) (parole revoked after eight years; 15 years remaining on original term).

having parole revoked because of erroneous information or because of an erroneous evaluation of the need to revoke parole, given the breach of parole conditions. And society has a further interest in treating the parolee with basic fairness: fair treatment in parole revocations will enhance the chance of rehabilitation by avoiding reactions to arbitrariness.

* * *

III

We now turn to the nature of the process that is due, bearing in mind that the interest of both State and parolee will be furthered by an effective but informal hearing. In analyzing what is due, we see two important stages in the typical process of parole revocation.

(a)   Arrest of Parolee and Preliminary Hearing. The first stage occurs when the parolee is arrested and detained, usually at the direction of his parole officer. The second occurs when parole is formally revoked. There is typically a substantial time lag between the arrest and the eventual determination by the parole board whether parole should be revoked. Additionally, it may be that the parolee is arrested at a place distant from the state institution, to which he may be returned before the final decision is made concerning revocation. Given these factors, due process would seem to require that some minimal inquiry be conducted at or reasonably near the place of the alleged parole violation or arrest and as promptly as convenient after arrest while information is fresh and sources are available. Such an inquiry should be seen as in the nature of a "preliminary hearing" to determine whether there is probable cause or reasonable ground to believe that the arrested parolee has committed acts that would constitute a violation of parole conditions.

In our view, due process requires that after the arrest, the determination that reasonable ground exists for revocation of parole should be made by someone not directly involved in the case. * * * The officer directly involved in making recommendations cannot always have complete objectivity in evaluating them.[14] * * *

This independent officer need not be a judicial officer. The granting and revocation of parole are matters traditionally handled by administrative officers. * * * It will be sufficient, therefore, in the parole revocation context, if an evaluation of whether reasonable cause exists to believe that conditions of parole have been violated is made by someone such as a parole officer other than the one who has made the report of parole violations or has recommended revocation. A State could certainly choose some other independent decisionmaker to perform this preliminary function.

---

[14]   This is not an issue limited to bad motivation. "Parole agents are human, and it is possible that friction between the agent and parolee may have influenced the agent's judgment."

With respect to the preliminary hearing before this officer, the parolee should be given notice that the hearing will take place and that its purpose is to determine whether there is probable cause to believe he has committed a parole violation. The notice should state what parole violations have been alleged. At the hearing the parolee may appear and speak in his own behalf; he may bring letters, documents, or individuals who can give relevant information to the hearing officer. On request of the parolee, a person who has given adverse information on which parole revocation is to be based is to be made available for questioning in his presence. However, if the hearing officer determines that an informant would be subjected to risk of harm if his identity were disclosed, he need not be subjected to confrontation and cross-examination.

The hearing officer shall have the duty of making a summary, or digest, of what occurs at the hearing in terms of the responses of the parolee and the substance of the documents or evidence given in support of parole revocation and of the parolee's position. Based on the information before him, the officer should determine whether there is probable cause to hold the parolee for the final decision of the parole board on revocation. Such a determination would be sufficient to warrant the parolee's continued detention and return to the state correctional institution pending the final decision. * * * "[T]he decision maker should state the reasons for his determination and indicate the evidence he relied on . . ." but it should be remembered that this is not a final determination calling for "formal findings of fact and conclusions of law." No interest would be served by formalism in this process; informality will not lessen the utility of this inquiry in reducing the risk of error.

(b) The Revocation Hearing. There must also be an opportunity for a hearing, if it is desired by the parolee, prior to the final decision on revocation by the parole authority. This hearing must be the basis for more than determining probable cause; it must lead to a final evaluation of any contested relevant facts and consideration of whether the facts as determined warrant revocation. The parolee must have an opportunity to be heard and to show, if he can, that he did not violate the conditions, or, if he did, that circumstances in mitigation suggest that the violation does not warrant revocation. The revocation hearing must be tendered within a reasonable time after the parolee is taken into custody. A lapse of two months, as respondents suggest occurs in some cases, would not appear to be unreasonable.

* * * Our task is limited to deciding the minimum requirements of due process. They include (a) written notice of the claimed violations of parole; (b) disclosure to the parolee of evidence against him; (c) opportunity to be heard in person and to present witnesses and documentary evidence; (d) the right to confront and cross-examine adverse witnesses (unless the hearing officer specifically finds good cause for not allowing confrontation);

(e) a "neutral and detached" hearing body such as a traditional parole board, members of which need not be judicial officers or lawyers; and (f) a written statement by the factfinders as to the evidence relied on and reasons for revoking parole. We emphasize there is no thought to equate this second stage of parole revocation to a criminal prosecution in any sense. It is a narrow inquiry; the process should be flexible enough to consider evidence including letters, affidavits, and other material that would not be admissible in an adversary criminal trial.

We do not reach or decide the question whether the parolee is entitled to the assistance of retained counsel or to appointed counsel if he is indigent.

* * * The few basic requirements set out above, which are applicable to future revocations of parole, should not impose a great burden on any State's parole system. * * * Obviously a parolee cannot relitigate issues determined against him in other forums, as in the situation presented when the revocation is based on conviction of another crime.

* * *

MR. JUSTICE BRENNAN, with whom MR. JUSTICE MARSHALL joins, concurring in the result.

* * *

The Court * * * states that it does not now decide whether the parolee is also entitled at each hearing to the assistance of retained counsel or of appointed counsel if he is indigent. *Goldberg v. Kelly,* 397 U.S. 254 (1970),[a] nonetheless plainly dictates that he at least "must be allowed to retain an attorney if he so desires." As the Court said there, "Counsel can help delineate the issues, present the factual contentions in an orderly manner, conduct cross-examination, and generally safeguard the interests of" his client. The only question open under our precedents is whether counsel must be furnished the parolee if he is indigent.

MR. JUSTICE DOUGLAS, dissenting in part. [Opinion omitted.]

QUESTIONS AND POINTS FOR DISCUSSION

1.   In Young v. Harper, 520 U.S. 143, 117 S.Ct. 1148 (1997), the Supreme Court held that a "preparole conditional supervision program" under which certain prisoners were released from prison early in order to alleviate prison crowding was sufficiently like parole to give rise to a liberty interest. Under this program, when crowding in the prison system reached a certain level, the parole board could release on "preparole" prisoners who had served 15% of their prison sentences. After serving one third of their sentences, the

---

[a]   *Goldberg v. Kelly* dealt with the procedural safeguards that must attend the termination of welfare benefits.

preparolees then became eligible for parole. But except for what the Supreme Court considered minor differences, release on preparole was like release on parole. Both preparolees and parolees were subject to similar restrictions on their freedom, such as the requirement that they meet at regular intervals with their parole officer. Consequently, participants in the preparole program, according to the Court, could not be sent back to prison unless they were afforded the due-process protections set forth in *Morrissey v. Brewer*.

2. In Gagnon v. Scarpelli, 411 U.S. 778, 93 S.Ct. 1756 (1973), the Supreme Court concluded that before individuals on probation can have their probation revoked, they must be afforded the procedural protections outlined in *Morrissey v. Brewer*. The Court in *Gagnon* also addressed a question left unanswered in *Morrissey*—whether indigent individuals have the right to be represented by appointed counsel during parole- or probation-revocation hearings. Pertinent portions of the Court's opinion discussing this issue are set forth below:

[W]e think that the Court of Appeals erred in accepting respondent's contention that the State is under a constitutional duty to provide counsel for indigents in all probation or parole revocation cases. While such a rule has the appeal of simplicity, it would impose direct costs and serious collateral disadvantages without regard to the need or the likelihood in a particular case for a constructive contribution by counsel. In most cases, the probationer or parolee has been convicted of committing another crime or has admitted the charges against him. And while in some cases he may have a justifiable excuse for the violation or a convincing reason why revocation is not the appropriate disposition, mitigating evidence of this kind is often not susceptible of proof or is so simple as not to require either investigation or exposition by counsel.

The introduction of counsel into a revocation proceeding will alter significantly the nature of the proceeding. If counsel is provided for the probationer or parolee, the State in turn will normally provide its own counsel; lawyers, by training and disposition, are advocates and bound by professional duty to present all available evidence and arguments in support of their clients' positions and to contest with vigor all adverse evidence and views. The role of the hearing body itself, aptly described in *Morrissey* as being "predictive and discretionary" as well as factfinding, may become more akin to that of a judge at a trial, and less attuned to the rehabilitative needs of the individual probationer or parolee. In the greater self-consciousness of its quasi-judicial role, the hearing body may be less tolerant of marginal deviant behavior and feel more pressure to reincarcerate than to continue nonpunitive rehabilitation. Certainly, the decisionmaking process will be prolonged, and the financial cost to the State—for appointed counsel, counsel for the State, a longer record, and the possibility of judicial review—will not be insubstantial.

* * *

We thus find no justification for a new inflexible constitutional rule with respect to the requirement of counsel. We think, rather, that the decision as to the need for counsel must be made on a case-by-case basis in the exercise of a sound discretion by the state authority charged with responsibility for administering the probation and parole system. Although the presence and participation of counsel will probably be both undesirable and constitutionally unnecessary in most revocation hearings, there will remain certain cases in which fundamental fairness—the touchstone of due process—will require that the State provide at its expense counsel for indigent probationers or parolees.

It is neither possible nor prudent to attempt to formulate a precise and detailed set of guidelines to be followed in determining when the providing of counsel is necessary to meet the applicable due process requirements. The facts and circumstances in preliminary and final hearings are susceptible of almost infinite variation, and a considerable discretion must be allowed the responsible agency in making the decision. Presumptively, it may be said that counsel should be provided in cases where, after being informed of his right to request counsel, the probationer or parolee makes such a request, based on a timely and colorable claim (i) that he has not committed the alleged violation of the conditions upon which he is at liberty; or (ii) that, even if the violation is a matter of public record or is uncontested, there are substantial reasons which justified or mitigated the violation and make revocation inappropriate, and that the reasons are complex or otherwise difficult to develop or present. In passing on a request for the appointment of counsel, the responsible agency also should consider, especially in doubtful cases, whether the probationer appears to be capable of speaking effectively for himself. In every case in which a request for counsel at a preliminary or final hearing is refused, the grounds for refusal should be stated succinctly in the record.

Id. at 787–88, 790–91, 93 S.Ct. at 1762–63, 1763–64.

After *Gagnon,* the question still remains whether probationers and parolees have the right to be represented by a retained attorney in probation- and parole-revocation hearings where an indigent would have no right to appointed counsel. Id. at 783 n.6, 93 S.Ct. at 1760 n.6. How would you resolve this question?

3.   Since *Morrissey,* the Supreme Court has concluded that a parolee has no right to an initial preliminary hearing before being transferred back to prison for a suspected parole violation when he or she has already been convicted of the crime upon which the parole revocation is based. The conviction itself provides the requisite probable cause to believe the parolee

has violated the terms and conditions of parole. Moody v. Daggett, 429 U.S. 78, 86 n.7, 97 S.Ct. 274, 278 n.7 (1976).

The Court in *Moody* also clarified the meaning of its observation in *Morrissey* that the opportunity for a final revocation hearing must be afforded a parolee "within a reasonable time after the parolee is taken into custody." The parolee in *Moody* had pled guilty to two crimes—manslaughter and second-degree murder—committed while he was on parole for rape. For these two homicides, he was sentenced to ten years in prison. Following his convictions, the United States Board of Parole issued, but did not execute, a parole-violator warrant. The issuance of the warrant simply held the parolee's rape sentence and parole term in abeyance while he served his other sentences.

Hoping that he could serve any imprisonment resulting from the revocation of his parole at the same time that he was serving the prison sentences for the homicides, the parolee asked the parole board to immediately execute the parole-violator warrant and decide whether to revoke his parole. The parole board refused. The parolee then filed a habeas corpus action contending that any revocation of his parole was barred by the board's failure to afford him the prompt parole-revocation hearing guaranteed by *Morrissey*.

The Supreme Court disagreed, holding that a parolee has no right to a parole-revocation hearing unless and until he is taken into custody as a parole violator. The Court also opined that delaying the parole-revocation hearing made sense in a case such as this one because the parolee's conduct while in prison might be revealing to a parole board later deciding whether revocation of parole was warranted.

4.   According to most courts, due process only requires that probation and parole violations be established by a preponderance of the evidence. State v. Shambly, 795 N.W.2d 884, 897 & n.53 (Neb.2011). In your opinion, should statutes mandate, as some do, application of a higher standard of proof in revocation proceedings? See, e.g., Neb. Rev. Stat. § 29–2267(1) (violation of probation must be established by clear and convincing evidence). Why?

5.   Most courts agree that an acquittal on criminal charges generally will not bar the revocation of probation or parole for the crime of which a probationer or parolee was acquitted. See, e.g., State v. Wetzel, 806 N.W.2d 193, 196–97 (N.D.2011). The courts reason that even if the government was unable to prove the probationer's or parolee's guilt beyond a reasonable doubt, the government may be able to meet the diminished standard of proof applicable in revocation proceedings. Nor does the revocation of probation or parole following an acquittal violate the Fifth Amendment's double-jeopardy prohibition. A revocation proceeding is not considered a new criminal prosecution for the offense of which the probationer or parolee was acquitted but rather an adjunct to the original criminal prosecution that had led to the individual's placement on probation or parole. Cf. Johnson v. United States, 529 U.S. 694, 700–01, 120 S.Ct. 1795, 1800–01 (2000) (noting that reimprisonment after the revocation of supervised release is punishment for

the original offense for which the individual was serving a term of supervised release, not punishment for the violation of release conditions).

Some people might think that if the government decides to proceed first with a revocation hearing and is unable to meet its burden of proof at that hearing, collateral-estoppel principles would bar a subsequent criminal prosecution based on the same alleged underlying conduct. Most of the courts that have addressed this issue, however, have concluded that the outcome of a revocation hearing should not dictate whether a criminal prosecution can go forward. State v. Gautier, 871 A.2d 347, 358 n.5 (R.I.2005) (listing cases). Some of these courts have reasoned that applying collateral-estoppel principles to foreclose a criminal prosecution would frustrate the government's interest in responding quickly to probation and parole violations. Krochta v. Commonwealth, 711 N.E.2d 142, 148 (Mass.1999). In order to avoid a finding against the government at a revocation hearing that would have the effect of barring a future criminal prosecution, the government often might have to delay revocation proceedings.

Critics of the majority view, however, charge that it allows the government to use a revocation proceeding as a "fishing expedition" where it can obtain a preview of the defendant's defense before the criminal trial. State v. McDowell, 699 A.2d 987, 991 (Conn.1997) (Berdon, J., dissenting). These critics contend that permitting the government to treat revocation hearings as a " 'Heads I win, tails I flip again' proposition" will undermine the public's confidence in the justice system. Id. at 992 (quoting Lucido v. Superior Court, 795 P.2d 1223, 1243 (Cal.1990) (Broussard, J., dissenting)). Nor, they add, is an immediate revocation hearing needed to protect the public's safety; if a probationer or parolee charged with criminal conduct poses a threat to the public's safety, that threat can be abated by denying release on bail or imposing appropriate pretrial-release conditions. State v. Brunet, 806 A.2d 1007, 1018 (Vt.2002) (Johnson, J., dissenting).

In your opinion, do public-policy considerations support or weigh against barring a criminal trial after a revocation hearing that resulted in factual findings inconsistent with the defendant's guilt?

6.   A parole-revocation proceeding may raise several issues, including the following: (1) Did the parolee violate a condition of his or her parole? See, e.g., Arciniega v. Freeman, 404 U.S. 4, 92 S.Ct. 22 (1971) (per curiam) (construing a condition that the parolee not associate with other people with criminal records as not encompassing contacts with people employed at the same restaurant). (2) Did the parole board have the statutory authority to impose the condition? (3) Is the condition violated constitutional? (4) Does the violation of the condition warrant the revocation of parole and the parolee's return to prison? Similar questions may arise during probation-revocation proceedings except that a judge, rather than an administrative board or official, generally will decide whether probation should be revoked because of the violation of a condition of probation. For a discussion of statutory and

constitutional constraints on probation and parole conditions, see notes 1 through 6 on pages 267–270 and Chapter 8, Section B.

7.   Sometimes the failure of an individual to abide by the conditions of probation or parole will warrant the modification of those conditions rather than the incarceration or reincarceration of the individual. The question is: When, if ever, does due process accord a right to certain procedural safeguards before the restrictions to which a person is subject as a condition of probation or parole are augmented? How would you answer this question? In doing so, consider the import, if any, of the Supreme Court decisions holding that transfers of inmates to prisons with more onerous conditions of confinement typically do not deprive them of a liberty interest, thereby triggering the protections of due process. See, e.g., Meachum v. Fano, 427 U.S. 215, 96 S.Ct. 2532 (1976).

If you believe that the modification of probation or parole conditions can or does spark the protections of due process, what procedural safeguards, in your opinion, must attend that modification process? Most courts have held that a probationer generally has no due-process right to a court hearing or to the assistance of counsel before the conditions of probation are modified. See, e.g., Stephens v. State, 716 S.E.2d 154, 161 (Ga.2011). If you concur with this view, does it necessarily mean that a probation officer's directive that a probationer be subject to electronic monitoring or participate in a sex-offender treatment program comports with due process?

8.   It always behooves us to remember that procedural safeguards can be extended to an individual even when not mandated by due process. Federal Rule of Criminal Procedure 32.1(c), for example, generally requires that before a court modifies the conditions of probation or supervised release, a hearing be held at which the person who may be subject to more stringent conditions has the rights to counsel, to make a statement, and to present mitigating information to the court.

9.   Many people confined in the nation's prisons and jails are there because their probation or parole has been revoked. Bureau of Justice Statistics, U.S. Dep't of Justice, Prisoners in 2016, at 10–12 (2018) (probation, parole, and other conditional-release violators comprised over a quarter of those admitted to prisons in 2016). A number of these revocations are for nonviolent crimes or for what are called "technical violations" of probation or parole conditions. Technical violations are typically noncriminal violations, such as failing to report, as required, to a probation or parole officer.

The American Bar Association's Model Adult Community Corrections Act, which can be found on pages 282–291, calls for a different approach to probation and parole violations. The Act establishes a rebuttable presumption that a community-based sanction is the appropriate penalty for a violation of a condition of probation or parole that is either noncriminal or constitutes a misdemeanor or a nonviolent felony. Do you agree with the Model Act's recommended approach to probation and parole violations?

10. Title 18 U.S.C. § 3583(e)(2)–(4) is an example of a statute providing judges with a range of options when responding to a defendant's violation of a supervised-release condition. The judge can extend the period of supervised release if the defendant was not sentenced previously to the maximum supervised-release term, or the judge can modify the conditions of the supervised release. Alternatively, the judge can revoke the supervised-release term and require the defendant to serve some or all of the remainder of the term in prison, with no credit for the time already served under postrelease supervision. Finally, as an alternative to incarceration, the judge can order the defendant's confinement at home during nonworking hours, with the confinement monitored electronically or telephonically if the judge so orders.

11. Some states utilize one or more tools to guide responses to violations of release conditions. Some tools classify the violation's severity, specifying whether it warrants a sanction in the low range (e.g., a verbal reprimand), medium range (e.g., a curfew), or high range (e.g., placement in a treatment center or incarceration). Other tools include the person's risk level, as well as the severity of the violation, in the grid used to determine the response-level category into which the violation falls. For examples of instruments developed by states to promote proportional and consistent responses to violations of release conditions, see Memorandum from the Vera Institute of Justice, Center on Sentencing and Corrections, to Public Safety Performance Project, Pew Center on the States (Nov. 26, 2012), available at https://www.appa-net.org/eWeb/Resources/SPSP/State-Response-Guide.pdf.

2. THE FIFTH AMENDMENT PRIVILEGE AGAINST SELF-INCRIMINATION

The Fifth Amendment to the United States Constitution provides in part that "[n]o person . . . shall be compelled in any criminal case to be a witness against himself." This amendment, which directly constrains the federal government, also applies to the states via the Due Process Clause of the Fourteenth Amendment. Malloy v. Hogan, 378 U.S. 1, 6, 84 S.Ct. 1489, 1492 (1964).

Assume that a defendant is convicted of a sex offense, sentenced to probation, and as a condition of probation, required to participate in a sex-offender treatment program. For successful treatment to occur, experts who run the program agree that a person must admit having committed the sex offense of which he or she was convicted. The defendant, however, refuses to admit criminal culpability or discuss the circumstances surrounding the offense. Can the defendant's probation constitutionally be revoked for failure to cooperate in the treatment program? Consider how, if at all, the Supreme Court's analysis in the following case has a bearing on this question.

McKUNE V. LILE

Supreme Court of the United States, 2002.
536 U.S. 24, 122 S.Ct. 2017, 153 L.Ed.2d 47.

JUSTICE KENNEDY announced the judgment of the Court and delivered an opinion, in which THE CHIEF JUSTICE, JUSTICE SCALIA, and JUSTICE THOMAS join.

In 1982, respondent lured a high school student into his car as she was returning home from school. At gunpoint, respondent forced the victim to perform oral sodomy on him and then drove to a field where he raped her. * * * Although respondent maintained that the sexual intercourse was consensual, a jury convicted him of rape, aggravated sodomy, and aggravated kidnapping. * * *

In 1994, a few years before respondent was scheduled to be released, prison officials ordered him to participate in a Sexual Abuse Treatment Program (SATP). As part of the program, participating inmates are required to complete and sign an "Admission of Responsibility" form, in which they discuss and accept responsibility for the crime for which they have been sentenced. Participating inmates also are required to complete a sexual history form, which details all prior sexual activities, regardless of whether such activities constitute uncharged criminal offenses. A polygraph examination is used to verify the accuracy and completeness of the offender's sexual history.

While information obtained from participants advances the SATP's rehabilitative goals, the information is not privileged. Kansas leaves open the possibility that new evidence might be used against sex offenders in future criminal proceedings. In addition, Kansas law requires the SATP staff to report any uncharged sexual offenses involving minors to law enforcement authorities. * * *

Department officials informed respondent that if he refused to participate in the SATP, his privilege status would be reduced from Level III to Level I. As part of this reduction, respondent's visitation rights, earnings, work opportunities, ability to send money to family, canteen expenditures, access to a personal television, and other privileges automatically would be curtailed. In addition, respondent would be transferred to a maximum-security unit, where his movement would be more limited, he would be moved from a two-person to a four-person cell, and he would be in a potentially more dangerous environment.

Respondent refused to participate in the SATP on the ground that the required disclosures of his criminal history would violate his Fifth Amendment privilege against self-incrimination. He brought this action under 42 U.S.C. § 1983 against the warden and the secretary of the Department, seeking an injunction to prevent them from withdrawing his prison privileges and transferring him to a different housing unit.

* * * [T]he United States District Court for the District of Kansas entered summary judgment in respondent's favor. The District Court noted that because respondent had testified at trial that his sexual intercourse with the victim was consensual, an acknowledgement of responsibility for the rape on the "Admission of Guilt" form would subject respondent to a possible charge of perjury. After reviewing the specific loss of privileges and change in conditions of confinement that respondent would face for refusing to incriminate himself, the District Court concluded that these consequences constituted coercion in violation of the Fifth Amendment.

The Court of Appeals for the Tenth Circuit affirmed. * * *

* * *

When convicted sex offenders reenter society, they are much more likely than any other type of offender to be rearrested for a new rape or sexual assault. States thus have a vital interest in rehabilitating convicted sex offenders.

Therapists and correctional officers widely agree that clinical rehabilitative programs can enable sex offenders to manage their impulses and in this way reduce recidivism. An important component of those rehabilitation programs requires participants to confront their past and accept responsibility for their misconduct. * * * Research indicates that offenders who deny all allegations of sexual abuse are three times more likely to fail in treatment than those who admit even partial complicity.

* * *

* * * The SATP lasts for 18 months and involves substantial daily counseling. It helps inmates address sexual addiction; understand the thoughts, feelings, and behavior dynamics that precede their offenses; and develop relapse prevention skills. Although inmates are assured of a significant level of confidentiality, Kansas does not offer legal immunity from prosecution based on any statements made in the course of the SATP. According to Kansas, however, no inmate has ever been charged or prosecuted for any offense based on information disclosed during treatment. There is no contention, then, that the program is a mere subterfuge for the conduct of a criminal investigation.

As the parties explain, Kansas' decision not to offer immunity to every SATP participant serves two legitimate state interests. First, the professionals who design and conduct the program have concluded that for SATP participants to accept full responsibility for their past actions, they must accept the proposition that those actions carry consequences. Although no program participant has ever been prosecuted or penalized based on information revealed during the SATP, the potential for additional punishment reinforces the gravity of the participants' offenses and thereby aids in their rehabilitation. If inmates know society will not punish them for their past offenses, they may be left with the false impression that society does not consider those crimes to be serious ones. The practical effect of guaranteed immunity for SATP participants would be to absolve many sex offenders of any and all cost for their earlier crimes. This is the precise opposite of the rehabilitative objective.

Second, while Kansas as a rule does not prosecute inmates based upon information revealed in the course of the program, the State confirms its valid interest in deterrence by keeping open the option to prosecute a particularly dangerous sex offender. * * *

* * *

* * * The Fifth Amendment Self-Incrimination Clause, which applies to the States via the Fourteenth Amendment, provides that no person "shall be compelled in any criminal case to be a witness against himself." * * * [T]he Court has insisted that the "constitutional guarantee is only that the witness not be *compelled* to give self-incriminating testimony." The consequences in question here—a transfer to another prison where television sets are not placed in each inmate's cell, where exercise facilities are not readily available, and where work and wage opportunities are more limited—are not ones that compel a prisoner to speak about his past crimes despite a desire to remain silent. The fact that these consequences are imposed on prisoners, rather than ordinary citizens, moreover, is important in weighing respondent's constitutional claim.

* * *

* * * The compulsion inquiry must consider the significant restraints already inherent in prison life and the State's own vital interests in rehabilitation goals and procedures within the prison system. A prison clinical rehabilitation program, which is acknowledged to bear a rational relation to a legitimate penological objective, does not violate the privilege against self-incrimination if the adverse consequences an inmate faces for not participating are related to the program objectives and do not constitute atypical and significant hardships in relation to the ordinary incidents of prison life.

* * *

In the present case, respondent's decision not to participate in the Kansas SATP did not extend his term of incarceration. Nor did his decision affect his eligibility for good-time credits or parole. Respondent instead complains that if he remains silent about his past crimes, he will be transferred from the medium-security unit—where the program is conducted—to a less desirable maximum-security unit.

No one contends, however, that the transfer is intended to punish prisoners for exercising their Fifth Amendment rights. Rather, the limitation on these rights is incidental to Kansas' legitimate penological reason for the transfer: Due to limited space, inmates who do not participate in their respective programs will be moved out of the facility where the programs are held to make room for other inmates. * * *

* * *

Respondent also complains that he will be demoted from Level III to Level I status as a result of his decision not to participate. * * * An essential tool of prison administration, however, is the authority to offer inmates various incentives to behave. The Constitution accords prison officials wide latitude to bestow or revoke these perquisites as they see fit. * * *

* * *

The cost to respondent of exercising his Fifth Amendment privilege [is] denial of certain perquisites that make his life in prison more tolerable * * *. * * * [P]lea bargaining does not violate the Fifth Amendment, even though criminal defendants may feel considerable pressure to admit guilt in order to obtain more lenient treatment. See, *e.g., Bordenkircher v. Hayes*, 434 U.S. 357 (1978); *Brady* [*v. United States*], 397 U.S., at 751 [(1970)].

* * *

Respondent is mistaken as well to concentrate on the so-called reward/penalty distinction * * *. The answer to the question whether the government is extending a benefit or taking away a privilege rests entirely in the eye of the beholder. * * * The prison warden in this case stated that it is largely a matter of chance where in a prison an inmate is assigned. Even if Inmates A and B are serving the same sentence for the same crime, Inmate A could end up in a medium-security unit and Inmate B in a maximum-security unit based solely on administrative factors beyond their control. Under respondent's view, however, the Constitution allows the State to offer Inmate B the opportunity to live in the medium-security unit conditioned on his participation in the SATP, but does not allow the State to offer Inmate A the opportunity to live in that same medium-security unit subject to the same conditions. * * * Respondent * * * would have us say the Constitution puts Inmate A in a superior position to Inmate B solely by the accident of the initial assignment to a medium-security unit.

* * * Respondent's reasoning would provide States with perverse incentives to assign all inmates convicted of sex offenses to maximum security prisons until near the time of release, when the rehabilitation program starts. * * *

* * *

The Kansas SATP represents a sensible approach to reducing the serious danger that repeat sex offenders pose to many innocent persons, most often children. The State's interest in rehabilitation is undeniable.

There is, furthermore, no indication that the SATP is merely an elaborate ruse to skirt the protections of the privilege against compelled self-incrimination. Rather, the program allows prison administrators to provide to those who need treatment the incentive to seek it.

* * *

JUSTICE O'CONNOR, concurring in the judgment.

The Court today is divided on the question of what standard to apply when evaluating compulsion for the purposes of the Fifth Amendment privilege against self-incrimination in a prison setting. I write separately because, although I agree with Justice Stevens that the Fifth Amendment compulsion standard is broader than the "atypical and significant hardship" standard * * *, I do not believe that the alterations in respondent's prison conditions as a result of his failure to participate in the Sexual Abuse Treatment Program (SATP) were so great as to constitute compulsion for the purposes of the Fifth Amendment privilege against self-incrimination. I therefore agree with the plurality that the decision below should be reversed.

* * *

I do not believe the consequences facing respondent in this case are serious enough to compel him to be a witness against himself. * * * These changes in living conditions seem to me minor. Because the prison is responsible for caring for respondent's basic needs, his ability to support himself is not implicated by the reduction in wages he would suffer as a result. While his visitation is reduced as a result of his failure to incriminate himself, he still retains the ability to see his attorney, his family, and members of the clergy. The limitation on the possession of personal items, as well as the amount that respondent is allowed to spend at the canteen, may make his prison experience more unpleasant, but seems very unlikely to actually compel him to incriminate himself.

Justice Stevens also suggests that the move to the maximum-security area of the prison would itself be coercive. Although the District Court found that moving respondent to a maximum-security section of the prison would put him "in a more dangerous environment occupied by more serious offenders," there was no finding about how great a danger such a placement posed. Because it is respondent's burden to prove compulsion, we may assume that the prison is capable of controlling its inmates so that respondent's personal safety is not jeopardized by being placed in the maximum-security area of the prison, at least in the absence of proof to the contrary.

* * *

JUSTICE STEVENS, with whom JUSTICE SOUTER, JUSTICE GINSBURG, and JUSTICE BREYER join, dissenting.

* * *

* * * [T]he Fifth Amendment guarantees * * * the right of a person to remain silent unless he chooses to speak in the unfettered exercise of his own will, and to suffer no penalty . . . for such silence." * * * [W]e have found prohibited compulsion in the threatened loss of the right to participate in political associations, *Lefkowitz v. Cunningham*, 431 U.S. 801 (1977), forfeiture of government contracts, *Lefkowitz v. Turley*, 414 U.S. [70], at 82 [1973], loss of employment, *Uniformed Sanitation Men Ass'n, Inc. v. Commissioner of Sanitation of City of New York*, 392 U.S. 280 (1968), and disbarment, *Spevack v. Klein*, 385 U.S. 511, 516 (1967). None of our opinions contains any suggestion that compulsion should have a different meaning in the prison context. * * *

* * *

The plurality and Justice O'Connor hold that the consequences stemming from respondent's invocation of the privilege are not serious enough to constitute compulsion. * * *

It took respondent several years to acquire the status that he occupied in 1994 when he was ordered to participate in the SATP. Because of the nature of his convictions, in 1983 the Department initially placed him in a maximum-security classification. Not until 1989 did the Department change his "security classification to 'medium by exception' because of his good behavior." Thus, the sanction at issue threatens to deprive respondent of a status in the prison community that it took him six years to earn and which he had successfully maintained for five more years when he was ordered to incriminate himself. Moreover, abruptly "busting" his custody back to Level I would impose the same stigma on him as would a disciplinary conviction for any of the most serious offenses * * *. * * * This same loss of privileges is considered serious enough by prison authorities that it is used as punishment for theft, drug abuse, assault, and possession of dangerous contraband.

The punitive consequences of the discipline include not only the dignitary and reputational harms flowing from the transfer, but a serious loss of tangible privileges as well. Because he refused to participate in the SATP, respondent's visitation rights will be restricted. He will be able to earn only $0.60 per day, as compared to Level III inmates, who can potentially earn minimum wage. His access to prison organizations and activities will be limited. He will no longer be able to send his family more than $30 per pay period. He will be prohibited from spending more than $20 per payroll period at the canteen, rather than the $140 he could spend at Level III, and he will be restricted in what property he can keep in his cell. In addition, because he will be transferred to a maximum-security unit, respondent will be forced to share a cell with three other inmates rather than one, and his movement outside the cell will be substantially curtailed. The District Court found that the maximum-security unit is "a more dangerous environment occupied by more serious offenders."[9] Perhaps most importantly, respondent will no longer be able to earn his way back up to Level III status through good behavior during the remainder of his sentence. ("To complete Level I, an inmate must . . . demonstrate a willingness to participate in recommended programs and/or work assignments for a full review cycle").

* * *

* * * We have recognized that the government can extend a benefit in exchange for incriminating statements, but cannot threaten to take away privileges as the cost of invoking Fifth Amendment rights, see *e.g., Turley*, 414 U.S., at 82; *Spevack*, 385 U.S., at 516. * * *[10]

* * * The plurality contends that the transfer from medium to maximum security and the associated loss of Level III status is not intended to punish prisoners for asserting their Fifth Amendment rights, but rather is merely incidental to the prison's legitimate interest in making room for participants in the program. * * * [P]etitioners have not alleged that respondent is taking up a bed in a unit devoted to the SATP; therefore, all the Department would have to do is allow respondent to stay in his current medium-security cell. If need be, the Department could always transfer respondent to another medium-security unit. Given the absence of evidence in the record that the Department has a shortage of medium-security beds, or even that there is a separate unit devoted to participants in the SATP, the only plausible explanation for the transfer to maximum security and loss of Level III status is that it serves as punishment for refusing to participate in the program.

* * *

* * * The State's interests in law enforcement and rehabilitation are present in every criminal case. If those interests were sufficient to justify

---

[9] Respondent attested to the fact that in his experience maximum security "is a very hostile, intimidating environment because most of the inmates in maximum tend to have longer sentences and are convicted of more serious crimes, and, as a consequence, care less how they act or treat others." He explained that in the maximum-security unit "there is far more gang activity," "reported and unreported rapes and assaults of inmates are far more prevalent," and "sex offenders . . . are seen as targets for rape and physical and mental assault[s]," whereas in medium security, "because the inmates want to maintain their medium security status, they are less prone to breaking prison rules or acting violently."

[10] * * * While it is true that in some cases the line between enhancing punishment and refusing leniency may be difficult to draw, that does not mean the distinction is irrelevant for Fifth Amendment purposes. * * *

impinging on prisoners' Fifth Amendment right, inmates would soon have no privilege left to invoke.

The plurality's willingness to sacrifice prisoners' Fifth Amendment rights is also unwarranted because available alternatives would allow the State to achieve the same objectives without impinging on inmates' privilege. The most obvious alternative is to grant participants use immunity. Petitioners have not provided any evidence that the program's therapeutic aims could not be served equally well by granting use immunity. * * * In fact, the program's rehabilitative goals would likely be furthered by ensuring free and open discussion without the threat of prosecution looming over participants' therapy sessions.

The plurality contends that requiring immunity will undermine the therapeutic goals of the program because once "inmates know society will not punish them for their past offenses, they may be left with the false impression that society does not consider those crimes to be serious ones." The idea that an inmate who is confined to prison for almost 20 years for an offense could be left with the impression that his crimes are not serious or that wrongdoing does not carry consequences is absurd. Moreover, the argument starts from a false premise. Granting use immunity does not preclude prosecution; it merely prevents the State from using an inmate's own words, and the fruits thereof, against him in a subsequent prosecution. * * *

Alternatively, the State could continue to pursue its rehabilitative goals without violating participants' Fifth Amendment rights by offering inmates a voluntary program. * * * Indeed, there is reason to believe successful rehabilitation is more likely for voluntary participants than for those who are compelled to accept treatment. See Abel, Mittelman, Becker, Rathner & Rouleau, Predicting Child Molesters' Response to Treatment, 528 Annals N.Y. Acad. of Sciences 223 (1988) (finding that greater perceived pressure to participate in treatment is strongly correlated with the dropout rate).

Through its treatment program, Kansas seeks to achieve the admirable goal of reducing recidivism among sex offenders. * * * No matter what the goal, inmates should not be compelled to forfeit the privilege against self-incrimination simply because the ends are legitimate or because they have been convicted of sex offenses. Particularly in a case like this one, in which respondent has protested his innocence all along and is being compelled to confess to a crime that he still insists he did not commit, we ought to ask ourselves—what if this is one of those rare cases in which the jury made a mistake and he is actually innocent? And in answering that question, we should consider that even members of the Star Chamber thought they were pursuing righteous ends.

* * *

QUESTIONS AND POINTS FOR DISCUSSION

1.   In Minnesota v. Murphy, 465 U.S. 420, 104 S.Ct. 1136 (1984), the Supreme Court considered the admissibility in a criminal trial of incriminating statements made by the defendant during a meeting with his probation officer. At the time of the meeting, the defendant was on probation for the crime of false imprisonment, and one of the conditions of his probation was that he "be truthful" with his probation officer "in all matters." When questioned by his probation officer during the meeting about his suspected involvement in a rape and murder of a woman many years earlier, the defendant admitted committing the crimes.

The Supreme Court first rebuffed the defendant's argument that his incriminating statements should have been suppressed in his trial for murder because the probation officer failed to give him *Miranda* warnings before questioning him. The Court observed that when the defendant met with his probation officer in her office, he was not "in custody" within the meaning of *Miranda,* and therefore no *Miranda* warnings were necessary.

The defendant also argued that his incriminating statements should have been suppressed because when he was questioned by the probation officer, an unconstitutional burden had been placed on the exercise of his Fifth Amendment privilege against self-incrimination. He maintained that because of the probation condition requiring him to respond truthfully to his probation officer's questions, he faced a Hobson's choice: either respond to those questions, thereby providing evidence to be used against him in a criminal prosecution, or refuse to answer the questions and have his probation revoked. The Supreme Court, however, refused to construe the probation condition as requiring the defendant to answer questions when those answers might be incriminating in a criminal prosecution of the defendant. As the Court's discussion, set forth below, of some of the Fifth Amendment implications of probation interviews reveals, the result in the case would have been different had the Court found that the probation condition required the defendant, upon threat of revocation, to provide responses that could be used against him in a criminal prosecution:

> A State may require a probationer to appear and discuss matters that affect his probationary status; such a requirement, without more, does not give rise to a self-executing privilege. The result may be different if the questions put to the probationer, however relevant to his probationary status, call for answers that would incriminate him in a pending or later criminal prosecution. There is thus a substantial basis in our cases for concluding that if the State, either expressly or by implication, asserts that invocation of the privilege would lead to revocation of probation, it would have created the classic penalty situation, the failure to assert the privilege would be excused, and the

probationer's answers would be deemed compelled and inadmissible in a criminal prosecution.[7]

* * *

If Murphy did harbor a belief that his probation might be revoked for exercising the Fifth Amendment privilege, that belief would not have been reasonable. Our decisions have made clear that the State could not constitutionally carry out a threat to revoke probation for the legitimate exercise of the Fifth Amendment privilege.

Id. at 435 & n.7, 438, 104 S.Ct. at 1146 & n.7, 1148.

2.   In Ohio Adult Parole Authority v. Woodard, 523 U.S. 272, 118 S.Ct. 1244 (1998), a prisoner who had been sentenced to death contended that an interview in which he could participate as part of the clemency-review process impinged on his Fifth Amendment privilege against self-incrimination. By not affording him immunity for statements he made during the interview, the prisoner asserted that he was placed between the proverbial rock and a hard place. If he agreed to be interviewed and then made incriminating statements, he might doom his chances of obtaining postconviction relief from his conviction or death sentence. But if he refused to be interviewed, his silence might be used against him, thereby negating any prospect of obtaining a commutation of his sentence.

The Supreme Court rejected the prisoner's claim. Noting that the decision to participate in a clemency interview is a voluntary one, the Court held that the compulsion that would give rise to a Fifth Amendment violation was absent. According to the Court, the choice to participate or not in a clemency interview was no more difficult or constitutionally problematic than the choice

---

[7]   The situation would be different if the questions put to a probationer were relevant to his probationary status and posed no realistic threat of incrimination in a separate criminal proceeding. If, for example, a residential restriction were imposed as a condition of probation, it would appear unlikely that a violation of that condition would be a criminal act. Hence, a claim of the Fifth Amendment privilege in response to questions relating to a residential condition could not validly rest on the ground that the answer might be used to incriminate if the probationer was tried for another crime. Neither, in our view, would the privilege be available on the ground that answering such questions might reveal a violation of the residential requirement and result in the termination of probation. Although a revocation proceeding must comport with the requirements of due process, it is not a criminal proceeding. Just as there is no right to a jury trial before probation may be revoked, neither is the privilege against compelled self-incrimination available to a probationer. It follows that whether or not the answer to a question about a residential requirement is compelled by the threat of revocation, there can be no valid claim of the privilege on the ground that the information sought can be used in revocation proceedings.

Our cases indicate, moreover, that a State may validly insist on answers to even incriminating questions and hence sensibly administer its probation system, as long as it recognizes that the required answers may not be used in a criminal proceeding and thus eliminates the threat of incrimination. Under such circumstances, * * * nothing in the Federal Constitution would prevent a State from revoking probation for a refusal to answer that violated an express condition of probation or from using the probationer's silence as "one of a number of factors to be considered by the finder of fact" in deciding whether other conditions of probation have been violated.

faced by criminal defendants when deciding whether to testify at trial. Do you agree?

3.   Reconsider, in light of the Supreme Court decisions of which you have just read, the question posed earlier in this chapter: Would the revocation of the probation of an individual required, as a condition of probation, to participate in a sex-offender treatment program violate the Fifth Amendment privilege against self-incrimination when the revocation was based on the individual's refusal to discuss sex-related crimes? Are there any additional facts you would want to know before answering this question? Is it constitutionally relevant whether eligibility for participation in the treatment program required the probationer to discuss sex crimes with which he had not been charged and convicted or only the crime of conviction? Compare United States v. Antelope, 395 F.3d 1128, 1137–39 (9th Cir.2005) (holding that revoking probation, and later supervised release, because of defendant's refusal to divulge his sexual history, including sex crimes other than the crime of which the defendant was convicted, violated the Fifth Amendment privilege) with State v. Pritchett, 69 P.3d 1278, 1285–87 (Utah 2003) (requiring defendant, who received a five-year prison sentence, to admit committing the sex offense of which he was convicted to be eligible for probation and placement in a residential treatment center for people who have committed sex offenses did not violate the privilege against self-incrimination).

4.   It is important to remember that compulsion alone does not give rise to a Fifth Amendment claim. To prevail on such a claim, the person asserting it must face a "real and appreciable" risk of incrimination. Hiibel v. Sixth Judicial Dist. Court of Nev., Humboldt Cty., 542 U.S. 177, 190, 124 S.Ct. 2451, 2460 (2004). In Johnson v. Fabian, 735 N.W.2d 295, 310–11 (Minn.2007), the Minnesota Supreme Court found that two prisoners, both of whom had refused to participate in a sex-offender treatment program in which they had to admit committing the sex crimes of which they had been convicted, were confronted with the requisite risk of self-incrimination. One prisoner's criminal case was pending on appeal at the time he refused to participate in the treatment program. And the court concluded that the other prisoner faced a genuine risk during the treatment program of incriminating himself of the crime of perjury because at trial, he had denied committing the sex offense that he was supposed to admit committing as part of his treatment.

Do you agree with the court's conclusions? What if the first prisoner's case was no longer on appeal, but he was seeking postconviction relief from the conviction? What if a prosecution of the second prisoner for perjury was barred by the statute of limitations?

3.   THE FOURTH AMENDMENT

Not only are the rights of probationers and parolees limited because of the restrictions placed on them as conditions of probation or parole, but they are also limited because the Constitution affords them less protection than that afforded individuals not subject to probation or parole supervision. The following Supreme Court case is one of several that illustrate that the Fourth Amendment applies differently to probationers and parolees.

GRIFFIN V. WISCONSIN

Supreme Court of the United States, 1987.
483 U.S. 868, 107 S.Ct. 3164, 97 L.Ed.2d 709.

JUSTICE SCALIA delivered the opinion of the Court.

* * *

On September 4, 1980, Griffin, who had previously been convicted of a felony, was convicted in Wisconsin state court of resisting arrest, disorderly conduct, and obstructing an officer. He was placed on probation.

Wisconsin law puts probationers in the legal custody of the State Department of Health and Social Services and renders them "subject . . . to . . . conditions set by the court and rules and regulations established by the department." One of the Department's regulations permits any probation officer to search a probationer's home without a warrant as long as his supervisor approves and as long as there are "reasonable grounds" to believe the presence of contraband—including any item that the probationer cannot possess under the probation conditions. * * * Another regulation makes it a violation of the terms of probation to refuse to consent to a home search. And still another forbids a probationer to possess a firearm without advance approval from a probation officer.

On April 5, 1983, while Griffin was still on probation, Michael Lew, the supervisor of Griffin's probation officer, received information from a detective on the Beloit Police Department that there were or might be guns in Griffin's apartment. Unable to secure the assistance of Griffin's own probation officer, Lew, accompanied by another probation officer and three plainclothes policemen, went to the apartment. When Griffin answered the door, Lew told him who they were and informed him that they were going to search his home. During the subsequent search—carried out entirely by the probation officers under the authority of Wisconsin's probation regulation—they found a handgun.

Griffin was charged with possession of a firearm by a convicted felon, which is itself a felony. He moved to suppress the evidence seized during the search. The trial court denied the motion * * *. A jury convicted Griffin of the firearms violation, and he was sentenced to two years' imprisonment. * * *

* * *

A probationer's home, like anyone else's, is protected by the Fourth Amendment's requirement that searches be "reasonable." Although we usually require that a search be undertaken only pursuant to a warrant (and thus supported by probable cause, as the Constitution says warrants must be), we have permitted exceptions when "special needs, beyond the normal need for law enforcement, make the warrant and probable-cause requirement impracticable." * * *

A State's operation of a probation system * * * presents "special needs" beyond normal law enforcement that may justify departures from the usual warrant and probable-cause requirements. * * *

[Probation] restrictions are meant to assure that the probation serves as a period of genuine rehabilitation and that the community is not harmed by the probationer's being at large. These same goals require and justify the exercise of supervision to assure that the restrictions are in fact observed. * * * Supervision, then, is a "special need" of the State permitting a degree of impingement upon privacy that would not be constitutional if applied to the public at large. That permissible degree is not unlimited, however, so we next turn to whether it has been exceeded here.

* * *

A warrant requirement would interfere to an appreciable degree with the probation system, setting up a magistrate rather than the probation officer as the judge of how close a supervision the probationer requires. Moreover, the delay inherent in obtaining a warrant would make it more difficult for probation officials to respond quickly to evidence of misconduct and would reduce the deterrent effect that the possibility of expeditious searches would otherwise create. By way of analogy, one might contemplate how parental custodial authority would be impaired by requiring judicial approval for search of a minor child's room. And * * * [a]lthough a probation officer is not an impartial magistrate, neither is he the police officer who normally conducts searches against the ordinary citizen. He is an employee of the State Department of Health and Social Services who, while assuredly charged with protecting the public interest, is also supposed to have in mind the welfare of the probationer * * *. * * *

Justice Blackmun's dissent would retain a judicial warrant requirement, though agreeing with our subsequent conclusion that reasonableness of the search does not require probable cause. This, however, is a combination that neither the text of the Constitution nor any of our prior decisions permits. While it is possible to say that Fourth Amendment reasonableness demands probable cause without a judicial warrant, the reverse runs up against the constitutional provision that "no Warrants shall issue, but upon probable cause." Amdt. 4. * * *

We think that the probation regime would also be unduly disrupted by a requirement of probable cause. * * * First, even more than the requirement of a warrant, a probable-cause requirement would reduce the deterrent effect of the supervisory arrangement. The probationer would be assured that so long as his illegal (and perhaps socially dangerous) activities were sufficiently concealed as to give rise to no more than reasonable suspicion, they would go undetected and uncorrected. The second difference is * * * we deal with a situation in which there is an ongoing supervisory relationship—and one that is not, or at least not entirely, adversarial—between the object of the search and the decisionmaker.

In such circumstances it is both unrealistic and destructive of the whole object of the continuing probation relationship to insist upon the same degree of demonstrable reliability of particular items of supporting data, and upon the same degree of certainty of violation, as is required in other contexts. In some cases—especially those involving drugs or illegal weapons—the probation agency must be able to act based upon a lesser degree of certainty than the Fourth Amendment would otherwise require in order to intervene before a probationer does damage to himself or society. * * *

* * *

The search of Griffin's residence was "reasonable" within the meaning of the Fourth Amendment because it was conducted pursuant to a valid regulation governing probationers. * * *

JUSTICE BLACKMUN, with whom JUSTICE MARSHALL joins and, as to Parts I-B and I-C, JUSTICE BRENNAN joins and, as to Part I-C, JUSTICE STEVENS joins, dissenting.[b]

In ruling that the home of a probationer may be searched by a probation officer without a warrant, the Court today takes another step that diminishes the protection given by the Fourth Amendment to the "right of the people to be secure in their persons, houses, papers, and effects, against unreasonable searches and seizures." In my view, petitioner's probationary status provides no reason to abandon the warrant requirement. The probation system's special law enforcement needs may justify a search by a probation officer on the basis of "reasonable suspicion," but even that standard was not met in this case.

* * *

---

[b] Justice Brennan did not join the portion of Justice Blackmun's dissenting opinion asserting that a search of a probationer's home can be grounded on "reasonable suspicion," a level of suspicion lower than probable cause. Justice Brennan joined those portions of the dissenting opinion maintaining that a warrant is needed for this kind of search and concluding that there was no reasonable suspicion to support the search in this case. Justice Stevens agreed with this latter conclusion.

QUESTIONS AND POINTS FOR DISCUSSION

1.   In United States v. Knights, 534 U.S. 112, 122 S.Ct. 587 (2001), the Supreme Court even more narrowly construed the scope of probationers' Fourth Amendment rights, upholding a warrantless search of a probationer's apartment conducted by a detective from the sheriff's office who had a reasonable suspicion that the apartment contained evidence of several crimes. In balancing the intrusiveness of these kinds of searches against the need for them, the Court emphasized that their intrusiveness is diminished because the liberty of probationers already is restricted. The Court also said that because probationers have such a high recidivism rate, there is a significant need to permit law-enforcement officials to conduct warrantless searches of their residences. See also People v. Johns, 795 N.E.2d 433, 444 (Ill.App.Ct.2003) (Myerscough, J., dissenting) ("Law enforcement is armed and better equipped to conduct these searches.")

2.   Because the search at issue in *Knights* was grounded on reasonable suspicion, the Court did not address the question whether a search conducted without reasonable suspicion would pass constitutional muster. How would you resolve this question? However you resolve it, would a suspicionless search, in any event, be constitutional if, as a condition of being placed on probation, the defendant had agreed to have his residence searched without any reasonable suspicion?

In the case that follows, the Supreme Court explored some of the Fourth Amendment ramifications of a condition predicating parole release on a prisoner's agreement to be searched by parole or police officers without a warrant and without cause. As you read this case, consider its implications for probationers.

SAMSON V. CALIFORNIA
Supreme Court of the United States, 2006.
547 U.S. 843, 126 S.Ct. 2193, 165 L.Ed.2d 250.

JUSTICE THOMAS delivered the opinion of the Court.

California law provides that every prisoner eligible for release on state parole "shall agree in writing to be subject to search or seizure by a parole officer or other peace officer at any time of the day or night, with or without a search warrant and with or without cause." Cal.Penal Code Ann. § 3067(a). We granted certiorari to decide whether a suspicionless search, conducted under the authority of this statute, violates the Constitution. * * *

In September 2002, petitioner Donald Curtis Samson was on state parole in California, following a conviction for being a felon in possession of a firearm. On September 6, 2002, Officer Alex Rohleder of the San Bruno Police Department observed petitioner walking down a street with a

SEC. A   PROBATION AND PAROLE REVOCATION   443

woman and a child. Based on a prior contact with petitioner, Officer Rohleder was aware that petitioner was on parole * * *.

* * * [P]ursuant to Cal.Penal Code Ann. § 3067(a) and based solely on petitioner's status as a parolee, Officer Rohleder searched petitioner. During the search, Officer Rohleder found a cigarette box in petitioner's left breast pocket. Inside the box he found a plastic baggie containing methamphetamine.

The State charged petitioner with possession of methamphetamine * * *. The trial court denied petitioner's motion to suppress the methamphetamine evidence * * *. A jury convicted petitioner of the possession charge and the trial court sentenced him to seven years' imprisonment.

The California Court of Appeal affirmed. Relying on *People v. Reyes,* 968 P.2d 445 ([Cal.] 1998), the court held that suspicionless searches of parolees are lawful under California law; that " '[s]uch a search is reasonable within the meaning of the Fourth Amendment as long as it is not arbitrary, capricious or harassing' "; and that the search in this case was not arbitrary, capricious, or harassing.

* * *

"[U]nder our general Fourth Amendment approach" we "examin[e] the totality of the circumstances" to determine whether a search is reasonable within the meaning of the Fourth Amendment. Whether a search is reasonable "is determined by assessing, on the one hand, the degree to which it intrudes upon an individual's privacy and, on the other, the degree to which it is needed for the promotion of legitimate governmental interests."

* * *

[P]arolees are on the "continuum" of state-imposed punishments. On this continuum, parolees have fewer expectations of privacy than probationers, because parole is more akin to imprisonment than probation is to imprisonment. * * * "In most cases, the State is willing to extend parole only because it is able to condition it upon compliance with certain requirements."

* * * The extent and reach of these conditions clearly demonstrate that parolees like petitioner have severely diminished expectations of privacy by virtue of their status alone.

Additionally, * * * the parole search condition under California law—requiring inmates who opt for parole to submit to suspicionless searches by a parole officer or other peace officer "at any time"—was "clearly expressed" to petitioner. He signed an order submitting to the condition and thus was "unambiguously" aware of it. In *Knights,* we found that acceptance of a clear and unambiguous search condition "significantly diminished Knights' reasonable expectation of privacy." Examining the totality of the circumstances pertaining to petitioner's status as a parolee, "an established variation on imprisonment," including the plain terms of the parole search condition, we conclude that petitioner did not have an expectation of privacy that society would recognize as legitimate.[3]

The State's interests, by contrast, are substantial. This Court has repeatedly acknowledged that a State has an "overwhelming interest" in supervising parolees because "parolees . . . are more likely to commit future criminal offenses." Similarly, this Court has repeatedly acknowledged that a State's interests in reducing recidivism and thereby promoting reintegration and positive citizenship among probationers and parolees warrant privacy intrusions that would not otherwise be tolerated under the Fourth Amendment.

The empirical evidence presented in this case clearly demonstrates the significance of these interests to the State of California. * * * California's parolee population has a 68-to-70 percent recidivism rate. See California Attorney General, Crime in California 37 (Apr.2001) (explaining that 68 percent of adult parolees are returned to prison, 55 percent for a parole violation, 13 percent for the commission of a new felony offense). * * *

* * *

* * * Imposing a reasonable suspicion requirement, as urged by petitioner, would give parolees greater opportunity to anticipate searches and conceal criminality. This Court concluded that the incentive-to-conceal concern justified an "intensive" system for supervising probationers in *Griffin*. That concern applies with even greater force to a system of supervising parolees.

Petitioner observes that the majority of States and the Federal Government have been able to further similar interests in reducing recidivism and promoting re-integration, despite having systems that permit parolee searches based upon some level of suspicion. * * * Petitioner's reliance on the practices of jurisdictions other than California, however, is misplaced. That some States and the Federal Government require a level of individualized suspicion is of little relevance to our determination whether California's supervisory system is drawn to meet its needs and is reasonable, taking into account a parolee's substantially diminished expectation of privacy.

---

[3] Because we find that the search at issue here is reasonable under our general Fourth Amendment approach, we need not reach the issue whether "acceptance of the search condition constituted consent in the * * * sense of a complete waiver of his Fourth Amendment rights." * * * Nor do we address whether California's parole search condition is justified as a special need under *Griffin v. Wisconsin*, 483 U.S. 868 (1987), because our holding under general Fourth Amendment principles renders such an examination unnecessary.

* * * The concern that California's suspicionless search system gives officers unbridled discretion to conduct searches, thereby inflicting dignitary harms that arouse strong resentment in parolees and undermine their ability to reintegrate into productive society, is belied by California's prohibition on "arbitrary, capricious or harassing" searches.[5] The dissent's claim that parolees under California law are subject to capricious searches conducted at the unchecked "whim" of law enforcement officers ignores this prohibition. * * *

Thus, we conclude that the Fourth Amendment does not prohibit a police officer from conducting a suspicionless search of a parolee. * * *

* * *

JUSTICE STEVENS, with whom JUSTICE SOUTER and JUSTICE BREYER join, dissenting.

Our prior cases have consistently assumed that the Fourth Amendment provides some degree of protection for probationers and parolees. The protection is not as robust as that afforded to ordinary citizens; we have held that probationers' lowered expectation of privacy may justify their warrantless search upon reasonable suspicion of wrongdoing. * * * But neither *Knights* nor *Griffin* supports a regime of suspicionless searches, conducted pursuant to a blanket grant of discretion untethered by any procedural safeguards, by law enforcement personnel who have no special interest in the welfare of the parolee or probationer.

* * *

The suspicionless search is the very evil the Fourth Amendment was intended to stamp out. The pre-Revolutionary "writs of assistance," which permitted roving searches for contraband, were reviled precisely because they "placed 'the liberty of every man in the hands of every petty officer.'" While individualized suspicion "is not an 'irreducible' component of reasonableness" under the Fourth Amendment, the requirement has been dispensed with only when programmatic searches were required to meet a " 'special need' . . . divorced from the State's general interest in law enforcement."

* * *

Ignoring just how "closely guarded" is that "category of constitutionally permissible suspicionless searches," the Court for the first time upholds an entirely suspicionless search unsupported by any special need. And it goes further: In special needs cases we have at least insisted upon programmatic safeguards designed to ensure evenhandedness in application; if individualized suspicion is to be jettisoned, it must be

---

[5]   Under California precedent, we note, an officer would not act reasonably in conducting a suspicionless search absent knowledge that the person stopped for the search is a parolee.

replaced with measures to protect against the state actor's unfettered discretion.[c] Here, by contrast, there are no policies in place—no "standards, guidelines, or procedures"—to rein in officers and furnish a bulwark against the arbitrary exercise of discretion that is the height of unreasonableness.

* * *

Nor is it enough, in deciding whether someone's expectation of privacy is "legitimate," to rely on the existence of the offending condition or the individual's notice thereof. * * * [T]he loss of a subjective expectation of privacy would play "no meaningful role" in analyzing the legitimacy of expectations, for example, "if the Government were suddenly to announce on nationwide television that all homes henceforth would be subject to warrantless entry."[4]

* * *

Had the State imposed as a condition of parole a requirement that petitioner submit to random searches by his parole officer, who is "supposed to have in mind the welfare of the [parolee]" and guide the parolee's transition back into society, the condition might have been justified either under the special needs doctrine or because at least part of the requisite "reasonable suspicion" is supplied in this context by the individual-specific knowledge gained through the supervisory relationship. Likewise, this might have been a different case had a court or parole board imposed the condition at issue based on specific knowledge of the individual's criminal history and projected likelihood of reoffending, or if the State had had in place programmatic safeguards to ensure evenhandedness. Under either of those scenarios, the State would at least have gone some way toward averting the greatest mischief wrought by officials' unfettered discretion. * * *[6]

---

[c] Because of the absence of such "programmatic safeguards," the Supreme Court, for example, held in Florida v. Wells, 495 U.S. 1, 110 S.Ct. 1632 (1990) that the search of a suitcase as part of an inventory search of an impounded car violated the Fourth Amendment. The Court noted that since the jurisdiction in question had no policy governing containers found during inventory searches of vehicles, people were subject to police officers' "uncanalized discretion" when they were deciding whether to open the containers. Id. at 4, 110 S.Ct. at 1635.

[4] Likewise, the State's argument that a California parolee "consents" to the suspicionless search condition is sophistry. Whether or not a prisoner can choose to remain in prison rather than be released on parole, he has no "choice" concerning the search condition; he may either remain in prison, where he will be subjected to suspicionless searches, or he may exit prison and still be subject to suspicionless searches. Accordingly, "to speak of consent in this context is to resort to a manifest fiction, for the [parolee] who purportedly waives his rights by accepting such a condition has little genuine option to refuse."

[6] The Court devotes a good portion of its analysis to the recidivism rates among parolees in California. * * * Of course, one cannot deny that the interest itself is valid. That said, though, it has never been held sufficient to justify suspicionless searches. If high crime rates were grounds enough for disposing of Fourth Amendment protections, the Amendment long ago would have become a dead letter.

The Court seems to acknowledge that unreasonable searches "inflic[t] dignitary harms that arouse strong resentment in parolees and undermine their ability to reintegrate into productive society." It is satisfied, however, that the California courts' prohibition against " 'arbitrary, capricious or harassing' " searches suffices to avert those harms * * *. I am unpersuaded. The requirement of individualized suspicion, in all its iterations, is the shield the Framers selected to guard against the evils of arbitrary action, caprice, and harassment. To say that those evils may be averted without that shield is, I fear, to pay lipservice to the end while withdrawing the means.

* * *

QUESTIONS AND POINTS FOR DISCUSSION

1. Do you agree with the majority's conclusion that the search at issue in *Samson* comported with the Fourth Amendment? If not, would the alternative ways proffered by Justice Stevens to curtail officials' discretion in conducting searches of parolees obviate the Fourth Amendment problem?

2. A state court, of course, has the prerogative to interpret the protections afforded by the state's constitution more expansively than the Supreme Court's construction of the protections emanating from the United States Constitution. The Supreme Court of Iowa, for example, rejected the reasoning of *Samson* when holding that a police officer's suspicionless search of a parolee's motel room violated the state constitutional provision whose language mirrors the Fourth Amendment. See State v. Ochoa, 792 N.W.2d 260, 287–91 (Iowa 2010). This case serves as a reminder of the importance of raising both state and federal grounds for contesting the legality of the actions of government officials directed against one's client.

3. Even if the Fourth Amendment permits suspicionless searches of parolees, at least when parole release is conditioned on a prisoner's agreement to be subjected to such searches, and even if such suspicionless searches are permissible under the state's constitution, states and the federal government can choose to place additional constraints on parolee searches. As a matter of policy, what restrictions would you place on parolee searches and why?

4. People on probation, parole, or supervised release are often subject, by law, to DNA testing. See, e.g., 42 U.S.C. § 14135a(a)(2). The DNA information is then stored in a national or state database. Most courts have held that the mandatory DNA testing of such persons does not abridge their Fourth Amendment rights. See United States v. Mitchell, 652 F.3d 387, 402 n.13 (3d Cir.2011) (listing cases). Do you agree? Does your answer to this question hinge on the nature and severity of the crime of which a person was convicted? See United States v. Amerson, 483 F.3d 73 (2d Cir.2007) (upholding, in a case in which one defendant had been convicted of aiding and abetting wire fraud, the constitutionality of applying the DNA-collection statute to individuals on probation for nonviolent crimes).

While the Supreme Court has not considered the constitutionality of DNA testing in the probation, parole, or supervised-release context, it has, in a 5–4 decision, upheld a state statute authorizing the DNA testing of individuals arrested and booked into a detention center for specified violent crimes, burglary, or an attempt to commit one of these crimes. Maryland v. King, 569 U.S. 435, 133 S.Ct. 1958 (2013). The Court found that the DNA testing furthered the legitimate governmental interest in accurate identification of the person being detained, such as whether he or she was linked through DNA evidence to a heinous crime. The Court also emphasized that its holding was limited to DNA testing of arrestees detained for "serious" offenses. Id. at 465–66, 133 S.Ct. at 1980.

5.   As a general rule, evidence obtained in violation of the Fourth Amendment is inadmissible in a criminal trial. Mapp v. Ohio, 367 U.S. 643, 655–60, 81 S.Ct. 1684, 1691–94 (1961). But in a 5–4 decision, the Supreme Court held in Pennsylvania Board of Probation and Parole v. Scott, 524 U.S. 357, 118 S.Ct. 2014 (1998) that the Fourth Amendment exclusionary rule does not apply in parole-revocation hearings. As a result, the revocation of parole can be predicated partly or wholly on evidence procured in violation of the Fourth Amendment.

In determining whether the Fourth Amendment exclusionary rule applies in parole-revocation hearings, the Court, as it typically does when determining the exclusionary rule's scope, weighed the costs and benefits of applying the exclusionary rule in a particular context—in this case, during parole-revocation proceedings. The Court noted that since the government has an "overwhelming interest" in ensuring that parolees abide by the conditions of their parole and are returned to prison if they do not, the costs of excluding reliable and relevant evidence in parole-revocation hearings are quite high. In addition, the Court observed that importing the exclusionary rule into the parole-revocation context would transform the informal and, what the Court considered largely nonadversarial, revocation process into a "trial-like" proceeding not focused on what is in the parolee's and society's best interests. Id. at 366–67, 118 S.Ct. at 2021.

The Court then concluded that the costs of applying the Fourth Amendment exclusionary rule in parole-revocation proceedings were not counterbalanced by the benefits of deterring violations of the Fourth Amendment. The Court opined that since parole officers are not parolees' adversaries, they are less prone than police officers to violate the Fourth Amendment to find evidence of a crime or other violation of parole. And, according to the Court, even if parole officers were inclined sometimes to flout the Fourth Amendment, the potential prospect of being sued for damages or disciplined administratively would dissuade them from doing so.

The Court also was not persuaded that exempting parole-revocation hearings from application of the Fourth Amendment exclusionary rule would provide police offers with an incentive to ignore whatever constraints the Fourth Amendment places on parolee searches. The Court was confident that the knowledge that illegally seized evidence generally cannot be introduced at trial would propel police officers to comply with the Fourth Amendment. Suppression of the evidence at parole-revocation hearings, which are outside police officers' " 'zone of primary interest,' " therefore would have little, if any, additional deterrent effects. Id. at 368, 118 S.Ct. at 2022.

In his dissenting opinion, Justice Souter disagreed with the majority's assessment of the impact that applying the Fourth Amendment exclusionary rule in parole-revocation hearings would have in deterring violations of the Fourth Amendment:

> As to the benefit of an exclusionary rule in revocation proceedings, the majority does not see that in the investigation of criminal conduct by someone known to be on parole, Fourth Amendment standards will have very little deterrent sanction unless evidence offered for parole revocation is subject to suppression for unconstitutional conduct. It is not merely that parole revocation is the government's consolation prize when, for whatever reason, it cannot obtain a further criminal conviction, though that will sometimes be true. What is at least equally telling is that parole revocation will frequently be pursued instead of prosecution as the course of choice * * *.

> The reasons for this tendency to skip any new prosecution are obvious. If the conduct in question is a crime in its own right, the odds of revocation are very high. Since time on the street before revocation is not subtracted from the balance of the sentence to be served on revocation, the balance may well be long enough to render recommitment the practical equivalent of a new sentence for a separate crime. And all of this may be accomplished without shouldering the burden of proof beyond a reasonable doubt; hence the obvious popularity of revocation in place of new prosecution.

> The upshot is that without a suppression remedy in revocation proceedings, there will often be no influence capable of deterring Fourth Amendment violations when parole revocation is a possible response to new crime. Suppression in the revocation proceeding cannot be looked upon, then, as furnishing merely incremental or marginal deterrence over and above the effect of exclusion in criminal prosecution. Instead, it will commonly provide the only deterrence to unconstitutional conduct when the incarceration of parolees is sought, and the reasons that support the suppression remedy in prosecution therefore support it in parole revocation.

Id. at 378–79, 118 S.Ct. at 2027 (Souter, J., dissenting).

6.   The Supreme Court's decision in *Pennsylvania Board of Probation and Parole v. Scott* does not mean that illegally obtained evidence is always admissible in parole-revocation proceedings. Some state courts have held that when evidence is obtained in violation of their state's constitution, the evidence

is inadmissible in a parole- or probation-revocation hearing. See, e.g., Commonwealth v. Arter, 151 A.3d 149 (Pa. 2016) (exclusionary rule emanating from the state constitution applies in parole-revocation and probation-revocation proceedings).

B. PAROLE RELEASE

In the case which follows, the Supreme Court considered the implications of *Morrissey v. Brewer* for parole-release decisions. The Court addressed two questions: first, does due process require that certain procedures be followed when determining whether an inmate should be released on parole; and second, if so, what procedural safeguards are constitutionally mandated?

GREENHOLTZ V. INMATES OF NEBRASKA PENAL AND CORRECTIONAL COMPLEX

Supreme Court of the United States, 1979.
442 U.S. 1, 99 S.Ct. 2100, 60 L.Ed.2d 668.

MR. CHIEF JUSTICE BURGER delivered the opinion of the Court.

* * *

I

Inmates of the Nebraska Penal and Correctional Complex brought a class action under 42 U.S.C. § 1983 claiming that they had been unconstitutionally denied parole by the Board of Parole. * * * One of the claims of the inmates was that the statutes and the Board's procedures denied them procedural due process.

* * *

The procedures used by the Board to determine whether to grant or deny discretionary parole arise partly from statutory provisions and partly from the Board's practices. Two types of hearings are conducted: initial parole review hearings and final parole hearings. At least once each year initial review hearings must be held for every inmate, regardless of parole eligibility. At the initial review hearing, the Board examines the inmate's entire preconfinement and postconfinement record. Following that examination it provides an informal hearing; no evidence as such is introduced, but the Board interviews the inmate and considers any letters or statements that he wishes to present in support of a claim for release.

If the Board determines from its examination of the entire record and the personal interview that he is not yet a good risk for release, it denies parole, informs the inmate why release was deferred and makes recommendations designed to help correct any deficiencies observed. It also schedules another initial review hearing to take place within one year.

If the Board determines from the file and the initial review hearing that the inmate is a likely candidate for release, a final hearing is scheduled. The Board then notifies the inmate of the month in which the final hearing will be held; the exact day and time is posted on a bulletin board that is accessible to all inmates on the day of the hearing. At the final parole hearing, the inmate may present evidence, call witnesses and be represented by private counsel of his choice. It is not a traditional adversary hearing since the inmate is not permitted to hear adverse testimony or to cross-examine witnesses who present such evidence. However, a complete tape recording of the hearing is preserved. If parole is denied, the Board furnishes a written statement of the reasons for the denial within 30 days.

II

The District Court held that the procedures used by the Parole Board did not satisfy due process. * * *

On appeal, the Court of Appeals for the Eighth Circuit * * * modified the procedures required by the District Court as follows:

(a) When eligible for parole each inmate must receive a full formal hearing;

(b) the inmate is to receive written notice of the precise time of the hearing reasonably in advance of the hearing, setting forth the factors which may be considered by the Board in reaching its decision;

(c) subject only to security considerations, the inmate may appear in person before the Board and present documentary evidence in his own behalf. Except in unusual circumstances, however, the inmate has no right to call witnesses in his own behalf;

(d) a record of the proceedings, capable of being reduced to writing, must be maintained; and

(e) within a reasonable time after the hearing, the Board must submit a full explanation, in writing, of the facts relied upon and reasons for the Board's action denying parole.

* * *

III

* * *

Decisions of the Executive Branch, however serious their impact, do not automatically invoke due process protection; there simply is no constitutional guarantee that all executive decisionmaking must comply with standards that assure error-free determinations. * * *

* * *

IV

Respondents suggest two theories to support their view that they have a constitutionally protected interest in a parole determination which calls for the process mandated by the Court of Appeals. First, they claim that a reasonable entitlement is created whenever a state provides for the *possibility* of parole. Alternatively, they claim that the language in Nebraska's statute, Neb.Rev.Stat. § 83–1,114(1) (1976), creates a legitimate expectation of parole, invoking due process protections.

A

In support of their first theory, respondents rely heavily on *Morrissey v. Brewer,* 408 U.S. 471 (1972), where we held that a parole-revocation determination must meet certain due process standards. See also *Gagnon v. Scarpelli,* 411 U.S. 778 (1973). They argue that the ultimate interest at stake both in a parole-revocation decision and in a parole determination is conditional liberty and that since the underlying interest is the same the two situations should be accorded the same constitutional protection.

The fallacy in respondents' position is that parole *release* and parole *revocation* are quite different. There is a crucial distinction between being deprived of a liberty one has, as in parole, and being denied a conditional liberty that one desires. The parolees in *Morrissey* (and probationers in *Gagnon*) were at liberty and as such could "be gainfully employed and [were] free to be with family and friends and to form the other enduring attachments of normal life." The inmates here, on the other hand, are confined and thus subject to all of the necessary restraints that inhere in a prison.

A second important difference between discretionary parole *release* from confinement and *termination* of parole lies in the nature of the decision that must be made in each case. As we recognized in *Morrissey,* the parole-revocation determination actually requires two decisions: whether the parolee in fact acted in violation of one or more conditions of parole and whether the parolee should be recommitted either for his or society's benefit. "The first step in a revocation decision thus involves a wholly retrospective factual question."

The parole-release decision, however, is more subtle and depends on an amalgam of elements, some of which are factual but many of which are purely subjective appraisals by the Board members based upon their experience with the difficult and sensitive task of evaluating the advisability of parole release. Unlike the revocation decision, there is no set of facts which, if shown, mandate a decision favorable to the individual.
* * *

* * *

That the state holds out the *possibility* of parole provides no more than a mere hope that the benefit will be obtained. To that extent the general interest asserted here is no more substantial than the inmate's hope that he will not be transferred to another prison, a hope which is not protected by due process. *Meachum v. Fano,* 427 U.S. [215,] 225 [(1976)].

B

Respondents' second argument is that the Nebraska statutory language itself creates a protectible expectation of parole. They rely on the section which provides in part:

"Whenever the Board of Parole considers the release of a committed offender who is eligible for release on parole, it shall order his release unless it is of the opinion that his release should be deferred because:

"(a) There is a substantial risk that he will not conform to the conditions of parole;

"(b) His release would depreciate the seriousness of his crime or promote disrespect for law;

"(c) His release would have a substantially adverse effect on institutional discipline; or

"(d) His continued correctional treatment, medical care, or vocational or other training in the facility will substantially enhance his capacity to lead a law-abiding life when released at a later date."[5]

* * *

* * * We can accept respondents' view that the expectancy of release provided in this statute is entitled to some measure of constitutional protection. However, we emphasize that this statute has unique structure and language and thus whether any other state statute provides a protectible entitlement must be decided on a case-by-case basis. We therefore turn to an examination of the statutory procedures to determine whether they provide the process that is due in these circumstances.

* * *

* * * The objective of rehabilitating convicted persons to be useful, law-abiding members of society can remain a goal no matter how disappointing the progress. But it will not contribute to these desirable objectives to invite or encourage a continuing state of adversary relations between society and the inmate.

---

[5] The statute also provides a list of 14 explicit factors and one catchall factor that the Board is obligated to consider in reaching a decision.

Procedures designed to elicit specific facts, such as those required in *Morrissey, Gagnon,* and *Wolff*,[d] are not necessarily appropriate to a Nebraska parole determination. Merely because a statutory expectation exists cannot mean that in addition to the full panoply of due process required to convict and confine there must also be repeated, adversary hearings in order to continue the confinement. However, since the Nebraska Parole Board provides at least one and often two hearings every year to each eligible inmate, we need only consider whether the additional procedures mandated by the Court of Appeals are required * * *.

Two procedures mandated by the Court of Appeals are particularly challenged by the Board:[6] the requirement that a formal hearing be held for every inmate, and the requirement that every adverse parole decision include a statement of the evidence relied upon by the Board.

The requirement of a hearing as prescribed by the Court of Appeals in all cases would provide at best a negligible decrease in the risk of error. When the Board defers parole after the initial review hearing, it does so because examination of the inmate's file and the personal interview satisfies it that the inmate is not yet ready for conditional release. * * * At the Board's initial interview hearing, the inmate is permitted to appear before the Board and present letters and statements on his own behalf. He is thereby provided with an effective opportunity first, to insure that the records before the Board are in fact the records relating to his case; and second, to present any special considerations demonstrating why he is an appropriate candidate for parole. Since the decision is one that must be made largely on the basis of the inmate's files, this procedure adequately safeguards against serious risks of error and thus satisfies due process.[7]

Next, we find nothing in the due process concepts as they have thus far evolved that requires the Parole Board to specify the particular "evidence" in the inmate's file or at his interview on which it rests the discretionary determination that an inmate is not ready for conditional release. The Board communicates the reason for its denial as a guide to the inmate for his future behavior. To require the parole authority to provide

---

[d]   In Wolff v. McDonnell, 418 U.S. 539, 94 S.Ct. 2963 (1974), the Supreme Court outlined procedural safeguards that due process requires during prison disciplinary proceedings that lead to the revocation of an inmate's good-time credits.

[6]   The Board also objects to the Court of Appeals' order that it provide written notice reasonably in advance of the hearing together with a list of factors that might be considered. At present the Board informs the inmate in advance of the month during which the hearing will be held, thereby allowing time to secure letters or statements; on the day of the hearing it posts notice of the exact time. There is no claim that either the timing of the notice or its substance seriously prejudices the inmate's ability to prepare adequately for the hearing. The present notice is constitutionally adequate.

[7]   The only other possible risk of error is that relevant adverse factual information in the inmate's file is wholly inaccurate. But the Board has discretion to make available to the inmate any information "[w]henever the board determines that it will facilitate the parole hearing." Neb.Rev.Stat. § 83–1,112(1) (1976). Apparently the inmates are satisfied with the way this provision is administered since there is no issue before us regarding access to their files.

a summary of the evidence would tend to convert the process into an adversary proceeding and to equate the Board's parole-release determination with a guilt determination. The Nebraska statute contemplates, and experience has shown, that the parole-release decision is, as we noted earlier, essentially an experienced prediction based on a host of variables. The Board's decision is much like a sentencing judge's choice—provided by many states—to grant or deny probation following a judgment of guilt, a choice never thought to require more than what Nebraska now provides for the parole-release determination. The Nebraska procedure affords an opportunity to be heard, and when parole is denied it informs the inmate in what respects he falls short of qualifying for parole; this affords the process that is due under these circumstances. The Constitution does not require more.[8]

* * *

APPENDIX TO OPINION OF THE COURT

The statutory factors that the Board is required to take into account in deciding whether or not to grant parole are the following:

(a) The offender's personality, including his maturity, stability, sense of responsibility and any apparent development in his personality which may promote or hinder his conformity to law;

(b) The adequacy of the offender's parole plan;

(c) The offender's ability and readiness to assume obligations and undertake responsibilities;

(d) The offender's intelligence and training;

(e) The offender's family status and whether he has relatives who display an interest in him or whether he has other close and constructive associations in the community;

(f) The offender's employment history, his occupational skills, and the stability of his past employment;

(g) The type of residence, neighborhood or community in which the offender plans to live;

(h) The offender's past use of narcotics, or past habitual and excessive use of alcohol;

---

[8] The Court of Appeals in its order required the Board to permit all inmates to appear and present documentary support for parole. Since both of these requirements were being complied with prior to this litigation, the Board did not seek review of those parts of the court's order and the validity of those requirements is not before us. The Court of Appeals also held that due process did not provide a right to cross-examine adverse witnesses or a right to present favorable witnesses. The practice of taping the hearings also was declared adequate. Those issues are not before us and we express no opinion on them.

(i)   The offender's mental or physical makeup, including any disability or handicap which may affect his conformity to law;

(j)   The offender's prior criminal record, including the nature and circumstances, recency and frequency of previous offenses;

(k)   The offender's attitude toward law and authority;

(l)   The offender's conduct in the facility, including particularly whether he has taken advantage of the opportunities for self-improvement, whether he has been punished for misconduct within six months prior to his hearing or reconsideration for parole release, whether any reductions of term have been forfeited, and whether such reductions have been restored at the time of hearing or reconsideration;

(m) The offender's behavior and attitude during any previous experience of probation or parole and the recency of such experience; and

(n)   Any other factors the board determines to be relevant. Neb.Rev.Stat. § 83–1,114(2) (1976).

MR. JUSTICE POWELL, concurring in part and dissenting in part.

[For the reasons set forth in Justice Marshall's dissenting opinion, Justice Powell opined that when a state sets up a system of parole, it creates a liberty interest in parole release protected by the Due Process Clause, regardless of the language of the parole-release statute. In addition, Justice Powell concluded that the notice provided Nebraska inmates of their impending parole-release hearings did not comport with due process.]

MR. JUSTICE MARSHALL, with whom MR. JUSTICE BRENNAN and MR. JUSTICE STEVENS join, dissenting in part.

My disagreement with the Court's opinion extends to both its analysis of respondents' liberty interest and its delineation of the procedures constitutionally required in parole release proceedings. * * *

* * *

I

It is self-evident that all individuals possess a liberty interest in being free from physical restraint. Upon conviction for a crime, of course, an individual may be deprived of this liberty to the extent authorized by penal statutes. But when a State enacts a parole system, and creates the possibility of release from incarceration upon satisfaction of certain conditions, it necessarily qualifies that initial deprivation. In my judgment, it is the existence of this system which allows prison inmates to retain their protected interest in securing freedoms available outside prison. Because parole release proceedings clearly implicate this retained liberty interest, the Fourteenth Amendment requires that due process be observed, irrespective of the specific provisions in the applicable parole statute.

* * *

* * * [T]he Court discerns two distinctions between "parole *release* and parole *revocation*" * * *.

First, the Court finds a difference of constitutional dimension between a deprivation of liberty one has and a denial of liberty one desires. * * * Whether an individual currently enjoys a particular freedom has no bearing on whether he possesses a protected interest in securing and maintaining that liberty. The Court acknowledged as much in *Wolff v. McDonnell*[, 418 U.S. 539 (1974)] when it held that the loss of good-time credits implicates a liberty interest even though the forfeiture only deprived the prisoner of freedom he expected to obtain sometime hence. * * *

The Court's distinction is equally unrelated to the nature or gravity of the interest affected in parole release proceedings. * * * "[W]hether the immediate issue be release or revocation, the stakes are the same: conditional freedom versus incarceration."

The Court's second justification for distinguishing between parole release and parole revocation is based on the "nature of the decision that must be made in each case." The majority apparently believes that the interest affected by parole release proceedings is somehow diminished if the administrative decision may turn on "subjective evaluations." Yet the Court nowhere explains why the *nature of the decisional process* has even the slightest bearing in assessing the *nature of the interest* that this process may terminate. * * *

But even assuming the subjective nature of the decision-making process were relevant to due process analysis in general, this consideration does not adequately distinguish the processes of granting and revoking parole. Contrary to the Court's assertion that the decision to revoke parole is predominantly a " 'retrospective factual question,' " *Morrissey* recognized that only the first step in the revocation decision can be so characterized. * * * Moreover, to the extent parole release proceedings hinge on predictive determinations, those assessments are necessarily predicated on findings of fact.[8] Accordingly, the presence of subjective considerations is a completely untenable basis for distinguishing the interests at stake here from the liberty interest recognized in *Morrissey*.

* * *

---

[8]   The Nebraska statutes, in particular, demonstrate the factual nature of the parole release inquiry. One provision enumerates factual considerations such as the inmate's intelligence, family status, and employment history, which bear upon the four predictive determinations underlying the ultimate parole decision.

II

A

I also cannot subscribe to the Court's assessment of the procedures necessary to safeguard respondents' liberty interest. Although the majority purports to rely on * * * the test enunciated in *Mathews v. Eldridge,* 424 U.S. 319 (1976), its application of these standards is fundamentally deficient in several respects.

To begin with, the Court focuses almost exclusively on the likelihood that a particular procedure will significantly reduce the risk of error in parole release proceedings. Yet *Mathews* advances *three* factors to be considered in determining the specific dictates of due process:

> "First, the private interest that will be affected by the official action; second, the risk of an erroneous deprivation of such interest through the procedures used, and the probable value, if any, of additional or substitute procedural safeguards; and finally, the Government's interest, including the function involved and the fiscal and administrative burdens that the additional or substitute procedural requirement would entail."

By ignoring the other two factors set forth in *Mathews,* the Court skews the inquiry in favor of the Board. For example, the Court does not identify any justification for the Parole Board's refusal to provide inmates with specific advance notice of the hearing date or with a list of factors that may be considered. Nor does the Board demonstrate that it would be unduly burdensome to provide a brief summary of the evidence justifying the denial of parole. To be sure, these measures may cause some inconvenience, but "the Constitution recognizes higher values than speed and efficiency." Similarly lacking in the Court's analysis is any recognition of the private interest affected by the Board's action. Certainly the interest in being released from incarceration is of sufficient magnitude to have some bearing on the process due.

The second fundamental flaw in the Court's analysis is that it incorrectly evaluates the only factor actually discussed. The contribution that additional safeguards will make to reaching an accurate decision necessarily depends on the risk of error inherent in existing procedures. Here, the Court finds supplemental procedures to be inappropriate because it assumes existing procedures adequately reduce the likelihood that an inmate's files will contain incorrect information which could lead to an erroneous decision. No support is cited for this assumption, and the record affords none. In fact, researchers and courts have discovered many substantial inaccuracies in inmate files, and evidence in the instant case revealed similar errors.[15] * * *

Finally, apart from avoiding the risk of actual error, this Court has stressed the importance of adopting procedures that preserve the appearance of fairness and the confidence of inmates in the decisionmaking process. The Chief Justice recognized in *Morrissey* that "fair treatment in parole revocations will enhance the chance of rehabilitation by avoiding reactions to arbitrariness," a view shared by legislators, courts, the American Bar Association, and other commentators. This consideration is equally significant whether liberty interests are extinguished in parole release or parole revocation proceedings. * * *

B

Applying the analysis of *Morrissey* and *Mathews,* I believe substantially more procedural protection is necessary in parole release proceedings than the Court requires. The types of safeguards that should be addressed here, however, are limited by the posture of this case.[17] Thus, only three specific issues need be considered.

While the question is close, I agree with the majority that a formal hearing is not always required when an inmate first becomes eligible for discretionary parole. * * *

The Court of Appeals directed the Parole Board to conduct such a formal hearing as soon as an inmate becomes eligible for parole, even where the likelihood of a favorable decision is negligible * * *. From a practical standpoint, this relief offers no appreciable advantage to the inmates. If the Board would not have conducted a final hearing under current procedures, inmates gain little from a requirement that such a hearing be held, since the evidence almost certainly would be insufficient to justify granting release. * * * The inmates' interest in this modification of the

---

[15] In this case, for example, the form notifying one inmate that parole had been denied indicated that the Board believed he should enlist in a self-improvement program at the prison. But in fact, the inmate was already participating in all such programs available. Such errors in parole files are not unusual. *E.g., Kohlman v. Norton,* 380 F.Supp. 1073 (D.Conn.1974) (parole denied because file erroneously indicated that applicant had used gun in committing robbery); *State v. Pohlabel,* 160 A.2d 647 (1960) (files erroneously showed that prisoner was under a life sentence in another jurisdiction).

[17] In accordance with the majority opinion, I do not address whether the Court of Appeals was correct in holding that the Nebraska Parole Board may not abandon the procedures it already provides. These safeguards include permitting inmates to appear and present documentary support at hearings, and providing a statement of reasons when parole is denied or deferred. Because the inmates failed to seek review of the Court of Appeals' decision, I also express no view on whether it correctly held that the Board's practice of allowing inmates to present witnesses and retain counsel for final parole hearings was not constitutionally compelled. Finally, it would be inappropriate to consider the suggestion advanced here for the first time that inmates should be allowed access to their files in order to correct factual inaccuracies.

* * *

Board's procedures is thus relatively slight.[18] Yet the burden imposed on the Parole Board by the additional formal hearings would be substantial. Accordingly, I believe the Board's current practice of combining both formal and informal hearings is constitutionally sufficient.

However, a different conclusion is warranted with respect to the hearing notices given inmates. The Board currently informs inmates only that it will conduct an initial review or final parole hearing during a particular month within the next year. The notice does not specify the day or hour of the hearing. Instead, inmates must check a designated bulletin board each morning to see if their hearing is scheduled for that day. In addition, the Board refuses to advise inmates of the criteria relevant in parole release proceedings, despite a state statute expressly listing 14 factors the Board must consider and 4 permissible reasons for denying parole.

Finding these procedures insufficient, the District Court and the Court of Appeals ordered that each inmate receive written advance notice of the time set for his hearing, along with a list of factors the Board may consider.[19] Although the Board has proffered no justification for refusing to institute these procedures, the Court sets aside the relief ordered below on the ground that "[t]here is no claim that either the timing of the notice or its substance seriously prejudices the inmate's ability to prepare adequately for the hearing." But respondents plainly have contended throughout this litigation that reasonable advance notice is necessary to enable them to organize their evidence, call the witnesses permitted by the Board, and notify private counsel allowed to participate in the hearing * * *. Given the significant private interests at stake, and the importance of reasonable notice in preserving the appearance of fairness, I see no reason to depart here from this Court's longstanding recognition that adequate notice is a fundamental requirement of due process * * *.

Finally, I would require the Board to provide a statement of the crucial evidence on which it relies in denying parole. At present, the Parole Board merely uses a form letter noting the general reasons for its decision. In ordering the Board to furnish as well a summary of the essential facts underlying the denial, the Court of Appeals made clear that " 'detailed findings of fact are not required.' " The majority here, however, believes even this relief to be unwarranted, because it might render parole

---

[18] Although a formal hearing at the point of initial eligibility would reduce the risk of error and enhance the appearance of fairness, providing a summary of essential evidence and reasons, together with allowing inmates to appear at informal hearings, decreases the justification for requiring the Board to conduct formal hearings in every case.

[19] The courts below found that 72 hours' advance notice ordinarily would enable prisoners to prepare for their appearances. The Court of Appeals further determined that the statutory criteria were sufficiently specific that the Board need only include a list of those criteria with the hearing notices or post such a list in public areas throughout the institution.

proceedings more adversary and equate unfavorable decisions with a determination of guilt.

* * * [I]t is difficult to believe that subsequently disclosing the factual justification for a decision will render the proceeding more adversary, especially when the Board already provides a general statement of reasons. And to the extent unfavorable parole decisions resemble a determination of guilt, the Board has no legitimate interest in concealing from an inmate the conduct or failings of which he purportedly is guilty.

While requiring a summation of the essential evidence might entail some administrative inconvenience, in neither *Morrissey v. Brewer, Gagnon v. Scarpelli,* nor *Wolff v. McDonnell* did the Court find that this factor justified denying a written statement of the essential evidence and the reasons underlying a decision. It simply is not unduly "burdensome to give reasons when reasons exist. * * *" *Board of Regents v. Roth,* 408 U.S. 564, 591 (1972) (Marshall, J., dissenting). And an inability to provide any reasons suggests that the decision is, in fact, arbitrary.

Moreover, considerations identified in *Morrissey* and *Mathews* militate in favor of requiring a statement of the essential evidence. Such a requirement would direct the Board's focus to the relevant statutory criteria and promote more careful consideration of the evidence. It would also enable inmates to detect and correct inaccuracies that could have a decisive impact.[23] And the obligation to justify a decision publicly would provide the assurance, critical to the appearance of fairness, that the Board's decision is not capricious. Finally, imposition of this obligation would afford inmates instruction on the measures needed to improve their prison behavior and prospects for parole, a consequence surely consistent with rehabilitative goals. Balancing these considerations against the Board's minimal interest in avoiding this procedure, I am convinced that the Fourteenth Amendment requires the Parole Board to provide inmates a statement of the essential evidence as well as a meaningful explanation of the reasons for denying parole release.[25]

* * *

---

[23] The preprinted list of reasons for denying parole is unlikely to disclose these types of factual errors. Out of 375 inmates denied parole during a 6-month period, the only reason given 285 of them was: "Your continued correctional treatment, vocational, educational, or job assignment in the facility will substantially enhance your capacity to lead a law-abiding life when released at a later date." Although the denial forms also include a list of six "[r]ecommendations for correcting deficiencies," such as "[e]xhibit some responsibility and maturity," the evidence at trial showed that all six items were checked on 370 of the 375 forms, regardless of the facts of the particular case.

[25] This statement of reasons and the summary of essential evidence should be provided to all inmates actually eligible for parole, whether the adverse decision is rendered following an initial review or a final parole hearing.

QUESTIONS AND POINTS FOR DISCUSSION

1.   In Board of Pardons v. Allen, 482 U.S. 369, 107 S.Ct. 2415 (1987), the Supreme Court held that the following parole statute in Montana created a liberty interest in parole of which a prisoner could not be divested without due process of law:

> Prisoners eligible for parole. (1) Subject to the following restrictions, the board shall release on parole * * * any person confined in the Montana state prison or the women's correctional center * * * when in its opinion there is reasonable probability that the prisoner can be released without detriment to the prisoner or to the community[.]
>
> * * *
>
> (2) A parole shall be ordered only for the best interests of society and not as an award of clemency or reduction of sentence or pardon. A prisoner shall be placed on parole only when the board believes that he is able and willing to fulfill the obligations of a law-abiding citizen.

The Court refused to distinguish between parole statutes like Nebraska's that mandated parole release "unless" certain conditions were met and other parole statutes like Montana's that required release "if" or "when" certain conditions were met. The Court conceded that the standards governing parole release in Montana, which focused on whether release on parole would be detrimental to the prisoner or the community and in the best interests of society, were more general than the Nebraska standards that were before the Court in *Greenholtz*. The Court, however, rejected the argument in a dissenting opinion that Montana prisoners had no more than a hope of being released on parole, rather than a protected liberty interest in such release, when the parole statute failed to specifically and "meaningfully" limit the discretion of the Montana parole board. Id. at 384, 107 S.Ct. at 2424 (O'Connor, J., dissenting).

2.   Under the approach followed by the Supreme Court in *Greenholtz* and *Board of Pardons v. Allen* in determining whether a state has created a liberty interest in parole, would the following state statute create such an interest?

> The Board shall not parole a person eligible for parole if it determines that: (1) there is a substantial risk that he will not conform to reasonable conditions of parole; or (2) his release at that time would deprecate the seriousness of his offense or promote disrespect for the law; or (3) his release would have a substantially adverse effect on institutional discipline.

See Hill v. Walker, 948 N.E.2d 601, 605–06 (Ill.2011). Would a statute like the one set forth below create a liberty interest?

> No inmate shall be placed on parole until and unless the board shall find that there is reasonable probability that, if he is so released, he will live and conduct himself as a respectable and law-abiding person and that his release will be compatible with his own welfare and the welfare of society. Furthermore, no person shall be released on

pardon or placed on parole unless and until the board is satisfied that he will be suitably employed in self-sustaining employment or that he will not become a public charge.

See Sultenfuss v. Snow, 35 F.3d 1494, 1501–02 (11th Cir.1994).

3.   In Sandin v. Conner, 515 U.S. 472, 115 S.Ct. 2293 (1995), the Supreme Court confronted the question whether the transfer of a prisoner to a disciplinary-segregation unit because of his violation of prison rules deprived him of a state-created liberty interest. In the course of answering that question, the Court expressed reservations about conditioning the finding of a state-created liberty interest on the existence of certain "mandatory language" in a prison regulation. Id. at 481–84, 115 S.Ct. at 2299–2300. The Court noted that this approach had the perverse effect of discouraging prison officials from adopting regulations dictating how prison officials should carry out their duties. The Court proceeded to articulate a new test to be applied when determining whether prison officials have deprived a prisoner of a state-created liberty interest. Under that test, a court examines whether the state has created an interest in "freedom from restraint which . . . imposes atypical and significant hardship on the inmate in relation to the ordinary incidents of prison life." Id. at 484, 115 S.Ct. at 2300.

Since *Sandin* was decided, most courts have concluded that application of the test it enunciated for state-created liberty interests is confined to decisions bearing on conditions of confinement and does not extend to assessments whether inmates in a particular state have a liberty interest in parole derived from state law. See, e.g., McQuillion v. Duncan, 306 F.3d 895, 903 (9th Cir.2002). These holdings rest in part on the Supreme Court's reaffirmation in *Sandin* of its holding in *Board of Pardons v. Allen*. But in Wilkinson v. Austin, 545 U.S. 209, 229, 125 S.Ct. 2384, 2397 (2005), the Supreme Court said, though in dictum and in a case dealing with altered conditions of confinement, that "*Sandin* abrogated *Greenholtz*'s . . . methodology for establishing the liberty interest."

In your opinion, should the Supreme Court modify the test it has applied when determining whether a state-created liberty interest in parole exists? If so, how? For an insightful discussion of the "mandatory language" approach of *Greenholtz* and *Board of Pardons v. Allen* and the Supreme Court's critique of that approach in *Sandin*, see Ellis v. District of Columbia, 84 F.3d 1413, 1417–18 (D.C. Cir.1996).

4.   *Greenholtz* and *Board of Pardons v. Allen* should be contrasted with Connecticut Board of Pardons v. Dumschat, 452 U.S. 458, 101 S.Ct. 2460 (1981). In *Dumschat,* a prisoner who was serving a life sentence for murder contended that he was deprived of a liberty interest without due process of law when the Connecticut Board of Pardons denied his application for a commutation of his sentence. He argued that certain procedures should have been followed by the board when reviewing his commutation application.

Under the applicable Connecticut statute, the board was vested with unconfined discretion to commute sentences or grant pardons. The prisoner nonetheless contended that he had a legitimate expectation that his life sentence would be commuted, because the board commuted the vast majority—eighty-five to ninety percent—of the sentences of inmates serving life sentences. The Supreme Court rejected this argument:

> In terms of the Due Process Clause, a Connecticut felon's expectation that a lawfully imposed sentence will be commuted or that he will be pardoned is no more substantial than an inmate's expectation, for example, that he will not be transferred to another prison; it is simply a unilateral hope. A constitutional entitlement cannot "be created—as if by estoppel—merely because a wholly and *expressly* discretionary state privilege has been granted generously in the past." No matter how frequently a particular form of clemency has been granted, the statistical probabilities standing alone generate no constitutional protections; a contrary conclusion would trivialize the Constitution. The ground for a constitutional claim, if any, must be found in statutes or other rules defining the obligations of the authority charged with exercising clemency.

Id. at 465, 101 S.Ct. at 2464. See also Jago v. Van Curen, 454 U.S. 14, 102 S.Ct. 31 (1981) (rescission of parole-release decision that occurred before inmate's actual release and that was prompted by the discovery that he had provided false information to the parole board did not implicate a liberty interest; inmate's understanding that he would be released on parole did not give rise to a liberty interest).

5.   In Ohio Adult Parole Authority v. Woodard, 523 U.S. 272, 118 S.Ct. 1244 (1998), the Supreme Court considered whether its holding in *Dumschat* should be extended to a capital case. The prisoner in *Woodard* contended that he was not afforded due process of law during clemency proceedings. In particular, he complained that (a) he was told only ten days before of the impending clemency hearing, (b) he was given only three days' notice of the option of being interviewed before the hearing, (c) his attorney was not permitted to be present during the interview, (d) he was not permitted to testify or to present documentary evidence at the clemency hearing, and (e) the decision whether to let his attorney participate in the hearing fell within the parole board's discretion.

A majority of the Court concluded that in a capital case, where life is at stake, clemency proceedings implicate due process. But in a splintered decision, a majority of the Justices concluded that the due-process rights of the prisoner in this case had not been violated.

Justice O'Connor, in an opinion joined by Justices Souter, Ginsburg, and Breyer, observed that the procedural safeguards incorporated into the state's clemency process, including the notice provisions and the opportunity afforded the prisoner to be interviewed before the clemency hearing, met the requirements of due process. While agreeing that clemency proceedings in capital cases trigger the protections of due process, Justice Stevens voted to remand the case back to the lower courts for an assessment of what procedural safeguards are required by due process in this context.

Four of the Justices—Justices Rehnquist, Scalia, Kennedy, and Thomas— took a more narrow view, asserting that clemency proceedings simply do not implicate due process. According to these Justices, it is during the trial and sentencing in a capital case, not the clemency process, that a person is deprived of his or her interest in life. If the prisoner sentenced to death is granted clemency, he receives "a benefit." Id. at 285, 118 S.Ct. at 1252. If not, he is "no worse off than he was before" under the sentence that was imposed after affording him the procedural safeguards required by due process. Id.

6.   One of the questions left unresolved in *Greenholtz* was whether inmates have a constitutional right to have access to the information in their parole files reviewed by parole boards. These files may include a presentence report; reports of disciplinary infractions; medical and psychiatric records; the prisoner's criminal record; reports about the inmate's adjustment while in prison; letters from the sentencing judge, police officers, victims, family members, and friends; and other materials.

The lower courts have divided on the question whether inmates have a right of access to their parole files when they are being considered for possible release on parole. Some courts have held that they simply have no such right. See, e.g., Worden v. Montana Bd. of Pardons and Parole, 962 P.2d 1157, 1166 (Mont.1998). Others have analyzed inmates' access demands on a case-by-case basis. See, e.g., Coralluzzo v. New York State Parole Bd., 566 F.2d 375, 380 (2d Cir.1977) (where parole board's statement of reasons for deferring parole consideration revealed that it had relied on information a state court had ordered stricken from the inmate's file, prisoner had a right of access to the file to confirm whether the information was still in it). Still other courts have crafted more general rules providing for or denying access to files in defined circumstances. See, e.g., Ingrassia v. Purkett, 985 F.2d 987, 989 (8th Cir.1993) (prisoners have no right of access to parole files when they are denied parole because their release would depreciate the seriousness of their crimes); Walker v. Prisoner Review Bd., 694 F.2d 499, 503–04 (7th Cir.1982) (inmates have right of access to documents considered by the parole board); Williams v. Missouri Bd. of Probation and Parole, 661 F.2d 697, 700 (8th Cir.1981) (inmates up for parole have a general right to be apprised of information in their files that may adversely affect their parole prospects).

When, if ever, do you believe that people being considered for parole release have a constitutional right of access to their parole files?

7.   Because of the many procedural safeguards already afforded prisoners being considered for parole in Nebraska, the Supreme Court in *Greenholtz* did not have to decide whether those procedures were constitutionally mandated. In your opinion, which of the following procedures, if any, does due process require in a state where the denial of parole implicates a liberty interest? A right to appear before the parole board? A right to present

documentary evidence? A right to call witnesses to testify on the inmate's behalf? A right to cross-examine adverse witnesses? A right to be represented by an attorney or to receive some other form of assistance? A right to receive a statement of the reason or reasons for a parole denial? A right to a "neutral and detached" decisionmaker? And whether or not these rights are subsumed within the protections afforded by due process, which, if any, of them and any other rights would you extend, for policy reasons, to prisoners during parole proceedings?

8.   Assuming that inmates have the right to a written statement outlining the reason or reasons why parole was denied, would a statement that release would depreciate the seriousness of the offense of which the inmate had been found guilty and engender disrespect for the law suffice? What would prevent a parole board from routinely reciting such reasons? How much more specific could the parole board be in relating its reasons for the parole denial?

9.   As was mentioned at the beginning of this chapter, parole has been supplanted in some jurisdictions by what is called "supervised release." One of the key distinctions between parole and supervised release is that the supervised-release term is imposed by the court as part of the defendant's sentence. Sometimes statutes require that a period of supervised release be included as part of the sentence for a particular type of crime, and sometimes the decision whether to include a supervised-release term in a defendant's sentence is left to the court's discretion. See, e.g., 18 U.S.C. § 3583(a). Statutes also typically define the maximum length of supervised-release terms, providing for longer periods of supervision for people convicted of more serious crimes. See, e.g., id. § 3583(b) (no more than five years for Class A and B felonies, no more than three years for Class C and D felonies, and no more than one year for most other crimes).

Another significant difference between parole and supervised release is that judges, rather than parole boards, often determine the conditions of defendants' supervised-release terms. These sentencing decisions must conform with the requirements of statutes outlining the permissible and mandatory conditions of supervised release. See, e.g., id. § 3583(d).

10. A number of states and the federal government have developed special release mechanisms to enable terminally ill prisoners meeting defined criteria to be released early from prison, whether through a court order or decision of the parole board, department of corrections, or other administrative entity. See, e.g., Cal. Penal Code § 1170(e)(2) (authorizing the resentencing and release from prison of a person with a terminal illness that a doctor employed by the department of corrections has determined will cause death within six months, provided the release will not jeopardize public safety and the prisoner was not sentenced to death or life in prison without possibility of parole). Some "compassionate release" statutes extend to prisoners other than those who are terminally ill. The California statute just cited, for example, also permits a court to resentence and release a prisoner when the following preconditions are met: (1) the prisoner is "permanently medically incapacitated" by a medical

condition that necessitates "total care" twenty-four hours a day and has rendered the prisoner forever incapable of performing the activities that attend "basic daily living"; (2) this incapacitation did not exist when the prisoner was originally sentenced; (3) the release will not threaten the public's safety; and (4) the prisoner did not receive a death sentence and is not serving a sentence to life in prison without the possibility of parole. See also 18 U.S.C. § 3582(c)(1)(A)(ii) (upon motion of the director of the Bureau of Prisons, court can modify sentence of certain prisoners who are at least seventy years old, have served at least thirty years in prison on their current mandatory life sentences, and pose no danger to others).

The Model Penal Code provides for the judicial modification of a sentence due to a prisoner's "advanced age, physical or mental infirmity, exigent family circumstances, or other compelling reasons warranting modification of sentence." Model Penal Code: Sentencing § 305.7(a) (2017). When, if ever, do you believe incarcerated people should be eligible for compassionate release? Should prisoners convicted of certain crimes be ineligible for such release?

CHAPTER 10

ENMESHED PENALTIES ("COLLATERAL CONSEQUENCES")

■ ■ ■

A. THE REINTEGRATION OF PERSONS RELEASED FROM PRISON: PRACTICAL OBSTACLES

Each year, over 600,000 people are released from prison in this country. Bureau of Justice Statistics, U.S. Dep't of Justice, Prisoners in 2016, at 10–11 (2018). Eventually, almost all prisoners return to the community. See Bureau of Justice Statistics, U.S. Dep't of Justice, Felony Sentences in State Courts, 2006—Statistical Tables 7 (2009) (less than 1% of people sentenced to state prison in 2006 for felonies received life sentences).

Generally bereft of resources and money, many people upon their release from prison are given, at most, a new change of clothing and a small amount of spending money and then sent on their way. Jeremy Travis et al., Urban Inst., From Prison to Home: The Dimensions and Consequences of Prisoner Reentry 19 (2001). Their prospects of finding a job with which to support themselves and any family members are dim. See Christy Visher et al., Urban Inst., Employment After Prison: A Longitudinal Study of Releasees in Three States 6 (2008) (55% of released prisoners in three states on which study focused—Illinois, Ohio, and Texas—were unemployed eight months after release). Many prisoners function at the two lowest literacy levels, with a large number of them unable to perform such mundane tasks as locating an intersection on a street map or determining the date of an appointment from an appointment slip. Bobby D. Rampey et al., Nat'l Ctr. For Educ. Statistics, Highlights from the U.S. PIAAC Survey of Incarcerated Adults: Their Skills, Work Experience, Education, and Training 3, 6 (2016); Elizabeth Greenberg et al., Nat'l Ctr. For Educ. Statistics, Literacy Behind Prison Bars: Results From the 2003 National Assessment of Adult Literacy Prison Survey 2–8, 13 (2007). The majority of imprisoned people do not receive vocational training while they are incarcerated, and over a third of them do not have job assignments. Rampey et al., supra, at 15, 30. And most of the available jobs involve tasks, such as laundry and janitorial work, designed to facilitate the operation of the prison rather than prepare people for reentry. Amy L. Solomon et al., Urban Inst., From Prison to Work: The Employment Dimensions of

Prisoner Reentry 16 (2004). In addition, few of the people returning to their communities from prison have been groomed on such basics as how to fill out a job-application form or dress for an interview, or even on the need to be punctual for an interview or job. And for those who are unable to procure a job upon release, there is no unemployment compensation and often no welfare assistance upon which to fall back temporarily.

People who are fortunate enough to secure a job upon their release from prison generally find that the jobs are low-paying and often accompanied by poor working conditions. It is little wonder then that the impulse to return to a life of crime may frequently prove irresistible. Studies have found that individuals who are unemployed following their release from prison generally are more likely to commit new crimes. Dallan F. Flake, When Any Sentence is a Life Sentence: Employment Discrimination Against Ex-Offenders, 93 Wash. U. L.Rev. 45, 63 (2015). The unemployment and underemployment of formerly incarcerated people may therefore explain, at least in part, the very high recidivism rates in this country. One study of released prisoners conducted by the Bureau of Justice Statistics revealed that half of them were reimprisoned within three years of their release, though some of these returns to prison were due to noncriminal violations of release conditions, such as not keeping an appointment with a parole officer. Bureau of Justice Statistics, U.S. Dep't of Justice, Recidivism of Prisoners Released in 30 States in 2005: Patterns from 2005 to 2010, at 1, 15 (2014). Recidivism studies have found, not surprisingly, that recidivism rates are highest during the first year after a person's release from prison. Id. at 7.

Upon their release from prison, individuals face other challenges that compound the difficulty of readjusting successfully to life outside prison. Substance-abuse problems are prevalent amongst prisoners, but the vast majority of them receive no treatment for those problems while they are in prison. Nat'l Ctr. on Addiction & Substance Abuse at Columbia Univ., Behind Bars II: Substance Abuse and America's Prison Population 23, 25, 40 (2010) (while 65% of state prisoners and 55% of federal prisoners met the medical criteria for a "substance use disorder" in 2006, fewer than one in five inmates with the disorder received substance-abuse treatment). A high percentage of prisoners also have mental-health problems, yet most of these prisoners receive no mental-health treatment while incarcerated. Bureau of Justice Statistics, U.S. Dep't of Justice, Indicators of Mental Health Problems Reported by Prisoners and Jail Inmates, 2011–12, at 1, 8 (2017) (while one in seven prisoners reported symptoms indicating an existing mental-health problem, close to half had received no mental-health treatment since their admission to prison). In addition, incarceration exacts a psychological toll on inmates, both those who are mentally ill and those who are not, that can further impede their adaptation to life outside prison. The tight controls exerted over prisoners make many of them highly dependent on others to make choices for them, leaving them poorly equipped to initiate the steps needed to reenter society as productive and law-abiding citizens. Other corrosive side effects of what is known as the "prisonization process" can include loss of trust in others, social withdrawal, feelings of degradation and low self-worth, a greater willingness and tendency to exploit others, and posttraumatic stress disorder. Craig Haney, The Psychological Impact of Incarceration: Implications for Postprison Adjustment, in Prisoners Once Removed: The Impact of Incarceration and Reentry on Children, Families, and Communities 40–46 (Jeremy Travis & Michelle Waul eds., 2003).

Finally, people released from prison typically return to fractured neighborhoods and communities plagued by unemployment, poverty, and high crime rates. These areas generally lack the jobs, resources, and family and other support systems that can foster individuals' reentry into the society from which they have, in effect, been exiled. Amy L. Solomon et al., Urban Inst., From Prison to Work: The Employment Dimensions of Prisoner Reentry 1, 13 (2004).

B. THE REINTEGRATION OF PERSONS RELEASED FROM PRISON: LEGAL OBSTACLES

In addition to the practical obstacles that impede released individuals' successful reintegration into the community, there are legal obstacles that stand in their way. Impediments to reintegration that stem from the law, but are not part of the sentence officially imposed for a crime, are most commonly called the "collateral consequences" of a conviction. This term has been criticized for being "woefully inaccurate and misleading," both for ignoring the direct link between criminal convictions and penalties triggered by them, even though not specified in the sentence, and for depreciating the severity of these penalties' adverse effects. See McGregor Smyth, From "Collateral" to "Integral": The Seismic Evolution of *Padilla v. Kentucky* and Its Impact on Penalties Beyond Deportation, 54 How. L.J. 795, 802–03 (2011) "Enmeshed penalties" and "hidden sentences" are examples of terms that, it has been argued, more accurately depict the direct, and often severe, adverse effects the law provides can or must follow from a criminal conviction, above and beyond the court-imposed sentence. Id. at 802; Joshua Kaiser, Revealing the Hidden Sentence: How to Add Transparency, Legitimacy, and Purpose to "Collateral" Punishment Policy, 10 Harv. L. & Pol'y Rev. 123, 127, 144–56 (2016). As you read the ensuing discussion in this section of the chapter, consider what term is the most apt—collateral consequences, enmeshed penalties, hidden sentences, or some other term.

The Collateral Consequences Resource Center maintains a database on federally imposed "collateral consequences" of a conviction. See

Collateral Consequences Resource Ctr., Compilation of Federal Collateral
Consequences, at http://federal.ccresourcecenter.org. The "National
Inventory of the Collateral Consequences of Conviction" is another
database of statutes, both federal and state, that place restrictions on
employment, housing, voting, and other opportunities due to a prior
criminal conviction and sometimes simply an arrest. See Justice Center,
The Council of State Governments, National Inventory of the Collateral
Consequences of Conviction, at https://niccc.csgjusticecenter.org/
description. Some of these enmeshed penalties are profiled below.

1.   EMPLOYMENT RESTRICTIONS

The countless enmeshed penalties (collateral consequences) that can
ensue from a conviction typically extend not only to prisoners but to others
convicted of crimes. For example, restrictions on the employment of people
with felony convictions abound, with a number of federal and state statutes
requiring or permitting barring them from specified jobs. Just a few
examples, drawn from the National Inventory of the Collateral
Consequences of Conviction, of jobs from which individuals with a felony
conviction can or must be excluded include barbers, beauticians,
electricians, landscape architects, livestock dealers, nurses, sign-language
interpreters, and teachers. Some statutes bar people with certain felony
convictions from working for a union. See, e.g., 29 U.S.C. § 504(a)(2). See
also De Veau v. Braisted, 363 U.S. 144, 157–60, 80 S.Ct. 1146, 1153–55
(1960) (upholding the constitutionality of a state law that had the effect of
disqualifying people with felony convictions from serving as officers of any
waterfront labor union unless they had been pardoned or received a
certificate of good conduct from the parole board). And the country's armed
forces are forbidden from enlisting people with felony convictions, although
exceptions can be made in "meritorious cases." 10 U.S.C. § 504(a).

2.   RESTRICTIONS ON GOVERNMENT BENEFITS

As was discussed in Chapter 6, judges may in some instances include
a ban on the receipt of certain government benefits as part of a defendant's
sentence. For example, individuals convicted of felony drug offenses can,
and sometimes must, be barred by the sentence from receiving certain
federal benefits, such as small-business loans and student financial aid. 21
U.S.C. § 862. While this sentencing provision currently exempts some
federal benefits from its scope, including retirement, welfare, Social
Security, health, disability, public-housing, and veterans' benefits, people
convicted of drug offenses can lose some of these exempted benefits under
other federal statutes. For example, persons convicted of a felony drug
crime are ineligible for food stamps and Temporary Assistance for Needy
Families benefits, id. § 862a(a), although states can opt out of this
exclusion or limit the length of the ineligibility period. Id. § 862a(d)(1)(A)–

(B). In addition, public-housing officials have broad discretion to evict or deny housing to persons whom they conclude are involved in criminal drug-related activity, and a drug-related conviction can be treated as evidence of such illegal activity. 42 U.S.C. § 1437d(l)(6).

Students convicted of possessing or selling a controlled substance and whose criminal conduct occurred when they were receiving federal financial aid for college are also ineligible for that aid, including student loans, for periods of time contingent on the nature and number of their drug convictions. 20 U.S.C. § 1091(r)(1) (ineligibility period for a first conviction for possession of a controlled substance is one year, two years for a second conviction, and an indefinite period for additional convictions; ineligibility period for a first conviction for selling a controlled substance is two years and an indefinite period for additional convictions). Students can regain their eligibility for financial aid by successfully completing a drug rehabilitation program or passing two unannounced drug tests administered by such a program. Id. § 1091(r)(2)(A)–(B).

Do you support the withholding of government benefits due to a criminal conviction and if so, what benefits and when? Should the denial of benefits be automatic or discretionary upon conviction? If discretionary, to whom should be remitted the question whether an individual will be denied a government benefit, and what factors should be considered in determining whether to withhold it?

3. RESTRICTIONS ON POLITICAL RIGHTS

Restrictions on political rights are another example of the legal impediments that make it difficult for people with criminal convictions to put their errant pasts behind them. One of the most common forms of this kind of restriction curtails voting rights, the subject of the Supreme Court case which follows.

RICHARDSON V. RAMIREZ

Supreme Court of the United States, 1974.
418 U.S. 24, 94 S.Ct. 2655, 41 L.Ed.2d 551.

MR. JUSTICE REHNQUIST delivered the opinion of the Court.

The three individual respondents in this case were convicted of felonies and have completed the service of their respective sentences and paroles. They filed a petition for a writ of mandate in the Supreme Court of California to compel California county election officials to register them as voters. * * *

Article XX, § 11, of the California Constitution has provided since its adoption in 1879 that "[l]aws shall be made" to exclude from voting persons convicted of bribery, perjury, forgery, malfeasance in office, "or other high crimes." At the time respondents were refused registration, former Art. II, § 1, of the California Constitution provided in part that " * * * no person convicted of any infamous crime * * * shall ever exercise the privileges of an elector in this State." * * * Sections 383, 389, and 390 [of the California Elections Code] direct the county clerk to cancel the registration of all voters who have been convicted of "any infamous crime * * *." Sections 14240 and 14246 permit a voter's qualifications to be challenged on the ground that he has been convicted of "a felony" * * *. * * *

Each of the individual respondents was convicted of one or more felonies, and served some time in jail or prison followed by a successfully terminated parole. * * * All three respondents were refused registration because of their felony convictions.

* * *

* * * The petition for a writ of mandate * * * contended that California's denial of the franchise to the class of ex-felons could no longer withstand scrutiny under the Equal Protection Clause of the Fourteenth Amendment. * * *

* * *

Unlike most claims under the Equal Protection Clause, * * * respondents' claim implicates not merely the language of the Equal Protection Clause of § 1 of the Fourteenth Amendment, but also the provisions of the less familiar § 2 of the Amendment:

> "Representatives shall be apportioned among the several States according to their respective numbers, counting the whole number of persons in each State, excluding Indians not taxed. But when the right to vote at any election for the choice of electors for President and Vice President of the United States, Representatives in Congress, the Executive and Judicial officers of a State, or the members of the Legislature thereof, is denied to any of the male inhabitants of such State, being twenty-one years of age, and citizens of the United States, or in any way abridged, *except for participation in rebellion, or other crime,* the basis of representation therein shall be reduced in the proportion which the number of such male citizens shall bear to the whole number of male citizens twenty-one years of age in such State." (Emphasis supplied.)

Petitioner contends that the italicized language of § 2 expressly exempts from the sanction of that section disenfranchisement grounded on prior conviction of a felony. She goes on to argue that those who framed and adopted the Fourteenth Amendment could not have intended to prohibit outright in § 1 of that Amendment that which was expressly exempted from the lesser sanction of reduced representation imposed by § 2 of the Amendment. This argument seems to us a persuasive one * * *.

* * * The legislative history bearing on the meaning of the relevant language of § 2 is scant indeed * * *. Nonetheless, what legislative history there is indicates that this language was intended by Congress to mean what it says.

* * *

* * * [R]espondents argue that our recent decisions invalidating other state-imposed restrictions on the franchise as violative of the Equal Protection Clause * * * support the conclusions of the Supreme Court of California that a State must show a "compelling state interest" to justify exclusion of ex-felons from the franchise and that California has not done so here.

As we have seen, however, the exclusion of felons from the vote has an affirmative sanction in § 2 of the Fourteenth Amendment, a sanction which was not present in the case of the other restrictions on the franchise which were invalidated in the cases on which respondents rely. * * *

Pressed upon us by the respondents, and by *amici curiae,* are contentions that these notions are outmoded, and that the more modern view is that it is essential to the process of rehabilitating the ex-felon that he be returned to his role in society as a fully participating citizen when he has completed the serving of his term. We would by no means discount these arguments if addressed to the legislative forum which may properly weigh and balance them against those advanced in support of California's present constitutional provisions. But it is not for us to choose one set of values over the other. If respondents are correct, and the view which they advocate is indeed the more enlightened and sensible one, presumably the people of the State of California will ultimately come around to that view. And if they do not do so, their failure is some evidence, at least, of the fact that there are two sides to the argument.

We therefore hold that the Supreme Court of California erred in concluding that California may no longer, consistent with the Equal Protection Clause of the Fourteenth Amendment, exclude from the franchise convicted felons who have completed their sentences and paroles. * * *

* * *

MR. JUSTICE MARSHALL, with whom MR. JUSTICE BRENNAN joins, dissenting.

* * *

* * * The Court construes § 2 of the Fourteenth Amendment as an express authorization for the States to disenfranchise former felons.

Section 2 does except disenfranchisement for "participation in rebellion, or other crime" from the operation of its penalty provision. As the Court notes, however, there is little independent legislative history as to the crucial words "or other crime"; the proposed § 2 went to a joint committee containing only the phrase "participation in rebellion" and emerged with "or other crime" inexplicably tacked on. * * *

* * *

It is clear that § 2 was not intended and should not be construed to be a limitation on the other sections of the Fourteenth Amendment. Section 2 provides a special remedy—reduced representation—to cure a particular form of electoral abuse—the disenfranchisement of Negroes. There is no indication that the framers of the provisions intended that special penalty to be the exclusive remedy for all forms of electoral discrimination. * * *

* * *

* * * [D]isenfranchisement for participation in crime was not uncommon in the States at the time of the adoption of the Amendment. Hence, not surprisingly, that form of disenfranchisement was excepted from the application of the special penalty provision of § 2. But because Congress chose to exempt one form of electoral discrimination from the reduction-of-representation remedy provided by § 2 does not necessarily imply congressional approval of this disenfranchisement.[24] * * *

* * *

In my view, the disenfranchisement of ex-felons must be measured against the requirements of the Equal Protection Clause of § 1 of the Fourteenth Amendment. That analysis properly begins with the observation that because the right to vote "is of the essence of a democratic society, and any restrictions on that right strike at the heart of representative government," voting is a "fundamental" right. * * * "[I]f a challenged statute grants the right to vote to some citizens and denies the franchise to others, 'the Court must determine whether the exclusions are *necessary* to promote a *compelling* state interest.' "

* * * The State has the heavy burden of showing, first, that the challenged disenfranchisement is necessary to a legitimate and substantial state interest; second, that the classification is drawn with precision—that it does not exclude too many people who should not and need not be

---

[24] To say that § 2 of the Fourteenth Amendment is a direct limitation on the protection afforded voting rights by § 1 leads to absurd results. If one accepts the premise that § 2 authorizes disenfranchisement for any crime, the challenged California provision could * * * require disenfranchisement for seduction under promise of marriage, or conspiracy to operate a motor vehicle without a muffler. Disenfranchisement extends to convictions for vagrancy in Alabama or breaking a water pipe in North Dakota, to note but two examples. Even a jaywalking or traffic conviction could conceivably lead to disenfranchisement, since § 2 does not differentiate between felonies and misdemeanors.

excluded; and, third, that there are no other reasonable ways to achieve the State's goal with a lesser burden on the constitutionally protected interest.

I think it clear that the State has not met its burden of justifying the blanket disenfranchisement of former felons presented by this case. There is certainly no basis for asserting that ex-felons have any less interest in the democratic process than any other citizen. Like everyone else, their daily lives are deeply affected and changed by the decisions of government. As the Secretary of State of California observed in his memorandum to the Court in support of respondents in this case:

> "It is doubtful . . . whether the state can demonstrate either a compelling or rational policy interest in denying former felons the right to vote. The individuals involved in the present case are persons who have fully paid their debt to society. They are as much affected by the actions of government as any other citizens, and have as much of a right to participate in governmental decision-making. Furthermore, the denial of the right to vote to such persons is a hindrance to the efforts of society to rehabilitate former felons and convert them into law-abiding and productive citizens."

It is argued that disenfranchisement is necessary to prevent vote frauds. Although the State has a legitimate and, in fact, compelling interest in preventing election fraud, the challenged provision is not sustainable on that ground. First, the disenfranchisement provisions are patently both overinclusive and underinclusive. The provision is not limited to those who have demonstrated a marked propensity for abusing the ballot by violating election laws. Rather, it encompasses all former felons and there has been no showing that ex-felons generally are any more likely to abuse the ballot than the remainder of the population. In contrast, many of those convicted of violating election laws are treated as misdemeanants and are not barred from voting at all. It seems clear that the classification here is not tailored to achieve its articulated goal, since it crudely excludes large numbers of otherwise qualified voters.

Moreover, there are means available for the State to prevent voting fraud which are far less burdensome on the constitutionally protected right to vote. * * * [T]he State "has at its disposal a variety of criminal laws that are more than adequate to detect and deter whatever fraud may be feared." * * *

Another asserted purpose is to keep former felons from voting because their likely voting pattern might be subversive of the interests of an orderly society. * * *

Although, in the last century, this Court may have justified the exclusion of voters from the electoral process for fear that they would vote to change laws considered important by a temporal majority, I have little doubt that we would not countenance such a purpose today. The process of democracy is one of change. Our laws are not frozen into immutable form, they are constantly in the process of revision in response to the needs of a changing society. The public interest, as conceived by a majority of the voting public, is constantly undergoing re-examination. * * * Voters who opposed the repeal of prohibition could have disenfranchised those who advocated repeal "to prevent persons from being enabled by their votes to defeat the criminal laws of the country." Today, presumably those who support the legalization of marihuana could be barred from the ballot box for much the same reason. The ballot is the democratic system's coin of the realm. To condition its exercise on support of the established order is to debase that currency beyond recognition. * * *

* * *

* * * I think it clear that measured against the standards of this Court's modern equal protection jurisprudence, the blanket disenfranchisement of ex-felons cannot stand.

* * *

QUESTIONS AND POINTS FOR DISCUSSION

1.   The Supreme Court distinguished *Richardson v. Ramirez* when holding a voting restriction unconstitutional in Hunter v. Underwood, 471 U.S. 222, 105 S.Ct. 1916 (1985). The restriction at issue in that case, set forth in the Alabama Constitution, precluded persons convicted of "any crime . . . involving moral turpitude" from voting. The Alabama Constitutional Convention of 1901 adopted this provision in order to disenfranchise African Americans whom, it was felt, were convicted of these types of crimes with greater frequency than white people. Because of the discriminatory intent which prompted the enactment of the disenfranchisement provision and because it continued to have a disproportionately adverse effect on African Americans, the Supreme Court, in a unanimous opinion written by Justice Rehnquist, struck down the provision on equal-protection grounds.

2.   The decision of the Supreme Court of Canada in Sauvé v. Canada, 3 S.C.R. 519 (2002) stands in stark contrast with the United States Supreme Court's decision in *Richardson v. Ramirez*. At issue in *Sauvé* was the constitutionality of a statute that barred people serving prison sentences of two years or longer from voting while they were incarcerated. The constitutional provision invoked by the Canadian Supreme Court in striking down this statute is worded quite differently than the Equal Protection Clause construed by the Supreme Court in *Richardson* in tandem with section 2 of the Fourteenth Amendment. Section 3 of the Canadian Charter of Rights and Freedoms specifically accords "[e]very citizen of Canada" the right to vote, subject to the caveat in section 1 that "reasonable limits" can be placed on a

right when shown by the government to be "demonstrably justified in a free and democratic society."

The Supreme Court of Canada concluded that the government had failed to meet its burden of proving that the voting restriction was "demonstrably justified" in a democracy like Canada's. The Court rebuffed the government's argument that the disenfranchisement of certain prisoners served an educational purpose, teaching both inmates and the general public about the value of respecting the law. Describing disenfranchisement as, in fact, "bad pedagogy," the Court remonstrated that the denial of voting rights would have the opposite of its intended effect, promoting disrespect for the law and a disregard of civic responsibilities:

> Denying citizen law-breakers the right to vote sends the message that those who commit serious breaches are no longer valued as members of the community, but instead are temporary outcasts from our system of rights and democracy. More profoundly, it sends the unacceptable message that democratic values are less important than punitive measures ostensibly designed to promote order.

Id. at 548.

The government also asserted that allowing the disenfranchised prisoners to vote would "demean" the political process. But the Court found the notion that some people are less worthy to vote—whether because of their gender, race, socioeconomic status, or conduct—to be an obsolete vestige of the past, one not in keeping with the respect for the dignity of each human being that is a core value of Canadian democracy.

The government furthermore argued that stripping people serving prison sentences of two years or longer of their voting rights was a legitimate way of punishing them for their crimes. Writing for the majority of the Court, Chief Justice McLachlin spurned this asserted justification for disenfranchising prisoners:

> The argument, stripped of rhetoric, proposes that it is open to Parliament to add a new tool to its arsenal of punitive implements— denial of constitutional rights. I find this notion problematic. I do not doubt that Parliament may limit constitutional rights in the name of punishment, provided that it can justify the limitation. But it is another thing to say that a particular class of people for a particular period of time will completely lose a particular constitutional right. * * * Could Parliament justifiably pass a law removing the right of all penitentiary prisoners to be protected from cruel and unusual punishment? I think not. What of freedom of expression or religion? Why, one asks, is the right to vote different? * * *

Id. at 550, 552–53.

Other countries' higher courts have ruled that voting bans imposed on prisoners are unconstitutional. In one case, for example, the Supreme Court of Israel upheld the right of the imprisoned assassin of Prime Minister Yitzak

Rabin, as well as other prisoners, to vote, citing the need to accord "respect for his right" to vote despite "contempt for this act." See Marc Mauer, Voting Behind Bars: An Argument for Voting by Prisoners, 54 Howard L.J. 549, 564 (2011). Courts have also found such blanket bans in violation of certain international human-rights agreements. In Hirst v. United Kingdom, 38 E.H.R.R. 40 (Eur.Ct.H.R.2004), for example, the European Court of Human Rights held that a statute in Great Britain prohibiting virtually all prisoners from voting contravened the European Convention on Human Rights. In some countries, such as Israel, polling places are located in prisons and detention centers to facilitate voting by prisoners and detainees. Pamela S. Karlan, Convictions and Doubts: Retribution, Representation, and the Debate Over Felon Disenfranchisement, 56 Stan. L.Rev. 1147, 1148 n.8 (2004). For additional details about prisoners' right to vote in other selected countries, see Penal Reform Int'l, The right of prisoners to vote: a global overview (2016).

3.   Felon-disenfranchisement laws vary from state to state in this country. In 2016, forty-eight states barred prisoners convicted of a felony from voting, with only Maine and Vermont according them the right to vote. Thirty-four states excluded parolees from the franchise, while thirty disenfranchised felony probationers. Twelve states prohibited some or all felons who had completed serving their sentences from voting. The Sentencing Project, 6 Million Lost Voters: State-Level Estimates of Felony Disenfranchisement, 2016, at 4 (2016). Approximately 6.1 million people—one out of every forty adults—were ineligible to vote in 2016 because of a felony conviction. Over half of these disenfranchised people (3.1 million) had completed serving their sentences. Less than a quarter of those disenfranchised due to a felony conviction were confined in prison or jail. Id. at 3–4, 6.

Felon-disenfranchisement laws have had a particularly significant adverse impact on African-Americans. In 2016, over 2.2 million African-Americans—one out of every thirteen old enough to vote—were ineligible to vote because of a felony conviction. Half of these disenfranchised people had completed serving their sentences. Id. at 3, 14, 16.

4.   Some researchers have concluded that the disenfranchisement of people with felony convictions has affected the outcomes of elections, including the 2000 presidential election. The Democratic candidate in that election, Al Gore, won the popular vote, beating the Republican candidate, George W. Bush, by over a half a million votes. But Bush won the Electoral College after carrying the state of Florida by a very close margin—537 votes. At the time, Florida had more people disenfranchised because of felony convictions than any other state in the nation, with over 600,000 of the estimated 827,000 individuals in that state barred from voting having fully served their sentences. After calculating the estimated turnout rate (27.2%) and the party preferences (68.9% Democratic) of the people disenfranchised due to felony convictions, two prominent sociologists concluded that Gore would have defeated Bush by 80,000 votes in Florida and won the presidential election if these individuals had been eligible to vote. Even if the estimated turnout rate was cut in half and only people who had served their sentences had been

permitted to vote, Gore reportedly would have carried the state of Florida by 30,000 votes. Jeff Manza & Christopher Uggen, Locked Out: Felon Disenfranchisement and American Democracy 192 (2006).

5.   Under what circumstances, if any, do you believe that the conviction of a person of a crime should lead to his or her disenfranchisement? For a comparative analysis of the disenfranchisement of felons in Germany, see Nora V. Demleitner, U.S. Felon Disenfranchisement: Parting Ways with Western Europe, in Criminal Disenfranchisement in an International Perspective 85–86 (Alec Ewald & Brandon Rottinghaus eds., 2009) (deprivation of voting rights for a period of time ranging from two to five years following release from prison can be ordered, in the judge's discretion, as part of the sentence for election-related crimes, such as voting fraud, and crimes, like treason, that imperil the "foundation of the German state").

6.   Like felon-disenfranchisement laws, other governmental policies pertaining to prisoners have political repercussions. These policies, which include those that affect how many and which people will be imprisoned, where they will be incarcerated, and the community they will be deemed residents of during the time they are incarcerated, have two particularly noteworthy effects. First, the Census Bureau counts prisoners as residents of the community in which they are incarcerated, not the community from which they came and typically will return following their release from prison. Since electoral districts are based on population size and since most prisons are located far from the inner-city areas from where most prisoners come and will return, the end result is a tipping of political power towards more rural areas, where the nonprisoner population is predominantly white, and away from urban areas heavily populated by minorities. Responding to what is commonly termed "prison-based gerrymandering," several states have enacted statutes deeming prisoners' residences for redistricting purposes to be their last known residence before they were incarcerated. See Erika L. Wood, One Significant Step: How Reforms to Prison Districts Begin to Address Political Inequality, 49 U. Mich. J.L. Reform 179, 192 n.69 (2015) (citing California, Delaware, Maryland, and New York statutes).

Second, the amount of some of the federal and state aid that a jurisdiction receives hinges on the size of its population as well as the median income of its residents. Since prisoners typically are counted as residents of the place they are imprisoned and make no or little money, urban areas lose money when people from those areas are incarcerated elsewhere. See Pamela S. Karlan, Convictions and Doubts: Retribution, Representation, and the Debate Over Felon Disenfranchisement, 56 Stan. L.Rev. 1147, 1159–60 (2004) (reporting that the incarceration of approximately 26,000 people from Chicago in downstate prisons at the time of the 2000 census would result in a loss to the city of $88 million in federal and state aid over the ensuing decade).

The aggregate effects of the Census Bureau's residency rules, government funding formulas, the location of prisons, and the disenfranchisement of prisoners have been analogized by some commentators to the "Three-fifths

Clause" that was part of the Constitution when it was first enacted. Id. at 1160. Under that provision, slaves, who had no right to vote, were counted as three-fifths of a person, thereby enhancing the political power of the slave states. U.S. Const. art. I, § 2, cl. 3. Do you find this analogy apposite? Where, in your opinion, should prisoners' domicile be for census purposes, which, as mentioned earlier, affects electoral districting, the level of federal funding, and in many states, the distribution of some state funds? If prisoners were accorded the right to vote, where should their domicile be for voting purposes? See Debra Parkes, Ballot Boxes Behind Bars: Toward the Repeal of Prisoner Disenfranchisement Laws, 13 Temp. Pol. & Civ. Rts. L.Rev. 71, 104–05 (2003) (positing the option of establishing a "default rule" under which prisoners' domicile, for voting purposes, is the place where they lived before their incarceration unless they change their domicile to the prison). What are the benefits and drawbacks of each domicile option?

7. In addition to possibly losing the right to vote, released prisoners and other people with criminal convictions may find that they are barred from serving on juries. Almost all states and the federal government have statutes authorizing or requiring certain people with criminal convictions to be barred from juries, though these statutes vary greatly in terms of, for example, the crimes triggering the disqualification and the duration of the disqualification period. Anna Roberts, Casual Ostracism: Jury Exclusion on the Basis of Criminal Convictions, 98 Minn. L.Rev. 592, 593, 595–99 (2013). In your opinion, should a prior criminal conviction ever bar a person who is not currently incarcerated from serving on a jury? Why or why not?

4. RESTRICTIONS ON DRIVERS' LICENSES AND THE POSSESSION OF FIREARMS

A criminal conviction sometimes can trigger the suspension or revocation of a person's driver's license. Some of these suspensions and revocations are for convictions not stemming from driving. One federal statute, for example, provides for a reduction in federal highway funds unless a state adopts and enforces a law suspending for at least six months the driving privileges of individuals convicted of drug offenses. 23 U.S.C. § 159(a)(3)(A). This statute, though, allows states to opt out from the automatic suspension requirement, id. at § 159(a)(3)(B), and in recent years, an increasing number of them have begun doing so. Joshua Aiken, Prison Policy Initiative, Reinstating Common Sense: How driver's license suspensions for drug offenses unrelated to driving are falling out of favor 1 (2016). When, in your opinion, should driving privileges be curtailed because of a criminal conviction?

All of the states place some restrictions on the possession of firearms by people with felony, and sometimes other, convictions. Some states prohibit all people with felony convictions from possessing any type of firearm. Other states limit firearms restrictions to those convicted of specified crimes, such as drug offenses or violent felonies. For a list of the restrictions on firearms privileges imposed by each state after a conviction, see Collateral Consequences Resource Ctr. et al., Restoration of Rights Project, State Law Relief from Federal Firearms Act Disabilities, at http://ccresourcecenter.org/state-restoration-profiles/50-state-comparisonstate-law-relief-from-federal-firearms-act-disabilities (last visited Feb. 13, 2018).

Federal statutes also place restrictions on the possession of firearms for certain criminal convictions. The interplay between state and federal firearms' restrictions can raise complex questions, as the Supreme Court's decision in Caron v. United States, 524 U.S. 308, 118 S.Ct. 2007 (1998) illustrates.

At issue in that case was a federal statute that provides for an enhanced sentence when a person who has three prior convictions for violent felonies or "serious" drug offenses possesses a firearm. 18 U.S.C. § 924(e). A prior conviction generally does not count, however, if the individual has had his or her civil rights restored for that offense. Only if the restoration of rights was limited, precluding the person from possessing or otherwise dealing with firearms, would the prior conviction count towards imposition of an enhanced sentence under the federal statute. Id. § 921(a)(20).

The problem that the Court confronted in *Caron* stemmed from the fact that a state law had restored the right of the defendant, who had previously been convicted of several violent felonies, to possess most, but not all, firearms. Under that law, the defendant could not possess handguns outside his home or business. When rifles and shotguns were later seized from his house, the question was: Was he subject to an enhanced sentence because, under state law, he could not possess handguns in certain places, or was he not subject to an enhanced sentence because a state law had restored his right to possess the kinds of firearms—rifles and shotguns—that were found in his home?

The Supreme Court concluded that the defendant was subject to the enhanced sentence under federal law. Although most of his "gun rights" had been restored, state law still prohibited him from possessing at least some firearms. Consequently, his sentence was enhanced under the federal statute for possessing rifles and shotguns that, under state law, he was permitted to possess.

5. RESTRICTIONS FOR SEX OFFENSES

a. Registration and Community-Notification Laws

In 1994, New Jersey enacted what is known as "Megan's Law," named after a seven-year-old girl who was raped and murdered by a man with two previous convictions for sexually assaulting children. N.J.Rev.Stat. §§ 2C:7–1 to –23. The law has two primary components: first, a requirement, backed up by criminal sanctions, that people convicted of certain sex offenses register at the local police department; and second, a requirement that local law-enforcement officials notify certain individuals and entities in the community about a registered individual's presence within the community.

The type of notification required under the community-notification provision depends upon the individual's level of risk of reoffense, as determined by the county prosecutor in the county in which the registered person was convicted, the prosecutor in the county in which he or she will reside, and any law-enforcement officials that the prosecutors pull into the assessment process. If the reoffense risk is low, only law-enforcement agencies likely to encounter the registrant need to be notified. If the risk is moderate, certain entities in the community, such as schools and youth organizations, must also be notified. And if the reoffense risk is high, members of the public "likely to encounter" the registrant must be notified as well. Id. § 2C:7–8(c)(3). As interpreted by the New Jersey Supreme Court, the latter group to be notified includes people in the registered person's immediate neighborhood; all schools within the community, depending on its size; and schools in nearby communities, depending on how close they are to places where the registrant lives, works, or goes to school. Doe v. Poritz, 662 A.2d 367, 385 (N.J.1995).

All of the states have now adopted sex-offender registration and community-notification laws. See United States v. Kebodeaux, 570 U.S. 387, 413 n.2, 133 S.Ct. 2496, 2513 n.2 (2013) (Thomas, J., dissenting) (listing state statutes). A federal statute referred to as SORNA (Sex Offender Registration and Notification Act) requires states to adopt such laws to be eligible for certain federal funding and mandates that information about registered individuals be available to the public on-line. 42 U.S.C. §§ 16912–16929. A corresponding criminal statute makes a person's failure to comply with the Act's registration requirements a federal crime. 18 U.S.C. § 2250.

In your opinion, are these registration and community-notification laws sound or unsound from a policy perspective? Are they constitutional?

The Supreme Court has adjudicated several questions concerning the constitutionality of sex-offender registration and notification laws. The question before the Court in Connecticut Department of Public Safety v. Doe, 538 U.S. 1, 123 S.Ct. 1160 (2003) was whether people with sex-offense convictions living in Connecticut had a due-process right to a hearing, at which it would be determined whether they were "currently dangerous," before information about them was included in a sex-offender registry that could be perused in certain state offices and on an Internet website. The state statute whose constitutionality was at issue in the case did not predicate the dissemination of personal information, including names, addresses, and photographs, on a finding that a registrant was currently dangerous. Instead, a conviction of certain crimes, by itself, triggered the statute's public-notification provisions. Consequently, the Supreme Court held, in a unanimous opinion, that there was no due-process right to a hearing on the question of the existence of a criterion—current dangerousness—that was irrelevant under the statute's public-notification provision.

In Smith v. Doe, 538 U.S. 84, 123 S.Ct. 1140 (2003), the Supreme Court considered another constitutional question about a sex-offender registration and public-notification law: whether Alaska's Sex Offender Registration Act violated the constitutional prohibition of *ex post facto* laws. The registration and notification provisions of that Act applied retroactively—to persons convicted before the statute's enactment. Individuals convicted of a nonaggravated sex offense were subject to the statute's registration provisions for fifteen years, and they had to update the information provided to the Alaska Department of Public Safety, such as their place of employment and physical description, once a year. Individuals convicted of two or more sex offenses or of an aggravated sex offense were subject to the reporting requirements for life and had to update the registration information every three months. Most of this registration information was disseminated to the public via the Internet.

The Supreme Court found the registration and notification provisions to be nonpunitive measures designed to protect the public's safety rather than a punishment that cannot be imposed retrospectively. Unmoved by the fact that the registration provisions had been placed in the state's criminal code, the Court remarked: "The location and labels of a statutory provision do not by themselves transform a civil remedy into a criminal one." Id. at 94, 123 S.Ct. at 1148. Nor was the Court's conclusion that the restrictions were nonpunitive altered by the fact that Alaska's Rules of Criminal Procedure required courts to both apprise certain people of the registration and notification provisions before accepting their guilty pleas and to spell out the provisions' requirements in the written judgments for specified crimes. Notifying individuals of the civil consequences of their convictions, observed the Court, did not make those consequences punitive. Such notification, the Court added, served the laudable, nonpunitive goal of ensuring that they complied with the registration requirements.

In a dissenting opinion, Justice Stevens argued that the registration and notification provisions had all of the hallmarks of a criminal punishment. "[A] sanction that (1) is imposed on everyone who commits a criminal offense; (2) is not imposed on anyone else; and (3) severely impairs a person's liberty is punishment," he contended. Id. at 113, 123 S.Ct. at 1158. In discussing the latter component of a criminal punishment—how the registration provisions substantially curtailed the liberty of people with sex-offense convictions living in Alaska, Justice Stevens pointed out that those subject to the law could not take such mundane actions as changing the color of their hair, shaving their beards, or switching employers without notifying authorities.

In a separate dissenting opinion, Justice Ginsburg, joined by Justice Breyer, opined that the registration and notification requirements were simply modern counterparts to age-old shaming punishments like whipping, branding, the pillory, and banishment. But the majority, for two reasons, found the analogy inapposite: first, the colonial punishments involved either a "direct confrontation" between the person being punished and the public or that person's expulsion from the community; and second, the primary purpose of these primeval punishments was to stigmatize the offender. Id. at 98, 123 S.Ct. at 1150. By contrast, the notification provision's purpose and "principal effect" were "to inform the public for its own safety, not to humiliate the offender." Id. at 99, 123 S.Ct. at 1150.

The Court did not consider this purpose belied by the fact that a registered person's picture and other personal information were posted on an Internet website. The Court felt that utilizing the Internet was simply an efficient means through which the public could protect itself. The Court emphasized that this notification mechanism was "passive" since individuals had to visit the website to obtain the information they wanted or needed about people convicted of sex crimes. Id. at 105, 123 S.Ct. at 1153. In finding that this notification system was much more akin to visiting an archive to view criminal records than it was to the penalties designed to incite public opprobrium in colonial times, the Court stated: "Our system does not treat dissemination of truthful information in furtherance of a legitimate governmental objective as punishment." Id. at 98, 123 S.Ct. at 1150.

After the Supreme Court rendered its decision in *Smith v. Doe* rebuffing the federal constitutional challenge to the Alaska Sex Offender Registration Act, the Alaska Supreme Court held that the Act, as applied to someone whose sex crime preceded the statute's enactment, violated the Ex Post Facto Clause of the state's constitution. See Doe v. State, 189 P.3d 999, 1019 (Alaska 2008). In your opinion, do registration and notification requirements inflict punishment on people convicted of sex offenses, raising *ex post facto* concerns if those requirements are applied retroactively?

b. Civil-Commitment Laws

KANSAS V. HENDRICKS

Supreme Court of the United States, 1997.
521 U.S. 346, 117 S.Ct. 2072, 138 L.Ed.2d 501.

JUSTICE THOMAS delivered the opinion of the Court.

* * *

I

A

The Kansas Legislature enacted the Sexually Violent Predator Act (Act) [Kan. Stat. Ann. § 59–29a01 *et seq.*] in 1994 to grapple with the problem of managing repeat sexual offenders. Although Kansas already had a statute addressing the involuntary commitment of those defined as "mentally ill," the legislature determined that existing civil commitment procedures were inadequate to confront the risks presented by "sexually violent predators." In the Act's preamble, the legislature explained:

> "[A] small but extremely dangerous group of sexually violent predators exist who do not have a mental disease or defect that renders them appropriate for involuntary treatment pursuant to the [general involuntary civil commitment statute]. . . . In contrast to persons appropriate for civil commitment under the [general involuntary civil commitment statute], sexually violent predators generally have anti-social personality features which are unamenable to existing mental illness treatment modalities and those features render them likely to engage in sexually violent behavior. The legislature further finds that sexually violent predators' likelihood of engaging in repeat acts of predatory sexual violence is high. * * * The legislature further finds that the prognosis for rehabilitating sexually violent predators in a prison setting is poor * * *."

As a result, the Legislature found it necessary to establish "a civil commitment procedure for the long-term care and treatment of the sexually violent predator." The Act defined a "sexually violent predator" as: "any person who has been convicted of or charged with a sexually violent offense and who suffers from a mental abnormality or personality disorder which makes the person likely to engage in the predatory acts of sexual violence."

A "mental abnormality" was defined, in turn, as a "congenital or acquired condition affecting the emotional or volitional capacity which predisposes the person to commit sexually violent offenses in a degree constituting such person a menace to the health and safety of others."

As originally structured, the Act's civil commitment procedures pertained to: (1) a presently confined person who, like Hendricks, "has been convicted of a sexually violent offense" and is scheduled for release; (2) a person who has been "charged with a sexually violent offense" but has been found incompetent to stand trial; (3) a person who has been found "not guilty by reason of insanity of a sexually violent offense"; and (4) a person found "not guilty" of a sexually violent offense because of a mental disease or defect.

The initial version of the Act, as applied to a currently confined person such as Hendricks, was designed to initiate a specific series of procedures. The custodial agency was required to notify the local prosecutor 60 days before the anticipated release of a person who might have met the Act's criteria. The prosecutor was then obligated, within 45 days, to decide whether to file a petition in state court seeking the person's involuntary commitment. If such a petition were filed, the court was to determine whether "probable cause" existed to support a finding that the person was a "sexually violent predator" and thus eligible for civil commitment. Upon such a determination, transfer of the individual to a secure facility for professional evaluation would occur. After that evaluation, a trial would be held to determine beyond a reasonable doubt whether the individual was a sexually violent predator. If that determination were made, the person would then be transferred to the custody of the Secretary of Social and Rehabilitation Services (Secretary) for "control, care and treatment until such time as the person's mental abnormality or personality disorder has so changed that the person is safe to be at large."

In addition to placing the burden of proof upon the State, the Act afforded the individual a number of other procedural safeguards. In the case of an indigent person, the State was required to provide, at public expense, the assistance of counsel and an examination by mental health care professionals. The individual also received the right to present and cross-examine witnesses, and the opportunity to review documentary evidence presented by the State.

Once an individual was confined, the Act required that "[t]he involuntary detention or commitment . . . shall conform to constitutional requirements for care and treatment." Confined persons were afforded three different avenues of review: First, the committing court was obligated to conduct an annual review to determine whether continued detention was warranted. Second, the Secretary was permitted, at any time, to decide that the confined individual's condition had so changed that release was appropriate, and could then authorize the person to petition for release. Finally, even without the Secretary's permission, the confined person could at any time file a release petition. If the court found that the State could no longer satisfy its burden under the initial commitment standard, the individual would be freed from confinement.

B

In 1984, Hendricks was convicted of taking "indecent liberties" with two 13-year-old boys. After serving nearly 10 years of his sentence, he was slated for release to a halfway house. Shortly before his scheduled release, however, the State filed a petition in state court seeking Hendricks' civil confinement as a sexually violent predator. * * *

Hendricks subsequently requested a jury trial to determine whether he qualified as a sexually violent predator. During that trial, Hendricks' own testimony revealed a chilling history of repeated child sexual molestation and abuse, beginning in 1955 when he exposed his genitals to two young girls. At that time, he pleaded guilty to indecent exposure. Then, in 1957, he was convicted of lewdness involving a young girl and received a brief jail sentence. In 1960, he molested two young boys while he worked for a carnival. After serving two years in prison for that offense, he was paroled, only to be rearrested for molesting a 7-year-old girl. Attempts were made to treat him for his sexual deviance, and in 1965 he was considered "safe to be at large," and was discharged from a state psychiatric hospital.

Shortly thereafter, however, Hendricks sexually assaulted another young boy and girl—he performed oral sex on the 8-year-old girl and fondled the 11-year-old boy. He was again imprisoned in 1967, but refused to participate in a sex offender treatment program, and thus remained incarcerated until his parole in 1972. Diagnosed as a pedophile, Hendricks entered into, but then abandoned, a treatment program. He testified that despite having received professional help for his pedophilia, he continued to harbor sexual desires for children. Indeed, soon after his 1972 parole, Hendricks began to abuse his own stepdaughter and stepson. He forced the children to engage in sexual activity with him over a period of approximately four years. Then, as noted above, Hendricks was convicted of "taking indecent liberties" with two adolescent boys after he attempted to fondle them. As a result of that conviction, he was once again imprisoned, and was serving that sentence when he reached his conditional release date in September 1994.

Hendricks admitted that he had repeatedly abused children whenever he was not confined. He explained that when he "get[s] stressed out," he "can't control the urge" to molest children. Although Hendricks recognized that his behavior harms children, and he hoped he would not sexually molest children again, he stated that the only sure way he could keep from sexually abusing children in the future was "to die." Hendricks readily agreed with the state physician's diagnosis that he suffers from pedophilia and that he is not cured of the condition; indeed, he told the physician that "treatment is bull——."

The jury unanimously found beyond a reasonable doubt that Hendricks was a sexually violent predator. The trial court subsequently determined, as a matter of state law, that pedophilia qualifies as a "mental abnormality" as defined by the Act, and thus ordered Hendricks committed to the Secretary's custody.

Hendricks appealed, claiming, among other things, that application of the Act to him violated the Federal Constitution's Due Process, Double Jeopardy, and *Ex Post Facto* Clauses. * * *

* * *

II

A

Kansas argues that the Act's definition of "mental abnormality" satisfies "substantive" due process requirements. We agree. * * *

* * *

* * * Commitment proceedings can be initiated only when a person "has been convicted of or charged with a sexually violent offense," and "suffers from a mental abnormality or personality disorder which makes the person likely to engage in the predatory acts of sexual violence." The statute thus requires proof of more than a mere predisposition to violence; rather, it requires evidence of past sexually violent behavior and a present mental condition that creates a likelihood of such conduct in the future if the person is not incapacitated. * * *

A finding of dangerousness, standing alone, is ordinarily not a sufficient ground upon which to justify indefinite involuntary commitment. We have sustained civil commitment statutes when they have coupled proof of dangerousness with the proof of some additional factor, such as a "mental illness" or "mental abnormality." These added statutory requirements serve to limit involuntary civil confinement to those who suffer from a volitional impairment rendering them dangerous beyond their control. * * *

Hendricks nonetheless argues that our earlier cases dictate a finding of "mental illness" as a prerequisite for civil commitment * * *. He then asserts that a "mental abnormality" is not equivalent to a "mental illness" because it is a term coined by the Kansas Legislature, rather than by the psychiatric community. * * *

[W]e have never required State legislatures to adopt any particular nomenclature in drafting civil commitment statutes. Rather, we have traditionally left to legislators the task of defining terms of a medical nature that have legal significance. * * * Often, those definitions do not fit precisely with the definitions employed by the medical community. The legal definitions of "insanity" and "competency," for example, vary substantially from their psychiatric counterparts.

To the extent that the civil commitment statutes we have considered set forth criteria relating to an individual's inability to control his dangerousness, the Kansas Act sets forth comparable criteria and Hendricks' condition doubtless satisfies those criteria. The mental health professionals who evaluated Hendricks diagnosed him as suffering from pedophilia, a condition the psychiatric profession itself classifies as a serious mental disorder. Hendricks even conceded that, when he becomes "stressed out," he cannot "control the urge" to molest children. This admitted lack of volitional control, coupled with a prediction of future dangerousness, adequately distinguishes Hendricks from other dangerous persons who are perhaps more properly dealt with exclusively through criminal proceedings. Hendricks' diagnosis as a pedophile, which qualifies as a "mental abnormality" under the Act, thus plainly suffices for due process purposes.

B

We granted Hendricks' cross-petition to determine whether the Act violates the Constitution's double jeopardy prohibition or its ban on *ex post facto* lawmaking. The thrust of Hendricks' argument is that the Act establishes criminal proceedings; hence confinement under it necessarily constitutes punishment. He contends that where, as here, newly enacted "punishment" is predicated upon past conduct for which he has already been convicted and forced to serve a prison sentence, the Constitution's Double Jeopardy and *Ex Post Facto* Clauses are violated. * * *

The categorization of a particular proceeding as civil or criminal "is first of all a question of statutory construction." We must initially ascertain whether the legislature meant the statute to establish "civil" proceedings. If so, we ordinarily defer to the legislature's stated intent. Here, Kansas' objective to create a civil proceeding is evidenced by its placement of the Sexually Violent Predator Act within the Kansas probate code, instead of the criminal code, as well as its description of the Act as creating a *"civil commitment procedure."* Kan. Stat. Ann., Article 29 (1994) ("Care and Treatment for Mentally Ill Persons"), § 59–29a01 (emphasis added). Nothing on the face of the statute suggests that the legislature sought to create anything other than a civil commitment scheme designed to protect the public from harm.

Although we recognize that a "civil label is not always dispositive," we will reject the legislature's manifest intent only where a party challenging the statute provides "the clearest proof" that "the statutory scheme [is] so punitive either in purpose or effect as to negate [the State's] intention" to deem it "civil." * * * Hendricks, however, has failed to satisfy this heavy burden.

As a threshold matter, commitment under the Act does not implicate either of the two primary objectives of criminal punishment: retribution or deterrence. The Act's purpose is not retributive because it does not affix culpability for prior criminal conduct. Instead, such conduct is used solely for evidentiary purposes, either to demonstrate that a "mental abnormality" exists or to support a finding of future dangerousness. * * * In addition, the Kansas Act does not make a criminal conviction a prerequisite for commitment—persons absolved of criminal responsibility may nonetheless be subject to confinement under the Act. * * *

* * *

Nor can it be said that the legislature intended the Act to function as a deterrent. Those persons committed under the Act are, by definition, suffering from a "mental abnormality" or a "personality disorder" that prevents them from exercising adequate control over their behavior. Such persons are therefore unlikely to be deterred by the threat of confinement. And the conditions surrounding that confinement do not suggest a punitive purpose on the State's part. The State has represented that an individual confined under the Act is not subject to the more restrictive conditions placed on state prisoners, but instead experiences essentially the same conditions as any involuntarily committed patient in the state mental institution. * * *

* * *

Finally, Hendricks argues that the Act is necessarily punitive because it fails to offer any legitimate "treatment." * * *

* * *

Accepting the Kansas court's apparent determination that treatment is not possible for this category of individuals does not obligate us to adopt its legal conclusions. We have already observed that, under the appropriate circumstances and when accompanied by proper procedures, incapacitation may be a legitimate end of the civil law. * * *

* * *

Although the treatment program initially offered Hendricks may have seemed somewhat meager, it must be remembered that he was the first person committed under the Act. That the State did not have all of its treatment procedures in place is thus not surprising. What is significant, however, is that Hendricks was placed under the supervision of the Kansas Department of Health and Social and Rehabilitative Services, housed in a unit segregated from the general prison population and operated not by employees of the Department of Corrections, but by other trained individuals. And, before this Court, Kansas declared "[a]bsolutely" that persons committed under the Act are now receiving in the neighborhood of "31.5 hours of treatment per week."[5]

Where the State has "disavowed any punitive intent"; limited confinement to a small segment of particularly dangerous individuals; provided strict procedural safeguards; directed that confined persons be segregated from the general prison population and afforded the same status as others who have been civilly committed; recommended treatment if such is possible; and permitted immediate release upon a showing that the individual is no longer dangerous or mentally impaired, we cannot say that it acted with punitive intent. We therefore hold that the Act does not establish criminal proceedings and that involuntary confinement pursuant to the Act is not punitive. Our conclusion that the Act is nonpunitive thus removes an essential prerequisite for both Hendricks' double jeopardy and *ex post facto* claims.

1

The Double Jeopardy Clause provides: "[N]or shall any person be subject for the same offence to be twice put in jeopardy of life or limb." * * * Hendricks argues that, as applied to him, the Act violates double jeopardy principles because his confinement under the Act, imposed after a conviction and a term of incarceration, amounted to both a second prosecution and a second punishment for the same offense. We disagree.

Because we have determined that the Kansas Act is civil in nature, initiation of its commitment proceedings does not constitute a second prosecution. Moreover, as commitment under the Act is not tantamount to "punishment," Hendricks' involuntary detention does not violate the Double Jeopardy Clause, even though that confinement may follow a prison term. * * * If an individual otherwise meets the requirements for involuntary civil commitment, the State is under no obligation to release that individual simply because the detention would follow a period of incarceration.

* * *

2

Hendricks' *ex post facto* claim is similarly flawed. The *Ex Post Facto* Clause, which " 'forbids the application of any new punitive measure to a crime already consummated,' " has been interpreted to pertain exclusively to penal statutes. As we have previously determined, the Act does not impose punishment; thus, its application does not raise *ex post facto* concerns. * * *

---

[5] * * * [T]o the extent that treatment is available for Hendricks' condition, the State now appears to be providing it. By furnishing such treatment, the Kansas Legislature has indicated that treatment, if possible, is at least an ancillary goal of the Act, which easily satisfies any test for determining that the Act is not punitive.

III

We hold that the Kansas Sexually Violent Predator Act comports with due process requirements and neither runs afoul of double jeopardy principles nor constitutes an exercise in impermissible *ex post facto* lawmaking. * * *

JUSTICE KENNEDY, concurring.

* * *

* * * A law enacted after commission of the offense and which punishes the offense by extending the term of confinement is a textbook example of an *ex post facto* law. If the object or purpose of the Kansas law had been to provide treatment but the treatment provisions were adopted as a sham or mere pretext, there would have been an indication of the forbidden purpose to punish. * * *

* * * In this case, the mental abnormality—pedophilia—is at least described in the DSM–IV. American Psychiatric Association, Diagnostic and Statistical Manual of Mental Disorders 524–525, 527–528 (4th ed.1994).

* * *

On the record before us, the Kansas civil statute conforms to our precedents. If, however, civil confinement were to become a mechanism for retribution or general deterrence, or if it were shown that mental abnormality is too imprecise a category to offer a solid basis for concluding that civil detention is justified, our precedents would not suffice to validate it.

JUSTICE BREYER, with whom JUSTICES STEVENS and SOUTER join, and with whom JUSTICE GINSBURG joins as to Parts II and III, dissenting.

[In Part I of his opinion, Justice Breyer explained why he agreed with the majority of the Court that Kansas's Sexually Violent Predator Act does not violate due process.]

II

Kansas' 1994 Act violates the Federal Constitution's prohibition of "any . . . *ex post facto* Law" if it "inflicts" upon Hendricks "a greater punishment" than did the law "annexed to" his "crime[s]" when he "committed" those crimes in 1984. * * *

Certain resemblances between the Act's "civil commitment" and traditional criminal punishments are obvious. Like criminal imprisonment, the Act's civil commitment amounts to "secure" confinement and "incarceration against one's will." See Testimony of Terry Davis, SRS Director of Quality Assurance (confinement takes place in the psychiatric wing of a prison hospital where those whom the Act confines and ordinary prisoners are treated alike). In addition, a basic objective of the Act is incapacitation, which, as Blackstone said in describing an objective of criminal law, is to "depriv[e] the party injuring of the power to do future mischief." * * *

Moreover, the Act, like criminal punishment, imposes its confinement (or sanction) only upon an individual who has previously committed a criminal offense. And the Act imposes that confinement through the use of persons (county prosecutors), procedural guarantees (trial by jury, assistance of counsel, psychiatric evaluations), and standards ("beyond a reasonable doubt") traditionally associated with the criminal law.

These obvious resemblances by themselves, however, are not legally sufficient to transform what the Act calls "civil commitment" into a criminal punishment. Civil commitment of dangerous, mentally ill individuals by its very nature involves confinement and incapacitation. Yet "civil commitment," from a constitutional perspective, nonetheless remains civil. Nor does the fact that criminal behavior triggers the Act make the critical difference. The Act's insistence upon a prior crime, by screening out those whose past behavior does not concretely demonstrate the existence of a mental problem or potential future danger, may serve an important noncriminal evidentiary purpose. Neither is the presence of criminal law-type procedures determinative. Those procedures can serve an important purpose that in this context one might consider noncriminal, namely helping to prevent judgmental mistakes that would wrongly deprive a person of important liberty.

* * *

* * * I would place particular importance upon those features that would likely distinguish between a basically punitive and a basically nonpunitive purpose. * * *

* * *

* * * First, the State Supreme Court here * * * has held that treatment is not a significant objective of the Act. * * *

* * *

* * * Indeed, were we to follow the majority's invitation to look beyond the record in this case, an invitation with which we disagree, it would reveal that Hendricks, according to the commitment program's own director, was receiving "essentially no treatment." Dr. Charles Befort in State Habeas Corpus Proceeding, App. 393; 912 P.2d, at 131, 136.

* * *

Second, the Kansas statute insofar as it applies to previously convicted offenders, such as Hendricks, commits, confines, and treats those offenders after they have served virtually their entire criminal sentence.* * * But why, one might ask, does the Act not commit and require treatment of sex offenders sooner, say soon after they begin to serve their sentences?

* * * And it is particularly difficult to see why legislators who specifically wrote into the statute a finding that "prognosis for rehabilitating . . . in a prison setting is poor" would leave an offender in that setting for months or years before beginning treatment. This is to say, the timing provisions of the statute confirm the Kansas Supreme Court's view that treatment was not a particularly important legislative objective.

* * *

Third, the statute, at least as of the time Kansas applied it to Hendricks, did not require the committing authority to consider the possibility of using less restrictive alternatives, such as postrelease supervision, halfway houses, or other methods * * *. * * *

This Court has said that a failure to consider, or to use, "alternative and less harsh methods" to achieve a nonpunitive objective can help to show that [the] legislature's "purpose . . . was to punish." * * *

Fourth, the laws of other States confirm, through comparison, that Kansas' "civil commitment" objectives do not require the statutory features that indicate a punitive purpose. I have found 17 States with laws that seek to protect the public from mentally abnormal, sexually dangerous individuals through civil commitment or other mandatory treatment programs. * * * Only one State other than Kansas, namely Iowa, both delays civil commitment (and consequent treatment) and does not explicitly consider less restrictive alternatives. But the law of that State applies prospectively only, thereby avoiding *ex post facto* problems. See Iowa Code Ann. § 709C.12 (Supp.1997) (Iowa SVP act only "applies to persons convicted of a sexually violent offense on or after July 1, 1997"). * * *

* * *

* * * [A] State is free to commit those who are dangerous and mentally ill in order to treat them. Nor does my decision preclude a State from deciding that a certain subset of people are mentally ill, dangerous, and untreatable, and that confinement of this subset is therefore necessary * * *. But when a State decides offenders can be treated and confines an offender to provide that treatment, but then refuses to provide it, the refusal to treat while a person is fully incapacitated begins to look punitive.

* * *

* * * [T]he Act as applied to *Leroy Hendricks* (as opposed to others who may have received treatment or who were sentenced after the effective date of the Act) is punitive.

* * *

III

To find that the confinement the Act imposes upon Hendricks is "punishment" is to find a violation of the *Ex Post Facto* Clause. * * *

To find a violation of that Clause here, however, is not to hold that the Clause prevents Kansas, or other States, from enacting dangerous sexual offender statutes. A statute that operates prospectively, for example, does not offend the *Ex Post Facto* Clause. Neither does it offend the *Ex Post Facto* Clause for a State to sentence offenders to the fully authorized sentence, to seek consecutive, rather than concurrent, sentences, or to invoke recidivism statutes to lengthen imprisonment. Moreover, a statute that operates retroactively, like Kansas' statute, nonetheless does not offend the Clause *if the confinement that it imposes is not punishment*—if, that is to say, the legislature does not simply add a later criminal punishment to an earlier one.

The statutory provisions before us do amount to punishment primarily because, as I have said, the legislature did not tailor the statute to fit the nonpunitive civil aim of treatment * * *. * * *

* * *

QUESTIONS AND POINTS FOR DISCUSSION

1. Do you agree with the Supreme Court's constitutional analysis in *Hendricks*? If so, from a policy standpoint, do you support or oppose the enactment of sexually violent predator acts? Is there any additional information you would want before resolving this latter question?

2. In Kansas v. Crane, 534 U.S. 407, 122 S.Ct. 867 (2002), the Supreme Court elaborated on the nature of the mental abnormality needed for the civil confinement of a sexually violent predator to be constitutional. In addition to proving that the abnormality makes it likely that the defendant will commit acts of sexual violence in the future, the state must prove that the defendant has "serious difficulty," although not necessarily total incapacity, controlling his or her behavior. Id. at 413, 122 S.Ct. at 870. The genesis of this limitation on the mental abnormalities that will permit the civil confinement of sexually violent predators was the Court's obvious concern that because so many prisoners have mental disorders, civil commitments triggered solely by a finding of dangerousness and some kind of mental problem could be used as a matter of course to extend the confinement of vast numbers of prisoners. See id. at 412, 122 S.Ct. at 870 (citing one report that 40 to 60% of male prisoners have an antisocial personality disorder).

In a dissenting opinion, Justice Scalia, joined by Justice Thomas, excoriated the majority for concluding that due process requires a volitional impairment—a substantial inability to control one's behavior—before a person can be confined as a sexually violent predator. Justice Scalia objected:

> It is obvious that a person may be able to exercise volition and yet be unfit to turn loose upon society. The man who has a will of steel, but who delusionally believes that every woman he meets is inviting crude sexual advances, is surely a dangerous sexual predator.

Id. at 422, 122 S.Ct. at 875 (Scalia, J., dissenting).

3.   Alcohol-use disorder is one of the mental disorders listed in the American Psychiatric Association's *Diagnostic and Statistical Manual of Mental Disorders* (5th ed., 2013). After *Hendricks* and *Crane*, would it be constitutional to civilly commit a person about to be released from prison for a fourth drunk-driving conviction under a state statute providing for the civil commitment of certain dangerous alcoholics who are unable to control their drinking? Why or why not?

4.   In Seling v. Young, 531 U.S. 250, 121 S.Ct. 727 (2001), the Supreme Court considered a constitutional challenge to the implementation of the Washington statute after which the Kansas Sexually Violent Predator Act had been patterned. The petitioner in that case was committed as a sexually violent predator after serving a prison sentence for his sixth rape conviction. Placed in the custody of the state's social-services department, he was then confined in a Special Commitment Center located on the grounds of a state prison.

In his petition for a writ of habeas corpus, the petitioner contended that the purportedly "civil" statute under which he had been committed was applied in such a punitive way that his rights under the Double Jeopardy and *Ex Post Facto* Clauses of the Constitution were violated. The petitioner cited the pervasive involvement of the Department of Corrections in the day-to-day operations of the Special Commitment Center and claimed that he was treated even more harshly than a prisoner.

The Supreme Court assumed that the Washington statute, like the Kansas Act, was civil in nature. The Court then rejected the petitioner's argument that a statute providing for the civil commitment of sexually violent predators can be challenged on double-jeopardy and *ex post facto* grounds because of the punitive way in which it is being implemented. Concluding that such "as applied" challenges would be unworkable because conditions of confinement constantly change, the Court observed: "The civil nature of a confinement scheme cannot be altered based merely on vagaries in the implementation of the authorizing statute." Id. at 263, 121 S. Ct. at 735.

The Supreme Court hastened to add that civilly committed sexually violent predators are not left remediless to challenge the conditions of their confinement. If those conditions do not comport with state law, such as a mandate to provide them with individualized treatment, they can seek enforcement of the state statute in a state court. Noting that due process requires that the conditions and length of a person's confinement bear a "reasonable relation" to the purpose for which the person was confined, the

Supreme Court also seemed to suggest that sexually violent predators subject to civil confinement might mount, in some circumstances, a successful due-process challenge to their confinement conditions. Id. at 265, 121 S. Ct. at 736. Finally, the Court underscored that the Special Commitment Center itself was operating under an injunction issued in a different case brought under 42 U.S.C. § 1983 to enjoin certain unconstitutional conditions.

In *Seling*, the Supreme Court left open an issue that it said it had not yet "squarely addressed": the relevance of conditions of confinement to the threshold question whether a statute providing for the confinement of sexually violent predators is civil or punitive. Id. at 266–67, 121 S. Ct. at 736–37. In your opinion, how should this issue be resolved?

c. Residency and Other Restrictions

States have imposed other restrictions on people convicted of sex offenses that are not part of their sentences. For example, a majority of states have enacted laws restricting where people convicted of sex offenses can live. See John Kip Cornwell, Sex Offender Residency Restrictions: Government Regulation of Public Health, Safety, and Morality, 24 Wm. & Mary Bill Rts. J. 1, 6 n.18 (2015) (listing statutes). Typically, these statutes make it a crime for these individuals to live within a prescribed distance, ranging usually from 300 to 3000 feet, of places where children congregate, such as schools, playgrounds, and daycare centers. Id. at 6–7. Do you favor or oppose such restrictions on where people with convictions for sex offenses can live? Why?

Some courts have, for varied reasons, found such residency restrictions to be unconstitutional. For example, the California Supreme Court held that a blanket ban barring all registered people on parole from residing within 2000 feet of a school or park where children gather regularly abridged due process. In re Taylor, 343 P.3d 867 (Cal.2015). The court said that for residency restrictions to be constitutional, they must be imposed on a case-by-case basis based on the "particularized circumstances" of each individual. Id. at 882. The Sixth Circuit Court of Appeals, on the other hand, held that the retroactive application of a residency restriction to people convicted before the law's enactment violated the constitutional prohibition on ex post facto laws. Does v. Snyder, 834 F.3d 696 (6th Cir.2016).

Some states have also placed restrictions on the access people with sex-offense convictions have to the Internet. In Packingham v. North Carolina, 137 S.Ct. 1730 (2017), the Supreme Court struck down one such law, a North Carolina statute that made it a felony for a person on the sex-offender registry to "access a commercial social networking Web site where the sex offender knows that the site permits minor children to become members or to create or maintain personal Web pages on the commercial social networking Web site." In holding that this statute violated the First

Amendment's Free Speech Clause, the Court assumed, without deciding, that the statute was a content-neutral restriction on the place where speech can occur, triggering "intermediate scrutiny" under the First Amendment. Id. at 1736. To be constitutional under this test, the statute had to be "narrowly tailored to serve a significant governmental interest." Id. In concluding that the restriction on access to social networking sites like Facebook, LinkedIn, and Twitter curbed more speech than necessary to protect children from sexual abuse, the Court observed:

> By prohibiting sex offenders from using those websites, North Carolina with one broad stroke bars access to what for many are the principal sources for knowing current events, checking ads for employment, speaking and listening in the modern public square, and otherwise exploring the vast realms of human thought and knowledge. These websites can provide perhaps the most powerful mechanisms available to a private citizen to make his or her voice heard.

Id. at 1737.

In a noteworthy aside in its opinion, the Supreme Court also expressed concern that the North Carolina statute imposed "severe restrictions" on people who had completed serving their sentences. Id. But noting that the implications of this "troubling fact" were not before the Court, the Court did not address its significance. Id.

C. RESTORATION OF RIGHTS AND OTHER STEPS TO LIMIT OR ELIMINATE ENMESHED PENALTIES

There are a number of ways in which the adverse effects of criminal convictions, outside those imposed by the sentence, can be dissipated. Several key mechanisms and means to limit the harmful effects of enmeshed penalties or eliminate those penalties altogether are highlighted below. For additional information about steps jurisdictions have taken to provide relief from enmeshed penalties, see Collateral Consequences Resource Ctr., Forgiving and Forgetting in American Justice: A 50-State Guide to Expungement and Restoration of Rights (2018).

1. PARDONS

Some have described the exercise of the power of executive clemency as an "executive act of mercy." Kathleen Ridolfi & Seth Gordon, Gubernatorial Clemency Powers, 24 Crim. Just. 26, 26 (Fall 2009). A pardon is one of the means through which this clemency power is wielded. (A commutation of a sentence—an executive reduction of a sentence—is another example of executive clemency.) All of the states and the federal government have procedures in place for issuing pardons to people who have committed crimes. In some states, the governor makes the pardoning decision; in others, the decision is made by the parole board or a board of pardons; and in still others, the decision is made by the governor in conjunction with, or after consultation with, the parole or pardon board. Id. at 31 & app. In the federal system, the power to grant pardons is vested in the President. U.S. Const. art. II, § 2, cl. 1.

A person who receives an unconditional pardon will generally be relieved from at least many of the legal disabilities that attend a criminal conviction. He or she will, for example, be able to vote and sit on a jury. In most jurisdictions, however, there are limitations on the ability of a pardon to fully restore the rights of individuals convicted of crimes. In accepting a pardon, people are, according to many courts, implicitly acknowledging their guilt of the crimes for which they are being pardoned. See, e.g., Burdick v. United States, 236 U.S. 79, 94, 35 S.Ct. 267, 270 (1915). The following observation of the Florida Supreme Court reflects this majority view: "A pardon is the equivalent of forgiveness for a crime; it does not declare the pardoned individual innocent of the crime." R.J.L. v. State, 887 So.2d 1268, 1281 (Fla.2004).

Since a pardon does not, in most jurisdictions, erase a person's guilt of a crime, many courts have concluded that individuals who receive pardons are not entitled to have the records of their criminal convictions expunged. See, e.g., Robertson v. State, 158 So.3d 280, 282–83 (Miss.2015). In addition, the conduct underlying a criminal conviction can be considered when a person who has received a pardon applies for a position that requires that applicants meet certain character requirements. For example, in Hirschberg v. Commodity Futures Trading Commission, 414 F.3d 679, 682–84 (7th Cir.2005), the Seventh Circuit Court of Appeals held that while it would violate the Pardons Clause to deny registration as a commodities broker (who acts as a fiduciary for others) because of a mail-fraud conviction for which a presidential pardon had been issued, denying the registration because of the conduct underlying that conviction would not. And criminal conduct resulting in a prior conviction may lead to a determination that an individual is unfit to practice law, even though he or she has been officially pardoned for the crime. See, e.g., Grossgold v. Supreme Court of Illinois, 557 F.2d 122, 125–26 (7th Cir.1977) (attorney can be suspended from the practice of law, despite a presidential pardon, because the pardon "did not wipe out the moral turpitude inherent in the factual predicate" supporting the conviction).

One of the common criticisms of pardons is that the pardoning power is exercised so sparingly in most jurisdictions that it is an ineffectual means of restoring convicted individuals' rights and reintegrating them into society. See Justice Kennedy Comm'n, Am. Bar Ass'n, Reports with Recommendations to the ABA House of Delegates 70 n.9 (2004) (noting that President George W. Bush granted eleven pardons during the first three years of his presidency while denying 601 pardon applications in that time period). Political considerations, particularly a fear of appearing "soft on crime," suffuse the pardoning process, discouraging its use as a reintegration tool. In addition, many people lack the resources or knowledge needed to pursue a pardon or the political connections that often are needed to obtain a pardon in many jurisdictions. See Margaret Colgate Love, Reinvigorating the Federal Pardon Process: What the President Can Learn from the States, 9 U. St. Thomas L.J. 730, 733 n.7 (2013) (noting President George W. Bush's acknowledgement, after he left the presidency, that he "came to see the massive injustice" of a system that granted those with "connections to the president" special access to pardons). For details on the pardoning structure and the frequency with which pardons are granted in each state and at the federal level, see Collateral Consequences Resource Ctr. et al., Restoration of Rights Project, Characteristics of Pardon Authorities, at http://ccresourcecenter.org/state-restoration-profiles/ 50-state-comparisoncharacteristics-of-pardon-authorities (last visited Feb. 13, 2018).

2. RESTORATION-OF-RIGHTS PROCEDURES

A number of states have adopted statutes that enable certain people with felony convictions to get some or all of their civil rights lost as a result of their convictions restored. Many of these statutes provide for the automatic restoration of certain rights at a defined time after completion of a sentence. Other statutes require that an application for restoration of rights be made to a court, administrative agency, or executive official. For a list of the differing mechanisms in each state for securing restoration of civil rights, such as the right to vote or serve on a jury, and firearms rights and for citations to the statutes providing for the restoration of these rights, see Collateral Consequences Resource Ctr. et al., Restoration of Rights Project, Loss and Restoration of Civil Rights & Firearms Rights (2017), at http://ccresourcecenter.org/state-restoration-profiles/chart-1-loss-and-restoration-of-civil-rights-and-firearms-privileges.

Restoration-of-rights statutes are often like pardons in the sense that even people whose civil rights have been fully restored may be denied professional or occupational licenses because of the conduct that led to their criminal convictions. Margaret Colgate Love, Starting Over With a Clean Slate: In Praise of a Forgotten Section of the Model Penal Code, 30 Fordham Urb.L.J. 1705, 1719–20 (2003). In addition, individuals whose rights have been restored, like some people who have received pardons, still may be obliged to reveal their criminal records on job-application forms. One of the differences between pardons and statutes providing for the automatic restoration of rights is that the former are discretionary while the latter are triggered automatically by the occurrence of a certain event.

3.   RESTRICTING ACCESS TO CRIMINAL RECORDS

The expungement or sealing of criminal records is another way of reducing the adverse effects of a criminal conviction. State statutes providing for the expungement and sealing of criminal records vary widely in their effects, including what the terms expungement and sealing even mean. Often though, the expungement of records of a criminal conviction means that "the slate is wiped clean"—that the conviction no longer exists. Alessandro Corda, More Justice and Less Harm: Reinventing Access to Criminal History Records, 60 How. L.J. 1, 22 (2016). Upon expungement, criminal records may be destroyed under some states' laws, with electronic records deleted. By contrast, if records are sealed, access to them is limited, but the records themselves are generally preserved. Typically, sealed records are still available for use by law-enforcement officials and courts. They may be considered, for example, when sentencing a person for a subsequent crime.

State statutes also differ as to who is eligible to have criminal records expunged or sealed. Some statutes, for example, extend only to people convicted of nonviolent crimes. Others generally prohibit people with more than one felony conviction from getting records of their convictions expunged or sealed. For a state-by-state comparison of sealing and expungement statutes, see Collateral Consequences Resource Ctr. et al., Restoration of Rights Project, Judicial Expungement, Sealing, and Set-aside, at http://ccresourcecenter.org/state-restoration-profiles/50-state-comparisonjudicial-expungement-sealing-and-set-aside (last visited Feb. 13, 2018).

For people with criminal convictions, the potential advantage of having criminal records expunged or sealed is that they then may be entitled, depending on the state's law, to refrain from mentioning their criminal convictions on job-application forms. But commentators have pointed to some drawbacks in relying on the expungement and sealing of criminal records as means of enabling people with criminal convictions to put their misdeeds behind them and move forward with their lives. The concealment of facts that occurs when criminal records are expunged or sealed and the ensuing license sometimes given people to deny the existence of their convictions, it has been argued, do not comport with a legal system grounded on a commitment to truth. In addition, with the evolution of technology, the expungement and sealing of records can be ineffectual in suppressing the circulation of information about a person's criminal history. See Margaret Colgate Love, Starting Over With a Clean Slate: In Pursuit of a Forgotten Section of the Model Penal Code 1705, 1726 (2003). Under what circumstances, if any, do you believe that statutes should provide for the expungement or sealing of criminal records?

4. CERTIFICATES OF REHABILITATION AND GOOD CONDUCT

Some state laws authorize courts or a correctional agency to issue what is sometimes called a "certificate of rehabilitation," "certificate of good conduct," or some alternatively named certificate. Whatever the name of the certificate issued to a person who has met certain specified requirements, such as completion of a sentence for a criminal conviction, one of its principal purposes is to help enable that person overcome the stigma of the conviction when, for example, seeking employment. For details about the certificates of rehabilitation and other certificates available in some states, see Collateral Consequences Resource Ctr. et al., Restoration of Rights Project, Judicial Expungement, Sealing, and Set-aside, at http://ccresourcecenter.org/state-restoration-profiles/50-state-comparisonjudicial-expungement-sealing-and-set-aside (last visited Feb. 13, 2018).

When exercising what he considered the court's inherent authority to issue a "federal certificate of rehabilitation" to someone he had sentenced thirteen years before, one federal district judge observed:

> There are two general approaches to limiting the collateral consequences of convictions: (1) the "forgetting" model, in which a criminal record is deleted or expunged so that society may forget that the conviction ever happened; and (2) the "forgiveness" model, which acknowledges the conviction but uses a certificate of rehabilitation or a pardon to symbolize society's forgiveness of the underlying offense conduct.

Doe v. United States, 168 F.Supp.3d 427, 442 (E.D.N.Y.2016). Which of these two models do you prefer and why? Are there more than two models to consider adopting when tackling questions about enmeshed penalties and how to limit other adverse repercussions of criminal convictions? Consider this question as you read the materials in the following subsection.

5. DISCRIMINATION BANS AND LIMITS ON ENMESHED PENALTIES

Another way of mitigating the adverse effects of a criminal conviction is through laws that limit the enmeshed penalties that can ensue from a conviction. The ABA Standards for Criminal Justice: Collateral Sanctions and Discretionary Disqualification of Convicted Persons (3d ed. 2004) contain standards that can be incorporated in statutes and court rules to achieve this purpose. The ABA Standards are designed to diminish in three ways the adverse effects of criminal convictions not stemming from the sentence itself: one, by placing limits on the rights and privileges that can be lost because of a criminal conviction; two, by outlining certain procedures that must be followed when imposing what the Standards refer to as a "collateral sanction" or a "discretionary disqualification"; and three, by providing for the establishment of mechanisms to relieve individuals from the burdens of collateral sanctions and discretionary disqualifications. Some of these standards and portions of the commentary explaining them are set forth below.

ABA STANDARDS FOR CRIMINAL JUSTICE, THIRD EDITION: COLLATERAL SANCTIONS AND DISCRETIONARY DISQUALIFICATION OF CONVICTED PERSONS

© 2004 by the American Bar Association.
Reprinted with permission. All rights reserved.[*]

INTRODUCTION

Persons convicted of a crime ordinarily expect to be sentenced to a term of probation or confinement, and perhaps to a fine and court costs. They also understand that they will bear the social stigma of a criminal conviction. But what they often do not appreciate is that their convictions will expose them to numerous additional legal penalties and disabilities, some of which may be far more onerous than the sentence imposed by the judge in open court. These "collateral consequences of conviction" include relatively traditional penalties such as disenfranchisement, * * * as well as newer penalties such as felon registration and ineligibility for certain public welfare benefits. They may apply for a definite period of time, or indefinitely for the convicted person's lifetime. To the extent they occur outside the sentencing process, they may take effect without judicial consideration of their appropriateness in the particular case, without notice at sentencing that the individual's legal status has dramatically changed, and indeed without any requirement that the judge, prosecutor, defense attorney or defendant even be aware that they exist.

* * *

These Standards proceed from a premise that it is neither fair nor efficient for the criminal justice system to label significant legal disabilities and penalties as "collateral" and thereby give permission to ignore them in the process of criminal sentencing, when in reality those disabilities and penalties can be the most important and permanent results of a criminal conviction.

* * *

The criminal justice system must also concern itself with unreasonable discrimination against convicted persons. "Discretionary disqualification"

---

[*]   This information or any portion thereof may not be copied or disseminated in any form or by any means or stored in an electronic database or retrieval system without the express written consent of the American Bar Association.

from benefits or opportunities on grounds related to [a] conviction, while not a "sanction" that must be considered at sentencing, may just as surely prevent or discourage convicted persons from successfully reentering the free community, and impose on the community the costs of their recidivism. * * *

* * *

PART I.
DEFINITIONS AND OBJECTIVES

Standard 19–1.1 Definitions

For purposes of this chapter:

(a) The term "collateral sanction" means a legal penalty, disability or disadvantage, however denominated, that is imposed on a person automatically upon that person's conviction for a felony, misdemeanor or other offense, even if it is not included in the sentence.

(b) The term "discretionary disqualification" means a penalty, disability or disadvantage, however denominated, that a civil court, administrative agency, or official is authorized but not required to impose on a person convicted of an offense on grounds related to the conviction.

Commentary

"Collateral sanctions" are those penalties that automatically become effective upon conviction even though not included in the court's judgment of conviction or identified on the record. The term signifies a direct and immediate change in an offender's legal status that does not depend upon some subsequent additional occurrence or administrative action, and that would not have occurred in the absence of a conviction. Examples include disenfranchisement, automatic loss of firearms privileges, per se disqualification from employment or public benefits, and mandatory felon registration. To the extent a non-citizen's immigration status changes as a result of a criminal conviction, so that the offender becomes automatically deportable without opportunity for discretionary exception or revision, deportation too must be regarded as a "collateral sanction."

* * *

"Collateral sanctions" are to be distinguished from discretionary penalties or disabilities based on conduct underlying a criminal conviction, which could occur whether or not the person has been convicted. These Standards deal with this more attenuated effect of conviction as a "discretionary disqualification." The disqualifying conduct might be established by the conviction, but it might also be established in some other way, such as by a civil action or administrative determination. An example of a discretionary disqualification is the law that excludes persons who engage in "drug-related criminal activity" from federally funded housing benefits. * * *

* * *

PART II.
COLLATERAL SANCTIONS

Standard 19–2.1 Codification of collateral sanctions

The legislature should collect, set out or reference all collateral sanctions in a single chapter or section of the jurisdiction's criminal code. The chapter or section should identify with particularity the type, severity and duration of collateral sanctions applicable to each offense, or to a group of offenses specifically identified by name, section number, severity level, or other easily determinable means.

Standard 19–2.2 Limitation on collateral sanctions

The legislature should not impose a collateral sanction on a person convicted of an offense unless it determines that the conduct constituting that particular offense provides so substantial a basis for imposing the sanction that the legislature cannot reasonably contemplate any circumstances in which imposing the sanction would not be justified.

Commentary

* * *

There are certain situations in which a collateral sanction will be so clearly appropriate given the nature of the offense that case-by-case evaluation at the time of sentencing would be pointless and inefficient. Examples might include exclusion of those convicted of sexual abuse from employment involving close contact with children, loss of public office upon conviction of bribery, denial of licensure where the offense involves the licensed activity, and prohibition of firearms to those convicted of violent crimes.

Examples of collateral sanctions that would not be justified under this Standard are denial of student aid and loss of a driver's license upon conviction of a drug offense. It might well be appropriate to provide for automatic suspension of a driver's license where the offense conduct is related to driving or motor vehicles, or to exclude from educational institutions those who sell drugs there. And, it may be appropriate to revoke a driver's license or exclude from aid on a case-by-case basis, subject to Standard 19–3.1. But it is unreasonable and counterproductive to deny all drug offenders access to the means of rehabilitating themselves and supporting their families, thereby imposing a cost upon the community with no evident corresponding benefit.

* * *

When the legislature identifies a close connection between the offense and the collateral sanction, the Standards provide that relief from the sanction should be available if warranted. Standard 19–2.5. * * *

Standard 19–2.4 Consideration of collateral sanctions at sentencing

(a) The legislature should authorize the sentencing court to take into account, and the court should consider, applicable collateral sanctions in determining an offender's overall sentence.

(b) The rules of procedure should require the court to ensure at the time of sentencing that the defendant has been informed of collateral sanctions made applicable to the offense or offenses of conviction under the law of the state or territory where the prosecution is pending, and under federal law. Except where notification by the court itself is otherwise required by law or rules of procedure, this requirement may be satisfied by confirming on the record that defense counsel has so advised the defendant.

* * *

Commentary

Standard 19–2.4(a) requires a sentencing court to take into account applicable collateral sanctions in fashioning a package of sanctions at sentencing. * * * [T]he sentencing court should ensure that the totality of the penalty is not unduly severe and that it does not give rise to undue disparity.

* * *

Standard 19–2.5 Waiver, modification, relief

(a) The legislature should authorize a court, a specified administrative body, or both, to enter an order waiving, modifying, or granting timely and effective relief from any collateral sanction imposed by the law of that jurisdiction.

* * *

(c) The legislature should establish a process by which a convicted person may obtain an order relieving the person of all collateral sanctions imposed by the law of that jurisdiction.

* * *

Commentary

Standard 19–2.5(a) provides that collateral sanctions should be subject to waiver, modification, or "timely and effective relief" from a court or a specified administrative agency if the sanctions have become inappropriate or unfair based on the facts of the particular case. Jurisdictions could choose to allow the waiver authority to be exercised at the time of sentencing, or only at some later date. Waiver or modification of a collateral sanction under Standard 19–2.5, whether at the time of sentencing or at some later time, would not preclude a court or administrative agency from taking action based on the conduct underlying the conviction, pursuant to Standard 19–3.1.

* * *

Standard 19–2.5(c) differs from 19–2.5(a) * * * insofar as it contemplates a judicial or administrative process for obtaining relief from *all* collateral sanctions imposed by the law of that jurisdiction. * * *

* * *

Standard 19–2.6 Prohibited collateral sanctions

Jurisdictions should not impose the following collateral sanctions:

(a) deprivation of the right to vote, except during actual confinement;

(b) deprivation of judicial rights, including the rights to:

(i) initiate or defend a suit in any court under one's own name under procedures applicable to the general public;

(ii) be eligible for jury service except during actual confinement or while on probation, parole, or other court supervision; and

(iii) execute judicially enforceable documents and agreements;

(c) deprivation of legally recognized domestic relationships and rights other than in accordance with rules applicable to the general public. Accordingly, conviction or confinement alone:

(i) should be insufficient to deprive a person of the right to contract or dissolve a marriage; parental rights, including the right to direct the rearing of children and to live with children except during actual confinement; the right to grant or withhold consent to the adoption of children; and the right to adopt children; and

(ii) should not constitute neglect or abandonment of a spouse or child, and confined persons should be assisted in making appropriate arrangements for their spouses or children;

(d) deprivation of the right to acquire, inherit, sell or otherwise dispose of real or personal property, except insofar as is necessary to preclude a person from profiting from his or her own wrong; and, for persons unable to manage or preserve their property by reason of confinement, deprivation of the right to appoint someone of their own choosing to act on their behalf;

(e) ineligibility to participate in government programs providing necessities of life, including food, clothing, housing, medical care, disability pay, and Social Security; provided, however, that a person may be suspended from participation in such a program to the extent that the purposes of the program are reasonably being served by an alternative program; and

(f) ineligibility for governmental benefits relevant to successful reentry into society, such as educational and job training programs.

Commentary

* * *

* * * [A] jurisdiction's ability to suspend a convicted person from a necessity of life program should be limited to cases presenting a clear risk to public safety and/or opportunity for recidivism.[57] * * *

PART III.
DISCRETIONARY DISQUALIFICATION
OF CONVICTED PERSONS

Standard 19–3.1 Prohibited discretionary disqualification

The legislature should prohibit discretionary disqualification of a convicted person from benefits or opportunities, including housing, employment, insurance, and occupational and professional licenses, permits and certifications, on grounds related to the conviction, unless engaging in the conduct underlying the conviction would provide a substantial basis for disqualification even if the person had not been convicted.

Commentary

* * *

[T]he line between a mandatory collateral sanction and discretionary disqualification is not always a bright one: * * * The key distinction is whether disqualification decisions are made on a bona fide case-by-case basis, taking into account the equitable merits of each case. If convicted persons are the *only* people disqualified, and if *all* convicted persons are disqualified without consideration of the merits, then under the principles of administrative law, the failure to exercise discretion might constitute an abuse of discretion that could be remedied on appeal or through judicial review.

---

[57] For example, all persons who have been convicted of rape or sexual abuse of a minor could be automatically suspended from participation in a public housing program, but only so long as they have reasonable access to alternative low-cost housing. In the absence of alternative housing, individuals convicted of such crimes could be excluded from public housing upon case-by-case determinations that the conduct underlying their convictions constituted grounds for discretionary disqualification (see Standard 19–3.1).

Standard 19–3.2 Relief from discretionary disqualification

The legislature should establish a process for obtaining review of, and relief from, any discretionary disqualification.

Commentary

Standard 19–3.2 requires that some mechanism be available for obtaining review of, and relief from, any discretionary disqualification imposed by an administrative agency, civil court or other government official. On review, an individual might seek to argue that engaging in the conduct underlying the conviction is not a substantial basis for imposing the penalty; or that individuals who engage in the conduct but are not convicted are not subject to the same penalty. * * *

Standard 19–3.3 Unreasonable discrimination

Each jurisdiction should encourage the employment of convicted persons by legislative and executive mandate, through financial incentives and otherwise. In addition, each jurisdiction should enact legislation prohibiting the denial of insurance, or a private professional or occupational license, permit or certification, to a convicted person on grounds related to the conviction, unless engaging in the conduct underlying the conviction would provide a substantial basis for denial even if the person had not been convicted.

QUESTIONS AND POINTS FOR DISCUSSION

1.   How, if at all, would you revise the ABA Standards?

2.   Charging that the "collateral consequences" of a criminal conviction (referred to in this book as "enmeshed penalties") often serve no penological purpose and impede rehabilitation by relegating people with criminal convictions to the status of "second-class citizens" and "social outcasts," Professor Nora Demleitner has proposed the following restrictions on their imposition: First, collateral consequences should only be imposed as part of a court-ordered sentence. Second, sentencing guidelines should guide courts' decisions regarding the inclusion of a collateral consequence as part of the sentence. Third, collateral consequences generally should be imposed only when necessary to prevent future crimes or, in limited situations, when needed to effectuate the retributive goals of the law or to communicate society's disapprobation. Fourth, laws imposing collateral consequences should contain sunset provisions, thereby necessitating legislative review of the laws' effectiveness. Nora V. Demleitner, Preventing Internal Exile: The Need for Restrictions on Collateral Sentencing Consequences, 11 Stan. L. & Pol'y Rev. 153, 154, 158 (1999). Do you concur or disagree with Professor Demleitner's recommendations?

3.   People with criminal convictions face an array of employment barriers, including the unwillingness of employers to hire someone with a criminal record. Standard 19–3.3 of the ABA Standards set forth above calls

for overcoming this unwillingness by offering employers financial or other incentives to hire individuals with prior convictions. Some states take a different tack, generally barring employment discrimination because of prior convictions. See, e.g., Wis. Stat. § 111.321 (prohibiting employment discrimination based on "conviction record," subject to some exceptions found in Wis. Stat. § 111.335). To avert such discrimination, a Hawaii statute generally forbids an employer from inquiring about and considering a job applicant's criminal record until after the employer has tendered a conditional job offer to an applicant. Haw. Rev. Stat. § 378–2.5(b). And even then, the employer can withdraw the job offer only if the conviction has a "rational relationship" to the duties and responsibilities of the job. Id.

The first safeguard instituted in Hawaii, barring an employer from asking about and considering a job applicant's record of criminal convictions until after the person has been deemed qualified for the job, is known as "ban the box"—the box on employment applications for applicants to indicate whether they have a prior criminal conviction. Many states, counties, cities, and employers have adopted ban-the-box policies. See Beth Avery & Phil Hernandez, Nat'l Employment Law Project, Ban the Box: U.S. Cities, Counties, and States Adopt Fair-Chance Policies to Advance Employment Opportunities for People with Past Convictions (2017) (describing the ban-the-box laws and policies adopted in 29 states and over 150 cities and counties). In your opinion, what other steps could and should government officials take to induce employers to hire persons with criminal records?

4.   Refusing to hire someone because of a past criminal conviction may violate Title VII of the Civil Rights Act of 1964, a federal statute that, in part, prohibits employment discrimination due to a person's race or national origin. 42 U.S.C. § 2000e–2(a). The Equal Employment Opportunity Commission (EEOC) has explained that the denial of employment due to a person's criminal record can have a disparate impact on African-Americans and Hispanics. EEOC Enforcement Guidance No. 915.002, Consideration of Arrest and Conviction Records in Employment Decisions Under Title VII of the Civil Rights Act of 1964 §V.A.2. (2012). This disparate impact generally violates Title VII unless the employer proves both that the exclusion from that position was "job related" and "consistent with business necessity." Id. § 2000e–2(k)(1)(A).

5.   In addition to statutory restrictions, the Constitution may sometimes constrain governments from denying government employment to individuals simply because of their criminal records. The Supreme Court has observed that due process requires at least a "rational connection" between the type of job for which the applicant applied and the criterion which led to the applicant's rejection. See, e.g., Schware v. Board of Bar Examiners, 353 U.S. 232, 239, 77 S.Ct. 752, 756 (1957). This rational-relationship test may not be met in certain circumstances when an applicant's criminal conviction serves as the basis for denial of a government job. In addition, state constitutions may prohibit public as well as private employers from denying a person a job because of a criminal conviction. See, e.g., Nixon v. Commonwealth, 839 A.2d 277, 288–90 (Pa.2003)

(statute prohibiting the hiring of certain individuals with convictions for specified crimes, including burglary, forgery, and felony drug crimes, at facilities providing care to senior citizens violated the state constitutional right to pursue an occupation).

6. SENTENCING ADVOCACY

The following article describes the role that defense attorneys can play in avoiding or mitigating the adverse effects of enmeshed penalties on their clients. As you read this article, written by a defense attorney known for his expertise in "holistic defense," consider what could be done so that defense attorneys more readily know which enmeshed penalties are implicated in a particular case.

MCGREGOR SMYTH, "COLLATERAL" NO MORE: THE PRACTICAL IMPERATIVE FOR HOLISTIC DEFENSE IN A POST-*PADILLA* WORLD . . . OR, HOW TO ACHIEVE CONSISTENTLY BETTER RESULTS FOR CLIENTS

31 St. Louis U. Pub. L.Rev. 139 (2011).
Reprinted with the permission of the author.

* * * Defense attorneys can use knowledge of these enmeshed penalties, so-called "collateral" consequences, as a direct advocacy tool to win better dispositions in the criminal case and improved life outcomes for clients. An investment in these strategies will return measurable results in four major areas * * *.

1.   Improved Criminal Dispositions

Experience has taught that defenders can obtain more favorable bail, plea, and sentencing results—and even outright dismissals—when they are able to educate prosecutors and judges on specific and severe consequences for the clients and their families. When raising these consequences with prosecutors and judges, keep in mind that they typically respond best to consequences that offend their basic sense of fairness—those that are absurd, disproportionate, or harm innocent family members.

We have found these four categories of penalties most powerful in advocating for alternative dispositions:

• *Immigration.* Deportability, inadmissibility, or ineligibility for a waiver as the result of a plea.

* * *

• *Housing.* Loss of public housing or [housing subsidies] as the result of a plea.

Jake was wheelchair-bound and suffering the degenerative effects of cerebral palsy. A victim of a home invasion in his public housing development, he got an illegal handgun for protection. One day soon after, he was handling the gun and it accidentally fired—straight through the wall into his neighbor's apartment. Jake faced years of prison time from multiple felony charges. Even a felony plea with a non-incarceratory sentence would have triggered an eviction from public housing and rendered Jake homeless. His defense attorney found critical leverage by describing Jake's personal circumstances, and by demonstrating the devastating impact of not only incarceration but any felony plea on Jake's permanent, affordable housing. After significant advocacy, the defender convinced the prosecutor to offer a misdemeanor plea with no jail time, preserving Jake's home in the process.

• *Employment & Military Service.* Loss of a job or employment license, particularly for a breadwinner.

* * *

• *Student Loans.* Loss of a federal student loan eligibility and educational opportunity.

* * *

Other serious penalties intimately related to criminal charges include sex offense registration and its attendant consequences, civil commitment, loss of voting rights, ineligibility for government benefits, and prohibition on firearms possession.

Incorporating these penalties into negotiation strategy gets consistently improved results even by traditional criminal justice measures. * * *

2.   Risk Management

Knowledge of so-called "collateral" consequences is also a key risk management tool for defenders. Clients facing criminal charges will often have to face ancillary civil or administrative proceedings in housing court, family court, or with employment licensing agencies. * * *

* * * Clients will often testify or give written statements as part of these ancillary proceedings about the underlying facts of the pending criminal case, or they are penalized for invoking their right to remain silent, usually without ever telling their defense attorney. When agencies suspend employment licenses after an arrest, they usually require licensees to provide additional information about the charges and offer a procedure for challenging the suspension. Most people jump at any opportunity to keep their jobs and give extended explanations, in writing or on the record, of the events that led to the charges. Prosecutors in New York City routinely force landlords to initiate eviction proceedings while the related drug charges remain pending, and then send Assistant District Attorneys to Housing Court to observe and record. Defense attorneys must

be familiar with these civil consequences so they can anticipate these proceedings, plan for them, and properly advise clients of the impact on their criminal case.

3.   More Equitable Discovery

Proper risk management has another significant benefit: as a result of being prepared for these ancillary proceedings, defense attorneys can use them for additional discovery not available in the criminal case. Eviction cases, employment licensing proceedings, DMV [Department of Motor Vehicles] hearings, school suspension hearings—these are all venues where important witnesses might testify and where an administrative or lower court judge, or even an attorney, is likely to have subpoena power, allowing defenders to obtain a wide range of documents or testimony otherwise unavailable in the criminal case. With proper planning, a defense attorney can cross-examine an arresting officer or complaining witness.

Expansive use of these entirely legal litigation tools provides an obvious benefit in the criminal case, but it can also create positive pressure that avoids or mitigates the civil penalty or suspension for the client. A prepared defense attorney can have significant impact in these venues that are not used to dealing with represented parties. More indirectly, a prosecutor who sees the criminal case litigated and advanced outside of his or her control will exert significant pressure on agency and private actors to lift suspensions or otherwise benefit the client simply to remove the defense discovery tool. We have seen both outcomes routinely in our defense practice. Either way, the client benefits.

4.   Improved Life Outcomes for Clients

* * * Implementing these strategies quite literally preserves homes, saves jobs, and keeps families together. * * *

* * *

* * * It also empowers clients to choose outcomes based on their own priorities. Help clients think about these long-term hidden effects of strategy or plea decisions before they make them. * * *

What is more important—jail or prison time (the liberty interest)? Custody of children? Immigration status? Housing or a job? There is no universal answer; only each client can decide for herself. The collateral damage of being arrested often falls most heavily on family members. When given the option, our clients will often choose the outcome that minimizes the impact on their families. This is where we start to find meaning in being "client-centered" rather than "case-centered."

* * *

D. THE REINTEGRATION OF INCARCERATED PEOPLE INTO SOCIETY: AN INTEGRATED APPROACH

To facilitate a person's reintegration into the community upon release from prison, Jeremy Travis, the former director of the National Institute for Justice, called for the creation of "reentry courts," which are patterned after drug courts. His description of one way in which reentry courts could operate follows.

JEREMY TRAVIS, BUT THEY ALL COME BACK: RETHINKING PRISONER REENTRY

National Institute of Justice (2000).

* * *

Judges as reentry managers

If a new vision were written on a clean slate, the role of reentry management would best be assigned, in my view, to the sentencing judge, whose duties would be expanded to create a "reentry court." At the time of sentencing, the judge would say to the offender, "John Smith, you are being sentenced to X years, Y months of which will be served in the community under my supervision. Our goal is to admit you back into our community after you pay your debt for this offense and demonstrate your ability to live by our rules. Starting today, we will develop, with your involvement, a plan to achieve that goal. The plan will require some hard work of you, beginning in prison and continuing—and getting harder—after you return to the community. It will also require that your family, friends, neighbors, and any other people interested in your welfare commit to the goal of your successful return. I will oversee your entire sentence to make sure the goal is achieved, including monitoring your participation in prison programs that prepare you for release. Many other criminal justice agencies—police, corrections, parole, probation, drug treatment, and others—will be part of a team committed to achieving the goal. If you do not keep up your end of the bargain, I will further restrict your liberty, although only in amounts proportionate to your failure. If you commit a crime again after your release, all bets are off. If you do keep up your end of the bargain, it is within my power to accelerate the completion of your sentence, to return privileges that might be lost (such as your right to hold certain kinds of jobs or your right to vote), and to welcome you back to the community."

At the time of sentencing, the judge would also convene the stakeholders who would be responsible for the offender's reentry. They would be asked to focus on that day, perhaps years in the future, when John returns home. How can he be best prepared for that day and for a successful reentry? What does his support network commit to doing to ensure that success? A "community justice officer" (who could be a police officer, probation officer, or parole officer) would also be involved, since there might be special conditions, geared to the neighborhood, that the offender would have to meet.

The judge-centered model described here obviously borrows heavily from the drug court experience. Both feature an ongoing, central role for the judge, a "contract" drawn up between court and offender, discretion on the judge's part to impose graduated sanctions for various levels of failure to meet the conditions imposed, the promise of the end of supervision as an occasion for ceremonial recognition.

Incarceration as a prelude to reentry

If John goes to prison, a significant purpose of his activities behind bars would be preparation for reentry. What does that mean? It depends on the type of offender and the offense, and could include sex offender treatment, job readiness, education and/or training, a residential drug treatment program, and anger management. These activities would also involve people, support systems, and social service and other programs based in John's neighborhood. Drug treatment in prison should be linked to drug treatment in the community, job training should be linked to work outside, and so forth. In other words, mirror support systems should be established so that John can move from one to the other seamlessly upon release.

Even while in prison, John would continue to pay restitution to his victim or to the community he has harmed—tangible, measurable restitution. A lot of time would be spent with John's family, to keep family ties strong and to talk about what John will be like when he returns home. As the release date approached, the circle would widen, as the support system was brought into the prison to discuss how to keep the offender on the straight and narrow after release. Buddy systems would be established and training in the early warning signs of relapse provided. Again, the community justice officer could broker this process. All the while, the judge would be kept apprised of progress.

Setting the terms of release

When released, John would be brought back to court, perhaps the same courtroom where he was sentenced. A public recognition ceremony would be held, before an audience of family and other members of the support team, and the judge would announce that John has completed a milestone in repaying his debt to society. Now, the judge would declare, the success of the next step depends on John, his support system, and the agencies of government represented by the community justice officer.

The terms of the next phase would be clearly articulated. If John's case were typical, he would have to remain drug free, make restitution to his victim and reparation to his community, work to make his community safer, participate in programs that began in prison (work, education, and the like), avoid situations that could trigger relapse, and refrain from committing crime. He would be required to appear in court every month to demonstrate how well the plan was working.

Making the contract work

The judge presiding over a reentry court would be responsible for making sure that John held up his end of the bargain and that the government agencies and the support system were doing their parts. As in drug courts, the court appearances need not be long, drawn-out affairs; the purpose of invoking the authority of the court would be to impress on John that he has important work to do and to mobilize the support network. The power of the court would be invoked sparingly when John failed to make progress. The court would view relapse in its broadest sense and would use the powers at its disposal (to impose prison sentences, greater restrictions on liberty, fines, and similar sanctions) to ensure that John toes the line. His family and other members of his support system would be encouraged to attend these court hearings. The community justice officer would keep the court apprised of neighborhood developments involving the offender. To the extent John became involved in programs that made his community safer, there would be occasion for special commendation. The judge would be empowered by statute to accelerate the end of the period of supervision, to remove such legal restrictions as the ban on voting, and to oversee John's "graduation" from the program—his successful reentry into the community.

This approach would have several benefits. It cuts across organizational boundaries, making it more likely that offenders are both held accountable and supported in fulfilling their part of the reentry bargain. By involving family members, friends, and other interested parties in the reentry plan, it expands the reach of positive influences upon the offender. By creating a supervisory role for judges, the approach gives them far greater capacity to achieve the purposes of sentencing. Most important, by focusing on the inexorable fact that the prison sentence will one day be completed and the offender will come back to live in the community, the approach directs private and public energies and resources toward the goal of successful reintegration.

* * *

QUESTIONS AND POINTS FOR DISCUSSION

1. Some jurisdictions have begun to utilize reentry courts. Reentry courts can now be found, for example, in a number of federal-court districts. Rodney Villazor, Reentry Courts: An Examination of the "Provocative Proposal" in Practice, 28 Fed. Sentencing Rep. 253, 255 (2016). Do you support

the use of reentry courts? Why or why not? If you favor their establishment, would you structure them in the way described above? As a practical matter, what obstacles might impede the development and operation of reentry courts?

2.   Programming and planning for reentry are now commonplace, with some states undertaking to institute reentry-related programming and planning statewide. See Cheryle Lero Jonson & Francis T. Cullen, Prisoner Reentry Programs, 44 Crime & Just. 517, 534 (2015). In 2008, Congress enacted the Second Chance Act of 2007, Pub. L. No. 110–199, 122 Stat. 657, which authorizes federal funding to spur the development of such reentry plans and programs.

What steps do you believe should be taken, both while people are incarcerated and after their release, to facilitate their successful return to society and reduce recidivism rates? After identifying these steps, compare your ideas with the thirty-five recommendations contained in the Report of the Re-Entry Policy Council: Charting the Safe and Successful Return of Prisoners to the Community (2005), available at https://csgjusticecenter.org/wp-content/uploads/2013/03/Report-of-the-Reentry-Council.pdf.

INDEX

References are to Pages